D0891773

To my research assistant, Céline

The Children and the Nations

The Story of Unicef

Maggie Black

With Forewords by Peter Ustinov and Sir Robert Jackson

The contents of this book reflect the views
of the author, and do not necessarily reflect
the views of the United Nations Children's
Fund or any other United Nations organization.

ISBN 92 1 100302 4

Library of Congress Catalog Card Number 86-14674

Produced for Unicef by P.I.C. Pty Ltd, Box 797 GPO,
Potts Point, Sydney, Australia 2011

Jacket design by Colin Bond
Designed by Elizabeth Douglas and Bill Reed
Typeset by ProComp Productions Pty Ltd, Adelaide
Printed in Hong Kong

Contents

Acknowledgements

Many people, knowingly and unknowingly, have made this book possible, and I acknowledge their contributions with deepest appreciation.

My first debt is to Tarzie Vittachi, whose idea it was that I should undertake the assignment, and who thereby demonstrated the kind of master's confidence in the student which makes the student wish to do the very best she can.

My second debt is to James Grant, who gave the idea his blessing, and personally assured me at the outset that my independence of view would be respected. For an author undertaking a history of any member organization of the United Nations system, to be given such an assurance is already remarkable; not only has it been consistently upheld, but also both Mr and Mrs Grant have given me a great deal of personal encouragement during the course of the book's development.

My third debt is to the staff of the Unicef history project, led by Jack Charnow, who have been throughout the past year-and-a-half friends and supporters of my work and myself: Alex Allard, Joan Bel Geddes, Joan Dydo, Gladys Felpeto, Dorothy Lewis, Nikolle Solomone, Laura Lopez-Lising, Khurram Mirza. In this group also belongs Lily Solmssen Moureaux, who undertook the photo research.

My ideas about social and humanitarian co-operation in and with Third World countries have been fashioned not only within Unicef, where I have worked since 1977 in Africa and in New York, but also over the entire course of fifteen years of learning and writing about development issues. My first group of mentors and co-learners were at Oxfam UK or associated with it; my second were in East Africa, including the Community Development Trust Fund of Tanzania; my third were at the *New Internationalist* magazine, Oxford, UK. Many people associated with these organizations and with Unicef have taken part in the process which has woven within my mind the perspectives which find frequent—some will think too frequent—expression in these pages. Some of these people are scholars and experts; some are people whose hearts and careers have been committed to improving the lives of the poorest members of Mankind, and who have shared the riches and the frustrations of their experience; some are the people whom this great humanitarian endeavour is all about—the people out there in the dusty compounds and winding tracks of the Third World village or shanty town; those whose views, in the end, make or break all efforts on their behalf. The people who, in a symposium, a conference, a discussion, an argument, a tête-à-tête, or under the shade of the proverbial tree, have helped to shape this book are too many to name, and to single out some would be invidious. There are also others who have given me personal support during its writing and helped me through its many minor crises. I hope that in the above description, a number of those who deserve to find themselves there will know that I am grateful.

In the exhaustive process of revising the manuscript, many retired and current Unicef staff members, and others who over the years have been closely associated with the organization, reviewed and commented on certain chapters or sections of the manuscript.

Many changes—some minor, many major—have been incorporated as a result of their labour; their contributions have added a great deal to whatever merit the final text contains. In this context, I would like to thank: Manzoor Ahmed, Estefania Aldaba-Lim, Sasha Bacic, Grace Barbey, Jacques Beaumont, Martin Beyer, Newton Bowles, Susan Cole-King, Hans Conzett, Bill Cousins, Al Davidson, Karin Edstrom, Jan Eggink, Roberto Esguerra-Barry, Pierre Fazzi, Barney Fraser, Reinhard Freiberg, Margaret Gaan, Ken Grant, John Grun, Perry Hanson, Virginia Hazzard, Ron Hill, Johannes Holm, Betty Jacob, Alfred Katzin, Sam Keeny, Malcolm Kennedy, Ulf Kristoffersson, Boguslaw Kozusznik, Paul Ignatieff, Michel Iskander, Kurt Jansson, Harry Labouisse, Eve Labouisse, Otto Lehner, Jack Ling, Michael Lubbock, Gertrude Lutz, James McDougall, Raymond Mande, Tony Meager, Sherwood Moe, Edward Marks, Canon Joseph Moerman, Helenka Pantaleoni, Moberly Rajendran, François Rémy, Mike Sacks, Martin Sandberg, John Saunders, Alice Shaffer, Hans Singer, Datus Smith, Victor Soler-Sala, Herman Stein, Arne Stinus, Peter Taçon, Rupert Talbot, Les Teply, Nils Thedin, Tarzie Vittachi, Ma Yansheng.

The following took the time and trouble to read and comment on the entire manuscript, or on almost all of it: Gordon Carter, Jack Charnow, Ralph Eckert, Charles Egger, James Grant, Dick Heyward and Sir Robert Jackson. I am indebted to all of them, but I am particularly indebted to three not otherwise singled out above. Firstly to Sir Robert Jackson, the only principal at the birth of Unicef who is still among us, and who has given unstinting encouragement to the project from the moment he became involved. Secondly to Dick Heyward, for reasons that will be understood by all who know Mr Heyward or who have worked with him; I value his comments on my work more highly than those of any other single person. Where I have made a mess of economic theory, or nutritional science, or the lifestyle of the *anopheles* mosquito, he has eased me onto a different track, sometimes even taking the trouble to research and draft more accurate versions unsolicited, saving me much time and many agonies.

Lastly, I have to thank Jack Charnow. To him, more than to anyone else, I owe whatever accomplishment this book represents. Not only has he been my constant reader, friendly critic and filler-in of gaps; he has given me personal help and encouragement with a constancy at which I can only marvel.

Maggie Black
New York

Introduction

There are those in our world whose pleasure it is to speak ill of the United Nations, as though that organization were the source of all their frustrations, a barrier to what they regard as a healthy nationalism, and as money down the drain.

It is always difficult to argue with such people, since by nature they are more adept at expressing opinions of their own than at listening to those of others, and therefore have difficulties with the rules of debate, and the fundamental principles of democracy.

Because of this, they regard themselves as essentially political animals, always alive to any quirk of national policy not to their liking, forever writing to newspapers and to Congressmen in order to express their outrage at this or that. As often as not, they are members of pressure groups to right real or imagined wrongs, and to protect themselves against often peaceful folk who do not happen to share their views.

It stands to reason that once such people find it hard to stomach internal democracy, any form of democracy tinged with (or, in their views, tarnished with) internationalism is bound to act as an intolerable provocation.

A sophisticated idea such as the United Nations, born of the world's deceptions, and the errors of the League of Nations, which, on top of other novelties, gives small nations the illusion of being as worthy of attention as the greatest powers on this planet, is the ultimate of impertinences to them.

It stands to reason, therefore, that the agencies of the United Nations—the shop as opposed to the shop window of the General Assembly—have come in for their own share of misconception and abuse.

The International Labour Organization and UNESCO have had more than the usual share of marching and countermarching, of threat and of gesture. Even Unicef, the organization with the least controversial of platforms, comes in for its regular ration of suspicion and abuse.

'Haven't we enough undernourished and poor children of our own without bothering with those of other countries?' The cry usually emanates from rich parts of the developed world, and one must admit that, while one is often saddened by the degree of poverty in developing countries, one is sometimes shocked by the prevalence of poverty in wealthy countries. But it surely does not need an international organization to help solve problems which are not those of dire necessity, but of policy.

Unicef directs its energies and ideas towards those who are born where history and geography have precluded a natural or available affluence, and it is right that this should be so. Its strength as an organization is the very fact of its independence from religious or political colour. One remembers that in Nigeria, Unicef was encouraged to continue its mission of mercy immediately after the conclusion of the civil war over breakaway Biafra at a time when other organizations were denied this urgent access. One may also recall the appeals from the Governments of both South and North Vietnam, as well as from the Viet Cong, for Unicef to become active even before the cessation of hostilities in order to save as many young lives as possible as the chaos of the final debacle engulfed them.

Nowadays, the initials remain, even though Unicef is no longer called the United Nations International Children's Emergency Fund, but merely the United Nations Children's Fund—no doubt because the emergency is ongoing and perpetual. There are always conflicts, famine and tragic migrations in the news. There has never been so much for Unicef and its sister organizations with overlapping interests, such as the UN High Commissioner for Refugees and the World Health Organization, to face up to.

At a time in which it is fashionable to reduce national contributions to international organizations in order to find funds for sections deemed imperative, such as defence, the ingenuity and will to survive of these servants of humanity are put to a severe test. It is remarkable with what resilience they have met the challenge.

Unicef has helped develop, and is now promoting worldwide, a cure for diarrhoeal dehydration, that great killer of babies, which costs the equivalent of 11 cents US a packet . . . hardly an extravagance. Unicef has also estimated that it is possible in this day and age to immunize all the children in the world against the handful of lethal diseases which affect childhood for a cost amounting to less than that of three strategic bombers.

Now, certainly to its pilot and to its designer one of these aircraft is a thing of beauty—and as an object of sheer design, it may well awaken feelings of aesthetic admiration in many of us. But let us compare it to a child. First of all, for all its extraordinary technical complication, it is far less sophisticated than a child. Its capacities are all destructive, and it cannot develop. It can merely age. That a child can do also, but a child can grow, in size and in experience. It can even, if it has the inclination, become the master of such a machine, or its victim, if we all lose control over the monsters we never cease creating.

Think, every time that such a machine falls from the sky by accident or design, that the supply of vaccine which could have protected millions of the world's children has been splashed uselessly over the landscape.

The time has come in the development of the human animal for a decision to be reached. Which are more important, people or things? Despite the fact that we spend infinitely more on things, on the pretext that these things are for the ultimate benefit of people, those who regard a particular nation as being above the rest instead of part of the rest must forgive me if I vote for people. People of every colour, every race, every belief. People.

Peter Ustinov

Peter Ustinov is known worldwide for his accomplishments as an actor, producer, novelist, playwright, designer and film star. He has been a Goodwill Ambassador for Unicef since the late 1960s, representing Unicef in television specials and other benefit events in various parts of the world and has travelled extensively for Unicef, both officially and unofficially, to a large number of countries.

Foreword

by Sir Robert Jackson, A.C., K.C.V.O., C.M.G., O.B.E.

It gives me a special pleasure to write this foreword for I have had the good fortune to be associated with this remarkable organization, Unicef, since it was first conceived in 1946.

Maggie Black has emphasized that this is not an official history. However, from my own personal knowledge both of Unicef and of official histories published by various organizations within the UN system, I doubt very much if any other record will ever provide a more comprehensive, clearer, or more readable description of Unicef's wonderful work.

Not only today's generation of children, but also their parents have no recollection of the unbelievable horrors and endless human suffering which gave rise to the idea of a special UN organization for children, tens of millions of whom suffered so terribly during the second World War. I would therefore like to recapitulate the events that led to the creation of this institution, whose work over the last forty years has expanded continuously until it is now vitally concerned with children and their mothers in over 100 countries.

Anyone who served in the second World War and helped to deal with its aftermath witnessed death, destruction and suffering on a scale beyond human comprehension. Great cities were reduced to rubble, towns and villages were obliterated. Vast tracts of eastern Europe and the USSR were subjected again and again to the devastation of 'scorched earth'. The tornadoes of war swept through the Pacific islands and African deserts which were left once more silent and empty, littered with graves, rusted guns and armour. Finally, to crown the incredible saga of horror, came the climax of Hiroshima which cast a lasting shadow of fear and foreboding over the entire world.

And while all this destruction took place, there were other more terrible, hidden horrors. Millions of men and women were herded into concentration camps, tortured, used as living experiments, exterminated. Even more became human flotsam and jetsam scattered all over Europe by turbulent forces of an intensity never before experienced in this world; ultimately they became known officially as 'displaced persons'—homeless, hungry, bereft of hope.

Within this maelstrom of terror, tens of millions of children struggled to

1

survive. Not for them the simple pleasures of childhood; all they knew was constant hunger, constant fear and, all too often, no homes and no-one to love or protect them. Great numbers were orphans; others had been separated from their parents as a deliberate act of government policy.

Having personally observed this unending grief and misery in every theatre of war, I was left with one absolute conviction: nothing was more important in the postwar world than to try to do everything possible to succour these children, the most innocent and most heart-breaking of all the victims of that terrible conflict.

As the Allied forces began to liberate occupied countries from 1944 onwards, it was the disclosure of the concentration camps that produced, understandably, the most sensational effect on people all over the world. Their first reaction was one of horror and disbelief, followed immediately by a desire to do everything possible to help the survivors. Yet, to those of us who were responsible for providing relief and rehabilitation, the needs of those millions of children in the war-torn countries and in the camps for displaced persons were equally urgent, for the children represented the next generation in whose hands would rest the possibility of creating a better world.

What could be done to restore a war-ravaged planet? Winston Churchill and President Roosevelt, with their principal advisors, had shown great foresight and imagination during 1941 and 1942. During these most difficult war years, they took action that led to the creation in 1943 of an international organization deliberately designed to provide relief and rehabilitation, immediately hostilities came to an end, to all countries. UNRRA—the United Nations Relief and Rehabilitation Administration—became the first of the many institutions that now make up the modern UN system. Its first Director-General was Governor Herbert Lehman, a distinguished American statesman and philanthropist, whose Senior Deputy I had the honour to become towards the end of 1944.

UNRRA began operations in 1944 as Allied forces were liberating countries in the Mediterranean and the Balkans, and progressively assumed greater responsibilities until the Armistice in May 1945. It was then inundated with an avalanche of requests from governments all over Europe in desperate need of assistance. In addition, the Allied forces, wishing to demobilize as quickly as possible, turned over to UNRRA responsibility for the pathetic survivors of the concentration camps, and also for some 8,500,000 men, women and children displaced by the ravages of unrestricted warfare. The Governments of the Ukraine and Byelorussia—the two countries most devastated by the war—also asked for assistance, and shortly afterwards, when hostilities with Japan ended, war-torn countries in Asia—China, Korea, and the Philippines—joined the chorus in need.

In the immediate aftermath of the conflict, action by UNRRA was a matter of life and death. Despite the political and practical difficulties that often impeded its work, and with the invaluable support of the Allied forces, hundreds of millions of people survived as a result of its operations. Three special responsibilities were invariably given absolute priority: the survivors of the concentration camps, the displaced persons and, above all, the children. The success with which it shouldered its task is illustrated by the fact that, in dramatic contrast to 1918–1919 when it is estimated that over thirty million people perished from influenza and typhus, there were no major disease epidemics during the very harsh winter in Europe of 1945–1946.

By early 1946 UNRRA was moving essential relief supplies to over twenty countries on a scale that exceeded the movement of munitions by the Allied forces during the war. The preservation of life dominated every action and speed was the constant order of the day. A remarkable range of goods was procured, shipped and distributed: every form of basic food stuffs; clothing (new and second-hand provided as a result of voluntary appeals); materials that could provide shelter (military surpluses were a goldmine, and provided at bargain prices); medical and dental supplies and equipment, vaccines, hospital equipment; seeds, fertilizers, agricultural machinery (tractors were flown into Yugoslavia during the early months of 1945 in a desperate effort to secure a harvest soon after the war ended); industrial machinery; telecommunications in every form; aircraft for transport, and for malaria spraying; large numbers of locomotives, thousands of railway wagons, tens of thousands of trucks (many provided by Allied forces); fishing trawlers and nets; Bailey bridges; sewing machines; about a quarter of a million horses and mules (the latter used for distribution of food in mountain areas); tens of thousands of dairy cattle (with their rumps branded UNRRA); and innumerable fowls and chickens—the range was endless. All those supplies preserved the lives of those hundreds of millions of people in three continents, and they were also of critical importance in UNRRA's work of looking after the survivors of the concentration camps, the displaced persons and, above all, the children. In today's currency, UNRRA had about $20 billion at its disposal—and there was never enough—and employed about 15,000 professional staff and some 35,000 local staff.

While UNRRA was doing everything in its power to provide the supplies essential for the preservation of life, it was simultaneously making every effort to nurse and endeavour to restore strength to those who, miraculously, still survived from the horrors of the concentration camps. Many of the millions of displaced persons had also undergone great suffering and hardship. Wherever possible, the obvious thing was to get them back to their homelands, and here again the US Air Force and the Royal Air Force played a decisive role with UNRRA in moving six million people. Over two millions, alas, remained and UNRRA therefore initiated an operation designed to find new homes for them in other parts of the world. Although nearly two million were resettled, still more refugees from eastern Europe arrived during the period 1945–1948.

UNRRA had realized from the outset that this work would extend beyond its own lifetime, and it therefore advanced proposals to the first General Assembly of the UN in 1946 for the establishment of a new and more permanent agency which, in due course, could take over UNRRA's responsibilities. The proposals were adopted, and the International Refugee Organization (IRO) came into being, which would later become the UN High Commission for Refugees (UNHCR).

It is worth noting that UNRRA's operations in relation to displaced persons led to an acute political confrontation, for certain governments claimed that they alone could decide the future of those of their nationals in UNRRA's care. UNRRA resisted this claim successfully on the ground that the individual alone could decide what he or she wished to do, and in that process UNRRA laid the foundation of what became the UN Universal Declaration of Human Rights.

UNRRA's performance was impressive. But then came a bombshell. Sir Winston Churchill, who had played such a critical role in the creation of UNRRA, also prepared its death warrant. On 6 March 1946, he gave his famous 'Iron Curtain' speech at Fulton, Missouri. The Cold War had become so intense that UNRRA's days were numbered. Probably the most difficult political aspect of UNRRA's operations was the fact that so much of its assistance went to the Socialist countries in eastern Europe, while it depended for its funds almost entirely on the US and its Western allies. Under these circumstances it was most improbable that future financial support could be mobilized. Nevertheless, UNRRA carried on for another two years, continuing to preserve great numbers of lives in many parts of the world, to provide for the survivors of the concentration camps and for the displaced persons, and to safeguard the children—its most important responsibility.

In many respects, the suffering of the children provoked the deepest reaction of all. Their deeply-sunken eyes, reminiscent of small, frightened animals, and their emaciated little bodies can never be forgotten. Malnutrition was starkly apparent everywhere, but even more heart-rending was the ever present sadness and sense of hopelessness. You rarely saw a smile, and the eyes were always fearful and all too often suspicious. These were not children as we know children; they barely existed. They could well be regarded as the ultimate victims of that global conflagration: they had lost the most precious years of their lives. And the picture was the same wherever one travelled—in the displaced persons camps in Germany, in Poland, in Austria; in the refugee camps in the Middle East (whose inhabitants were almost all Poles); in China, in the Ukraine, in Greece, everywhere. Obviously they needed a proper diet; they needed medical attention; they needed proper homes. But, above all, my deepest impression was that they needed love.

Most of those children, thank God, had one priceless asset. They were resilient. Of course, the effects of malnutrition would take some time to correct (in some cases, alas, permanent damage had been done); but once they were treated as all children should be treated, the response was wonderful. There were still tens of thousands who were orphans, and large numbers separated from their parents. As more normal conditions returned to the war-devastated countries, local organizations and local families were able to give invaluable help, thus reinforcing the efforts of UNRRA's medical and welfare staffs, and of the many nongovernmental organizations that made such a vital contribution to this aspect of UNRRA's work.

Gradually, some degree of order appeared out of chaos. Once it was clear beyond doubt that a child was an orphan, possibilities for adoption could be explored (carefully), and many new homes were found. But the problem of children separated from their parents was the most complex of all those we faced, and aroused more profound emotions than any other. From the outset it was realized that there could be no complete solution; tens of thousands of children were scattered in camps spread all over Europe, nearly as many parents had been swept into other parts of the continent by the merciless force of that warfare. It was a matter of doing everything possible to reunite as many as could be traced.

If the problem is likened to a criminal investigation (and, indeed, the substance of the problem represented one of the greatest crimes committed during the war) then it would have tested all the professional skill, imagination and commitment of the finest detective force in the world. The only written evidence that could help to solve it was, at best, small bits and pieces. In a few camps there might be a register or some kind of record; by a miracle the child might have some means of identification. But all too often the children did not even know their full names. As for the parents, there might be a document or, vitally important, a photograph. Oral evidence? Little could be expected from the children. Much more, of course, from the parents, but very frequently the circumstances they described had totally changed as a result of the war.

And who were the detectives who devoted themselves to this, the most moving of human challenges? The great majority were women from national Red Cross societies and voluntary organizations, working within the framework of UNRRA. During the war, women had frequently demonstrated their superiority over men in conducting research and in analyzing the results of photo-reconnaissance, for they were more painstaking, pertinacious and patient. Those qualities were demonstrated to the full when it came to dealing with the infinitely detailed and incomplete jigsaw puzzle represented by those thousands of children; in addition, the profound emotion of maternal care exercised a compelling influence. Without exception, everyone involved in that work demonstrated dedication, remarkable imagination, and seemed never to rest from their labour of love. Photographs were a vital factor in the process of reunion; sadly, it was often a case of attempted reunion. Virtually all children were photographed, and, where possible, compared with earlier pictures in the possession of parents. Frequently, parents were brought to inspect photographs in the hope that they might be able to recognize a child. The work never ceased, it just went on and on.

It is difficult to conceive of a greater emotional experience than to have witnessed that moment of contact, after years of separation and suspense and sorrow, between the child and the possible parent or parents. If it was, in reality, the reunion of the child with its mother and father, the reaction was ecstasy—not only for the family, but also for those who had the wonderful good fortune to bring it about. If, tragically, it became clear that it was not a reunion of a family, the reaction, if anything, was even more searing. It was an experience that was almost beyond description: a few moments of hope, of expectancy, of shining eyes, and then the look of total despair, the retreat, and the return to numbing sadness. My memories of those occasions, often on the central railway station in Vienna—memories which bring back those moments of ecstasy and of heartbreak—are as vivid today, forty years later, as they were then. Over the years many successful reunions were brought about as a result of the extraordinary efforts and dedication of those wonderful women, whose work must have remained with them always as the most profoundly satisfying experience of their lives.

Another very clear memory of UNRRA's efforts to help children remains. After the completion of the great operation to return to their national homes all those displaced persons who were eligible for repatriation, negotiations were initiated with governments all over the world to accept those who were either stateless or feared to return to their own countries of origin. Unbelievably, for over a year, not one government—even those of countries that had not been combatants during the war—would receive any of these unfortunate people. However, in July 1946 the Prime Minister of Australia, the Hon. J. B. Chifley, agreed, as a major act of policy, to accept immediately 100,000 of them, including many children. This began a great immigration programme which was ultimately to provide new lives for many hundreds of thousands of people, and to bring great benefits to their newly-adopted country. Australia having broken the log-jam, discussions were held a few days later with the Prime Minister of New Zealand, the Hon. Peter Fraser, and they, too, were successful. This made it possible to bring pressure on countries in North and South America, and some in Europe, to follow suit. Ultimately, new homes were found for some two million of these displaced persons.

Within that great sea of misery, there was one particular tragedy which aroused the world's sympathy. In September 1939, over a million Poles fled east in the face of the Nazi onslaught. Ultimately, less than 100,000 arrived on the northern border of Iran, the remainder having perished during their long and perilous journey. As the war progressed, the survivors became the responsibility of the British authorities who accommodated them in settlements in Karachi, Nairobi and Ismailia. These were administered by a new organization, the Middle East Relief and Refugee Administration (MERRA) based in Cairo.

A census determined that there were precisely 999 orphans in the settlements: not 998 nor 1000, but precisely 999! Somewhat naturally, those orphans became famous simply because of their number. As soon as it was possible to do so (in late 1944) UNRRA took over responsibility from MERRA for those refugees, not all of whom wished to return to their homeland. How to ensure that everything possible was done to give those 999 orphans love, protection and new lives? As soon as they were mentioned to Mr Fraser he exclaimed: 'Of course we'll take them' — and where better in the world could they start new lives than in New Zealand? By then, the famous 999 had been in my life continuously for nearly five years, and when the Prime Minister gave his approval my reaction can easily be imagined. It was natural that a careful record should be kept of their future progress and without a single exception they developed into splendid New Zealanders, to the delight of all concerned. (About a year later, Mr Wladyslaw Gomulka, who was then Vice-Premier of Poland, complained good naturedly that UNRRA had 'stolen' some of his children, but UNRRA's reputation in Poland was remarkable — 'To us, UNRRA is a holy word' — and he quickly agreed that they could not have gone to a better country.) That tiny little operation within a vast worldwide enterprise remains one of the best memories of UNRRA's most rewarding involvement with children.

These recollections underline how deep and widespread was UNRRA's involvement with children. Within the framework of the fundamental principle of preserving human life, the well-being of children was always UNRRA's paramount concern. Unintentionally, Churchill's 'Iron Curtain' speech in March 1946 planted the first seed of a unique tree that would one day grow into Unicef as we know it today. Churchill's speech meant that UNRRA's life was limited; how to preserve the most essential of its functions? One action of critical importance was to ensure that, whatever happened, other UN institutions could carry on the most important elements of its work. Within a month, UNRRA's senior staff prepared a policy document, describing how its residual functions could best be preserved. Some of its work could be transferred naturally to the UN itself (then just coming to life), and to the UN Food and Agricultural Organization (FAO), the UN Educational, Scientific and Cultural Organization (UNESCO), and to the Interim Commission of the World Health Organization (WHO). As a result of UNRRA's foresight, an International Refugee Organization had been approved by the General Assembly a few months before in February 1946, and it would be relatively easy to transfer staff and sufficient funds ('seed money') to get the new institution on its feet. But what of the most important responsibility of all, children?

When the policy memorandum of 25 June 1946 went to governments, it made a special plea that effective child feeding should be continued in every country in which UNRRA had been operating, and that continuity of UNRRA's work would be preserved. The memorandum ended with an unmistakable warning to all governments: 'These matters cannot be left in abeyance.' That part of the memorandum provided the seed with which Unicef was conceived.

The memorandum was considered by UNRRA's Governing Council at its Fifth Session in August 1946, where various representatives of governments gave it impressive support under the leadership of Fiorello La Guardia, who had succeeded Governor Lehman as Director-General a few months earlier. The Governing Council adopted a Resolution (103) which recommended that an International Children's Fund should be created and, indeed, embodied a suggestion advanced by UNRRA (informally to avoid difficulties with the specialized agencies) that any funds remaining at the end of its operations should be transferred to the new children's organization.

After that, the Economic and Social Council gave its blessing, and then finally, the General Assembly on 11 December 1946 approved the creation of a United Nations International Children's *Emergency* Fund. The word 'emergency' was of vital importance in securing the support of some governments that were not keen to see any new institution established which resembled even part of UNRRA's work. In one form or another, the 'emergency' has continued for forty years. Long may it continue!

Shortly after the passage of the resolution, Maurice Pate was appointed the first Executive Director of Unicef. It was an inspired choice. During the next two years, as UNRRA gradually wound down its operations, both staff and funds were transferred to Unicef. The passage of the resolution in the Governing Council, and all the subsequent development gave great pleasure and satisfaction to all those of us in UNRRA who had been involved with children. We were confident that our precious human legacy was in safe hands.

With the passage of time, and Unicef's success, it was understandable that many individuals should feel that they played a special role in its creation. Undoubtedly several men and women made outstanding contributions once the recommendation for continuing assistance to children was put before UNRRA Governing Council, and stimulated the process that enabled the seed of Unicef to be fertilized and nurtured. But there would never have been a Unicef if there had not been an UNRRA, a fact in which many of us who lived through the postwar UNRRA experience feel a special kind of pride.

*   *   *   *   *   *

All these early developments in Unicef's life are admirably described by Maggie Black, who then goes on to tell the story of Unicef's first forty years. It is a fascinating record of the evolution of an international organization which has succeeded in making the whole world aware of its responsibilities for safeguarding its most priceless asset: children. The book is divided into five distinct parts, each of which deals in chronological order with a particular period in Unicef's life. This arrangement has the advantage of showing clearly how the organization has adjusted itself successfully to the constantly changing political forces since the second World War—indeed it has been a period of both political and scientific revolution—while simultaneously taking initiatives and exploring new methods which might improve children's lives.

The first part deals with Unicef's first four years when it could be regarded as a direct offshoot of UNRRA, although its resources at that time were, of course, tiny in comparison. It soon began to move in new directions and, as its work progressed, new experience was gained and the organization was consolidated. Unicef developed a very distinct character of its own. It was most fortunate that such was the case, for in 1950 the US—incredible as it may seem today—led a campaign to terminate Unicef's existence. This action, of course, reflected the same attitude that had brought an end to UNRRA's invaluable work. Fortunately, this attack was repulsed, and Unicef was able to survive, thus enabling innumerable children all over the world to benefit from its aid in the years to come.

Having overcome that crisis in its existence, Unicef continued to undertake new programmes during the decade of the 1950s, which forms the second part of the chronicle. Many of these grew out of programmes which began in Europe in the postwar era, some—malaria control, campaigns against treponemal disease—with links tracing back to UNRRA programmes. Assistance was given to an international onslaught against tuberculosis, first in Europe and then in other countries; support was also provided for campaigns against yaws, leprosy and trachoma throughout Asia, Latin America, Africa—the parts of the world then known as 'underdeveloped'. All these activities achieved much success, but the great campaign to eradicate malaria, while making notable progress, met an exceptionally tough opponent in the *anopheles* mosquito who, despite massive attacks, often 'lived to fight another day'.

All this activity by Unicef in the field of health naturally brought it into close contact with WHO. As a result of opposition in the US Congress, WHO had got off to a slow start; two years elapsed before sufficient governments ratified the agreement negotiated by the Interim Commission in 1946 and thus brought the organization to life. Every specialized agency within the UN system is very sensitive about its independence and its constitutional responsibilities, and it was natural that at times strains should develop between the two organizations as to where the responsibilities of each in the field of child health began and ended. However, commonsense, professional interest in the substance of each problem and, above all, recognition that both institutions existed to help children and mothers in need, steadily led to an effective partnership that has brought benefit to all concerned.

During this period, the General Assembly confirmed (in 1953) Unicef's existence indefinitely, at the same time recognizing that its primary focus should be the children who suffered not from the temporary calamity of war, but the permanent disaster of poverty and underdevelopment. The words 'international' and 'emergency' were dropped from Unicef's title, but the acronym was retained because it had by now become so well-known. The need for Unicef's existence has never again been challenged, and it is now most improbable that it ever will be.

Maggie Black very appropriately selects for the third part of her record the first Development Decade, 1960 to 1970. This was a time of great political and economic activity, with the Third World literally exploding into existence as country after country in Africa attained its independence. The effect of this political revolution on the UN itself, and on the UN system, was profound; the entire character of the system was changed as new voices were heard, and appeals were made to consolidate political independence by economic and social development. In one sense, the 'balance of power' in the UN was changed for all time. When the UNRRA Agreement was signed on 9 November 1943, there were forty-four member States; today there are 159. The governments of the older, industrialized nations, now outnumbered, were compelled to listen to the claims of the new, and adjust their policies accordingly.

All these developments naturally had a very direct effect on Unicef, and its Executive Board and senior officials sought to define new policies. After much debate, it was agreed (rightly) that children should be regarded as a resource—and, indeed, the most precious resource of all—and as a vital element in national development. Quite apart from the essential needs of the child in Asia and in Latin America and in some parts of Europe, the needs in Africa had a special significance. In large parts of that continent food production has always been hazardous as a result of climatic conditions. The fragility of the family food supply as well as shortages of nourishing proteins and vitamins have resulted in widespread malnutrition. These conditions placed great numbers of children at risk, and Unicef soon found itself forging new partnerships with the FAO and the World Food Programme.

During this period, there were at least three other important events in Unicef's life. First, the UN itself and all relevant institutions within the UN system, became actively concerned with population growth, Once more, Unicef found itself involved with a global problem, particularly from the point of view of the negative impact of the large families, poorly spaced, on the health and well-being of the individual child. Second, the Nobel Peace Prize was awarded to Unicef (in 1965) – an honour which was well-earned, and one which served to consolidate the organization's role and reputation still further. The only sadness was that Maurice Pate, whose contribution to Unicef is unsurpassed, died shortly before the award was announced.

The third event was the tragedy of the Nigerian civil war and here Unicef played the key role in providing humanitarian relief. That it was able to do this during a civil war within a member State was made possible by what might be described as 'a fluke of history'. When the resolution that brought Unicef into existence was being drafted for the General Assembly, much of the work was undertaken by UNRRA's legal staff. During one meeting, a senior UNRRA official, exasperated and frustrated by the politics that were bringing the organization's operations to an end, exclaimed: 'For God's sake, keep governments out of this as much as you can. Make it possible for the new show to give help to mothers and children direct'. While the basic resolution on Unicef requires that governments agree to Unicef operations, in some delicate political situations successive Executive Directors have been able to interpret this provision flexibly. The art is *not* to persuade governments to agree that Unicef should undertake activities, but to ensure that the government does not say no and then, in the absence of a prohibition, to get on with the job as quickly and discreetly as possible. That flexibility was of great value in making it possible to provide assistance for mothers and children in rebel-held territory during the Nigerian civil war. Some years later it would prove to be the key that enabled Unicef to open the political door, and so take the lead in alleviating the effects of what some regard as the greatest individual tragedy in history: that in Kampuchea in 1979–81.

The next decade (until 1980) represents the fourth part of the story, and is described by the author as 'The Era of Alternatives', a period when still further dimensions were added to Unicef's increasing range of activities. Particular attention was paid to the availability of clean drinking water, and great progress was made in rural areas. In 1974, the Sixth Special Session of the General Assembly reflected with dramatic clarity the great change in the composition of member States, and what the new nations felt should be their place in the world. This led to the definition of a new international economic order which gave great impetus to alternative approaches to development. Unicef articulated its own version, 'the basic services strategy', in 1976. Hitherto, the transfer of knowledge and experience had been almost entirely from the older, industrialized countries to the new nations. Now the knowledge and the expertise that had always reposed in the Third World was recognized. Another expression of the search for alternatives could be seen in a major change in the philosophy of what was meant by 'health care for all'. At a meeting of ministers of health in Alma Ata, USSR, in 1978, a new 'Primary Health Care' model was designed, based on pioneering work in rural communities. The concept of Primary Health Care, whose most important implications were for the health of mothers and children, was one which Unicef helped WHO to develop.

Twice in the 1970s, Unicef found itself heavily involved in major disaster operations co-ordinated by the UN. Bangladesh became independent at the end of 1971 and during the next three years the UN carried out the largest relief and rehabilitation operation ever undertaken for a single country since the days of UNRRA. Throughout that operation Unicef provided invaluable assistance, and on its completion on 31 March 1974 Unicef reverted to its normal work. Towards the end of the UN operation, it became apparent that a substantial sum of money would be available for transfer to other UN agencies to continue parts of the rehabilitation programme. Naturally each of them did all they could to secure these funds, but bearing in mind the precedent by which UNRRA provided Unicef with the financial support that brought it to life, no prizes would be offered for guessing which agency became the beneficiary!

By the middle of 1979, Unicef became involved with what could be regarded as one of the most notable operations in its remarkable record. In early January 1979, Pol Pot and his forces were driven out of what is now known as Kampuchea, and a new regime was established in Phnom Penh. During the next few months, some of the obscene atrocities practised by Pol Pot gradually became known to the outside world. For nearly four years, from 1975 onwards, the people of Kampuchea had been subjected to one of the most ruthless revolutions ever known; in some respects it was even more bestial than the horrors of the concentration camps. This had been preceded by the effective collapse of the political, economic and administrative structure of the country by its involuntary entanglement in the Vietnam war. The US Air Force, which commenced bombing secretly in March 1969, dropped on Kampuchea bombs whose destructive power was equivalent to 120 times that of the atomic bomb dropped on Hiroshima. All this created death and destruction on an almost unbelievable scale. Yet, for some extraordinary reason, it is a tragedy that is now forgotten by most of the world, but certainly not by the Kampuchean people.

About the middle of 1979, in conditions of great political difficulty, Unicef and the International Committee of the Red Cross managed to make contact with the new authorities, and about the same time FAO and voluntary agencies such as Oxfam also succeeded in visiting Phnom Penh. After many weeks of delicate, and often frustrating, negotiations Unicef and ICRC were able to initiate a relief programme, and Oxfam also began to provide assistance. The expansion of Unicef's programme within Kampuchea in 1980 and 1981—which was of critical importance in preserving life—and its equally valuable work with ICRC and the World Food Programme in looking after the great number of Khmers who had taken refuge on the border between Thailand and Kampuchea, is recounted clearly and with sensitivity by the author.

In September 1979, because of Unicef's established record of working in co-operation with administrations which the UN General Assembly did not recognize, the Secretary-General designated Unicef the 'lead agency' for humanitarian relief inside Kampuchea. Thanks to the flexibility with which Unicef's Executive Directors had always interpreted the basic resolution governing Unicef's work, it was able with the ICRC to spearhead the relief operation in circumstances of great political sensitivity. Unicef was able to draw on the resources of the relevant specialized agencies—FAO, WHO, UNESCO—and from UNDP and WFP, their role, so to speak, being that of subcontractors. The efforts of the UN system to do its best to alleviate at least some of the unbelievable suffering of the Khmer people evoked harrowing memories in anyone who had been concerned with the Nazi concentration camps. Unicef's outstanding work in Kampuchea represents one of the finest chapters in its history.

Maggie Black then moves on to the fifth and concluding part of her book which deals with the five years from 1980 onwards. During that period, in which what is described by Unicef as 'A revolution for Child Survival' began, great changes took place. Unicef became more directly concerned with the women's movement (itself gathering momentum), as well as the phenomenon of uncontrolled urban growth in Third World cities. The world scene darkened with an economic recession, and drought and famine again struck many countries in Africa (to which Unicef responded with its customary speed and efficiency). Not only did Unicef succeed in adjusting its work to these constantly changing conditions, but it embarked on a great and ambitious campaign designed to secure the immunization of all children by 1990, and boost other measures for their survival and development.

It is essential that Unicef should continue to sink deeper roots and flourish. During the last forty years Unicef has accomplished great things; perhaps the most significant has been its success in making people of the world aware that the most important reason for living their own lives is to cherish and safeguard the lives of the children who will make the world of tomorrow.

Clearly a great deal has been done, but it is almost insignificant compared to what is still waiting to be done. One statistic is enough; a statistic that Unicef has emphasized again and again. Forty thousand children are still dying unnecessarily each day, and Mankind has the power to save them. Obviously, Unicef cannot resolve this vital global problem by itself, but it can undoubtedly play a unique role. Indeed, it is already pointing the way to solutions. For that reason, all who believe in the future of the human race and the preservation of this planet will pray that Unicef will continue to go from strength to strength.

*   *   *   *   *   *

I should like to end this Foreword on a personal note. Looking back on a long involvement with the UN system, I know of nothing, apart from the effectiveness of UNRRA's operations, that has given me greater pleasure than to have participated in the earliest steps that led to the creation of Unicef, to have been able to provide assistance with UNRRA staff and funds, and to have observed with admiration and respect its subsequent work both in headquarters and in the field.

Unicef has been blessed with three outstanding Executive Directors, and I have had the good fortune to be their friend: Maurice Pate from the time he was first considered for the appointment until his death, Henry (Harry) Labouisse from the time of our work together during the second World War, James (Jim) Grant who started his international career with the UNRRA Mission in China in 1945. More friendships with Unicef's staff were forged during the Bangladesh, Indo China and Kampuchean operations, when the Secretary-General entrusted me with the responsibility for co-ordinating each of them. It is therefore natural that Unicef should occupy a special position in my life, and leave me with constant feelings of affection and gratitude.

Maggie Black has written an excellent account of Unicef's first forty years, and it is a book which is not only full of interest for anyone who is interested in children, or the way in which international organizations work, but one which will undoubtedly give pleasure and satisfaction to all those who have been fortunate enough to have any association with Unicef's work and its dedicated staff.

Sir Robert Jackson, currently Senior Advisor to the United Nations, first served with the incipient UN system as Senior Deputy Director-General of the United Nations Relief and Rehabilitation Administration from 1944 to 1947. He had previously served in the Navy and British Army, and was later Director-General of a large Anglo-American paramilitary organization—the Middle East Supply Centre—which became the model for the Economic Commissions in the UN. When UNRRA completed its work he became Assistant Secretary-General for Co-ordination at Lake Success, and after that held a variety of appointments in the UK, India, Pakistan, Australia and West Africa. From 1961 he has held several senior appointments in the UN and has been involved with development plans and projects in some sixty countries. He was married to Barbara Ward (Baroness Jackson of Lodsworth, D.B.E., F.R.S.) who died in 1981.

Chapter 1

Founding Fathers

The story of Unicef is a story about children in the poorer parts of the world, children whose lives were touched at some point—maybe a vital point, maybe not—by a particular organization trying to fulfill its humanitarian mission. The lives of those children are important in this story not as objects of pity or as trophies of international goodwill, but because ideas about how to touch those lives for the better have changed fundamentally in the postwar and post-colonial era.

With hindsight, much that was done in the name of the children of the developing countries forty, thirty, or even twenty years ago now seems naive. It was done with the best intentions, and often with the help of the best wisdom of the day. In twenty years time, the same will be said of what is being done today, and it will probably prove as sobering and instructive.

Nothing sounds simpler than helping improve the lives of children. In fact, as every parent knows who stops to think about it, nothing could be more challenging or more complex. The only simple part is that everyone agrees, nowadays, that the child has a right to that help. 'Mankind', says the Declaration of the Rights of the Child, 'owes the child the best it has to give'. The governments of the developing nations, which carry out the programmes and deliver the services that Unicef exists to help, all subscribe to that Declaration.

Despite all differences of colour, creed, income, nationality and ideology, and despite the many forces of division in a troubled world, the innocence of the child transcends all boundaries. In an ideal world, every adult wants the best for every child, whether the child belongs to a camel caravan in the Sahara Desert, a ghetto in a decaying inner city, a village in the high Sierras, or a humble homestead in the steppes of Asia. No government delegate or political leader, no economic planner or social reformer—whatever the real implications of the policies they espouse—repudiates the claim of every child to be protected, nurtured, fed, clothed, educated and raised in familial love. The child is everyone's tomorrow, and tomorrow must be brighter than today.

Unicef, the United Nations International Children's Emergency Fund, was created on 11 December 1946 by resolution of the UN General Assembly. In the aftermath of the second World War, the desire to tie more tightly the bonds uniting the family of man and to share the fruits of economic and technological progress more liberally among the people of the world led to a great experiment in international co-operation: the United Nations. Unicef's creation was a part of that experiment.

Created to help war-shattered countries mend the lives of their children, Unicef stayed in being to help developing countries improve lives undermined by hunger and ill-health. Unicef never abandoned the children of crisis—of war, conflict, drought, famine or other emergency—but within five years its mission changed. The international movement to put an end to poverty and underdevelopment around the world demanded of the new experiment in international co-operation that a special effort be made for the children. Unicef took on that special effort, shaped it and was shaped by it.

Within the UN, Unicef is a unique organization. Its mandate is for a particular group of human beings defined only by their lack of years, rather than for an area of human activity, such as health, agriculture, employment, education, or for an underprivileged group with a common predicament. Children can never be simply another cause because they are already part of every cause. Wherever you find the hungry, the sick, the ill-fed, the poorly-clothed, the homeless, the jobless, the illiterate, the destitute, there you find children. And because children are more vulnerable than adults to any kind of deprivation, they suffer worse the effects of all these things because they are children. So Unicef's mission sounds neat and self-contained, but is the opposite: helping the nations to help their children demands that it engage in many areas of human activity, accumulate many kinds of expertise, work with every underprivileged group, and do so alongside many other UN and voluntary organization partners.

Even to reach the lives of children in the poorer parts of the world, let alone to touch them for the better, is far from simple. Most children in the industrialized world regularly spend time in a play group, a day-care centre, a schoolroom; when they are small, they are regularly taken to the doctor or the clinic for a check-up. The absence of such institutions and services is a mirror image of a society's condition of underdevelopment.

Thanks to the progress of the past thirty-five years, more children in the developing world now attend classrooms and clinics. But in the majority of cases, particularly in the poorer countries of Asia, Africa and Latin America, the critical context in which to touch children's lives is still at home, in the family. That is the setting in which the child lives or dies, is hungry or well-fed, clean or ragged, languishes or bounces with good health.

Unicef therefore tries to touch the lives of children by helping to shape health, education or nutrition services which touch those of their families and communities. The most important person in the child's early life is the child's mother. The mother's own health and well-being have a critical impact on that of her children. And her capacities as a mother depend on the way the family earns its living, what that living amounts to, and how the family's decision-makers translate it into food, shelter, clothing, health care and education. These are the decisive factors in a child's present condition and future prospects. Therefore, almost every effort to improve the well-being of children has a context for our society at large almost identical to efforts to create employment and work, and run health, education, and social welfare services. Every policy decision that affects work places, neighbourhoods, homes has an impact on the child.

Because the child has no vote and no political say in the issues which affect the life of the family and the community, the illusion is preserved that the fate of the child is an object of humanitarian concern and not one that affects political figures, administrators or economic policy-makers. Fortunately, the illusion is often strong enough to provide a shield for the child when one is needed. Unicef has been an architect of that shield at certain critical moments during the past forty years, when civil disturbance or international crisis has combined with food shortage to remove children almost beyond the reach of help. That strand of the Unicef story is the most visible and the most widely reported because it concerns wars and emergencies which throw a spotlight onto their victims.

In its other context, that of social and economic progress, the story of Unicef reflects the many debates which have characterized the whole evolution of development thinking in the postwar era. The response to the problems of children in the poorer parts of the world is, inevitably, part of the story of the response to world poverty itself. In four decades, that response has undergone many changes. Every setback has produced its new insights and understandings, but the chequered process of change for the better has moved slowly, inexorably forward.

In the 1950s, the menace of widespread disease—tuberculosis, yaws, syphilis, malaria—succumbed in large measure to medical science and the mass campaign. In the 1960s, the UN's first Development Decade, the coming of independence to many new nations sparked an international crusade to bring to an end centuries of rural stagnation and neglect. In the 1970s came disillusion and self-doubt within the growing international development community generating alternative visions, wiser and more thoughtful remedies for the ancient problems of hunger and disease. In the 1980s, global recession and debt, and the spectacle of large parts of Africa gripped in almost constant distress, have presented a challenge of new dimensions.

An ideal of international co-operation came of age because of the wholesale human destruction of the second World War. Unicef, the first arrangement between the nations to do something specifically for children, was almost accidentally conjured into existence as a result. This is the story of where that impulse led.

*　　　*　　　*　　　*　　　*　　　*

The idea of an international mechanism to look after the specific needs of children was not without antecedents. During the first World War, Eglantyne Jebb, a remarkable Englishwoman, set up an organization in London called the 'Save the Children' fund and sent relief to children on the continent throughout the British blockade of Germany. In 1920, when Europe was in the grip of postwar famine, she prevailed upon the International Red Cross in Geneva to support a 'Save the Children International Union', in order to raise and spend voluntary donations on behalf of the children.

Many other voluntary organizations which had their roots in nineteenth-century missionary and philanthropic zeal were already active on behalf of the victims of disaster—fire, flood, epidemic; and of impoverished women and children. The abandoned and indigent mother and her child, the widowed and the orphaned, those who were otherwise a burden on poorhouse and parish, had a natural place among the main beneficiaries of both religious and secular charitable works. But the idea of international relief was a twentieth-century novelty. And the idea that children were a special kind of people whose well-being transcended partisan considerations only began to gain currency when Eglantyne Jebb defied the British courts in declaring the principle that there was no such thing as an 'enemy' child: a curious notion by the standards of the time.

These ideas were refinements of an ethic born on the battlefields of Europe during the mid-nineteenth century as a result of the terrible sufferings inflicted on soldiers by modern instruments of warfare. In 1864, the Geneva Convention was ratified, conferring neutrality upon voluntary relief workers tending the wounded, the dying, and those taken prisoner. From now on, the red cross on a white background, the colours of the Swiss flag in reverse, became a familiar emblem of a new principle: human life was too precious to be entrusted solely to political or national self-interest. For the time being, this idea was only applied to those carrying arms, but once established, it took a comparatively small leap of the imagination to apply it to defenceless civilians, particularly children who could never be thought to bear the blame for hostilities declared by their country's leaders.

Meanwhile, the philanthropic impulse was being spurred from another direction. The industrialization of Europe and America was inflicting upon the poor a destitution far more degrading and ugly than the familiar, age-old rural poverty of the agricultural world. The cholera outbreaks in the slums of the new cities, the miseries suffered by children and women working in mines and sweat-shops, the poor diets of those on wage labour . . . these were the product of the factory age.

The changing face of society produced new tools for social progress, as well as an ideological and political flood of ideas. Democratic notions about universal education and universal suffrage gained ground. Socialist ideas about equality and the distribution of wealth joined them. Out of urban squalor came the science of public health. Out of material prosperity came technological progress of all kinds. Benevolence and capitalism joined forces to push forward the medical, social, and humanitarian frontier. In the USA, trusts and foundations endowed by Rockefeller, Carnegie, and other benefactors of The Gilded Age invested hundreds of millions of philanthropic dollars in preventive and constructive, as well as ameliorative, tasks. People were beginning to set a higher price on human life at all social levels, whether they believed in John D. Rockefeller's 'business of benevolence', or Karl Marx's doctrines on the class struggle. Many secular organizations like the Red Cross supported an ideal of voluntary service to Mankind rooted in the Christian tradition but nominally purporting to be quite differently inspired; while other voluntary organizations which owed their existence to Christian piety—the YMCA, the Society of Friends— began to gain high reputations for secular good works.

When the first World War broke out, the growing humanitarian community faced a challenge of entirely new dimensions. War on this scale, affecting so many combatants and so many civilians, had never been known before. The protracted agony of the war, and the equally protracted misery of postwar famine and epidemic, represented a watershed in human affairs. The suffering it caused in the trenches and among 'innocent' civilians left a generation 'scorched in mind and character'. Not only did the extraordinary circumstances of suffering elicit extraordinary responses, such as that of Eglantyne Jebb, but the mobilization of voluntary resources for relief reached a phenomenal level. The war reached into people's hearts and minds in a way that helped to reshape social attitudes. Among all the other things the war did, it also launched the careers of a whole generation of people who carried the banner of international co-operation forward, through the Depression and a second world war, to the birth of a United Nations and beyond.

At the outset of the war, the Red Cross began to run its by-now familiar field hospitals for the care of sick and wounded combatants. But it soon became clear that medical help for wounded soldiers paled into insignificance beside the relief needs of the civilians in occupied territory. The British and French blockaded Channel and North Sea ports, shutting off all imports of food into Germany and Belgium. Within a month, the normally-thriving Belgian population of 7·5 million was reduced to hunger and destitution. A new kind of international humanitarian effort was needed: the relief of a civilian population in time of war, through the mediation of neutral parties.

Within a week of the alarm being sounded in the autumn of 1914, the Commission for Relief in Belgium (CRB), an unofficial private and philanthropic organization, was set up in London at the initiative of an American engineering magnate, Herbert Hoover. Inspired by his Quaker conscience and his passionate belief in the ideal of voluntary co-operation, Hoover used his influence with the US Ambassador and other neutral diplomats to negotiate an agreement with the warring parties. Food and relief supplies for the starving Belgian civilians could go through the blockade, as long as they were not diverted to the German occupation forces. The new chapter he opened in organizing international relief also led his own career up a ladder of public service and power which took him into the White House.

The task undertaken by the CRB was to acquire by purchase or by gift the thousands of tons of food, clothing and other supplies needed to sustain the Belgian people—and later the people of German-occupied northern France—and to assemble, transport, and distribute these supplies. Contingents of bright young men—one of them a Nebraskan, Maurice Pate, the future first Executive Director of Unicef—were recruited to act as Hoover's envoys, overseeing the distribution of relief through civilian committees and making sure that nothing was diverted to the occupying forces. The enterprise went relatively smoothly, and won the warm support of voluntary organizations and private individuals worldwide. Drawing upon Belgian government deposits abroad—as well as British, French and US loans, together with $52 million in private contributions—the CRB had dispensed supplies worth $1 billion by 1919.

If the achievements in Belgium were surprising, they were outmatched after the Armistice by the man who had now become the major domo of international relief, the 'food czar' himself. Hoover performed even more Herculean feats of organizing and executing international aid during 1919–22. Millions of people in central and eastern Europe were suffering from the worst famine in 300 years. The US had quantities of surplus agricultural produce which it was willing to send overseas. Hoover, who was simultaneously head of the US Food Administration, the US Grain Corporation, the American Relief Administration, and Director-General of relief in Europe for the Allied governments, turned the official American Relief Administration into a private charitable organization. Once more he enlisted the support of religious and humanitarian organizations, as well as his former CRB bright young men, including Maurice Pate, and began to buy and ship supplies to Germany, Austria, Poland, and Russia. The toll during these years from typhus epidemics, undernutrition, influenza, and all the pestilences of war, mounted above thirty million.

In 1920, Hoover estimated that between four and five million homeless and orphaned children faced imminent death from starvation. But if many died, millions were saved. Hundreds and thousands of children lined up daily to receive special rations of nutritionally fortifying milk and soup, nicknamed 'Hooveria'. It is ironic that Hoover's name similarly applied in the USA during the years of the Great Depression has such opposite connotations—'Hoovervilles': packing-case dwellings; 'Hoover blankets': old newspapers. In Europe, Hoover was known as a great humanitarian, not someone whose name was identified with distress. The soup kitchens established an enduring model for emergency relief. In parts of Europe, a generation of children grew up regarding Herbert Hoover as their saviour.

One of the outcomes of the new spirit of internationalism engendered by the first World War and enshrined in the Treaty of Versailles was the League of Nations. On its formation in 1919, the League became immediately caught up in the programmes of emergency relief needed in postwar Europe. In association with the Red Cross and many voluntary organizations, the League sent food and supplies to the victims of the terrible Russian famine of 1921–22, under the direction of Dr Fridtjof Nansen, the Norwegian explorer and politician, who later served the League as High Commissioner for Refugees. During the turmoil of the Russian civil war, not only was there widespread hunger and starvation, but troops and refugees infested with lice spread a great epidemic of typhus fever. At this time, no effective treatment existed. There were over twelve million cases, and at least one million people died.

In 1921, the fledgling health organization of the League took a leading role in preventing the epidemic from invading the rest of eastern Europe. A 'cordon sanitaire' from the Baltic to the Black Sea had been imposed, but could not be tightly enough sealed to contain the outbreak. The situation demanded closer co-operation between the countries affected.

The chief medical official of the League's health secretariat was a Polish doctor and epidemiologist, Ludwik Rajchman. Rajchman managed to negotiate a sanitary convention between Russia and Poland which was widely regarded as the turning point in the fight to prevent typhus engulfing the whole of Europe.

At a conference in Warsaw in 1922, all the European countries threatened by epidemics, whether League members or not, agreed to pool epidemiological intelligence. This was an important precedent, not only for international action in the field of health, but also for other areas where the sharing of scientific knowledge or human experience was of mutual benefit to all Mankind. Under Rajchman's brilliant and active leadership, the health secretariat organized international commissions and conferences on common health problems; solicited the financial support of such organizations as the Rockefeller Foundation; advised certain countries, notably China, on how to run public health services; and established a skeleton of international order in disease control.

These solid achievements by the League were eclipsed by its failures in political and economic affairs. Its performance was flawed from the start by the refusal of the US, and the long reluctance of Russia or Germany, to join it. Despite its inability to contain the repudiation of treaties and the acts of aggression of its members, the League was nevertheless more than just a symbol of a new tide in the affairs of men. Although the League had lost most of its prestige by 1939 when the outbreak of European hostilities sounded its death knell, it had provided a nursery where governments took their first hesitant steps towards trying to put in place an international safety net under Mankind.

In humanitarian and welfare affairs—the least obviously contentious of international activities—the League had done well. Dr Nansen had been a distinguished Commissioner for Refugees; Rajchman an outstanding pioneer of international public health; some of the League's institutions were merely put into mothballs for the war, awaiting a future in the international arrangements of the postwar world.

Although much of the influence the League had tried to bring to bear on economic and social questions was still-born during its lifetime, during its final days Viscount Bruce of Melbourne, a former Prime Minister of Australia, delivered a report distilling twenty years of its experience and proposing the creation of a new kind of international regulatory mechanism. Six years later, this system came to life as the United Nations Economic and Social Council.

Besides the League, other forces were at work between the two world wars shaping and refining the twentieth century's humanitarian conscience. After the first World War, no crisis, no invasion, no aggression between the countries of a still-colonial world took place without eliciting a reaction from the forces of modern humanitarianism. Voluntary organizations ran soup kitchens and shelters for the victims of the Great Depression. Their inability to cope with the underlying causes of such widespread social distress eventually gave way to Franklin D. Roosevelt's New Deal in the US—and in Britain and elsewhere to economic interventionism and the welfare state advocated by John Maynard Keynes and other revisionist thinkers. Humanitarian effort spilled over into public service, and public service now began to be seen as the service that governments were expected to provide. Overseas, the voluntary organizations, and many of the heroes of postwar European famine relief, went off to rescue victims of the Spanish Civil War. Or they raised funds for the settlement of Jews in Palestine. Or they promoted medicine and education in the countries of the Far East. While the storm clouds gathered over Europe, protest against totalitarianism and militarism was closely linked with a kindling of spirit in the humanitarian community.

Then came the second World War. Its destructive force was unlike anything ever seen before. Even the sufferings of the first World War belonged to a different order and another scale. As early as August 1940, Winston Churchill in the British House of Commons recognized that exceptional arrangements would be needed to bring relief to the populations of Axis countries after the war was won. The last world war had given an indication of the hunger, misery, and pestilence to be expected; but the price of victory in this one would be far more pervasive and devastating of civilian life. On the day of their liberation, millions of people would be hungry, sick, and homeless; not only emergency relief, but rehabilitation of their homes, communities, and countries would be needed.

On 9 November 1943, at a time when the term 'united nations' was still being used to describe the alliance between the USA, USSR, and Britain, the United Nations Relief and Rehabilitation Administration—UNRRA— was set up in Washington with a membership of over forty countries and dominions. UNRRA was the organization which would stand ready to move in behind the Allied armies and begin the task of mopping up the detritus of war. No-one had envisaged, not even Churchill, quite what that task would actually encompass.

As the Allied armies moved across continental Europe in 1944 and the scale of devastation began to unfold, UNRRA began to shoulder the largest and most complex international relief effort ever mounted. Cities had been levelled. Industrial plant lay in ruins. Trade was at a standstill. Agriculture and food production were in disarray. Educational and health services had collapsed. Millions of people had been uprooted from their homes and had nowhere to go and nothing to live on. All basic commodities—food, fuel, clothes, medicines—were in critically short supply. Some countries had endured such sustained and systematic devastation that their whole economic and social fabric lay in tatters and somehow had to be restored. And in many of these, the ranks of those in managerial and professional occupations—those whose leadership was now needed to restore government, administration, manufacture, trade, transport systems and services— had been drastically, even deliberately, thinned.

Infinitely more shocking and incomprehensible than the physical damage—the worst of which was carried out by scorched earth policies and Allied bombing—was the scale of the human disaster. That around twenty million people had been displaced by the war, either because they had fled their homes or had been forcibly taken away to a destination outside their country, was known long before the war ended. But what, in stark reality, this might turn out to mean had not been understood. As the armies of liberation moved into Europe, the deepest evils of a system of terror, torture, and extermination were discovered by the opening of the prison camps and the revelations about what had gone on inside them. Apart from the atrocities visited on slave labourers and war prisoners, the world understood for the first time that a systematic attempt had been made to extinguish forever the Jews of Europe. Five or six million people had perished. The closing of the camps, the succour of those found there still clinging precariously to life, the attempt to identify family members and bring relatives together again, the care of orphans and the homeless, the repatriation of around 8·5 million displaced people . . . this was the task assigned to UNRRA, with vital help from voluntary organizations. For many of the personnel involved, dealing with this tragic residue of the war was among the most heartbreaking experiences of their lives.

Care of those reduced by war to a state of almost indescribable misery was only one part of UNRRA's mission. A larger and even more complex task was to bring in enough food and emergency supplies to fan the embers of economic and social life until national efforts for self-help and reconstruction could take over. Exactly when that critical moment was reached was a matter of fine judgement, and one that could — and did — quickly run foul of national sensitivities. Herbert Lehman, ex-Governor of New York and UNRRA's first Director-General, delicately explained the approach: 'Nations no less than individuals desire to live in dignity and self-respect. They wish to become self-reliant members of the world community. To this end they seek the opportunity to work, to produce, to trade. They turn to us with no idea of long-continuing relief . . . they merely ask for our help in order that they may overcome a dire national emergency'.

Although the US was the main reservoir of funds and supplies, UNRRA was not intended to be a charitable operation run by the victors for the victims of war. It was a genuine international partnership, in which even countries which received its help provided whatever they could spare in surplus foodstuffs or commodities for the relief of others. The guiding principle of the financial plan was that countries which had not been invaded would contribute one per cent of national income: 'to each according to their needs; from each according to their resources'. In this respect, UNRRA set a new pattern in mechanisms for international humanitarian effort.

During the three and a half years of its life, UNRRA provided essential relief and rehabilitation supplies to around twenty-five countries, including China, the Philippines, Korea, Ethiopia, and the countries of central and eastern Europe. In doing so, it helped in small or large measure the lives of several hundred million people. In 1945 and 1946, the peak period of operations, UNRRA had 15,000 international staff and 35,000 local employees on its own pay-roll, and spent nearly $4 billion on aid.

One of the first priorities was to rebuild communications and transport systems so that relief could be distributed. Trucks, locomotives and rolling stock, boats, horses and mules poured out of UNRRA cargo holds into European ports. During the winter of 1945–46, before the first postwar harvest was in, UNRRA supplies of fats and cereals kept millions of people alive. Seed, fertilizer and agricultural machinery arrived to help revive food production. Imported cattle and livestock restocked slaughtered herds. Raw materials and tools helped local industries to re-start. During 1945 and 1946, UNRRA procured and moved twenty million tons of supplies into Europe, a larger amount than the US Army's total wartime shipments across the Atlantic.

But despite this achievement, UNRRA met constant criticism in the US. In 1944 and early 1945, this vast international apparatus to run a massive supply and recovery operation had been very quickly assembled. In the chaos of postwar Europe and Asia—a chaos whose full dimensions were never fully appreciated by many US policy-makers—UNRRA's efforts were bound to come occasionally unstuck, even though Lehman's Deputy Director, Commander Robert Jackson—an Australian who had distinguished himself in the wartime British forces running supply operations in the Middle-Eastern theatre—was widely regarded as an organizational genius. Lehman's own reputation was above reproach. Yet public and official opprobrium on the American side of the Atlantic dogged UNRRA with constant accusations of mismanagement, both among its own officials and among the officials of governments who received UNRRA goods. Some stemmed from misunderstanding of the Keynesian principle governing UNRRA operations: a country receiving goods free of charge was entitled to sell them on the market to accumulate resources for other UNRRA-approved rehabilitation projects. No doubt the system did leave room for abuse; some UNRRA goods found their way onto a black market awash with army surplus. This and other anomalies made little serious difference to national recovery, but certainly fuelled bad publicity, and UNRRA proved to be not adept at defending itself from attack.

Herbert Lehman blamed its poor reputation on the governments of member countries who failed to arouse public applause. In the US, little effort was made initially to broadcast the organization's good work for fear of the charge that it was taking bread out of American mouths. Xenophobia and the deepening political distrust between East and West exacerbated the problem; most of UNRRA's European clients were in the eastern countries, and nearly three-quarters of what they were receiving came from the US.

UNRRA was always intended to have a temporary life, to exist for no longer than whatever period of time it took for Europe and Asia to be set on the path to full-scale recovery. But few imagined that UNRRA's life would be abruptly and prematurely curtailed before that period had run its course. By the end of 1945, the widening rift between the wartime allies was already beginning to alter the dynamics of postwar recovery. As UNRRA failed to shake off its US critics, the Truman Administration, buttoning up against the early chills of the Cold War, began to see its operations in an exclusively negative light. By early 1946, the writing was already on the wall. The iron curtain which Churchill described as descending on Europe in his speech at Fulton, Missouri, in March 1946 was about to ring down on UNRRA relief. Commander Jackson and other senior UNRRA officials began to speed up their preparations for handing on essential functions—agricultural rehabilitation, support to medical and educational institutions, care for the displaced and the refugees, safeguards for children—to other incipient organizations of the new United Nations. On 25 June 1946, a detailed aide-memoire was sent to all the member governments of UNRRA describing the plans for this transferral. Having pointed out the need for a continuity in all operations, the aide-memoire stated: 'In considering future needs it is earnestly hoped that the United Nations will include arrangements which will enable effective child feeding to be continued in all the countries in which UNRRA has been operating'. Here was UNRRA's avowal that, whatever else happened, the children of Europe must not be forgotten.

Meanwhile, President Truman decided on a course of action which would shift the emphasis in postwar relief away from an impartial, international context and place it more closely under an all-American wing. The 1945 European harvest had been extremely thin, and by the early spring of 1946, alarmists were describing 800 million people around the world as threatened by famine. Truman, the Democrat, therefore invited the man he said knew more than anyone about feeding nations to undertake an advisory mission on his behalf: Herbert Hoover, the Republican ex-President and 'food czar' of days gone by.

Hoover was an outspoken critic of UNRRA and was itching for a chance of public service. His life-long enmity with President Roosevelt, the Democrat who had driven him from the White House in 1933, had denied him any recent opportunity to put his talents for organizing wartime relief at the disposal of the US Administration. He gladly accepted Truman's request.

Herbert Hoover, now seventy-three years old, flew off on a world tour to assess global food supplies and to see how surpluses from the Americas and Asia might be deployed. The 50,000-mile tour of thirty-eight countries in eighty-two days was an extraordinary feat, given the discomforts of travel at the time. In an unpressurized plane he landed at Paris, Rome, Berlin, Quito, Tokyo, Warsaw, Caracas, London, Prague, Delhi, Ottawa, Cairo, on a whirlwind schedule. Accompanying him was a handful of aides, veterans of Belgian relief and the ARA famine and epidemic missions of the early 1920s. Among them was Maurice Pate, still one of his devoted protégés, who was assigned to assess the condition of children. Hoover's mission had little in common with the typical UNRRA operation. Everywhere the grand old man descended from the skies there were banquets and receptions, kings and presidents, prime ministers and ambassadors, lined up to discuss food shortage and national destitution with the distinguished representative of the US President. From the plane, a secretary sent daily reports back to Washington, describing the miseries of ration centres where mothers and children lined up in rags, babies wrapped in newspapers instead of blankets, food riots, medical shortages, malnutrition. All were issued to the press: a main part of the mission's purpose was to unlock the frozen conscience of North America and regain public support for postwar relief. In this, the mission was an unqualified success.

Everywhere, Hoover made speeches. On the radio, at meetings, to the press, he called for an all-out campaign against famine. He wanted people in the US to self-ration themselves—the average American was currently eating 3500 calories a day—so that food could be given to others. 'The first expression of famine is to be found among the children', he told an audience in London on 5 April. 'From the Russian frontier to the Channel, there are today 20 millions of children who are not only badly under-nourished, but steadily developing tuberculosis, rickets, and anaemia. If Europe is to have a future, something must be done about these children. . . . (They) will grow up with stunted bodies and distorted minds (and) furnish more malevolents in the world.' For malevolents, Hoover meant totalitarian warmongers, fascist and communist alike. He recalled how he organized meals for millions of hungry children after the last world war and regretted that an organization had not been set up then to carry on with the task. As the days went by he began to develop this theme.

On 19 May, he spoke to the American people from Chicago. This was vintage Hoover, a noble appeal to the voluntary spirit, and his words echoed through Unicef's literature for years. 'Of the Four Horsemen of the Apocalypse, the one named War has gone. But Famine, Pestilence and Death are still charging over the world. Hunger is a silent visitor who comes like a shadow. He sits beside every anxious mother three times a day. He brings not alone suffering and sorrow, but fear and terror. He carries disorder and the paralysis of government. He is more destructive than armies; not only in human life, but in morale. All of the values of right living melt before his invasion and every gain of civilization crumbles. But we can save these people from the worst—if we will.'

A few days later, he addressed the new UN Food and Agricultural Organization in Washington. He called upon the UN to supply every underfed child with an extra daily meal of 500 restorative calories. He told the conference that this was the most important reconstruction effort in the world, and that if governments working together wanted to bring peace and order, food and children was where they should start. He also began to promote his idea in the US State Department and Congress, and on the travels he continued to undertake. He tried to enlist Argentina's General Juan Peron and the First Lady, Eva. He did enlist Prime Minister Mackenzie King of Canada who assured Hoover that he would instruct his representatives at the UN to support any such proposal.

When the Hoover food survey mission was announced, many UNRRA officials were dismayed. However useful the publicity of Europe's plight might be, it was clearly not going to be useful to UNRRA's continuing efforts to relieve it. Commander Jackson, who visited Hoover in his suite in the Waldorf Towers both before and after the mission, was sceptical that a whistle-stop survey could reveal more about the problems facing Europe than the UNRRA mission chiefs had already reported; he was bound, however, to live with the mission and its political implications. Herbert Lehman did not feel the same way. For him the political implications were more personally significant: he was a Democrat, Hoover a Republican. He resigned as UNRRA's Director-General, disheartened by the turn US policies had taken. His place was taken by Fiorello LaGuardia, former Mayor of New York City.

LaGuardia, who took up his appointment anticipating the quick acceleration of UNRRA's end, was horrified to discover the depth of the trauma from which Europe was only beginning to emerge. A passionate man, his tour of war-torn countries on the far side of the Atlantic convinced him that he had been thoroughly misled about the desirability of UNRRA's demise. From mid-1946, he did his best to prolong UNRRA's life. Not only did he recognize that much of Europe was still in desperate need of help, but that the death of UNRRA could only exacerbate Cold War tensions. He was already seriously ill, and his particular brand of fire-and-brimstone anger exhausted him to no avail. It was already too late. The US Administration had made its decision.

Simultaneously, UNRRA was moving ahead with plans to transfer its functions to other organizations within the United Nations. The Food and Agriculture Organization had already been established in October 1945, and plans were already far advanced for the establishment of Unesco—the United Nations Educational, Scientific, and Cultural Organization. By resolution of the first UN General Assembly, the International Refugee Organization had been set up in February 1946, to take over where UNRRA would leave off.

UNRRA had originally taken over the functions of the League of Nations' defunct health section; in July 1946, an 'interim commission' of the new World Health Organization was set up while technical and political problems over the shape and mandate of the permanent international health body were resolved. But at this point, nothing clearly guaranteed the continued feeding and medical care of the children of Europe—children whose plight daily confronted many a UNRRA official and epitomized the continuing needs of war-shocked Europe. Children, always, are most vulnerable to any sudden new calamity.

Commander Jackson believed that a too-abrupt termination of UNRRA's operations might endanger the benefit so far achieved and plunge people and countries back into the state of desperation in which the organization had found them. The precarious state of children's well-being bore visible witness to this risk, as the aide-memoire of the previous June had pointed out.

The timetable of UNRRA's demise was finally settled at its fifth Council session in August 1946. Shortly before it took place, Commander Jackson flew around the world to muster last-ditch support for a new round of financial commitments and a stay of execution. Most of the countries receiving UNRRA aid were desperate that the supplies should continue: conditions were still extremely grim. Having gained the support of almost every other member UNRRA state, the British government proved the stumbling block. Clement Attlee's government was only prepared to support UNRRA if, by doing so, it did not interfere with a forthcoming US loan of $3·75 billion. It did.

The UNRRA Council delegates from nearly fifty member states assembled in Geneva in the old League of Nations headquarters, requisitioned by the UN just in time to provide a setting for another doomed venture in international co-operation. LaGuardia presided. Unhappily, he stated that UNRRA's emergency task was over, although the needs in Europe and Asia continued. He described plans for the procurement and transhipment of supplies to complete the programme, outlined the preliminaries of UNRRA's demobilization, and asked to be relieved of his duties. William L. Clayton, the US delegate, then informed the Council that the US Administration believed that UNRRA was no longer needed. At the moment of their liberation, certain countries had not had the means to sustain themselves; most now did. Those governments still in difficulties could obtain loans on concessionary terms from friendly countries. Here, nine months before the Marshall Plan was first proposed, was the new US approach to post-war recovery.

The US had provided over seventy per cent of UNRRA's income; with the UK and Canada, the joint proportion amounted to over ninety per cent. If the US was determined, and the UK and Canada followed suit, the end of UNRRA was a *fait accompli*. Many delegates were appalled at the news and pleaded their unreadiness to manage without UNRRA assistance. They were not much reassured to hear that other UN bodies would be at their disposal: many were still in their infancy or not yet born. Aake Ording, the Norwegian delegate, made a plea that a last, more modest, round of contributions be made to fill the time gap between the end of UNRRA and the readiness of other UN bodies to assume its programmes. He spoke eloquently of the children who would be unfed and medically untreated in the coming months. The US and its supporters were not to be moved.

The meeting turned to the business of wrapping up UNRRA's affairs. A series of resolutions based upon the aide memoire sent out in June designated the inheritors of UNRRA's vital functions: health to the World Health Organization or its Interim Commission; displaced people to the new International Refugee Organization; agriculture to the FAO; other functions to the UN itself or bodies responsible to its Economic and Social Council. Among them resolution number 103, which signalled a determination that UNRRA's feeding programmes for children should go on, and that funds left in the UNRRA account at the end of the year—when the rest of the supplies operation closed down—be used to finance this special emergency venture for children. The resolution stated that 'such assets as . . . may be available after completion of the work of UNRRA shall be utilized for the benefit of children and adolescents; that such purpose might effectively and appropriately be served by the creation of an International Children's Fund'.

Fiorello LaGuardia, always an enthusiastic supporter of children's causes, was already deeply committed along with Jackson and many members of UNRRA's staff; so in his personal capacity was Philip Noel-Baker, the UK representative, a veteran of 1921–22 famine relief in Russia; George Davidson, the Canadian delegate, along with some others, felt that such a proposal upset the tidy UN organizational pattern. But they conceded to the mood of the moment and the intense lobbying effort carried on in support of the resolution by Ludwik Rajchman, the Polish delegate to the UNRRA Council.

Thus, the first formal move within a United Nations context had been made towards establishing a special organization for children. A number of factors and a number of powerful individuals favoured the idea. But it took more than their goodwill to bring it into being. It took, first, legislative action; second, financial support; third, executive leadership which could transform an idea into a practical reality. The person who relentlessly pursued all three was Ludwik Rajchman, the extraordinary and brilliant figure who before the war had headed the League of Nations health secretariat.

When hostilities broke out in Europe, Rajchman had left the crumbling edifice of the League of Nations to help his Polish countrymen on the run from Hitler's armies. At first he went to France; when France fell, he went to Washington, where he represented Poland on certain diplomatic and US Administration circuits. He naturally took a close interest in the conferences at which the new mechanisms for international co-operation in the postwar world were designed: Bretton Woods, Dumbarton Oaks, San Francisco; and he represented Poland at all the UNRRA Council meetings.

A few weeks before the fifth UNRRA Council in Geneva in August 1946, the International Health Conference took place in New York and gave birth to the Interim Commission of WHO. For Ludwik Rajchman personally, the outcome of this conference had been a bitter disappointment. Rajchman had given his career to the cause of international public health. He had earned a high reputation as a medical visionary, was held in awe among peers at the Rockefeller Foundation and other prestigious institutions, and had almost unparalleled expertise in the international politics of health affairs. Quite understandably, he had hoped to play a leading role in the UN organization due to inherit the mantle of his old League of Nations operation in Geneva. But he had discovered that his services would not be required.

Rajchman was in the forefront of those who believed in social medicine, who wanted to apply knowledge about bacteriology and epidemiology to the control of diseases among society at large. He was also an enthusiast for incorporating child nutrition and maternal care into regular medical practice—ideas which were still viewed as revolutionary by more conservative, clinically-oriented members of the health profession. During the course of his career, Rajchman's views and his thrusting operational style had not endeared him in every quarter: he was too much of a pusher and a doer. Those who wished to discredit him used his nationality and the political climate of the time against him, branding him as a doctrinaire left winger. As a key figure in WHO, Rajchman was unpalatable to the USA. Dr Thomas Parran, Surgeon-General of the US Public Health Service and President of the International Health Conference, was opposed to Rajchman's involvement and made sure he was rejected.

The man chosen to head the WHO Interim Commission, and who became the first Director-General of WHO in 1948, was Dr Brock Chisholm. Chisholm was Canadian.

If Rajchman could not put his long years of international service at the disposal of the new UN health organization, at least he could put them at the disposal of children. The well-being of children had first and foremost to do with their health and nutrition; an international children's fund within the UN system would have to be involved in public health. In the autumn of 1946 Rajchman invested a great deal of energy in the pursuit of a UN 'ICEF'. In so doing, he played a vital role in bringing the organization into existence and shaping its early years. For Rajchman, the needs of children became as important a cause as public health had previously been; and he never drew any very definite line between the two. This did not endear him to some of the senior people in WHO Interim Commission, which during the next few years looked upon Rajchman's 'ICEF' exploits with deep mistrust.

The UNRRA resolution to create an international children's fund was as yet no more than a statement of pious intent. A committee was set up to put flesh on its bones. On 30 September, its suggestions came before the Economic and Social Council (ECOSOC). 'Politics and international difference took a rare holiday here today', reported the *New York Times* from Lake Success, 'as the delegates vied with each other in eloquent and unanimous support of an international children's fund'.

Fiorello LaGuardia was a leading champion. 'I am keeping an eye on the final phase of UNRRA to see that there is something left in the till when we close shop', he assured the delegates. He had earmarked a $550,000 donation and would 'hand it over the minute this new organization for children is given life'. ECOSOC invited the UN Secretary-General to present detailed proposals to the General Assembly. In October, the Committee on Social and Humanitarian Affairs—the Third Committee of the General Assembly—set up a subcommittee of delegates from Europe, the USSR, the US, China and Brazil to draft the proposal which would go before the full meeting of the Assembly in December.

In all these tortuous and bureaucratic procedures, Rajchman was the leading player. He was the rapporteur, and essentially the executive secretary, of this international committee responsible for elaborating the fund's mandate and operating procedures. Not surprisingly, therefore, they were largely his work. He also worked out the strategy for making them internationally palatable. Here, he exercised his lobbying skill, which combined endless consultation with the accumulation of allies. He visited Washington frequently and made every effort to involve the US Administration as closely as possible. If he could manage to co-opt the State Department into drafting the resolutions which had to navigate various UN committees and assemblies, US support would be guaranteed. Both in political and financial terms, that support was critical. Support for an 'ICEF' at the United Nations was also taken up enthusiastically and championed in Washington by some of the voluntary organizations which had been active in postwar relief under the UNRRA umbrella.

As the weeks went by, the support of the US Administration became increasingly crucial. Rajchman began to fear that the residual assets of UNRRA—on which the children's fund was not the only UN claimant—would offer a slim financial base for meeting the needs of twenty million children, the number in need in Europe alone.

Earlier in the year, $100 million had not seemed fanciful. Now it seemed possible that UNRRA might expire with considerably less. Even if there was something substantial left, the accounts might take years to wind up, and in what proportions the inheritance would be divided between WHO IC, the refugee organization, and the children's fund was uncertain. Rajchman was thinking in terms not of millions, but of hundreds of millions, of dollars. There was no other possible source than the US government. But the people at the State Department were careful to make no commitments to Rajchman as to how large a contribution they might recommend—or if indeed they would recommend one at all. They did, of course, appreciate that the fact of any 'ICEF' ultimately depended on the support of the US Congress and Administration. At this moment in history, when most other potential government supporters were trying to recover from the wounds of war, this was no more than a fact of life for any new mechanism of international co-operation trying to struggle into existence.

Gradually, opinions about the scope of the children's fund and its terms of reference began to coalesce. Like Rajchman, US State Department officials believed that it must consist of something more than the soup kitchen for children, designed according to the Hoover model. Nutrients were important, but children's needs did not begin and end with a reasonably full stomach. Ideas about the range of children's needs had considerably advanced during the first half of the twentieth century, courtesy of advances in medical, psychological, and educational science.

Within the US, a federal agency for children—the Children's Bureau—had been set up as early as 1912 to act as an advisory body on legislation and government policy on all matters concerning children's well-being. The current director of the Bureau, Katherine Lenroot, had frequently served as a US representative in international conferences on children's issues. Now her views were sought on the establishment of an equivalent international body for children within the new mechanisms of United Nations co-operation. She became a keen advocate and an important influence. Many of the ideas incorporated into the resolution for the creation of the 'ICEF' derived from the Children's Bureau expertise. The abandoned child and the child suffering from emotional disturbance must not be ignored; thorough surveys of the extent and nature of childhood nutrition and health should be envisaged; support to mothers was critical.

One of the young State Department officials who spent much energy on the paperwork was Jack Charnow; he found the experience useful when he joined Unicef's staff the following year.

On 7 December 1946, the final proposals for the new fund came before the General Assembly. They reflected concern with children both in Europe and Asia; the preamble was an eloquent statement of why the organization was needed: 'The children of Europe and China were not only deprived of food for several cruel years but lived in a state of constant terror, witness to massacres of the civilians, to horrors of scientific warfare and exposed to progressive lowering of standards of social conduct. The urgent problem facing the United Nations is how to ensure the survival of these children ... With the hope of the world resting on the coming generation, the problem of caring for children is international in scope and its solution must be found on an international basis'. It was proposed that, in every country where children were hungry, the government should set a target of providing 700 extra calories to all children in schools, orphanages, clinics, hospitals, and day-care centres. Each country would have to develop its own overall plan to do this, co-ordinating the existing work of local authorities and voluntary agencies. Their work at present . . . 'only touches the fringe of the problem, hence the necessity for an International Emergency Fund'. The years 1947 to 1950 would be the critical period: 'Upon the success of the international assistance proposed will depend to a large degree the future of the children of Europe, and of China, and thus the future of the world'.

On 11 December the UN General Assembly unanimously established the UN International Children's Emergency Fund or Unicef by adopting resolution 57(I). The mandate this resolution conferred on Unicef was deliberately broad. For the sake of flexibility, the broader the better. It spoke of 'children's rehabilitation' and 'child health purposes generally'— terms vague enough to legitimize almost anything the organization wanted to do. It could receive voluntary contributions from any source, and spend them on virtually any kind of supplies, technical assistance, or services, as long as it monitored their 'proper utilization and distribution'—a conscious effort to keep Unicef free of the criticisms levelled at UNRRA. A very important provision laid down that all assistance should be given 'on the basis of need, without discrimination because of race, creed, nationality, status, or political belief'. No limits should be set on which children might be eligible for help: ex-enemy children were, therefore, explicitly included, as were children in any and every part of the world.

The administration of the Children's Fund was to be carried out by an Executive Director according to policies determined by its Executive Board. Members of the Board would be chosen by ECOSOC from among the UN member governments, but nonmember states could be included. The twenty-five members of the Executive Board were named in the resolution; they included the US, the USSR, Australia, Brazil, Britain, Canada, China, France, Poland, Sweden, and Yugoslavia. Switzerland—a nonmember state—was added soon afterwards. An Executive Director would be appointed by the UN Secretary-General in consultation with the Executive Board. Staff and facilities would also be provided by the UN secretariat, and Unicef was expected to draw on the services of the specialized agencies, in particular WHO, to keep separate budget and personnel requirements to a minimum.

The Unicef Board held its first meeting a week later on 19 December, and elected Ludwik Rajchman as its Chairman. The first item on Rajchman's agenda was the appointment of the Executive Director. He had long had a candidate in mind.

Months before, Rajchman had decided who he wanted to occupy the chief executive slot at Unicef. His own experience had shown how easily any international organization or its leadership could be jeopardized by the political currents of the Cold War. Storms were ahead, and the best insurance against their destruction was a leadership which would draw no opposition from the US and its Western allies. For preference, the Executive Director should be an American with established Republican sympathies. Political positions over the past half century showed that the risk of a US Administration retreating into the old isolationist stance emanated from the Republican rather than the Democratic camp. The more Americans of Republican sympathy there were in senior UN positions, the less likely the US Administration was of withdrawing its co-operation from the new UN machinery.

Among the US candidates for Unicef's leadership, Herbert Hoover's stable of aides with their experience of famine relief in Europe were among the most striking; moreover, as Hoover protéges, they were decidedly Republican. One of them was a special acquaintance of Rajchman.

Maurice Pate, who had first served on Hoover's staff in Belgium, had spent thirteen years in Poland between the wars. During 1939–45 he had been active in Polish relief in Washington, in which capacity Rajchman had come to know him. The idea of Pate at the head of Unicef appealed to Rajchman. Pate had played no part in the various preparatory committees and conferences out of which the UN and its component parts were born; unlike Rajchman, he had no 'enemies' on the circuit.

While he was visiting New York in September 1946, Pate was sounded out by Rajchman, both on his views about an 'ICEF' and on his attitude towards becoming its chief executive. Before giving Rajchman an answer, Pate consulted the man he always called the 'Chief'. Hoover thoroughly approved, and from that point onwards both Pate and—by association—the 'Chief' were members of Rajchman's informal circle of advisers. When Rajchman received's Pate's provisional assent that his name be put forward, he proceeded to lobby Trygve Lie, the UN Secretary-General, and enlist the support of friends in the UN delegations.

The only resistance came from the US Administration. Pate, a business-man from the Midwest, was not on any obvious list for State Department selection as their man for the leadership of a UN organization. Pate seemed too limited, too Hoover-esque, good at logistics and knowledgeable about child-feeding, but hardly the modern internationalist. Eleanor Roosevelt, chief US representative at the UN for social and humanitarian questions and an 'ICEF' supporter, thought that he was too old; his association with Hoover cannot have been much of an attraction in her eyes. Eventually, mainly due to Rajchman's lobbying, opposition to Pate's appointment gave way before the support his name mustered from other UN delegates. This hardly seemed an important diplomatic issue to the US Administration, particularly as the Children's Fund would remain a very insignificant body for the duration of what was expected to be its limited life. A more helpful assessment could not have been made; Maurice Pate turned out to be a choice of genius.

Maurice Pate received his letter of appointment from Trygve Lie on 8 January 1947. The $550,000 from UNRRA that LaGuardia had promised was handed over, and arrangements were also made for Unicef to employ the services of some of the staff whose jobs at UNRRA were coming to an end. The immediate task was to start pressing Washington for financial support on the generous scale that he and Rajchman regarded as essential. The last shipments of UNRRA food were due to arrive in Europe in March. There must be a minimal pause before Unicef cargoes arrived to take their place.

Within a few days of his assumption of duties, Maurice Pate wrote to General George C. Marshall, then Secretary of State, and asked for $100 million towards the costs of 'a glass of milk and some fat to be spread on bread for six million hungry children in Europe and China'.

Unicef, the special UN effort for children, was launched.

Main sources

The Dynamics of International Organization by Philip E. Jacob, Alexine L. Atherton, Arthur M. Wallenstein; The Dorsey Press, 1972.

'International Union for Child Welfare, 50 years'; Special Edition of the International Child Welfare Review; No. 7, June 1970.

A History of the League of Nations by F. P. Walters, former Deputy Secretary-General of the League of Nations; published under the auspices of the Royal Institute of International Affairs; OUP, 1952.

UNRRA, The History of the United Nations Relief and Rehabilitation Administration, George Woodbridge, Columbia University Press, 1950; Vols I, II, III.

An Uncommon Man: The Triumph of Herbert Hoover by Richard Norton Smith, Simon & Schuster, 1984.

Interviews, memoirs, and papers of Sir Robert Jackson, Senior Deputy Director of UNRRA 1945–48.

Published obituaries and reminiscences of Dr Ludwik Rajchman; and interviews carried out for the Unicef History Project by Jack Charnow and Sherwin Moe, 1983–85.

Resolutions of the UN Committee on Social and Humanitarian Affairs; the UN Yearbook; Resolutions of the General Assembly; Unicef Executive Board documentation 1947–50, and summary records of discussions.

Some notes on trip with the Hoover Mission (March–June 1946); Maurice Pate, 1 August 1946; papers of Maurice Pate; unpublished memoir by Maurice Pate, 1958.

Department of State, US government: memoranda and position papers; Committee on Voluntary Foreign Aid and other State Department papers, 1946–47.

Chapter 2

Some Milk and Some Fat, on Bread . . .

Maurice Pate, a businessman with a humanitarian record of helping the victims of two world wars, was the perfect choice for Unicef's Executive Director. This was not because of his qualifications—which were more than adequate—but because he had something else: a remarkable quality of personality, an aura, a touch of something people could only describe as saintliness.

Herbert Hoover called him 'the most efficient human angel I have ever met'. Speaking of the UN system, Secretary-General Dag Hammarskjold once said: 'The work of Unicef is at the heart of the matter, and at the heart of Unicef is Maurice Pate'. Pate's height, his distinctive crest of silver-white hair, his gentle manners, and his slow, deliberate way of speaking helped implant a memorable impression. But the physical presence was only a part of what came across to colleagues and associates. The charisma was hard to define, and never apparently consciously exercised. But it was what people most noticed and remembered about Maurice Pate.

Pate was born in Nebraska in 1894, the first child of a Midwestern banker and businessman. Three of his six brothers and sisters died in infancy: one from polio, one from diphtheria, one from intestinal infection caused by drinking unpasteurized milk—a classic pattern of family loss in places where child health care standards as yet gained little from modern medical science. Pate was a keen and conscientious student, who discovered during his years at Princeton that while he was not marked out for the highest academic or intellectual distinction, he had a flair for business and for establishing the kind of associations with people which somehow made successful living a pleasant and straightforward proposition.

After graduation, he began work in a family concern in Iowa, but became restless when the first World War broke out. He wanted to sign up in the Canadian forces, but his father suggested that he seek service instead with Herbert Hoover's Belgian Relief Commission. He was young—twenty-two years old—and not fluent in French. But he managed to be signed on, and late in 1916, he was put in charge of food distribution in the Belgian county of Tournai. Here he received his first lesson in how to make an operation work by devolving responsibility onto other people, in this case local relief committees. This influenced his management style throughout his career. He also earned Hoover's personal notice and esteem. Typically for Pate, he credited the success of his work with the confidence the 'Chief' had placed in him, and this, too, became a model he tried to copy.

After the war, he again served Hoover in famine relief in Europe. He went to Poland for the American Relief Administration (ARA), where he organized feeding for more than a million children. In 1922, when the ARA disbanded, Pate decided to remain in Warsaw as a representative of various US banking and business firms. In 1927, he married Jadwiga Monkowska, the daughter of an old Polish landowning family. Pate stayed in Poland until 1935, and these thirteen years later had a profound effect on the rest of his life. By the mid-1930s events in Europe had become ominous, and Pate decided to return to the US. His wife did not accompany him, but he remained—at least in his mind—married to her until she died in 1960. Back home he led an unpretentious life as a bachelor, and continued to prosper.

In September 1939, when the German army invaded Poland, Pate went at once to Washington and volunteered his services to help the Polish people. With Hoover's backing, he became president of a private organization, the Commission for Polish Relief. In this context, he came to know Ludwik Rajchman. Another person who also became a lifelong friend at this time was Helenka Pantaleoni, a Polish-American deeply committed to women's and children's causes and who later became Pate's staunch associate.

Pate put to work the old Hoover combination of neutral ethics and efficiency, purchasing supplies and parleying with the German authorities to deliver them to the beleaguered Polish people. These efforts came abruptly to an end with the US entry into the war. Pate then joined the American Red Cross as director of relief to prisoners of war in Europe and Asia. This involved a large and complex programme of supplies purchase and shipment, via neutrals and through enemy lines; it saved the lives of many thousands of prisoners trapped in a disintegrating Germany. After the war was over, he joined Hoover's entourage for the grand old man's food survey on behalf of President Truman. By this stage he had already begun to resume his life as a businessman in the Midwest. He did not intend to continue a humanitarian career, unless the 'Chief' asked for his help in some other special tour of duty.

The request to head the 'ICEF' did not come from Hoover, but it meant serving an organization that his food-mission broadcasts had helped to create, and it received his keen endorsement. Pate did not envisage that the 'ICEF' would live longer than the few postwar emergency years; after the earlier war, the child feeding kitchens had closed down once life returned to normal. He therefore accepted what he saw as an urgent assignment, something which would keep him occupied for a while before he went back to his business life in the Midwest. He stipulated only one condition: there must be no discrimination against children of any nationality, least of all the 'ex-enemy'. In the spirit of the UN, all Unicef's founding fathers were thoroughly agreed on this point. He also insisted that he should have a clear line of authority from the UN Secretary-General Trygve Lie himself, and that he should be completely responsible for the choice of his own personnel and the direction of Unicef's activities. Lie assured him that the Executive Board was not intended to run the organization, but to meet occasionally and discuss policies and programmes.

Early in January 1947, Pate set up an office in Washington and hired a secretary at his own expense. He was relatively well-off and hesitant to take a personal salary; friends persuaded him to the contrary. He then began to put to use both his businessman's skills and his diplomatic ingenuity. Estimating what it would cost to feed the twenty to twenty-five million needy children in Europe, plus another thirty million in Asia, Pate and Rajchman initially thought in terms of an all-sources budget of $450 million: they were, it seemed, almost single-handedly taking on the task of saving the lives of an entire generation. That rather larger task than anything Unicef then, or since, could conceivably have managed to accomplish was an integral part of the whole process of European recovery, whose chief engine was shortly to become the Marshall Plan. In early 1947, it was still not easy to see that the role of private philanthropy had significantly changed in the new international order. Pate's and Rajchman's sense of urgency that the despatch of additional food supplies must not be delayed and that European children depended on Unicef, was very real. Pate spent much of his first few months trying to ensure that Unicef would be awarded a large contribution from the US Congress, and exploring other avenues of support in the belief that the balance of UNRRA residues could not possibly go as far as needs demanded.

Maurice Pate was the most modest of men, self-effacing almost to the point of obsession. He only ever admitted to having usefully brought two qualities to his leadership of Unicef: one was the ability to pick the right people for his staff; the other was his talent as a fund-raiser. Others would have cited his ability to make things happen, not because he was a mover and shaker in the Rajchman style, but because he slowly and inexorably pushed ahead without ever entertaining the notion that they could do anything else. If an obstacle, which to others might appear insuperable, appeared in his path, he simply neglected to notice it until it went away.

His negotiating style was similar; he was patient and gentle, but he seemed to have difficulty in hearing obstructive opposition. This was not contrived; it was part of that otherworldliness he possessed, innate rather than accomplished. Pate's ability to inspire support and financial generosity from individuals and governments alike was the most important factor in the creation of Unicef as an organization rather than as an idea.

His talent for attracting money was far from being an obvious attribute. With his slow, sometimes painfully slow, way of speaking, he did not have the usual kind of salesman's charisma. He did not have a flair for rhetoric nor for publicity, except of the solid and traditional kind. He credited his ability to his experience in business, which had given him a keen sense of financial values and helped him arrive at a formula for combining risk with caution. But there was more to it. Like his mentor the 'Chief', he believed in the self-evident moral duty of everyone who could to give a helping hand to those who were less fortunate. The way in which he projected this belief conveyed a conviction which few could resist. He did not indulge in populist slogans or intellectual arguments. He just behaved as though everyone else had the same beliefs and generous nature as his own. It was not naïve; it was utilitarian. It worked as well with statesmen as with school children. Even if he did not really think that everyone was an angel, he certainly believed that everyone had some capacity to be one, and his attitude towards people tended to make them want to try, at least while they were in his company.

Pate never forgot that Unicef was dependent on the goodwill of citizens and their governments. In early 1947, the government of the country of which he himself was a citizen was the only possible source of large infusions of financial aid; but as other countries recovered from the war, their governments and citizens might become generous. Pate's idea of how to build up Unicef's fortunes was very pragmatic. The organization should constantly be in the thick of action, and when the dust settled it should be judged on its achievements. If the results for children were convincing and cost-effective, Unicef's reputation would be its own best advertisement.

Pate set up an organization designed to take action, he unflinchingly took it even in circumstances which were uncomfortably close to the edge of its existing competence. He relied on carefully-chosen lieutenants, to whom he gave a very free rein. The organizational atmosphere he thought most conducive to success was that of a family, and his kindly and avuncular figure lent itself to the role of *pater familias*. He took a personal interest in all his staff, and he did the same with Executive Board delegates, political allies, and professional experts, placing great importance in cultivating close relationships with all those who were Unicef's actual or potential givers and takers.

Maurice Pate, who never became a father himself, was an honorary father of the world's children, and a friend to everyone who knew him. He was that rarest of human beings, someone of whom it could genuinely be said that he never had an enemy in his life.

Maurice Pate's feeling for the Polish people after his years in Warsaw, together with Rajchman's nationality, created a special relationship between

Unicef and Poland. Apart from the Ukraine, Poland had suffered longest and worst. Accompanying Hoover to Warsaw in March 1946, Pate had discovered at first hand what this had meant. He was deeply struck by the poverty visited on a country which held for him many associations of graceful living, solid warmth and family comfort. The evil unleashed on Poland, and on much of the European heartland, would require years of reconstruction, human and physical, to dispel.

Although then it was more than a year since the Allied armies had liberated Poland from Hitler's occupation, the people were still short of many basic essentials. During the war, six million Polish lives—almost a fifth of the population—had been lost. The savagery of the German occupation was a retaliation against the Polish people's refusal to co-operate with their invaders. Throughout the countryside, agriculture had been destroyed; cattle and herds had been slaughtered; horses led away; machinery smashed; and land ground under the heels of invading armies. Industrial plant was mostly wrecked or at a standstill. Hundreds of thousands of the country's professional and administrative classes had been systematic-ally murdered, or led away to concentration and forced-labour camps. Over one million children—the best specimens—were taken to Germany from towns and cities, and sent into special child camps for slavery. All uni-versities and medical schools had been forcibly closed; giving or taking educational instruction in this period of darkness had been made a crime punishable by death. By the end of the war, half the country's doctors were dead and the health services decimated. Infant death had soared, along with the spread of communicable disease. Hunger and exhaustion, and the crowding of fragmented families into camps and ghettoes had taken a heavy physical and psychological toll. After the Warsaw uprising had been put down in October 1944, the entire city had been razed to the ground. In Poland, Hitler's apocalyptic dream about what he would do to the world had been all but fulfilled: 'We shall leave an inheritance of ruins, stone heaps, rats, epidemics, starvation, and thereby western civilization will perish'.

In March 1946, Pate had discovered the children of Poland in a pitiful condition. 'The food of many poor families is little more than watery soup, carried from a nearby kitchen', he reported. 'In some parts of the country, families are living on potatoes. The women walk miles each day, begging and foraging for food.' Problems were not confined to diet. The destruction of housing meant that many families occupied buildings which constantly threatened to collapse. In ruined Warsaw, some were living underground in the sewers, and in cellars which were dark, damp and rat-infested. Everywhere were pale faces and undersized bodies. Clothing too was short. In winter, many children were too poorly clad to go out of doors, nor could they go to school for lack of shoes. Most tragic of all was the destruction of families. Among Poland's children and young people, more than one-seventh had lost one or both parents. The tremendous dis-locations of the years when family members were forcibly removed to the death camps was still pathetically in evidence. On the walls of abandoned buildings little messages fluttered: 'To So-and-So. Your grandmother is the only survivor. She is at So-and-So'.

As the war ended, UNRRA relief supplies arrived in Poland via the Black Sea. Altogether two million tons of supplies were imported into Poland before the end of 1946. Food—and trucks, locomotives, even horses for its distribution—helped stave off hunger at a critical period, and medical supplies prevented epidemics of typhus and typhoid. During 1946, the Polish authorities ran a supplementary feeding programme for over one million children and mothers on the basis of UNRRA rations.

At the end of that year, UNRRA folded up its operations. A few cargoes, delayed by Baltic ice, arrived in the spring of 1947. After this, the feeding programme closed down. In the early summer, a team from FAO went to Poland to carry out a survey of agricultural needs. So alarmed were they by the degree of chronic nutritional deficiency among the children that Sir John Boyd Orr, FAO's Director-General, wrote at once to Ludwik Rajchman with an appeal: 'There is an urgent need for immediate help for Polish children. Your organization is the only one I know which can act immediately'.

In the pre-television era, the full enormity of the wartime devastation not only in Poland, but in southern Italy, Germany, the Ukraine, and many other countries in eastern and central Europe was not fully appreciated, particularly in North America, either by the public or by administrators and policy-makers. UNRRA had released a film in 1946 called *Seeds of Destiny* to portray the misery endured by the children, and its brutalizing effect on their personalities. This film was too late to do anything to keep UNRRA in existence, but it was widely shown for fund-raising purposes by many of the voluntary organizations. It enabled them more than anything to send aid to war-torn Europe, and helped raise $200 million.

The film showed the thin bodies and white faces of children living in bombed-out buildings, sleeping in dank bunkers—the only shelter their homeless families could find against the terrible cold of the 1946–47 winter. The first two postwar harvests were a disaster everywhere; drought compounded the problems facing countries trying to reclaim battlefields from weeds—and trying to plant crops with little seed, less fertilizer, and no draught animals to help plough or reap. Food was only one of the problems visible everywhere. In southern Italy, young boys lived in caves and roved the streets like packs of wild creatures. In Czechoslovakian villages, children who had never had a proper pair of shoes or a warm coat ran barefoot in the winter cold. In parts of Germany, rubble and shell craters were the children's playgrounds. Every country had its orphanages overflowing with the victims of war, some of whom were maimed both physically and psychologically. The most makeshift arrangements were made to care for the sick; in every household, the sound of coughing might remorselessly herald another small tragedy.

During the spring of 1947, Maurice Pate began to assemble the first members of his Unicef team—many of whom brought valuable UNRRA experience with them—and to plan the shipment of food to the children of Europe. At this stage, he did not envisage that any elaborate organizational network would be required to support their delivery and use in the countries of destination. But he thought it would be useful if Alfred Davidson, previously UNRRA's legal counsel and now helping to set up the International Refugee Organization (IRO) in Geneva, opened up a small liaison office for Unicef in Paris. Davidson had larger ideas. He accepted Pate's invitation and immediately set about developing the strong Unicef network in Europe he believed the programmes would need, backed up by a Paris headquarters of some administrative and operational sophistication.

In many European countries, as in Poland, Greece, and Italy, Unicef was able to take over many of the existing UNRRA staff, as well as its office facilities, bank accounts, vehicles; even its stationery. But there were some countries, such as Bulgaria and Rumania, where UNRRA had not been operational, but whose children were also in serious need. Davidson negotiated agreements with governments all over Europe to prepare the way for the administration of Unicef supplies and new or resurrected feeding programmes. He also hired chiefs of mission, some of whom were destined to work in countries where conditions were becoming increasingly politically sensitive. Davidson also recruited some people of considerable prestige from Rajchman's network of old League of Nations contacts, as well as some of UNRRA's European staff. As his deputy, Davidson was fortunate to be able to use the services of one of Rajchman's long time associates, Dr Berislav Borcic.

Borcic was a Yugoslavian public health expert who had worked in China for the League of Nations during the 1930s and more recently as a senior UNRRA/WHO official. In 1948, at Unicef's request, he was seconded from WHO to give technical advice on medical programmes and liaise between the two organizations. He became an important Unicef figure, not least because in the early days he formed a bridge between WHO reservations about Rajchman's ambitions and his legitimate desire that Unicef become involved in programmes which would contribute some lasting benefit to children's well-being.

The immediate priority in summer 1947, however, was the poor nutritional condition of millions of European children. The food shortage thought to be most damaging for children was that of milk. Throughout Europe, war and occupation and their effects on farming life had depleted the number of milk cows and lowered their yields. In some countries, milk production had been lowered by as much as forty or fifty per cent. The first priority in restoring agricultural production were the staples: grain for bread and animal feed, and root crops such as potatoes. All the foods regarded by the best nutritional wisdom of the day as 'protective' of children's health—not only milk, but fat, meat, and other sources of protein and vitamin—were everywhere in short supply, and impoverished countries short of foreign exchange could not afford to import them.

At Unicef's request, an expert group of paediatricians and nutritionists from FAO and WHO met in July 1947 to offer advice on the prospective food shipments for children, the best and most economical ingredients, and how rations should be computed. They recommended that supplies should consist of animal protein, calcium and vitamins. One of the group, Dr Martha Eliot, Associate Chief of the US Children's Bureau, became Unicef's principal technical adviser for child feeding. Eliot travelled all over Europe to all the thirteen countries where Unicef was about to begin food deliveries, and her surveys of needs had a critical influence on the development of the local programmes.

The main ingredient was milk, whole and skim, in the form of powder, still a relatively recent food-processing technology; whole milk was for infants, and skim milk for pre-school and school children. As well as milk there was fat in the form of margarine, lard or coconut fat; vitamins A and D in the form of cod- and shark-liver oil; and small amounts of fish, meat, and cheese. These nutritionally rich ingredients were calculated in quantities of 250–300 calories per child per day. The receiving countries provided grains, potatoes, and vegetables from their own resources to combine with the protective foods in a supplementary meal which children ate at school, nursery, kindergarten, sanatorium, or summer camp. For small babies, whole milk rations were given out to their mothers at health clinics to take home.

At the end of August 1947, Unicef's first shipment of three million pounds of powdered milk left New York by sea for destinations in Austria, Greece, Poland, and Yugoslavia. Already, programmes had been approved by the Unicef Executive Board in these four countries and seven others: Albania, China, Czechoslovakia, Finland, France, Hungary, and Italy. Other shipments followed over the course of the next weeks. On 6 October the SS *Mark Hanna* from New York docked at Gdynia in the Baltic Sea to offload 450 tons of whole powdered milk for the children of Poland. A welcoming ceremony took place on the quay, which was attended by Unicef's Chief of Mission from Warsaw, Earl Bell, officials from various Polish ministries, and 800 school children. A Polish Councillor gave gracious thanks 'to the noble donors—the United Nations and the American people'. The children sang songs, recited poems, and gave a speech, after which they were invited on board by the captain and crew who gave them sweets and oranges—treats never seen by them before.

Within a few weeks, children's feeding programmes in Poland and in other countries were moving into action.

By mid-1948, Unicef was providing rations for 4·5 million children to eat a daily meal in around 30,000 locations in twelve countries. This only represented an average of nine per cent of the children in any country, although in several—particularly in Austria, Bulgaria and Greece—the proportion was much higher. The largest programme was in Italy, where over a million school children received a daily drink from their local 'milk bar'.

Maurice Pate, returning from a visit to Bulgaria, Czechoslovakia, France, Hungary, Italy, Poland and Rumania, reported that even in remote villages and tiny feeding stations the name of Unicef was known and supplies were getting through. Constant reassurance to the American public was considered vital to Unicef's success; the unhappy publicity surrounding the work carried out by UNRRA was too recent a memory for comfort. The scale of Unicef's feeding schemes never grew beyond the relatively modest. Unicef was not bringing an entire generation of children back from the brink of starvation, although sometimes the glow surrounding Unicef's name gave this very exaggerated impression. A great number of children, however, were unquestionably gaining in health and strength from an effort in which Unicef played an important part.

The way the feeding programmes were run varied from country to country, but in their essentials they were similar. All the schools, kindergartens, orphanages, and health clinics to which rations were delivered were under the supervision of a government ministry charged with co-ordinating its efforts in joint committees at national, district, and local level. Unicef did not operate autonomously, picking this or that school or health institution to receive its assistance. According to its agreement with the country in question, it channelled its supplies into a programme whose authority came from the government and which was carried out by government officials, often with help from local committees of parents, teachers, or volunteers. It was a format from which, in its essentials, Unicef has never subsequently deviated. The task of the Unicef mission was to try and see that the right supplies were procured and delivered, to monitor their use, and to help local officials iron out problems they ran into.

Unicef tried to give assistance so as to stimulate permanent enthusiasm for the protective virtues of milk and mass feeding for children. Enthusiasm for dried milk was greater among those who did not have to eat it: at this stage in its development, the product was not easy to reconstitute and had a strong flavour. It had to be carefully cooked with other ingredients to make it palatable. The distribution of recipes to schools whose teachers were not equipped with culinary imagination was just one of the extra tasks the feeding entailed. Also, some officials were not enamoured by the odder ingredients that sometimes appeared among Unicef cargoes; it required the serving of a gourmet dish of whalemeat at their next meeting to convince one national co-ordinating committee that this ingredient was usable. These and the many organizational problems having been overcome, Unicef hoped that countries would sustain their feeding programmes indefinitely. Some—Austria, Finland, Czechoslovakia, and Poland—did so, continuing to provide a regular meal in schools long after Unicef supplies ceased to arrive.

Other basic essentials besides food were in desperately short supply. Everywhere in villages and towns, children were running around barefoot and in rags. There was almost no soap, no clothing available, and no shoes. For many mothers of newborn infants, there was nothing except newspaper to use for a diaper, and rags and paper also had to serve as blankets in the depths of winter. Unicef purchased raw materials—cotton and wool, leather for shoes—which were imported, and manufactured on the spot. In Poland, Warsaw's National Research Institute for the Mother and Child, set up in 1948 as part of the programme for health care recovery, offered every mother of a newborn baby a layette with diapers, shirts, and blankets. With each came a message of congratulations, and advice about the baby's care. 'A clean and satisfied child never cries', the booklet stated optimistically. Mothers were encouraged to breast-feed and to take their babies regularly for a check-up. In Germany, where food rations were already provided by the postwar occupation forces, help took the form of cod liver oil, wool for warm underclothing, and leather for shoes.

In 1948, the harvest in most European countries finally recovered. Dread of famine receded thankfully into the past. Unicef continued to send some 'milk and fat to be spread on bread . . .' for the next two years, reaching six million children through 50,000 schools and other locations in the spring of 1950. But by then, Unicef's chief preoccupation with milk had moved on from the imported variety to the home-grown.

In October 1947, Unicef's Executive Board had directed Maurice Pate and his staff to start thinking about how to secure 'the maximum amounts of safe milk for children from indigenous production'. Information about dairy herds and milk-processing equipment was solicited from a number of European countries. The verdict was that many of them not only suffered from a shortage of cows, but that the sanitation of milk was poor, and dairy factories had little in the way of equipment for pasteurization and bottling. In the late spring of 1948, dairy experts from various governments sat down with FAO specialists at a conference in Paris. They were aware that, during what was known as the 'flush' season, there was often a milk surplus which children in non-dairy areas and in other seasons badly needed. The problem was how to conserve the milk and redistribute it to those children most in need.

Unicef took part in these discussions, and soon afterwards established a joint Unicef/FAO Milk Experts Panel which could advise a country's agricultural ministry and dairy industry. In July 1948, $2 million was set aside for support to milk conservation projects. This was the first step in a new Unicef direction. Before long, Unicef had started to recruit engineering consultants for its Milk Conservation Programme. Although their presence in a children's organization appeared an anomaly at first glance, they filled a special gap at a useful moment when no other UN organization was in a position to help.

The head of the team was Donald Sabin, an American who had served UNRRA in Poland and had previously been on the staff of the US Department of Agriculture. Most were dairymen of the technical variety, men who knew about the manufacture of dairy produce, and could advise on equipment—pasteurizers, dryers, coolers, and bottling chains—and the construction of plant.

While Unicef's assistance to milk conservation was intended to revitalize and speed up the rehabilitation of dairies, so as to make more milk more cheaply available to consumers and therefore to children, it had a much more specific focus. The milk which emerged from a piece of dairy equipment provided by Unicef was primarily intended to replace the milk currently imported by Unicef for child feeding programmes. Plans to distribute milk products to children and nursing mothers either free, or heavily subsidized, must therefore form a part of any country's milk conservation agreement with Unicef. Where possible, there should be an actual link with an existing feeding scheme.

The Milk Conservation Programme in Europe was Unicef's first attempt at combining idealism with a carefully limited investment in industrial enterprise. Its success paved the way for later attempts of a similar kind which were not so wise nor so economically viable. In Europe, the dairy industries were relatively well-established; the small boost that Unicef tried to give them in the direction of children was easy to accommodate within their existing pattern and their plans for rehabilitation and growth. Although it was a modest programme, it was imaginative, and it received widespread acclaim from recipient governments.

In certain milk-flush areas, the best way of preserving milk was by drying. One type of assistance offered by Unicef was the imported machinery needed in order to set up milk-drying plants. In Czechoslovakia, Unicef provided the equipment to set up three such plants, while the government built the extra dairy buildings needed to house them, and met all the costs of local freight and labour, and provided all materials which could be furnished from within Czechoslovakia: an investment fifteen times the value of Unicef's. The dried milk produced was given free to all children in orphanages and hospitals, and sold at a fixed low price to mothers of infants under one-year-old. The number of the children in these categories amounted to 320,000. Any supplies left over went into the school feeding programme, currently reaching 510,000 children. This arrangement was typical of those drawn up with Yugoslavia, Bulgaria, and Poland for similar investments.

One of the Polish enterprises selected for help was at Wrzesina, a small town some 150 miles west of Warsaw. During the war, the factory had been run by Germans, who set milk quotas for local farmers and used the milk for the German Army. When the war ended, they killed all the cows or took them away. A few were hidden by their owners. The factory buildings at Wrzesina were in disrepair, and there was no milk for them to process. The owners re-started milk production from a herd of goats, and gradually the local cows calved and multiplied; but it took several years before milk again began to flow from the factory. By 1949, the dairy at Wrzesina was producing a small surplus. It became the site of the first of five powdered-milk plants in Poland. All five were completed by December 1950 and, by June 1951, their combined monthly production was 400 tons.

In most countries—including Poland—the national dairy authorities were fully aware that, however hard they tried to instil in the public mind a respect for dried milk, what most people wanted was milk from the cow.

The problem was that raw cow's milk was often unsafe. In many countries, therefore, Unicef provided sterilizing and pasteurizing equipment for fluid milk. Its provision was tied to what was described as a 'sound milk policy'. Pasteurized milk from a dairy was bound to cost more than raw milk taken from a cow tethered in a back yard. If both were available, it would be difficult to ensure that the poorest children—those Unicef's aid was meant for—received the benefit of the safe milk. Unicef's agreement with the Greek government, for example, stipulated that in the places where its equipment was installed, pasteurized milk at the same price as raw milk would be supplied to local children. In France, where the dairy industry was more developed, the undertakings went much further. Legislation was passed to outlaw the sale of raw milk in cities where Unicef equipment was installed; a ban followed on the sale of raw milk in all towns with a population of more than 20,000. The dairies receiving Unicef equipment were also bound to supply milk to its value as part of the programme of free milk distribuion in schools. For a total of $700,000 from Unicef, France had been enticed into making landmark decisions affecting children's health.

By 1950, 2·5 million litres of milk a day were flowing through the equipment provided by Unicef in eight European countries. The milkmen had done a useful job. Their success encouraged Unicef to look for new cows and new dairies further afield—in the Middle East, central America and Asia.

*   *   *   *   *

Not only was there a postwar nutritional emergency among children, but a health emergency as well. During the war years, infant death rates had risen dramatically in many countries; in some of those areas still affected by famine in the terrible winter of 1946–47, nearly half the babies born alive died before their first birthday. Mothers' own debility from lack of good nutrition lowered the average weight of their babies at birth, and premature and still-births were common. Children of all age groups were underweight for their years, and their unrobust condition made them prey to many diseases whose infection rate had rapidly increased: rickets was increasing; dental decay and skin disease were common; in countries of occupation venereal disease was widespread; and the rate of infection from the 'white plague' — tuberculosis — had soared.

Typhus had stamped the aftermath of the first World War; by the end of the second, although typhus was still an epidemic disease in certain areas of central Europe, dusting bodies and clothes with DDT provided an effective barrier to its fearful capacity to run loose. In the baggage train of the second World War, the disease whose control was most elusive was tuberculosis, particularly in its most dangerous forms: miliary tuberculosis and tubercular meningitis.

Everywhere in Europe, as the horrors of death and destruction began to recede, tuberculosis rates were found to have multiplied. In Yugoslavia, death from tuberculosis in 1946 was between 350 and 400 per 100,000 population, a rate ten times higher than in countries where there had been no enemy occupation and measures for tuberculosis control were in operation. In some parts of Poland, the child death rate from tuberculosis had risen by four times in seven years; half a million people were infected.

From Schleswig Holstein, alarming reports reached the Danish authorities that German children were suffering from epidemics of tuberculosis in its most lethal forms. The Danish Red Cross set up dispensaries for special treatment and sought help from the State Serum Institute in Copenhagen; its director, Dr Johannes Holm, was a leading tuberculosis specialist. He immediately recommended a mass immunization campaign using *Bacillus Calmette-Guerin* or BCG. This is a vaccine named after the two French scientists who developed it early in the century. In France, it had fallen into disrepute when the wrong strain was used during a vaccination campaign in 1929 and a number of people died. As a result of this disaster, its use in some countries, including the US, was prohibited. Trials in the Scandinavian countries gradually vindicated the vaccine, and by the time war broke out it had become common in both Denmark and Sweden to vaccinate newborn infants with BCG. Using it under clinical conditions, however, was very different from using it in a mass public-health campaign. This had never been done before.

Towards the end of 1946, with help from Dr Holm and his staff, the Danish Red Cross began to prepare immunization campaigns against tuberculosis in Poland and Yugoslavia. Requests soon arrived for similar efforts in Czechoslovakia, Hungary, and Germany. In November 1947 Count Folke Bernadotte, the President of the Swedish Red Cross, visited Denmark to discuss a joint anti-tuberculosis campaign, and by the end of the year it had become an international Scandinavian Red Cross venture with Swedes and Norwegians taking part.

Ludwik Rajchman, simultaneously considering how Unicef might best support an anti-tuberculosis drive, contacted Johannes Holm in December 1947. A few days before, Unicef's Executive Board had set up a committee to consider support to medical projects under the chairmanship of Professor Robert Debré, a prominent French paediatrician and friend of Rajchman. Holm convinced Rajchman and Debré that Unicef should participate in the Scandinavian tuberculosis campaign. Their plans were already well advanced and had Danish government backing; but they were facing problems, partly due to strict foreign exchange controls in the Scandinavian countries. Their mobile vaccination vans needed replacing, equipment was in short supply, staffing costs would be high. Unicef's assistance could dramatically expand the programme's reach. Rajchman and Debré enthusiastically agreed.

The story of Unicef's involvement in what became the International Tuberculosis Campaign (ITC)—the largest vaccination campaign ever undertaken up to this time—illustrates Rajchman's supreme grasp of how to manipulate political and administrative machinery to do something for popular health. At this time, the WHO Interim Commission was preparing to become, finally, the World Health Organization, the body formally constituted by UN member states as the single worldwide international health organization of the United Nations. There was a deliberate emphasis on 'single'; the League of Nations' health organization had never been able to assert its direction over a predecessor in international health affairs, the International Office of Public Hygiene, set up in Paris in 1909. Failure to effect a merger between these two bodies had limited the effectiveness of both. Rajchman, a main protagonist in the earlier stand-off, understood very clearly the difficulties Unicef might face from WHO—and from many member states of the United Nations—if it assumed a major role in an international health programme over which WHO had no control.

This was a moment when all the new specialized agencies of the UN—of which WHO was the one with the most protracted birth—were trying to establish their territory and their credentials. Unicef was not a permanent UN body—not the international repository of technical expertise and wisdom on any subject—but an emergency fund to rush relief supplies to children and mothers in need. According to any strict definition, it had no business getting involved with mass disease campaigns run under international auspices. But Holm's suggestion that Unicef join in an anti-tuber-culosis venture was irresistible to Rajchman; it was a campaign after his own heart, exactly the kind of operation he would have desired to lead at the League of Nations. It was also true that Unicef could help in ways that WHO could not. WHO was not in a position to pay for supplies, vaccines, and equipment, in a disease campaign: it was an advisory body set up to offer expertise, not an organization with medical goods on the shelf to give out to prevent children and mothers becoming sick.

Rajchman knew that if Unicef was to be a partner in any health pro-grammes at all—and its founding resolution had specified that it could lend assistance for 'child health purposes generally'—it must do so in a relationship of co-operation with WHO, deferring correctly to WHO's international supremacy in health matters. Neither his own overpowering reputation in public health, nor the distance some senior medical people preferred to keep from him personally, must become an inhibition to cordial partner-ship between the two organizations.

Borislaw Borcic's role as liaison officer in Unicef's European headquarters was the first important piece of the jigsaw puzzle. Now he saw an equally important role for Johannes Holm. Holm had recently been appointed chairman of WHO's expert panel on tuberculosis. If the same Dr Holm was the director and technical adviser of a tuberculosis control programme supported by Unicef, potential conflict with WHO could be avoided. Holm could also join Unicef's medical committee, the group that Rajchman envisaged undertaking a regular process of consultation with WHO technical experts. In late 1947 and early 1948, Rajchman put tactful but persistent pressure on Brock Chisholm, head of WHO, to help establish arrangements for WHO/Unicef co-operation: he could not be faulted for leading Unicef into autonomous action.

In March 1948, the idea of a joint enterprise for BCG immunization between Unicef and the Scandinavian Red Cross was discussed at Unicef's Executive Board. Holm was invited by Rajchman to present the case in its favour. Some of the delegates were not happy about the proposal: they did not believe that Unicef was the competent body to conduct programmes in the medical field. Mixed feelings within WHO IC about the use of BCG had an effect on some of the delegates. In favour of Unicef's involvement was the fact that the tuberculosis threat could definitely be described as a postwar emergency; that WHO IC itself was not in a position to offer the campaign the relevant supplies and services; and that machinery for consultation with WHO was in the making. Together these arguments carried the day. The possibility was envisaged that, at some future date, the children's fund might hand over its part in the BCG campaign to WHO. The Executive Board agreed to the expenditure of $4 million from Unicef's resources, and the joint enterprise was underway.

On 7 April 1948, the World Health Organization came into formal existence. A few months later, in July, the first World Health Assembly met. Among the many other items on its agenda was the subject of WHO's relations with Unicef. A resolution was passed which was intended to put Unicef gently but firmly in its place. All international health projects should be planned and administered jointly with WHO, so that any of a continuing nature rather than just emergency band-aid should be handed over at the earliest opportunity. Pending WHO's assumption of all medical projects aided by Unicef, a Joint Committee on Health Policy would be set up with representatives from the two organizations to 'regulate' these projects; this Joint Committee was a purely temporary body, and would cease existence once the handover had been effected. In the case of the BCG campaign, the Assembly recognized that special circumstances pertained, namely the existence of agreements between certain nongovernmental organizations, governments, and Unicef. Rajchman had squeezed the joint enterprise under the wire.

When the new Joint Committee on Health Policy held its first meeting a few days later, the main item on its agenda was to resolve the differences in perspective between the WHO and the Unicef participants about the two organizations' areas of authority. The WHO representatives were, understandably, worried that a second UN agency operating in the area outlined in the WHO constitution—family health, environmental health, sanitation, disease control—might develop out of Unicef. Their assumption, as it transpired, was essentially correct: that is exactly what Unicef eventually became, but not with any independence of action until many years had passed and territorial boundaries had ceased to preoccupy either organization. In its first year or two of life, very few of those observing Unicef and its operations thought of it as anything more than an organization created to deal with a short-term emergency. Another of WHO's understandable worries was that Unicef might enter into long-term financial arrangements to carry out an international campaign—such as the ITC—and then expire, leaving WHO with the bill for something over which it had not been properly consulted and did not fully support. Rajchman and his Unicef colleagues assured their counterparts that Unicef would not obligate itself for health projects it could not fully finance from its own resources. In 1948, this essentially meant the BCG campaign; but other campaigns were also in the air.

Although reservations such as these continued to be aired in the Committee's meetings until the end of the decade, particularly as Unicef showed no inclination to curtail its health activities (rather the reverse), the relationship between colleagues from the two organizations was one of strong mutual respect. The Unicef representatives—Debré, Rajchman, Holm—were, after all, medical men of long experience. The purpose of both organizations was to further health among the peoples, the nations and the children, and issues of territory were minor compared with the overall goal. In time, it became easier to define the roles of the senior and junior UN partners: WHO was the technical arbiter and adviser; Unicef offered goods and equipment, drugs, vaccines, and medical supplies. Unicef also paid for training fellowships for health personnel, and the advice of WHO experts on specific programmes when it was needed. For many years, Unicef felt under an obligation to seek WHO approval for any assistance it offered to health care programmes. At a point when this no longer seemed appropriate, the practice was dropped. Meanwhile, the Joint Committee on Health Policy did not turn out to be such a transitory mechanism. It still meets.

The ongoing frictions between WHO and Unicef did not inhibit Johannes Holm from pushing ahead with the various national BCG campaigns. BCG vaccination programmes on a modest scale had started in Poland and Germany in April 1947, and by mid-1948 had extended to Hungary, Czechoslovakia, Italy, Greece, and Austria. Holm gradually built up the Scandinavian teams of doctors and nurses and, on the strength of Unicef's contribution, was able to equip them with vehicles, medical supplies, fluid for tuberculin testing, vaccines, laboratory equipment, X-rays for diagnostic work, and streptomycin for tuberculosis therapy. In countries where mass vaccination was to be carried out, arrangements were made for educational and publicity materials. More and more countries began to request assistance from the ITC, including countries in North Africa, the Middle East, and far away in Asia.

Holm, who was inexperienced in mounting such a vast international exercise, consulted closely with Rajchman and Borcic. Rajchman advised him to decentralize authority for the programme as far as he could, and to choose young doctors with obvious leadership qualities to head the various teams. He impressed upon Holm the need to select and train the kind of young men and women who could become part of a new international cadre to serve organizations such as WHO and Unicef in the coming years. One of Holm's recruits was Dr Halfdan Mahler, a young Danish tuberculosis specialist who went to India to head the largest of the campaigns. This experience deeply influenced Mahler's ideas about health care in the developing world, and launched him on a career which took him in time to be the Director-General of WHO.

During 1948 and 1949, the anti-tuberculosis drive was concentrated in Europe. In most of the countries, the campaign's purpose was to vaccinate with BCG all children under 18 years old not infected with the tubercle bacillus. Such a campaign required a considerable degree of organization at national, district, and local level. Usually, all the medical teams concentrated in one province or district, and proceeded systematically to the next until the entire country was covered. This helped to blanket an area with information about the campaign and its purpose.

Two visits to each town and village were necessary. On their first, the vaccination team carried out a test on all the children by injecting a few drops of tuberculin fluid into the arm. On their second, they would check every child for a reaction to the test; only those whose reaction was negative could receive a BCG shot. Not all of those whose reaction was positive would later develop tuberculosis; to detect active cases, further diagnostic work was necessary. In most parts of Europe, around half of the children tested positive; therefore the BCG campaign could expect to protect definitively the other half.

The teams found that the best way to reach every child was to start with the school children, and then test the pre-schoolers and post-schoolers at public vaccination posts: the school children were the best propagandists for assuring a good turn-out of the rest. The most difficult areas were deep in the countryside, where it was hard to inform people, let alone persuade them to travel long distances to bring their children on an appointed day. To be efficiently and thoroughly run, the campaigns required an almost military degree of planning and preparation.

In Poland, the BCG immunization campaign was enthusiastically welcomed and tuberculin testing began in July 1948. The campaign was the largest undertaken in Europe. Sixty Scandinavian doctors and nurses were joined by roughly the same number of Polish counterparts and many more auxiliaries and volunteers to carry out the testing. The vaccine was brought to Warsaw every week from Copenhagen by a special ITC airplane. In village after village, parents responded. Farmers took precious time off from working their land to wrap up their children and take them by horse-drawn cart to the village store or restaurant, temporarily transformed into a tuberculosis testing station. The teams worked fast: 400 tests an hour was the target. They went to schools, to orphanages, and to factories employing adolescents. By December 1949, the teams had tested nearly 5·5 million children, and vaccinated more than half of them. Once the mass campaign was over, Polish doctors and nurses continued carrying out BCG vaccination on a regular basis.

The results of the immunization campaign bore fruit everywhere. Doctors began to report a much lower incidence of tuberculosis among children. Special clinics which had been set up to treat babies with miliary tuberculosis and tubercular meningitis, at first besieged by parents with small patients, began to see their numbers decline. Medical circles throughout Europe were positive about the campaign's results, and began to move ahead with other measures to control and treat TB. Anti-tuberculosis centres were set up; laboratories equipped; diagnostic facilities improved; training courses were run for medical staff. In these projects to upgrade tuberculosis control and treatment in a number of countries, WHO offered technical advice, and Unicef furnished equipment in what was becoming a familiar pattern. Meanwhile, vaccination continued. By the time the ITC phase ended in mid-1951, almost 30 million persons had been tested and 14 million

Ludwik Rajchman, an international public-health pioneer whose experience and lobbying were crucial to the founding of Unicef in 1946. (*Unicef*)

In 1946, refugees returning to Poland travelled in boxcars provided by the United Nations Relief and Rehabilitation Administration. (*UN Archives*)

The fight against
malnutrition:
Guatemala. Here a
child waits for free
milk provided by
Unicef as part of a
supplementary
feeding scheme.
(*UN Archives*)

Trick or Treat for
Unicef'—American
children collecting
money to help
children in poor
countries.
(*US Committee for
Unicef/Avakian*)

When the refugees
had to leave their
homes in Palestine
in 1948, their first
and vital need was
shelter. Tents were
flown in as an
emergency measure.
(*UNWRA*)

China, August 1946.
An abandoned baby
found on a city street
by a UNWRA welfare
worker is near death.
(*UN Archives*)

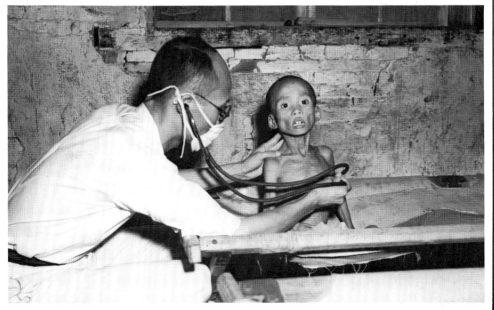

This husky Chinese youngster has just received his daily ration of milk. An UNWRA-trained male student nurse tips the scale. (*UN Archives*)

Flip charts are used to give mothers malaria lectures in N'Djamena, Chad. (*Unicef/Danois*)

vaccinated. Thousands of children and babies with the disease had been treated with streptomycin.

During the postwar years, the largest proportion of Unicef's assistance to medical programmes went to maternal and child health. Several countries were rehabilitating and upgrading their antenatal, maternity, and infant health services. They needed equipment—baby scales, thermometers, laboratory supplies, incubators, oxygen tents—and they needed training for their personnel. Unicef provided the first and sponsored the second, defraying the costs of short courses in social paediatrics for child-care staff from the countries whose own training programmes had been set back by the war. In 1950, the French government set up an International Children's Centre under the leadership of Robert Debré to provide the kind of courses that staff from Europe and elsewhere needed to improve health services for children. These initiatives were taken with the technical approval of WHO, and under the guidance of the WHO/Unicef joint health-policy committee. They were the basis for much of Unicef's later assistance to health care services in other parts of the world.

For drama, however, it was the disease campaigns which attracted notice. The ITC was the largest but not the only co-ordinated onslaught on communicable disease.

Syphilis had also reached epidemic proportions in occupied countries, and the medical authorities in Poland, Czechoslovakia, and Yugoslavia were particularly anxious to bring it under control. Some of the victims were newborn children whose mothers were infected; others were teenagers. Penicillin had recently made syphilis a much easier disease to cure. Its availability at a reasonable price made anti-syphilis campaigns a practical possibility. Unicef became a supplier to the campaigns; by the end of 1949 the Polish government had eliminated syphilis as a major public-health problem, and in Yugoslavia the numbers of children affected by endemic syphilis were decreasing rapidly.

Unicef also took over UNRRA's role in supplying vehicles, sprayers, and insecticides for the control of malaria, typhus, and other insect-borne diseases. The scientific advances of the past generation had reduced the cost and revolutionized the prospects of anti-epidemic campaigns. They were popular, effective, and demonstrated international co-operation at its best. In the wake of the second World War when European services were being rebuilt, the success of the disease campaigns was the harbinger of a new era in international public health.

In the postwar emergency, most of Unicef's assistance went into feeding and other emergency programmes in Europe. But the children of Asia had also suffered from the war. Among the 'countries victims of aggression' on the other side of the world, China was the largest. Millions of the Chinese people had suffered from occupation longer even than the Austrians, Czechs, and Slovaks.

Japanese forces had begun their occupation of Manchuria in 1931; in 1937, they extended their control southwards across The Great Wall until they had overrun an area as large and even more populous than that eventually occupied by German armies in Europe. After Japan's surrender in August 1945 and the withdrawal of its forces from northern China, the Western Allies hoped that peace would open a chapter of Chinese stability and economic recovery under a broad political coalition. Instead, it unleashed the final phase in the long power struggle between the Nationalists under Chiang Kai Shek and the Communists under Mao Tse Tung.

In late 1945, civil war erupted in Manchuria. For over twelve months, General Marshall, the US envoy, tried to mediate a reconciliation. In January 1947, he gave up. In spite of US support to Chiang's superior forces, his control of mainland China was slipping. The Communist campaign in Manchuria had begun as a guerilla offensive in the countryside; against all expectations it was gradually isolating Chiang's military strongholds. A tide had turned; the Communists were winning.

In November 1944, UNRRA had opened an office in Chungking, Chiang's wartime capital in the south, and began to organize the largest relief and rehabilitation programme ever undertaken in a single country. By the end of 1947, when UNRRA closed down its vast network of operations in areas on both sides of the civil war, its expenditures had amounted to $670 million, and over 2·5 million tons of supplies had been imported and delivered. By early 1947, the Nationalist economy was collapsing rapidly and demoralization and confusion had overtaken Chiang's Administration. UNRRA officials preparing for departure at the end of the year informed Maurice Pate that in the circumstances it had become almost impossible to run an effective relief operation. At the same time, UNRRA estimated that there were at least 29 million children in desperate need of emergency help.

Pate decided to press ahead with a programme and, in April 1948, $5 million was approved for China by Unicef's Board. At the suggestion of Dick Heyward, the Australian delegate, $500,000 was designated for use in Communist-held areas: although a representative of Chiang's government sat on the Unicef Board, the principle of nonpartiality was upheld.

Pate invited Marcel Junod, an eminent Swiss surgeon and the chief wartime delegate of the International Red Cross in Asia, to head the Unicef mission. Junod arrived in China in February 1948 and set up an office in Nanking, the Nationalist capital. He reported to Pate that the circumstances in which the mission had to function were 'unbelievable': social and economic administration was disintegrating. He took on a number of staff from UNRRA, worked out shipping and supply routes, and managed to start child-feeding programmes in seven cities: Peking, Tientsin, Tsingtao, Hankow, Nanking, Shanghai, and Canton. In each city, respected community leaders were asked to serve on a committee charged with the setting up and the running of feeding centres to which supplies were consigned. A Unicef staff member in each city acted as liaison and executive secretary. Over the course of the next year-and-a-half, 60,000 children in day-care centres were given dried milk and other protective rations according to the standard Unicef pattern. Against the needs, it was an infinitesimal effort; but in the circumstances, Junod and his staff were proud of it.

The feeding programme absorbed most of Unicef's resources for China. But the injunction to offer help to children in Communist, or 'liberated', areas was not overlooked. Junod opened up contacts with CLARA, the Chinese Liberated Areas Relief Association in Hong Kong. In summer 1948, he negotiated permission for a Unicef team to pass through no-man's-land to the town of Shih Chia Chuang in Hebei Province. As his emissary to northern China, Junod recruited Dr Leo Eloesser, a thoracic surgeon from San Francisco currently working under Berislav Borcic in the UNRRA health division. Eloesser, a 67-year-old veteran of humanitarian adventure, had already made one irregular foray into Communist-held territory earlier in the year. He had spent some weeks living in a mountain village near Yenan, Mao's capital, working alongside the Communist forces' medical personnel. Their health system was fragmentary; most of the staff knew little more than the basics; but Eloesser had been impressed, and fascinated, by the health service potential of training large numbers of ordinary people in simple medical and public-health tasks. Eloesser convinced Marcel Junod that feeding programmes for children were not necessary or suitable for the rural areas under Communist control, and that a health-training programme would be more useful.

In August 1948, Eloesser set off for Shih Chia Chuang with Perry Hanson, an ex-UNRRA China staff member now serving Unicef. In the midst of Nationalist bombing raids, they negotiated an agreement with CLARA officials. A Unicef supply centre would be set up for the receipt of drugs and medical equipment transhipped through the fighting lines. Eloesser's training proposals were accepted. His ideas reflected not only the preventive health and first aid techniques evolved by Mao's troops on The Long March, but also corresponded with similar ideas about rural medical practice which had emerged in China in the 1930s. Various pioneers had then begun to recognize that hospitals and clinical medicine could hardly touch the surface of health problems among millions of mothers and children in the Chinese countryside. In due course, these ideas were to crystallize in the rural health-care system popularly known by the epithet applied to its practitioners: the 'barefoot doctors'. At the time that Eloesser reached his Unicef agreement with CLARA, however, there had been no programme of this kind previously tried in Hebei province.

Eloesser's agreement with the CLARA medical authorities laid down that the new training school would run courses for middle school graduates from local communities in maternal and child health, sanitation, control of communicable disease and first aid. Courses for groups of twenty would last three-months and, as more trainees graduated, teams would gradually be deployed so as to cover all the districts in the liberated areas. Since the population in the area was eighty-two million, the scheme was ambitious, to say the least.

To help bring communicable disease under control, Unicef would provide the equipment for a new vaccine production plant under the directorship of Dr Li Chih Chung, head of the local anti-epidemic bureau. Li became Eloesser's most active colleague. His headquarters were in what had once been a Trappist monastery; it now also became the site of the training school. Conditions were primitive. Li kept small herds of cows and Manchurian ponies for cultivating vaccination lymph and toxoids; bacteriological incubators had to be warmed by kerosene lamp; light, heat, water, and fuel were as precious as gold; essential equipment—watches, thermometers, syringes, jars, and bottles—were so scarce as to be almost irreplaceable. The hardship and constant improvisation demanded in this environment appealed to Eloesser. With great enthusiasm, he organized the erection of a modest building, and assembled a faculty of staff for the programme, including Dr Li. The first course began in November 1948, and proceeded smoothly.

It was not long before the progress of the civil war began to affect Eloesser's project and Unicef's programme throughout China. Late in 1948, the Communist advance began to roll forward at a speed which caught everyone by surprise. As the Nationalist armies began to collapse, all UN personnel—except Unicef's—evacuated Nanking. Tientsin and Peking fell in January 1949; Nanking and Shanghai followed in April and May. The Unicef-assisted child-feeding programmes continued to function for a while, using supplies which were stockpiled before the Red Army arrived. But once these supplies were exhausted, the Unicef staff found that the new authorities were not willing to let feeding continue. This was perplexing; the relations with CLARA had been cordial. The programme in the north had been greeted enthusiastically, so there had been every reason to expect that the new government would look with favour upon an impartial international organization helping children.

Early in the year, Junod returned to New York to discuss the shape of Unicef's assistance to the new China. The WHO/Unicef Joint Committee on Health Policy met in Geneva in April 1949 and discussed support for long-term child welfare: health training, disease campaigns, tuberculosis control, milk promotion. Plans and funds were tentatively approved, but discussions with the new Chinese authorities proceeded to make little headway.

By mid-1949, only the Nanking and Peking offices remained open. The health training courses had been moved to a centre at Tungchow, just outside Peking; they expanded the student intake and began to achieve solid results. Three Unicef-sponsored faculty members stayed on until January 1950. But everything else ground slowly to a halt. The crucial point at issue was the degree of control Unicef should retain over its supplies once they had landed on Chinese soil; in all countries with Communist regimes, this question and others like it had started to become an issue. In September, after months of discussion, Eloesser judged that an impasse had been reached and left for home. Perry Hanson stayed on in Nanking, still perplexed by what had soured a once-flourishing relation and hoping to break the deadlock.

On 1 October the People's Republic of China was declared. The United Nations refused recognition. By now, US backing for the Nationalist cause was affecting China's relations with every representative of the US, individual or organizational or perceived as either. Into this category fell the UN and its works. Attacks on Eloesser and Unicef began to appear in the Chinese press. From this point onwards, efforts to negotiate a programme and a presence were doomed. Nationalist China was still a member of Unicef's Board. Late in 1950, Premier Chou En-Lai nominated a representative of the People's Republic to take the seat instead; this was a critical test of Unicef's acceptability to the new regime. The vote in the Board was tied, so the delegate from Taiwan stayed on. On 1 December 1951, Hansen received instructions to suspend Unicef's operations and withdraw. The effort to stay in China had failed.

Eloesser's ideas left their mark on Unicef. What mark they left on China is more difficult to judge. The pioneers of the 1930s are rightly credited with designing the model for the 'barefoot doctors' who, two decades later, inspired the admiration of the world. In one thing he was certainly correct: that this was the future shape that maternal and child-health care services must take in the rural communities of the developing world.

As the postwar emergency drew to an end in Europe, Unicef began to phase out its cargoes and terminate its operations. By the end of 1950, seven out of the original thirteen country missions had closed, leaving only Austria, Czechoslovakia, Germany, Greece, Italy, and Yugoslavia in operation, of which the first two were already in the process of closing down. In some of these countries, those whose children's services were less well-established before the war, Unicef continued to provide assistance throughout the 1950s and even the 1960s, mostly to milk conservation and to the spread of maternal and child health care. But in those eastern European countries whose governments were in political and economic alliance with the USSR, the increasing chill gust of cold war precipitated Unicef's withdrawal. If events had allowed, the same, more modest amounts of assistance which continued to be welcome elsewhere could have been provided. But the international climate was not conducive.

Within the United Nations, the divisions that were beginning to polarize the former wartime allies into rival camps of 'West' and 'East' had emerged as early as the first General Assembly in 1946. Very quickly, the immediate postwar climate in favour of strong international organizations had given way to moves to restrict their role and discretionary authority. With the declaration of the Truman Doctrine in March 1947, the corner in US postwar relations with other States had been turned: support had been pledged to assist free peoples in their struggles against 'armed minorities' or 'outside pressures'.

Bipolarity was strengthened when the Marshall Plan for the recovery of Europe was announced and the USSR rejected its terms, encouraging its eastern European allies to do the same. Long before the outbreak of the Korean War in 1950, and the intervention of UN troops on the South Korean side, the USSR had begun to regard the UN and all its member bodies with increasing distrust.

Attitudes on both sides of the ideological divide began to harden to the point where even Unicef, the purely impartial humanitarian organization for children's relief, was affected. It became more and more difficult to persuade the US Congress that Unicef's operations in eastern European countries offered neither material nor moral assistance to the cause of Communism. Meanwhile, within those countries, these same operations were increasingly looked at askance, particularly the activities of staff who travelled around the countryside checking up on the use of Unicef goods. Most of the officials working with Unicef thought of nothing more than the good of children and the need to help them. But at the ideological upper reaches of national administrations, the idea that such an organization could be run by a truly international cadre of officials, sincere to an oath they would not seek or take instructions from their own governments, seemed neither plausible nor trustworthy. Quite a number of the staff employed by Unicef and other such organizations were North American and British, apparent proof that the organizations were Western-biased.

The distrust cut both ways. Many US citizens who served on the staff of UN relief operations in eastern Europe in the postwar years were later investigated by McCarthy tribunals, and suffered serious career and personal harassment simply because of the geographical accident of their posting. Yet some of the local staff they left behind were harassed or imprisoned for their UN associations.

For many of those committed to the UN, and the brave new world of international peace and goodwill it was supposed to stand for, this was a profoundly depressing interlude. Some of Unicef's missions in eastern European countries closed abruptly following the expulsion of the international staff. An example was Hungary; a period in which heavy overt and secret surveillance made it more and more difficult to operate led eventually to the government's declaration that a resident office was unnecessary. Accordingly, the whole programme was wound up in November 1949.

Within Unicef, views differed over whether a permanent Unicef presence in a country should be a precondition of continuing to provide assistance; Davidson insisted that it should, while Rajchman disagreed. The Executive Board went along with Davidson. This decision late in 1949 essentially meant that the winding up of Unicef operations in eastern Europe was only a matter of time. Czechoslovakia was the last of the Comecon countries with a Unicef mission on its soil; it closed in March 1951. Poland was the second last. Both retreats took place in a spirit of mutual co-operation.

In May 1949, Gertrude Lutz, a Swiss national who had been working in Poland for Don Suisse, a voluntary organization, was appointed Chief of Mission in Warsaw. Lutz was warmhearted and skillful—and she was a woman. She therefore provoked less suspicion than a male as a staff member of an organization for children. By January 1950, Unicef was the only international organization with a mission still operating on Polish soil: all others had been invited to withdraw. The atmosphere in which the staff worked was very different from the days when Unicef ships had docked in Gdynia and festivities had taken place on the quay. Visas for visitors were increasingly hard to obtain, as was permission to travel in the countryside to visit feeding stations or prospective milk plants. In spite of all her best efforts, and in contravention of the agreement between the Polish government and Unicef, none of the press releases or the few posters she put out were used to tell the Polish people that Unicef was helping their children. This was not a question of Unicef's vanity but of the need for public recognition, without which international co-operation under the auspices of the UN was thought to be in serious jeopardy. As practical expressions of an ideal, the UN organizations were still in their infancy.

Gertrude Lutz closed the mission in Warsaw in December 1950, and handed over its outstanding duties and deliveries to a liaison officer appointed by the government. A few months later, she wrote in reflection: 'In an upheavaled world, ravaged by war, friendly relations must be maintained and humanity respected. Possibilities for co-operation in social welfare and health are very great. There should be no reason why people interested in the same thing and with a common aim should not get together. In materialistic days such as ours, we cannot abandon idealism. While it should be an essentially keen and practical idealism, it must never lack faith'.

Main sources

'At the heart of Unicef': A profile of Maurice Pate in *The New Yorker* magazine, 2 December 1961.

Memoirs of Helenka Pantaleoni, Oral History Research Office, Columbia University, 1977.

UNRRA, The History of the United Nations Relief and Rehabilitation Administration, Volume II; George Woodbridge et al, Columbia University Press, 1950.

Notes on the trip of the Hoover food mission, Maurice Pate; 1 August 1946.

The History of Unicef in Poland, by Gertrude Lutz, Chief of Mission in Warsaw, May 1949 to December 1950; April 1951.

Unicef Executive Board: Final Report of the First Executive Board, E/1908; E/ICEF/160; 22 January 1951; documentation on milk conservation and medical projects presented to the 1949 and 1950 Board meetings.

Monograph on Unicef's Milk Conservation Programme, Ronald A. Hill, 24 June 1984.

The Origins and Policy Basis of WHO/Unicef Collaboration in the International Health Field: A Look at the Official Record (1946–1983). Prepared by WHO, Geneva, June 1983.

Final Report of the International Tuberculosis Campaign, issued by Unicef, Copenhagen, October 1951; The History of the International Tuberculosis Campaign; notes prepared by Johs. Holm, May 1984.

Leo Eloesser MD, Eulogy for a Free Spirit, Harris B. Shumacker Jr, MD. Philosophical Library 1982.

Unicef in China, 1947–51. Paper prepared for the Unicef History Project by Perry O. Hanson Jr, August 1984.

Chapter 3

Rites of Passage

Pate's efforts during his first few months in his new position yielded dividends from the US Congress, although not on the scale he and Rajchman had originally hoped. He had asked Secretary of State George Marshall for $100 million. On 15 May 1947, Congress agreed to an appropriation of $350 million for relief in Europe; Herbert Hoover himself had appeared before the House Appropriations Committee to plead for a generous share for Unicef. The amount of $40 million was earmarked, of which $15 million could be taken up immediately, and the rest as and when other governments contributed. Unfortunately, few showed any alacrity to do so. Only the Canadians came forward with a donation of $5 million. Pate was undaunted. He thought that there were plenty of other good fund-raising candidates: in Europe, Switzerland, Norway, and Sweden looked hopeful; Australia and New Zealand in the Pacific; and in Latin America, he set his sights on Argentina. Still, Unicef's financial health was hardly robust at the moment when the first cargoes of milk and cod liver oil set off for the Baltic.

During Unicef's first few years of operation, financial crisis constantly threatened. To move ahead with an expanding programme of assistance in countries ever further afield required courage and faith. Pate spent his time with one eye looking over his shoulder to see where the next cargo of supplies was coming from, and the other looking forward to see whether the next move might itself generate some bright and hopeful new source of income. Apart from the US and Canadian contributions, Unicef's other immediate source of funds was the residual assets of UNRRA. As the financial skein of UNRRA's outstanding debts and credits in various currencies was unwound, Unicef became an inheritor. The sums were neither so vast as had been hoped, nor so trifling as had been feared. By October 1947, UNRRA had handed over $6 million; by the end of 1950, $32·3 million, in thirteen different currencies.

Meanwhile, Pate had begun to build on the financial keystone of the US contribution. To release the $25 million left in the US allocation, he set out to stimulate other contributions. This was a dishearteningly slow process. By October 1947, two months short of Unicef's first full year of operation and at roughly the moment when the first cargoes were being unloaded, only two more governments had made contributions: France had volunteered francs worth $900,000, and Norway some cod liver oil. Another $3·85 million was pledged, mostly from Australia.

Argentina, to Pate's regret, had bowed out. His optimism on that score had been dashed by the rider attached to an offer of $10 million. The money would be only forthcoming if Madame Eva Peron could go on a pilgrimage throughout Latin America as an official Unicef representative, thus satisfying Argentina's 'moral and spiritual aspirations'. The UN had carefully replied that they would be delighted for Madame Peron to undertake such a voyage, but that it would be more advisable for the wife of a Head of State to do so in her national capacity. No more was heard from Buenos Aires about the $10 million.

In the meantime, another UN initiative to raise money on behalf of children was gathering steam. This was the brainchild of Aake Ording, the Norwegian delegate who had tried to find a formula to head off UNRRA's collapse at the Geneva Council meeting of August 1946. Ording had served as Norway's Deputy Foreign Secretary under Trygve Lie, now UN Secretary-General, and was a man of great individuality. Ording had an idea for helping the children of Europe, whom he regarded as abandoned by the UNRRA Council at a critical moment.

A spontaneous voluntary movement had sprung up in the south of Norway to raise money and organize relief for the war-devastated north. If this could happen across the geographic barrier within Norway, why not across borders throughout the world? In December 1946, at the same General Assembly which established Unicef, Ording proposed that the UN endorse the idea of soliciting 'one day's pay' from salaried people everywhere for programmes on behalf of children. The UN would declare the 'day'; voluntary organizations would gather in the proceeds. A joint effort of peoples and governments would give force to the idea of the United Nations, and do much to alleviate the suffering of children.

As with many visionary ideas which defy practical obstacles, the idea of a 'United Nations Appeal for Children' was greeted with considerable scepticism. The UN could not compel member governments to declare a 'one day's pay' donation from people in their own countries; nor did it have at that time any systematic means of collecting donations from individual citizens, except through governments. Collecting and spending were two sides of one coin: if the UN was to invite the voluntary organizations to do the work of collecting the money, it could hardly expect to relieve them of it to spend on schemes outside their control. Nevertheless, the persistence of the Norwegians eventually won qualified approval for the idea. The UN agreed that an Appeal for Children in its name could be a worldwide non-governmental drive for contributions from the general public, taking the form of a 'day' in each country and asking people to levy themselves for one day's pay.

The problem of who would actually disburse the proceeds was solved by agreeing that as much as half the money collected could be used for children's programmes run by national voluntary organizations; and that half, or more, would go to Unicef. This formula was not to the satisfaction of Ludwik Rajchman, who thought Unicef should receive all proceeds. Ording, and all those with experience of the private charitable world, knew very well that this would doom the Appeal in most of the countries where it needed to succeed: in North America and the better-off European countries. In each country, the Appeal would be run by a national committee made up of representatives of organizations such as Save the Children, the Red Cross Society, and other voluntary bodies. Presidents, princes, and priests would be asked to endorse the 'one day's pay' appeal. None of these national figures or bodies would be keen to throw their weight behind a popular drive if their own children were not to benefit. Rajchman's persistent refusal to accept this reality was unhelpful to Ording and dogged the Appeal with an unnecessary problem.

Ording was designated the Appeal's co-ordinator by Trygve Lie, and put his energies into obtaining the endorsements of governments, and of consumers', farmers', and businessmen's organizations. In June 1947 at Maurice Pate's suggestion, he took on Michael Lubbock, an Englishman who had worked for UNRRA in Greece, to build up a European UN Appeal for Children (UNAC) network. By this stage it was clear that the Appeal could not take place successfully without preparation.

Lubbock managed to visit most crowned heads in Europe and interest quite a few of them, as well as recruit a variety of enthusiastic officials and professional people to serve on national UNAC committees. In February 1948, Ording reported to the UN that national committees had been formed in twenty-one countries, and that twenty-three other countries were following suit. In each case, an agreement between the Secretary-General and the country concerned settled the question of who would administer UNAC funds and what proportion would go to Unicef. Meanwhile, an International Advisory Committee had been formed under the chairmanship of Chester Bowles, an American public figure. 1948 was a leap year and Bowles advised the Secretary-General to select 29 February as 'the day' for UNAC throughout the world.

In some countries, UNAC committees observed 'the day' but carried out their fund-raising later. In many European countries, the campaign produced a lot of publicity, which brought home for the first time to officials, voluntary organizations, trade unionists, and all the citizens' groups that participated, what—in its humanitarian guise—the UN was, or could be, about. By the end of 1948, campaigns had been held or launched in forty-five countries and thirty territories, and had altogether raised just short of $30 million. Unicef received just over one-third of the total.

The most lucrative appeals were those in Australia and New Zealand, which both raised over $2 million; Canada, South Africa and Britain each raised $1·5 million. Iceland was the star; there the appeal raised nearly $500,000, or $4·39 from each person. There was also a warm response in Denmark, Sweden and Norway, where the proceeds went to the International Tuberculosis Campaign. In eastern Europe, Czechoslovakia ran a very successful appeal.

In the US the results of UNAC were disappointing. Under $1 million was raised against a target of $60 million. The appeal dragged its feet because of lack of official enthusiasm, and because of the friction which accompanied its birth and pursued its career. The American voluntary agencies were very jealous of any invasion of their territory, and demanded that their equal partnership with Unicef in UNAC be constantly underlined. Much more energy was spent arguing about who would receive and spend the proceeds than setting up a strong co-operative arrangement for raising them. The creation of a US Committee for Unicef in December 1947 did little to resolve these problems.

This committee came into existence at the instigation of Katherine Lenroot, the Director of the US Children's Bureau and the US delegate to Unicef's Executive Board. She felt that support from a group of influential citizens might bolster US government commitment, and would help push through Congress a sizeable Unicef appropriation. A distinguished slate of Committee members was enlisted with help from the State Department. The chairperson was Mrs Mary Lord, a leader in prominent social circles with an impeccable career in voluntary service. The Committee's first meeting was held on 19 January 1948 in no less a venue than the White House, at the invitation of Mrs Harry Truman.

The contacts the group could command paid off. The *New York Times* ran an editorial on the same day, called 'The Appeal for Children', one of several around this time which lamented the hard-pressed financial fortunes of the United Nations children's fund. But the US Committee for Unicef stood aloof from any kind of fund-raising activity. Mary Lord did not feel the committee could raise funds or get involved in explaining to the American public what UNAC was without antagonizing key supporters of the Unicef appropriation in the US Congress.

The failure in the US was discouraging. In spite of its many successes, the UN decided not to allow UNAC to carry on for another year in its existing form, as Ording had hoped. He made his disappointment and anger public. In December 1948, the General Assembly passed a resolution that UNAC should continue, but that in future all funds raised should go to Unicef. Ording himself was repudiated. The battle had finally gone Rajchman's way.

Alfred Katzin, lately a senior official of UNRRA, took over the Appeal as a personal favour to Trygve Lie and Maurice Pate. He found it difficult to pick up the pieces. Except in a handful of countries, notably Australia and New Zealand, where the idea of voluntary association in support of UN efforts for children faced little opposition from humanitarian interests, UNAC's productive days were over. During 1949 and 1950, $1·5 million was raised: less than a tenth of the amount raised in 1948.

UNAC left an important legacy, however. It was the first time that the UN appealed for contributions to private citizens as opposed to governments, and this imbued it with some of the aura previously reserved exclusively for charitable and voluntary effort. In many countries United Nations Associations and national committees for Unicef became successor organizations.

With his banker's instinct, Maurice Pate did not allow any expectations from UNAC to get in the way of pursuing other sources of revenue, particularly governments'. During Unicef's early years, the outcome of the annual legislative circus on appropriations in Washington effectively meant the difference between the organization's life and death. As each year's discussions on the federal budget began, Pate maintained as much pressure on the US as he was able. He kept closely in touch with Herbert Hoover, and though he was too delicate to ask him to use his senior Republican connections on Unicef's behalf, Hoover did so voluntarily to good effect.

Independently of what could be managed on the various political circuits—and Pate himself spent considerable time in Washington trying to muster support—public pressure could make a difference. At this stage, the US Committee for Unicef was a body designed to act with maximum decorum and was quite unsuited to conducting vigorous popular campaigns. Here, Pate's friend Helenka Pantaleoni stepped into the breach. Through the network of women's and other organizations with which she was active, Pantaleoni managed to arrange that Congressmen were showered with letters of support.

An even more important arena was Washington itself. One of Pate's earliest recruits to Unicef was Betty Jacob, previously a special assistant to the Directors-General of UNRRA and active in relief work during the war. Jacob knew the Washington legislative circuits inside out, and moved around them in a way that quite set the State Department's teeth on edge; they found it impossible to plead that Congress would not support anything more than a modest financial appropriation when Jacob could produce a bevy of legislators to say the opposite.

In 1948, Congress agreed an appropriation for Unicef of $35 million. This compared to $40 million the previous year, but the reduction was more apparent than real. Of the $40 million voted for 1947, it had been stipulated that, beyond an initial $15 million, other governments must provide 'matching' contributions according to a formula of $43 to $57 before more could be released. So far, the response of other governments had not allowed Unicef to take up the entire amount.

In 1948, a more liberal 'match' of $28 to $72 from the US was stipulated. In spite of this generous enticement, support from other governments was still slow to pick up. At the end of June 1949, there was $13 million left untouched, which only did not disappear altogether because at the last moment, under more orchestrated pressure, Congress voted that Unicef could draw on it for another year.

Pate was constantly trying to widen the net of donors, not only to take up the money sitting idle in the US treasury, but to internationalize the base of Unicef's support. Some governments—Australia, Switzerland, and France were the most generous—did begin to give to Unicef as a habit. Others— Italy, Czechoslovakia, Poland, and Yugoslavia—gave generous contributions in kind considering that they were among the countries worst hit by war. But for all Pate's hard work, it took until June 1950 to squeeze out of governments around the globe enough to draw the entire $75 million voted by the US.

Unlike other UN organizations which received their financial allocations from member states on an assessed basis as part of their membership dues, Unicef was conceived from the start as a fund towards which governments and people gave voluntarily. This characteristic was one much valued by Pate. In these first few years, his small band of staff and helpers produced a series of ideas for raising money. One of these has done more than anything else to make Unicef a household name around the world: Unicef greeting cards.

The story of how the greeting cards began is part of Unicef folklore. The first design was a picture of a maypole painted on glass by a seven-year-old Czechoslovakian girl. Dzitka and her classmates were regular drinkers of Unicef milk, and the paintings they produced were a 'thank-you', sent off to Unicef's bureau in Prague by their teacher. From there, the glass picture of children dancing round the maypole went to Vienna, where one of Pate's bright young women—Grace Holmes Barbey, sent out on an information gathering mission—wrapped it up and took it back to New York. In October 1949, small numbers of a card using Dzitka's design were produced as a modest fund-raiser.

In spite of Pate's reservations about attaching Unicef's name to anything remotely commercial, comments were so favourable that the experiment was repeated the following year. This time, the design was completely pedestrian, a concession to his concern that the project should be purely 'educational'. The card showed the new UN building in Manhattan and a barge laden with Unicef supplies setting off down the river. However hard he wished it not to make money, the card defeated Pate by raising $4200!

These experiments led to the formal establishment of the Unicef Greeting Card Operation in 1951. Care was taken to avoid tying the cards either in picture or words exclusively to the Christian idea of the Christmas season. The greeting was printed in the official UN languages; everything was done to create as much of an international flavour as possible. Pate's scruples were met by printing on each card that its production and sale were for the benefit of the world's children.

Using the promotional network of the UN family and the many voluntary organizations in the US with which Jacob, Barbey, Pantaleoni, and others had established Unicef connections, 600,000 cards were sold. The designs for the cards were donated by Dagmar Starcke, a Danish artist, establishing a tradition for the future. In the next few years, Raoul Dufy and Henri Matisse donated designs, giving the operation useful publicity. In 1953, the greetings cards started to sell on the other side of the Atlantic and raised nearly $100,000. The sales operation was run by volunteers; their increasing numbers and the increasing sales of cards went hand-in-hand through the 1950s and 1960s with the growth of Unicef's national committees.

If millions of people were introduced to Unicef by cards at Christmas, families in the US began to hear of it at Halloween. On 31 October, as the pumpkin pie bakes in the oven, the custom all over North America is for children to go out and accost people with a threat: 'Trick or Treat'. A cookie or a candy bar is the 'treat' they are looking for; if it is not handed over, due warning has been given that a 'trick' — a prank — may be played. In October 1950, the Reverend Clyde Allison of Bridesburg, Pennsylvania, introduced a 'trick or treat' variation to the members of his Sunday School. Instead of demanding treats for themselves, the children of Bridesburg asked instead for nickels and dimes to send to Unicef.

In subsequent years, other churches and schools took up the idea, fostered originally by Betty Jacob and promoted actively after 1953 by the US Committee for Unicef, by then under the chairmanship of Helenka Pantaleoni. 'Trick or Treat for Unicef' provided a perfect vehicle for educating children in school and at home about children in other lands, how they lived and what their problems were. Many years down the road, with the help of Unicef's Ambassador-at-Large, Danny Kaye, the annual Halloween campaign for Unicef was to play a major part in etching Unicef's name indelibly on the map of popular support.

During the course of 1948 and 1949, Unicef began to take its first, then imperceptible, steps towards metamorphosis into an entirely different kind of organization. Most of these steps took place in Asia.

To begin with, Unicef's programme of assistance to countries in Asia other than China followed quite naturally from its concern for the children of all 'countries victims of aggression'. Japan had, after all, managed for a while to hold almost universal sway from Korea in the east to Burma in the west. But the emergency circumstances which confronted the children of Asia were so very different from those in Europe that, as was evident from the start, the essentially neat and tidy package—the 'food parcel plus'—that most assistance to Europe represented could not sensibly be copied. In groping around, trying to find out how to do something useful in this vast and heterogeneous chunk of the planet, Unicef began to be reshaped by the responses it produced. The alternative to the 'food parcel plus' in what were then called the underdeveloped regions eventually became the fundamental purpose of Unicef—and the reason why its existence was prolonged, at first temporarily into the early 1950s, and later indefinitely, to the present day. When Unicef first began in 1947 to contemplate assistance for 'the Far East other than China', this course of events was certainly not foreseen.

In the late 1940s, most of Asia was in a state of political and social upheaval. The second World War had permanently damaged the authority of ancient or traditional regimes, as well as that of the colonial powers. New political arrangements were gradually emerging, some accompanied by protracted turmoil. The Philippines gained their long promised independence from the US in 1946. The British extracted themselves from a divided Indian subcontinent the following year, and extended independence to Ceylon and Burma in less agonising circumstances. Fighting broke out against the French in Indo-China in late 1946 after they tried to reassert their control. In Indonesia, the days of the Dutch were numbered. In Korea, rival claims for sovereignty over the peninsula threatened violent confrontation. Everywhere from the plains of the Punjab to the streets of Saigon, the region presented a spectacle of profound uncertainty and teeming confusion.

By any standards, the prospect of running a useful assistance programme with a handful of dollars in an area containing 450 million children was extremely daunting. Under the circumstances there were some in Unicef's ranks who doubted whether the effort was worth making. However, as with China, Pate pushed ahead. Unicef was an international organization, and in his view it should behave like one. Its contribution might make a more measurable and significant difference in a European environment, but that did not justify ignoring others of a more problematic kind.

Superficially, there were some comparisons to be made between postwar Asia and postwar Europe. Many countries occupied by Japan had suffered intense wartime destruction. Manila had received more war damage than any European city except Warsaw. Food production was disrupted, and in many countries virtually nothing was left of pre-war health institutions and training schools. Public health had deteriorated; tuberculosis, insect-borne and venereal disease had increased.

Unquestionably, there was plenty of emergency relief and rehabilitation work to be done for children, specially in areas still affected by strife. But there was a very significant difference between the temporary nature of emergency needs in most of Europe and the permanent nature of those in most of Asia. Relief was intended to tide people over, and rehabilitation to restore the *status quo ante*. This, in most of the countries of Asia, was a state of affairs in which millions of mothers and children endured chronic, everyday hunger and ill-health outside the reach of any medical treatment or social service. It was not possible for Unicef to start discussing even an emergency programme for any of these countries without considering the underlying problems which would remain once the emergency was over. Asia defied a definition of the word 'emergency'.

In April 1948, in an attempt to try to establish a suitable policy for assisting in Asia, Unicef invited two authoritative public health figures to undertake a survey of thirteen Asian countries—Dr Thomas Parran, former Surgeon-General of the US Public Health Service, and Dr C. K. Lakshmanan, Director of the All-India Institute of Hygiene and Public Health in Calcutta. They travelled in British North Borneo, Burma, Ceylon, Hong Kong, India, Pakistan, Indo-China, Malaya, the Netherlands East Indies, the Philippines, Thailand and Singapore, meeting with senior health officials and trying to pinpoint child-health problems to which Unicef's slender resources might be applied. In July, they filed their report.

Their first conclusion was that it would be impossible to attempt any large-scale feeding of hungry children. Hunger, malnutrition, even starvation, were chronic conditions. But the size of the territories involved, the huge populations, the lack of communications and trained administrators—not to mention the political difficulties many new and inexperienced governments were facing—precluded food rationing schemes on any but the most local scale. If not food, then what? The high rate of infant death was striking in almost all the countries they visited. Only one country—Thailand —had a rate lower than 100 per thousand live births. Elsewhere, a rate of 200 was common, and in certain countries there were pockets where 300 was the norm.

Parran and Lakshmanan had everywhere sought to identify the best ways of making a small investment in child health. They began to focus on disease control. In spite of the lack of reliable statistics, the extent of certain diseases particularly affecting mothers and children was well-known. Many were more widespread as a direct result of war and civil disruption. Malaria was the number one killer in most countries: in India alone there were around 100 million cases a year, and two million deaths. Tuberculosis was not far behind: one country had carried out a recent survey which showed that fifty per cent of children at six years old were tuberculin positive. Syphilis was widespread; in places where occupying troops had been present over a long period, the rate among pregnant women was as high as fifty per cent. In Indonesia and Thailand, yaws—a dreaded and disabling disease which, like syphilis, was caused by treponema or spiral-shaped bacteria and manifested itself in painful lesions—had also reached epidemic proportions. In addition to these diseases, dysentery, intestinal parasites and malnutrition in various degrees of severity were so prevalent as to be the rule rather than the exception among small children.

Parran and Lakshmanan drew up provisional lists of assistance for all the countries they visited. The main emphasis was on laboratory equipment, and drugs and vaccines, for programmes of disease control. They were pinpricks of assistance compared to the scale of the problems. But they were useful pinpricks and essential components in any scheme trying to begin the process of bringing health problems under control.

There were, too, supplies of milk and other protective foods, the backbone of Unicef assistance. While child feeding on any large scale was impracticable, some situations invited the provision of nutritious food rations. Armed conflict was casting up hapless populations of refugees on shores and on frontiers. In the refugee camps of India, Pakistan and Hong Kong, as well as in orphanages and welfare institutes, organized feeding of children in care was not only possible but essential, according to Parran. 'Milk, under such circumstances, is medicine', he reported. 'How precious it is is proved by the willingness of mothers to stand in line, literally for hours, in order to get a small can.'

The main obstacle to better control of infectious disease and improving child health generally was the lack of health and social welfare services, and of people trained to run them. Doctors and nurses were in short supply. Specialists were almost non-existent. There weren't even any paramedical staff capable of performing simple medical and sanitary tasks. In October 1948, Unicef's Board agreed that seventy-three fellowships for overseas training might be granted, with advice from WHO about the selection of candidates and courses.

The results of these fellowships, most of which were in the fields of midwifery, public health nursing, paediatrics and tuberculosis control, taught Unicef an important lesson. Although the fellows marginally improved their performance when they returned home, most of what they had been taught in institutions reflecting the state of the art in Western medicine was inapplicable at home. Recognizing that training the different categories and echelons of personnel needed to run child-health services was ultimately even more essential than sending equipment and supplies, from this point onwards Unicef directed its assistance for professional training to institutions in the part of the world where trainees would later practise. One of its first moves in this direction was to provide $930,000, matched by a similar sum from the Indian government, to set up a regional training centre for maternal and child-health care workers at the All-India Institute of Hygiene and Public Health in Calcutta.

In November 1948, Dr Michael Watt who had just retired as New

Zealand's Director of Health Services, received a letter from Maurice Pate offering him the post of Unicef's Regional Director in South-East Asia. Watt had never heard of Unicef, but adventurously chose to accept. For the next twelve months he flew all over the southern seas and laid the groundwork for what became the largest and most dynamic of Unicef's programme networks. He was present in Colombo in March 1949 for the inaugural shot in the Ceylonese anti-tuberculosis campaign, one of three Asian countries to invite the Scandinavian teams of the ITC to vaccinate their children.

In Djakarta, Watt tried unsuccessfully to persuade the wartime Republican government to accept a consignment of Unicef milk powder from the hands of the Dutch. In Rangoon he visited a large maternity hospital and found it equipped with only two pairs of forceps. In a hospital in Karachi, he was introduced to the first group of young women to abandon purdah to join the nursing course. In the Philippines, where a feeding programme used milk, fish, rice, beans, and shark oil capsules from his own New Zealand, the authorities were sufficiently impressed with results to introduce school meals as a government policy.

Watt decided to set up Unicef's headquarters in Bangkok. Thailand seemed like a rock of stability in a troubled region, and Bangkok's position at the hub of South-East Asia also made it a suitable position for an office whose realm covered millions of square miles and almost as many millions of children. FAO and the UN had made the same decision about the location of their regional offices. Watt hired staff and began to establish the embryonic network of an operation fanning out in an arc from Karachi in the east, through Ceylon, Java, the Philippines, to Korea in the north-west. Gradually, a small band of Unicef representatives were taking up posts in New Delhi, Manila, Djakarta and elsewhere to supervise a steady flow of supplies arriving from all points of the compass.

Watt himself, for health reasons, decided not to stay. His replacement was an ebullient American, Spurgeon Milton Keeny. Sam Keeny, the emperor of Unicef in Asia for the next thirteen years, probably did more than any single person to prove that Unicef's work in countries outside Europe was worthwhile for not some, but all, the world's children.

It had been a British delegate to Unicef's Board, J. A. A. C. Alexander, and his concern for an area of traditional British interest, which had provided the decisive encouragement for Unicef to start seriously considering assistance for Asia. In the case of Latin America, the equivalent push came from the US delegate, Katherine Lenroot, along with allies from the Latin American member States themselves.

Early in 1947, when Maurice Pate and Ludwik Rajchman were concentrating most of their attention on the burning issue of fund-raising, they both looked upon the countries of Latin America primarily as sources of income, not as potential recipients of Unicef assistance. They were not, after all, countries gravely damaged by war, and some—notably Brazil—had given considerable support to UNRRA.

Very soon after Unicef's creation, a series of meetings took place with the Latin American member countries of the Executive Board to discuss the best way of soliciting funds from the region. The strategy adopted was to recruit distinguished Unicef emissaries to carry out educational and fund-raising missions to the most likely countries. Dr Domingo Ramos of the University of Havana and Dr Howard Kershner, a US philanthropist of international renown, were among the first. Their efforts were rewarded by a resolution passed at the Inter-American Conference on Social Security in Rio de Janeiro in November 1947 which endorsed the governments' support for Unicef and other UN organizations. Except for Uruguay, which gave $1 million in 1948, this resolution did not prompt any immediate, large-scale generosity. President Trujillo of the Dominican Republic handed Pate a cheque for $20,000 during a bizarre visit to the UN. Venezuela, Cuba, Costa Rica and Guatemala provided similar sums the following year. Potentially much larger donors held back, in spite of all Pate's efforts to woo them.

Some of the Latin American countries did not like to be perceived merely as a source of funds. The Brazilian delegate to the Unicef Board, Roberto Oliveira de Campos, was particularly vocal in pointing out that there were many children in the region greatly in need of assistance. To begin with, Unicef resisted the idea of becoming involved. There was a range of other international agencies in a better position to furnish advice on child health or welfare in the region. Especially to begin with, Unicef was stretched to provide a realistic programme for children in war-torn Europe.

But Katherine Lenroot saw the issue in a different light. She regarded Unicef as the international equivalent of the US Children's Bureau of which she was chief; in that capacity, she had considerable experience of children's welfare issues in Latin America, a part of the world quite unfamiliar to both Pate and Rajchman. She had been a US delegate to various Pan-American Child Congresses, and was closely associated with the International American Institute for the Protection of Childhood, based in Montevideo. Its ninth Congress took place in Caracas in January 1948; Dr Martha Eliot, Lenroot's deputy, attended for the Children's Bureau and played a prominent part. A resolution was passed inviting Unicef to pay attention to the needs of children in the Americas, and Lenroot took care to raise the issue in New York.

During 1948 attitudes within Unicef began to change. Campos began to get through to Rajchman and others the very real needs of Latin American children. In the rural areas of some countries, he pointed out, infant death rates were nearly as high as in parts of Asia: between 100 and 200 per 1000 births. In late summer, rumblings of serious dissatisfaction from Latin American member states began to circulate around the UN about Unicef's refusal to heed their requests. In their view, European recovery meant that their own children's needs were now as, or more, pressing than those in Europe. Anxious to avoid an attack on Unicef in the General Assembly, Rajchman began to elaborate a set of principles to govern some limited assistance to children's programmes in Latin America.

Before any specific requests were entertained, it would be useful to have more information about the specific health and nutrition problems of children in the region. FAO was organizing a conference on nutritional problems in Latin America scheduled for July 1948, so Rajchman invited Dr Reginald Passmore, a lecturer in the departments of Public Health and Social Medicine in Edinburgh University and an ex-member of the Indian Medical Service, to attend the conference on behalf of Unicef.

Passmore used the opportunity to consult other international organizations already active in the Americas and to visit various countries. His report was an important step forward. He witnessed little of the kind of starvation he was used to seeing in Asia, but there was plenty of malnutrition—for which he mainly blamed the lack of milk—and much infant sickness and death from tuberculosis and insect-borne diseases, specially malaria and typhus.

Soon after Passmore's return, Maurice Pate sent a letter to every Latin American UN delegation outlining the kind of programmes Unicef was willing to support: supplementary feeding, anti-tuberculosis and anti-syphilis campaigns, insect control to reduce malaria, milk conservation, and scholarships in social paediatrics.

In March 1949 the Executive Board made a block allocation of $2 million to be spent as and when specific projects came forward. By the end of the year, several were under discussion and the amount was upped to $3·8 million. Dr Leo Eloesser, who had returned from China, was sent off to Latin America to look at the possibilities for disease control and maternal and child-health services. Dr Johannes Holm from Copenhagen was another of several consultants who travelled to various Latin American countries. Close co-operation took place with the Pan-American Sanitary Bureau (PASB), the international health organization for the Americas affiliated with WHO and headed by Dr Fred Lowe Soper, a veteran of many famous disease control campaigns on the American continent.

Many of the earliest programmes to win Unicef's support were those of the most familiar kind: feeding programmes in schools. Unicef's experience in, and enthusiasm for, putting milk into children's mouths propelled it naturally in this direction. An Institute of Nutrition for Central America and Panama (INCAP) had been recently established in Guatemala City, under the direction of Dr Nevin Scrimshaw of the PASB. Because of

INCAP's presence, Guatemala City was chosen as the first location of a Unicef office in the region and, in September 1949, Alice Shaffer of the US Children's Bureau was recruited to serve there as Unicef's first representative. INCAP, whose governing body consisted of Public Health Ministers of the member countries, was beginning to tackle the shortage of reliable information on the scale of child malnutrition and the dietary practices of poor families. To begin with, Scrimshaw did not welcome Unicef's dried powdered milk for school lunch programmes. He was a critic of basing a nutrition programme for any length of time on an imported food, and preferred local sources of cheap vegetable protein. Some of the Health Ministers were, however, more enthusiastic and Unicef milk was imported for use in small-scale demonstration projects intended to prove that mass feeding in classrooms and institutions was a sound investment in child health. Scrimshaw simultaneously pursued his quest for a cheap nutritious vegetable-based food which could be locally promoted instead of milk as an antidote to child malnutrition. This initiative was a long time maturing.

The largest proportion of Unicef's early assistance to Latin American countries was spent on disease control. Early in 1950, two countries— Mexico and Ecuador—played host to the International Tuberculosis Campaign and carried out the first mass tuberculin testing and BCG vaccination in the hemisphere. Other support for disease control included supplies of DDT for use against malaria and other insect-borne disease; and penicillin for the cure of syphilis and yaws in eight countries of the Caribbean, including a mass effort in Haiti during the years when Dr Francois Duvalier became the popular maestro of health and earned the nickname 'Papa Doc'.

Unicef also provided equipment for maternal and child-health centres, and for laboratories to produce whooping cough and diphtheria vaccine. Over the first year-and-a-half of Unicef assistance in the region, the emphasis was on programmes that could develop rapidly and yield immediate results; Unicef's own future was too uncertain over the longer term.

Unicef's engagement in the countries of the eastern Mediterranean region was inspired by very different circumstances. After the second World War, the turmoil in the Middle East which had first been inspired by Jewish immigration to Palestine in the 1930s re-erupted. The pressure to create a homeland for the Jewish people grew to a crescendo, and the UN accepted the idea. When the British mandate in Palestine expired in May 1948, a new state of Israel was declared. The Arab countries refused recognition, and war engulfed the whole area. Hundreds of thousands of people fled their homes.

In August 1948, Count Folke Bernadotte, the special UN mediator in Palestine, made an international appeal for assistance. Unicef, under its mandate for providing help to children irrespective of political considerations, was able to respond relatively quickly. For many weeks, its food supplies were the mainstay of rations for refugee children; blankets and other essentials were supplied throughout the following eighteen months, along with a daily meal for half a million Palestinian and Israeli mothers and children. Distribution was handled through the Red Cross and the Friends Service Committee. These arrangements were eventually superceded by the creation of the UN Relief and Works Agency (UNRWA), which after 1 May 1950 co-ordinated all UN relief for Palestinian refugees. Unicef contributed over $10·5 million during the crisis period.

The first country in the region to seek Unicef assistance for regular, as opposed to emergency, child health and feeding was Israel. X-ray units, drugs and vaccines were sent, opening a warm relationship between Unicef and Israel which long survived the spirit of Arab/Israeli hostility pervading many other UN fora. By mid-1949, the tentacles of the International Tuberculosis Campaign began to reach other countries, including Egypt, Syria and Lebanon, and some of the countries of northern Africa, as well as the Palestinian refugees. Taking a cue from the anti-tuberculosis onslaught, Iraq then sought Unicef's help for an attack on bejel, another treponemous disease like syphilis and yaws. Thus began Unicef assistance in the eastern Mediterranean region, a programme much more primitive at the end of 1950 then either of those in Asia or Latin America. No programme yet existed in Africa south of the Sahara, a part of the world still almost entirely under the domination of the colonial powers.

In April 1949, Pate recruited a deputy. E. J. R. Heyward was a 34-year-old Tasmanian economist who had come to New York as First Secretary to the Australian mission and represented Australia on Unicef's Board. His first assignment for Unicef was in 1947 when, responding to a complaint from the Greek delegate, Pate asked him to go to Greece and to find out whether Unicef supplies were being used to support the Communist rebellion. This allegation proved to be spurious. Heyward thereafter took an active part in Unicef policy discussions, and his dissections of programmes commanded the attention of both Pate and Rajchman, towards whom the much younger man felt great respect. He also happened to be the delegate of the country which was Unicef's second largest government donor and its largest voluntary donor through UNAC. When the organization grew to a point where Pate felt over-extended, he asked the Australian Ministry of Foreign Affairs whether Dick Heyward could be loaned temporarily: at this stage, there was still no serious idea that the organization had more than another year or two to live.

Heyward brought to Unicef an intellectual strength never subsequently outmatched and, coupled with an outwardly shy and retiring personality, a bulldog tenacity which was to serve the organization through thick and thin during the course of nearly thirty-three years. He joined Pate's staff at a critical period. Over the course of the next few months, the idea of keeping the organization alive and consolidating rather than disbanding its work for children began to gain ground, both among senior staff and certain Board members. Heyward, together with Jack Charnow, Secretary to the Executive Board, were the key members of the team who helped Pate shepherd Unicef through more than eighteen months of dispute and uncertainty.

As the emergency in Europe began to recede, the specific purpose for which a temporary emergency fund for children had been set up under UN auspices no longer existed. By mid-1949, however, Unicef's programme already extended far beyond the original purpose, both in geographical extent and in character. Inevitably, as it began to face the challenges posed by 'emergency' requirements in Asia, children's health and nutritional needs had been revealed which would persist far beyond the next year or two, and for which some cargoes of food, drugs, and essential supplies were not needed merely as a vital protective stop-gap.

Unicef had followed to the letter a principle laid down for it by the Economic and Social Council in early 1947: 'Emergency measures shall be so developed and administered as to utilize and strengthen the permanent health and child welfare programmes of the countries receiving assistance'. For countries outside Europe, Unicef had transformed the 'food parcel plus' of traditional emergency relief into vaccinations for disease control, midwifery kits and health-centre equipment, milk-drying plants, training fellowships in social paediatrics, and other items—the latest under discussion were plant for Asia's first penicillin and DDT factories—for which need was most unlikely to disappear. The lack of foreign exchange to purchase such things was not a temporary phenomenon caused by war, but a product of underdevelopment, or poverty, which would stretch into the foreseeable future. Many Unicef people were beginning to feel distinctly unhappy about what would happen to replace their work when the organization closed down.

In June 1949, Maurice Pate proposed to the Executive Board that a study on 'the continuing needs of children' be carried out. This study would pave the way for a UN policy about how its assistance could in the future be used to help meet those needs. Ostensibly, this proposal envisaged Unicef's demise and the assumption of its responsibilities towards children by other, permanently-established parts of the UN system. But it raised the possibility, implicitly if not explicitly, that one way of helping to meet the continuing needs of children was through continuing the life of Unicef. The proposal was a litmus test to find out which countries might seek to prolong Unicef's life and which would resist such a move.

The answer was immediately forthcoming. Both the US and Canada supported the idea of such a study, but saw its essential purpose as the establishment of a timetable for the demise of Unicef and an early and orderly transition of its useful functions elsewhere. Switzerland and Australia also supported the idea of the study, but thought it unnecessary at this point to destroy public confidence in Unicef by talking openly of a 'dying organization'. The North Americans strongly disagreed; they wanted there to be no doubt in anyone's mind that Unicef was a temporary organization and that its days were numbered. Theirs was the view that prevailed.

Other UN organizations — notably WHO — were also beginning to call for such a 'study', which had now become a transparent euphemism for organizing the dismemberment of Unicef and dividing the spoils between various inheritors. A working group was set up 'to co-ordinate the work of UN organizations in regard to children'; it included representatives of the United Nations Secretariat, WHO, ILO, FAO, IRO, UNESCO, and Dick Heyward on behalf of Unicef.

He and Charnow began to pull together material from field offices around the world and wage a propaganda campaign on Unicef's behalf. In December 1949, the group produced its results. That children were in need around the world was not in dispute; that all the specialized agencies had a role to play in international assistance on their behalf was equally uncontentious; but they had failed to reach agreement on where each role began and ended and whether a specific fund for children in some shape or form was needed.

During the course of the next several months, in a series of different UN fora, the number and complexity of various suggestions for assuming the task of helping children was only paralleled by the number and complexity of the dissenting positions against them. If the secretariats of the organizations could not agree — and it was clear that at least between WHO and Unicef there would be no meeting of minds — the government delegates in their various commissions and committees did no better. Inevitably, as time went by the question began to be asked whether it would not be simpler — not to mention more beneficial for children — to leave Unicef to continue doing what it had begun.

Some preparatory moves were made to open the way for such a suggestion to come before UN decision-making bodies. On 2 December 1949 — the same day that the inter-agency working group reported on its inconclusive deliberations — the General Assembly passed a resolution congratulating Unicef for 'its great humanitarian effort in Europe and in the Middle East, now being extended to Asia, Latin America, and Africa, in bringing substantial aid of lasting value . . . to millions of mothers and children'. In the way of such resolutions, the wording might sound mild to the point of banality. But to those involved, it was the opening salvo of a counter-attack to rescue Unicef and keep it alive.

The areas of dispute were essentially three. The first area was money. Naturally this issue was most important to the US government which had played the role of the organization's postwar paymaster, and did not think it could go on persuading Congress to underwrite the children's fund once the emergency in Europe had disappeared. In early 1949, the Congress had stated its unwillingness to appropriate further funds for Unicef until plans for its termination had been formulated. Sadly, many Americans did not feel so deeply concerned about the fate of children in Asia, Africa, and Latin America as they had about those in Europe. The State Department therefore believed that it would be better to legislate for a small, additional sum to be given to the UN Secretariat budget by all member states to offset the cost of a permanent children's section within it. This could be guaranteed to survive the vagaries of government generosity, and its costs would be borne more fairly by other governments: instead of providing half Unicef's total income as it had to date, the US would provide one-quarter according to the standard cost-sharing formula between the nations.

The second issue was territory. WHO, and to a lesser extent FAO and the UN Bureau of Social Affairs, did not and had never appreciated the idea of a separate UN organization for children. The mandate of an organization which existed to help an age-group rather than a professional and governmental sector overlapped with their own. They wanted to be the inheritors of Unicef's programmes; the most they were prepared to concede was that a United Nations fund-raising and supplies organization would be useful. It should, of course, be properly under their wing from a technical point of view. Children could be put on posters and their smiles and tears used for UN promotional and publicity purposes; but there should be no separate mechanism for planning programmes on their behalf or safeguarding their special interests.

The third issue at dispute was much more confused. It had to do with the difference between 'technical assistance' and 'material assistance'; between the idea, not quite yet fully formulated, of participating in a country's 'development' and merely offering 'emergency relief'. At this time, the only engines of 'development' yet accorded recognition by the international community were capital investment and technical assistance. Within the new network of international mechanisms, capital investment was the domain of the institutions set up at Bretton Woods, particularly the World Bank. Technical assistance—or advice and scientific know-how in agriculture, health, nutrition, education, employment, or social welfare—was the service the specialized agencies had been set up to provide.

'Material assistance'—donated goods, which Unicef provided by raising funds and buying supplies—was a thoroughly inferior kind of affair. Provided in any circumstances other than the classic emergency, material assistance was seen as a welfare hand-out, the antithesis of the kinds of investment which would enable underdeveloped countries to move ahead. Unicef had begun to prove that this need not be so; and WHO, in suggesting that Unicef's expertise in supply procurement should be retained in its truncated offspring, had recognized that equipping a health centre or providing machinery for a penicillin plant did not necessarily mean helpless dependency on the part of the recipients. However, the idea that providing supplies was somehow by definition a nondevelopmental thing to do and that any organization which did this as a primary function did not deserve any permanence or independence greatly complicated the dispute about Unicef's survival. Unicef was seen as a humanitarian upstart of an organization with milk powder, penicillin and popular appeal but no serious role to play in the business of development. Some people persist in this view to the present day.

Maurice Pate took time to reach a point of inner conviction that Unicef in its existing form ought to continue. In his Hoover days, all the relief organizations he served automatically closed down when the emergency was over: this was almost essential to their ideological purity. In May 1949, when the US Congress had been considering the appropriation, Pate had testified before the Committee on Foreign Affairs that Unicef was closely collaborating with WHO and FAO with a view to handing its functions over to them. By January 1950, he had begun to waver. He told Mary Lord, Chairman of the US Committee, that he had reached the conclusion that the UN should embark on a 'second chapter' of work for children. He felt that Unicef had given great impetus to governments and individuals everywhere, and that 'in the world in which we live today I consider it enormously important to keep this kind of spirit highly alive'.

The first indication that sizeable opposition could be marshalled against the firm intention of the US and its supporters—Britain, Canada, South Africa, China (Taiwan), Netherlands, and the Scandinavian countries—to bow Unicef off the UN stage came in the spring. The revolt came in the Social Commission of the UN, which recommended that Unicef continue its mission in uninterrupted form. The vote came about because the majority of countries represented in the Social Commission were on the receiving end of Unicef supplies. This development greatly boosted the morale of Unicef's own people, and hardened the resolve of key supporters— the Australians, French, New Zealanders, and Yugoslavs.

Pate himself now adopted a much less ambiguous position, and began to present the case in Washington and elsewhere of the millions of deprived children and mothers in Asia and Latin America, where work had only just begun in earnest. There were also the thousands of children in countries such as Greece, Lebanon, Jordan, Japan, India, Pakistan, and now in Korea, whose suffering was still a vestige, direct or indirect, of postwar crisis. But his efforts made little impact at the State Department.

The US delegation was helping the UN Secretariat draft yet another compromise formula for submission to the UN General Assembly; it was a variation on the theme of a children's section within the UN Secretariat, but essentially no different from the earlier proposal which the Social Commission had rejected.

Aware that there would be energetic opposition, Pate went to see Eleanor Roosevelt, the chief US delegate to the UN Committee on Social and Humanitarian Affairs. To this disappointment, she proved as unmovable as the rest. A lifelong champion of children's causes and a keen supporter both earlier and later in Unicef's career, she allowed herself to believe that the children of the world would be best served by Unicef's demise. She was persuaded by the State Department that Congress would not be prepared to vote more funds and wanted a permanent arrangement within the UN for children. She refused to see that Unicef could ever be anything but a temporary organization sending emergency relief supplies, and she felt that its very existence was a hindrance to the establishment of something better. She did not understand the viewpoint of the underdeveloped countries about the value they attached to material assistance; nor the programme formulae that Unicef was developing for its work outside Europe.

The critical debate on Unicef's future took place on 6 October 1950 at Lake Success. Unicef's leading champion was Professor Ahmed Bokhari, a well-known figure in the US literary and academic world and Pakistan's permanent representative to the UN. Bokhari, who was known for his eloquence, dismissed totally the proposal presented by the UN Secretary-General. He described the notion that the 'emergency' was over as an illusion; this was the basis of the case that a separate UN children's fund was no longer needed. 'This illusion conveys the impression that, apart from possible future emergencies such as the occasional earthquake, all is well in the world and that the United Nations should concern itself not with aid to children in 1950 or 1951, but with long-range goals such as aid in the year 2000.

'Pakistan, as well as other countries in Asia', Bokhari continued, 'was shocked to see in pamphlets distributed by Unicef, photographs of emaciated European children, victims of the war. We received, however, a second shock on realizing that those European children still appeared to be in a no-worse state than millions of children living so-called normal lives in the underdeveloped countries.' He deplored the cold language of the proposal under discussion, 'according to which children suffering from endemic cholera might well be denied cholera vaccines, unless their illness is the result of an emergency. Instead, blueprints for the production of vaccines will be provided to the government concerned, and the United Nations will wash its hands of the fate of the children pending their local production'.

Bokhari delivered his speech on the first afternoon of the debate. His appeal, backed by other delegates from the Middle East and Latin America, turned the tide in Unicef's favour. After days of debate, no amount of amendment had made the UN proposal sufficiently palatable to enough of those present. The donor countries began to desert Mrs Roosevelt's side. After nearly two weeks, the Australian delegation proposed a simple way through the impasse. Unicef in its existing form should be extended for two more years and its life then be reconsidered; the Yugoslavs amended the proposal to add an extra year. The three-year extension was finally agreed by forty-three votes to eight.

On 1 December 1950, this resolution was laid before the full General Assembly. Pate, hopeful that he could still persuade the US delegation not to vote against its adoption, wrote at length to Mrs Roosevelt. She was not present on 1 December; her alternate was instructed to abstain. No-one else did so; Unicef had survived intact by what was a near-unanimous vote. To Pate, even one abstention was painful. The US delegate, Edith Sampson, was gracious in defeat: 'This is not the time to emphasize the misunderstandings which characterized so much of the debate on this issue. There are hundreds of millions of children in need, and we cannot forget them'. She went on: 'It is our earnest desire that ways and means will be found to ensure that the economically disinherited children of the world will receive effective United Nations aid over the years to come'.

The debates of 1950 were not the end of the story of Unicef's fight to survive; formally, all that had been won was a three-year stay of execution. But it was in 1950 that the die was cast. This was the debate that marked the watershed between one era and another. From this point onwards Unicef was to direct its full energies to the needs of the children in the underdeveloped world.

The question of Unicef's continuing existence was not finally settled until 5 October 1953, when the General Assembly unanimously agreed to prolong its temporary life indefinitely, or 'without reference to a time limit', dropping the words 'international' and 'emergency' from the name, but retaining the well-known Unicef acronym. During these three years, although the final UN verdict was still a nagging question, a much more real sense of insecurity came from Unicef's poor financial fortunes. The fears expressed in 1950 that international public and private generosity for children would dry up turned out to be fully justified.

In 1952, Unicef reached its financial nadir: only $9·4 million was received from governments worldwide, $6·7 million of which was from the USA. The following year, Helenka Pantaleoni and Betty Jacob kept up public and legislative lobbying campaigns to maintain US generosity at a time when the Eisenhower Administration was facing great Congressional opposition towards aid of all kinds. Unicef's $10 million appropriation was salvaged only after Eisenhower personally endorsed it as 'an integral part of our programme for America's security'. This vocabulary, applied to a fund for children, could only belong to a particular era: McCarthyism.

As the reverberations of the Cold War began to reach an emotional pitch in the US at the turn of the decade, Unicef did not remain untouched. Anti-UN feeling was so strong that no story about it could be reported outside the context which dominated the day-to-day interpretation of current affairs. Under the headline 'Reds Walk Out At UN Group's Child Aid Talks', the *New York Herald Tribune* of 7 March 1950 described how Unicef—'a non-political body that feeds children and mothers on both sides of the iron curtain—was hit by big power politics today when Russia and two satellites walked out'.

Ludwik Rajchman, Chairman of the Board, represented Poland, one of the 'satellites'; the other was Czechoslovakia. The problem was the continued seating of the Nationalist delegate of China (Taiwan) instead of the delegate of the People's Republic. The USSR regarded the continued recognition of the Nationalist government by the UN as illegal, and throughout 1950 and beyond it adopted tactics designed to underline its point of view and enjoined its allies to do likewise. It did not exempt the children's fund from these displays. Unicef had worked hard to uphold the principle that there was no such thing as an enemy child. In the climate of the times it was difficult to maintain the position that children were always above politics.

Ludwik Rajchman was in a particularly uncomfortable position. During the 1930s, at the head of the League of Nations mission to China, he had been closely associated with T. V. Soong and other senior officials of the Chiang Kai Shek administration. While in Washington during the war he had worked for his old associates, trying to tie down US commitment to the Nationalist cause. Now, he felt obliged to make a public display of support for their detested opponents, China's new Communist regime. Politics had caught up with Rajchman's commitment to humanitarian affairs. The year of 1950 was the last year of his chairmanship of Unicef's Board. All his experience of focusing on the task in hand and leaving the ideological fight to others was of no avail against the tide of anticommunist feeling.

Rajchman belonged neither on one side of the iron curtain nor on the other. Yet to sustain his position, he had to function on both. Poland was now run by a Communist regime allied to Moscow. He had not lived in Poland for more than twenty years, and was a long-time expatriate whose family now lived in the US. He was not a candidate likely to recommend himself to the new Polish administration as their representative to a UN organization. But he was also a man of international standing who had done much to gain US aid for Poland during the war years, and international assistance in its aftermath. Furthermore, he was still a Pole and a patriot, whatever the ideological orientation of his motherland's latest regime. His own ideological reputation down the years, particularly in his visionary approach to public health, was that of a left-winger, but no-one who knew him well regarded him as a Communist. On the other hand neither friend nor foe could say for certain where his political sympathies lay. He kept whatever views he had firmly to himself; that however was no longer a protection.

Rajchman managed for a while to walk a tightrope. He was chairman of a UN organization almost entirely dependent on US generosity, while his credentials for any formal involvement at all were provided by a Communist government. During the years of his chairmanship, he played an important—some said too important—role in the management of Unicef: he maintained an office in both New York and in Paris, and worked tirelessly without remuneration.

If Rajchman's style was often impatient and autocratic, Pate was tolerant and humoured his relentless scrutiny. But some other senior Unicef officers and mission chiefs were less ready to stomach Rajchman's proprietory attitude towards every Unicef nook and cranny he chose to enter. The time was coming for Rajchman to recede into the background as a distinguished elder statesman. While this was happening, the tightrope on which he had balanced successfully for so long was beginning to unravel. In 1950, when he found himself obliged to walk out of Unicef Board meetings in support of the USSR position on Nationalist China, it finally gave way.

After this, Rajchman was unable to play any important lobbying role in Unicef's fight for survival. By this stage, whatever he did was open to political interpretation of an unhelpful kind. He did make sure that the report of Unicef's activities during his chairmanship, on which its performance between 1946 and 1950 would be judged, provided a convincing record of achievement. But as far as his own involvement was concerned, the question of whether Unicef's lifespan would be extended was academic. If he had resisted the idea of relinquishing the chairmanship of the Board, the US delegation would have seen that he was voted out. In the current political climate, a chairman from a country with a Western alliance would be more suitable. Early in 1951, Mrs Adelaide Sinclair, the delegate of Canada, was elected the Board's second chairperson.

By this stage, Rajchman was no longer even welcome on US shores. During various US Senate subcommittee hearings targeted at those who were alleged to have 'betrayed' Nationalist forces in China into the hands of the Communists, Rajchman's name came up. His involvement in some of the international discussions surrounding the transformation of old League of Nations departments into new UN agencies was also regarded with suspicion. As the holder of a visa which described him as a delegate of the Polish government, he was branded a *de facto* Communist.

Towards the end of 1950, while visiting New York, he was served with a Congressional subpoena. As the citizen of another country and its diplomatic representative, this was a gross breach of international etiquette. He ignored the subpoena, and flew to France. He was never granted an entry visa again.

Rajchman did not return to Poland. He lived out his retirement close to his old associate Professor Robert Debré and the International Children's Centre, thus maintaining a link with his cherished Unicef. Maurice Pate kept him in touch with activities throughout the years, and visited him when trips to Europe permitted.

Ludwik Rajchman, a truly extraordinary individual, died in 1965, at the age of eighty-four.

Main sources

Final Report of the First Session of Unicef's Executive Board, 11 December 1946–31 December 1950. E/ICEF/1908; E/ICEF160, 22 January 1951; other Unicef Board documentation including report of the Survey Mission to the Far East, July 1948; excerpts from a report by Dr R. Passmore on nutrition and health of children in five Central American countries, November 1948.

Reports to ECOSOC by UNAC and Unicef; interviews for the Unicef History Project with ex-UNAC officials and retired staff members; articles in the 'United Nations Bulletin', 1948–51.

US Department of State memoranda and other US government papers, 1948–50.

Unicef comes to Asia; chapters from the memoirs of Dr Michael Watt, ex-Director of Health Services, New Zealand, March 1964.

Unicef in the Americas: For the Children of Three Decades, by Ken Grant, ex-Unicef Representative, prepared for Unicef's History Project, May 1985.

The Origins and Policy Basis of WHO/Unicef Collaboration in the International Health Field: A Look at the Official Record (1946–1983); WHO, Geneva, June 1983.

Official records of the UN General Assembly, Fifth Session, meetings of the Third Committee, nos. 278 through 287, 6–18 October 1950.

'My Day', a daily newspaper diary column by Eleanor Roosevelt; United Feature Syndicate Inc.

Personal reminiscences and commentaries on the life of Ludwik Rajchman; Hearings before the Subcommittee to investigate the administration of the Internal Security Act and other Internal Security Laws; United States Senate; 82nd Congress, 2nd session.

Chapter 4

The Mass Onslaught Against Disease

In its early efforts to help children in underdeveloped parts of the world, Unicef proceeded by trial and error, mixed with a spirit of adventure and a good measure of simple faith. With the help of established experts in the field of public health—Drs Parran, Lakshmanan, Eliot, Debré, Holm, Passmore, Rajchman himself and many others—it did its best to adapt its formulae for 'material assistance' to suit conditions in parts of the world far removed from those in Europe. Still, with the most expert advice and the greatest goodwill, the process of adaptation was initially somewhat crude. In common with similar organizations setting out on a new kind of humanitarian mission in the decolonizing world, Unicef could only do what it knew how to do, re-shaping and re-designing as it went along policies and programmes originally conceived for countries whose economic, social and cultural circumstances were very different.

From the outset, it was self-evident that certain precepts did not apply: no activity to improve child health or nutrition, whether mass feeding or something else, could be carried out in schools, clinics and day-care centres which did not exist. The poor health and poor nutrition among children in Asia, Africa and Latin America were greatly exacerbated because few such institutions were in place; yet without some organized social network, it was hard to reach either them or their mothers.

This was the conundrum of underdevelopment, what the 'emergency' in a country, such as India, Ethiopia or Guatemala, was all about.

Most of those who made up Unicef's new constituency lived in rural communities where life had hardly changed for generations. Families produced, or harvested wild, most of what they needed to live on; cash only passed through their hands in tiny amounts. Their food supply was uncertain, depending on the abundance of nature, the size of their land holding, the greed of their landlord, and the weather. Their exclusive social support system for dealing with the everyday crises of living and dying was their family and their kin.

Most of the governments of the countries they lived in had very little to spend on extending their networks of health and social services to touch such people's lives, even where the idea of so doing appealed to them. The inhabitants of far-flung villages only recognized the emissaries of 'government' in the shape of tax collectors or security forces: no other representative had yet come their way. Trying to help governments wanting to change this picture was a very daunting proposition. Even to describe the task in such terms begged all sorts of questions.

In those days, it was far from clear to Unicef or to many other external or international organizations what kind of useful role their assistance could play in such regions. Thirty-five years on, the debate is better informed and many of the issues are clearer; but there still are no definitive answers. To help some other country or government build a health and social network, even for children, has many implications: it is an act, potentially, of charitable gift or enlightened self-interest; it can promote social justice or exert invisible control. These implications are, and remain, major dilemmas of international activity in the postwar world, although they are often projected in other terms—financial and economic interests, political and strategic alliances, ideological conflict. In the early 1950s, however, theories about and models for 'development aid' were few and far between.

Unicef was not a specialized agency, whose task was to offer technical advice; nor was it a financial organization offering loans and credit, although it was called a 'fund'. These were roles belonging to other UN organizations set up to address the conundrum of 'underdevelopment', and both fitted within recognizable parameters, at least superficially. Unicef was an organization with a purely humanitarian mandate. But relief and rehabilitation—the UNRRA role—was no longer sufficient; something new had to emerge. If it did not emerge quickly and convincingly, Unicef would probably disappear, either because impecunity forced it out of business or because the temporary stay of execution won in 1950 from the General Assembly would eventually be rescinded.

In trying to arrive at an understanding of its new role towards the world's children, Unicef had what turned out to be a useful advantage. Since it was about giving 'material assistance', or supplies, and since it prided itself on making sure that its supplies reached their target, it was obliged to plunge itself up to its neck in 'underdevelopment'; to tramp around the remote corners of its vast parish and get its feet dirty—and, incidentally, its fingers burnt. During the 1950s, Unicef's staff travelling in what from this point onwards was called 'the field' learned a great deal about development aid, even though few would have attached such a label to their efforts.

The most immediately obvious problem to an organization whose mandate stated that its resources should be administered 'for child health purposes generally' was that millions of children in underdeveloped countries suffered from infectious disease; and that much of this disease could be prevented or cured with modern therapies.

The medical breakthroughs of the last half century suggested a strategy for dealing with disease which did not depend on the spread of doctors, hospitals and health centres. For the first time in history, mass onslaughts on various age-old scourges were a practical possibility; and they were a distinct advance on the nineteenth century and early twentieth century equivalent—quarantine and the *cordon sanitaire*.

The idea of the mass-disease campaign was not a novelty; certain national or regional campaigns against typhus, malaria, yellow fever and hookworm had paved the way in the past thirty years; and smallpox and diphtheria vaccination had long been around. But the end of the second World War offered not only new challenges but also new solutions: better technologies, cheaper costs, and the communications and transport systems which made it possible to move through a population and have a measurable impact on health in a relatively short space of time. In spite of the residual scepticism about BCG, the International Tuberculosis Campaign was now the worldwide vaccination front-runner. The properties of DDT had promoted it to the pre-eminent killer of mosquitoes, lice and other disease-carrying insects, and was everywhere in hot demand. Large-scale production of penicillin, only achieved during the war, was beginning to offer miracle treatments not just to a handful of the élite, but also to the general population. Mysterious agents of diseases which invaded the body and would not go away now succumbed to the toxic powers of drugs which were otherwise obligingly benign.

The new drugs, vaccines and compounds were getting cheaper all the time; they represented the threshold of a global advance in public health. Used on a mass scale according to a systematic geographical coverage and timetable, they could be applied in such a way as to relinquish the hold of an infectious disease over a whole population. Once the caseload of the disease they carried descended below a certain level, mathematical probability reduced the life chances of certain parasites and bacteria to a point where the disease they spread would disappear for good. Therefore, over a relatively short period of years, a special investment in a disease campaign could produce permanent health dividends, even where there was no sophisticated health network to back it up. That at least was the vision of those brave and confident enough to embrace it.

One such individual was Sam Keeny, Unicef's Regional Director in Asia from 1950 to 1963. Keeny was a great believer in public health campaigns. He had been a relief worker in Siberia during the first World War and witnessed the horrors of a protracted typhus epidemic; he had served in Poland after that war, trying to prevent typhus crossing the *cordon sanitaire* from Russia into Europe. After the second World War, when he was chief of UNRRA in liberated Italy, he had asked Dr Fred Soper of the Rockefeller Foundation to mastermind a successful attempt to eradicate malaria from Sardinia.

The particular style of leadership and inspiration Keeny brought to

Unicef in Asia was specially suited to the era of the mass disease campaign. He combined acute intelligence with earthy common sense, behaving as if he was an ex-officio minister of health for millions of children in his surrogate care. He was comfortable with authority and exercised it with impunity, yet he made it his business to learn as much about his job from people in the villages of Asia as from any Minister or senior government official, and he expected others to do the same. Many of those who worked under him in the thirteen years he spent in Asia for Unicef, men and women who themselves went on to positions of leadership, thought that Keeny played a more important role than any other person in establishing Unicef's credibility and reputation in the field.

At the time Keeny arrived in Bangkok in 1950, WHO—which guided Unicef closely during these years—had already established mass-disease control as the priority for international health assistance in Asia. Lowering the huge caseload of 'killer' diseases was regarded as the first essential task; but fledgling health networks were thin on the ground, poorly equipped, understaffed and overwhelmed by the magnitude of need. Success in combating the diseases which afflicted people and children in their millions would pave the way for other things: more clinics, better midwifery, sanitation, improved nutrition and child care. Disease control en masse would also introduce the idea of health services to people who had never seen a white-coated doctor before and whose only idea of medical treatment was the local healer or herbalist. The campaigns would act as an advertisement and an advance guard.

During Michael Watt's brief Unicef tenure in the region, the first steps in Unicef's support to disease control had already been taken. DDT was being supplied to India, Pakistan and Thailand for spraying in experimental anti-malaria campaigns. BCG vaccination campaigns—in India the ITC campaign was by far the largest in the world—were also already underway. So were two national campaigns against yaws in Indonesia and Thailand. During the next few years, Keeny and his staff were to put much of their efforts into disease control, supplying campaigns with drugs and vaccines, with vehicles and equipment, with the costs of training local staff and the salaries of international experts.

Guided technically by WHO, managed and run by the national health staff of the countries concerned, these campaigns were to have many remarkable successes in saving lives and relieving human misery around the world. The most dramatic effects would be seen in Asia, where their profound demographic implications also most quickly raised concern.

Unicef was only one player in this huge and theatrical health exercise, but an important one. Its most obvious role was as a mass supplier of drugs, vaccines, compounds—the magic ingredients; but in countless other ways, especially in Asia and mostly because of the way Keeny operated and taught his staff to do likewise, Unicef did much to make the technical promise of the campaigns a practical reality. The spectacle of millions of children cured or protected from dreadful diseases was exciting to Unicef's recipients and donors alike. As a result of its contribution to these campaigns, Unicef's credibility grew, dispelling any lingering doubt that a United Nations fund for children could not find a niche in countries whose problem was underdevelopment, rather than the damage of war.

Yaws was the disease which fell earliest and most spectacularly to the mass campaign.

A disease confined to a tropical belt within twenty degrees of the equator, yaws was mostly found in hot, humid, poor, dirty, and almost invariably remote rural areas. The saying was that yaws began where the road ended. Because it was off the beaten track, estimates about the number of cases varied widely; in the early 1950s, there were thought to be around twenty million worldwide, of which over half were in Asia. As the mass campaigns moved ahead, the figures were revised upwards. By the end of the decade, the yaws map of the world had been re-drawn: in most places, yaws had ceased to be a major public-health problem. Except for some parts of Africa, where yaws today is making a comeback, the mass campaigns had had an astonishing success.

In the great majority of cases, the victims acquired the disease in early childhood. In many tropical rural areas, small children ran about barefoot and scantily clad, scratching their legs and feet on the spiky twigs and stones found on every village path. Yaws' tiny twisted micro-organism, or treponema, is not transmitted venereally like its close relation, syphilis, but by contact with broken skin; it therefore spread easily from child to child, particularly where few received a regular scrub with soap. Its first manifestation was a highly infectious raspberry-coloured sore rather like a boil. After a while, the sore would come to a head, burst, and heal. But gradually others erupted all over the body, sometimes attacking the membranes of the nose and the roof of the mouth. Often they turned up in the palms of the hands or on the soles of the feet, making it impossible to work in the fields, or to walk except in an awkward crab-like gait balancing on the sides of the feet. As the child grew up, the disease became entrenched in the body and its scars destroyed the skin. Joints became locked and the body immobilized. The nose and mouth were eaten away and deformities like those in leprosy developed. What began in childhood as a painful sore could become a permanently disabling condition by adulthood.

Penicillin had transformed the prospects for sufferers of treponemal diseases. Until the mid-1940s, arsenicals offered the only treatment for the treponemal diseases: yaws, syphilis, bejel and pinta—a skin disease mostly found in tropical America. This toxic, expensive and unreliable treatment required constant repeat dosages which could never be trusted to evict the disease entirely. Now this remedy had been outdated by modern antibiotics. The most effective treatment was a procaine penicillin in oil known as PAM, which acted slowly and stayed in the blood for several days after injection.

In the case of yaws, one shot would clear up the painful lesions within days, and only a limited number of doses were needed to rid the body of the disease for good. The experts of WHO, which had named the control of venereal and treponemal infections as among the original priority targets of the organization's activities, were careful to counsel that 'penicillin is not public health'; that supplies of the wonder drug were not the beginning and end of the story. But in the light of both its preventative and curative properties, it did in fact come close to being just that; more so than any vaccine or insecticide with only preventative properties.

The pioneering mass campaign against yaws was in Haiti. All the people living in the country's rural areas—around eighty-eight per cent of a population of three million or so in 1950—were at risk of catching yaws; more than half of them either had the raspberry insignia of the disease or scars indicating where they had been.

With help from the Pan-American Sanitary Bureau, a national effort had been underway to bring the disease under control since the early 1940s. In 1949, a new project was inaugurated with WHO advice and Unicef supplies of PAM. To begin with, mobile clinics were set up and the population invited to attend them on an appointed day. In the areas covered during the first year of the project, a little more than half the people attended. Unsatisfied with this turnout, the campaign moved into a new phase in 1951, aiming for blanket coverage. Every single rural household would be visited by teams going house-to-house; every single case would be tracked down. Each victim would receive one dose of penicillin; each contact of a victim would receive a protective shot of half the amount. Although Haiti was a small country, this still meant checking up on 2·7 million people, most of whom lived not 'at the end of the road', but nowhere near a road of any kind. The strategy adopted for reaching everyone had an important bearing on future mass campaigns.

For any mass disease campaign, the most important ingredient was competent personnel to run and manage the campaign teams in what was essentially a labour-intensive exercise. In most parts of the underdeveloped world, fully-trained professional medical personnel were as scarce as gold dust. Each campaign therefore had a serious manpower problem to resolve; and each one, in its own way, came up with the only possible solution. Auxiliary staff, or lay medical workers, were recruited and trained for the specific purpose of the campaign. In Haiti, these personnel were called 'lay inspectors'. Their wages were quite attractive: equivalent to those of a skilled labourer.

Haiti's terrain is mountainous and rugged and in the early 1950s, nothing better than rutted tracks connected village to village and one cluster of huts to another. The most important skill needed by a lay inspector on the yaws programme therefore was the ability to drive a jeep and keep it in running order. Educational qualifications were regarded as secondary. Yaws was a singularly easy disease to diagnose: it took no particular skill to recognize the raspberry lesions. Most people could be taught to give an injection properly, and to keep the necessary records. They must, however, be healthy, vigorous and conscientious; checking out every house high in the hills often meant a hard trek on foot.

Haiti's campaign organizers were proud of their corps of jeep-driving yaws inspectors. By the summer of 1953, the entire country had been covered and 1·6 million people treated. A spot recheck in certain areas the following year produced hardly a case of the disease. Within a further period of continuous checking and treatment, yaws was fully eradicated from Haiti. This success opened up the hope of global eradication.

The next area of yaws onslaught was Asia, where the problem was on a vastly magnified scale. Both Thailand and the Philippines had black spots of yaws in their rural areas, as did India; but the main reservoir of the disease was Indonesia, where there were thought to be perhaps as many as ten million cases. Indonesia, unlike Haiti, was a huge archipelago, with some large and heavily-populated islands, and thousands of smaller ones. Its total population at independence in 1949 was seventy-five million, of which fifty-four million lived on Java. Around seventeen per cent of the Javanese people appeared to be afflicted by yaws, making Java at that time the home of the largest congregation of yaws sufferers in the world.

The first efforts to bring the disease under control in central Java began in the 1930s. Dr Kodijat, a district health officer destined to become a national hero in the fight against yaws, found that the rural health clinics under his charge were overcrowded with yaws patients. He elaborated a systematic way of treating them with arsenicals. This was beginning to attract national and even international notice at the time when war broke out. During the war, all work in yaws control completely ceased, and the incidence of the disease rose sharply. In the late 1940s, even before the struggle between the Nationalists and the departing Dutch reached its conclusion, discussions began about a national yaws campaign.

In 1950, the Indonesian Ministry of Health launched such a programme with agreement from WHO and Unicef that they would provide international assistance. The campaign was to start in the densely populated Javanese districts of Djakarta and Jogjakarta, and gradually extend throughout other parts of Java, as well as North Sumatra, parts of Kalimantan (Borneo), and the Lesser Sunda Islands.

Kodijat was placed in charge of the yaws campaign. His headquarters was in Jogjakarta, where his handful of staff ran a serology laboratory, a small hospital for yaws patients, all the training for the campaign, and masterminded the activities of the teams of campaign personnel. Kodijat had a reputation as the mildest and softest-mannered person; but he also had an iron will and a conviction that methods must be carefully tried and developed before being applied in the field. It took a while to persuade him of the efficacy of penicillin against yaws: only when he had tried it himself in his hospital at Jogjakarta and carefully analyzed its effects did he agree to accept it as the agent for the attack on yaws in Indonesia.

This was only the first of many issues on which Kodijat refused to be rushed by pressure from his international helpers; but as he was the longest-serving and most experienced yaws protagonist in the world, his painstaking experiments in all aspects of conducting the campaign and his immaculately-kept field data and survey maps were a model which less patient field marshals knew they ignored at their peril.

Kodijat's strategy, tried over many years and endorsed by Dr C. J. Hackett, a senior WHO expert on yaws who became an admirer and collaborator of his Indonesian colleague, involved the use of mobile teams of male nurses—*mantris*—headed in each case by a doctor. The teams of eight went out on the road and systematically covered the countryside, village by village. Their impending visit would be announced ahead of time by the village elders, who summoned the villagers at the appropriate moment. A temporary clinic was set up in the house of a headman, and a throng of mothers and children assembled. With the help of the elders, each team tried to ensure they examined as many of the village population as possible.

In most of Java, where census data were thorough, it was relatively easy to work out what proportion of people attended. In villages where the disease was very common—as many as one-third of the people might be infected—attendance was often nearly total. Each yaws sufferer was given a penicillin shot; a few days later the team would reappear and give each person a second injection.

The national campaign gradually covered more and more territory, surveying over 2·5 million people in 1952 and treating nearly 300,000 cases. Impressive though the progress was, it was not enough for Sam Keeny: at this rate, the elimination of yaws from all of Indonesia would take thirty years.

Keeny visited Kodijat at Jogjakarta at least once a year, and was an imaginative and energetic purveyor of ways to overcome the various obstacles to what he saw as the campaign's slow momentum. A major problem was the low budget for health services generally in Indonesia, a country still emerging from civil war and struggling with many other post-colonial problems besides health. Keeny was adept at juggling Unicef allocations to match the particular areas of shortfall in the national yaws campaign and other parts of the health budget, and at negotiating these solutions high up the national health command. Keeping down the costs of any mass-disease campaign was a critical factor which rarely left the back of Keeny's mind: it had implications for every other campaign of its kind.

When Dr Soetopo, a health officer in eastern Java, came up with a solution for the campaign's most intractable problem—manpower short-age—Keeny did a great deal of juggling and manoeuvring to make it financially possible to put it quickly and widely into action.

The limitations of the use of the mobile teams of *mantris* had become obvious by early 1952. Kodijat's staff at Jogjakarta had so far trained around 150 for the campaign; even diluting the teams by replacing some by health clerks for record-keeping did not greatly increase the number of teams, and the health services could spare no more *mantris* from other tasks.

Dr Soetopo brought existing 'polyclinics' into the yaws campaign picture. These small bamboo and thatch health posts, each manned by a *mantri*, were relatively common throughout the countryside of the larger islands. In eastern Java, Soetopo assigned assistant nurses, *djurupateks*, to work under the polyclinic *mantris* specifically on yaws control. The *djurupatek* visited local communities, identified yaws cases, and arranged a day for treatment with the village leaders and the local doctor.

Initially Kodijat was reluctant to accept this method as nationally applicable; he was anxious to avoid putting too much responsibility on relatively uneducated and lowly health personnel. This was a legitimate concern, especially given his determination that, above all, Indonesia's yaws campaign must be thorough. With persuasion, however, he came round.

In late 1952, with the enthusiastic backing of Keeny and Hackett, full-scale training of *djurupateks* began. The medical part of their job was easy; although, unlike Haiti's lay inspectors, *djurupateks* were not allowed to give injections. In Indonesia, candidates were not expected to be so generally able or professionally skilled. Bright young boys with primary school certificate were given six weeks' training, a bicycle from Unicef, and paid the princely salary of twenty-five dollars a month to become yaws canvassers.

By early 1953, thirty-five 'simplified' disease campaign teams were already in the field. By the end of 1954—a year earlier than anticipated—the number of cures per year in Indonesia had reached one million; and, due also to a drop in the world price of penicillin, the cost of each cure had gone down from around three dollars in 1952 to around eighty-five cents. In the meantime, the campaign had become the world's largest of its kind, and the most famous. It seemed that a ten-year eradication target was not unrealistic, if the rate of progress could be maintained.

The other Asian country with a sufficiently-high incidence of yaws to demand a mass campaign was Thailand. The problem was not nearly so daunting as in Indonesia: the disease was concentrated in certain particularly poor and remote rural areas. Out of the country's population of eighteen million, the total number of cases was thought to be around 1·4 million. A campaign assisted by WHO and Unicef began in April 1950; its target was to build up to the point where its mobile teams surveyed two million people a year, eventually covering all nine million in the yaws-affected areas. Hopefully, by the end of the decade the incidence of yaws would have declined to the point where existing health services could deal with the remaining cases without fear of any new major outbreak.

Thailand was not as overstretched for medical personnel as either Indonesia or Haiti. The Public Health Department was able to depute eighty-eight sanitary inspectors to undertake all the surveys and examinations, supplemented by Thailand's version of the lay health worker: high school graduates trained as 'lay injectors'.

Mass-disease campaigns have aspects in common no matter what the particular disease. These are the mass mobilization of communities; the teams of health personnel with drops or drugs or injections; the endless counting of heads and cases; the checking and rechecking and spot checking to catch those who were left out the first time round. Yet each type of campaign has particular problems associated with the particular organism causing the trouble, and the particular features of its antidote, the preventive or curative therapy. Until a certain amount of experience has accumulated and been scientifically examined, campaigns addressing an ancient problem with a new technique—as in the case of yaws and penicillin—are run along experimental guidelines which require constant revision and are the subject of endless debate and enquiry. In March 1952, WHO laid on the world's first international yaws symposium in Bangkok in a palace borrowed from the King of Thailand for the purpose.

In spite of the increasing evidence that yaws had become an almost miraculously easy disease to conquer from a technical point of view, there were a number of problems still to solve. One was dosage: in Haiti, a much smaller dosage was being given, in one shot only, than in Indonesia and Thailand. The amount of penicillin, and the number of times the team had to visit a given community or household had an important bearing on the cost and speed of a campaign. Then there was the question of contacts: WHO's experts were more and more convinced that it was important to give all family members of yaws patients a half-dosage as a protection. The other critical question was that of survey coverage of the target population. WHO insisted that ninety per cent of the community must be reached in order to be certain of catching enough cases to prevent transmission. Only by going house-to-house could a team manage to reach this proportion, and in some areas where homes were scattered and hard to reach, this was extremely difficult. As the Indonesian campaign moved out of Java towards smaller and more inaccessible islands, this became more problematic, and costs and time involved correspondingly higher.

A successful mass-disease campaign, against yaws or any other disease, had to balance on a knife edge between the thoroughness required to hunt down almost all the victims and carriers in a given community, and the speed required to reach all the problem communities before the still-infected could re-infect the cured. Judging this knife-edge balance from region to region and country to country was critical to the long-term outcome of any campaign, particularly where the vital ingredients— manpower resources, transport and fuel, fresh supplies of drug, vaccine, or chemical compound, and their costs—were thinly stretched by the nature of the underdeveloped part of the world in which it was occurring. Making the calculations come out right, not only on the back of an envelope or in a vehicle log or on a survey map or against a local census, but also in the villages where the current and future cases among children and adults were to be found, was what mass-disease campaign management was all about.

The campaign was an intensive effort designed to deal a short sharp blow; its absolute expense, as well as its temporarily disproportionate consumption of a large part of a national or district health budget, were only justified if the blow was decisive. The campaign could not go on for a much longer period than foreseen without putting at risk other important health priorities which it had temporarily crowded out.

Even in attacking a relatively simple disease such as yaws, different campaign managers computed these equations in different ways depending on the circumstances in which they were operating. At the end of 1952, following many of the recommendations emerging from the Bangkok symposium, the Thai authorities made various changes in their approach, many of which had the effect of slowing down the campaign but of guaranteeing better results over the long term. Kodijat, who always scrupulously consolidated the Indonesian efforts, was reluctant to do anything to speed up his campaign or cut any corners on cost if, in his opinion, such a step might jeopardize its ultimate success. Slowly each campaign evolved, according to its own findings, similar in many characteristics, differing in others.

In 1955, the second international conference on yaws took place in Nigeria. By this time, it was becoming evident that a far higher number of cases existed in Africa than had been previously thought: between twenty and twenty-five million. Campaigns along the familiar WHO- and Unicef-assisted pattern had begun in many west African countries during the previous two years and were just getting into their stride. Meanwhile, tremendous and striking results could be reported from Asia, particularly from Indonesia where the teams of *mantris* and *djurupateks* were managing to treat over 100,000 yaws cases a month. In Thailand, even though the numbers of examinations thought to be necessary had been revised upwards by a large margin, the campaign was ahead of schedule. Nearly one million cases had been cured, and the mass campaign was expected to end by mid-1959. Other campaigns in the Philippines and India had begun; full eradication in Asia was becoming an increasingly hopeful prospect. Meanwhile, the almost miraculous nature of the cure had made the campaigns so popular with yaws victims that they had acted as a 'spearhead' for other public-health programmes, conferring an aura on doctors, nurses, injectors, Unicef, WHO and everyone in any way associated.

Amidst the general rejoicing, however, a report prepared in 1954 by the WHO expert committee on the control of treponemal diseases for the WHO/Unicef joint health policy committee sounded a more cautious note. Essentially, it repeated the warning that penicillin was not public health.

The primary aim of the control programme was to interfere with the spread of the disease; dramatic scores of treatments given and cases cured was not the same thing as killing off enough yaws treponemae within a population to ensure that their hold was destroyed for good. Although the widespread use of penicillin had dramatically reduced yaws in a number of areas, no definitive means had yet been established for consolidating these gains. In Thailand, the plan was to hand over the task to the stationary rural-health services once the mass campaign phase was over. In some of the other campaign areas—yaws was after all a disease 'at the end of the road'—there were no rural polyclinics or their equivalent. Who was to check and recheck the villages to make sure that no children with lesions were running along the paths; or treat the few leftover cases that had hidden or been dormant when the teams came through? Without ninety per cent coverage in the mass-campaign phase, some odd cases were bound to persist; a few odd cases could quickly become an outbreak, an outbreak an epidemic, and the phenomenon of mass childhood infection appear all over again. This problem of the take-up of the residual prevention and treatment of a disease in an underdeveloped area once a mass campaign was over was to preoccupy many public-health experts for years to come.

Whatever the fears of the mid-1950s, yaws campaigns continued to make dramatic progress throughout the decade. Few diseases have ever given in to such an onslaught in such a short period. By the end of 1958, less than ten years after the first mass campaign began, thirty million cases of yaws had been cured worldwide. Of the 200 million people in the tropical areas thought to be at risk, seventy million in Africa, the Americas, South-East Asia and the western Pacific had been checked on the first surveys of mass campaigns assisted by WHO and Unicef—and ninety million had been checked on resurveys. Campaign techniques had been refined and improved; WHO now recommended that where five per cent of a community was infected, every single child under the age of puberty should be given a protective penicillin shot. In all campaigns, the preventive properties of penicillin were now given as much weight as the curative. The results everywhere were a cause of much satisfaction.

In South-East Asia, the grip of yaws was effectively broken by the end of the 1950s. In Thailand and the Philippines, the campaigns had covered all the yaws-affected areas and examined almost everyone at least once. The 'lay injectors' of Thailand had become 'yaws supervisors', joined the staff of the health centres and now carried out yaws surveillance work alongside sanitarians and school-health visitors. In three other countries with fewer victims—Malaya, India and Cambodia—yaws teams were operating. Six islands in the Pacific had successfully eradicated yaws. Only in Indonesia, where the scale of the problem had always been of another order altogether, did relatively large numbers linger on.

On Java, the huge yaws treponema congregation had been decimated. Here, by 1957, Kodijat had scored a triumph, and had been nationally honoured for his work. So difficult was it to find a raspberry sore that his training programme in Jogjakarta could scarcely carry on for want of being able to teach *djurupateks* to identify the disease. One thousand of the risk areas plotted on his maps had been declared virtually yaws free. His efforts to consolidate gains in existing campaign areas were as thorough as ever. But his efforts to extend the campaign to the outer islands of the archipelago were frustrated.

Kodijat was defeated by circumstances outside his control, the worst enemy of public health: political disturbance and military disruption. There were serious revolts against the government of President Sukarno in Sumatra and the eastern islands. The breakdown of security effectively stopped the yaws campaigns, like everything else, in their tracks. Staff were summoned away to military service; salaries went unpaid; ships with penicillin supplies were unable to dock or unload; transport was unavailable. By the end of 1958, insurgencies had grounded the campaign entirely.

Kodijat did not give up his dream of eradicating yaws from Indonesia. In 1963, still campaigning at the age of seventy-two, he requested help from Unicef to continue the campaign, and received it. By this stage, there was no further need for a mass campaign in Java and the other large islands of Indonesia; the few remaining cases could be treated in rural clinics, and public understanding about the disease had advanced to the point where sufferers freely sought out treatment.

Campaigns against yaws were still going on in parts of Africa. But the era of the mass onslaught against its painful lesions had passed its peak and begun to recede into history.

Yaws was the early success story among the many great disease campaigns of the second half of the century. Others achieved even more remarkable gains measured in terms of the absolute numbers of people they saved from illness or death; and in terms of the far more difficult obstacles placed in their path by more wily and elusive adversaries.

Throughout most of the 1950s, until the malaria extravaganza edged it from the limelight, the largest and most complicated international health campaign continued to be that against tuberculosis. Every month, WHO and Unicef published the figures of children and teenagers tested by tuberculin and vaccinated with BCG; by 1960, the tallies had reached the respective totals of 265·4 million and 105·7 million, and campaigns had been completed or were being carried out in sixty-four countries and territories.

The peak of this vast numbers game—in which Sam Keeny was one of the most prolific players—came between 1956 and 1959, when around 3·5 million children were tested each month, and around one million vaccinated. Over four-fifths of these were in Asia; within Asia, more than two-thirds were in India.

When in 1948 Unicef's Board stipulated that half the $4 million for the ITC must be spent in countries outside Europe, they did so mainly because of the rise in tuberculosis in all 'countries victims of aggression'. But in the underdeveloped countries, the aftermath of war had far less to do with the spread of tuberculosis than did the more remorseless process of social and economic change.

Tuberculosis began to strike such countries just at the time that its importance in the west declined. In Europe, the disease reached its peak in the nineteenth century. Although genteelly associated with consumptive pallor and early death among literary and artistic figures, tuberculosis was chiefly a disease of the slums and workshops of the Industrial Revolution. Densely-packed housing and urban squalor provided the bacillus with a perfect breeding-ground. In most parts of Asia, Africa and Latin America, tuberculosis was almost unknown until mines and factories spawned their surrounding shanty towns; then it took off on a virulent rampage.

There was no treatment for the victims, no sanitoria where they could be kept from infecting anyone else, nor any systematic improvement of housing or sanitation—the factors that had gradually cut down the tubercular toll in the West. In Europe, the war had temporarily reversed a positive trend of tuberculosis decline; elsewhere it boosted a negative one. Only one of its characteristics seemed to give the disease an edge over certain others as a reachable and conquerable scourge. Instead of being 'a disease at the end of the road', it was thought to be confined to the crowded areas; this proved sufficiently faulty to throw off some planners' calculations.

For an attack on tuberculosis in parts of the world where the average patient's chances of bed rest, fresh mountain air, and treatment in isolation from possible contacts were absolutely nil, there was no alternative to a mass campaign with BCG. Diagnosis by lung X-ray for suspected pulmonary cases was complicated and expensive enough in countries with the most minimal health facilities; but, as the authorities had pointed out to Drs Parran and Lakshmanan, treatment remotely akin to the standards of

Western care was way beyond the bounds of economic possibility.

At that time certain drugs had been developed which might prove to have the same miracle properties against tuberculosis as penicillin had against treponemal disease; but none had yet demonstrated an ability to destroy the tubercle bacillus with such killing effect. In the absence of a means of mass treatment, protection against those most at risk of the bacillus' invasion—children and young people—was the only option, whatever its shortcomings and imponderables. When questioned by Unicef in 1948 how he would conduct a BCG campaign in a non-European country, Johannes Holm had replied pragmatically that he would use the same techniques as were then in use in Scandinavia, and make the necessary adaptations as he went along. 'Adaptations' turned out to be something of an understatement.

When WHO took over the technical direction of the ITC in 1951, and Unicef retreated to its by-now established partnership role as principal international financier and supplier, there were still lingering doubts within the medical profession both about the efficacy of BCG vaccine and its suitability for widescale public-health campaigns. Even those confident in the vaccine's protective properties had to admit that the credentials of the tuberculin test were looking increasingly shaky. In 1949, WHO had set up a Tuberculosis Research Office in Copenhagen. As the international tuberculosis effort grew and spread, the TRO became responsible for the scientific investigation needed to re-design key technical elements of the campaigns. The data they used was collected by special WHO assessment teams based in different parts of the world and paid for by Unicef.

Operational problems were expected. The numbers of those the teams must reach were enormous: in India alone, the target was to reach 180 million children and adolescents—half the country's population. No serious doubts could any longer be entertained about using lay health workers to help staff the mobile teams; without large commitments of national medical personnel, professional, auxiliary and lay, the prospects of running any campaign on this scale were non-existent.

The other operational problem was that of reaching all the BCG candidates twice, once with the test, once for the results and, if applicable, the vaccine. In Europe, most children were captive. Babies could be reached conveniently in a maternity ward or a health clinic; older children could be found sitting behind a desk at school. In few areas of the under-developed world did any but a small proportion of better-off families use such amenities.

All campaigns in such areas, therefore, had to take place in a non-institutional setting, and people had to make the effort to bring their children. In many cases, a fifth of those who received the test never came back for the results . . . all the more reason to ensure that those who did take the time and trouble to attend received a technically-immaculate product. If the children later developed tuberculosis, their parents would distrust not only this health campaign but others.

The first discovery to shake the medical foundation of the campaign was that the tuberculin test used in Europe did not divide people everywhere else in the world into neat categories of 'positive'—and therefore not to be vaccinated—and 'negative'—in need of protection from BCG. The pattern of reaction to it was turning out to be very different among different populations, and its results were open to all sorts of different interpretations.

How some people came to be slightly insensitive to tuberculin was a mystery; it did not seem as though they could be suffering from the disease and would therefore be at risk from a BCG vaccination, but nothing could be taken on trust. What to do about cases of 'low sensitivity' or 'non-specific sensitivity' preoccupied the researchers at the Tuberculosis Centre in Copenhagen for many years until they settled on the precise degree of sensitivity below which they felt a BCG vaccination was not only safe but highly desirable. Meanwhile, because of the cost and complication of case-finding and sure diagnosis, the results of applying the tuberculin test were often used to gauge the prevalence of tuberculosis in a population. The uncertainties surrounding its results obviously threw out such calculations. WHO began to insist that a proper tuberculosis survey was essential before any campaign was mounted.

Even more threatening to the reputation of the international campaign was the discovery that the vaccine was not potent enough.

A second round of tuberculin testing after BCG vaccination in some north African and Asian countries revealed that it had 'taken' in no more than fifty or sixty per cent of cases. This compared with ninety or even ninety-five per cent of the children vaccinated in the European campaigns.

Dismayed, the ITC mentors—Holm, Debré and others in WHO and Unicef—considered all possible causes. The immediate deduction was that BCG vaccine was sensitive to a tropical climate. This realization inspired the invention of the 'cold chain': a system whereby vaccine and tuberculin could be kept at a low temperature from the moment they left the State Serum Institute in Copenhagen and other WHO-approved manufacturers until the moment when they entered the body of the child.

At the production centre, the vaccine was packed into insulated boxes before it was taken by airplane to its destination. Upon arrival at the airport, the insulated boxes were installed in jeeps; later they were strapped to the back of health workers and vaccinators. Unless the vaccine could be kept cool until it entered the syringe and passed through the needle, the whole operation was pointless.

Within a few years, techniques for freeze-drying vaccines were developed. This cut down the number of links in the cold chain; but, beyond the laboratory where the bulk supply was reconstituted into liquid form, the vaccine still needed to be transported in ice and stored in a refrigerator. These items added to the costs of the campaigns; and they became, and remain, standard parts of the equipment supplied for vaccination programmes by Unicef.

Further research revealed that the intense light of the tropical sun caused at least as much damage to the potency of the vaccine as did the heat. Halfdan Mahler, the senior WHO medical officer for the Indian BCG campaign between 1951 and 1961, was among the first to realize that at all times the vaccine had to be shielded from strong light; and that, if light was so destructive to the vaccine, it must also destroy the live bacillus expectorated by a patient.

Since the tubercular cough of the patient was the main means of passing on the disease, Mahler concluded that he or she only threatened other family members and workmates during the hours of darkness. If tuberculosis victims could be persuaded always to cough into a handkerchief and not to sleep in the confined space of the typical one-room house shared with all the members of the family, there was no reason, Mahler believed, that public health would be endangered by their continuing to lead a normal life during the daytime. These ideas were a breakthrough, since they offered at least some kind of alternative strategy to the impracticability and cost of hospital care in isolation.

In 1957, the WHO expert committee on tuberculosis examined at length the technical and operational experience of the many campaigns WHO and Unicef were assisting and assessed their overall results. Their recommendations marked a turning point in the way mass BCG campaigns were conducted. From its inception, the ITC had been very popular with governments and its assistance much sought after. Whatever the setbacks it had encountered, very real gains for public health had been made. The vaccine as a means of mass protection had now definitively proved itself, and health authorities and BCG campaign personnel had shown that even in the most adverse circumstances and the most difficult terrain, it was possible to take a vial of fresh vaccine across thousands of miles, and do whatever was necessary to put it to work in the bodies of children. BCG was doing much to popularize international health assistance. But the total process of solving the riddle of tuberculosis control, and the role of the mass campaign within it, was still evolving subject to scientific trial and error.

Some campaigns, on close examination, were going all out to chalk up the maximum numbers of tests and vaccinations without paying enough attention to the proportion of children they were reaching. The results of the numbers game were impressive; but they were masking the fact that the coverage in many places was not all that it ought to be.

Setting targets for each team, jeep and vaccinator to reach every month, and reckoning progress by their success or failure to do so was good to a point; it provided a built-in check on all the elements which could delay things, from punctures to religious feast days to personnel shortages. But it could also have the effect of discouraging teams to hunt down all the children whose houses it took time to reach, or whose mothers were busy the day they called, in favour of going on to an easier location.

Even the best-operated campaigns had not managed to reach more than half the children under the age of seven. Many children about seven years old were in school and the proportion was higher: around two-thirds. But the younger ones were the most important: the earlier a child was reached, the less chance there was that the tubercle bacillus would get there first. If the campaign had to slow down to reach more of the younger children, then it should do so. Here again was the knotty balancing act between speed and thoroughness, both of which were vital.

Much more careful attention had to go into selecting the places where the campaign teams should go. When international help with BCG vaccination was first offered to countries outside Europe, there had been a tendency to accept requests from every government which asked. Assumptions were made that tuberculosis was prevalent throughout their countries without carrying out a survey. The upshot was that precious resources had been wasted carrying out BCG vaccination in areas where the chances of contracting the disease were very low. Repeat campaigns in places where the risk was high were more useful than deploying teams in far-flung areas where the chances of contagion were very remote. In many high-tech areas, the coverage was not what it might have been. In all such areas, the report recommended, campaigns should be held every three years to vaccinate the children who had been born since the last time around or had then been left out. Some voices were already suggesting that BCG vaccination should be incorporated into the regular health services and the mass campaigns phased out. Not yet, declared the WHO experts. Teams which went out to obtain mass coverage with BCG were still an essential part of the armoury against tuberculosis.

Although this was true in 1957, the days of the mobile BCG teams were already numbered. Tuberculosis control was already moving into a new phase. The diagnosis of suspects by radiography and the complications of treating confirmed cases had made the curative part of the attack slow, difficult and expensive. Now the moment had come when a simple means of mass treatment could meet both the need of the patient for a cure, and the need of the community that the patient present no risk to others. In 1951, a drug had been discovered which was effective, cheap, could be taken orally and caused few complications.

Isoniazid appeared to be the breakthrough that everyone had been waiting for, but it took time and careful testing to prove it. Although isoniazid sent the disease into recession, it did not kill off all the infective bacilli. Not only could these take hold again if the patient stopped treatment, but also they seemed to develop isoniazid resistance, threatening to become a master race of infectious tubercle bacilli. Until it could be shown that the cough of a patient taking the new drug was not more hazardous to others than before, isoniazid had to be used only with great care in controlled circumstances and not given out in the community at large. By the end of the decade, the drug was conclusively shown not to offer a public health risk, and could then come into wider public use. The ground in tuberculosis control had shifted.

In 1964, WHO declared a new era in the continuing effort to defeat the disease worldwide. BCG vaccination of all young children was still one of the two main weapons, but it was now no longer regarded as necessary to administer a tuberculin test in advance. This dramatically reduced costs and logistical complications. The other weapon was home treatment of patients with an improved version of isoniazid. The best way to advance this strategy was no longer to build clinics, sanitoria, send out mobile X-ray units and BCG vaccination teams, but to incorporate prevention, diagnosis, and cure within the general health services. Although some countries at first proved reluctant to accept that this was the way WHO and Unicef now saw things, the days of international support for the mass tuberculosis campaign were over.

Another disease on the original WHO and Unicef campaign lists was trachoma, a painful and disabling eye complaint.

The trachoma virus flourished in dirty and poverty-stricken surroundings, and attacked young children mainly in the hot season when dust was permanently in the air. If left untreated, inflammation on the undersides of the eyelid became progressively more acute, which could in time damage the cornea and cause the eye to retract into the socket. In poor societies, the human consequence of blindness is often to be found on the corner of the street holding a begging bowl; sightlessness has denied him or her any useful role in family or community.

In the early 1950s, trachoma was regarded as another disease which need no longer be taken for granted as part of the general tapestry of ill-health. Rising living standards and improved hygiene had expelled the disease from Europe and north America; but with the degree of variation common to all calculations concerning diseases of poverty, it was thought that there were 100 to 400 million cases in the world. Now modern drugs had transformed the prospects of destroying the virus.

Two antibiotic eye ointments—aureomycin and terramycin—had come on the market at a price which made large-scale campaigns against trachoma affordable. In 1952, WHO established an expert advisory panel on trachoma, and the international attack began.

The first country to receive Unicef support for a trachoma campaign was Morocco. The Director-General of Health in what was then a protectorate of France was Dr Georges Sicault, a bold and successful adventurer in public health. Sicault had been in Morocco for many years and was responsible for campaigns against smallpox, malaria and typhus— from which he once himself came so close to death that his life was given up as lost.

Sicault was always in the vanguard of new disease control drives and had been the first senior public health official in north Africa to start mass BCG vaccination, with the help of the ITC. In 1952, Unicef provided the Moroccan health services with supplies of antibiotic ointment for an experimental four-year attack on trachoma.

Sicault's strategy was to cover the affected population systematically by sending mobile medical teams to each village at the beginning and end of the hot epidemic season. The teams applied ointment to the eyes of every person, gave out tubes free of charge and instructions for its use. From year to year, free ointment was gradually phased out in the belief that once they had understood its value, people would buy it; tobacco sellers and tea shops were encouraged to carry stocks. Both trachoma and conjunctivitis, its advance guard, gradually declined each season. But self-treatment did not work as well as expected.

There had been some misgivings within WHO and Unicef about trachoma campaigns from the beginning. No-one doubted the technical efficacy of the remedy. But up to this time, antibiotic ointments had mainly been used in the clinic, not as an instrument of public health. Far from providing a one-shot remedy, the ointment had to be applied three or four times daily over the course of months. This demanded of parents and children a great deal more than that they should present themselves once or twice for a test or an injection. Theoretically, any mother could learn how to put ointment on her child's eyes. In practice, clumsy fingers might squeeze too much from the tube at a time and quickly exhaust its contents; or the top might be lost or the goat eat it and the ointment dry up. Applying it regularly anyway seemed a curious routine to an unlettered mother in a dusty back street to whom modern medicine was a totally alien idea. Without someone to encourage, help and admonish her, she would not easily become its practitioner on behalf of her children.

This kind of observation was little more than common sense; it did not require an anthropologist to work it out. But it eluded those campaign experts whose own world was very remote from the one in which their carefully-planned operations were supposed to take place, and who did not think that their time should be spent bumping around in jeeps and sitting for hours in dusty village compounds chatting with the great unwashed. Yet for any campaign which demanded people's co-operation such factors as the vagaries of human behaviour could make the difference between success and failure.

The pioneer trachoma programme in Asia, which WHO, Unicef and especially Keeny, saw as the guinea-pig for others, took place in Taiwan. Two million people were thought to be infected. It began in the schools. Doctors and nurses from all health centres were taught how to identify the disease. School superintendents organized the schedule of doctors' visits, and the teachers were taught how to apply the ointment. They had a classroom drill with basin and soap for hand-washing, marked tubes of ointment, squares of tissue paper for each child to press over the eyelids and fix the ointment in the sockets. In eighteen months beginning in 1954, 1·3 million children were tested, of whom about half had trachoma, and another quarter conjunctivitis. Among a captive and disciplined child population, the campaign was a success.

In 1956, the campaign began to embrace children outside the schoolroom. Taiwan had a higher proportion of children in school than in most other Asian countries; nonetheless, trachoma was a disease of poverty and a campaign to get rid of it had to reach deeper into the community. The schools invited people to come for eye examinations and issued tubes of ointment for use at home. The teachers and students kept records and visited in the community to see that the ointment was correctly applied. But for all its precise organization, the trachoma campaign in Taiwan was a disappointment. Although the incidence of the disease had dropped, it did not decline nearly so far as had been expected.

By the end of the decade 6·5 million Asian children had been treated. Worldwide, millions of children's eyesight had been protected, but new trachoma cases continued to appear at the same pace.

Both the behaviour of people and the behaviour of the virus were responsible. The virus had proved a more changeable adversary than anyone had expected. Without a careful study of the way it behaved in each different environment, no single version of antibiotic treatment could be guaranteed as effective. There was no one drug, applied in a set pattern of doses, which could be recommended as the standard global cure. In Taiwan, a variety of treatment schedules, continuous and interrupted, were tried in what was a more organized society than many, but still the rate of relapse was high. The Taiwanese campaign, a model by comparison with some others, was a poor proposition by normal cost-benefit standards. Assistance to this and other campaigns was wound down while more comprehensive research was undertaken. Trachoma was not after all a suitable case for the mass campaign.

If, at one level, the technical problem had proved more complex than had been expected, at another it was so simple that it ought to be possible to banish trachoma without recourse to such complex and expensive manoeuvres. The virus—like so many other unpleasant organisms— flourished in conditions of poverty and squalor. Quite simple measures of cleanliness would keep almost all of them at bay. Yaws and trachoma were diseases unlikely to strike those who frequently came into contact with a bar of soap, a basin of water, and a clean set of clothes. In the case of yaws, it had been possible to substitute an antibiotic therapy because it offered a prompt and final solution. In the case of trachoma, it did not.

Unfortunately, most of the people of rural Asia, Africa and Latin America did not regard dirt as an enemy. On the contrary, most thought of 'dirt', indistinguishable from 'earth', as a close friend. The earth grew their food; earth, packed together, made floors, walls, houses, even furniture; people worshipped the earth as life itself. They knew nothing about the microscopic germs and parasites it harboured, organisms which swam in their drinking water, inhabited their homes, attached themselves to their skin, and wafted in the air they breathed. For perhaps more than half the world's people, disease came from somewhere else altogether. Its laws were mysterious, even mystical, immutable as the rising and setting of the sun. Sickness was to do with the Spirits or the wrath of the gods.

A clinical concept of health was often greeted with scepticism. It was hard to convince mothers that barefoot toddlers playing in muddy yards were leading a hazardous life. Or that eating rice with fingers that had just tended the buffalo was a dangerous practice. Even where people were persuaded that dirt was not on their side, that cleanliness was next to healthiness, they could not easily separate themselves from its invasion. Water was far from the house and had to be carried. Soap was expensive. But if only people could be persuaded to understand their significance, the expense and organizational complications of the mass campaign as a method of disease control would be bypassed. In the end the success of disease control depended as much on people's behaviour as it did on all the drugs and vaccines.

This elementary truth took some time to sink in. Most of the mass campaigns did not require much active co-operation from their targets, who simply had to line up — or be lined up — to receive their preventive or curative treatment. It was not easy to be certain that everyone who should be was in the line. But once in it, they became the passive recipients of what the health team delivered. The trachoma campaigns — except when the teacher was in control — were different. A tube of ointment was not an injection. People had to want to use it enough to spend time, effort, and sometimes their own money to buy it. That meant they had to make a judgement about its value against other priorities in their lives.

In every campaign, people — parents, teachers, children, adolescents — had to be willing participants to some degree or other. The greater the degree of independent action that had to be taken by people with little previous contact with the goods, services, and ideas of the modern world, the more unpredictable the outcome became. They often responded in ways which confused the health authorities, or the situation led to the kind of arbitrary action that more appropriately belonged to the days of quarantine and the *cordon sanitaire*. Disease control posed questions about individual freedom and governmental action. In time, health propaganda and education programmes were developed to try and bridge the gap. But in the era of the mass campaign, they were still a weapon of the future.

In 1952, when at Unicef's request, WHO first tendered an opinion on what kind of assistance might be offered to countries trying to control or cure leprosy, the verdict was discouraging. Leprosy, the disease which had inspired the world's earliest and most notorious *cordon sanitaire*—the leper colony—was another disease of poverty and poor standards of hygiene. It, too, had been driven out of Europe as standards of living improved. Unlike so many others, in 1952 there was still no drug or vaccine which WHO could recommend for the mass treatment of this particularly-detested disease.

The leprosy bacillus invaded the nerves through the membranes of the skin, producing patches of completely insensitive light-coloured skin. The infection could be fast and virulent, or very slow-acting, lying dormant in the body for years. Its most conspicuous effect was that since it destroyed the feelings of pain which protect the body, injuries and burns easily occurred and deformity was progressive. The great ugliness of the disease, the lack of any treatment, and the belief that it was highly infectious meant that, down the centuries, the community continued to insist on the outcast status of the leper, and on his or her segregation with other similarly-cursed individuals.

The bacillus had first been identified in the laboratory in 1874, but its elusive behaviour in the human body and its refusal to be cultured in the Petri dish had slowed the pace at which it yielded its secrets to medical enquiry. The stigma which since time immemorial had attached to leprosy's victims seemed to invade even the scientific laboratory. By the early 1950s, it was known that most patients contracted leprosy only after a long and close association of the kind that a mother has with a child. But the exact circumstances of transmission were still not understood, nor how long or in which stages of the disease a patient was infectious. In the absence of such knowledge, it was still thought that segregation was inevitable in leprosy treatment. The children of a mother with leprosy, in keeping with a more primitive era of public health, were quarantined neither with their mother nor with healthy children and were therefore deprived of both normal family and school life. In Asia and Africa, most known patients were confined to leprosaria which, apart from the more humanitarian principles by which in the twentieth century they were run, did not mark a significant advance on medieval times.

Fortunately, the picture was rapidly changing. In 1953, soon after Unicef had agreed to provide its first assistance to a leprosy project in Nigeria, WHO came up with some encouraging findings. A new drug—diammo diephemyl sulphone—looked promising. Therapy took time; marked improvement took several months, and reducing the chances of infection to a negligible point might take years. The drug was, however, cheap and easily administered. If a patient received treatment every week or every month, over time the patches of leprous skin, the sources of infection, would disappear. Meanwhile family members, specially children, could be kept under observation and themselves be treated for any symptoms. With a cure, even one whose time span was so protracted, the prospects for leprosy control were transformed. No longer need a victim hide suspected lesions, fearing banishment once they were discovered. Health authorities could go out and look for cases with some hope that they would identify themselves.

Once leprosy became a prospect for the special campaign, many requests for WHO and Unicef assistance came forward. By 1955, Unicef was assisting eight programmes of which four were in Africa, the largest leprosy reservoir. Estimates of the number of sufferers, now that people were asking for treatment, were revised upwards from two million worldwide to ten or twelve million. The new therapy, on the other hand, meant that the costs of tending leprosy had dropped even more dramatically: treatment for 20,000 leprosy outpatients in Africa now cost the same as setting up a segregated farming colony for 2000. Most programmes depended on medical auxiliaries, the foot soldiers of disease campaigns, to travel a weekly or monthly circuit, hand out sulphone tablets at appointed places, and make regular reports on patients' progress.

By the end of the 1950s, trends in leprosy treatment had crystallized. Taking sulphone tablets over a long period had not proved toxic, as had been feared. Since there was no further need for the compulsory segregation of patients, the leprosarium could be relegated to the pages of history, and pressure was put on countries to repeal the relevant legislation. WHO and Unicef were no longer willing to provide help for segregated treatment. Medical opinion now even held that infectious mothers should keep their babies, who thus received a prophylactic dose of sulphone with their mothers' milk. A few settlements for those too elderly, and no longer able or willing to manage on their own, lingered on; nowadays, they have all but disappeared. Some facilities were converted into hospitals for surgical cases or rehabilitation of the disabled.

Alongside these encouraging developments, efforts were needed to keep up the momentum of the new kind of control programme. The three years it took to cure a patient—and sometimes it took twice as long—proved a stumbling block. During the first six months, patients rapidly improved. Once they felt better, it was difficult to persuade them to go on collecting and consuming pills for years on end. If they were in close touch with a health centre, they could be easily given their regular dose of drugs and persuasion. But if, as was common in Africa, patients had to travel many miles on foot to pick up their supply, the effort was arduous and interfered with urgent farming and domestic tasks. Yet, without treatment, the disease would continue indefinitely on its slow and destructive course.

By 1960, it was thought that one-third of the leprosy patients in the world were undergoing treatment. The question then became how to ensure that patients not only started treatment, but went on until they were fully cured. Leprosy victims, as well as all those who came in contact with them, have been candidates for the public-health propaganda campaign. Although there is still no vaccine or quick-acting cure, what has been achieved in the generation since is truly remarkable. The stigma of leprosy, physically and socially, has all but disappeared.

By the end of the 1950s, almost half of Unicef's aid—$12·2 million out of a total of $25 million a year—was committed to mass campaigns against the insects, parasites, viruses and bacteria responsible for so much ill-health in so many poor communities and among so many children around the world. The campaigns made headlines; they were popular; they raised funds. But, as the experts were increasingly coming to realize, not everything about the mass campaigns was quite so perfect as their public relations image. After a decade of intense activity on many technical and geographical fronts, important lessons had been learned, some of whose implications had yet to sink in.

A lesson that had been fully absorbed was that rushing in with an expensive and difficult operation in a part of the world where there was still little in the way of organized institutional development could be wasteful and unwise. It was very difficult to make campaigns work in places where administration was weak or almost non-existent, where communications were poor and transport frequently broke down, where the number of trained professional staff was always fewer than it needed to be. Before any campaign was launched in such an environment, a survey must be carried out in advance to establish the pattern and amount of the disease in the specific place it was thought to be a problem; then the campaign must start on a small, experimental scale until procedures which would work among the whole population—or at least had a reasonable chance of doing so— were operational.

Another important lesson was one that everyone had always paid lip service to, but which now began to come home with fuller force. Mass campaigns against disease were conceived as interim solutions for reducing huge caseloads of infectious disease until such time as regular health services could be set up throughout the community. They were supposed to provide a short cut, a means of lifting the stranglehold of ill-health on families and children, and on fragile networks of health centres and medical personnel shouldering too many overpowering burdens at once. The problem was that the mass campaign, in the way typical of short cuts, had other in-built hazards which threatened to turn it into a long cut after all. If the sharp and decisive stroke the mass-disease campaign was meant to deliver became long, repetitive and inconclusive, then its justification was more difficult.

In many countries of the underdeveloped world, the mass campaigns were achieving remarkable successes in their early stages. But they were not able to sustain them to the point where the threat posed by parasite, vector, virus or bacillus was insignificant.

As the decade progressed, there was more and more talk about 'consolidation': to the need to incorporate disease control into basic health services so that the cases which had been dormant, the survey candidates who had been away, the infants who had not yet been born at the moment when the teams came round, could still be looked after. Until this point was reached, it was argued, the mobile teams would have to go on plying their rounds.

Here was a serious contradiction. While disease campaigns absorbed heavy proportions of a country's health budget, not just for a short period but for many years, there were fewer resources for building health services. Yet no campaign manager wished to withdraw his troops from the field if to do so might mean a resurgence of the disease they had spent many years trying to roll back.

Another important lesson from efforts which were in many cases the first, vital point of contact between a government's health services and far-flung communities was the response of the people themselves.

Where they found painful sores disappearing as if by magic, they would celebrate and invite their saviours to join them. But cause and effect was not always so clear-cut. Every programme which sets out to alter people's behaviour, even if the benefits are apparently self-evident, runs into resistance. Among communities in traditional societies, the resistance is greater because over the years people whose margins for error are very narrow have devised solutions to life-threatening problems which they depend on and are most unwilling to give up.

They have no guarantee that 'help' from outside will not dry up as quickly as it appeared — if it was useful in the first place. The teams arriving in the jeep may understand neither the nature of their true problems, nor the new problems their apparently foolproof solutions will create. Only the mutual understanding which develops when there is some kind of permanent medical presence in the community can allow the health service to interact properly with the ill-health it is trying to combat. In the end, not just for first aid and for the general care of the mother and child, but also for preventing and treating cases of communicable disease, services in the community were to prove more important than flying visits from mobile teams.

The days of the mass application of the mass campaign were drawing to an end. But there was one campaign, the largest of them all, which did not learn the lessons soon enough: the campaign against the malarial mosquito.

Main sources

WHO/Unicef Joint Committee on Health Policy; papers by WHO expert consultants produced for deliberation by the Committee, and reports of its recommendations; 1952–1961; other Unicef Executive Board documents of the period.

Unpublished History of Unicef by Jack Charnow and Margaret Gaan; prepared in 1964–65.

40.000 Enfants par Jour: vivre la cause de l'Unicef, by Dr Francois Rémy; published by Robert Laffont and Michel Archimbaud, Paris, 1983.

Half the World's Children: a diary of Unicef at work in Asia; a book excerpted from the monthly reports of S. M. Keeny, Unicef Regional Director for Asia, 1950–1963; published by Association Press, New York, 1957; Memoirs of Spurgeon Milton Keeny; Columbia University Oral History Project, 1977.

Unicef News; other publications and articles issued by the Unicef Information Division; articles in *World Health*, the magazine of WHO.

Interviews undertaken by Jack Charnow and others for the Unicef History Project 1983–85.

Chapter 5

The Perfidious Mosquito

At the midpoint of the century, the disease with the highest incidence in the world was malaria. Every year, malaria was thought to strike 350 million human beings and cause one in every 100 deaths.

Most of both deaths and non-lethal bouts of fever were among children: those who lived in places where malaria was endemic and survived their early contests with it developed some degree of immunity. Even so, they stayed vulnerable to the coming and going of the parasite in their bloodstream, and spent their lives sporadically impaired by the severe headache, chills and sweats; the swollen spleen and anaemia; and the deep lassitude malaria induced. For pregnant women, it was a special threat since it could cause the loss of the child in their womb.

The malaria parasite takes two common forms: *vivax*, which debilitates and causes great sickness; and *falciparum*, fulminating and more often deadly. Malaria can be bewildering in its speed of devastation, especially among people not previously exposed. During the second World War, malaria hospitalized 378,000 US soldiers in the Far East, and was rated by General MacArthur as an enemy as dangerous as any Japanese force. In Egypt, *anopheles gambiae*, the most virulent malaria-carrying mosquito, appeared from Sudan at the height of military activity in the western desert region, and the parasites it brought killed 180,000 people before the carrier was wiped out.

Malaria was capable of depopulation. It had such serious implications for economic productivity that many malarious countries took it more seriously as a public health problem than any other.

The trick of malaria's transmission was discovered just before the turn of the century. The female of a blood-sucking *anopheles* mosquito species ingested the parasite while feeding on an infected person, gave it a home in her body for a part of its growth cycle, and then deposited it during another 'meal' into the bloodstream of someone else. Before the discovery of the man-insect-man transmission cycle, the only antidote was a therapy: quinine. After it, prevention was possible. Instead of killing the disease in the victim's bloodstream, it could also be killed in the mosquito.

Techniques for the mosquito's mass elimination were pioneered by William Gorgas, a US Army physician who led a famous battle against yellow fever and malaria in the Panama Canal zone, making possible the Canal's construction. General Gorgas had many inheritors in both North and South America. They drained swampy land, larvicided standing water with copper-arsenic dust, and introduced larva-eating minnows into ponds. The armoury against the mosquito steadily grew, not only in the Americas but also in the malarious parts of Europe and in the colonial possessions of Britain and France, along with experience in the management of insect-borne disease control. The problem was that everything in the armoury was laborious and expensive.

Then came DDT. Dichlorodiphenyltrichloroethane was synthesized in 1874, but it took until 1939 for its lethal effect on insect life to be appreciated. Today, the reputation of DDT has been tarnished. But when it was first used during the second World War for public-health purposes against typhus and malaria, the way it stayed lethal to insects for months after being dusted into clothes or sprayed onto surfaces was seen as miraculous. By 1943, the compound was in mass production and its future in both public health and agriculture seemed limitless.

The first demonstration that DDT spraying, house by house, could dramatically reduce malaria was carried out near Naples in 1944 by two long-time warriors against insect-borne disease: Drs Fred Soper and Paul Russell from the Rockefeller Foundation. Their success prompted Dr Alberto Missiroli, Director of the national antimalaria service, to try and eradicate malaria from the Italian peninsula; this was achieved within five years. It also led to an effort to banish both mosquito and disease from Sardinia, a campaign whose merits Soper and Russell sold to Sam Keeny, then heading UNRRA in Italy. The campaign, using UNRRA-supplied DDT, did eliminate malaria; it did not eliminate the mosquito. Other DDT spraying campaigns followed in Europe and the Mediterranean, initially supplied by UNRRA, later by Unicef.

Spraying the inside walls of people's homes with insecticide was a well-established technique of malaria control. By the 1940s, it was regarded as preferable to larviciding since it specifically singled out those mosquitoes which were causing the problem. It was based on certain rules of *anopheles* behaviour. After a mosquito had taken her blood meal, she found it awkward to fly and landed on a surface nearby to help her digestion. Since she pursued her quarry at night, this was often the wall of the room in which the victim was sleeping. If that surface was toxic, the mosquito would die before the parasite could mature.

Soper had used this technique with deadly effect against *anopheles gambiae* in both North-East Brazil in 1939–40, and in Egypt during 1944–45. The weapon then had been insecticide made from the pyrethrum daisy.

The reason that DDT opened up such dizzying new vistas in public health was that it only had to be sprayed on a surface once or twice a year, enormously reducing manpower and insecticide requirements. Regular

DDT spraying of all households in a malarious area therefore became an affordable proposition and quickly eclipsed other antimalaria strategies.

Unicef's first assistance to countries trying to bring malaria under control went to various countries in Europe, including Hungary, Poland, Yugoslavia. Missiroli, the malaria victor of Italy, advised as to methods. When WHO came into being in 1948, the attack on malaria was cited as one of its top priorities. WHO, in the usual relationship between the two organizations, then became the technical adviser to national campaigns seeking international help, with Unicef as supplier—in this case, DDT and spraying equipment. As both organizations became more closely involved with health problems in the underdeveloped world, malaria control projects quickly expanded and DDT and spray equipment were in hot demand. By 1953, Unicef was spending around $6 million a year on providing enough DDT to protect 13·5 million people in thirty countries and helping set up two factories for local DDT production in the Indian subcontinent.

The incidence of malaria—and, as a consequence, the disease and death rate generally—dropped dramatically once spraying began. In Ceylon, where a national control programme began in 1945, the number of cases dropped from the millions to the thousands, and then to the hundreds, in a few years. In Mauritius, the number of deaths ascribed to malaria in 1948 was 1500; seven years later, it was three, and the infant mortality rate dropped from 186 to sixty-seven per thousand. Unicef, involved in more modest programmes, could also cite impressive results: in Thailand, experimental spraying for one year in a malarious area reduced new cases among infants to zero, and the number of children with malaria parasites in their blood by eighty per cent. For economic planners, the savings were equally impressive. In one area of the Himalayan foothills, food production rose by fifty per cent as a result of Unicef-assisted spraying. In El Salvador, the cost of the insecticide, sprayers, spraymen, vehicles, and campaign management came to around fifty cents per person protected per year—a great deal less than the cost of land unused, crops unplanted, and people unwell. From 1951, the US Government began to invest large amounts in malaria control worldwide. Nationally and internationally, DDT spraying was a mass-campaign hit.

The euphoria was punctured in the early 1950s. Certain species of *anopheles* mosquito were becoming resistant to DDT. In Greece, a country where DDT spraying had been going on for several years, it was no longer a certain weapon against the three critical mosquitoes. An Indonesian species had developed resistance; so had two African and two American. The prospect that the *anopheles* could defeat DDT's effect by biological adaptation seemed to spell disaster to malaria control. Within a few short years, it was possible not only that all the recent progress would be undone, but also that malaria carried by the super-mosquito would re-appear in areas from which it had long since departed and cause unbelievable havoc.

Alarmed by this grimmest of prospects, the most prestigious combatants of insect-borne disease proposed a decisive strategy: a short, sharp stroke not merely to bring malaria under control, but to end transmission and eliminate the disease for good.

With the enemy daily increasing its defensive power against DDT, mere control was self-defeating; only eradication would do. Malaria was different from the other diseases currently under attack: the mosquito had imposed a deadline for achieving results. It took six years for the *anopheles* to develop resistance to DDT. Therefore, the choice was between indefinite malaria and indefinite control; and eradication within the next six years. At least, that was the choice presented in 1955 by Fred Soper, Paul Russell, E. J. Pampana, chief of WHO's malaria section, and veterans of other campaigns in Europe, Asia and Latin America. Soper, in particular, presented his case with great conviction; at this stage in the history of public health, there was no-one who knew more than he about what it took to eliminate malaria's vector.

Fred Lowe Soper came from Kansas and spent much of his career fighting mosquitoes in Brazil. He was originally sent there by the Rockefeller Foundation to attack hookworm, and in time gained a reputation for masterminding a brilliant and conclusive campaign against yellow fever and its vector, *aedes aegypti*; and for wiping out, in North-East Brazil and in Egypt, the lethal malarial interloper from tropical Africa, *anopheles gambiae*.

Soper was a forceful personality whose style of leadership was driving, zealous, and brooked no interference. He was one of the great names in disease warfare, a spiritual successor to Gorgas of the Panama Canal, and by the 1950s was already something of a legend.

In 1947, as the candidate of US Surgeon-General Dr Thomas Parran, Fred Soper became the Director of the Pan American Sanitary Bureau in Washington, the international public-health organization for the Americas. In 1949 the PASB also became the regional bureau of WHO, and was later renamed the Pan American Health Organization (PAHO). Soper, having given a lifetime of service to the control of disease in the Americas, fought hard to preserve for the PASB an independence of action for its activities in the hemisphere. During his twelve-year directorship, he considerably expanded the budget and size of its programme, giving much weight to the eradication of communicable disease and, in the case of yellow fever, to the eradication of *aedes aegypti*, its vector.

While the experience of Sardinia had proved that it was difficult, if not impossible, to eradicate a malarial mosquito from its indigenous habitat, it had also proved that it was possible to vanquish the plasmodium itself— the parasite. All Fred Soper required to commit himself to the unversallydesirable goal of the eradication of a specific disease was proof of technical feasibility. Operational feasibility, in his view and according to his example, could be managed; it only needed full jurisdiction, by which he meant full authority uncluttered by bureaucratic red tape and backed at the highest political level; adequate financial resources; and meticulous administration.

In October 1954, the fourteenth Pan American Conference meeting in Santiago, taking its cue from Soper and from Pampana of WHO, instructed the PASB to do everything in its power to eradicate malaria in the Americas. Belief in the possibility was fortified by the experience of Venezuela, where a national eradication campaign led by Dr Arnoldo Galbadon, another malaria maestro, was closing in successfully on its goal.

Soper had been pushing for continental eradication since 1950; but in the past few years, the early success of DDT spraying in malarious areas had lulled ministries of health into a sense of security. Just when the DDT-resistant *anopheles* mosquito was about to strike back, they had reduced their budgets for malaria control and relaxed their efforts. This was common to almost all disease-control campaigns: when a type of illness which had been common disappeared from a locality, it was difficult to persuade both inhabitants and health administrators that a campaign's momentum should be maintained. Determined to swing the pendulum back, Soper had become a forceful salesman for an invigorated international malaria-action plan in the hemisphere, for which he had full WHO support.

On 15 March 1955, Soper addressed Unicef's Executive Board in New York. His belief that the threat of DDT-resistance made it imperative to declare a regional countdown against malaria carried great conviction. Since the 1954 Conference in Santiago, American ministries of health were committed in principle; but to carry out national campaigns they needed international help. The PASB could offer technical advice on the disease and its vectors and on how to run campaigns against both, but it could offer much less help with the hardware: DDT, spraying equipment, and vehicles. Hence the appeal to Unicef's Executive Board. Here was a unique opportunity, Soper suggested. A permanent solution to a disease which affected fifty million people, most of them children, could be achieved by a small investment of capital over a short period.

Soper's belief that malaria eradication was technically feasible was based not on the idea of destroying every last *anopheles* mosquito—which had failed in Sardinia—but the mathematics favouring the extinction of the parasite. If the mosquito and parasite were kept apart, parasites could not be taken from, nor deposited in, the human bloodstream. If existing parasites waited in vain for an *anopheles* bite to take them onto the next stage of evolution, their life cycles could not progress. The parasite would die out and the bite of the *anopheles* would eventually become harmless. Since a person's bloodstream divested itself of the parasite after three years, malaria would disappear from an infected area during this time unless reintroduced from elsewhere.

Because of the uncontrollable to-ings and fro-ings of mosquitoes and human beings across boundaries, eradication in a country, let alone a continent, was only feasible if campaigns were co-ordinated between contiguous malarious areas simultaneously. This was Soper's boldest leap: from a local campaign in a geographically self-contained area, such as the island of Sardinia or the Italian peninsula, to a rather larger land mass; not just a country or even a continent, but a hemisphere. Once a malarious area had been sprayed into harmlessness, the most solid defence had to be erected against the possibility of the parasite in either of its vectors—man or mosquito—re-entering.

Soper's plea for Unicef support was strongly backed by its own Director for the Americas, Robert Davée. Davée proposed that Unicef spend $3 million a year for four years on malaria eradication in the region, mostly in Mexico where the problem was worst. This represented a very large allocation for one particular type of programme, but he believed it was worthwhile.

Many delegates did not agree. They were by no means convinced that Unicef should throw such a disproportionate amount of its scarce resources—about a quarter of the total—into one continental programme. Not only might other projects in the Americas suffer, but also there would be less money available for other parts of the world.

Some felt that Unicef was forgetting its mandate. This campaign would certainly help children; but were its benefits specific enough to justify the volume of support? Others were sceptical that the costs and technical aspects had been fully appreciated. They wanted more answers before committing Unicef to such an ambitious venture, and asked that the WHO/Unicef joint health-policy committee consider the idea and make recommendations.

Senior delegates from the two organizations' governing bodies met in New York on 6 May 1955 for the health-policy committee meeting. Some of the world's leading experts on malaria took part. Their support for replacing the goal of malaria control with that of eradication was persuasive. The committee discussed the implications, and unanimously signalled a green light not just for the Americas, but also for malaria eradication everywhere.

The arguments pushing in this direction were partly scientific and partly emotional. The last five years had seen spectacular successes in breaking transmission and bringing malaria under control. It had been possible to achieve what ten years ago would have been dismissed as a fantasy: to protect from malaria 300 million people, or half the world's total then estimated to be living in malarious areas. The number of malaria cases had dropped globally by at least one-third.

It did not seem over-optimistic to imagine that an all-out effort could complete the job within another five years or so, especially as more of the same would produce diminishing returns as DDT resistance grew. Only in Africa south of the Sahara, where the disease was endemic but where spraying had not yet shown the same results, was eradication recognized to be impracticable at present.

The experts recommended a 'revolutionary' approach, which was essentially that developed by Soper. Malaria eradication should consist of an 'attack' phase, and a 'consolidation' phase. 'Attack' would last no longer than four years: one year in which to stop transmission, and three years for the parasite to disappear from the local bloodstream. At this point, consolidation would take over: a system of surveillance would make sure that every time a case of malaria occurred, measures were taken to treat it and stop the disease spreading. Although the attack phase would be expensive, there were cost advantages in the strategy: surveillance would be cheaper than attack since it would merely treat a few cases and keep an eye on danger zones. After another four years, surveillance would be wound down. Allowing for preparatory time and inevitable delays, the two phases would last around ten years, which was therefore the period for which a national malaria service would be needed. After that, malaria would be a rarity and could be treated by 'maintenance': the ordinary health care network.

Reaching the maintenance phase did require an initial all-out effort and investment. Both national governments (on whom most of the burden would fall) and international organizations would have to pledge themselves to commit the financial resources necessary to carry the campaign through to the end. Once started, any going back in any country would threaten the potential for success in a neighbouring one. The absolute nature of the moral obligation and the long-term financial commitment to malaria eradication made this mass campaign different from any other, including its own precursor, malaria control; DDT resistance and the deadline it imposed appeared to constitute such a threat that there seemed no alternative but to accept their terms.

First signalled in 1954 not only by the Pan American Sanitary Conference, but also from a regional WHO conference in Asia, international momentum was gathering behind the call for malaria eradication. When the World Health Assembly met in Mexico shortly after the joint WHO/Unicef committee meeting, it took its cue on malaria from their discussions. One of the most famous resolutions in WHO history was passed, urging governments in malarious regions to abandon malaria control for malaria eradication and to speedily re-design their programmes accordingly. Those who felt sceptical found their voices stilled by the fervour of the moment. The entire world health community was bent on committing itself to an all-out crusade.

Few of the delegates realized quite how much they were demanding of themselves and others. As Fred Soper liked to observe, 'perfection is the minimum permissible standard' for a successful eradication campaign. In the social and economic circumstances of most malarious parts of the world, perfection was a very tall order.

Now that the green light had been given, Unicef enthusiastically advised its staff around the world of the new emphasis in malaria assistance, and pressed them to make its case to governments. In Africa, where no-one as yet had managed to interrupt malaria's transmission, control could still be supported if its purpose was to act purely as an interim step.

Elsewhere, existing malaria efforts should be re-planned as quickly as possible to match the new 'attack' and 'consolidation' format. Before requesting further supplies of insecticide or sprayers from Unicef, governments should show their commitment to eradication by setting up a national malaria service and by pledging financial support to complete the programme to the bitter end. They would also have to pass the necessary laws; malaria had to become a compulsorily notifiable disease and spraymen have the legal right of entry to people's houses.

Of all disease campaigns conceived as something done to a passive population, this feature made those which attacked insect-borne disease the most oblivious to people's attitudes. A leprosy lesion or a yaws sore could be hidden; it was more difficult to hide a house. They were also the most intrusive; people had no choice about whether or not they co-operated.

The regional eradication programme in the Americas was now assured of Unicef's whole-hearted support. First in the field was Mexico, where nineteen million people lived in malarious areas. The Mexican Government intended to mount a four-year mass eradication campaign, and asked Unicef to meet the $8 million costs of insecticides, transport, and sprayers— a request which the earlier hesitations had put on hold. In September 1955, fortified by the WHO resolution, the Unicef Board voted a first instalment of $2·4 million for Mexico's antimalaria drive, the largest amount of money allocated to a single project in Unicef's nine-year history.

A campaign to spray, one-by-one, on a regular basis over three million houses required herculean feats of organization. The Mexican authorities were already deep into plans for their attack phase, having set up a national malaria eradication commission to run the autonomous operation under the health authorities which Soper and other veterans regarded as critical to success. Under its guidance, surveys were being carried out on the *anopheles* species and their guests, the plasmodia, and their various living, reproductive, and dietary habits. Hospitals, health centres, and private medical practitioners in malarious areas had been instructed to report every case of fever. Mobile teams of sprayers were in training.

Houses were being numbered and mapped, and itineraries prepared. The army was in charge of logistics, adding real military presence to a campaign characterized by the vocabulary of war.

The campaign was launched on 7 September 1956 in an atmosphere of high excitement and with every visible sign of political support. President Adolfo Ruiz Cortines reviewed his national malaria combat troops at a grand military parade on the central avenue in Mexico City. In the line-up there were 300 senior officers, 1650 spraymen, and a column of 600 campaign vehicles, donated by Unicef, painted bright yellow and stamped with the malaria-campaign emblem. Soper was present, as were Maurice Pate and Robert Davée. Nationwide radio broadcast the presidential proclamation. Newspapers carried banner headlines. Cinemas screened a film about the campaign, which opened with tanks careering over a hill to the sound of martial music.

The 'attack' was planned to last three years. The 200 mobile malaria squads visited areas where malaria was a year-round problem twice a year. Where it was only a problem during the rainy season and the months following, they visited once a year, timing their spraying to precede the mosquitoes' busiest periods of feeding on human blood. A precise schedule covering three million houses, taking into account weather and road conditions as well as all local variations of mosquito and human behaviour, would be difficult to plan anywhere in the world; but where people were not living in a close-knit and organized society it was more than difficult.

Some of the villages up in the Sierras were so remote that they could only be reached by packhorse. The 'mounted cavalry' of the campaign—khaki-clad spraymen in paratroop boots and helmets—forded rivers and climbed paths carrying malaria flags. As they sprayed each house, often over the objections of bewildered householders, they attached a sign with the date. In towns and villages and jungle clearings, they put up posters to appeal for co-operation. In schools, meeting-places, and churches, the campaign was explained. Vigilance against the mosquito was endlessly preached.

The attack phase of the Mexican campaign encountered operational problems typical of many campaigns. Map-making and census-taking revealed early on that the number of households in malarious areas had been under-estimated by a considerable margin: 500,000 or one-sixth. In 1958, heavy rains caused flooding and spread malaria to parts of the country previously spared, once again increasing the numbers of houses to be sprayed. These setbacks lengthened the period of attack, and substantially increased the costs of the campaign, causing considerable headaches to both the Mexican authorities and their international partners. In other ways the attack moved ahead satisfactorily; the teams of spraymen managed to beat their target of ten households a day; the supply chain of insecticide and equipment held up; logistics and transport ran smoothly.

By 1959, the epidemiologists could report that the most prevalent of the malaria parasites—*falciparum*—had disappeared for more than eighteen months in areas inhabited by more than half the population at risk.

These results were extremely impressive. They were also worrying. In the other malarious half of Mexico—in the warmer, more humid and low-lying coastal areas where the mosquito was most in its element—vector and plasmodium had defeated the attack. The same disconcerting news was beginning to filter in from a number of other countries.

Malaria eradication had been predicated on the theory that one or at most two years of blanket spraying would be enough to prevent more than a completely insignificant number of new malaria cases developing. The rest of the attack phase was to keep mosquitoes away until the parasite had left the local bloodstream. In many places, transmission had been broken in the time set; in others, after spraying for eighteen months or longer, it had not. One alternative was to change the insecticide: in some places this was tried and worked. In others the problem was not so clear-cut. Was it the lack of organizational perfection? Or was there something wrong with the underlying theory? At this stage, most people were still convinced that, with the right backing, financial resources, trained personnel, administrative perfection, and warlike vocabulary, the malaria parasite would have to succumb.

As malaria eradication campaigns progressed in countries all over the world, they evolved on the basis of information thrown up by their own activities, like other mass disease campaigns. This was information that was previously unavailable for many of the areas into which the attempt at universality was carrying health services and medical personnel for the very first time. Also for the first time, this information was being systematically pooled through the international organizations involved. It was a phenomenon of all mass campaigns that they discovered a much larger spread of their disease than expected, and that its epidemiology always turned out to be much more complex than any map with coloured, hatched, and shaded patches could ever imply.

In 1959, just before the five-year mark and the moment at which the attack phase of many campaigns should be closing down, if everything was proceeding according to the symmetry of maps and theories, WHO's malaria experts produced an exhaustive technical appraisal of what the campaigns had accomplished.

In a handful of countries—most of them in Europe or the Caribbean—eradication had been achieved; in many others it had been 'commenced' or was 'in preparation'. Five years before, 600 million people had been thought to be living in malarious areas. Now the figure was amended to 771 million, of whom 516 million were living in areas where attack was underway. A few years before, this definition would have been: 'protected from malaria', indicating tremendous progress. But because more than three years had passed—and three years had a witching connotation in malaria eradication—the discovery that 516 million people were living in the attack phase and that only sixty-four million had progressed to the consolidation phase sounded rather less encouraging.

The upwards revision of numbers meant that attack would have to continue for longer; the short, sharp, spraying phase was turning out, in a way sadly familiar to disease campaigners, to be neither so short nor so sharp as expected. The effect of turning malaria control into malaria eradication had become psychologically hard to handle. The veterans of insect-borne attack now fighting what, for them, was the world war of all time tended to remain optimistic. To men like Soper, setbacks were only to be expected and would be overcome. But their upbeat tone about campaign refinements were beginning to jostle with dissonant voices.

Problems were far from confined to the increase in numbers that surveys and spraying operations had thrown up. Each review of the campaigns recited the same litany of organizational defects. Some governments had embarked on the attack phase with more enthusiasm than appreciation of what was involved for parts of the country where censuses and maps were nonexistent. Malaria services lacked both the administrative calibre and the autonomy regarded as vital; many were understaffed, underskilled, and underpaid.

The analyses of many campaigns persistently upbraided governments for being 'unwilling or unable' to devote sufficient financial resources, and for failing to pass the necessary legislation—or at least to put it firmly into effect. Emphasis was mostly placed on organizational and financial short-comings in the early analyses. Some recognition was also given to the 'technical' and 'social' problems posed by the behaviour of the creatures involved—man, mosquito, and plasmodium—whose respective contrariness had been greatly underestimated. Mosquitoes did not always ingest blood at the prescribed place or time or alight on walls having done so. Human beings did not all spend their evenings and nights indoors; some were nomadic and moved backwards and forwards across huge distances, taking their houses, their animals, and their plasmodia with them. Again, the analyzers chided those in charge: they had not carried out a geographical survey; they had started their campaigns with far less than the necessary epidemiological and entomological information at their fingertips.

The standard list of operational shortcomings spoke volumes as much about the over-optimistic expectations of those who drew it up as it did about the campaigns themselves. The fact was that many of the malaria men had writ large a campaign in Italy, Sardinia, the plantations of Malaya and the US army camps of the Pacific, but they had simply not bargained for conditions on the ground symptomatic of gross underdevelopment, covering huge areas and large, remote, spread-out populations whose ways of life, like those of their zoological companions, were not fully understood.

To level these kinds of criticisms against many of the countries in question was tantamount to criticizing them for being malarious. If their public-health authorities had been able to reach such administrative perfection and budgetary reliability, lacking only technical advice and DDT, their populations would probably not have been suffering from such a massive disease problem in the first place. Some very large countries—India, for example—understood what they were taking on when they 'converted' from malaria control to malaria eradication, and did so only when they were ready. In Asia, anyway, the organizational problems were not so deeply confounded by serious technical problems—mosquito and plasmodium perversity—as they were in Africa and Central America. For a long time, however, it was difficult to disentangle one set of problems from another.

Once governments and their various international helpers had committed themselves and their resources down the line, and in the absence of any conclusive evidence that anything had happened other than a postponement of the goal, it was natural to hope that an extension of the effort would resolve the problems. Time had by no means yet run out; in many parts of the world *anopheles* had not yet developed unmanageable resistance. WHO's 1959 appraisal rang with conviction that the goal was as attainable as ever, that the strategy was sound, that the principles remained intact, and that a more refined understanding of the complexities involved only proved that no slackening of effort was justified. In this report Soper, who was by then on the verge of retirement from PAHO, had a considerable hand; another irrepressibly-optimistic Unicef colleague, Sam Keeny, was on his team. But Unicef as a whole was beginning to balk; reaching the end of the attack phase, let alone the ultimate goal, was obviously going to entail much greater expense over a much more extended time frame than was originally thought.

In 1955, when the drive for eradication began, Unicef had agreed to provide weaponry and transport for the attack phase—DDT and other imported supplies—primarily in the Americas and the eastern Mediterranean. The US Government, through the International Co-operative Administration (ICA), the precursor to USAID, had become the largest international donor to malaria eradication, providing the external supplies needed for the programmes in the larger programmes of Asia—India, Pakistan, Indonesia—and for Brazil. WHO offered technical advice, co-ordination of the global effort, and evaluation; and PAHO offered technical advice and regional co-ordination in the Americas. The costs to Unicef of becoming the quartermaster for its share of worldwide spraying campaigns had been calculated on the basis of existing malaria-control projects, then averaging twelve cents per head of population protected per year. The target population in the countries destined for Unicef assistance was estimated at forty million; the costs were expected to be $5 million a year over five years.

Within a year these estimates had risen substantially. In 1956, the Unicef Board accepted that they had been too conservative, but imposed a ceiling for the rest of the decade: not more than $10 million could be spent on attacking mosquitoes in any one year. The Board had not been very enthusiastic that almost half of Unicef's total programme budget might be absorbed on campaigning against one disease, but the temporary high cost had been accepted because it was seen as a worthwhile long-term investment in children's health. By 1960, it was assumed, most attack phases would be over and aid would phase out: it had not been imagined that Unicef's help would be needed during the consolidation phase.

On the verge of the new decade, however, a long-term investment for a few years only was becoming an abnormally high recurrent cost: $8 million a year. In the disused language of malaria control, the numbers of mothers and children freed from the misery of malaria—the homes of over thirty million people were sprayed in 1959—the campaign's results were exemplary; but the only recognized gauge of success was progress towards eradication.

For all the reasons outlined in WHO's report, the attack phase was still going on and looked as though it would do so for some time to come. Instead of peaking in 1957–58 and then declining, demands on Unicef resources were likely to rise unless an effort was made to check them. Unicef did not question WHO's view of eradication's technical feasibility, nor the likelihood of its ultimate achievement. But other considerations intruded, many of them raised back in 1955 before the eradication policy had been adopted. Unicef, the organization which existed to help promote 'child health purposes generally' could not be indefinitely distracted by malaria eradication. Whatever the merits of trying to reach the goal, the time had come for Unicef to establish a timetable for the reduction of its annual expenditures on this one disease in such a way as would be least damaging to promising projects and to its relations with governments and other international organizations.

In 1959, the Unicef Executive Board took a careful look at the information available, and attached stringent conditions to Unicef's future aid for malaria eradication.

No new projects would be helped except in very exceptional circumstances. The renewal of assistance for existing programmes would depend on their being able to demonstrate that their operations were technically, financially and administratively sound, and that the prospects of eventual eradication appeared good. If it was necessary to extend the attack phase for a year or two beyond the original timetable, support would probably continue; but if malaria transmission had not been halted by the fourth year of spraying every house in a malarious area, spraying should cease and the entire basis of the campaign be re-considered.

Assistance to malaria control would be limited to pilot schemes and preliminary surveys; there must be reason to think that these 'pre-eradication' projects would lead to full-scale eradication in due course, although Unicef in no way committed itself to supporting such projects when they decided to do so. Under these terms, Unicef hoped to lower its assistance to malaria campaigns from $9·5 million in 1960 to around $3 million in 1964.

In one respect alone, the policy laid down in 1959 was more lenient than before: some limited assistance could be given to consolidation, including supplies of drugs and of insecticide needed to stamp out any remaining 'foci' of disease. By this stage, ideas of what consolidation should constitute, and what resources were required for it to work, had undergone a transformation. This was one more way in which the strategy for achieving malaria eradication had evolved. Ultimately, it was the most significant evolution of all.

The consolidation phase in malaria eradication was the phase at which spraying in a given area could cease when the number of people with the parasite still in their bloodstream had gone down to one in every 2000. The only way to find out when this magic moment was reached was by an effective surveillance system, a system which every national malaria eradication service was expected to put into place within two or three years of starting the attack.

At the beginning of the eradication drive, when the spraygun had seemed invincible, surveillance had not received much attention; everyone had concentrated on the drama and difficulties of attack. As attack began to yield less-than-perfect results in certain countries and areas, surveillance turned out to be a much more critical indicator of progress than any house count or spray schedule, and the importance attached to it began to grow. The ultimate test of any campaign was the number of plasmodia in the local bloodstream; and if there were still a fair number present after attack had been going on for a while, the results of surveillance were needed to help redesign the battle formation so that its pattern would have the desired effect.

Effective surveillance had to be based on the systematic collection and analysis of blood smears from malarious areas—not an easy proposition in places where there were few doctors, health centres or laboratories. The search for plasmodia in most of the countries was too large and expensive a task to be carried out by the full-time staff of the malaria service.

In some countries a familiar solution was employed: lay people were invited to volunteer as reporting agents. In Mexico, these were known as *notificantes*, and over 30,000 from many walks of life were enrolled; school teachers and community leaders, as well as pharmacists, laboratory technicians and health staff in hospitals and clinics took part. The national malaria staff trained the volunteers in how to take blood smears and prepare slides, and gave them supplies of malaria drugs. Villagers and townspeople with symptoms of fever sought out their local *notificante*, gave a blood smear, and received treatment in return. Staff from the Malaria Commission visited regularly to give supervision and investigate the cases' origins. With certain modifications, this pattern of surveillance was used in countries all over Latin America.

While the system worked adequately in parts of the world with a relatively high degree of social organization and where the national malaria service could provide effective supervision, in most places the use of volunteers was not sufficiently reliable for watertight surveillance. The reporting of fever cases, the taking of blood-slides, their transport to the laboratory, their analysis, the follow-up of positive cases back in the village, required just the same degree of military precision as the attack phase. Surveillance operations were just as complex as spraying, but with less of their excitement or dramatic results.

Instead of battalions of combat troops to send out on a mosquito and disease destruction mission, there was an interminable pile of blood slides—it had to represent between three and ten per cent of the population in the malarious area—to collect and analyze. Hunting down and despatching the handful of remaining malaria plasmodia was unexpectedly turning out to be just as expensive as preventing the first thousands and tens of thousands of fever cases. Chemotherapy, a weapon against malaria which had not originally been expected to play any major role in eradication, was now hauled up from reserve. Not only did patients who had endured the invasions of the spraying teams without effective result need to be treated; but if the plasmodium could not be definitively killed off inside the mosquito, killing it also in the human bloodstream was the second line of attack. In some places where attack had not produced the expected results, spraymen were given supplies of malaria drugs to give out to household members as a preventive dose.

Gradually, as it became clear that the post-attack consolidation phase played an essential part in reaching the point of definite and certifiable eradication in a given area, it also became clear that the presence of a static and permanent network of health services, however rudimentary, was a pre-condition of eradication. In accordance with the unwritten laws of public health, the most malarious areas were by definition those where such health networks were skeletal or non-existent.

Advancing the basic health-service network into the countryside alongside the malaria spray squads therefore became a vital adjunct to a successful campaign. In some of the countries of Asia—India and Ceylon, for example—this realization of the symbiotic relationship between the spearhead attack and the regular health-security forces prompted the faster growth of the latter. In most of Africa, and in larger or smaller parts of other countries, the installation of such networks was years, even a generation, away. Sponsors of malaria eradication were therefore forced to recognize that there were certain countries where eradication simply could not happen within the foreseeable future; and others where malaria could be banished from large areas, but where eradication from the entire country would remain elusive.

By 1961, Unicef's expenditure on malaria eradication had declined to $5·5 million a year. This represented over a quarter of all programme expenditure, still too high a proportion in the view of most Unicef policy-makers. The Unicef stance was growing progressively tougher towards the standards of the campaigns it was supporting and others for which its support was requested. Part of the reason was its own organizational evolution and a desire to face the challenges of the UN's first 'Development Decade' by moving into broader programme areas and concentrating less on being a supplier of drugs, vaccines and other material to the narrow objective of disease control. The other part was that many of the pro-grammes for malaria eradication it had originally supported were not doing well. Most were in poorer, and therefore more problematic, countries—or in countries which, despite the most resolute attempts to overcome setbacks, had not managed to end spraying operations in all malarious areas.

In the face of Unicef's palpable determination to reduce its support for malaria eradication, WHO showed concern. WHO Director-General, Dr Marcolino Gomez Candau of Brazil, was very committed to malaria eradication: his enthusiasm had been fuelled by Fred Soper while employed in his country's insect-borne disease service. Candau attended the June 1961 session of the Executive Board to ask Unicef to maintain its financial support. Although the Board re-affirmed the $10 million ceiling for malaria projects, in practice no effort was made thereafter to reach it.

Unicef's disenchantment was strongly influenced by what was seen as the lack of commitment displayed by certain governments whose vigour in trying to eradicate malaria dwindled when serious problems emerged. It argued that where insufficient interest and support was displayed within the country itself, there was little Unicef could do. In certain countries like India, Ceylon and Taiwan, malaria eradication was proceeding convincingly towards its goal because commitment and resources were assured, and the mechanisms for consolidation were receiving due attention. Elsewhere, there was simply no point in throwing money away, especially as a poor effort at malaria eradication might succeed in reducing a population's acquired immunity to the disease and make them even more vulnerable to its resurgence. After 1961, Unicef began to withdraw from a number of 'pre-eradication' programmes in Africa which were not preventing the transmission of malaria and therefore could not lead to national eradication campaigns.

In January 1964, the Unicef Board again stiffened the organization's policy on malaria eradication. Apart from ongoing commitments to well-run programmes in which Unicef had been involved from the outset, such as that in Mexico, or campaigns for which there were other long-standing commitments, the conditions attached to new support for malaria programmes were so stringent as to mean that it was almost unobtainable. Unicef had effectively given notice to malaria eradication.

From this point onwards, it preferred to combat malaria and other diseases by supporting the spread of basic health services, particularly those for maternal and child health. If a ministry of health requested supplies of chemoprophylaxis or other antimalaria weapons to be used by health centres alongside other curative and preventive therapies for infectious disease, Unicef was willing to assist. But no more support was forthcoming for autonomous malaria services with their squads of spraymen and convoys of vehicles. What had once been their much-vaunted autonomy now became a black mark against them in countries which had more medical personnel dealing with malaria than with anything else. 'Integration' of malaria personnel into the mainstream of health services now became the favoured policy. Sometimes these shifts in New York and Geneva were hard for Unicef and WHO staff in the field to explain to the governments they had cajoled into carrying out the original strategy.

Whatever Unicef felt about the necessity for reducing its own commitments, as the 1960s wore on the enthusiasts for malaria eradication could still point to significant progress towards their goal. By the middle of the decade, the attack phase finally passed its peak. In 1960, forty per cent of the target population were under attack. By 1964, that proportion had declined to twenty-five per cent, or 372 million people; forty-six per cent, or 686 million, were living in areas which had reached consolidation or from which malaria had been finally eradicated. It was a tremendous advance, even if it was not the kind of advance the prophets of eradication had promised. Except in Africa—and it was a large exception—malaria was firmly in retreat.

The question now appeared to be the cost and complexities of going the last mile. It seemed to many that there was no 'last mile', just endless expensive and possibly-irrelevant miles beyond each last one, and that the equation between investment and results had become hopelessly unbalanced. Even the threat of the DDT-proof super-mosquito—the original justification for the goal—appeared less compelling.

There was also the inevitable school of thought which felt that, having got so far, the goal should not be abandoned at the critical moment. For some who had believed in the dream of a world free of a vicious disease, there was a deep emotional resistance to the idea that, after all, when science and mathematics said it was possible and when the best wills had been put to discovering the best ways, the dream was not attainable. Opinions were deeply divided—within ministries of health and between them, within the international assistance organizations and between them.

Unicef had by this stage given up agonizing over whether eradication was practicable or not. It was not willing to commit more than a certain proportion of its resources to any one disease and that was that. Although it was never explicitly stated, in the early 1960s Unicef psychologically abandoned malaria eradication. The essence of eradication was that it was an all-or-nothing proposition. As the insect-borne pioneers had demonstrated over and over again, whatever weapon you flung against a mosquito and its occupying parasite it would cause them to retreat; and if you flung it en masse, they would retreat en masse. But when you relaxed, even by a small amount, you allowed vector and plasmodia their chance of come-back—which invariably they took. If you discontinued the onslaught in one country, infected man or infected mosquito would sooner or later cross the border from another.

Fred Soper went to his grave still believing that throughout the world a generation of children was being sacrificed to malaria on the spurious grounds that local health units must first be put in place before the plasmodia could be banished. But the experiences of Soper and others like him were garnered in a different world—one where authority and autonomy, exercised with the panache of a superb field marshal, could inflict health on a population whether they chose to co-operate or not. By the 1960s, those halcyon days had vanished.

In the end, it was not the organizational and administrative failures on the battlefield which drove home the nail in the coffin of malaria eradication. It was certainly true that many governments, which really could not have done otherwise once the real demands of effective consolidation through a health service network were understood, did not commit the necessary financial resources, nor did they organize their operations to the 'minimum' standard of perfection. Ultimately, however, the technical problems turned out to be more than a match for organizational perfection.

The boldest international public-health endeavour of all time was defeated by the creatures of the living world. Mosquito and parasite, particularly *anopheles gambiae* and *plasmodium falciparum*, were able to adapt their biological or behavioural performance too fast for the campaign strategists to catch up. Conniving in their victory was the other malaria vector, man, who did the opposite. He did not adapt his social behaviour to the campaigns, and the strategists' notion that the law—backed up if necessary by the police—could make him do so proved naive. Such ideas might have worked in a plantation economy or in a highly-organized society, but most malarious areas were neither. The unwitting bond between man and mosquito proved as strong as that between mosquito and parasite in defeating the goal of malaria eradication.

Certain species of *anopheles* mosquito, as forecast, developed resistance to DDT and other chlorinated hydrocarbon insecticides. What had not been anticipated, however, was that some mosquitoes would find the poison irritable and unpleasant and learn to avoid it. Others had marked tendencies towards 'exophily' and 'exophagy', terms which began to appear in the literature and meant that they preferred the outdoor life, particularly alfresco feeding.

In Africa's savannah regions, *anopheles gambiae* was a persistent non-conformist, which was why no 'pre-eradication' scheme ever defeated it. Even where the chances looked hopeful—for example in the islands of Zanzibar and Pemba off the East African coast—all efforts to design a spraying programme to defeat the mosquito failed: it hid in the coral. Man helped it elude its attackers. New dwellings sprouted up without permission; itinerant workers with plasmodia in their bloodstream arrived from the mainland for the clove-picking season. The man-mosquito alliance proved unbeatable—and in 1968 Unicef withdrew its assistance.

Man was not deliberately perverse. Most of the people whose flesh the mosquitoes greedily sought could not be expected to understand fully upon what precise mathematical formulations malaria eradication depended. In tropical countries, many people took the advantage of the cool of the evening to sit and socialize out of doors; and some preferred to sleep outside rather than in the cramped and airless interior of a modest dwelling. Some spent virtually their whole lives out of doors, living in tents and migrating with their livestock and the season. Among nomadic peoples, no amount of understanding of the feeding habits of mosquitoes could have made a difference. In southern Iran, for example, not only did the mosquito become DDT-resistant, but the movements of nomad groups between grazing grounds made it impossible to carry out surveillance and case detection. This was another programme from which Unicef eventually phased out.

In many parts of Africa, even sedentary peoples moved with the farming season. When the time came for planting or harvesting, they went to live in a different hut on a distant patch of land. If migration was part of people's way of life and their food supply depended on it, they were unlikely to change it because of visits from antimalaria sprayers. Among people who did stay in their village all year round, house repairs—plastering or filling in cracks in the walls—did not stop because of DDT. Some materials used for building—mud for example—absorbed insecticide and deprived it of its potency. In many places, once the insect population was decimated, people refused entry to the spray teams, law or no law. They did not see why strangers should upset their lives and violate their privacy to no useful purpose.

The malaria eradication campaign in Mexico, the largest to receive Unicef assistance, made great progress in its early years. But Mexico was one of the countries whose 'problem areas' defeated all the government's administrative excellence and, by the mid-1960s, seemed to indicate that the technical feasibility of malaria eradication might after all be an illusion. Over 4·5 million people lived in problem areas where the local *anopheles* resolutely held out against DDT and its alternative, dieldrin.

Every variation of attack was tried: the spray cycle was stepped up to four times a year; 84,000 people were routinely given antimalarials; larvicides were brought into use; where people slept outside to escape bugs in their bedding, the spray tea ns attacked the bugs to tempt people back inside.

The detection of a hard core of persistently smouldering malaria transmission was a setback in Mexico and elsewhere, which WHO described in 1966 as a 'greater challenge than might at first appear'. At the least, it meant more expense. In Mexico, Unicef agreed in 1965 to spend a final $3·5 million to bring problem areas into consolidation. The effort was inconclusive. In the late-1960s, Unicef withdrew assistance even from Mexico. By this time USAID had also begun to back-pedal on its commitments.

Malaria eradication had lost its glamour. In 1968, it received a mortal blow. Ceylon, whose drop in malaria from 2·7 million cases in 1946 to seventeen in 1963 was among the most phenomenal successes of any programme, ceased spraying altogether in 1967. In 1968–69, malaria came back with a vengeance: over a million people were infected.

While this disaster was still fresh in everyone's mind, DDT was becoming the prime target of conservationist groups in the US and Europe. Its miracle property—the toxic residue which did not go away—had become a symbol of man's determination to poison his planet. As a result of the opprobrium poured upon DDT, its manufacture went into steep decline and many countries banned its use altogether.

US support for malaria eradication also rapidly declined. In 1970, WHO carried out a soul-searching review of the strategy, and laid its conclusions before the World Health Assembly. Current methods for malaria eradication, the report stated, 'demand a degree of efficiency often unobtainable under existing conditions in certain malarious areas of the world'. Until simpler and cheaper methods could be devised, WHO recommended malaria control. Fifteen years on, with many painful lessons learned, the original prescription was reinstated. Nearly 1000 million people had been reached and protected from endemic malaria; but reaching the 360 million still unprotected by any form of specific programme—most of whom were in Africa—was still beyond the horizon. Psychologically, the corner had been turned.

There are few people today who believe that with money, men and administration, malaria could have been, or could yet be, globally eradicated. For some, there is a painful memory of an endeavour to which they committed their best working years and were forced to abandon in the face of overwhelming evidence that it could not succeed. A particular circumstance—the threat of what might happen as a result of *anopheles* resistance to DDT—had allowed the goal to be set. By the time perceptions changed about the relative importance of the interaction between mosquito and DDT to the epidemiology of malaria and attempts to interfere with it, there seemed to be no going back. But going forward meant that when all the high hopes were finally dashed, disenchantment replaced them. Disillusion with the attempt was out of proportion to its failures.

The decline in resources for malaria programmes was one reason for the resurgence of the disease in the 1970s. Since then, governments and international organizations have not shown the same will to mount a joint strategy against it. The spread of better and cheaper antimalarial drugs via the health services was the chosen approach; to some of the old malaria campaigners it seemed a tame and passive creature beside the heroic efforts of days gone by. Now a new breakthrough—an equivalent to the genuine miracle of DDT in its time—is eagerly awaited and close at hand: a vaccine against the wily and changeable malaria plasmodia. When it comes, strategic and organizational orchestration, backed up by a network of basic health services, will still be needed for any new eradication effort. Perhps next time it will succeed.

In the meantime, the malaria wheel has gone full circle: from a quinine cure to control; from control to eradication; from eradication back to control; and now back to cure. The early identification of a case of malaria and its prompt treatment is regarded as the first essential of antimalaria services. Spraying with residual insecticide as a means of keeping the vector at bay is a long way down the list, the old-fashioned mosquito net or incense coil being less likely to invite biological adaptation. The use of antimalarial drugs as a means of prevention in endemic areas is no longer recommended except for pregnant women: in children, it prevents development of natural immunity and encourages resistance in the parasite. Quick treatment at the first onset of fever, even without a professional diagnosis, is the surest means of saving life and health and of keeping natural selection working against the disease.

The drugs are cheap; the problem is to put them within reach of poor and remote rural families. This still depends on 'surveillance', although that is not the term which would nowadays be used to denote that there is a volunteer in the community trained to look out for tell-tale signs and to do something about them.

In Taiwan alone, more than half the school children used to suffer from painful trachoma. A little girl rubs her eyeballs and lids with soothing antibiotic ointment provided by Unicef in a major antitrachoma drive in the late 1950s. (*Unicef/Ling*)

In the early 1950s, some sixty-five million Indonesians lived in yaws-infected areas. The target: one million penicillin injections a year to cure the disease. (*Unicef/Ling*)

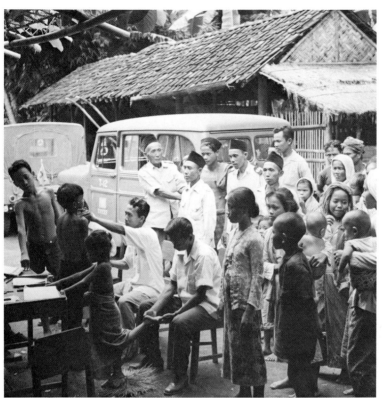

Indonesia mounted the world's largest campaign against yaws in the 1950s, employing great numbers of mobile male nurses working in the field. (*Unicef/Ling*)

India, 1950: Bombay received much of its milk from buffaloes kept in congested, unsanitary cattle sheds within the city. (*Unicef/Ling*)

A baby is born in the highlands of Puno, Peru, under the trained hands of a traditional midwife equipped with a Unicef kit who walked three days to reach her 'client'. (*Unicef/Rosler*)

A literacy class in Endeber, Ethiopia: part of a national campaign that increased the literacy rate from thirteen per cent in 1974 to thirty-five per cent in 1981. (*Unicef/Campbell*)

In primary schools in Pakistan, Unicef supplies of slates, chalks and other educational equipment help get learning underway. (*Unicef/Vajrathon*)

Equipment and supplies are needed for day-care centres. By 1981, more than 550 such centres had been established in the poorer areas of Puno, Peru, with Unicef assistance. (*Unicef/Frank*)

Malaria was not eradicated; but, except for the countries of Africa where little progress was made, the effort to bring malaria under control was not a colossal failure. Much was achieved, much was learned, much was built upon both strengths and weaknesses.

In India, eight years of the campaign reduced 100 million malaria cases a year to 80,000. Huge numbers of auxiliary medical personnel engaged in the campaign were then retrained to become multi-purpose health workers. In every malarious country to reach consolidation, infant mortality rates dropped from the hundreds to double digit figures. In a few, the effect of the campaign was to purchase for a few dollars a head a life expectancy equivalent to that of a modern industrialized society. In Mexico and elsewhere, large tracts of previously-unused land were opened up for settlement and brought under cultivation. In many countries, the anti-malaria drive was responsible for underlining the importance of a basic health-service network to consolidate the gains of any disease-control campaign, and setting its growth on track.

In one sense, malaria control was an extraordinary success. It saved so many lives, especially children's, that it created a population explosion. By the late 1960s, this problem—one that some saw as a monster unleashed by thoughtless progenitors of disease-control campaigns—was occupying far more of the world's attention than malaria ever had.

The eradication of malaria awaits a vaccine. The disease for which the technique of vaccination was first developed was smallpox. With great difficulty, Edward Jenner, a late eighteenth-century English physician, persuaded medical and scientific contemporaries to accept the evidence he had put together in support of an observation made to him by country folk: that those exposed to cowpox did not contract smallpox. He also believed that the use of the technique could banish the dreaded and disfiguring disease for good. Jenner was right; but it took nearly 200 years and a concerted global onslaught led by WHO to bring his prophecy to fruition.

A worldwide programme to eradicate smallpox began in 1958. The campaign was revitalized in 1967 following the realization that without a co-ordinated and carefully-designed international effort, even the eradication of a disease technically ideally suited to definitive prevention would not happen.

Launched twelve years after the antimalaria drive began, the smallpox eradication campaign gained from many of its lessons—in particular the need for effective surveillance, and the complications of case-finding in places where health services barely existed. It required a considerable act of faith to go for the world's first organized disease eradication at a time when mass-disease campaigns, with their tendency for a decisive burst to turn into an endless drain on hard-pressed health budgets, had earned themselves a bad name. Smallpox eradication recouped some of disease control's lost reputation, and provided the world with a spectacular and popular world health success story.

Most of the credit for smallpox eradication rightly went to WHO. The brunt of the expense and the national mobilization of personnel behind the campaigns was borne by the afflicted countries; but the technical weapons and the strategy which put them to work came from WHO's smallpox eradication team. The hideous reputation of the disease and its extreme contagiousness also helped bring in support from countries spending considerable sums on vaccination and travellers' health checks so as to protect their own populations.

Among the international donors, the US, USSR and Sweden were substantial givers of vaccine, fuel and transport. Unicef helped some countries set up their own production units for freeze-dried vaccine and provided vehicles for mobile teams, but it never identified itself closely with the smallpox effort. This was mainly because enthusiasm for the control of specific diseases had given way to helping develop multipurpose mother-and-child health services. Unicef was also influenced by the searing experience of malaria eradication, and the considerable scepticism in its wake over whether any disease was globally eradicable.

Smallpox was, however, a very different proposition from almost every other disease for which a means of prevention lay ready to hand. Compared with malaria (such a frequent cause of death because such a frequent cause of sickness), the smallpox caseload was relatively small; but the effect of contracting the disease was much more likely to be fatal, or at the least, permanently disfiguring. Like leprosy, therefore, it was a disease which struck terror, especially as no cure was available. Unlike leprosy, the incubation period was short—two weeks—and the course of the disease swift and decisive. Outbreaks occurred most often and with greatest destruction in crowded, urban slums into which an outsider had introduced the virus. In the worst of its two forms, *variola major*, the death rate was forty per cent. Since so many victims died, epidemics of this kind of smallpox were usually small-scale and swiftly burned themselves out.

There was another reason why smallpox was exceptionally containable. The virus was neither harboured nor contracted by any animal or insect, and could only be passed from person to person within a relatively short infectious period. During the two weeks or so that the actual pox erupted on the skin, a victim's clothing or bedding or infected skin was highly contagious; but those who survived, ugly though they might have become, could at least reassure themselves that they were permanently immune and non-infectious. This was the characteristic of smallpox which, ultimately, made it susceptible to all-out attack.

The existence of preventive vaccination was the most obvious critical ingredient, for if a high enough proportion of the population could be successfully immunized, the disease would spontaneously die out. Unfortunately it was discovered in the early 1960s that, because smallpox was so contagious, in highly endemic areas this proportion had to be virtually 100 per cent. In many afflicted countries, 100 per cent coverage for any disease control campaign was known to be out of the question. But because of the stability of the virus and its fixed pattern of transmission, the smallpox eradicators could use a back-up strategy. Instead of blanket vaccination, they concentrated on finding cases, isolating them, vaccinating every contact, and quarantining them until the danger of incubation was over. Smallpox was thereby trapped and could go no further. Once the patients in a family or community died or recovered, the source of infection was eliminated.

When the real push for global eradication began, the number of reported smallpox cases in the world was fluctuating between 50,000 and 100,000 a year, and this was thought to represent only a fraction of the total. In 1967, the first year of the newly-intensified campaign, it rose to 132,000: a sign that the campaign, as tended to happen, was flushing its target's dimensions into the open. Apart from a reservoir in Brazil, which also threatened countries on its borders, smallpox was nearly eradicated from the Americas. The main reservoirs were in certain countries of Asia— Afghanistan, Burma, India, Indonesia, Pakistan and Nepal— where *variola major* was common; and in most of the countries of Africa south of the Sahara, where the usual form was *variola minor*, a virus somewhat less terrifying since the death rate was only one in a hundred.

Most countries with endemic smallpox had already embarked on vaccination programmes; now WHO proposed that these be stepped up for three- or four-year periods. The weapons for vaccination were specially streamlined. Vaccinators used either bifurcated needles for scratching the skin, which conserved vaccine more carefully, or jet injectors in areas where there was a shortage of fully-trained personnel. Stringent tests guaranteed the potency of vaccine whether imported or locally-produced. WHO recommended that mass vaccination be carried out by mobile teams in all endemic areas; once this was completed, the existing health services should maintain the coverage by vaccinating travellers and the newborn.

The strategy for malaria eradication had viewed surveillance as a campaign element which overlapped and followed the attack phase. With smallpox eradication, although mopping up intractable 'foci' was originally the identical intention, surveillance quickly overtook attack and became the cornerstone of campaign strategy. During the campaign in Nigeria, a shortage of vaccine inspired planners to concentrate on tracking down cases and confining them, if necessary by a policeman at the door. The available vaccine could then be sparingly applied to contacts only. Even in areas where vaccination coverage rates were low, this method stopped transmission in its tracks. 'Surveillance-containment'—a gentler term for the modern version of quarantine—was then introduced in countries with similarly spread-out populations; it was successful in both Brazil and Indonesia, whose last smallpox cases were detected in 1971 and 1972 respectively.

The strategy was further refined in 1973 for the densely-populated countries of Asia. First in India, and later elsewhere, thousands of teams of case-finders, working with the co-operation of health institutions and schools, and with the knowledge of where the last outbreak had occurred, tracked down every possible and actual smallpox victim.

The disease gave itself away by its ugly pox both during and after infection. The discovery of a possible case—it might turn out to be something less serious, such as chickenpox—would prompt 'flying squad' action to make a diagnosis, identify all contacts, and swiftly contain the spread of infection. In India, over 150,000 searchers took part in active surveillance, and the public was offered a financial reward for sightings of pox.

By 1975, the number of smallpox cases in the world had dropped to 2130 and, in less than ten years, the number of countries where the disease could still be found had dropped from thirty to three: India, Bangladesh, and Ethiopia. By the end of the year, the last case of *variola major* was reported in Bangladesh.

The resources for a concentrated attack on *variola minor*'s last redoubt were shifted to Ethiopia, where the lack of roads and any kind of health or social service infrastructure in most of the countryside presented organizers with great logistical difficulties. Smallpox left Ethiopia in August 1976; unfortunately not before nomads in the south-east had carried the virus across the border into Somalia, where an epidemic occurred in mid-1977. In October, the last case of *variola minor* was reported in the town of Merca; in 1979, the victim was declared to have been the last smallpox case in the world!

In May 1980, the World Health Assembly declared the disease extinct. Vaccine supplies have since been kept in laboratories around the world against the possibility of an outbreak. The only known cases since 1977 were the result of a laboratory accident. WHO's offer of $1000 reward for the report of a confirmed case in any part of the world still awaits collection.

In the case of smallpox, due to the behaviour of the disease, the technical means to hand and the relatively low caseload, the equation of investment against results made eradication possible.

The costs of going the 'last mile' even with smallpox were not inconsiderable; during the final outbreak of the disease in Somalia in June 1977, twenty-four WHO epidemiologists and 3500 national staff—a huge proportion of the health personnel in such a poor country even including semitrained auxiliaries—were employed full-time on the exclusive task of looking for cases. Between 1977 and 1979, there continued to be 1500 Somali personnel and twenty WHO staff on nothing but smallpox hunting duties. At the same time, there were 1200 searchers in neighbouring Ethiopia, and 265 in neighbouring Kenya. Surveillance was also initiated in Djibouti, North and South Yemen, and during the annual pilgrimage to Mecca.

This kind of mass effort to make absolutely sure of the enemy's conquest could only be justified by the technical certainty of the methods used to obtain the result. The investment of around $300 million, one-third of which came from international sources and two-thirds of which was borne by the afflicted countries, saved the world around $1000 million annually in vaccine, vaccine administration, applying international health regulations and other costs. Most of that saving has, however, been to the budgets of industrialized countries which can afford upfront investments against a hoped-for, but nonetheless risky, target.

Devoting proportionately much larger amounts of the health budgets of developing countries to mass campaigns for disease control is not a strategy necessarily vindicated by the success of smallpox eradication. So far, WHO has not advocated any further mass eradication onslaughts; polio is the only disease talked of as a possible candidate.

The mass-disease campaigns which did so much during the 1950s and 1960s to relieve the fears and the sufferings of the family of man taught the practitioners of international public health a number of lessons. Not the least important was that disease control cannot be consolidated without a network of health services and health personnel reaching out into every nook and cranny of the land. Another was that people have to want to join in. People have to want to be cured of a particular disease, which is usually easy; they also have to want to understand how to prevent it, which is extremely difficult among the poor, usually ill-informed and sometimes superstitious inhabitants of dusty and distant villages.

When the pendulum swung away from the disease-control campaign, it was this conundrum that the public-health experts began to address, and it is the conundrum they are still trying to unlock today.

Main sources

Unicef Executive Board; general reports, statements, summary records, and specific evaluations of the regional, country and global progress towards the goal of malaria eradication; in particular, the technical appraisals prepared by WHO for the Unicef Board in 1959, 1961 and 1963; accompanying documentation by Unicef on financial implications of malaria eradication projects; project recommendations for Mexico and elsewhere; reports of the WHO/Unicef Joint Committee on Health Policy, 1955–1970.

Articles in *WHO Bulletin*, *World Health*, and *World Health Forum*, and other publications of WHO; in particular *A Re-examination of the Global Strategy of Malaria Eradication*; Official Records of the World Health Organization, Offprint No. 176, December 1969.

Unicef in Latin America for the Children of Three Decades by Ken Grant; prepared for the Unicef History Project, May 1985.

The Plague Killers, Greer Williams, published by Charles Scribner & Sons, New York, 1969.

Ventures in World Health; the Memoirs of Fred Lowe Soper; published by the Pan American Health Organization, Washington, 1977.

Articles in *Unicef News* and other Unicef information materials.

Chapter 6

Civilization Follows the Cow

In the early 1950s, the instinctive reaction to the problem of the hungry or malnourished child took one exclusive form: milk. The importance attached to its particular blend of animal fat and protein, vitamins and minerals, eclipsed all other solutions. In the Unicef mind, the virtues of milk could no more be questioned than the virtues of motherhood. In the eyes of both beneficiaries and supporters, Unicef remained for many years a kind of gigantic organizational udder, distributing a daily cup of safe, hygienic, nourishing milk to as many children in the world as possible.

When Unicef was created, its main purpose had been to provide extra rations for feeding hungry children in war-torn countries, and the axiomatic ingredient was skim milk in dried and reconstitutable form. Once the postwar crisis was past, the argument for keeping the organization alive had mainly hinged on the existence of hungry children all over the world, and it therefore continued to think about how to feed them health-giving foods.

Milk from a cow was not the most common or most obvious item of diet for children in many tropical countries. Unicef recognized this; yet for a long time it continued to regard the problem as one to be overcome by making milk more common and its virtues more obvious; or by doing the same for something as close to milk as nature and scientific invention would permit. Adulation for milk governed Unicef's attitude towards child nutrition in a profound and long-lasting way.

The science of milk conservation had made great progress in the first half of the twentieth century. In many milk-drinking parts of the industrialized world, milk drunk straight from a cow of uncertain health tethered in the backyard had been replaced by the pasteurized or otherwise hygienized contents of a bottle. The importance of milk in the infant's and child's diets were sacrosanct principles of nurturing; and this was the period when a synthetic formula based on cow's milk was believed by some paediatricians to be as good as human milk, if not better.

Changes in social behaviour, among them the emancipation of women, contributed to the move for sanitized milk and milk-based infant food products. Unicef itself, using whatever leverage it could wield through its own milk conservation programme, encouraged European governments to establish 'a safe milk policy'; it also supported the manufacture of dried milk products for children's consumption. Safe liquid milk and powdered milk in a packet were, by definition, more expensive milk than milk from an udder in a stable; some countries subsidized the price through their milk marketing boards to be sure that safe milk would be within reach of poorer families. As public health regulations became more stringent, the dairies expanded, and as the number of urban consumers grew, the price would drop of its own accord, it was hoped.

The milk breakthrough with the biggest impact on Unicef's activities was the technology for roller-drying, and later for spray-drying, still a recent invention in the postwar world. Because these developments in dairy production allowed milk to be preserved and moved around without refrigeration, they held out the promise of a health bonanza even among children remote from any dairy cow. Skim milk contained all the same body-building elements as full cream milk, and since it was a residue from the production of expensive foods like cream, butter, and cheese, it was also very cheap. In the past, skim residues were usually fed to farm animals or thrown away; now they could be conserved, as could milk surpluses in the flush season. Unicef purchased nearly two million pounds of skim milk surplus from US stocks during 1949 and 1950, the years when the feeding schemes in European countries reached their peak.

After 1950, when Unicef began to concern itself almost entirely with children whose hunger and ill-health had less to do with the impact of cataclysmic emergency than to do with age-old rural poverty, it faced a very different set of nutritional circumstances. So much was made clear by the early surveys carried out in Asia and elsewhere, and by the international experience brought to Unicef by people of the calibre of Ludwik Rajchman, Berislav Borcic, Martha Eliot, and many others. But as Unicef moved into parts of the world not very familiar to its organizational culture, its mind still inevitably ran along lines developed during the period when most of its assistance went to Europe.

In the context of child feeding, the intimate connection between child health and milk was seen as universally valid, even if its universal applicability was impracticable for a number of reasons, not least the lack of cows and a dairy industry in most parts of the tropical world. Some compensation might be made by continuing to import skim milk for mother and child feeding programmes; but this strategy had inherent limitations. However cheaply milk surpluses could be procured from North America and elsewhere, no amount nor means of transhipment could make it reach all the hungry and malnourished children in need. Their numbers were one problem; but a much greater problem was that supplementary feeding required a high degree of organization and a functioning social network—schools, health institutions, community groups—which in many such countries was all but non-existent. A disease campaign team might be able to arrive in a place and accomplish its mission in one visit, or in a series of occasional visits; supplementary feeding had to continue day in, day out, for weeks and months and maybe even years on end.

At the beginning of Unicef's new phase of existence, therefore, it was no more than realistic to envisage the use of skim milk powder as mainly confined to children and mothers in relief or refugee camps, orphanages or welfare institutions, and as a medicine for children showing clinical signs of severe malnutrition, either in hospital or maternal and child health care centres. But Unicef did allow itself to hope that, specially in countries which were economically further advanced, feeding programmes similar to those in European schools and health institutions could have a broader purpose. Wherever possible, milk powder distribution should be more than a hand-out; it should be a practical demonstration of the vital connection between nutrition and health. Its consumption should be accompanied by education about proteins and vitamins, which in time would foster new eating habits.

In Central and South America the policy appeared to pay off. The largest programme was in Brazil: it reached 500,000 children and mothers altogether, some through mother's clubs which promised to become mini 'milk co-operatives', purchasing a cow or a few goats to provide their own alternative source of dairy goodness. The supply of Unicef skim milk was popular in many American countries, and since the feeding schemes involved a wide variety of people— teachers, parents, community leaders, medical personnel— the idea of special meals for children began to catch on. Both Unicef and FAO were gratified when certain governments adopted child-feeding as part of public welfare policy.

Meanwhile, the prospects that cargoes of skim milk powder could make an equivalent dent in the fortunes of malnourished children appeared much bleaker on the other side of the world. Returning from a visit to Burma, India, Pakistan, and Thailand in 1951, Dick Heyward described himself as 'baffled and disappointed' by the lack of enthusiasm he had encountered among ministries of health for taking over full responsibility for child-feeding schemes currently supplied by Unicef. Malnutrition was an underlying, or direct, cause of so much ill-health among Asian children; and, with the important exception of India, most countries had more than enough food to meet their overall needs. Yet it seemed that, until the disease-control programmes had begun to roll back sickness from a different direction, scant attention or financial resources could be spared for organizing the nutritional protection of child health. This made it very important to try and find some alternative approaches. Quite what these should be in social and economic circumstances so different to those in Europe, and even than Latin America, was difficult to determine.

The plight of the hungry and malnourished child was then, and will always remain, the mainspring of international humanitarian compassion.

Yet of all the problems confronting the international organizations as they began to take their first steps in social and economic co-operation, less precise information was available about the nature of this problem than probably any other. Infant and child death rates in underdeveloped countries were known to be very high, maybe eight or twelve times those of industrialized countries, and it was assumed that a high proportion were caused by nutritional deficiency; but what proportion, among which children, and why, let alone what to do about it, were still largely a matter of conjecture.

During the course of the past twenty years, certain pioneering individuals had tried hard to gain for nutrition a prominent role within the field of international public health. One of these was Wallace Aykroyd, a British nutritionist who had served under Ludwik Rajchman in the League of Nations Health Section and had extensive experience in India. As head of FAO's Nutrition Division, Aykroyd now began to initiate moves at the highest levels of the UN system to make good the lack of a detailed scientific grasp on the worldwide child nutrition problem. In Unicef, his closest and keenest ally was Dick Heyward, who alongside his role as Maurice Pate's Deputy Director, began a life-long quest for solutions to what has turned out to be at one and the same time the most central, and most elusive, of all the problems of underdevelopment.

In the meantime, there was milk. After the supplementary feeding programmes in Europe began to close down, Unicef did not envisage a long continuing involvement in the mass movement of milk around the world. Events decreed otherwise. In 1953 the US Government made an offer that could not be refused: 100 million pounds of skim milk at a giveaway price. Unicef was guaranteed that this was not merely a sudden windfall which would not be repeated. Surplus milk would be available in quantity and on similar terms for several years to come, barring drought or other agricultural disaster. The following year, 1954, the US Congress passed Public Law 480, whereby various voluntary US overseas aid organizations were offered grain, milk and other surplus US farm produce free of charge from the port of exit. The amount of skim milk made available to Unicef was enough over the next few years to give a daily cup of milk to between two and four million children and nursing mothers. The cost of freight— the sole cost to Unicef— was less than two cents a pound.

Giving surplus milk to countries where milk was not an ordinary item of local diet was not without its critics. Nevin Scrimshaw, Director of INCAP in Guatemala City, was a strong exponent of the view that only foodstuffs locally grown and available in quantity were suitable for programmes meant to inform people about what caused malnutrition in children and provide them with long-term solutions. If people could not buy or 'grow' milk, they should not be encouraged to idolize its properties. Unicef disagreed. It believed in milk as an advertisement for the values of nutrition as a principle. US food generosity appeared to offer the prospect of doing something not merely instantly charitable and humanitarian, but useful over a longer period; it offered a gratuitous extension to the period during which, it was hoped, the epidemiology of malnutrition would become better understood and some new preventive and therapeutic solutions materialize which were not so inextricably connected with the output of the dairy cow.

While Unicef shippers and programme staff in countries such as Korea, Japan, India, Brazil, Pakistan, Israel, Jordan and many others continued to grapple with barrels and kegs of powdered milk from milk-surplus USA, its 'milkmen' continued to look at 'indigenous' sources of milk. Unicef's milk conservation programme had been set up to provide the dairy industries in war-torn Europe with the odd critical piece of equipment which would speed up its development in such a way as to get more milk more quickly into more under-sized children.

This programme continued in operation throughout the 1950s in Greece, Italy, Yugoslavia and many other European countries, mostly those around the northern and eastern shores of the Mediterranean where the develop- ment of the dairy industry lagged behind that in more northerly climes. Not only did Unicef help equip plants and liquid milk factories; it also helped pay the training costs for dairymen and dairy managers. A new phase of the programme opened towards the end of the decade, when Spain joined the list of recipients and when certain countries in eastern Europe— including Poland and Bulgaria— revived their postwar interest in receiving dairying and other assistance from Unicef.

By 1960, Unicef had provided over 150 milk processing plants to European dairies; some help continued until nearly the end of the decade. The overall effect of this effort was as important in its policy as its practical implications. In many countries, the authorities became— at least partly because of Unicef's influence— so convinced of the permanent health advantages of boosting milk consumption that such measures were enshrined in national policy, and the plants helped by Unicef a ready source of cheap nutritional goodness.

Unicef's new orientation towards the countries in less developed regions of the world did not initially appear to hold out any such milk conservation opportunity. The outlook for replacing imported skim milk powder given to schools and health centres with the contents of a bottle milked from a local cow and processed in a local dairy plant appeared extremely limited.

It was widely assumed that the cow's udder—even where its contents were a regular item of local diet—could only become the basis of a dairy industry in a temperate zone. Many tropical countries had their own cows and cattle breeds; but they bore little relation to the Jerseys and Holsteins chewing the cud in the clover fields of Europe and North America. They were tough and hardy, suited mainly to draught and burden, for which they were principally bred; they gave little milk, and in a hot climate such little they did give was highly perishable. A dairy industry is a sophisticated industry, requiring scientific breeding, pasturing, stabling and sanitary milking methods; also elaborate and dependable systems of milk collection, cooling, pasteurization, packaging, distribution and sales. In most of the countries outside Europe where the Unicef milk team and their FAO advisors now began to set foot, such dairy industries as existed only produced luxury foods for a tiny élite.

The most hopeful prospect was in the Americas. Scrimshaw's protests to Unicef about the use of imported skim milk as the basis for nutrition programmes had an unquestionable validity unless a local supply could be developed as the future substitute. On an exploratory visit to Central America and Brazil in 1951, Don Sabin and Dr Joseph Edwards, an FAO expert from Britain's Milk Marketing Board, found that government leaders, thanks to Unicef, had become greatly impressed by the alchemy performed by the dairy cow on a mangerful of such unpromising materials as herbage, straw and oil seed residues. In Costa Rica, at a meeting attended by no less than four Ministers and the President of the National Bank, the Minister of Public Health solemnly declared: 'It is remarkable what a glass of milk can do. The Unicef child-feeding programme has been responsible not only for starting the milk-drinking habit among children, but for bringing together, for the first time, the many interests in the country which are bound to be concerned in the establishment of a permanent milk policy'.

In his report on this visit, Joseph Edwards, commented with homely wisdom that 'civilization follows the cow'; there seemed to be more promising signs about the possibility of setting up dairy industries in less developed regions than had previously been envisaged. Edwards explained his philosophy: 'Compared with single-crop farming which exhausts the soil, dairy farming, properly encouraged and organized, can make an immense contribution to the health of children, while at the same time enriching the countryside'. The indications in Central America were that, as in Europe, milk's connection with child health would soon become an established part of national consciousness, and that local resources would carry on what schemes assisted by Unicef had begun.

Soon afterwards, Unicef agreed to provide equipment for dairy plants in Brazil, Chile, Nicaragua and Ecuador. These were experimental ventures: the intention was that each plant would serve as a test and a demonstration in its country of the viability of dairy enterprise. As always in the case of Unicef's involvement in milk conservation, the agreements stipulated that part of the plants' output was to be used for child feeding, to the value of one-and-a-half times Unicef's contribution. These agreements sparked requests from elsewhere in Latin America; by 1955, Unicef had committed support to eleven dairy factories in the continent.

There was also a country in Asia, a very large country with a very large number of hungry children, where there was an indigenous supply of milk and the beginnings of a dairy industry: India. Perhaps, in India at least, the problem of promoting the use of milk in supplementary child feeding in the hungriest part of the world might not prove so 'baffling and disappointing' after all.

In the early 1950s, India contained one-third of the world's cattle and half the world's buffaloes—one milkable bovine for every six people. Milk, fresh or soured, and *ghee*—clarified butter—played an important part in the traditional Indian diet; they were the only form of animal protein permitted under the strict rules of Hindu diet. The cow was seen as so benificent a beast that Indians treated it as holy, never slaughtering one past its prime but letting it loose to wander around and feed where it might. In the countryside, a farming family often kept a cow, mostly for breeding animals for ploughing and draught, and sold whatever tiny milk surplus was left after meeting the family's needs. In the cities, milch animals were kept as a business. Milk was a popular food, and there was plenty of room for improved dairying. The milk yield of the average Indian cow was one-twentieth that of an exotic breed—and that of the average buffalo, one-tenth.

Bombay is an island city. In the mid-1940s, its growing population was beginning to burst its seams. Anxiety about poor public health was exacerbated by the presence in the city of a large bovine population and the uncontrolled sale of dirty and adulterated milk. Urban construction had swallowed the local pastureland, and the owners of the city's milk buffaloes kept their animals in common stables whose squalor was of Augean dimensions. The stalls contained many hundreds of animals; each stall was constantly awash with ordure, and each animal's owner or his lessee guarded his charge from a hammock swung above. He sold his milk from house to house, carrying a wooden yoke around his neck from which dangled two open brass pitchers. The milk was a sea of bacteria and customers routinely boiled it. A Unicef document of the time modestly described these conditions of milk production and distribution as 'lacking in elements of hygienic control'.

In 1946, D. N. Khurody, the Milk Commissioner of Bombay, began to put into place elements of the kind of 'safe milk policy' Unicef was soon to champion in Europe. Restaurants and hotels were bound by law to use only imported skim milk powder, sold to them at a profit by the government. With the proceeds, Khurody realized a new concept in Indian dairying: a buffalo colony.

Cowsheds were laid out in acres of rolling parkland twenty miles away at Aarey, and buffalo owners were enticed into exiling their beasts to a new and sanitary existence. For a small monthly licence fee, the owner received stabling, breeding services and accommodation, and contracted to sell all the animal's output to the State government at agreed rates and standards of quality. The supply of milk from Aarey allowed Khurody to implement the other part of his milk scheme: the high-fat buffalo milk was 'toned' with water and skim milk powder to produce a milk as rich as cow's but saleable at half the price. Not only did this make cheaper milk available to more city people, but it provided a free supply for the schools. A survey had revealed that a quarter of Bombay's school children were badly undernourished, and blamed the lack of milk in their diet. By the early 1950s, 40,000 of them drank a daily cup of 'toned' Aarey milk.

By 1953, when the first emissaries from Unicef arrived to discuss dairying with Khurody, Aarey colony had become the showpiece home of 15,000 buffaloes and a regular tourist spot where the unlikely sight of calves being washed and combed among the flower gardens never failed to impress international visitors. Glan Davies, a Welshman recruited by Sam Keeny as his lieutenant in India, was looking for an opportunity to use skim milk to promote dairying. Khurody's milk scheme, the forerunner of others in India, was already a recipient of Unicef milk supplies. Davies was accompanied by Don Sabin and another milk conservation colleague, Ronald Hill. To begin with, discussions centred on Unicef's offer of new pasteurization and bottling equipment for Aarey, about to receive a new influx of buffaloes from the stews of bovine Bombay; but as other aspects of the city milk set-up were revealed, a more ambitious and more risky suggestion materialized.

The Unicef group was introduced to Verghese Kurien, the manager of a co-operative dairy union based at Anand, 260 miles to the north, where local farmers had long been producing milk for sale to Bombay. The milk co-operative, out in the countryside, was currently facing expansion problems directly connected to the Aarey buffalo colony's increasing milk output. Davies, Sabin, and Hill decided to extend their trip up-country. They took the train to what seemed like the most unprepossessing outpost of dairy enterprise, were impressed by Kurien and what he showed them, and thereupon embarked on what became one of Unicef's proudest partnerships. In time, Anand became a national and international byword for success in both tropical dairying and transforming the lives of the rural poor.

Anand was in Kaira District— a large, flat and fertile plain whose one-and-a-half million people depended entirely on farming. Each family kept a buffalo or two, and milk was a modest cottage industry. When Bombay's Milk Scheme was launched, the city's demand for milk from Kaira rapidly increased; but because of the perishability of their product, the small producers found themselves at the mercy of private contractors who bought and processed their milk and sent it to Bombay, pocketing the proceeds. In order to cut out the middlemen, the farmers in certain villages formed co-operative societies in January 1946; within a year, the societies formed a union. One of the most important elements in their success was the backing they had from prominent Gandhians and some key political figures, one of whom was V. Patel, shortly to become India's first deputy Prime Minister. Verghese Kurien, a young engineer with training in dairy management, was appointed as the co-operative union's manager in 1950. By this time, it had a small pasteurizing plant in Anand. Under Kurien's leadership, the union embarked on a process of rapid expansion.

Kurien had a visionary approach to the development of the dairy industry in India. He was inspired not by the idea of large gleaming milk factories in the cities and colonies of thousands of buffaloes ranged neatly in organized cowsheds, but of an industry based upon the tiny rural homestead, with the cow or buffalo in the family compound yielding every day to the fingers of the womenfolk no more milk than would fill a small brass pot.

The difficulties of collecting thousands of tiny amounts in a countryside with few roads and a fierce climate would have appeared insuperable to most dairy enthusiasts. But Kurien abandoned preconceived ideas about the conventional basis of dairy farming elsewhere in the world: the herd of cows, its collective pasturing and milking requirements, the quantities it produced which went en masse for processing and sale. That was not the pattern of milk production in the Indian countryside nor was it likely soon to become so. The main markets for milk were certainly in the cities; to Kurien the problem therefore became one of connecting the brass pot of milk in the village homestead with its urban customer. Modern cooling and conservation techniques seemed to offer the necessary connecting rod. The suburban buffalo colony might be a suitable means of keeping animals off the streets, with the added advantage of keeping the milk supply close to the city and therefore easier to keep fresh; but the cost of bringing in fodder from the countryside and taking cow-dung back to it was too high to make the milk economic.

The owners of most of the nation's bovines and the producers of more than half its milk were also the nation's poorest people: the small farmers and the landless. A fair price for their milk would still keep it cheap for the consumer, and if they could be inspired to feed their animals better and improve their yields, their own livelihood and the state of their children would be transformed.

By 1953, when Kurien first set out his ideas to Davies and Sabin, the Kaira District Co-operative Milk Producers' Union at Anand consisted of fifty-eight village societies, 10,600 member-farmers with 23,000 buffaloes, and milk collection centres in eighty villages. The State government had begun to construct 'milk collection roads' to link up with an all-weather highway passing through Anand, and had given grants for schemes to improve pasture, install water pumps, construct hygienic cattle standings, and offer veterinary and breeding services.

Among farming families there was a marked rise in living standards, health, and children's welfare. But the union's growth had reached an impasse: its own treatment plant was small, and Bombay could no longer guarantee to accept the 8000 gallons of milk being sent down by train from Anand every day. Countryside was competing with city, and the city was winning. With no alternative sales outlet, Kurien had been forced to introduce a system of denying a market to different village societies on rotation. At the season that their buffaloes were most productive, the village societies suddenly found themselves making a loss.

Kurien wanted the fortunes of the co-operative union to become less dependent on the whims of Bombay city milk drinkers and the handling capacity of the city dairies. The means he proposed for reversing the situation were audacious: a modern dairy plant right in the heart of traditional India.

He invited Unicef and FAO to join the New Zealand Government— offering assistance under the Colombo Plan— to become founder investors. Alongside a plant for the production of tinned butter and *ghee*, Kurien wanted a plant for spray-drying the residues into a buffalo skim milk powder: just the kind of machinery in which Unicef had appropriate expertise. The milk powder produced at Anand would be used to 'tone' buffalo milk, and thereby increase the volume of cheap, safe milk available to low-income families. No-one had ever previously attempted to dry buffalo milk; fortunately, its unusually high-fat content did not resist the process as some had feared it might. Once Don Sabin had satisfied himself that the enterprise was technically sound, Unicef agreed to supply the necessary equipment. Unicef's first assistance for milk conservation in India thereby linked a pasteurizing plant for Aarey with a spray-drying plant for Anand, and added a refrigeration plant in Bombay for preserving milk from both. As always, a pre-condition of support was free milk to more than its value for children both in Kaira district and Bombay.

At that time, Unicef's support for Kurien's dairy enterprise seemed a brave leap of faith. It was hard to picture that such a seemingly humble operation as that at Anand, whose only obvious assets were the flair and dedication of its leaders, had the organizational capacity or the financial backing to purchase land, erect buildings, install water supplies and electricity, hire and train dairy staff.

The leap of faith proved amply justified. The foundation stone of the dairy plant was laid in November 1954, and on 31 October 1955, Prime Minister Jawaharlal Nehru himself declared the new factory officially open. Anand could boast the largest dairy complex of its kind in India, including the first spray-drying plant for buffalo milk in the world. The most impressive feature of the factory was, however, not what it was but where it was and whose direct interests it served. Every day, thousands of men, women and children of all castes and creeds queued up with their pots at the village milk collection stations; their milk was measured and checked for its fat content, and they received cash on the nail. For these rural people of India, this represented a transformation in their lives.

The installation of the new dairy plant at Anand had far reaching consequences. Within five years, the co-operative union had expanded its membership to 40,500 village societies. The increased output of the hundreds of thousands of buffaloes supplying Anand meant that, between its own factory and the quantity still contracted to Bombay, the co-operative soon had a milk surplus once again. Between 1958 and 1960, Anand opened up more plants, to produce sweetened condensed milk, baby food— and another world 'first': buffalo cheese. The Kaira Union adopted the brand name Amul— Anand Milk Union Ltd— for all its products; 'amul' means 'priceless' in Sanskrit, and the label began to earn a reputation throughout India for top-quality dairy goods.

A few years later, on the basis of a grant from Oxfam and food wastes provided by the World Food Programme, a plant for cheap buffalo feed was opened; the local buffaloes soon began to yield 1000 litres of milk a year, more than twice the national average. By this stage, Anand had become not only a brand leader in dairy products, but a training centre for dairy management and a test tube for the expanding dairy industry not only in the region, but the country as a whole.

In the late 1950s, the Indian Government embarked on a nationwide city dairy upgrade to increase milk supplies for urban consumers. Unicef was an enthusiastic supporter. During the course of these years, assistance was extended to dairies in Rajkot, Ahmedabad, Bangalore, Calcutta, Kanpur, Hyderabad, Madurai, and others. The largest dairy Unicef helped to build was at Worli, near Bombay. In spite of its large, industrial nature, Unicef gave $1·5 million altogether towards the construction of Worli dairy, mainly out of loyalty to Khurody whose imaginative policies— buffalo colonies, the use of cheap or free imported skim milk to 'tone' milk and reduce the price permitting welfare and school distribution— had done so much to pave the way for improving the supply and quality of milk in urban India, and to promote the health of mothers and children. By 1965, Unicef had spent $7·4 million on milk conservation in India for thirteen milk plants and five dairy training institutes.

The rural milk producer co-operative at Anand was something of an anomaly in the regular pattern of Unicef assistance for milk conservation, which had a natural tendency to be city-bound. Unlike Verghese Kurien, whose primary target was the rural poor and who viewed the milk of their buffaloes as a means of transforming their livelihoods, Unicef was exclusively interested in milk production as a necessary precondition of its consumption by underfed children.

The basic assumption of the time was that the countryside looked after its own milk needs. In the city, milk was only available from a vendor, not 'free' from a cow tethered in the yard. City milk was not only a more costly food item, but also much more likely to be hazardous to health—unless, of course, it came from a clean dairy and had been sealed into a hygienic bottle. In the city, too, unlike in the countryside, there were schools, hospitals and large congregations of palpably-needy people, which meant that it was easier to find a means of reaching the Unicef customer.

In the early years of Unicef's milk-conservation experience in countries outside Europe, efforts to put more clean cows into milking stalls, more clean milk onto city streets, and more free milk into under-fed children were thought to be as significant as any transformation in rural well-being brought about by forming prosperous milk producer co-operatives. For some time there was a school of thought—fostered by some of FAO's leading nutritionists—which went so far as to believe that no dairy plant should be set up in a rural milk-producing area. Those of this persuasion were sceptical of Kurien's ideas and even found it indecent for Anand's factories to exploit the local buffaloes so efficiently; they held that the children of Kaira's farmers were actually being deprived of their 'free' source of milk. Khurody's milk scheme in Bombay, which not only fed children in school but which sold cheap, subsidized milk at kiosks in the city slums, was much more typical of the kind of welfare scheme visiting experts recognized from their European experience.

The Kaira milk union was a private enterprise; the Bombay milk scheme was run by the city authorities as a public welfare programme with an overtly humanitarian purpose. In Asia it was pioneering a policy of 'milk for the people', and it deserved the support and admiration it inspired. But its importance as a model was over-emphasized, partly because of the wishful thinking of its admirers, who attached a halo to any successful scheme distributing subsidized milk to the needy in the adverse social and economic circumstances of a country such as India.

Those who distrusted the nutritional benefits of the Kurien approach were in time roundly disabused. In Kaira district, the buffalo-owning families' milk consumption did not fall as their business boomed; it increased. Unicef's assistance had been provided with the usual strings attached: milk to one-and-a-half times the value of the plant was to be distributed to children free. The village societies set up their own feeding schemes, handing out rations every day at the milk collection stations.

This programme peaked in 1959, when more than 12,000 children received a daily cupful. Nutritional criticism of Kurien's approach had derived from nothing more scientific than the deep suspicions often aroused by the spectacle of commercial success in purveyors of humanitarian blessings. Time was to show that Kurien's marriage between the people's well-being and a profitable dairy enterprise was a much less awkward affair than the version Unicef and its milk-conservation partners mostly tried to bolster.

By 1959, after several years of milk-conservation experience outside Europe, Unicef's involvement in dairying had expanded way beyond the narrow welfare base of its original intention.

At the end of the decade, Unicef invited its technical partner, FAO, to analyze the results of its milk conservation projects in Central and South America, the eastern Mediterranean and in Asia. Not only was it important to find out whether the investment had directly helped mothers and children by trying to count the heads of those who had drunk the milk; but as Unicef had found itself plunging rather more deeply into other aspects of the dairy business than the local supply of milk for supplementary feeding, it wanted to consider the implications thoroughly.

FAO and Unicef had advanced the civilizing mission of the cow together. FAO's advisors had offered technical expertise about everything to do with dairy farming and management: fodder, breeding, pasturing, protection from disease, and other elements of care for the cow; as well as milk quality, pricing, collection, processing and marketing. Unicef's role was, initially at least, conceptually modest, even if financially more significant. It provided the equipment needed to secure a supply of safe milk for welfare programmes, and some training in how to run and manage it; its dairy engineers merely advised on the donated equipment's specifications and installation. However, in countries whose dairy industry was at best embryonic, the Unicef milkmen either had to do more than this or nothing at all. No longer could milk conservation assistance simply consist of supplying missing pieces in an all but fully-fledged operation; it had to help set up the whole affair. A pasteurization or drying plant, carefully selected, immaculately installed, could do nothing for child nutrition on its own. Self-evident though this was, how seriously deficient some countries would turn out to be in the various essentials for a dairy industry, let alone one that could inculcate the habit of milk-drinking among children, came as quite a shock to both Unicef and FAO.

By 1959, after some false starts and other delays at various project sites, a survey technique had been elaborated to eliminate all candidates for dairying help whose proposed processing plant would be a hopelessly uneconomic proposition. For the time being, this almost automatically included any drying plant: while huge stocks of free surplus skim milk continued to be available from North America, no drying plant set up to conserve a country's or locality's surplus—'surplus' being a misnomer anyway except in the flush season—could possibly compete. In fact, FAO's consultants suggested that it would be a good idea if more dairies would use the imported supplies in the way employed at Aarey—either for 'toning' very rich milk, or 'standardizing' full cream cow's milk to reduce the fat content and subsidize the sale of cheaper milk or its free distribution.

While it was unrealistic to judge many of the new dairies by regular standards of economic efficiency, the fact was that, in order to subsidize mother and child welfare (not just during their period of obligation to Unicef, but on a continuing basis, which was after all the ultimate purpose of helping them in the first place), they did have to become economically viable as quickly as possible. The only way this would happen was to help the dairies gather in a plentiful supply of cheap milk.

Careful cross-breeding would help fill the udders of animals whose primary purpose in the existing rural economy was burden or beef. That the existing milk-yielding cows in tropical places had a different genetic make-up from relations in temperate zones was not a surprise; but this was now seen as relatively insignificant. FAO's consultants were much more dismayed to discover that the cows' human minders had not the smallest notion of making hay or otherwise growing and conserving fodder. The same cow, unreconstructed from a biological point of view, might produce more milk if given more to eat; but such food would have to be grown or bought.

These were not familiar notions to many farmers in the new pastures in which FAO and Unicef were grazing. They quickly became familiar to the farmer and his wife if a good price was given for the milk their animals produced: the existence of a new dairy did appear to exert some pulling power of increasing milk production in the countryside nearby. But the price often remained relatively high from the dairy's point of view; only much increased volume would bring it down, and that in turn depended on better animal husbandry. Until the price of raw milk fell, the price of processed milk to the consumer stayed correspondingly high, and the cost of welfare distribution too prohibitive to be attractive to governments over the longer term.

At this stage, although a number of plants had been authorized for American, Indian and Middle Eastern destinations, only a handful—Aarey, Anand, drying plants in Nicaragua and Costa Rica, fluid plants in Iran, Israel, and Turkey—were yet in operation. Unicef did not now take fright at the risky nature of its milk conservation investment. It accepted the implications of trying to help provide milk in much more difficult surroundings, and broadened its policy accordingly. If agricultural extension services were needed in rural areas to put more food into the cow, Unicef was willing to assist; if skills and expertise in dairy management were needed to put the milk business onto a sounder basis, then Unicef would help fund further fellowships and training. Only at organized cross-breeding did Unicef draw the line. The purpose of its milk conservation policy was still to ensure a good supply of cheap milk for undernourished children and mothers but, if certain things had to be done to reach the ultimate goal, then so be it. The civilizing mission of the cow was too important to hold back.

Throughout the 1950s, Unicef continued to ship large quantities of US surplus skim milk around the world. The peak came in 1957, when 4·5 million children and pregnant and nursing mothers— mostly in Asia— were provided regularly with rations either in schools or in health facilities. This number represented a small proportion of those in need; nevertheless it not only gave direct nutritional help to some of those who needed it, but did so in a way that satisfied the international humanitarian impulse to put the world's surplus food to good use.

In places where the output of new dairy plants was expected soon to take its place, the skim milk was also seen as a useful stop-gap; elsewhere, it was hoped, it would at least have an educational side benefit. Meanwhile, every effort was made to develop a better-informed grasp of the scale and nature of the nutritional difficulties facing children around the world.

Early in the decade, the world's leading nutritionists narrowed down the field of malnutrition's victims and identified the chief dietetic culprit. Of great influence on contemporary thinking were the results of a nutritional exploration of the African continent undertaken by Professor J. F. Brock of the University of Cape Town and Marcel Autret, Aykroyd's deputy and, later, successor in FAO's Nutrition Division. Their report, published by WHO in 1952, focussed on 'kwashiorkor'. the condition in young children first described in 1930 by a British physician, Dr Cicely Williams, in the Gold Coast. Roughly translated, kwashiorkor meant 'the disease of the child deposed from the breast'; its victim was the child forced to make too sudden a transition from breast-milk to an adult diet because of the mother's next pregnancy. The condition was a relatively recent phenomenon in Africa; until missionaries inveighed against the practice of polygamy, lengthy spacing between child-bearing was an in-built feature of traditional family life and marriage custom.

Brock and Autret found that kwashiorkor was almost unknown among the children of cattle herders whose diet included milk and meat, and unusual among farming peoples whose staple food included grains and vegetables with a high-protein content. It mostly affected the children of peoples whose regular cuisine relied on starchy grains and tubers, particularly cassava which well deserved its reputation as a 'famine crop': it grew easily, plentifully, in poor soil, with little rain; but it was all bulk and almost no nutritional goodness. Kwashiorkor's symptoms were listlessness, swollen limbs and stomach, and reddish patches in skin and hair, which in time gave way to the unmistakable symptoms of frank starvation. Here was a specific, clinically definable, malnutrition 'disease' which illustrated vividly what happened when a small child was given no special regimen during the crucial period between the ages of six months and three years to compensate for the abrupt and definitive loss of proteins and other nutrients in breast-milk.

Although etymologically the disease belonged to Africa, in the early 1950s kwashiorkor came into wide use as a term describing similar manifestations of protein deficiency 'disease' in children all over the world. Research at medical and scientific research institutes in Asia and Latin America consistently confirmed that kwashiorkor in young children was a much more widespread public-health problem than previously realized, and was a contributing if not the clinically specified cause of death in many young children.

The growth and health of many others whose sickness was never caught in the medical searchlight was hindered by a lack of body-building proteins at an early age, sometimes permanently. Other ingredients required by the small body — vitamins A, D, B_1, and elements like iron whose absence was often responsible for anaemia in the mother and frailty in the newborn baby — also needed special attention; but the threat to health caused by the lack of protein in the younger child outclassed all other concerns. Filling this 'protein gap' became for a while the overwhelming nutritional pre-occupation.

Pinpointing the target — children in the age group between one and four years old — ought theoretically to have made the task of the food and nutrition policy-makers very much simpler. It actually did the reverse, for of all children this group was the hardest to reach. However thin the spread of health facilities and schools in certain countries and regions, at least some proportion of babies and school-age children could be found in clinics and classrooms. The only specific place to find the in-betweens was in the kindergarten or nursery school; but outside the industrialized world this was a very rare institution, and where it did exist was attended almost exclusively by the well-fed child of well-educated city parents.

There were few obvious alternative routes to the small child in the rural home, the child of the mother whose knowledge of food values and the symptoms of nutritional deficiency was marginal or governed by dietary taboos or plain ignorance. Gradually, this predicament forced the nutrition fraternity to rethink their strategies. The supplementary feeding programme — the mass welfare approach — was no use in the absence of an institutional framework.

During the second half of the 1950s, strenuous efforts were made to try and reduce the proportion of Unicef skim milk given out in school lunch programmes, and increase the amount distributed to mothers attending health clinics to feed to their younger children. Even if this re-orientation only touched the edge of the problem, it was the only choice. Other than hoping for, and doing their best to support, more rapid 'infrastructural

development'—more maternal and child health centres, more kindergartens, more women's clubs—Unicef and its partners in the skim milk
distribution business were at a loss. At least, they comforted themselves,
the programmes that did exist offered an opportunity for implanting ideas
about sound child nutrition, ideas whose obvious merit must appeal.

Unfortunately, nutrition education was not always such a convincing
benefit among those it was most supposed to impress. Busy health staff had
little time to give instruction, and mothers with squawling infants were
short of the patience and concentration needed to take the information in.
The typical nutrition talk and flip chart usually bunched foods into scientific
groups and extolled the protein content of milk, meat, fish and eggs, and
the delights of vitamins and other elements in vegetables and fruits. Even if
such notions were comprehensible, the fact was that in most parts of the
world, these were luxury ingredients consumed irregularly or only on
celebratory occasions, and rarely by children. It was difficult enough to put
across the idea that the scoop of skim milk powder, carried home in the
bowl the mother had brought for the purpose, was to be made up carefully
and fed to her younger children and herself. Whatever anyone told her to
do, she would make a decision dependent on fuel, utensils and cooking
amenities, and this might well be to add the powder to the family pot. Skim
milk could not be the force that would change the cooking and eating
arrangements of poor and ignorant mothers to suit the requirements of the
small child, especially if these were portrayed according to classic patterns
of western nutritional predilection. For most such mothers, skim milk
rations could only be skim milk rations, and if they ended, the average
mother could not or would not replace them with some other protein-rich
equivalent.

Part of the problem, especially in milkless zones, had to be that no such
equivalent existed. So, at least, the nutritionists reasoned. The narrowing
focus onto protein begged an obvious question: where milk could not fill
the 'protein gap', what was the alternative? In certain countries of the
developing world, no amount of optimism could colour the forecast for the
dairy industry; cows and buffaloes were simply too thin on the ground, and
short of a meteorological miracle, were likely to remain so for several
generations.

A substitute for milk was needed, something which could be easily and
cheaply produced, nourishing, digestible and palatable enough to command
dietary fashion. There were a number of vegetable sources of protein: the
beans and peas of the pulse family offering a specially rich supply. Many
foods had crossed oceans from other continents—maize, potatoes, sugar,
spices—to become part of the regular diet in an immigrant location;
changing basic food habits was not a rare historical phenomenon, quite the
contrary. It was not a quick nor an easy process to get a new food crop
widely grown and accepted; the agriculturalists, educators, nutritionists,

and paediatricians would have to join forces to make the foods well-liked and acceptable. With more and better nutrition education, more and better training for nutrition educators, food habits and culinary practice could— must— change in time.

Although cereal and legume proteins were still regarded very much as poor relations to proteins from the animal kingdom, recent experiments had shown that careful combinations of beans, peas and seeds could compensate for their individual deficiencies. In an age when food processing technology was altering what was eaten in which season by people all over the industrialized world, it was a small jump from the idea of processing and conserving milk for protecting children's health to the idea of pro-cessing combinations of vegetables and doing the same with the result.

R. F. A. Dean, a British nutritionist, had used a combination of barley, wheat and soy, malted together and spray-dried, as a supplementary food for malnourished children in postwar Germany; with ten per cent of skim milk added, the children had done very well. Already in 1950, Don Sabin in Unicef had begun to dream of equipping nondairy 'milk' factories to turn out white, creamy, vegetable liquids as a substitute. In an age when new technology was being applied so successfully to public health, it could surely be enlisted to blend peas and beans into cheap and nutritious foods to conquer widescale protein deficiency 'disease' in children. Thus began a nutritional Jules Verne period, a futuristic vision of harnessing food technology to conquer hunger, a vision to which at the time only a few cynics remained immune.

The closest approximation in the vegetable world to the magic of milk was the humble soya bean. In several eastern Asian countries, the soya bean— fermented, turned into a curd or a sauce, or eaten just after sprouting— was a familiar item of diet. By the 1950s, its possibilities as a milk substitute had already been analyzed quite extensively. The first soya milk 'dairy' was set up in Shanghai in the 1920s, and successor products, enriched with vitamins, were sufficiently successful to be sold in the US and Europe for infants allergic to cow's milk.

In Indonesia, cow's milk was virtually unobtainable and there was no foreseeable prospect of establishing a dairy industry. In the early 1950s the Indonesian Government requested UN advice on their national nutrition programme, and decided to act on the suggestion that a locally-manufactured soya milk might serve as a health-giving, body-building weaning food. In 1953, on the technical advice of FAO, the Indonesian authorities began construction of a $2·7 million factory in Jogjakarta for the production of 'saridele', a powdered soya milk. Unicef contributed $543,000. The enterprise had great appeal to food scientists and laymen alike, for 'saridele' appeared to hold out the promise of a child nutrition breakthrough for other countries where soya was already widely grown, or might without difficulty be introduced.

Unicef made one other early foray into the experimental manufacture of a milk substitute. In 1955, after three years of trials carried out with help from FAO, Unicef lent its support to the construction of a small fish-flour factory in the Chilean town of Quintero. As a source of protein, fish ranked very high in the nondairy pecking order, but, like milk, fish quickly lost its appeal in a hot climate; even smoked and salted it did not keep well. There were many countries around the world with a seaboard and a fishing industry where fish were underutilized as an item of local diet. The good fish went for export and landed up in cans on the larder shelves of Europe and North America; the lower class fish, pungent and strong-tasting, were ground into fishmeal and sold as a fertilizer or a feed for farm animals. To make fish a suitable supplement for children, it needed careful processing. Fishmeal, while extremely cheap and highly nutritious, was regarded as unfit for.human consumption.

Chile had an interminable coast and a surplus catch both of lean white fish and of the less palatable variety. The pilot plant at Quintero was therefore regarded as the ideal laboratory for similar enterprises elsewhere. In the season when there was surplus white fish, the plant would process it into powder; at other times it would deodorize and deflavourize fishmeal and 'flour' it instead. The results of the initial runs of both these substances were fully field-tested and found acceptable when mixed with other ingredients; since its protein content was at least seventy per cent, only a tiny amount was needed as a daily nutritional booster and the cost of adding it to primary school lunches was estimated at between twenty-five and fifty cents per child per year.

In the mid-1950s, the persistent efforts of a growing band of international devotees began to pay off; an explosion of excitement began to develop around the idea of processing locally-produced vegetable or piscine ingredients into milk's brave new alternatives. One group of ingredients had begun to take on a special allure: the by-products of the edible oil industry. Once the oil had been extracted from soya beans, coconuts, cottonseed, peanuts, sesame seeds and sunflowers, a 'cake' full of good quality protein remained. These presscakes were the world's cheapest supply of edible protein: like skim milk, they were a residue and, like skim milk before the invention of drying techniques, they were commonly fed to livestock. But unlike skim milk, their 'starting material'— the nut, bean or seed itself— was much less prejudiced by a hot sun and other hazards endured by the dairy cow in tropical climates; many oilseed crops thrived in the very parts of the world where protein deficiency in the preschool child was such a problem. Here was a foodstuff even less well utilized than fish in filling the 'protein gap', and certainly far cheaper than flour made from white fish or milk made from soya.

In 1955, the leading medical and nonmedical experts in food technology and nutritional science gathered for what turned out to be a landmark conference, sponsored by WHO and FAO. The chairman was Dr Charles Glen King, a leading US nutritionist whose enthusiasm for commandeering all conceivable goodness from plants and cowcakes on behalf of children was enhanced by a recent tour of Central American countries undertaken on behalf of Unicef. King was particularly impressed by Scrimshaw's work at INCAP, both in charting the problem of child nutrition and in pioneering the use of locally-grown vegetable protein as a solution.

The conference, held at Princeton University, opened a new phase in the working relationships on the child nutrition problem between FAO, WHO, and Unicef, and led to an international programme for food products research and testing, carried out by institutes, laboratories and university departments around the world. The purpose was to exploit cheap, locally-available sources of protein to develop prototype foods for mass production by the food industry and mass consumption by the malnourished child.

Any new food product intended for the consumption of infants and young children had to be thoroughly tested to ascertain its chemical composition and biological value. WHO set up a special Protein Advisory Group (PAG) of four nutritionists and paediatricians to advise on tests and testing methods; in time this group expanded its interests across the whole range of protein and other child nutrition problems, but its genesis was the processing of fishmeal and oilseeds into flours for filling the 'protein gap'.

The Rockefeller Foundation was the research programme's main donor, providing $550,000 in grants for tests carried out in various institutes. These funds were administered through the Committee on Protein Malnutrition of the US National Research Council, some of whose members were also members of the PAG. Unicef added $300,000, mainly to cover the costs of buying or making pilot batches of food products for testing on animals, and later, under controlled medical supervision, on humans. The foods' preservative qualities in hot climates also had to be discovered, as well as that vital and fickle element: their acceptability to the human palate. The programme became gradually more refined, eliminating products which could not be easily grown or caught in a net, or whose processing was complex or uneconomic.

By 1959, twenty-two investigators in thirteen countries had carried out laboratory and clinical testing of milks, flours and pastes, and the future weaning foodstuff field had been thoroughly surveyed. The ground was mapped geographically, biologically and technologically: when complete, the comprehensive body of knowledge it produced was supposed to enable an appropriate machine to be installed anywhere in the world to make the essential link between the local pulse, sardine, peanut and person. Technically, the programme's results were excellent. It was conclusively proved that many different nondairy mixtures could cure or prevent kwashiorkor in young children as efficiently as milk, and as acceptably. By the early 1960s, it seemed as though the final stages were in sight. The only missing link was a strategy for moving the foodstuffs off the laboratory bench into health centre rations for the under-fours and into the culinary repertoire of mothers keen to see their children grow and flourish when they left the breast. A great deal of interest had been aroused and many products were at a relatively advanced stage of development; others had already been launched on the market.

When the research and testing programme began in earnest in 1956, Unicef and FAO were already able to point to the two practical projects they were jointly supporting: 'saridele' in Indonesia and fish flour in Chile. At neither project did things go entirely according to plan. In Jogjakarta, technical hitches during the plant's construction meant that 'saridele' did not come on stream until 1957, and not until the following year did output reach the 300 tons target. Although the 'saridele' plant was still a mecca for protein enthusiasts from Unicef and elsewhere, its costs and the budgetary climate necessitated some serious rethinking. Originally the intention had been for the government to buy the whole output, and distribute it to hospitals, health centres, and in the school feeding programme. Instead, half the output was sold as a flavoured drink, imitating the milk conservation pattern Unicef promoted in the dairy industry: high-priced products subsidizing the welfare component. The fish flour plant did not go into full production until the early 1960s; here too the cost equations turned out to have been over-optimistic, and the market price of the foodstuff made it less appropriate as a welfare food or nutritional medicine than had been originally anticipated.

A product which did made a successful transition from the laboratory to the production phase was a weaning food developed by INCAP. In 1950, Scrimshaw and his colleagues had set about analyzing the nutritional value of every common locally-grown and edible plant. They started to blend various grains and legumes in 1951; it took them eight years to achieve a formula that was scientifically satisfactory, palatable, cheap and easy to prepare. The final recipe combined cornmeal, ground sorghum, cotton-seed flour, yeast, calcium and vitamin A in a powder whose taste was bland and inoffensive. INCAP mimicked a popular traditional drink called *atole*, a gruel made from ground corn, and marketed their version—'incaparina'— as a health-giving *atole* for children.

'Incaparina' was sufficiently successful to attract a sponsor from the food industry. In 1961, Quaker Oats of South America, based in Colombia, signed a licensing agreement with INCAP, and a few years later put the drink mix on the market for a price of ten cents for a week's supply. Unicef encouraged its use in schools and health centres and by 1966 total sales in Latin America had reached 4·5 million pounds. By the late 1960s, the product had established itself; it is still on sale in Central America today.

But by then it had become clear that however successful certain low-cost, high-tech, high-protein foodstuffs might be among families of a certain income level, the involvement of Unicef in their production could no longer be justified.

Processed substitutes for milk were not the salvation of the protein malnutrition problem because they could not become a common item of home consumption in the families whose children were most likely to be malnourished. Mesmerized by the promise of food technology, carried along by the enthusiasm of research institutes, paediatricians, government sponsors and popular applause, it took time for Unicef and its international and national partners to absorb this lesson. However biologically and technologically successful their efforts were, the advocates of processed weaning foods eventually ran up against the same old impenetrable barrier of the lack of an 'infrastructural' network among those they were trying to reach.

As with the promotion of safe and wholesome milk, Unicef had started by thinking in terms of supplementary feeding; but even if they were used exclusively as malnutrition 'medicines' or welfare foods in children's wards and school lunches, the budgets of most ministries of health in less well-off countries could not carry the expense on their own, as the experience with 'saridele' and fish flour showed. Even to use the products for organized welfare, they had to be put on sale to the public at large. Welfare on its own was, anyway, too limited an objective: mass programmes of supplementary feeding rarely reached the weanling child. If the new foods were to be widely eaten at home, the food industry had to be sufficiently interested to manufacture them and channel them down the distribution network for marketed goods. But as time went on, and few companies in the food industry expressed enthusiasm, Unicef began to discover an irreconcilable tension between its own welfare motivation and the products' economic viability.

Cheap ingredients and the miracle of food technology could only resolve the first generation of problems connected with putting synthetic foods into the mouths of children. In 1963, at a meeting in Rome with food company representatives, Unicef and FAO pointed out that the industry had so far made only a few timid attempts— mostly in Latin America— to fulfill their nutritional duty to the next generation by producing and marketing protein-rich weaning foods. The reply was not encouraging. The introduction of a new foodstuff onto the market in a developing country was such a precarious proposition, the industry's representatives pointed out, that even with assistance from government or international organizations, few companies could find the risk worth taking. All sorts of information must be collected— sociological, medical, dietary, economic— before such a proposition could even be contemplated. Even if thought to be sound, a loss could be anticipated over a relatively long period; and even if a market for the new food was eventually established, the profit margin on a product intended for consumption by poor families would always remain very low. The commercial food producers could not invest in a foodstuff they did not believe would keep a factory running. Profit and nutritious food for the poor were very uneasy companions.

Even where the food industry did become involved, their best efforts could not shift the processed weaning food much beyond the standard network of retail outlets, all of which were in the towns, and most of which served the better-off. The 'infrastructure' needed to distribute consumer products from the modern world to the world inhabited by most of the malnourished children was little better developed than that of health, education or social services. There were few shops for such families because they had little purchasing power and were not customers for more than a handful of manufactured products—salt, soap, matches, kerosene, a utensil or two. In a word, such people were poor. Malnutrition was a 'disease' suffered by the children of the poor, and since the poor were poor they could not buy their protective way out of it, by two cents a day worth of *atole* or any other biologically impeccable alternative. If an egg, a cup of milk, a fish, or a slice of beef was for them a luxury ingredient, even more so was a powder in a packet.

To put a factory between the poor and their food supply was unhelpful, to say the least. Most of the people in the rural parts of Asia, Africa and Latin America grew their food, trading any surplus in the market. The limit of their food processing experience was to spread certain grains or berries in the sun to dry—and to winnow, to scrape, to grind, to pound, to mill, sometimes to ferment, the crops they harvested and stored in their granaries. In a family living on the edge of subsistence, money was a rare commodity. Even urban people in the lowest social strata spent as little as possible and that meant by definition mostly cheap natural produce from the market. Only the better-off could afford a can, a packet, a 'convenience' food. A woman in the town who bought her family's food supply in a store might put a processed weaning food on her metaphorical shopping list; some would be able to afford the new food where they could not afford an imported equivalent. But those did not include the really poor, the families whose children were most likely to be malnourished.

In 1967, twelve years after the testing and research programme began, Unicef began to adjust itself to the irrefutable evidence that processed foods with a high-protein content had a limited application to the public health problem of child malnutrition. Unicef did not actually withdraw its support from all efforts to develop high-protein foods; certain well-thought-out, economically-hopeful enterprises continued to gain support in India, Algeria, Peru, and other places. But stringent conditions were laid down about the pricing and distribution structure which would have to be guaranteed before support would be forthcoming. As in the case of malaria eradication, Unicef made the conditions of its support so difficult to fulfill that without ever having to say so explicitly, it effectively pulled out of manufacturing local foods. It had finally recognized the naivety and ethnocentricity of trying to use the food-processing technology developed in industrialized countries to help the poor and hungry child living in a totally different consumer world.

By this time, the dimensions of the 'protein gap' had also been redefined. The focus which narrowed so tightly onto protein in the early 1950s had been broadened: protein deficiency and food deficiency were now regarded as close neighbours to one another, and the notion of 'medicinal' response to a 'disease' was seen to be far too limited.

Large-scale supplementary feeding through schools and institutions was by now also regarded as an anachronistic approach, except for victims of emergency or complete indigence. For these, as for children in hospital wards or nutrition rehabilitation units seriously ill from kwashiorkor or other diseases of nutritional deficiency, milk or a close substitute was still an optimal therapy.

During the late 1960s, when surplus skim milk was no longer available in large quantities for donation to welfare programmes, the US began to experiment with CSM, a protective food for small children composed of corn flour, soy flour and skim milk, with added vitamins and minerals. CSM, unlike most of the locally-processed mixes, had a future; but it was a future paralleled by the use of dried skim milk in the supplementary feeding schemes of earlier years, not a solution to the more intractable everyday problem of child malnutrition as a problem akin to respiratory or diarrhoeal infections. The new approach to child malnutrition as a public health problem was 'applied nutrition'; its emphasis was on growing nutritious foods and keeping chickens and other small livestock in the family or village backyard.

In the second half of the 1950s, as the food technologists ground and mashed and powdered their ingredients in the laboratory and proved that combinations of this with that produced biological formulae nearly akin to the nutritious elixir produced by the dairy cow, it occurred to some of them that the same chemical transformation would as well occur in a cooking pot as in a test tube. It did not need the intervention of a scientist, any more than a laboratory or a factory, to make a home mix of vegetable and animal protein which would do the same for the small child as any powdered version in a packet. With the right information, people who grew their own food could do the whole thing themselves.

What was true for milk substitutes also turned out to be true for milk. A dairy was also a factory; and a factory product was bound to remain out of reach of the poor, at least for the foreseeable future. The milk conservation programme had been set up to speed up the moment at which underfed children could be supplied with free or subsidized milk. In Europe, making that moment arrive more quickly had required some deft topping up of equipment, or training, or giving a fillip to safe milk policies. As the years went by, it became clear that any remotely similar basis for a welfare programme based on milk conservation only existed in a handful of countries outside Europe: India, Pakistan, Chile and a few others. In most parts of the underdeveloped world, no amount of speeding up could make the moment arrive at which the really underfed child of preschool age would daily consume a nourishing drink of pasteurized milk from a city dairy, in the home or anywhere else.

When Unicef first offered assistance for milk conservation in the less well-off countries, no-one anticipated that upwards of 600 million pounds of skim milk powder would be made available to such countries free of charge every year. Since Unicef's share went to welfare programmes, there was no clash—theoretically at least—with efforts to boost local milk production; Unicef believed the contrary, that such programmes helped create a taste and demand for milk. But all the free milk floating round the world was bound to have an effect on many countries' incipient dairy industries. However exciting the prospect of processing the product of local cows in gleaming new equipment, in the cold light of day much of the effort turned out to be expensive and complicated. Meanwhile free, clean, already packaged, nearly unperishable milk powder was readily available. In many Central American countries the fledgling milk industry could not stand the competition. Unless governments took steps to control the marketing of low-priced skim milk from overseas—which sometimes they did and more often they did not—the market for domestic milk was virtually destroyed and milk production seriously discouraged.

In such circumstances, the basis on which Unicef had provided assistance to the dairy industry fell apart. Where there was no domestic surplus, there was no possibility of subsidizing the provision of low fat or skim milk for welfare distribution out of the profits on cream and butter. Many of the processing plants assisted by Unicef were still operating way below capacity seven or eight years after their original installation. Unicef's agreements with government authorities were optimistically based on the idea that within a few years the new plant would have 'catalyzed' dairy production, and the price of milk would have dropped to the point where it was much more widely affordable.

In practice, this rarely happened. Meanwhile the new dairy faced all the problems of establishing itself economically during a period when its output was supposed to subsidize welfare feeding. Not surprisingly, when the period of obligation came to an end, many governments were either unable or unwilling to absorb indefinitely the costs of the supplementary feeding programme.

While in certain countries the availability of free skim milk powder disrupted the prospects of the dairy industry and undermined Unicef's milk conservation assistance, in Asia it temporarily did the opposite: in India its availability for 'toning' high-fat buffalo milk was central to the economic viability of welfare schemes. While imported skim-milk powder was available in quantity, free or cheap milk distribution from many Indian city dairies was practicable. But if the supply dried up—as it did in 1965—the output of toned milk was drastically cut back. The customers for free or subsidized milk distribution were the first to suffer.

Unicef's milk conservation activity continued through most of the 1960s, and in some parts of the world—notably in Africa where the dairy industry was more embryonic than elsewhere and special consideration was given to helping it get started—it went on into the early 1970s. But from around the midpoint of the decade, milk conservation as a way of making an important contribution to child nutrition suffered an eclipse. Many countries had been inspired to formulate national dairy policies, dairy managers had been trained to put them into effect, and dairy industries launched. Unicef had contributed nearly $24 million altogether to this effort; but enthusiasm for milk as the universal food for children was beginning to appear misguided.

After all, it seemed, those who benefited most directly and in the largest numbers from the Unicef milk conservation schemes were the families who supplied milk to the dairies. The focus on production rather than consumption, the focus which years before Verghese Kurien had adopted at Anand, was the one that proved most successful in using the dairy industry to help the children of the Unicef target family. The success of the Amul enterprise afforded the most striking example of the improvements in diet and living standards which followed a rise in the incomes of the owners of milkable beasts.

Kurien's whole multimillion rupee industry was firmly based on the buffalo owner in the village. The system of organization was, if not unique, uniquely successful: its tiers of buffalo owners, societies, unions, and State-level federations assured a regular income to its members, and supplied cheap and high quality products to its consumers. Better family fortunes could be seen in better child health, better dress and housing, enthusiasm for education, and the acceptance of change. Co-operative profits were ploughed into running schools, dispensaries, health centres, youth clubs, and improving roads and other community services. In 1963, a special accolade was accorded Anand's success. An autonomous body, the National Dairy Development Board, was set up under the aegis of the federal government to promote milk producer co-operatives all over India. Prime Minister Shastri appointed Kurien Director. Anand had become a model not only for the milk industry, but for the national struggle against rural poverty.

In 1969, dairy development in India was propelled by Kurien into a phase called 'Operation Flood'. To finance the programme, the government used the same device which had been applied on a more modest scale in Bombay in the 1940s: India procured quantities of world surplus dairy products as gifts, sold them domestically, and invested the profits in its dairies.

Operation Flood was so-called after the 'flood' of milk it intended to produce from the rural areas by stimulating production in the country's milksheds. In its first phase, milk markets in the four metropolitan cities of Bombay, Calcutta, Delhi and Madras were linked to twenty-seven milksheds in their hinterland through a network of co-operatives. By 1981, 1·5 million families had joined rural groups and the national milk output had nearly doubled.

Many international organizations played a role in Operation Flood: the World Bank, FAO, the World Food Programme, the EEC. Unicef also offered support, partly for old times' sakes. By this time such a project was no longer a risky proposition in humble surroundings seeking donors prepared to make a leap of faith. On the contrary, it could command more financial and political support than it usefully knew what to do with. By 1970, Unicef was moving away from the dairy cow. As the answer to the problem of child nutrition, milk from an animal had finally been discarded.

Main sources

Unicef Executive Board documentation between 1952 and 1969; in particular memoranda prepared by FAO Nutrition Division; reports on survey missions by Dr Charles Glen King; reports of the FAO/Unicef Joint Committee; evaluations of the Skim Milk Distribution programme, the Milk Conservation programme, and the programme for the Research and Testing of High-protein Weaning Foods.

On milk conservation in India: *India Milk 1983*, a publication of the National Dairy Development Board; project recommendations prepared for the Unicef Executive Board; Oxfam project write-ups; articles in *Unicef News* and other Unicef information publications; 'Semi-industrial projects assisted by Unicef in India'; assessment prepared for Unicef by Tata Economic Consultancy Services, December 1984.

On milk conservation and high-protein weaning foods elsewhere: *Kwashiorkor in Africa* by Brock and Autret, WHO 1952; *A History of Unicef in Latin America* by Ken Grant; Unicef Board documentation and information materials; monthly reports of S. M. Keeny, Regional Director of Unicef in Asia 1950–1964.

Chapter 7

A Mother and Her Child

If the health and well-being of the child are at the heart of an organization's concern, then, however dramatic the impact of any mass campaign against disease, ultimately it must hold most dear the effectiveness of those parts of the health services which look after the expectant mother and her foetus; the mother in labour and at the moment of delivery; the mother and her newborn baby; and, with the co-operation of the mother, her small and growing child.

There are particular hazards associated with reproduction in women and with the growth of the child before and after birth for which special types of health and nutritional care are needed. And because of the love which every mother feels towards her child—and because of the hopes she and her husband, her parents, her inlaws and the entire family of Mankind entertain for their children's survival and future well-being—the time of pregnancy and early motherhood offer unique opportunities for influencing the kind of care a mother gives her child through the first risky months and years of life.

In postwar Europe, once the first moves had been made to get emergency feeding underway, Unicef offered help to ministries of health trying to rebuild and at, the same time, improve the parts of their health services which catered to everything connected with conception, childbirth and the vulnerabilities of the foetus and small child. These were usually separate and self-contained branches of the medical world with their own practitioners and settings: gynaecologists, obstetricians, paediatricians; maternity wards, children's hospitals, and baby clinics.

In many countries, the immediate needs—needs met initially by UNRRA's much larger programme for restocking hospitals, clinics and laboratories—were still for drugs and other expendable supplies without which even rudimentary medical care could not be administered. But there were many other items—instruments, diagnostic tools, basic medical equipment—which were still in very short supply and were critical to the delivery of any acceptable standard of care in maternity and paediatric wards. Under the rubric of assistance to 'maternal and child welfare', Unicef took over from UNRRA the task of supplying items such as these to hospitals and clinics. Before long, the list began to extend to more sophisticated items such as

X-ray equipment and incubators.

When WHO came into formal existence in 1948, maternal and child health, or MCH, was designated as one of its top priorities. Its focus was narrower than Unicef's only by the use of the word health instead of welfare; Unicef wanted to be sure that social work among handicapped children and other activities extracurricular to health in its narrow sense were not omitted from its definition. But to all intents and purposes, the two organizations began to pursue the identical goal of helping build up permanent maternal and child-health services within their usual partnership: guidance from WHO's technical experts; material assistance from Unicef. During the next decade the partnership between the two organizations was extremely close, particularly out in the places where together and in close collaboration with local medical services and ministries of health, WHO and Unicef people wrestled as a team with the problems of developing programmes of MCH in the unfamiliar landscape of underdevelopment.

The most visible and tangible items in any MCH programme were the supplies. Medical supplies, both because of their range and because of the permutations of different designs and manufactured costs, presented much more of a challenge than the milk powder and cod liver oil capsules needed for supplementary feeding. Finding, packaging or having specially-manufactured the right therapy or equipment was as complex as meeting the specifications for milk plants—even though items like pills, thermometers and enamelware seemed a great deal less glamorous.

The requirements of the International Tuberculosis Campaign, followed by the other mass campaigns against yaws, leprosy, malaria and others multiplied by many times the complications and dimensions of the supplies procurement and shipping functions gradually taken on by Unicef under the guidance of WHO. The chief of Unicef's supplies operation during these years was Ed Bridgewater, a Canadian who had originally worked in the grain business and joined Unicef from UNRRA in 1947. Bridgewater and his staff quickly developed an expertise in medical procurement which eventually had an important impact on the niche the organization carved out for itself within the UN family.

As important as any medical consumable or diagnostic tool was the need to provide a high standard of training to all the kinds of professional personnel whose work impinged on child care. In the postwar phase, this mostly meant the retraining of people whose wartime experiences had cut them off from any contact with developments in their field, and even in some cases from performing in it altogether. In 1948–49, some 900 fellowships were organized for public-health workers, paediatricians, nurses and social workers on the strength of donations from Britain, France, Sweden and Switzerland. In 1950, Unicef co-operated with the French Government in setting up in Paris an International Children's Centre (ICC) with the idea that it would provide a permanent training, research and documentation service for the best and the latest in the promotion of child health. Professor Robert Debré, the ICC's philosophical architect, had special views about what constituted the right kind of training for the well-set-up child-health promoter. He fused the specialization of paediatrics with the idea of public health in a discipline of which he was one of the key inventors: 'social paediatrics'. The social or preventive paediatrician not only knew how to care for mothers and children in the hospital ward, but also held 'well-baby' clinics and undertook other kinds of preventive maternal and child care in the community.

The early programmes or support for MCH in postwar Asia were almost a mirror image of forebears in Europe: 'shopping lists' of drugs, diet supplements, medical instruments, children's ward furniture, items expendable and nonexpendable, for clinical use and for training purposes, were drawn up in collaboration with ministries of health to replace those destroyed or worn out in the war, or which had never existed before it. Fellowships were offered for doctors, public-health workers and paediatricians; within the All-India Institute of Hygiene and Public Health in Calcutta a new centre was offered support similar to that given the ICC in Paris to provide postgraduate training in MCH, serving India and other countries in the region. But it was clear from the start that the scope of this assistance was inherently very limited, not to mention its minute quantity in relation to needs. In parts of the world where the permanent network of public-health services was embryonic, the immediate prospects of developing any extensive system of catering specifically for the health and welfare needs of mother and child were very dim.

An MCH service was a much more complicated affair than a mass treatment or vaccination campaign. For both a baby clinic, and for a vaccination, mothers might well line up with their small children under a tree or on a verandah in the expectation of some kind of health-promoting therapy; but there the similarities ended. Every pregnant mother and every child had to be treated as an individual case and their specific problems, actual or potential, identified. Only fully-trained professional staff were equipped to make this kind of judgement; the only service the lay worker or the auxiliary could reliably perform was to hand out whole milk powder to nursing mothers or carry out other straightforward diagnostic or preventive routines. Not only were professional staff needed, but they were needed on a regular basis; a pregnant mother needed several check-ups before giving birth, domiciliary or hospital care during labour, and her small child needed regular monthly check-ups thereafter.

In most Asian, American, and Mediterranean countries, eighty per cent of the people lived in the rural areas where there were few permanent health installations; some were hospitals and health centres set up courageously, but in a piecemeal fashion, by church and voluntary organizations, at a remove from the embryonic national health network. Unicef and

WHO set out to equip existing facilities, most of which were in the towns and larger population centres, to carry out pre-natal and baby clinics; and to set up model MCH centres for training and practical purposes. These were supposed to illustrate what a good MCH service meant; some performed valuable service in finding out which methods transposed well from more developed parts of the world and which did not.

Although Unicef might wish it to be otherwise, a relatively small proportion of its assistance went towards maternal and child welfare in the years following its reorientation towards the underdeveloped countries. This was seen as undesirable, and efforts were made to reverse the trend, particularly in Asia. But this was the era when disease control was widely regarded as the public-health priority, and the mass campaigns as the vanguard of permanent services following along more slowly in their wake. The campaigns were quicker and easier to mount than any service intended to be left permanently in place, and their instant results made them exciting and popular. The international organizations were carrying the banner of disease control higher every year throughout the 1950s; under these pressures it was unfair to expect hard-pressed ministries of health to divert more attention, and a substantially larger share of their budgets, to promoting MCH services and training workers in the various child-care disciplines.

Health budgets were small—minute in relation to needs—and under many competing strains. Lip service was often paid to their importance, but MCH was invariably a poor contender. Even where ministries were sincerely committed, the expense and the lack of trained personnel reduced progress to a snail's pace. Time was to show that the only chance of speeding up progress was to develop models for health care systems which incorporated MCH and looked and functioned very differently from most counterparts in the industrialized world.

Meanwhile, one of the first pieces of the maternal and child health jigsaws to be singled out by WHO's and Unicef's enthusiasts was the most obvious: the moment, place and circumstances of a child's delivery into the world.

The most risky moment in the natural course of a person's life is the moment of being born. The moment of giving birth—a moment which some women experience many times—is also fraught with risk. Before the advent of modern medicine, it was commonplace to lose either or both participants in their joint moment of jeopardy. In many countries, the death of mother or baby, or both, in childbirth or shortly afterwards was not uncommon in the postwar world, and in some of the world's remotest corners the same holds true today.

No society, however remote, however 'primitive', is without its maternity service, even if it does not resemble the wardfull of obstetrical paraphernalia and personnel in which most modern mothers expect to undergo a confinement. In the 1950s, modern methods of childbirth were not even remotely available for the great majority of women living in Asia, Africa and Latin America; in many countries, especially in the countryside, this is still the case today. Their children come into the world in the privacy of their grandmother's or mother's humble home, with only the village 'grannie' or 'auntie' in attendance to help ease their passage: the *dukun*, as she is known in Indonesia; the *dai* in India and Pakistan; the *matronne* in French-speaking Africa; the *empirica* in Latin America. These were, and are, the 'traditional birth attendants' whose profession is one of the oldest known to Mankind: women who have passed down through many generations the mysteries of how to tend a woman in labour and deliver her baby safely into the world.

Many professional health practitioners and educated people used to classify the traditional birth attendant as a creature closely related to the witch: an illiterate crone who chewed herbs and brewed potions and whose superstitions and unclean ways were irredeemable. This school of thought believed that she must be displaced as swiftly as possible from her position as the village godmother, and mothers must deliver either in a hospital ward, or at home tended by a trained midwife. Her clients often saw the matter differently. They were deeply attached to the customs surrounding the birth of a baby, the careful protection and privacy in which the mother and her newborn child must be shielded. Even where an alternative was available, these were not lightly abandoned for the questionable advantages of being attended at a time of great stress by a stranger, especially away from home. The lack of importance the *dai* attached to particles of dirt lodged in her finger-nails or on the blade of the knife with which she cut the umbilical cord did not cause her clients anxiety: no connection was made with any later onset of a fatal sickness. If she had good hands and a soothing voice, if her knife was sharp and her movements deft, all would be well— God willing. If things went badly, then it was assumed that God, for some reason, was not willing. For the midwife's pains, she would take home a chicken, some fruits or a length of cloth for a scarf. Her advice, with that of grandmother or grandmother-in-law, would guide an inexperienced mother in how to nurse her child through the first risky weeks of life.

In the late 1940s, some progressive and pragmatic health practitioners, recognizing that the skills of the birth attendants were well-trusted and that in many places any version of the modern maternity ward was at least a generation away, began to advance the idea that the traditional midwives should be courted instead of discouraged from plying their trade. They were likely to command a clientele whatever the professionals thought of their methods. If they could be persuaded to add some notions of hygiene to their existing skills, and were linked to some kind of MCH supervision and back-up, they could be co-opted into a relationship with regular MCH programmes. Not only could they then perform better their existing vocation, but they could summon professional help if a birth turned out to be more complicated than they could manage. They could also keep a track of pregnancies and births, informing the health centre, encouraging pregnant women to go for prenatal care and mothers to take their newborn babies for routine weighing and check-ups.

By the early 1950s, despite lingering scepticism, the image of the traditional midwife was already improving. Certain countries in Asia were starting to give some a weekly day of instruction or were persuading them to come to the health centre for a brief residential course. One way to help this process along was to provide a stock of the items they were teaching the midwives to use. A supply of medicaments and some better tools than the rusty old knife she currently used for cutting the umbilical cord would offer an enticement for *dais* and *dukuns* to join the training programmes, as well as improve their performance afterwards. Some modified versions of a standard midwifery kit had already been tried out in various places; on his return from China, Leo Eloesser started to experiment with assembling a range of items— sharp knife, basin, gauze, gloves, plastic sheet, bottle of antiseptic fluid— which could be supplied as a standard kit that the traditional birth attendant could carry in a canvas bag over the fields to wherever the woman in labour was waiting.

The kit was a simple but inspired notion. The product that resulted became eventually almost as well-known and as intimately associated with Unicef as powdered milk. Its final shape— not a canvas bag, but a cheaper and more durable aluminium box— and the final list of its contents was determined by Dr Berislav Borcic, with help from many WHO and Unicef colleagues. Borcic, with his long experience in China and other parts of the world, had a sharp eye for, and a strong disposition against, the complicated or extravagant medical accessory. With the help of friendly manufacturers enlisted by Ed Bridgewater and the supplies people, he pared the kit as close to the bone as possible: the total cost of box and ingredients was around $12. Apart from the financial savings of standardization, the practical advantage of a pre-assembled kit— or what came to be a series of three standard kits designed for midwifery services of different degrees of sophistication— was the ease with which they could be ordered and despatched to destinations all over the world. Their contents could also be adapted according to the requirements of different health services.

The midwifery kits made possible an immediate expansion in Unicef's support for MCH services. The upsurge was most remarkable in Asia, where they became standard issue at the end of programmes to train several thousand *dukuns* each year in Indonesia and growing numbers of *dais* in India and Pakistan. One of the countries quick to make full use of Unicef's support was the Philippines, whose *hilots*—'old ones'—still provided the backbone of maternity services in rural communities. When Philippine health authorities began to extend maternal and child-health services along conventional lines into the countryside, they found that the local women refused to have their babies delivered by fully-trained midwives in the MCH centres. The only way to tempt the mothers into starting to use the centres was to give the *hilots* institutional recognition via training and a midwife's bag, and hope that they would become advertisers for the centres' postnatal services. This strategy was farsighted and worked well; in time the local women began to overcome their original prejudices.

The *hilots* attended twelve weekly training sessions. They were taught about normal pregnancy and delivery, with special emphasis on the risk of infection, the need to sterilize the knife before using it to cut the cord, and how to tend the wound with antiseptic so that there was less risk of tetanus. They were also told to report pregnancies and births to the health unit, send pregnant women along for prenatal care and encourage mothers to take their young infants to its well-baby clinics. At the end of their training a ceremony was held, and they received their new kit in a neat tin box with 'Unicef' stamped on the lid. If something broke or ran out, the *hilot* was supposed to seek a replacement from the health centre. In 1955, when the programme had begun to move into its stride throughout most of the islands, the Unicef representative in Manila recorded that the 2000 *hilots* trained so far averaged one delivery a week; which meant that over 100,000 infants a year would be brought into the world with a better chance of survival for a cost of around $20 for each midwife. As gratifying was their willing co-operation with the rural health centres, which they seemed not to perceive as a threat to their business. In some districts, *hilots* outside the programme had actually visited civic leaders to demand that they too be given training and a box of drugs and utensils.

The midwifery kit for the traditional birth attendant was just one small example of a process of refining and standardizing the supply of essential drugs and equipment for maternal and child services. This was not as easy as it sounds. 'Health centre'— as Sam Keeny frequently pointed out, and he made it his personal business to know— was a descriptor used indiscriminately to denote institutions engaged in functions so different in content and sophistication that it was almost misleading to think of them as generically related. The health-centre building could consist of open-air and a large tree, a bamboo hut with coconut matting walls and one tin chest, or a handsome brick structure with an operating theatre, wards with beds, and its own electricity plant. To reach the centre could require anything from a few minutes bus ride from a hotel in town, to a trek on foot along miles of paths, a boat ride upriver for several hours, or a steep mountain climb and a precarious scramble across a rope bridge. The staff in charge ranged from the auxiliary nurse-midwife proud of her competence at reading the labels on the bottles, to a fully-trained specialist at the frontier of tropical paediatrics. This, then, was the 'health centre' which Unicef was trying to equip.

Supplies available from Unicef consisted firstly of expendables—cod liver oil capsules, basic drugs, iron tablets, vitamin A, and milk powder. These consumables were only supposed to supplement, not replace the provision of drugs and dietary extras by the health service, and then only for an initial period; but in many places they often consisted of the only supplies available. In practice therefore their function was far from supplementary; they were the only things more concrete than advice that midwives and nurses had to offer mothers who had often walked for miles with one baby on their back and another at the hip and lined up patiently for several hours on a crowded verandah.

These items increasingly came to be seen as an important draw, making of mothers a captive audience for talks on nutrition, or for preventive care such as a prenatal examination which they might not otherwise have sought. WHO gave technical advice about what should be supplied; this approach later led to the suggestion that health services depend on a basic stock of cheap 'essential drugs', and to the development of specific therapies for common complaints such as diarrhoea.

The range of possible items of equipment needed by health institutions from the grandest to the humblest was overwhelmingly varied, depending on the centre's staff, size and sophistication. To streamline costs and complications, lists of standard equipment were developed by WHO and Unicef to guide health officials and programme officers in drawing up 'shopping lists' as part of their MCH extension plans. Criteria emerged about what was reasonable and what was not; where a doctor was in charge, diagnostic equipment and even surgical instruments could be included; where midwives or nurses were in charge, the package was appropriately scaled down. Where an auxiliary nurse/midwife was expected to undertake home visiting and attend home deliveries, she might be provided with a bicycle; where a doctor ran an outreach programme of mobile clinics or subcentre supervision, a car or four-wheel-drive vehicle could be provided. Refrigerators—kerosene, gas, or electricity—were needed to keep vaccines fresh and other perishables from spoiling in hot temperatures; the specifications of every centre and the kind of service it was capable of running had to be known in order not to make mistakes over such critical factors as the existence or otherwise of a power supply.

Quite elaborate safeguards were set up to keep a check on what kind of health institution received what kind of equipment, and how well or badly it was put to use. Inevitably, stories abounded about refrigerators with the wrong specifications, the vehicle of a make for which no spare parts were available in the country, the equipment which was locked in a cupboard and brought out only for inspection by visiting officials. There were also the centres where staff were so overworked that equipment was used long past the time when it should have been replaced; and others whose feedback enabled designs to be modified so as to make equipment more durable and better suited to its functional setting. One of the problems was how to set up a reporting system which was thorough, but which was not too complex, costly or time-consuming to carry out. On the basis of the information gathered, a great deal could be learned not only about whether the co-operation of WHO and Unicef was used and useful; but about what kind of ailments were most common; which staff in outlying places needed more supervision, or more training, or perhaps a promotion; which modest subcentre deserved upgrading, and which was serving no good use at all. These procedures, developed co-operatively with the authorities, were often incorporated into government practice.

Meanwhile, Unicef's own supplies operation outgrew its facilities in the basement of the UN building in New York. In 1962, it moved to special warehousing premises and packaging facilities in Copenhagen at the invitation of the Danish Government. There, as UNIPAC (the Unicef Procurement and Assembly Centre), it remained, expanding its operations more than tenfold over the next twenty years. As an instrument for the improvement of maternal and child-health care around the world, and a service to many other UN and non-UN organizations, UNIPAC became a phenomenon in its own right.

The other side of the maternal and child-health care coin was personnel. Shortage of staff, and of the wherewithal to pay the costs of training and employing them, was usually a greater barrier to the penetration of services into the rural landscape than any shortage of supplies and equipment. But in the early 1950s, there were still strong limitations on what Unicef could offer ministries of health to overcome this problem.

It was still widely held that funds donated for international humanitarian purposes could not fittingly be spent on doing anything to further people's expertise; furthering expertise was the domain of 'technical assistance'. An exception had been made after the war to allow students to be sent overseas to undertake courses of advanced study that, because of the wartime hiatus, were not available at home. In these cases other international considerations applied—considerations of healing international wounds, making desirable international exchanges, and how to make use of contributions in nontransferable currencies. But in order to do something so self-evidently sensible as pay for the training or in any way remunerate nurse/midwives for the day-to-day services they rendered to village women in Pakistan or Burma, Unicef had first to whittle down entrenched and outdated ideas.

The argument against such a use of funds was ideological: the development of national resources— personnel or other— was a matter for national budgets and national planners, using whatever technical advice and extra financial investment they could negotiate from international partners. Humanitarian goodwill was only for the 'mercy mission' or its equivalent; it could not be used for something which was by its very nature ongoing and had nothing to do with a hiatus due to war or other emergency. Humanitarian donors—both governments using taxpayers' money and private individuals making charitable contributions—are as fussy about what happens to their money as any investor in business enterprise. They expect a certain return, and they are suspicious when it is difficult to measure in straightforward ways. In the case of a training programme, it was, and is, difficult to quantify exactly how the training of one person has benefited others supposed to live better as a result. Donors tend to prefer (it has taken many years to wean some of them away from such preferences) the reassurance of concrete actions like malaria control or feeding schemes; they like results which can be counted: milk rations, sprayguns, drugs, bicycles, baby scales—and kidney basins ordered, delivered and put to use. The problem in the 1950s—and in some places it is still the problem in the 1980s—was that without people properly trained to carry out the programmes, the equipment could be ordered and delivered, but could not be put to use. Not ordering it and not delivering it seemed an equally bad way of helping improve maternal and child health.

At that time, while ideas about international co-operation in the postwar world were still crystallizing and the philosophy of 'development' was yet to be fully articulated, attitudes about international humanitarian effort were still dominated by narrow definitions of welfare for the indigent or those dispossessed of some part of the physical or mental equipment human beings need to lead a 'normal' life. Remnants of such notions still persist; they are a holdover from an era in which humanitarian aid and social development were regarded as two quite separate and unconnected areas of human endeavour. During the 1950s, alleviating human distress and advancing human progress gradually came to be perceived as inextricable from one another. As both the intergovernmental and voluntary humanitarian organizations enhanced their experience of working with people in different economic, social and cultural circumstances, it became clear that no useful effort to do something 'humanitarian' could escape the implications of doing something 'developmental'.

At the beginning of the era in which Unicef began to wrestle with problems of underdevelopment, the stock on its metaphorical shelf fell within quite a narrow perceptual range: nutrition called for milk; health for disease control and MCH services. Gradually, the limitations of this stock-in-trade became obvious. Unicef offered 'material' rather than 'technical' assistance; at its best it not only went looking to see what was happening to the milk rations, cotton swabs, and enamelware delivered to the health centre out in the rice paddy or perched on the mountainside but also ruminated constructively on what it had seen. Because of this, its arguments for breaking away from convention and getting involved in new fields of activity were pragmatic, and ultimately unanswerable.

The most serious bottleneck, in every area, was the lack of trained personnel to carry out programmes. It was originally to help develop MCH that Unicef began to push out the frontiers of its assistance for training. A series of decisions were taken during the 1950s— decisions inched through the resistance of certain major donor countries— on what kind of manpower development in underdeveloped countries could be supported in the cause of improving child health. These decisions had the full backing of WHO. In a very important sense, they paved the way for Unicef's evolution into a very different creature than the one it was at its inception.

The first step came in 1952, when Unicef adopted the policy of meeting the training costs for 'auxiliary' health personnel. This category excluded personnel receiving professional training at a school or college; it included those who had little formal schooling but who, on the basis of a short training course, were expected to play a vital role at the furthermost tip of the health services: traditional midwives, nursing assistants, sanitary inspectors, lay vaccinators and other members of mobile teams. Such training courses did not need to be long in duration nor expensive, but instructors and trainees needed stipends to make it possible for them to travel to the place of training and stay away from home for a while. This decision was the crack in the door; it led to Unicef's entry into a wide range of health-training assistance, for it soon became obvious that low calibre staff could not augment the health services on their own. What was more, if no-one followed them back to the villages to see how they were doing, it was impossible to judge whether their training had had any effect, let alone improve upon it. In 1954, it was agreed that Unicef might defray the regular MCH training costs of professional nurses, midwives, and public health workers, as well as the costs— travel and stipends— of giving auxiliaries supervision.

In 1957, another considerable leap was taken in the area of more senior professional training. It was agreed that grants-in-aid might be given for periods of up to five years to help establish departments of child health in teaching institutes in parts of the world where these were few or nonexistent. One of the outcomes of this decision was the establishment of a Unicef chair in Paediatrics at Makerere University in Uganda. This was ably filled by Derrick Jellife, an English paediatrician who quickly developed an international reputation in child nutrition. By the end of the decade, still in close co-operation with WHO, Unicef had become involved in almost every aspect of health training related to maternal and child care in the underdeveloped world, providing at one end of the scale stipends worth a few dollars for members of the ancient profession of midwifery; at the other, grants and fellowships designed to create an élite of health professionals to head the evolving MCH services in their countries.

By this time, a new theme was emerging, one that was to dominate health service development throughout the next decade and beyond. All efforts to improve the health of the entire community, including disease control campaigns, should embrace MCH; and MCH should embrace activities other than the strictly medical for the overall improvement of family life. Assessments of MCH progress had begun to show that too many nurses, midwives and public health workers were not extending the concept of MCH as far as WHO and Unicef had hoped. The numbers of health centres equipped and the numbers of personnel trained were mounting; but their impact left a lot to be desired. Too many so-called MCH activities were isolated from any other public health service and their scope often did not extend beyond routine maternity care.

The effort made to support MCH was too haphazard; more should go into setting up networks of MCH services which themselves were part of larger health-care networks. Somehow, more must be done, both inside the health centre and outside it, to reach mothers and children at all their moments of vulnerability. MCH must advance in a synchronized fashion with disease prevention, health education, nutrition, and public hygiene. Such ideas had implications for the training curricula of MCH workers, the contents of kits, the structures in which MCH was carried out— even the very nature of MCH itself.

Meanwhile, the health and well-being of the mother and her child could also be influenced from other directions. The MCH clinic might be the most obvious place to find Unicef's target customers congregated and ready for tangible assistance, but it was not the only one. In quite a few parts of the world there were also women's mutual support groups, such as the ones in Brazil which had been encouraged to take up mini-dairying. These networks belonged somewhere in between the traditional and the modern worlds; the idea of the mothers' union, of which they were in some places a copy and in others a deviation, was imported by the missionaries; but it was an idea that fell on fertile ground in places where there was a strong tradition of mutual help between women of a kin, caste or an age-set. It was among the women of Africa south of the Sahara, the last major part of the world to become a beneficiary of Unicef assistance, where this form of co-operation began.

In the early postwar years, the colonial powers did not welcome UN overtures to become involved in the parts of Africa where they were the responsible authorities. In the years when African aspirations for political autonomy were growing, Ralph Bunche and other senior UN officials concerned with non-independent territories were anxious to prepare the ground for the UN's future role in what was destined to become an array of new, and struggling, independent African states. In the early 1950s, Bunche began to sound out WHO, FAO and Unicef on their willingness to offer, and the colonial powers on theirs to accept, a modest amount of technical and humanitarian assistance. Britain, France and Belgium responded positively.

Unicef opened negotiations with Paris, Brussels and London in 1951. The first allocation for Africa south of the Sahara—milk powder and medical supplies worth $1 million—was despatched to destinations in French and Belgian territories in Western, Northern, and Equatorial Africa, and Liberia, late in 1952. Unicef at this stage was woefully ignorant about the 'dark continent', no Unicef programme person having yet set foot on its soil. This shortcoming was soon remedied by Charles Egger, director of Unicef's European headquarters in Paris, in whose domain Africa fell in the light of the need for close contacts with the metropolitan authorities.

Egger, a young and ebullient Swiss who had first served Unicef in postwar Bulgaria, was seized with enthusiasm by the idea of shaping a programme in what seemed like a vast, mysterious and virgin land. The first Unicef representative to live and work in Africa was another Swiss, Dr Roland Marti. Marti had served the International Red Cross for most of his career, was a veteran of arduous assignments, and brought to his interminable safari a conviviality which did much to make Unicef welcome throughout the continent. Marti arrived in Brazzaville in September 1952, was given a corner of the WHO regional office out of which to work, and worked from the outset in closest co-operation with colleagues from both WHO and FAO.

As always, Unicef's instinctive reaction in any place where it was offering assistance for the first time was child feeding. Brock and Autret's FAO/WHO sponsored study on 'Kwashiorkor in Africa' had recently appeared, and they had specifically singled out skim milk from milk-surplus countries as a remedial strategy. But the attempt to mount protective feeding programmes for the under-fives in various corners of French Equatorial Africa and the Belgian Congo was not an entirely fruitful experience—except in terms of lessons learnt. Little account had been taken of the distances which had to be travelled in Africa, the lack of roads, the fact that most people did not live in convenient clusters of dwellings in settlements akin to the notion of 'village' or 'hamlet', but in homesteads scattered far and wide throughout the bush. The complications and expense of distributing rations on a regular basis, and the difficulty of reaching the children most in need, made nonsense of giving out powdered milk as a kwashiorkor preventive.

There were other more banal but just as important reasons why milk powder made little impact on nutritional deficiency in rural Africa—reasons which made Marti laugh at his own and others' naiveté. The instructions for reconstituting milk powder demanded that it be heated, and then rapidly cooled. But how, far off in the bush, was a large cauldron of milk, brought to the boil only after hours of heating over a brush fire, to be rapidly cooled? The women waited in the mornings for the milk to heat, and in the afternoons for it to cool. After a few sessions, bored and fed up and obliged to return to work in their fields, they stopped coming. Charles Egger described these results diplomatically to Executive Board delegates in New York: 'It may be necessary to reconsider certain elements', he reported, given 'the simplicity of existing facilities'. In due course, the milk powder was sent to schools, and to hospitals and health centres as a medicine for the specific treatment of kwashiorkor patients. Milk had a very limited application to the amelioration of child health in most of Africa.

Throughout the 1950s, by far the largest proportion of Unicef's modest assistance in Africa went to disease-control campaigns, particularly to schemes intended to prepare the way for malaria eradication. In the early 1960s, when WHO had reported that only in a few upland areas of Africa had it proved possible to kill enough malaria-carrying *Anopheles gambiae* mosquitoes to stop malaria transmission, almost all these projects were abandoned. The campaigns against yaws were much more successful: the susceptibility of yaws to penicillin made it very much easier to attack than malaria, particularly as any regular follow-up was so problematic.

Africa turned out to have a much larger reservoir of yaws than originally anticipated: twenty-five million cases, mostly in the West. Campaigns were mounted in Nigeria and in French Equatorial Africa, reaching a peak of three million treatments in 1958. In French territories the campaigns were carried out with a high degree of efficiency by the French Army's mobile epidemic disease units. The other targeted disease was leprosy. By the early 1960s, sulphone drugs had transformed the prospects of leprosy patients by ending the need for segregation and reducing the stigma attached to the disease. The missionaries looked after most of Africa's leprosy victims, and indeed were the only source of medical care in many parts of the vast hinterland.

In Africa south of the Sahara, more absolutely than anywhere else, programme models originally designed for circumstances of temporary social breakdown were hopelessly inadequate. Many believed that the deadweight of endemic and epidemic disease which cursed large parts of the continent—smallpox, typhus, yellow fever, sleeping sickness, river blindness, bilharzia, blackwater, as well as malaria, yaws, and leprosy—had to be tackled before anything else. Even though results were not always encouraging, disease control was one of the few options open in a part of the world where the only pervasive system of health care depended on self-employed practitioners dispensing a mixture of herbal concoctions, magic, ritual and promises of supernatural intervention. Except for the missionaries' brave little hospitals in the bush, it was nearly impossible to find a functional health centre running any kind of MCH service outside the towns.

If the French authorities relied on the army's mobile teams for public health in the African countryside, the British both in West Africa— Gold Coast and Nigeria— and in East Africa— Kenya, Uganda, Tanganyika— had a different approach, envisaging the gradual spread of permanent services run by locally-trained and locally-stationed African health personnel.

When Unicef programme support for Kenya began in 1954, midwives and sanitary inspectors were spending some part of their training visiting rural communities and giving talks and demonstrations. As yet, almost no effort had been made to improve the skills of traditional birth attendants: even that kind of programme, however simple the course and relatively inexpensive, required an existing MCH service to give the training and follow it up with supervision. Training schools turning out the kind of professionals and auxiliaries needed for MCH were gradually increasing their number and the range of their curricula, but they were still very few and far between. In French West Africa, Dakar had a school for African midwives; but the French tended to concentrate on giving a high level of sophisticated training to medical personnel, almost invariably in institutions in France itself. Unicef's first contribution for MCH in French West Africa was in 1958, when the authorities in Senegal decided to transform their midwifery programme into full-blown MCH and give it a much wider spread.

The paucity in Africa of academic training institutions offering any grounding in paediatrics or courses in the public health subjects most strategic to the well-being of children was the main reason for Unicef's decision in 1957— a decision endorsed by WHO— to offer fixed-term grants-in-aid to medical colleges and university faculties. The chair in Child Health at Makerere was the most striking outcome of the new Unicef policy; other grants were made to institutes in Dakar, Senegal, and Ibadan, Nigeria. The work undertaken at these institutes, particularly at Makerere by Jellife and his team, helped begin the process of shedding the ethno-centric attitudes which afflicted social development policies in Africa— a process which, in the 1980s, is still far from complete.

Until teachers and students working in Africa itself began to develop a body of professional knowledge and experience about the way different societies bore and raised their children, the vacuum in child-health policy, personnel and practice could not be properly filled. This entailed studying family life, health and diet, in a wide range of different settings. In large parts of Africa, the life style of the people was shaped by the environment in a way that people living in a consumer society find hard to imagine. Responses to problems of health or nutritional deficiency suited to nomadic pastoralists living in the desert or semidesert were not applicable to settled agriculturalists living scattered in the plains; their diet and health problems would differ again from those of close-knit societies living among the verdant greenery of cooler highlands. In colonial times, these differences were more often studied by anthropologists than by public health officials. Now times were changing.

In the absence of rural health centres and MCH services, the search for other organizational entities in which to put across to mothers information about child care, nutrition, domestic hygiene and family welfare, led Unicef to the women's groups. While traditional associations— among women circumcised in the same group, among the market women of western Africa— existed in many parts of the continent, the first formally-constituted women's movement to achieve recognition and support from what were then the colonial authorities was in Kenya. In 1956, Unicef offered assistance to the women's group movement in Kenya and to that in Uganda the following year.

The Kenyan movement for the progress of women— *Maendeleo ya Wanawake*— was established in 1951 to provide training for the leaders of women's clubs. A handful of these had sprung up at the initiative of rural women whose husbands had received some training in community development. But, as happened elsewhere in Africa, the real forcing ground of the women's movement in Kenya was the political struggle for freedom. Between 1952 and 1955, the years of the Mau Mau uprising against white settlers occupying the ancestral land of the Kikuyu people, thousands of women lost their husbands and fathers, and with them, their right to land, to occupation, even to legal existence as individuals. Shaken out of the set pattern of life by circumstances beyond their control, the women of Kenya began to demand something of a world which was offering change to men— training, education, jobs, money— but was leaving them in age-old servitude as men's appendages. *Maendeleo ya Wanawake*, by providing leadership and a co-ordinating structure, channelled what was essentially a grass-roots movement born of personal and economic hardship into a network of associations trying to improve the lives of members in many different ways. In five years the movement took off among rural women all over the country; by 1956, there were 500 clubs with a membership of over 30,000. Some clubs defied the law and bought land to farm co-operatively. Many hired themselves out to large farmers as contract labour, cutting grass and harvesting produce. The income they earned was used on a rotating basis between members, often for home improvements. A tin, or *mabati*, roof in place of thatch was the heart's desire of many, and as tin roofs began to dot the landscape, the groups became known as the *mabati* women.

In 1956, when Unicef first supported the women's club movement in Kenya, its assistance for training in mothercraft and homecraft reflected an idealized image of women's lives and ways of rearing children which had little connection with the realities of rural Africa. It was taken for granted that a demand for classes in cooking, nursery care, sewing, knitting and handicrafts—the typical occupations of the mothers' union or women's guild in the Western world—were the principal reason why African women were clamouring for training and material assistance. At an elementary level, the need to educate women was beginning to be recognized; if they remained trapped in a fatalistic predetermined world, bound by the unchallenged authority of fathers, husbands and mothers-in-law over every aspect of their lives, then they would not embrace change, and therefore would not consider improving the way they raised their children and managed their family affairs. The same perspective also recognized the need to engage them in society, and to encourage in them qualities of independent judgement. But the vital part African women played in growing, harvesting and storing the family's food supply was only very vaguely understood, as was the amount of time and energy they spent on gathering fuel and collecting water, tasks as essential to the functioning of the household as any performed by men. Gathering sticks from the bush and loading them on one's back did not deserve attention in the standard text on 'homecraft'. Nevertheless, whatever the narrow perception of women's needs as mothers and homemakers which then prevailed not only at Unicef but also throughout the humanitarian community, the enthusiasm for supporting them was an enlightened step forward which, in time, opened the door to a broader view of the role of women in development.

Both the women's group movements in Kenya and Uganda were promoted under the rubric of 'community development', an approach which had developed a considerable following by the end of the 1950s. These were to be found among the policy makers in countries other than those in British East Africa: India, for example, whose rural administrative structure was refashioned in 1959 specifically to help community development along; and also in the circles where international assistance policies were shaped. 'Community development' was an approach with great appeal, particularly among those who thought of themselves as reformers and progressives and who were frustrated by the agonizingly slow pace at which conventional methods were transforming underdeveloped rural economies and—or—improving the lot of the rural poor.

The coming of community development marked a new chapter in ideas about poverty and underdevelopment, because its philosophical and practical characteristics distinguished it from any approach that had gone before. Its starting point was the growing realization that the problems of low productivity, hunger, ignorance and ill-health, were interlocking, particularly among those experiencing them; and therefore that they required a multidisciplinary response.

The multidisciplinary response demanded new things of people taught to refine and concentrate their attention on applying their own programme speciality and on leaving things outside their competence to the professional attention of others. The problem with trying to improve the well-being of the rural poor from one direction only was that in the absence of other programmes or services, the good to be had was often promptly nullified. A nutrition lesson about the proteins in legumes or fish or eggs was not useful where no such foodstuffs were grown or found on sale at a reasonable price in the market; by the same token, a cure for malnutrition was useless if the child went home to the same starchy, protein-deficient diet. Doctors needed to concern themselves with nonmedical matters, like the food supply and water source; agriculturalists needed to think not only about crop varieties, seeds and fertilizers, but also about diet and health; educators needed to think of how to put all these things across to those who ought to be able to put such information to good effect. Community development tackled the family's and community's many different problems in tandem, usually by a team of people from a number of different government departments: local government, health, education, agriculture, forestry, public works, social services.

Not everything could be tackled at once, and no order of priorities was pre-defined from country to country or district to district; according to the ideal model, each team was supposed to establish their own. This element was associated with the other major novelty of the community development concept: a glimmering of recognition that the people on whose behalf schemes were devised were not simply their passive recipients, but had views and energies of their own to contribute. One piece of Unicef literature of the time commented: 'The community development process brings with it a new kind of vitality because it utilizes the felt needs of people'. The observation came from a review of the experience gained in supporting the women's groups movements in Kenya and Uganda. It conveyed the idea that people's sense of needing something was a resource to be harnessed; it did not suggest that their needs were other than self-evident—which meant in effect that they were defined by others. But at least the idea was admitted that they did have a sense of their needs, and that it could be important.

In Kenya the *Maendeleo* movement would not have spread so quickly—more quickly than any output of trained 'leaders' could possibly 'co-ordinate'—if it had not corresponded to something the women keenly wanted, even if they did not articulate their needs in terms of knitting and cooking lessons. To understand this was to move away from the one-dimensional view of poor people in underdeveloped countries as helpless and pathetic victims, and to begin to see the task of helping them as something other than a process of rhetoric and imposition, at the end of which they would have accepted something devised for their own good by someone who had never thought of asking their opinion.

Within Unicef, while there was no opposition to supporting mother-child welfare via the novel route of women's groups, there was some doubt about whether an organization dedicated to the well-being of children should become involved in a process so detached from their specific needs as community development. The viewpoint was similar to that which saw disease control as the polar opposite of MCH, arguing that the only right and true Unicef pursuit was an activity directly focused on the child. Community development, by definition, did not distinguish between age-group, sex, or between the needy and the not-so-needy; in fact it was a great deal more of a catch-all even than disease control because a main part of its inspiration was economic rather than social. But evidence was accumulating in favour of thinking 'community' as well as 'child'. Studies of recent declines in foetal, infant and early childhood mortality showed that improvements in child health had as much, or more, to do with measures affecting the family and community generally as they did with efforts to impinge directly on the health of mothers, infants and children themselves.

Disease control, a cleaner environment, better housing, the chance of education and an increased food supply, played as important a part as maternity care, vaccinations and supplementary feeding in lowering the death rates of the under-fives.

A policy to promote children's welfare could not be devised and carried out in isolation from a policy to promote the well-being of the family as a whole. A set of baby-scales could not do more for a child than a bumper harvest in the family granary; a vaccination could not take the place of better housing on land distinguishable from the municipal garbage dump; a daily cup of nourishing milk was not a substitute for a supply of bacteria-free drinking water and a place where human ordure could be hygienically contained. Nobody disputed that a mother and her child faced special health risks and needed special attention; but if those requirements were held as the one-and-only sacrosanct destination of assistance divorced from their economic and social context, results were bound to be dis-appointing. The tunnel vision which insisted on seeing the child's well-being as somehow separable from that of family and community mitigated against the child . . . just as every untreated family and community member in a campaign against yaws or malaria was a potential source of re-infection for the child. The overall condition of family and community had a decisive effect on the child's present health and future prospects.

Well-reasoned as such a position might be, it took some years for Unicef as a whole to find it convincing. Where the expansion of MCH services was a specific ingredient of a community development strategy, as in India from 1956 onwards, Unicef was delighted to support that particular ingredient; but mother-and-child welfare was the beginning and end of the story. Gradually, however, Unicef became less cautious and began to see the benefits of the strategy as a whole for mother-and-child health. In the language of the time, the techniques of community development delivered a 'psychological shock' which broke the fatalistic bonds imprisoning people

— mothers being the operative people from Unicef's point of view—in custom and superstition and enabled them to take their first steps towards a more enlightened sense of who they were and what they were capable of doing. When Unicef began to support *animation féminine* in Senegal in the early 1960s, it had come around to the point of view that the 'psychological shock' was what counted, the spark that ignited women's interest in doing things together to solve common problems. That what many of the groups did together was to run crèches for children whose mothers were busy with agricultural tasks during the planting season was thoroughly pleasing; but the fact that the women themselves had made the choice, not the authorities or the supporting international donor, was an important evolution.

If the tantalizing promise of community development was that it could reach into households and families, arouse an appetite for change, promote productivity and release people from ignorance and ill-health, there was one problem for which it seemed an ideally suited strategy: the attack on hunger and malnutrition.

Ever since the early 1950s, FAO, WHO, Unicef and other partners in international co-operation had been trying to unlock the puzzle of how to do more for the hungry and malnourished child. Hunger and malnutrition epitomized the condition of underdevelopment in a way that nothing else could do. The misery they induced in the small child was the impulse that conjured not only Unicef but literally hundreds of bodies with similar purposes into existence.

Yet assuring the hungry and malnourished child enough to eat, not just today but every day, turned out to be the most complex of all the things these organizations were trying to do. As each new initiative deplored the failures that went before, it gradually went through a process of discovering that the presence of food on a child's metaphorical plate or in their family's metaphorical larder depended on an endless multiplicity of factors which, however frequently they were re-arranged and re-interpreted, always ended up in one configuration: poverty.

Only when poverty ended would the threat of hunger and malnutrition finally vanish; but in the meantime the hungry child could not wait. For an organization such as Unicef the puzzle of what to do about the hungry and malnourished child was, therefore, how to find ways of tackling some of the many factors— food quantity, food quality, food storage, food preservation, food preparation, food consumption, knowledge and skills in all these areas— without first solving the problem of poverty.

The discipline for addressing the combination of these factors was nutrition. One thing that WHO, FAO and Unicef had been trying to do from the early 1950s onwards was to boost the image of nutrition itself. Nutrition was described in many a UN document as 'the bedrock of health', without which no sweeping prophylactic campaigns against disease and no maternal and child welfare activities would have much effect. Yet for all the rhetoric, nutrition was normally treated as an insignificant kind of subject, associated in the public mind with dieticians and vitamin pills. Depending on academic fashion, nutrition was passed around from the medical practitioners to the agriculturalists, to the social workers, to the economists; but wherever it landed— often half in and half out of many places at once— it tended to occupy a back seat.

With the advent of the new ideas of the late 1950s— 'community development', 'multidisciplinary responses'— nutrition finally came into its own. Hunger and malnutrition were the classic problems requiring a package of interlocking ingredients delivered by a combination of different players.

As far as Unicef's assistance was concerned, nutrition had already moved through the gamut of milk conservation, social welfare, MCH, school meals, education, dairy development and food technology. In 1959, a new kind of nutrition programme won approval: the actual cultivation of the protein and vitamins— in eggs, fish, fruits, green leafy vegetables— which the small child so badly needed. Support for 'applied nutrition' placed a heavy emphasis on training professional and auxiliary workers in how to balance carbohydrates with proteins, vitamins and minerals. Nonetheless its accompaniment— support for growing the ingredients in gardens, ponds and poultry houses— met with resistance from those who believed that agriculture was an economic activity and had little to do with helping children. The logic of applied nutrition was, however, inescapable: if Unicef funds could support the blending of legumes or fish into a manufactured weaning food, then why not the local cultivation of the legumes or the fish so that the mothers could do the blending themselves.

The community development pattern launched in India during the second Five-Year Plan (1956–61) provided applied nutrition with its test tube. In 1960, the year after India introduced a new administrative tier— the community development 'block' of around 100 villages— an experimental nutrition programme began in 240 villages located in thirty-two blocks of Orissa State. A communal poultry unit, school vegetable garden and fish 'tank' were planned for every village; poultry hatching units and veterinary services were provided at block level. Among the many items which Unicef provided were tube-well linings and hand pumps for water supplies, garden tools and seeds, poultry incubators and fishing nets. The community development staff of Orissa drew upon agricultural, fisheries and animal husbandry extension services, as well as education, health, and public information services, to help co-ordinate activities. This programme, which became a national blueprint for tens of thousands of Indian villages, provoked considerable excitement both within India and internationally from nutrition's growing band of professional enthusiasts.

Whatever else the school and village council might decide to do with the produce, some part of the fish, eggs, fruits, pulses and green leafy vegetables planted and nurtured in ponds, hutches and gardens was intended for a nutritious extra daily meal for the community's under-fives. Here was the classic pattern of support to supplementary feeding: a short-term investment intended to set in motion a long-term activity.

Many of the villages were already recipients of skim-milk powder from Unicef, so the idea of organizing a special meal for the children was not unfamiliar. As the gardens began to yield, the milk powder was to be replaced by local ingredients. From the point of view of the villagers, the difference was important: the milk powder simply materialized, but chickens would not lay nor gardens grow without effort from themselves. The fact that they could produce a surplus and make a profit was an incentive to make the effort; but there were questions about whether it would be a sufficient incentive and, if it was, whether the attraction of profit might not deprive the under-fives of their special portion.

The Orissa nutrition schemes were cajoled into existence with little difficulty: the response of many villages was spectacular. Local landowners gave land, the schools planted gardens, and the village—often the youth club—dug fish tanks. The poultry houses, initial stock of hens and feed and the salary of an attendant were paid for by the local government until such time as the units became self-supporting. But the critical factor in the success of the Orissa experiment was the involvement of the women—their women's clubs—the *mahila samiti*—the women village workers, the auxiliary staff known as *gram sevikas* working in teams in each block. The *mahila samitis* saw to it that food from the gardens and poultry units was used for the preschool children; they also began to take an interest in the importance of nutrition, dropping some of their old resistance to certain types of food and introducing different menus into the meals in their own homes. When visitors saw children of different castes sitting and eating together in the *balwadis*—the preschools, and the crowds of enthusiastic women of all ages attending training camps, they felt that they were truly witnessing the erosion of social and psychological fetters. In 1963, Unicef agreed to support an expansion of the programme in several other Indian States, and in subsequent years repeated its support. The story of applied nutrition in India had only just begun.

By the end of the 1950s, at the end of the first decade of international effort to come to terms with the endemic condition known as underdevelopment, and on the threshold of the first official development decade, great changes were in the air. In Africa, the tide of independence was running strong; in the Western world, a new and optimistic era was about to open in international relations; in what was becoming the international development community, new links were being forged across disciplines and sciences, and between them. The whole field of social and economic co-operation was opening up. In November 1959, Maurice Pate wrote a letter to around

100 of his staff seeking their views in answer to a question: *Quo Vadis?*. Unicef was in a process of metamorphosis. In the era of 'development', what role should it try to play in improving the well-being of a mother and her child?

Main sources

Unicef Executive Board documentation; reports of the WHO/Unicef Joint Health Policy Committee; reports of the Executive Board; studies on MCH development undertaken by WHO; statements by Sam Keeny and Charles Egger to the Unicef Executive Board.

Unicef Information Publications, including *Unicef News*.

Unpublished History of Unicef by John J. Charnow and Margaret Gaan, Unicef 1965.

Interviews with current and retired Unicef staff members and others associated with Unicef undertaken by the Unicef History Project, 1983–85.

Chapter 8

Development and the 'Whole' Child

In January 1961 the United Nations resolved that the decade of the sixties would be the Decade of Development. The actual declaration was made by President John F. Kennedy, the contemporary figure who most personified the new spirit in international affairs. The first US President since Harry Truman to identify himself closely with the fate of people in under-developed countries, Kennedy went to the UN General Assembly immedi-ately after his inaugural address to launch the first Development Decade.

The declaration was an expression of commitment to a new framework of international economic relations, a framework which took account of a Third World. This term designated a group of countries trying to assert a political and psychological distance from the Old World and the New, belonging neither to the Western alliance nor the Eastern bloc. This new force in geopolitics had begun to stir in the early 1950s, making its formal entry onto the world stage in April 1955 when President Sukarno of Indonesia invited the leaders of twenty-nine African and Asian countries to a conference in Bandung. The occasion midwifed the political association of the 'non-aligned'; the standing of its leading figures—men such as Jawaharlal Nehru of India and Kwame Nkrumah of Ghana—helped to unleash a tide of sentiment in favour of countries emerging from a status of dependence on the old Imperial powers and taking on the character of new nation-states.

The process was at its most dramatic in Africa. During the late 1950s, the 'winds of change'—a phrase immortalized by Prime Minister Harold Macmillan of Britain—blew down the continent in stormy gusts. As the appetite among African peoples for political independence steadily grew, the British, French and Belgian colonial authorities began to withdraw. By the end of the decade, the exit of the European powers had gathered such speed that what less than a century ago had been the European scramble to gain possession of large chunks of territory on the continent was now mirrored by a scramble to give them up.

The United Nations, where Dag Hammerskjold had raised high the flag in support of the self-determination of African peoples, provided a useful brokerage service for the elaboration of constitutions and other necessary handover arrangements. The watershed year was 1960, which, at the UN,

191

was known as The Year of Africa: fourteen former French colonies, the Belgian Congo, Somalia and Nigeria all achieved independence, and UN membership. Within the next few years, most of the rest followed suit. At the end of the critical phase of decolonization, only a few bastions of colonial power remained, mostly in the southern part of the African continent.

Decolonization changed the course of international affairs, altering not only the geographical, political and strategic map, but setting up new vibrations between the nations. It was a period of excitement and hope, a time in which the new kinds of links being forged within the community of free peoples were full of promise that the age of international peace and prosperity was finally at hand. The sense of euphoria was fuelled by the emergence of so many new countries and the sense that youthful vigour unfettered by the past was striding onto the world stage. But to emerge, the countries of the Third World must also develop.

In many, industrialization was still in a primitive phase. The majority of their populations—which together outstripped those of both the other 'worlds'—lived in grinding poverty. They must shake off this poverty along with their colonial status, and to do so they needed capital resources and technical know-how from their richer world neighbours. Thus was born the push for development, a concept which embraced moral and humanitarian fervour along with more conventional notions of political self-determination, investment and materialist expansion.

The UN provided a forum where these new dynamics gained strength. There, the newly independent nations had as much a right to prime time as the geopolitical heavyweights, and their new brand of rhetoric offered a welcome reprieve from that of East-West confrontation. The network of UN organizations had been founded in a burst of almost religious faith that the Allied powers could, through its offices, forestall another global conflagration. At a time when war wounds were fresh and the international climate still very volatile, the most important means of preventing war were seen as diplomacy, disarmament and international peace-keeping. But the almost immediate division of the Allies into two camps upset these prospects. The war in Korea, in which the US invoked UN patronage, revealed its inherent limitations as a peace-broker, and its reputation in that context never truly recovered. Other methods for keeping peace in the world therefore began to gain in importance just as the process of decolonization was gathering momentum.

Against the wishes of the colonial powers, who had reluctantly given in to pressure from the US and the British Dominions, the charter establishing the world body had also talked of 'the equal rights and self-determination of peoples', and of the UN's role in promoting higher standards of living and 'solutions of international economic, social, health and related problems' (Article 55).

During the 1950s, the major preoccupation within the UN shifted from international co-operation for mutual security to something very much broader but closely related: international co-operation for an assault on hunger, disease, poverty, economic instability and all the socially and economically disruptive forces likely to give rise to national and international turmoil. In the late 1940s and early 1950s the UN began to flesh out the organs it had devised for this part of its purpose.

Two types of co-operation were envisaged: a transfer of modern scientific know-how, and a transfer of financial resources. The principal sources of the know-how were the UN's specialized agencies, whose task was to tap the best advice and latest technology in a given field and put it at the disposal of member nations in the form of technical assistance.

The specialized agencies had originally been conceived more as universities than as operational consultancies, and they took time to adapt to the challenges facing them in the era of decolonization. All were autonomous from the UN proper with their own charters and governing structures. Coherent co-ordination for the attack on world poverty was not easy. Nonetheless, they were the repositories within the international community of the best scientific and technical wisdom the age could muster, and their usefulness in the new development scenario was therefore self-evident.

Other institutions designed to boost the role of the UN in the provision of technical assistance also began to emerge. In July 1950 the Economic and Social Council, itself in the process of assuming greater importance, set up a mechanism for co-ordinating technical assistance and gathering more resources behind it. This body, the Expanded Programme of Technical Assistance (EPTA), represented a joint operation of the UN and several of the specialized agencies, including FAO, ILO, WHO and UNESCO. The funds provided to EPTA by member countries were supplementary to the independent budgets of the specialized agencies although utilized through them; the effect of a common fund was to promote more co-operation and a greater interlocking of their affairs.

In the mid-1950s, an attempt to create a Special UN Fund for Economic Development (SUNFED) foundered because the industrialized countries had no desire to furnish large sums of money to a strong international development authority whose activities they could not control. Here was another indicator of the inherent limitations on what kind of responsibilities the nations were jointly prepared to take on or give up on each other's behalf. In 1957, with the SUNFED proposal still deadlocked, and awareness growing that something more was needed to respond to the economic plight of the up-and-coming parts of the world, a proposal for an alternative joint mechanism, the UN Special Fund, managed to gain approval. Over the course of the next six years, the Special Fund harnessed $450 million for what was called 'pre-investment'—the thorough checking of what seemed like good ideas for developing fisheries or forests, foundries or factories before taking the plunge and going ahead with the project in question. EPTA and the Special Fund placed the UN squarely in the forefront of international co-operation for development, partly thanks to the brilliant leadership provided respectively by an Englishman, David Owen, and an American, Paul Hoffman. The two organizations were the joint forerunner of the UN Development Programme, into which they were merged in 1966 under the leadership of the same two principals.

The mechanism within the UN system for the second type of transfer— capital investment—was the International Bank for Reconstruction and Development. The IBRD, usually known as the World Bank, was set up in 1945 by the international conference which met at Bretton Woods in the US; it was conceived as one means of helping countries to avoid the depressions of the 1920s and 1930s, such potent causes of international tension and breeding grounds for war. The task of the World Bank was to advance loans for projects of importance to a country's overall development; but the terms on which it made loans were not suited to the rather special purpose of investment in countries whose stage of development meant that returns and repayments would not be quickly forthcoming.

Two years later, in 1947, came the US Marshall Plan for European postwar recovery, in which for the first time large injections of public funds were used on concessionary terms to assist sovereign nations with economic regeneration. The invention of 'aid' and its successful application set a precedent; there was even talk of other US 'Marshall Plans' for Asia and Latin America, but the model was unsuitable for parts of the world where initial construction, not reconstruction, was needed.

Meanwhile, as the SUNFED proposal remained grounded, the underdeveloped countries clamoured even more loudly for better access to concessionary finance for major development projects. In 1959, a World Bank affiliate was created: the International Development Association. The IDA offered loans for similar types of projects as those supported by the World Bank, but on particularly 'soft' terms: low or no interest, and long repayment schedules.

Without the support of the US in the new, evolving and expanding international mechanisms for technical assistance and financial investment—and the identification of US foreign policy goals with economic security in the new nations—the movement for international development would have been stillborn. At the turn of the 1960s, as President Kennedy stepped into the White House with a vision of US support to free economically struggling peoples as the underpinning of world peace, US policy was as vital a precondition of the declaration of the first Development Decade as any careful build-up of UN and other multilateral channels.

Development was an idea whose time had come, and 'aid' from the better-off countries to the poorer was the means to bring development about. To many people, the twin ideas of aid and development were charged with idealism and recompense; they were the means of effecting economic stability and social opportunity in a just and peaceful world. In particular, aid through the unbiased multilateral machinery of the UN seemed an instrument untainted by any blemish of national self-interest of a strategic, political or economic kind, less easily applied with any other goal in mind than improvement in the human condition.

That such improvements were very much needed was beginning to penetrate the mass mind of the public in the industrialized world, courtesy of the spread of communications. Throughout the 1950s, North America and Europe had experienced uninhibited economic and material growth. With mass prosperity in the air, many of those tuned into the international network were stricken by the contrast presented by average living conditions in Asia, Africa and most of Latin America. The spectacle of misery and rural stagnation was familiar to those who had served overseas in their country's armed forces, to diplomats, colonial servants, missionaries, explorers, and anthropologists. But until the age of development, it was not presented in such terms.

Up to this time it was more usual—and this view was not confined to opinion in the Western world—to see the people of warrior tribes and ancient civilizations either as exotics or as primitives; perhaps as a source of fighting power or cheap labour; sometimes as the childlike subjects of missionary zeal. Great civilizations—in the Nile Valley, along the Indus and the Yellow River, in South America—had left their stamp on history, as explorers and archaeologists bore witness. But the societies they had created were outmatched in the crucible of modernization and therefore inferior.

With the advent of the first Development Decade, people in industrialized countries began for the first time to think of the average villager in Asia or Africa as a real person with the same rights and abilities as anyone else, only differing in that he lived in poverty, and that this poverty was susceptible to some kind of external intervention. In the contemporary state of understanding, the idea of social and economic opportunity for every human being with a toehold on the planet struck many people forcibly for the first time. It was a dramatic switch in human thinking.

The new lines of thought, in all their implications, demanded new efforts of study, research and policy formulation. In the years since the war, a new intellectual avant-garde had begun to analyze the root causes of under-development, had produced theories to explain the phenomenon, and had suggested means of overcoming it. Third World development was becoming an academic discipline, an off-shoot of economics and the social sciences, as well as a philosophy and a cause—a rallying cry for anticolonial political radicals and a focus for popular philanthropy. In its deepest sense, the movement for world development projected the idea of national social justice onto an international canvas and dreamed of a world made more humane by the rearrangement of wealth between the nations. The availability of aid, whatever form it took, was the context of a new international mutual benefit society. If resources of all kinds could be provided on a significant scale, so the reasoning went, the gap between the new prosperity of the industrialized countries and the poverty of the rest could speedily be narrowed.

When the UN declared the Development Decade in January 1961, and set a target of one per cent of gross national product for official Overseas Development Assistance (ODA) from every industrialized country, the idea that a decade would see the task almost through, fantastic as it now seems, did not then appear so far-fetched. Many a twentieth century miracle had been accomplished in less. No-one doubted the sense of urgency emanating from the developing countries or the commitment of their statesmen. The resources and political will were flowing. Within the international community, mechanisms for making it happen had evolved or sprung into life.

No organization which formed a part of that community could remain immune to the new currents of thinking, nor wish to stand to one side and leave the central mission of the era entirely to others. During the next few years, Unicef tried to absorb this maelstrom of ideas and events, and find its own niche in the story of international co-operation for development. The transformation it underwent in the process was the most critical in its history.

Unicef, unlike the specialized agencies with their technical expertise and the banks and Special Fund with their concessionary loans, was not a member of the group of agencies and organizations which loosely constituted the development club.

At the beginning of the Decade, most donors and recipients would not have thought of its operations as within the sightlines of the new perspective. Unicef was still mostly regarded as a benificent do-gooding organization which distributed goods to distressed mothers and children. The idea still prevailed that free imported supplies, even if they did solve problems of resource and foreign exchange shortage, could not claim more than a subsidiary developmental role.

No-one doubted that Unicef was a thoroughly good thing; practical, reasonably efficient, powered by disinterestedly humanitarian motivation. It had a reputation for expeditious supply procurement and delivery, a role still most visible at times of emergency. Its field and programme operations testified to a fine combination of missionary tradition with the new internationalism. But these attributes did not necessarily confer on it any role in development co-operation.

After more than ten years of activity in the developing countries, there were many who felt that Unicef's experience and institutional knowledge were more relevant to the mobilization for development than its image as an organization conveyed. The fields in which it was engaged—public health and nutrition—were at the heart of human development, even if they were usually to be found on national balance sheets in the debit column as a drain on resources rather than as a contribution. In several areas—drug and vaccine production, milk conservation, malaria eradication—Unicef's involvement had been developmental according to the standard definition of the term; and in the case of most disease campaigns and nutritional schemes the level of its investment had far exceeded that of either of its senior UN partners, WHO and FAO. Some of its resources had paid for technical advisers; others had been spent on supplies or equipment crucial to the existence of many projects whose mainstream development credentials were impeccable.

Unicef was a much more decentralized organization than the specialized agencies. The original reason for employing staff based in the countries receiving Unicef assistance had been to check that supplies went smoothly along the channels they were supposed to travel and reached the mothers and children for whom they were intended.

From the beginning of its operations most of Unicef's staff had been based in the 'field', and the representatives in country and regional offices had considerable autonomy and room for manoeuvre, not over policy itself but over its application as well. These aspects of its character were very different from the specialized agencies, most of whose expertise was located in their international or regional headquarters. During the fulfillment of their duties, Unicef's field officers had accumulated a good deal of wisdom and understanding about the face of Third World poverty. They had valid judgements to make about the design and execution of programmes, even if they ultimately depended on the finishing technical touches of experts, and they also had a much more continuous relationship than most specialized agency personnel with the government officials charged with day-to-day responsibility for administering them.

One of the critical features of the new way of looking at the problems of Third World poverty—a still somewhat shadowy feature in the early 1960s, but one coming gradually into clearer focus—was that lack of development could not be made good only by technical advice and cheap credit. Even supplemented in advance of project design by 'pre-investment', and following it by the provision of supplies, this formula for development co-operation was woefully inadequate. Problems of poverty have important political, social, cultural and administrative dimensions. Programmes to tackle the poverty of a given community, whether motivated by economic or humanitarian objectives, have to deal with many of the manifestations of poverty at once or each separate programme finds its own purpose frustrated. This was the lesson which had inspired the community development approach. It was a lesson to which Unicef, because of its decentralized institutional character, was privy at a relatively early stage. Some of those whose technical credentials were outstanding, but who did not have time to adapt their expertise to the local context, spent longer shaking off their preconceived ideas. In this, many officials in the newly-independent countries connived; they were keen to see their countries develop as fast as possible, and ideas about what this development should still look like reflected what passed for progress in Western industrialized society.

Unicef had no role to play in helping create mirror images of Western economic prosperity or social institutions. Its only interest was in finding ways to inject its resources where they might strategically do most for mothers and children. The vision of development it was keen to address was one in which the needs of the inheritors of the nations and the world— the children—took pride of place.

Elsewhere in the United Nations a different initiative for children began to make headway in the late 1950s. This was a protracted campaign to enunciate formally a Declaration of the Rights of the Child. The Universal Declaration of Human Rights, adopted by the UN General Assembly in 1948, singled out children for a special mention; but this provision had not satisfied the non-governmental lobby, which believed that it did not adequately reflect children's unique needs within the family of man.

The idea that children were individuals with rights of their own dated only from the nineteenth century. In most agricultural societies, particularly those living at the edge of subsistence, children were the least productive and therefore the most expendable members of the family. A child who died could be replaced; a weakling child was a drain on family and community. Early childhood therefore was often a survival course, in which the child received the least, rather than the most, food, care and consideration. Having weathered their first few years, children helped with household and agricultural chores to the extent of their ability from the time they could walk until the prescribed moment of maturity. At this juncture, marriage dictated the assumption of adult responsibilities and the cycle began again.

This situation still prevails in much of the rural developing world. Some children endured a far less benign upbringing; this, too, is not uncommon today in certain countries. In their helplessness against adult greed, sexual abuse, neglect or exploitation, children were—are—sometimes treated with great cruelty. The waif, the changeling, the foundling—words no longer in the vocabulary of Western child welfare—used to be familiar products of society. It was common to abandon children if unwanted; at the worst they might be sold into slavery, prostitution, or some other form of bondage.

In Europe and North America, the Industrial Revolution forced society to a reckoning with the fate of its children. Putting children to work at an early age to help support their families bore a very different complexion away from field, furrow, and the tough but not remorseless timetable of rural life. In Britain's mines and factories, children worked between twelve and fifteen hours a day for six days a week, usually in airless, unsanitary and confined conditions. Their bodies were stunted, their eye-sight impaired and their emotional repertory consisted of a catalogue of insults and savagery.

The sufferings of the children of the working poor prompted legal intervention on their behalf. Laws restricting their hours of labour and working conditions paved the way for others concerning their education and protection. As the century progressed, children were removed from adult prisons, special schools were opened for the handicapped and mentally retarded, orphanages run on caring and humanitarian principles were founded, and public education expanded. By the early twentieth century, rapid advances in medicine, nutrition and psychology in the countries reaping the benefits of scientific and technical modernization had fully established the fact that children were not simply miniature adults, but had special characteristics and needs of their own.

The chaos of the first World War was the genesis of the idea of the child above the political and military fray, the idea which underpinned the efforts by Herbert Hoover and others to deliver humanitarian aid to 'innocent victims' on both sides of a conflict. The attempt to carry the idea forward into a binding international agreement was initiated by Eglantyne Jebb, the Englishwoman who had defied the law on the basis that there was no such thing as an 'enemy child'.

In 1923, the organization she had set up in Geneva with the help of the International Committee of the Red Cross, the Save the Children International Union (SCIU), drafted and approved the first Declaration of the Rights of the Child. This marked the formal establishment of an international movement for children's rights. A year later, this document was adopted by the League of Nations and consecrated as the World Child Welfare Charter. The preamble to the Declaration repudiated once and for all the conventional wisdom of days gone by: 'Mankind', it stated, 'owes to the child the best that it has to give'. It was a simple document with five clauses, demanding for the child the means for material, moral and spiritual development; special help for the hungry, sick, handicapped and orphaned; first right to relief in times of distress; training to earn a living and protection from exploitation; and an upbringing which would instill in the child a sense of duty towards society.

In 1946, after the second World War, SCIU was merged with the International Association for the Promotion of Child Welfare into the International Union for Child Welfare (IUCW), a non-governmental federation whose member organizations joined forces to exert pressure at the international level for children's rights. The IUCW began to lobby the Economic and Social Council of the newly formed United Nations to emulate its predecessor, the League, and to endorse the 1924 Declaration. ECOSOC consulted with member governments and the non-governmental organizations involved, and approval was given in principle, subject to modifications and additions which would give more weight to recent developments in the child welfare field. Various drafts emerged, but the question was put on hold in the early 1950s while other covenants on human rights were being formulated. In 1957, the Human Rights Commission of the UN took up the task of reconciling various proposals, which by this stage included the idea of a binding convention rather than simply a statement of principle. In November 1959, they finally brought to the UN a new version of the original Geneva Declaration.

The 1959 Declaration included directly or indirectly all the earlier provisions, and added substantially to them. The first principle prohibited any kind of distinction or discrimination against a child 'on the grounds of race, colour, sex, language, religion, political or other opinion, national or social origin, property, birth, or other status'. The new version also confronted the postwar problem of the child refugee: 'The child shall be entitled from his birth to a name and a nationality'. The other major change was a much fuller elaboration of the child's social needs, including his dependency on his family, and his mother's needs on his behalf. The preamble stated that by reason of his physical and mental immaturity, the child needs special safeguards and care 'before as well as after birth'. Principle Six endorsed his need for love and understanding 'for the full and harmonious development of his personality', and emphasized the family as the best context for his upbringing. His rights to adequate nutrition, housing, recreation and medical services were specified, and principle Seven was devoted to his educational needs: 'He shall be given an education which will promote his general culture, and enable him on a basis of equal opportunity to develop his abilities, his individual judgement, and his sense of moral and social responsibility, and to become a useful member of society'.

The unanimous adoption by the UN General Assembly of the Declaration of the Rights of the Child represented another step forward in the continuing story of raising children and their needs higher on the national and international agenda. Unicef did not take any major part in the elaboration of the Declaration or in helping ease its passage; it took the position that helping with implementation, particularly in the fields of health, nutrition and welfare, was where its strengths and interests lay. The UN General Assembly, in its accompanying resolution, affirmed that aid provided by Unicef constituted a practical means of international co-operation to promote the Declaration's aims.

From the point of view of children's protagonists, the Declaration of the Rights of the Child was an important expression of principle. Hunger, poverty, disease and ignorance endured by countless children in the developing countries had been identified as an abrogation of their rights. A holistic view of the child as a creature with a complex of special but interlocking needs, and the right to have those needs addressed, was gaining international ground and intellectual recognition. The thinking simultaneously taking place in Unicef around the theme of children and development was converging in the same direction.

Maurice Pate's Quo Vadis? letter to professional staff all around the world asking for their views on where Unicef was going, rightly or wrongly was sent out in the same month as the passage of the Declaration of the Rights of the Child. For the past two or three years, what Pate described as a 'powerful ferment of ideas' had been stirring, and he hoped that an exercise in organizational soul-searching might reduce tensions at what was to prove a watershed in Unicef's career.

The 'ferment' was fuelled mainly by two individuals: Dick Heyward and Georges Sicault. Sicault, lately Director-General of Health Services in Morocco, joined Unicef in 1956 and became Deputy Executive Director for Planning in 1957. He brought a seasoned, pragmatic grasp of programme realities, an intellect unburdened by the restraints of orthodoxy, and a distinguished record in public health. Like Heyward, he was deeply caught up in the philosophical currents of the time, and his influence on policy development during the course of the next few years was decisive.

The most powerful of the new ideas was the perception of people's needs as interlocking parts of a puzzle, necessarily to be met only by interlocking responses. The theory of community development was that a multipronged programme with complementary ingredients could tackle the poverty problem of an entire community. By the same token, the interlocking problems affecting children could only be addressed by a mix of complementary ingredients; and as children were not a socially separate group, but intimately dependent on their families and the wider community, interlocking programmes for children must also interlock with those for other family members and the community at large.

The previous ten years of experience in the poorer countries had shown that it was not only very difficult to compartmentalize children's needs, but positively counter-productive. Therefore, according to the vision slowly edged forward by Heyward and Sicault, the needs of the 'whole' child must be taken into account, in the context of the needs of parents, teachers, nurturers and mentors. Unicef must gradually be steered into functioning as if the child was something other than a set of parts, only a few of which were Unicef's concern.

The immediate stumbling block to the realization of this way of seeing things was that certain categories of activity on behalf of children were ineligible for its assistance. The most conspicuous of these was education. The General Assembly resolution establishing Unicef in 1946 had laid down that aid might be given for 'child health purposes generally'.

As the years had gone by, this had been treated very much as a *tabula rasa* on which Unicef's Executive Board might write what it chose, and the definition had proved conveniently elastic. It did not, however, extend to slate, chalk, blackboard, classroom drill or any ingredient of formal schooling. Apart from the family, the school was the social institution with the most influence on the formation of the child, and the shedding of ignorance and superstition was a critical pre-condition of development. Nonetheless, there was considerable resistance to viewing education as within the spirit of 'child health purposes generally'.

In September 1958, it was suggested for the first time to the Executive Board that Unicef should in principle be as willing to promote the intellectual as the physical well-being of the child. The suggestion, made by the delegate of Pakistan, sparked off a controversy between those who had become convinced of the need to consider the 'whole' child in the context of the development of the whole community, and those who regarded Unicef as having a deliberately narrow humanitarian focus which must be fiercely defended from the heresy that children's needs were indistinguishable from those of the wider society.

Up to this point, the theme of interlocking elements within programmes had been exclusively articulated in terms of child health and nutrition programmes. Supplies must interlock with training; both must interlock with technical and logistical expertise. Good weaning practices must interlock with disease control, and both with MCH services. Now, at the suggestion that health and nutrition should interlock with education, the Executive Board baulked. Education in the form of stipends for traditional birth attendants and women's club leaders, or flip-charts with pictures of foods for lectures on nutrition, was one thing. Formal schooling was quite another. Opponents believed that the scant resources available for programmes—in the region of $25 million a year—could not possibly be put to any effective use in primary education.

The schools of just one large developing country would devour the entire amount at a gulp and show little for doing so. Their very inclusion within the categories of Unicef assistance would raise expectations impossible to satisfy, it was reasoned. In spite of the fact that UNESCO supported the notion of working with Unicef in much the same co-operative relationship as was already established with WHO and FAO, the spectre of overlap was raised. The view prevailed that it would be better for Unicef to persevere single-mindedly with its mandate for relieving child hunger and disease, problems for which complete solutions were still far distant.

The battle over whether or not Unicef should assist primary education was a battle about principle. Even the most convinced supporter of the new thesis did not anticipate a sudden rush of projects for classroom extensions and curriculum reform, nor the substitution of cargoes of first-grade primers for skim milk powder. But they did feel that the school classroom and everything academically associated with it should not be categorically excluded from support. Contemporary opinion attached a very high degree of importance to education as the key to economic development. Many Third World countries were not able to absorb large injections of capital because they were not yet equipped with a sufficiently large administrative class or the trained manpower to use it effectively. Education was the magic ingredient which would build up the 'human capital'. This notion of people as a natural resource, like a rich lode of ore waiting to be turned into a profit on investment, was very widespread. Development should give priority to human-capital formation; skills and expertise, conferred by professional diplomas and university degrees, were the building blocks of prosperity.

Such idioms infiltrated even Unicef phraseology. 'Children are a country's most precious resource' was the catch phrase which summarized the new outlook. Unicef's unwillingness to invest intellectually as well as physically in this 'precious resource' weakened its claim to champion the interests of the 'whole' child.

On their side, the developing countries were passionately keen on education in any and every shape and form. Education was the golden passport to a new life. Everywhere, people were hungry for learning. It was not only the economists and theoreticians who saw education and training as magic ingredients, but ordinary people in the town or the village who saw what a white-collar did to transform a man's fortunes. In Africa in particular, where learning institutions were thinnest on the ground, the appetite for education amounted to a craving. Many countries came to independence with no more than a handful of secondary school graduates, let alone the university variety. Maurice Pate, commenting on the UN's Year of Africa, told the Unicef Executive Board: 'Africans everywhere aspire to a future which, they feel, must inevitably be of their own making. ... It has become increasingly clear that the emphasis in future development plans will be on education, and on economic activities which will contribute to increasing the production potential'. Whatever reservations some of Unicef's leading government donors might feel, the demand from the developing countries for support to education was becoming very difficult to resist by the early 1960s. While international fora resounded with talk of the self-determination of peoples, to refuse to respect a country's own set of priorities for solving their children's problems was distinctly out of tune with the times.

The Quo Vadis? inquiry suggested a key to the problem. Out of 'the powerful ferment of ideas', one emerged which had particular appeal: to find out what the priorities for children were in different countries by carrying out a special survey. Ten years had elapsed since Unicef was directed by the General Assembly to focus its attention on the children of the developing world. Since that time policies had evolved on a pragmatic basis, sometimes with more regard to what the major donors and the leading technical experts of the day thought the priorities for children ought to be than to the priorities defined by those on the spot. This could on occasion produce quite bitter stand-offs between those immersed in the day-to-day realities—field staff who took their cue from local officials and ordinary people out in the villages—and those in the policy-making strata in Unicef and the specialized agencies who ultimately called the tune.

As general guidelines, the policies might be sound. But they might also be inhibiting Unicef from addressing critical issues which fell, deliberately or otherwise, outside their scope. There was a fine line between making sure that government officials and field staff knew how to design a project so that it would qualify for Unicef's co-operation and dictating to those government officials what was or was not a suitable project for them to set up. A survey on children's needs throughout the developing world, carried out in co-operation with the countries themselves and with the specialized agencies, would provide a proper basis for review. It would also help to re-weight the process of designing projects away from Unicef's centre.

There were some doubts when the proposal for such a survey was first put to the Executive Board in March 1960. Those who resisted felt that such an undertaking would be expensive, and that its findings were bound to raise expectations among governments for amounts of aid which Unicef would not be able to satisfy. Pate reassured the delegates that the survey would not be exhaustive, and that it would be carried out within Unicef's existing capacity. Among those delegates who warmly endorsed the idea were the Swedes; they had for some time been suggesting that Unicef's method of co-operation was much too piecemeal. Here was the coherent rethink for which they had been pressing.

The Survey on the Needs of Children was organized by Georges Sicault, and it took a year to complete. It was the turning point in a complete revision of Unicef's outlook on how to help the world's children. It was accompanied by state-of-the-art reports from the specialized agencies: the health needs of children (WHO), the nutritional needs of children (FAO and WHO), the educational needs of children (UNESCO), the social welfare needs of children (Bureau of Social Affairs), the labour needs of children (ILO); and by reports from twenty-four different countries (two of which were carried out with the assistance of the International Children's Centre), and two from other international children's organizations: the Inter-American Children's Institute in Montevideo, and the International Union for Child Welfare.

The Unicef report set out to prove the case for considering the needs of children within national development plans. Although its primary purpose was to analyze children's needs and make recommendations for practicable action, its intellectual scope was far broader. Children should not be the orphans of the development process; they should be a target of all policies and programmes directed at building up a country's human capital. The report interwove all the relevant social and economic strands concerning children's well-being in a way which had never been done before. A theory of development was presented in which the satisfaction of children's needs during the various phases of childhood and pre-adulthood mattered deeply. 'Children first' had gained currency during the past fifty years as a motto for times of war and sudden catastrophe. Now Unicef was articulating a new version of the same motto in the context of national development.

The report was presented to the Executive Board by Maurice Pate in June 1961, six months after the declaration of the Decade of Development. More resources from both multilateral and bilateral sources were becoming available for capital investment in developing countries. Unicef's task for the Decade therefore would be to try to ensure that a reasonable share of these resources were used to improve the well-being of children in an integrated and effective form.

Any new project should be planned and phased as a part of a broader multisectoral programme, itself part of a national plan for meeting children's needs. This thesis had implications for Unicef's own operational character: if governments were expected to look at the needs of their children in this light, Unicef would have to do the same. Many countries attached a high priority to certain activities—schooling, for example—which did not currently fall within approved categories of co-operation. It would hardly be consistent for Unicef to argue for pinpointing children's needs within a comprehensive plan and itself be willing to respond only in certain pre-determined areas. Therefore, as part of the new approach, the Executive Board was asked to agree to support virtually any kind of strategic inter-vention on children's behalf as long as it met a priority need. Unicef should also be willing to assist governments in establishing such needs, and be ready to support any part of the plan that emerged within which its advice, supplies or training stipends would usefully fit.

The new approach was greeted with favour. Many of the more influential Board members had been sounded out in advance, and the time was ripe for its acceptance. Those who had previously expressed reservations about moving into education—the US, the UK, Australia—now gave their approval for change. Although the thesis was advanced against a broad backcloth, the institutional changes proposed were actually quite modest.

Much of the existing checklist of questions against which project proposals were judged would remain extant; but a wider range of proposals would be considered, and commitments could be made to several interrelated projects at once, over a period spanning not just one year but several. There would be less stringent demands on governments to commit capital resources to projects several times the value of Unicef's own inputs; this matching principle had been devised for the circumstances of postwar Europe as a benchmark of a recipient government's long-term commitment to a programme, but was inhibiting programme development in the developing countries. There would be more flexibility about paying local costs, particularly where these were incurred in association with training.

Unicef would not only help finance surveys on children's needs, but would also be willing to offset some of the costs of thorough project preparation. Where there was a shortage of a particular expertise needed for planning or carrying out a programme, in the future Unicef could sponsor the services of technically qualified staff assigned to the government department in question. This was a step away from exclusive dependency on the experts of the specialized agencies. All in all, these changes reflected Unicef's quest for greater autonomy, its growing self-confidence as an organ of international co-operation, and its desire to make its funds go to work quickly at the pressure points in the development of better children's services.

The June 1961 Executive Board session was a turning point. Although the disease campaigns and the milk conservation programmes were still in operation and would remain so, the peak of their importance was psychologically past. From now on the emphasis would be on things which were less spectacular, more lasting and conceived in tandem with one another. Most of Unicef's staff, field representatives especially, were delighted. Maurice Pate and his senior colleagues, by taking their time, by treading cautiously and in harmony with their most important government backers, had negotiated the organization into the Development Decade. During the 1950s, it had discarded its original character as a carefully proscribed operation for child relief; now it was beginning a second metamorphosis from a humanitarian and welfare organization to an international mechanism for development co-operation.

When the organizations of the UN system began to address the problems of world poverty and underdevelopment in the early 1950s, one of the words that joined their vocabulary was 'infrastructure'. By infrastructure, they meant the architecture of society. Underdevelopment was a condition characterized by the absence of a recognizable social architecture.

The limits of any scheme promoting development are defined by the availability of social institutions into which a seed can be implanted and expected to bear fruit. Disaster creates its own institutions: the refugee camp, the temporary shelter, places where victims of war or famine flock to receive relief aid—institutions which are almost by their nature antithetic to self-help, operating in an artificial crisis-induced environment. Development, on the other hand, has both to create the kind of institutions which are organic to daily life, and cannot take place unless they are there. In the poorest society, the infrastructure—schools, roads, police stations, hospitals, factories, courts, town halls, social welfare agencies—is weak or non-existent and touches the lives of the fewest people. Any organization trying to help a society 'develop', can only bring its aid to bear on the poorest at the rate at which the society itself reaches out to them. In under-developed countries, this process can take a generation or more. And parts of it may not be at the top of a country's priorities, or simply cannot be undertaken before a great many other things have been 'developed' first.

The tension between obvious need in the form of acute poverty, high infant mortality rates, illiteracy, hunger and malnutrition and the lack of an institutional framework through which to meet those needs constitute what could be called the development trap.

In the post-colonial era, as this tension became more acutely felt, the need to build up a social and economic infrastructure became the theme of the development fraternity. Its absence, especially in large parts of Africa, was a source of great frustration to those trying to reach the poor. Without roads, transport, marketing arrangements, communications and administration, there was no way into a society, physically or metaphorically.

The development trap prompted a variety of reactions from those trying to find a way to release the spring. Some leaders of newly-independent countries were too impatient to wait for the infrastructure to grow, solidly, organically, at whatever painfully slow generational pace a country's treasury and international credit-rating would allow. They wanted development now, and so did their people, to whom they had made a political promise to deliver it. Artificial infrastructures were slapped down upon societies, politically enforced in the hope that short-term turmoil would quickly abate under the persuasive influence of their rewards.

Among the international funding organizations, there were many apostles of development who tried to compensate for the lack of an infrastructure by putting in their own organizational network to bypass or overtake halting and often inefficient official institutional growth. Here, the theory was that the self-evident benefits that ensued would twist the arm of government to take them over at a later date. Often these hopes were built on sand. How to force the pace of infrastructural expansion, with few resources and without creating something alien and resented by those who were meant to benefit, was a problem whose outlines gradually sharpened as the Development Decade progressed. At the beginning of the Decade, faith rested in the trinity of capital transfers, technical transfers and economic growth. The benefits of increased prosperity would, in time, trickle down to the poor through infrastructures they erected on the way.

So at least the theory ran.

At the beginning of the 1960s, the word infrastructure was mostly used to denote the physical features conventionally regarded as key ingredients of a modern economy: hydroelectric dams, industrial plant, cement factories, arterial highways, ports, railroads, cash-crop plantations, sewage and water works, universities and hospitals. This was the kind of infrastructural development which chiefly pre-occupied both the developing countries themselves, and most of the institutions developed by the UN and its member countries for the purpose of transferring resources from the rich world to the poor.

Humanitarian organizations such as Unicef whose sole focus was the poor and the vulnerable took up the issue of infrastructure from a different direction. Their concern was the social architecture at the level where the poor lived their lives: in the community, sometimes urban but usually rural, where even to apply the word 'community' tended to imply a far more sophisticated pattern of settlement and social organization than usually existed. Without some infrastructural network—schools, health centres, co-operative societies, women's clubs—there was nothing for the agents of progress to invest in, build onto, staff or equip.

During the 1960s, beginning with the Survey on the Needs of Children, Unicef tried in numerous ways to adapt its own culture and institutional style so as to help strengthen the range of social organizations at the community level which would enable children, especially pre-school children, to receive better care. Unicef itself, as an external funding organization, could never be a direct instrument for such a purpose; but it could fine-tune itself so as to be as responsive as possible to efforts designed by government departments and carried out by local officials towards that end.

The expansion in support of training schemes over the previous few years was one area in which Unicef had tried to help build up health and nutritional infrastructures; the growing enthusiasm for community develop-ment was another example of infrastructural emphasis. The changes in Unicef policy which first began to come about as a result of the 1960–61 Survey on the Basic Needs of Children, although they appeared superficially to be of a 'housekeeping' variety, were attempts to find a broader spectrum of ways to use Unicef's assistance to plug infrastructural nooks and crannies.

This was the underlying motivation behind the evolution towards the 'country approach': the design of a programme in which all the ways in which Unicef would co-operate in developing children's services—MCH, disease control, nutrition, social welfare, community development, edu-cation and training—were conceived as part of a whole, and negotiated as a package with the government in question. The same motivation was reflected in Unicef's enthusiasm for surveys on children's needs and, in circumstances where a country was short of necessary expertise, some of the costs of project preparation. It only took one short extra step to arrive at the concept which in 1962 emerged at the leading intellectual edge of Unicef's contribution to the Development Decade: planning to meet the needs of children.

In the era when development thinking was dominated by the economists and economic growth regarded as the precondition of all other manifestations of development—from the lowering of the infant mortality rate to the construction of schools and health centres—planning was the cardinal development discipline. Planning as the way to apply scarce national and international resources to problems of underdevelopment was being increasingly adopted by the developing countries, and was beginning to be demanded by external donors and creditors as a precondition for official aid. India was one of the first developing countries to adopt a succession of five-year plans. Many others followed suit. National plans laid down targets for economic and social development and defined the parameters for the allocation of national budgetary resources. If the plan was the arbiter, it was logical from Unicef's point of view that the masters of the plan were the point of leverage for influencing programme expenditures on children.

More important still was that, in the absence of co-ordinated national planning, policies thought to have nothing to do with children were actually having a profound, and sometimes negative, impact on their well-being. A country's ministry of agriculture might be busily engaged in bringing as much land under cash crop cultivation to raise export income, for example, while the ministry of health was preoccupied with providing clinical services to treat the consequences of hunger and malnutrition. If the planners looked at both policies in tandem, they might be able to ensure that the policy of raising export income was not over-emphasized at the price of the country's food production and the children's nutritional condition.

In June 1962, Unicef's Executive Board approved a declaration of policy for children in relation to the Development Decade which asserted the need to take children's and young people's interests into account when designing national development plans. The essence of this declaration was endorsed by special resolution of the UN General Assembly later in the year.

In October 1962, Edward Iwaszkiewicz, a Polish economist who had served with distinction in his country's Planning Commission, joined Unicef with a particular brief to incorporate the planning dimension into Unicef's work worldwide. Under the guidance of Iwaszkiewicz and a small staff of planners, momentum gathered behind the concept of 'Planning for Children'. Their main task was to convince governments that it was important to consider the needs of the 'whole' child within a comprehensive framework. To do this required that the idea be endorsed at an international level. Economists with national and international standing had to be persuaded that there were reasons far more cogent than sentiment or humanitarian concern for taking children's needs into account in the national scheme of things.

Iwaskiewicz was a skilful diplomat who knew how to promote the new thesis in the UN's regional economic commissions and among professionals and academics in research institutes in different parts of the world. Under his influence, together with that of Heyward and Sicault, Unicef began to spell out its new vision in a variety of fora.

An infusion of economic vocabulary entered Unicef's statements and publications, elaborating the notion of programmes for children as the creation of 'human capital': 'the key to self-sustaining growth is improvement in the quality of the oncoming generations'; 'economic development will be conditioned by the quality of the flow of young persons into the growth sectors of developing countries in the course of the next few decades'; 'of particular importance is the number of leaders they will produce for the extension of the development process'. Some of this language, so far removed from the inspiration for helping mothers and children in distress which many believed was the proper inspiration for a Unicef made some of Unicef's staff and Executive Board members a little uncomfortable. Not everyone was convinced that economic planning was the salvation of mankind.

The high point of articulation of the new thesis was reached at a round-table conference convened under Unicef's auspices at the Rockefeller Foundation Centre in Bellagio, Italy. Held in April 1964, the conference was called 'Children and Youth in National Development', and it was designed to put both Unicef and its vision on the planning map worldwide. It brought together a number of leading development economists and planning specialists—including Professors Jan Tinbergen, Alfred Sauvy and Hans Singer—and a high level of representation from developing countries: an indication of respect for the new axis of partnership in the post-colonial world.

The chairman of the conference was Professor V. K. R. V. Rao, a member of the Indian Planning Commission; also taking part were Tunisia's Secretary of State for Planning and Finance and Tanganyika's Minister for Development Planning. The planning expertise of the socialist countries was recognized by the presence of representatives from USSR, Poland and Yugoslavia. The dean of the Unicef Executive Board delegates, Professor Robert Debré of France, played a leading part. Two of the UN economic commissions sent high level observers, as did FAO, WHO, ILO and the Bureau of Social Affairs. From Unicef, Maurice Pate, Dick Heyward, Georges Sicault and Edward Iwaszkiewicz were the key participants, together with Professor Herman Stein of the Columbia University School of Social Work, an associate of Unicef's who acted as conference rapporteur.

For many of those connected with Unicef over the years, either on its staff or on its Executive Board, this round-table conference was the most important meeting in its seventeen-year history. Even those who were not entirely convinced by the swing of the pendulum which had led Unicef into planning and were still unsure about where it would lead appreciated the landmark the Bellagio Conference represented for an organization which had originally set out on the modest task of feeding children in postwar Europe.

It was a point of pride that Unicef could now sit down with senior government ministers and other luminaries and present its own development approach. In effect, Unicef was announcing in a nonconfrontational manner that it no longer wished to be regarded as very much the junior partner of the specialized agencies and other international development collaborators, and was presenting its credentials for joining the development club as a fully-fledged member.

In the succeeding years, the practice of seeking specialized agency approval for the technical aspects of projects supported by Unicef fell away, as did other arrangements for co-operation no longer suited to the changing relationships between Unicef and its fellow members of the UN family. The formal recognition by the system that Unicef was primarily a development rather than a humanitarian organization came eventually in 1972 when, for the first time, its annual report was considered in the Second Committee of the Economic and Social Council, on Economic and Financial Questions, rather than the Third, on Humanitarian and Social Affairs.

By the mid-1960s, the indivisibility of social and economic aspects of the problems of poverty and underdevelopment was becoming much more widely recognized. Unicef's new approach fitted this evolution of contemporary ideas. At the outset of the Development Decade, the conventional viewpoint saw planning principally as a tool for economic rather than social development. Where planning was a useful method for manipulating 'human capital', this was mainly because human resources were a necessary adjunct to productive capital investment. The educational, health and other social services which developed human capital and kept it in trim were obviously necessary from an economic point of view, and themselves required human resources and planners to deploy them. Gradually, however, this mechanistic view gave way to a better appreciation that human resources were not so easily manipulable to economic ends unless the framework within which they were to become so was convivial, and answered to their needs as human beings, family and community members. In this scenario, Unicef's suggestion that planning had as much to do with children as it did with irrigation works and public highways began to make more sense.

During childhood, Unicef pointed out, the adult was formed—physically, intellectually, and emotionally. Hitherto, any attention given specifically to children within the allocation of national budgetary resources had confined itself to the underprivileged and the handicapped, a kind of subspecies whose special problems the State addressed in default of their parents' and communities' capacities to do so. But all children had special problems, as recent generations of scientific inquiry had made clear. A national policy concerning children should therefore embrace the interests of all children, not just a few exceptional cases. And it should do so across all the appropriate sectoral lines—in health, education, agriculture, public works, labour and of course planning itself—not just within 'social affairs', always a poor relation when it came to command over resources. No-one was suggesting that children should become a sector of their own: children are an age group, not a discipline. But within the various sectors, their needs ought to be recognized not merely on humanitarian grounds, but on the grounds of society's own health and well-being, now and in the future.

The Bellagio round table was followed by similar conferences, held at levels progressively closer to programme planning design and implementation. In 1965 and 1966, conferences with similar agendas to the Bellagio meeting, were held in Santiago, for the Latin American region, and in Bangkok, for the Asian region. Both these conferences were jointly hosted with regional planning institutes and the respective UN Economic Commissions. In 1966, two less elaborate regional meetings were held to consider programmes for children and youth within national development in Africa—one in Paris for the French-speaking countries and one in Addis Ababa under the auspices of the Unicef Executive Board.

In 1967, Peru became the first country to organize a national conference along similar lines; other countries in Latin America and Asia, as well as the Arab States, began to follow suit. By 1969, it was becoming almost standard practice in certain Asian countries to undertake a systematic review of programmes for children and youth while discussing their next five-year plan. Iwaszkiewicz and his planning staff continued to reinforce their links with regional planning institutes, reimbursing faculties in Dakar and Bangkok for lecturers on social planning. At universities in both the industrialized and the developing world where development studies were being incorporated into the academic curriculae Unicef tried to identify allies who could help to gain intellectual respectability for the topic of children and youth in national development.

The last of the major Unicef-sponsored conferences on a similar theme was held in Lomé, Togo, in May 1972. The conference, in which ministers from eight francophone West African countries took part, was the final chapter in a three-year regional exercise to strengthen the countries' own capacities for planning for the needs of children. Unicef's Regional Director in Abidjan, Cheikh Hamidou Kane, previously Director of Senegal's Planning Commission, used his prestige to enlist the political backing of the heads of state in each country for this exercise. National studies on children, youth, women and economic development, inspired and partially financed by Unicef, were examined in an effort to define regional priorities for improving the lives of women and children.

In 1969, the year in which the Lomé studies were commissioned, Unicef reached the peak of its involvement in planning as a separate discipline. Iwaszkiewicz himself retired, and the small group of planners began to break up, absorbed into Unicef's regular programme staff.

At one level, they had worked themselves out of a job. The 'country approach' had been formally established as the required method of designing programmes in which Unicef's co-operation would play a part; and the idea of considering the needs of children and youth within national development plans had reached a degree of acceptability which meant that it was no longer necessary to have a special planning staff to make it happen. At another level, the elaboration of children's needs within national plans had not guaranteed that greater amounts of budgetary resources were put to meeting them. Planning was an important corrective of the haphazard methods of project formulation which had preceded its ascendancy; but it was by no means the master key for unlocking the development trap. Gradually, as the Development Decade drew to a close, that key was beginning to seem increasingly elusive.

The push for planning had served many purposes. The most important contribution it had made was to open up the debate about children and society, bringing within its range questions concerning children's rights, women's status, the break-down of traditional family structures, the forces that shape the 'good person' and encourage democratic values, as well as to give new emphasis to more conventional social issues of child health, nutrition and welfare. But in the end, it was extremely difficult to fuse all these elements together and describe a systematic planning method to deal with them.

With their endless ramifications and their overlaps into almost every branch of social and economic science, they escaped elaboration into a distinct set of principles. Perhaps the consciousness-raising effect was enough. Children as agents, and as symbols, of growth and change and a healthy society had gained a new legitimacy; so, in the eyes of many governmental and organizational collaborators, had Unicef itself.

The idea of meeting the priority needs of children as a target of national development plans had been a useful intellectual shock tactic. But in the fullness of its potential it was, and is, more of a dream than a reality.

Main sources

'Development Aid: A Guide to Facts and Issues', Leelananda de Silva; published by Third World Forum in co-operation with the United Nations Nongovernmental Liaison Service (Geneva).

The United Nations at Work, Joseph Marion Jones, Pergamon Press, Oxford 1965.

Unicef Executive Board; reports, summary records, progress reports to ECOSOC on Unicef's contribution to the Development Decade, etc. 1958–72.

'The Human Rights of Children', Cynthia Price Cohen; paper for a symposium on Children and the Law, reprinted in the Capital University Law Review, 1984; The United Nations and Human Rights, UN Department of Information, New York, 1984; International Child Welfare Review, Vol XXII, 1968.

'The Real Problems of Unicef', draft paper by E. J. R. Heyward, 15 December 1959; Unicef Quo Vadis? appraisal report, prepared by Sir Herbert Broadley, 1 April 1960.

Survey on the Needs of Children, ed. Georges Sicault, the Free Press of Glencoe, New York 1963.

'Children of the Developing Countries: a Report by Unicef', the World Publishing Company, Cleveland and New York 1963.

Interviews with past and present staff members, carried out by the Unicef History Project 1983–85.

'Planning for the Needs of Children in Developing Countries: Report of a Roundtable conference, April 1964, Bellagio, Italy, ed. Herman Stein, published by Unicef 1965.

40,000 Enfants par Jour: Vivre la Cause de l'UNICEF, Dr Francois Remy, Editions Robert Laffont, S.A., Paris 1983.

Settler children of
the Mahaweli
Development Project
in Sri Lanka
undertake some of
their studies
outdoors.
(*Unicef/Holbrooke*)

Children wander
aimlessly among
rubble in Wahdate
Camp, one of the
many refugee camps
in Amman, in Jordan,
1970. (*Unicef/Gerin*)

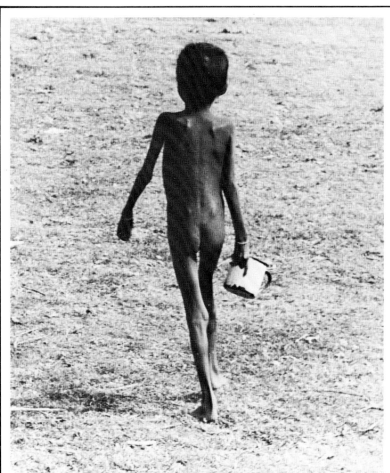

A boy and his ration cup. This malnourished child in drought-stricken India in 1974 is receiving a ration of milk at a special feeding programme. (*Unicef/Satyan*)

Food lines in Chimaltenango, Guatemala. On 4 February 1976, a massive earthquake killed 25,000 people and made a million homeless, including a half a million children. (*Unicef/Ling*)

A simple, dependable and maintainable water hand pump known as the India Mark II has been developed. These pumps have brought water supplies to thousands of previously-deprived communities. (*Unicef/Holbrooke*)

Collecting water consumes much of the time of rural women in the developing world. In Kenya, Kikuyu girls climb a steep hill to bring back their day's supply. (*Unicef/Matheson*)

A village co-operative sewing class in Ecuador. Children's well-being is affected not only by their mother's health and welfare, but by their ability to earn money too. (*Unicef/Wolff*)

A family planning lesson in the hills of Nepal. (*Unicef/Sassoon*)

Chapter 9

In a Popular Cause

Those who knew Unicef intimately in its early years often describe it as a family, with the benevolent patriarch, Maurice Pate, at its head. Throughout the 1950s, the numbers of its staff slowly increased along with the growth in income and programmes, but although its institutional form began to crystallize, its character did not radically change.

At a very early stage, Maurice Pate had obtained from the UN Secretary-General a certain amount of discretion in applying within Unicef the administrative rules and regulations of the UN system. These had been designed for a static Secretariat, chiefly servicing conferences and commitees. Pate, in contrast, was building an organization whose thrust was operational, and most of whose staff were based elsewhere. In addition, his personal dislike for bureaucratic nicety was intense; he belonged to the school of thought which holds that anything worth saying can be contained in a one-page memorandum. He relied a great deal on developing personal contacts, and he gave his senior staff considerable discretion in the exercise of their responsibilities. As a result of Pate's influence and organizational necessity, therefore, Unicef adopted a free-wheeling, decentralized type of organizational structure rather different from many other UN bodies whose locus of power rested absolutely in their headquarters.

By 1960, the number of staff on Unicef's payroll had risen to 426 from 275 at the beginning of the decade. Approximately half of them worked in twenty-nine field offices in Asia, Africa, eastern Mediterranean and Latin America, and most of the rest in either New York or Paris. Unicef's income had grown over the same period from $11·5 million to $26·5 million. The main government contributors were still the US, Canada and Australia; only $5 million altogether came from the European governments.

This was a lean organization with very modest resources to deploy on behalf of the millions of children of the developing world. Consciousness of the contrast between needs and funds available, coupled with the strong motivation of many of the first generation of Unicef employees, had established a tradition of frugal housekeeping. Pate spent freely from his own pocket in entertaining Board members and others who would be useful to the cause.

In the early days, before pay scales were systematically established and when Pate drew on his own network of friends and contacts to help him out, many people worked for a pittance, or on precarious short-term contracts with no guarantees of security. They were supposed to be buoyed by spirit and commitment—and they usually were. In the field, representatives expected staff to work six days a week, eschewed the pomp and circumstance UN status could have conferred, and kept their premises modest. The sense of mission was palpable, and it was the envy of other organizations within the UN system.

The zeal rubbed off. The most well-known recruit to Unicef's cause was the actor and comedian Danny Kaye. During a flight from London to New York, an airplane caught fire in mid-Atlantic and, in the hours while the plane limped back to the safety of Ireland, Maurice Pate took the opportunity to tell his fellow-passenger Danny Kaye all about Unicef. Something struck a chord with Kaye, whose gift for enthralling children both in person and on film had won him a worldwide reputation.

Some months after this chance encounter, a proposal was put to Danny that he take time out of an Asian holiday to visit some health and nutrition projects. He was entertained to lunch by UN Secretary-General Dag Hammerskjold, President of the UN General Assembly, Mrs Vijaya Lakshmi Pandit, and Maurice Pate. The idea emerged that he should take along a camera and a crew and film his encounters with the children of Asia. Paramount Pictures offered to underwrite the expense, release the result commercially, and donate the picture's profits to Unicef.

On the spring day in 1954 that Danny left on the first leg of his travels, Maurice Pate handed him a scroll at a crowded UN press conference, and appointed him Unicef's 'Ambassador at Large'. It was the first diplomatic mission of its kind. In later years two other entertainment personalities likewise became Unicef's 'ambassadors': Peter Ustinov and Liv Ullmann. Danny Kaye was the first, and the energy he threw into the role established the tradition.

The first film that Danny Kaye made for Unicef was called 'Assignment Children'. The project turned out to be one of those extraordinarily blessed ideas which confers delight on everyone. It set Danny en route to becoming 'Mr Unicef', the single most important personality in popularizing Unicef's name and endearing its cause to millions of people all over the world. His first port of call was New Delhi, where he was welcomed on home territory by Mrs Pandit, and attended a BCG vaccination session in a nearby village. From there he went to Burma, and joined DDT spray teams in a malaria control drive among the rice paddies. Then in Thailand he made friends with a small boy whose body was covered with the raspberry blotches of yaws. The tour wound up in Japan, where he spent an afternoon with 200 children from orphanages and nurseries who were regular Unicef milk drinkers.

The genius of the film was that the children—the stars, as Danny insisted, with himself in only a supporting role—were always laughing. Those who had asked what a comedian could contribute to the sad cause of endemic hunger and sickness among children in poor societies were given an answer: moments of sheer delight. His film showed that the appeal of children, however distant their home and however remote their predicament, was universal. Not only did it convey the parameters of Unicef's programme co-operation, but it did so with the charm and humour for which Danny Kaye was already so well-loved. He came back from the trip inspired to do much more. The Ambassador at Large put his talent to entertain at the disposal of the world's children through Unicef, and went on doing so for over thirty years.

During the course of the next two years, Danny appeared at gala launches for 'Assignment Children' in cities all over the world. The film was translated into eighteen languages, including Arabic, Danish, Hindi, Indonesian, Japanese, Mandarin, Persian and Tagalog. In 1954, at the prompting of the International Union of Child Welfare which was pushing for a UN Declaration of the Rights of the Child, the UN General Assembly declared that a Universal Children's Day should be celebrated in every country. In many countries, UN Associations found that Unicef—with Danny Kaye playing celluloid host for the world's children—was their most popular draw. In Australia, where the annual UNA Appeal for Children for many years raised more money for Unicef than any other nongovernmental source, cinema managements frequently showed the film as an accompaniment to the main feature, and took up collections for Unicef afterwards. Many years later, customers for greeting cards from the Unicef Australian Committee (established separately from UNA in 1966), described how their wish to help Unicef had first been inspired by 'Assignment Children'. Its worldwide audience was reckoned to have topped 100 million.

With this and other films and personal appearances, Danny Kaye helped to boost the fund-raising activities of many of Unicef's national affiliates— the national committees for Unicef—in the English-speaking parts of the world. By the late 1950s, the US Committee for Unicef, under the vigorous chairmanship of Helenka Pantaleoni, had flowered into a forceful campaigning network on behalf of the world's children. Although the fund-raising in which the Committee had been so reluctant to engage in its earliest days was now a purposeful activity, it was still very much perceived as incidental to the more important task of informing people about the conditions of life endured by less fortunate children in other lands.

Well-educated public opinion was the means of underpinning a generous US government contribution to Unicef and, until the end of the 1950s and the dawning of the Kennedy era, there was an urgent need to foster a climate of North American public opinion in favour of international understanding. The children's cause was one of the most popular with which to break down old isolationist attitudes and Cold War fears.

By the early 1960s, the annual Trick or Treat Campaign at Halloween had become one of the US Committee's most highly-developed instruments for public awareness, and for dimes-and-nickels fund-raising on a grand scale.

For three years in succession, Danny Kaye undertook a virtuoso effort to boost Trick or Treat for Unicef. He piloted his own plane on a country-wide tour to encourage youngsters everywhere to sport a black and orange 'help children help children' button, and collect money for Unicef instead of playing pranks on friends and neighbours. These whirlwind tours enlisted thousands of schoolchildren for Unicef and helped to turn the annual event into a national institution. They were the brainchild of Paul Edwards, Unicef's Director of Information, who had a gift for stunts and razzamatazz as a way of gaining public support, and contacts in Hollywood and in the showbusiness world whom he regularly enlisted. On Danny Kaye's first Trick or Treat tour in 1965, he and Edwards managed to visit thirty cities in three days. They zigzagged through time zones and darted in and out of one unfamiliar airport after another. Crowds of children came to cheer and the media was always out in force to catch a quip or a funny face from the comedian before he was whipped aloft again. In 1968, they visited sixty-five cities in five days.

By the mid-1960s, over three million children in 13,000 communities in the US were collecting more than $2.25 million in their orange Halloween boxes. The campaign was used as a peg on which educational materials about children in other lands were distributed to schools all over the country. In 1966, the Pope visited the UN in New York and met a group of children carrying their Trick or Treat boxes. This was the high-water mark of the Halloween programme in the US. Since those years, Trick or Treat has never quite recaptured the same momentum, although it is still a hardy perennial.

The Canadian Committee for Unicef followed the US lead in adopting the Trick or Treat idea as their major annual fund-raising and educational drive among children. This national committee was founded in 1955 under the auspices of the UN Association. A key mover was Adelaide Sinclair, at this stage still the delegate of Canada to the Unicef Executive Board, shortly to become Deputy Executive Director for Programmes on the retirement of Berislav Borcic in 1957. The first Halloween campaign in Canada, held to launch the Committee's fund-raising efforts, brought in $15,000. Within ten years the amount had risen to nearly $500,000. In 1967, Danny Kaye included Canadian cities on his pre-Halloween itinerary. By then the National Committee had put in place a country-wide network of provincial committees to service local volunteer support groups.

Whether in the US, in Canada or elsewhere, the men and mainly women who gave their time and energy freely to the cause of Unicef—some of them local pillars of the community, some of them salespeople for greeting cards, some of them teachers interested in children in other lands as an educational opportunity, some of them people who ran benefits or galas, or lobbied their legislative representatives during the budget season—were Unicef's most precious recruits. Their energy and dedication, sometimes taken too much for granted, often humbled those who worked closely with them.

The phenomenon of twentieth century volunteerism has launched and kept afloat many nongovernmental organizations. Within the UN family, no fund or agency has been as fortunate as Unicef in finding itself at the centre of a network of nongovernmental groups which have conveyed the appeal of Unicef and children to so many extra helping hands. Stars such as Danny Kaye, the first in a long line that included Marlon Brando, Cat Stevens, John Denver, George Harrison, Celeste Holm, Cecily Tyson, Mohammed Ali, Pelé, and many others who have made concert or sporting appearances, not only helped improve Unicef's prestige and credibility, but also gave other volunteers a boost both to their morale and to their fund-raising success.

In the US, this success has also had its unfortunate side effects. During the 1950s, when McCarthy era paranoia still attached deep-seated suspicion to the UN and all its works, Unicef's growing popular visibility attracted the venom of anti-Communist agitation. Lawrence Timbers, a fiercely patriotic American from Seattle, collected statements from various sources and issued a document entitled 'Red Influences In Unicef'. This was widely circulated among right-wing political circles and wherever he could find an audience, and caused a flood of propaganda. The Daughters of the American Revolution passed a resolution condemning Unicef, which was subsequently endorsed by the American Legion. Their main complaint was the godless and anti-Christian character of the Unicef greeting cards.

In the early years of the Greeting Cards Operation, the designs were carefully steered away from any kind of religious implications as a gesture to the spirit of internationalism. This encouraged the Daughters of the American Revolution to describe the cards as 'a Communist-inspired plan to destroy all religious beliefs'. In response to this attack, Jacqueline Kennedy, then First Lady, let it be known that she was a Unicef greeting cards customer. Sales of cards soared. Ironically, the DAR's public antagonism helped to promote Unicef's name. Their hate campaign faded during the 1960s, but the John Birch Society later took up the same kind of cudgels, and has periodically continued its attacks ever since. However unpleasant these attacks, they have never seriously damaged Unicef's credibility, either with the public or with any US Administration.

The US Committee was the first of the national support groups for Unicef. During Unicef's earliest years, the European countries were its chief beneficiaries. As their economies recovered, Maurice Pate began to consider how they might become a source of contributions. He attached at least as much intrinsic importance to support from citizens' groups as he did to government contributions. Pate's drive to create a reservoir of popular support for Unicef came from his lifelong adherence to the sentiment he imbibed from Herbert Hoover, which held that there was no more perfect ideal than that of voluntary service. He found it hard even to picture a Unicef which was not, at almost every level, an expression of people's selfless devotion to children.

In 1952, Pate asked Paul Henri Spaak, former Prime Minister of Belgium and the first President of the UN General Assembly, to tour Europe and make personal approaches on Unicef's behalf to government ministers, Heads of State, and leading personalities. Spaak agreed to do so, and was accompanied by Willie Meyer, a Swiss national who had first served Unicef as Head of Mission in Germany and then took over the management of external relations in the Paris office. The tour with Spaak was the beginning of Meyer's effort to create a network of Unicef national committees throughout Europe.

Meyer's particular gift was to identify individuals with sufficient enthusiasm and clout to set up an embryonic support group. Some were people who had originally helped with the 1948–49 UN Appeal for Children; many were already active in voluntary organizations with an interest in children, and occasionally on the fringes of government.

Meyer had a bulldog tenacity which did not endear him to everyone, but which regularly showed results. Within a year from the start of his efforts there were national committees for Unicef in Belgium and West Germany; in 1954 others followed, in Denmark, Sweden and Norway; in 1955, Italy and the Netherlands; in 1956, in the United Kingdom; and in 1958 in Luxembourg. The characters of the committees were very diverse. Some were totally independent of government; others were virtually a sub-department of the Ministry of Foreign Affairs. In Italy, the committee was under the patronage and leadership of Senator Ludovico Montini, a highly-placed government official in charge of liaison with international organizations, and brother of the Vatican Secretary of State who later became Pope Paul VI. Many other committees sought lofty patrons among presidents and royalty; few quite matched this degree of eminence.

Meyer's trump card with the new Unicef committees was that, in addition to whatever fund-raising or educational work they felt like undertaking, he had a ready-made activity on which they could instantly embark: the promotion and sale of greeting cards.

Meyer initially had great difficulty in establishing a Unicef committee in his native Switzerland, eliciting decidedly lukewarm responses to the idea from existing organizations concerned with child welfare. He finally called upon Dr Hans Conzett, an old school friend living on Lake Zurich. Conzett was a lawyer by background, and a printer and publisher by profession. He was also a member of Parliament and of its Committee on External Affairs. Meyer's suggestion fell in line with the politically neutral, humanitarian traditions of Switzerland and appealed to Conzett's personal commitment to international co-operation. Although not a member of the UN, Switzerland had always had a special place in Unicef's Executive Board, and from the beginning the Swiss delegation had been one of the most active. Pate, with the support of the Swiss Ambassador at the UN, Felix Schnyder, made an approach to the Foreign Minister, Max Petitpierre, asking his help in creating a Unicef committee. Petitpierre gave his approval, and informed Conzett that he could count on government endorsement.

The Swiss Committee for Unicef was established in June 1959 under Conzett's chairmanship. A few meetings each year were envisaged, and a little paperwork before and after. Willie Meyer had omitted to tell the Committee exactly what he had in mind. A few months before Christmas 13,000 boxes of greeting cards arrived from Paris. The Honorary Executive Secretary, a Swiss development aid official, was appalled. He had certainly not envisaged turning himself into a greeting cards sales agent, and promptly advertised for someone to come and get rid of the boxes of cards stacked in his office building. The saleswoman he recruited was Andrée Lappé, who had the kind of energy needed to move a mountain of Christmas cards onto the seasonal hearths of the citizens of Zurich. Working from an office in her home, with no resources of any kind, she managed to sell 11,697 boxes in two months. She persuaded the girl scouts and various business organizations to circulate a brochure and organized sales through bookshops and the Palais des Nations in Geneva. From these small beginnings, the Swiss Committee for Unicef gradually became a national institution.

As the network of national committees grew, mechanisms were set up to build links between these diverse members of the budding Unicef family. The first annual reunion of Unicef committees in Europe took place in 1955, and it became the forum in which the committees grappled with questions concerning their relationship with their international parent organization. On the financial side, the initial agreement was that committees should retain ten per cent of their proceeds from ordinary fund-raising to cover expenses, and fifteen per cent of their income from greeting cards. These extremely narrow margins were based on the assumption that most income would come from voluntary, virtually unsolicited, donations. As the years went by, the expansion and increasing sophistication of some of the committees led to a change in the character of fund-raising.

The late 1950s and early 1960s were the period when the conscience of the world was beginning to be aroused by the spectacle of hunger and malnutrition in the developing world.

In 1959, the Economic and Social Council of the UN endorsed a proposal from FAO that, in partnership with the UN and worldwide nongovernmental agencies, it should launch an international anti-hunger drive. 'Freedom from Hunger Campaign' was the fund-raising and public information vehicle which implanted the idea of the 'hungry millions' of Africa and Asia firmly into the mind of the public in the Western world. The aim of the campaign was ambitious and idealistic: 'To promote a climate of opinion throughout the world in which the problems of hunger and want would be faced realistically, their causes analyzed objectively, and appropriate remedies boldly and courageously applied'. A great volume of publicity offerings of all kinds, loaded with the images and statistics of hunger, were produced not only by FAO but by Unicef and others in an effort to create the new climate of opinion, which would in turn exert pressure on governments and organizations to do more about world hunger. They succeeded surprisingly well, a record rarely matched in similar UN 'years' or 'decades' for other great humanitarian causes.

The spirit of the times which infused the Freedom from Hunger Campaign also infected many of Unicef's national committees. Some began to play a part in promoting the new consciousness, helping implant the image of the hungry child in the national conscience. At this time, Unicef was still depending on the US and Canadian Governments to supply millions of pounds of dried skim milk to feed undernourished children and mothers through health centres and schools. In the latter half of 1959, the US Government unexpectedly found itself with a smaller dairy surplus than usual. The plight of the hungry pre-schooler, bereft of his nutritious Unicef cupful of milk, caught the imagination of several Unicef committees, among which the Swiss was particularly active. An approach was made to the Swiss Milk Producers' Association and, with its backing, Foreign Minister Friedrich Wahlen announced that 18 May would be 'Milk Day'. Wahlen, who by a happy coincidence was an ex-Director of FAO, appealed to the Swiss public to respond to the plight of the hungry child in Asia and Africa; they would not refuse a hungry child at their door, nor should they refuse one who could not come in person. Unicef 'milk tickets' went on sale for one Swiss franc at shops and other outlets throughout Switzerland. By the spring of 1961, nearly two million Swiss francs had been raised. This campaign launched the Swiss Committee, as well as the Dutch and other committees in dairy-conscious countries, beyond greeting cards and identified Unicef clearly in the national mind with the deprived child of the developing countries.

Most of the Unicef committees in Europe established themselves gradually, doing every year a little more successfully what Willie Meyer encouraged: promoting and selling cards. During the 1950s, most of the cards' customers were in North America, and to a lesser extent in Britain. A small sales office had been set up in London to handle the relatively insignificant European trade. In time, as a result of the committees' efforts, the volume of sales began to grow. The cards were the mainstay of their incomes, and increased sales their major opportunity of expansion. In 1959, they took over formal responsibility for sales of the cards in their own countries.

There were two areas of contention. One was the unrealistically narrow financial margins within which they were expected to operate. Everyone agreed that the maximum amount of income generated must go to help children, but there was no point in imposing such financial stringency that the committees could not compete with commercial companies. In 1964, the proportion the committees were allowed to keep was modified to twenty-five per cent.

The other problem was that the committees had very little voice in the way the greeting cards operation was run and no voice at all in the selection of the designs. Many complained that some were unsuited to their markets. The Europeans, like the North Americans, had problems with the decision to keep away from cards with a Christian motif and from culturally locked-in snow scenes, holly berries, and Santa Claus. As an international organization embracing donors and recipients of many different cultures and religious faiths, this was regarded as a point of principle. Hans Conzett, with his own background as a publisher and printer, was one of the voices raised in support of higher quality cards and a more sales-oriented outlook. Some committees proposed that each country produce its own cards for its own market. But this was resisted by Unicef headquarters, partly because of the loss of quality control and partly because it would eat into the profit margin. From 1967 onwards, a compromise was agreed whereby a group of national committee repre-sentatives took part in product design selection alongside artists and professional designers. It was also agreed that a committee could choose from among the full range of card designs and select only those ones they felt they could sell.

Many committees concentrated on building up networks of voluntary support groups, usually to market cards at Christmas time, as the heart of their fund-raising and public information strategy. In the early years, these often consisted of people who had taken part in postwar voluntary work or the UN Appeal for Children, who were inspired by the idealism of the UN and the twinning of children with peace. Many were influential people in business or their own community, and there was usually a royal or socially-eminent patron. This was the pattern in Holland, West Germany, Belgium, Britain—and later in France and Spain.

The Dutch Committee, for example, set up in 1955 by Jan Eggink, head of the National Council on Social Welfare, concentrated on building up committees all over the country and pitching Unicef's appeal to the young. On one occasion he imported 200,000 clay piggybanks from Sri Lanka and Princess Beatrix, the Committee's honorary chairman, helped promote them for sale as Unicef collecting-boxes. The Danish Committee organized sponsored walks. The Belgians ran hunger lunches, and the Austrians laid on gala benefits in Viennese concert halls.

By 1964, the number of Unicef national committees in Europe had reached a total of seventeen (including Turkey). The latest recruit was the French Committee. In 1963, Georges Sicault, now Director of the Unicef office in Paris, decided that the time had come to help set up a French National Committee to sell cards and undertake information work independently from the rest of the Unicef presence in Paris. Besides the French, the newer representatives at the annual reunion of 1964, meeting in Dublin, were the Irish, the Austrians, the Polish and the Spanish. Some of the committees had grown considerably. Few were any longer staffed by one person working at home with no proper facilities. Business executives and people with a strong professional background had come onto the scene. Certain committees were becoming much more self-confident and taking on their own special characters. These were formulated by the particular national and cultural climate in which they operated, as well as by the personalities of their leaders. The reunion was beginning to become less of a family get-together, and more of an occasion on which these national Unicef satellites flexed their muscles and sparred amicably—and sometimes less amicably—with representatives from headquarters in New York and Paris.

Apart from greeting cards and financial margins, the major problem area between the national committees and their international parent concerned public information. This could never be other than a battleground, for it is where one side of Unicef's dual personality competes with the other. The committees, with their networks of volunteer support groups, are the litmus paper of popular support for Unicef in the industrialized countries. They are the part of Unicef in touch with grass-roots support and, if they cannot succour it, not only do they wither, but so does the support. Without the popular support which underpins Unicef's worldwide reputation, many a donor government might fail to maintain the level, let alone raise, its own contribution. The idea that the cause of children can harness great reserves of compassion and goodwill in its service was good as far as it went. But simply to identify the cause of children with Unicef could not on its own sustain the existence and growth of volunteer networks and fund-raising events. The national committees needed a flow of information about projects, health campaigns, children whose lives had been transformed through their agency. Without this flow of information, no 'Milk Day', sponsored walk or hunger lunch could be profitable.

At one level, the need for information about projects in the developing world was a mechanistic requirement. Since the national committees themselves had no direct contact with programmes in the developing world, they depended on the international secretariat to supply them with publicity material vindicating Unicef's claims on behalf of the world's children. But at another level, the problem was more deep-rooted. As the committees became more self-confident, some—either consciously or subconsciously—began to want to cast Unicef in the image that most suited their fund-raising needs.

In its character as a UN organization, Unicef does not function like the typical voluntary overseas aid agency. It is an intergovernmental organization, co-operating with governments at their request in expanding services for mothers and children. In no sense does it run or manage projects or programmes. Some committees and supporters, even indeed those members of Unicef's staff who had not travelled widely in developing countries, found it difficult to distinguish between the idea of a 'Unicef project'—which did not exist—and a 'project assisted by Unicef'. On the ground, the difference is far from semantic. There is a vital distinction between an operational agency working independently from government bureaucracy and a funding agency trying to improve the situation of children by filling in some of the cracks—however significant those cracks—in a government's efforts to do so. Some of the frustration felt by committees towards the apparent inability to provide them with the kind of information they required had more to do with the inherent character of an organization working in partnerships with governments than with the mechanics of the information flow they found so inadequate.

In the early 1960s, when this problem first began to arise, Unicef's senior policy makers were trying to steer the organization away from its charitable image as a purveyor of milk powder and other supplies to ease distress, towards a more complex engagement with poverty and the development process. Some committees, reflecting what they felt their public would respond to, were trying to push in the opposite direction. The drama of an emergency—an earthquake, a flood, a famine—and the image of an international organization rushing relief supplies to its most pathetic victims were the moments at which the committees found the public most responsive to Unicef. Their need was for immediate bulletins, photos of Unicef cargoes unloading, children being fed with emergency rations, the sick being treated with Unicef medical aid. Meanwhile, policy makers back in headquarters were trying to build up a sense of partnership with the peoples in developing countries, and disliked any slippage into projection as a saviour of the helpless and ignorant. Where longer-term programmes were concerned, the committees wanted to be able to adopt a project so that their campaigners and givers could identify directly with the children on the receiving end of penicillin shots or milk rations.

In Unicef at this time, there were no circumstances in which a donor—most of which were governments—was permitted to specify that its money would go to one country or one project, rather than another. This was unhelpful to the committees. The idea that their carefully garnered donations simply disappeared into a pot called 'general resources' was unappealing from the fund-raising point of view.

Unicef had undergone, and continued to undergo, a constant educative process regarding the needs of children in the developing world and the best ways of responding to them. Not surprisingly, there was a time lag between the moment when those at the cutting edge of policy-making and programming first began to recognize the shortcomings of a particular shibboleth—the supremacy of milk as the answer to child nutrition problems, for example—and the moment at which others further away from the action became similarly attuned.

For the Swiss Committee, and for others which also organized 'Milk Funds' to help make up the unexpected shortfall in milk powder, the milk campaign of 1960 represented a tremendous advance in public understanding of children's needs and Unicef's attempts to respond to them. But at this stage, those leading the thinking on nutrition were rushing to Orissa State in India to look at poultry and fingerlings and fruit trees: applied nutrition was in fashion and milk was becoming passé. In Unicef, as in any evolving organization, certain outdated solutions, good in their time, tend to persist among staff, technical advisors, informed government opinion and public opinion at different distances from various centres of activity. The tendency for the committees and the public understanding they depended on to be out of step with the Unicef policy-making vanguard was inevitable, but it did—and still can—create tension.

Certain steps were taken to bridge the gap. In 1964, the Executive Board, meeting in Bangkok—the first occasion on which it had convened in a developing country—managed to agree upon a formula whereby projects or parts of programmes could be singled out for adoption. By this stage, the Freedom from Hunger Campaign had been underway for four years and the precedent of adopting projects had been established by FFHC committees in various countries: the success of the Freedom from Hunger Campaign—a partnership between voluntary effort and the UN system—would have been jeopardized if it had not proved possible to find a formula for raising and giving funds which did not detract from the multilateral character of an FAO or a Unicef. At the same Executive Board session, a set of guidelines were agreed which conceded to the national committees a co-operative relationship with the Board. From this point onwards, committee representatives could attend sessions as observers in their own right.

As the Development Decade progressed, the relationships between Unicef and the many satellite but virtually autonomous Unicef committees in the donor countries began to evolve and diversify. As the committees became more self-assertive and successful, the inherent tensions tended to become more difficult rather than less. The committees wanted to be not Unicef's agents, but its partners—at least where policy on fund-raising, greeting cards and information campaigns was concerned. But some members of the secretariat could never quite manage to pay more than lip service to such an idea, and sometimes did not even pay that. What is surprising in retrospect is not that there has been many a rough passage, but that no national committee has ever broken away and set itself up under an independent, non-Unicef banner. Nor has any closed its doors.

The relationship between Unicef and certain committees may temporarily come unstuck from time to time, but in the end the cement has always held. The cement is children. Whatever the arguments about means—arguments to be found in any organization however noble its purpose—the ends have never left any room for dispute. Helenka Pantaleoni, President of the US Committee and a life-long personal powerhouse for the cause of children, summed the matter up in her annual report of 1969: 'Whatever success we have been able to achieve—and much of it under duress—is, of course, due in large part to the magic of the focus on the child in need. However, I am convinced that in equal measure it is due to simple faith in our objective. Committee, staff, volunteers are motivated by their sincere belief that in working for an improvement in the lives of the children, they are working for a better future. As long as we keep this faith, we are bound to succeed'.

Unicef's national committees clearly had a number of common problems. Outside these, and their common association with Unicef, they were and are profoundly different from one another. At one extreme was a committee such as the Swiss, which took a decision from the outset to be entirely free and independent of government influence, and which concentrated on imaginative fund-raising campaigns. At another extreme was the Swedish Committee. The Swedish Committee for Unicef began life under the umbrella of Radda Barnen, the Swedish Save the Children. It was envisaged from the start as a body with close governmental links, and there was never any attempt to compete with Radda Barnen or any other organization for private donations. The Committee's task was to inform the Ministry of Foreign Affairs about Unicef, and lobby Unicef's policy makers concerning Sweden's priorities in the field of international development aid.

Both the Swiss and the Swedish Committees, with their very different backgrounds, have had a profound influence on Unicef's thinking down the years. In the case of the Swiss Committee, the chairman, Hans Conzett, who served as President of the Swiss Parliament in 1967–68, always had close links with his country's Ministry of Foreign Affairs and in 1964 became the leader of the Swiss delegation to the Unicef Executive Board. In the case of the semigovernmental Swedish Committee, the chairman, Nils Thedin, had no formal position in government or the civil service, but as a senior official in the Swedish Co-operative Federation, he was held in such respect by the Swedish Ministry of Foreign Affairs that he led the Swedish delegation to the Executive Board from 1961 until 1984. Thedin was elected Chairman of the Unicef Board from 1970 to 1972. Hans Conzett served as Chairman in 1975 and 1976. These two individuals, who straddled the divide between national committees and the senior decision-making body in Unicef, helped to pave the way for a closer connection between committees and official country delegations to Unicef and earn the voluntary sector a much enhanced credibility within Unicef's secretariat. In turn, they helped create a bridge to those in the committees who resented feeling like second-class Unicef citizens.

Nils Thedin was elected Chairman of the Swedish Committee at its first meeting in the Stockholm offices of Radda Barnen in August 1954. A journalist and magazine publisher by profession, Thedin had already served on the Swedish Commission to UNESCO and had a long record in the international labour movement. His first experience in relief work came during the Spanish Civil War, when he took a leave of absence from his job in the ILO in Geneva to work for the International Committee for the Assistance of Child Refugees in Barcelona. This organization was run by the British and American Quakers, and was devoted to feeding and caring for child victims on both sides of the conflict.

Thedin was deeply shaken by the plight of sick, undernourished and abandoned children. The experience ingrained in him a lifelong concern for the sufferings of children caught up in conflict. In 1954, when Radda Barnen was formally requested by the Ministry of Foreign Affairs to set up a mechanism for spreading information about Unicef in Sweden, and to advise the Swedish authorities on the policy, budget and activities of Unicef, Nils Thedin was Radda Barnen's Vice-President, and a natural choice for the Unicef Committee Chairman. The Swedish Red Cross was also represented, as were various government ministries. Over the years, many of the most prominent Swedish figures in international affairs and development assistance, a foreign policy area of growing importance to Sweden, served on the Unicef Committee.

Immediately, the Swedish Committee plunged into examinations of Unicef policy. Their interest focussed on maternal and child health care. When Sweden took a seat at the Executive Board from 1956 onwards, the official delegation began to draw heavily on its Committee as a resource for its statements. Unicef's policy of support to mother and child health expansion did not go far enough, in their opinion. They wanted health care to the preschool child to be the Unicef priority, building up the kind of welfare services which had given Sweden an international reputation for family care through day-care centres and paediatrics departments. The effect of their contribution to the debates was electric. No other national committee acted as an advisor on policy to an international delegation. Few national committees contained within their membership people equipped for any informed discussion of development issues. Unicef welcomed the seriousness and the enthusiasm with which the representatives of Sweden, both in their role as national committee leaders and Board delegates, began to engage in Unicef's affairs.

The Swedes have often been ahead in their thinking, even of Unicef's own vanguard, and unfazed by the awkward ripples set in motion by raising controversial issues. Some of these—family planning, women's rights—were raised by the Swedish delegation long before they were fashionable, and many eventually found their way into mainstream Unicef philosophy partly because of Sweden's persistence. The Swedes have taken certain issues very seriously, and pushed in certain directions much harder than the Unicef secretariat found it comfortable to move. Because of the excellent personal rapport between Nils Thedin and successive Executive Directors and deputies, the relationship between Unicef and Sweden has been closer and smoother than it otherwise might have been. The Swedish leverage over Unicef was reinforced by the steady rise in the official contribution to Unicef's general resources during the 1960s and 1970s. By 1965, Sweden—followed closely by Norway—was giving the highest contribution per head of population. In recent years, the absolute amount has usually been second only to that of the US, a remarkable record for a country with a population one thirtieth the size.

Among the Western donor countries, the character of the Swedish Committee is unusual. In eastern Europe, all the committees and commissions for Unicef are under the wing of government, not as advisory and educational bodies but as sub-branches of foreign affairs. The Yugoslav Commission for Co-operation with Unicef, established in 1947 to help channel Unicef assistance to children's programmes in Yugoslavia itself, is the oldest of all the European committees. It was the only Unicef operation in eastern Europe to survive the Cold War. Its purpose did not change markedly for the many years during which Unicef continued to give supplies and equipment for penicillin production, maternity and paediatrics facilities, for campaigns against endemic disease, and for programmes which included emergency relief after the Skopje earthquake in 1963. The Commission played host to the Unicef Programme Committee in 1953, and to the European reunion of national committees in 1962. Members of other committees were able to profit from what, for them, was a rare opportunity: visits to projects in which Unicef was involved. The Commission undertook the sale of Unicef greeting cards, took part in cultural and youth events, and collected donations on a modest scale; but its principal purpose remained the screening and co-ordination of Unicef assistance.

Towards the middle of the 1950s, Ludwik Rajchman's friend and old associate from the Polish delegation to UNRRA, Dr Boguslaw Kozusznik, began to discuss with colleagues in the Ministry of Health the idea of establishing a national committee for Unicef in Poland.

Kozusznik, who was Vice-Minister of Health, was much inspired by the Unicef Commission's example in Yugoslavia. During the early 1950s, with the exception of Yugoslavia, all the eastern Socialist countries had selectively withdrawn, not from membership but from close involvement in certain UN member organizations. Poland's retreat from Unicef was a source of great regret to Kozusznik. At a conference of Ministers of Health of eastern Europe, the question of re-engagement with UN organizations was raised, and Poland decided to rejoin the international health community.

In 1956, Poland sought election to the Unicef Executive Board, and Kozusznik led the delegation. In 1962, a Unicef committee was set up in Warsaw. It was a small advisory body under the wing of the Ministry of Foreign Affairs whose membership consisted of representatives from government and various social institutions. One of the most prominent was the National Research Institute of Mother and Child in Warsaw to which Unicef had given assistance in the immediate postwar years, and which later ran training courses attended by health workers from the developing countries under a programme of Unicef co-operation.

The committee sold greeting cards and undertook information activities, but its primary purpose was to foster discussion at the official level within Poland on children's issues, and to liaise between the Ministry of Foreign Affairs and Unicef. Kozusznik himself served as the committee's Chairman from 1962 to 1983. Its administrative head was a government official appointed by the Ministry of Foreign Affairs. Some token assistance from Unicef was agreed, mainly for spare parts for the milk conservation plants earlier installed with Unicef help, for which foreign exchange was scarce. During the late 1960s, Georges Sicault and Dr Kozusznik together toured eastern European countries to encourage the establishment of other Unicef committees. Between 1968 and 1974, Bulgaria, Czechoslovakia, Hungary and Romania all followed Poland's example. In the USSR, no separate Unicef Committee was established but the Soviet Red Cross and Red Crescent Societies began to undertake some of the liaison functions normally carried out by national committees. In time, the level of interest and involvement in Unicef's work in the other eastern European countries increased; a committee in the German Democratic Republic was established in the mid-1970s. But the links with other countries have never been so strong as with Yugoslavia or Poland, where for historical reasons Unicef has always enjoyed a special reputation.

Many of the voluntary organizations on which national committees for Unicef originally drew for their membership were those concerned with the problems of children in their own countries. In most parts of the industrialized world, the networks of professional, labour and youth organizations which formed an integral part of the social fabric were keen to function as active constituents of the new international society represented by the idea of the 'united nations'. The millions of individuals who gave their time and energy freely to such nongovernmental bodies had made possible the success of the UN Appeal for Children (UNAC) in 1948-49—and Unicef from its inception was a member of the UN family with whose interests many NGOs identified and sought a close relationship. A number had their own federated international structures, which already enjoyed consultative status with ECOSOC: the International Union of Child Welfare, the Friends World Committee for Consultation, the International Federation of Business and Professional Women, the World Confederation of Organizations of the Teaching Profession, the World Jewish Congress, the International Co-operative Women's Guild, and scores of others.

In some countries, as became clear during UNAC, the prospect that Unicef might become a competitor for philanthropic donations meant that existing voluntary organizations with programmes of overseas assistance looked upon Unicef national committees as rivals. In Sweden, by helping to create the Swedish Committee for Unicef, Radda Barnen made sure that this would not happen. Elsewhere, the relationship between Unicef committees and different kinds of NGOs was ambivalent and difficult to typify. In the US, friendly organizations willing to mobilize their members on behalf of the Unicef appropriation or to send out greeting cards brochures in their mailings had helped Unicef to survive its early struggles for existence. This pattern of mutual support was repeated elsewhere; members of women's organizations formed the backbone of the UK Committee, founded in 1956. But there were NGOs with whom there was no easy source of common identification. In certain European countries, the spread of development ideology in the 1960s helped nurture a new breed of voluntary activists, whose thinking about international social justice had more to do with anti-establishment radicalism than traditional humanitarian precepts; in the field, aims and programmes might converge, but at home the sense of common purpose might be rather more elusive.

Among the big league of international organizations with a social or humanitarian flavour and a loyal source of donations and subscriptions, there were many with aims broadly in line with Unicef's, and with money and goodwill. Some had affiliates in various countries which could be mobilized behind feeding and health care programmes with which Unicef was associated; while others were without an operational means of their own for helping children in other lands and so were pleased to be part of a network which did. Such organizations were natural allies; one of Pate's early recruits to the staff was a friend from his wartime days at the American Red Cross, Grace Holmes Barbey, whom he sent off on lecture tours and goodwill missions to cultivate the NGO constituency. Barbey was vibrant and outgoing and her efforts bore fruit.

In 1952, the Executive Board agreed that certain international NGOs with consultative status at ECOSOC, already grouped as an advisory body to Unicef, should be invited to form a higher committee whose members could attend and address Unicef Board sessions. The terms of reference of this NGO Committee were very general, referring mainly to 'forums for discussion' and 'exchanges of information'. Unicef hope was that the granting of consultative status to leading organizations within the non-governmental community would help swell the volume of public information and understanding about the needs of children in the developing countries and what was being done by Unicef and its partners on their behalf. This was all part of the strategy to popularize the children's cause; to encourage recipient governments to co-operate more energetically; and to exert a moral pressure on donors to boost their contributions.

Within the Unicef secretariat, attitudes towards the NGO community were mixed. Although the sense of common cause had been important during the years of postwar crisis, close liaison with many of the NGOs seemed less pertinent when the focus of attention shifted away from Europe and the victims of catastrophe towards the underdeveloped parts of the world and the victims of poverty.

In most such countries, there was scarcely an organized governmental network, let alone a nongovernmental one which in any way resembled the religious and secular infrastructure of the West. The NGOs in consultative status with Unicef believed that they had expertise to offer the design and execution of certain types of programmes; not everyone in Unicef was disposed to agree. In certain cases, their activities appeared to coincide only at the most superficial points with those of Unicef. Some were not interested in the specific problems of underdevelopment in Asia, Africa or Latin America, only with the plight of women and children in a more general context. Some did not have affiliates at the national or subnational level in the developing countries, and therefore were in a position to contribute little to the analysis either of problems or responses. Some NGOs—especially those with old-established and inflexible structures which had not adjusted to the pendulum swings of the times—did not appreciate the eclipse of their standing; nor did some of them make the adaptations required to recover it.

Quite apart from any sense of cultural and organizational divergence, the problem with trying to develop a unified method of relating to the NGOs was that their only common denominator was their interest in an association with Unicef—an association intended to serve their own interests as well as the other way around. If the national committees were full of dissimilarities, they were a close-knit kin compared with the array of NGOs looking for a common cause with Unicef. In 1958, Maurice Pate invited Norman Acton, previously the Executive Director of the US

Committee for Unicef, to examine in detail the current state of relationships between Unicef and NGOs and how they might be made more productive. Acton was held in high esteem both within Unicef and by many of the voluntary organizations in consultative status with Unicef, two of whom he already served in an advisory capacity. He had chaired the NGO Committee on Unicef from 1952 to 1954. Acton did his best to make sense of a state of affairs which was at the time fraught with conflicting expectations.

By the time of his 1958 survey, the membership of the NGO Committee had risen to fifty-seven international organizations ranging from Soroptimists to Veterans to Youth Hostels to Agricultural Producers. They represented thousands of member organizations in at least ninety countries and territories, all of whose public fora represented mechanisms whereby Unicef information could reach individuals and communities. They were, unquestionably, vehicles of potentially great significance to Unicef's cause.

Acton also reviewed the national committees for Unicef, many of which were themselves NGOs. He advocated that the national committees deserved special consideration from the secretariat, including staff services to help them organize themselves and their activities. He regarded the committees as the frontline of Unicef's support groups, and suggested that they be primarily responsible for contacts with NGOs other than at the international level. He recommended that criteria be laid down for the committees' formal recognition, in order to guide their work and prevent them getting too far out of line with Unicef's policy and purposes. The guidelines clarifying their relationship with their parent body, finally agreed in 1964, stemmed directly from this recommendation.

Acton, coming from an NGO background, did not fall into the trap of underrating the possibilities of NGOs, whether or not some of those in consultative status with Unicef were currently well-adapted to partnership in development co-operation. He registered the growth of organized citizen concern about poverty issues throughout the world—a concern that was to swell considerably during the Freedom from Hunger Campaign in the early 1960s. Acton believed that Unicef's focus on NGOs as fund-raisers for its own cause was not always conducive to fruitful partnership, and he also underlined the services Unicef could derive from certain NGOs on subjects within their specific competences.

For technical advice, Unicef normally relied on the specialized agencies within the UN system. But some of the NGOs, particularly at a time when Unicef was expanding its programme assistance to social welfare, had experience which could be drawn upon. The relative freedom enjoyed by NGOs working in developing countries—a freedom by definition denied to an intergovernmental organization—meant that they could experiment and pioneer, and do things on a personalized scale that large-scale pro- grammes did not have a fine enough mesh to catch. Although the main emphasis of his report was on the traditional areas of Unicef/NGO co-operation—education, public information, fund-raising, cultivating a common constituency—the idea of programme partnership in countries receiving Unicef assistance was articulated more forcefully than it had been for several years.

Out in the field, partnerships with local nongovernmental organizations— the women's clubs in Brazil, *Maendeleo ya Wanawake* in Kenya, its equivalent in Uganda, and their equivalents in India—were becoming a regular feature of programmes designed to reach into the nooks and crannies of rural society. The importance to Unicef of relationships with this kind of NGO was becoming more apparent to programme staff. The success of the partnership with the milk producers' co-operative at Anand in India was a classic illustration of what could be done by a nongovern-mental organization whose initiative remained untrammelled by govern-ment bureaucracy. This kind of grass-roots identification with small farmers was rarely achieved by low-level government officials carrying out instructions devised by policy makers in the capital city.

Charles Egger, travelling through Africa in the 1950s, had been similarly surprised by the quality of programmes run by many missionary societies. Some were the unique source of health, education, and social services in the communities they served. They might fear the intrusion of officialdom and be resistant to ideas that they dovetail their programmes with those run by the national health authorities, but they were a major avenue for Unicef assistance to mothers and children—sometimes the only one.

Certain projects directly in line with Unicef's objectives were run by the national branches of NGOs affiliated to Unicef at the international level: the YWCA, for example, was very active in the countries which had once been part of British East Africa. In some cases, where the parent body tried to create a new branch in a new country in the image of originals elsewhere, the voluntary support they drew upon came from the urban elite and projects they ran did not reflect any real concern with the problems of poverty. But this was not always the case. In Uganda, a nutrition education project run through eleven women's clubs was able to benefit from Unicef support in the form of transport and training provided through the Ministry of Community Development. This was a typical example of the welding of a partnership between a local NGO doing useful, if small-scale, work and the relevant government ministry, in which Unicef served as the go-between. There were, too, local groups and associations—the women's groups in parts of Africa and Asia, for example; the Gandhian inspired networks in the Indian subcontinent—which were far more concerned with local or national recognition and had little idea of international connections.

Many would not even have known that they belonged generically to an organizational type called NGO. They had been formed at the grass roots to solve specific local problems and, either by choice or by ignorance, their horizons did not extend to officialdom in their capital city, let alone to consultative status with an organization such as Unicef. But from Unicef's point of view, they were a valuable means of reaching the children of the rural poor. Among some field staff, the term NGO began to take on a different set of connotations from the ones they privately associated with good works and excellent intentions.

The 1964 Board session in Bangkok helped establish a renewed sense of NGOs as important Unicef partners. For three days prior to the Board meeting a seminar for NGOs was convened, jointly sponsored by Unicef and the International Council of Women, whose Vice-Chairman, Mrs Zena Harman, was also the senior delegate of Israel to the Unicef Executive Board and Chairman of its Programme Committee. The agenda of the seminar was to familiarize certain organizations with the kind of projects Unicef was favourably disposed towards, by visiting examples near Bangkok; and to try to convince those with a parochial focus that the task of upgrading the lives of children and youth required them to dovetail their efforts with government services and departments. This might also require them to upgrade their own competence, in order to command the respect of officialdom and play a role in national development planning. The notion of the 'whole' child as an object and subject of development, rather than that of charitable action on behalf of the specifically distressed—the handicapped or the refugee, for example—was introduced in some depth for the first time to many of those attending. The presence of many key national committee people in their governments' delegations—Hans Conzett, Nils Thedin, Boguslaw Kozusznik, Zena Harman, among others— helped to foster enthusiasm for modifying certain Unicef policies to make it easier for national committees and NGOs to harmonize their relationships with each other and with Unicef proper. In the era of development, Unicef's valuable, if occasionally vexed and vexing, partners in the non-governmental community had been accorded a new legitimacy and respect.

The year 1964 was a boom one for Unicef. It was the year in which the Executive Board for the first time met in a developing country; it was the year of the Bellagio Conference on Children and Youth in National Development; it was a year in which contributions rose, partnerships flourished, and a record number of greeting cards—thirty-five million— were sold. Unicef seemed to be on the threshold of a much larger future as a fully-fledged member of the international development community.

During 1964, at the instigation of Hans Conzett, a proposition was sent to Oslo from the Swiss parliament that Unicef should be nominated for the Nobel Peace Prize. Four years earlier, the Norwegian Committee for Unicef had wanted to nominate Maurice Pate, but he had let it be known that he would not accept the award on his own behalf, only on behalf of Unicef. The Swiss proposal bore fruit. But Pate did not live to know it.

On the evening of 19 January 1965, while taking a quiet walk on the streets of Manhattan, Pate collapsed. He was seventy years old. For some months the state of his heart had been uncertain and he had been taking things easy; when it came, the heart attack was massive. He was rushed to hospital, where he never recovered consciousness. The entire staff of Unicef, particularly his senior colleagues, were deeply stricken, for his passing represented so much more than an administrative hiatus. This was the end of an era, and it had descended with great suddenness. The whole organization was temporarily consumed with grief at the loss of a figure they had held in so much affection and respect.

Messages poured into Unicef headquarters from all over the world. The *New York Times* said in an editorial that relatively few people had heard of Maurice Pate but that 'scores of millions of children in well over 100 countries have been fed and clothed because he lived . . . No monument could be more imposing than Unicef'. The Executive Board met to pay him their last respects. The memorial service was thronged with ambassadors and UN dignitaries of many nationalities. Special tributes to his leadership of Unicef were paid by the President of the 19th UN General Assembly, Alex Quaison-Sackey; by UN Secretary-General U Thant; by Zena Harman, now Chairman of the Board; and by Dick Heyward. Among the many qualities they cited, one stood out: an innate, spiritual power, manifest in gentle humility, to bind people together in the common cause of humanity. He had made Unicef a family in a sense rarely found in large organizations. His very presence was a harmonizer. 'The passions that breed dissension, intolerance and distrust', said Zena Harman, 'were silenced in his presence, rendered impotent by the strength of his unquenchable faith in man's ultimate goodness, in the power of love and friendship. He believed that all people everywhere sought peace in a better world through the well-being of their children'.

On 25 October 1965, nine months after Pate's death and on almost the exact day that people all over the world were celebrating the twentieth anniversary of the founding of the UN, great news arrived from Oslo. Unicef had been awarded the 1965 Nobel Peace Prize. The ultimate honour had been conferred on the organization that Maurice Pate had built and cherished.

Main sources:

Memoirs of Helenka Pantaleoni, Columbia Oral History Project 1977, op cit.

People Who Care: Adventures of the Human Spirit, Alfred Lief, published by Appleton Century Crofts 1967.

Histories of Unicef National Committees: The Unicef Committee of Australia, 1963–1983; The United States Committee for Unicef; Canadian Unicef Committee, 1955–84; Swiss Committee, 1959–1985; The Swedish Committee for Unicef 1954–1983, and its contribution to the deliberations of Unicef's Executive Board, 1954–1985; United Nations International Children's Emergency Fund in Jugoslavia, 1948–1983, published by the Yugoslav Commission for Co-operation with Unicef, Belgrade, 1984; *Twenty Years of Work for Unicef*, 1964–1984, published in Les Enfants du Monde by FISE/French Committee for Unicef, November 1984.

'A Historical Perspective on National Committees for Unicef in Europe', prepared for the Unicef History Project by Doris Phillips, October 1984.

Interviews with Dr Hans Conzett, Nils Thedin, Dr Boguslaw Kozusznik and others, undertaken by Jack Charnow and Tarzie Vittachi for the Unicef History Project, 1982–1985.

'History of the Unicef Greeting Card Operation', prepared for the Unicef History Project by Margaret Sharkey.

Issues of *Unicef News*, in particular on Unicef in Europe (1977), on the death of Maurice Pate (February 1965), and the awarding of the Nobel Peace Prize (January/February 1966).

Unicef Executive Board: special papers, reports, project submissions etc, 1955–65.

Chapter 10

The Population Debate

On the death of Maurice Pate, the UN Secretary-General U Thant confirmed Dick Heyward as the Acting Executive Director of Unicef until arrangements could be completed for appointing Pate's successor. Conscious of his age and declining health, Pate had already begun to make preparations to stand down and make way for a new director some months before. The US Government, still the organization's largest donor and the most influential member of the Executive Board, had made it clear that it would like another US citizen. Although the formalities demanded that the appointment be made by the UN Secretary-General in consultation with the Executive Board, Pate himself played the key role in choosing the person to follow him.

The candidate he began to court, and to recommend to the small group of people he kept conversant with his plans, was Henry Richardson Labouisse. Labouisse was a Southerner by birth, from a family with French Huguenot forebears; by profession he was a lawyer, and had practised for many years in New York before the second World War. In 1941, he entered the US government service and from that time onwards his life's work was devoted to international affairs, mostly in positions where his strong sense of social responsibility was particularly suited.

In the era of the Marshall Plan, Labouisse worked as an economic minister in the US embassy in Paris, and was heavily involved in the shaping of the new mechanisms for economic co-operation in Europe. His courteous, non-dictatorial style, and his success at negotiation, brought him to the notice of many leading figures on the international circuit. In 1954, at the personal request of Dag Hammarskjold, then UN Secretary-General, Labouisse was released from US government service to head the UN Relief and Works Administration in the Middle East. UNRWA, whose headquarters were in Beirut, was the international body established to handle the human upheavals associated with the creation of Israel, and was then responsible for housing, feeding, clothing and caring for some 900,000 Palestinian refugees.

In 1958, Labouisse returned to the US; his experience now put him in line for a top position within the US Government. But he was a registered Democrat, and while the Eisenhower Administration ran its term, his prospects were blocked. Instead, he became a consultant to the World Bank and spent part of the next two years in Venezuela as the head of a survey team concerned with economic and social policy.

At the end of 1960 when John F. Kennedy was elected President, the outlook changed. Dean Rusk, soon to be installed as Secretary of State, invited Labouisse to become the head of the International Co-operation Administration in the new government. The ICA was the most prominent among a number of departments administering segments of US foreign aid, and Labouisse accepted. Kennedy wanted a major reorientation of the aid programme, away from explicit associations with the anticommunist effort, towards economic and social objectives more loosely tied to US ideological interests. It was therefore decided to restructure its administration and combine everything labelled as foreign aid in one agency. Labouisse was asked to head a task force to prepare the necessary legislation for Congress, which he accomplished successfully.

The US Agency for International Development (USAID) was created in 1962; but for various political reasons, Labouisse was not invited to become its head. Instead he was offered an ambassadorship. Greece was the country he settled upon, and where he went with enthusiasm.

In November 1964, when Maurice Pate began to sound out his views on becoming his heir apparent, Labouisse was halfway through his third year as US Ambassador in Athens. To begin with, he was somewhat taken by surprise, and unsure at the age of sixty whether he wished to cut short his tour to take up such a demanding position.

Labouisse had first come across Maurice Pate and Unicef in 1954. Shortly after he became head of UNRWA, he had enlisted Unicef's help with relief for children and mothers living in Jordanian border villages where UNWRA's official mandate did not extend. During the following years, Labouisse and Pate maintained their acquaintance, meeting occasionally when Labouisse was visiting New York. His leadership of UNWRA impressed Pate. He was a quiet but effective bargainer for funds, and he was astute in dealing with the web of sensitivities in which any initiative on behalf of Palestinians invariably became enmeshed. Another attribute that attracted Pate was his economic background, which was especially appropriate at a time when Unicef was using every opportunity to claim a place for children's well-being in the conference rooms and planning institutes where development issues were under discussion.

But the essential characteristic which weighed heavily with Pate was Labouisse's quality as a human being, which signalled to him a kindred spirit, the kind of person to whom Pate could comfortably hand over. Whatever the new fashion for talk of investing in children as an economic resource, Unicef was an organization with a heart and an essential humanitarian bias, not only in its mission but in its inherent character. Harry Labouisse was a Southern gentleman, soft-spoken, calm, and statesmanlike.

His career and his personal attributes indicated that he was a man of integrity and compassion.

Labouisse had one other admirable asset. His second wife—his first wife had died tragically in 1945—was Eve Curie, daughter of the world-famous discoverers of radium. Eve Curie-Labouisse was a dynamic woman who had given up her own writing career to devote herself to her husband's. Maurice Pate had lived alone for most of the years he headed Unicef. But after his Polish first wife died in Warsaw in 1961, he had married Martha Lucas, ex-President of Sweetbriar College, Virginia. She had been a forceful support in his final years, and the attribute of a first-class woman at his side no doubt seemed to him a great advantage for the Executive Director of Unicef.

In December 1964, Labouisse visited New York to discuss the possibility of his directorship with Pate and Heyward, Zena Harman, the current Chairman of Unicef's Executive Board, and U Thant. He also sounded out Paul Hoffman, Managing Director of the UN Special Fund, as well as Dean Rusk and other friends and contacts in Washington. In January 1965, Labouisse informed U Thant and Pate that he would accept the appointment if it was approved by the Executive Board, but that he would not be ready to take over until September. After the death of Pate later that month, Zena Harman visited Labouisse in Athens to express in person the Board's enthusiasm for his candidature, and try to persuade him to take up his appointment at an earlier date. He agreed to take over in June 1965, at the time of the annual session of the Executive Board.

The session was conducted essentially by Heyward. In the wake of Pate's death, still less than six months before, it was a sober and mostly uneventful session. Issues which might arouse controversy were handled *sotto voce* or put on hold, out of deference to Pate's memory, to Labouisse's début, and to Heyward's interim position as Acting Executive Director. On 14 June 1965, Labouisse addressed the Board delegates for the first time, explaining that he was 'somewhat out of breath' as a result of the speed with which events had unfolded. He had literally relinquished his ambassadorship only a few days previously. He also knew how hard it would be to follow in the footsteps of Maurice Pate, whose leadership over so many years had accomplished 'a sort of miracle, reflected by the outstanding record of Unicef and by its reputation in the world'.

Labouisse was not more than a few months into the process of taking over full control of his new responsibilities when that 'outstanding record' was recognized by the Nobel Committee in Oslo. On a dark, snow-bound December day Harry Labouisse led a strong Unicef contingent to collect the 1965 Nobel Peace Prize. With him were Zena Harman, Chairman of the Executive Board; Professor Robert Debré, delegate of France; Adelaide Sinclair, Deputy Executive Director for Programmes; Georges Sicault, Director of Unicef in Europe; Hans Conzett, Chairman of the Swiss Commitee for Unicef and delegate of Switzerland to the Executive Board; Helenka Pantaleoni, Chairman of the US Committee. Danny Kaye, Mr Unicef himself also attended while there for a Norwegian artists' gala for Unicef. On 10 December, in the Aula Hall at Oslo University in the presence of King Haakon, Labouisse stepped forward to receive the Nobel Peace Medal and Diploma from Gunnar Jahn, Chairman of the Nobel Committee of the Norwegian Parliament. The following day, coincidentally the nineteenth anniversary of Unicef's founding by the General Assembly, Zena Harman delivered the Nobel lecture at the Nobel Institute.

In Labouisse's speech of acceptance, he paid tribute to Maurice Pate as Unicef's architect and builder and as a great practical idealist, adding: 'We miss him poignantly in Oslo today'. The moment synthesized the record of everything Pate had stood for and everything Unicef had become. Labouisse spoke with eloquent sincerity: 'To me, the most important meaning of this Nobel award is the solemn recognition that the welfare of today's children is inseparably linked with the peace of tomorrow's world. Their sufferings and privations do not ennoble: they frustrate and embitter. The longer the world tolerates the slow war of attrition which poverty and ignorance now wage against 800 million children in the developing countries, the more likely it becomes that our hope for lasting peace will be the ultimate casualty . . .

'We accept the Nobel Prize for Peace with humility, knowing how little we are able to do and how immense are the needs . . .

'To all of us the prize will be a wonderful incentive to greater efforts, in the name of peace. You have given us new strength. You have reinforced our profound belief that, each time Unicef contributes, however modestly, to giving today's children a chance to grow into useful and happier citizens, it contributes to removing some of the seeds of world tension and future conflict.'

These words came to symbolize the most significant features of Labouisse's tenure at the head of Unicef in the political and economic turmoils of the first and second development decades.

During the mid-1960s, a new menace began to blight the prospects of social and economic development in the Third World. From this time, the analysis of population trends began to take on the character of an international *cause célèbre*, etching in the public mind images of overpopulation which pervaded contemporary thinking.

During the years following the second World War, dramatic declines in the death rates in many developing countries, unaccompanied by declines in their birth rates, played havoc with the traditional rules of demography. The lack of population data from such countries meant that the economic and scientific community took some time to absorb the full dimensions of what was going on. When it finally began to penetrate in the early 1960s, a heated search for explanations and responses began.

The onslaught against epidemic disease was held to be mainly responsible, especially the antimalaria campaigns whose effects in some countries were quite spectacular: in Ceylon between 1945 and 1960, for example, the death rate from malaria dropped from 1310 per million to zero and, as a result, the country's overall death rate dropped from twenty-two to eight per 1000. But other less tangible factors—political stability, economic prosperity, the expansion of communications which made possible the relief of famine—also played important parts in chasing mortality rates downwards.

The balance between these various factors has ever since been a subject of controversy; but its effect on the new nations' demographic profiles was undisputed and without historical precedent. A population growth rate of two-and-a-half per cent per year might sound harmless, but its effect over a short period was startling. Firstly, the population became younger, with as many as half a country's citizens under the age of fifteen. Secondly, the speed of growth was exponential: fifty per cent more citizens in sixteen years, double the number in twenty-five. The kind of increase which had taken three centuries to come about in Europe was taking place in parts of Africa, Asia and Latin America within fifty to seventy-five years, including in some of the most populous countries on earth.

In Europe and North America, declining death rates had been invariably accompanied by rising prosperity. The effects of improvements in living standards were mirrored in the increasing value, as well as cost, attached to individual children, and in corresponding drops in the birth rates. Since the rate of natural increase in the population was relatively low, national governments did not feel any need to take account of Malthusian prophecies; policies for curbing procreation were unknown and, to all intents and purposes, unimaginable.

Until the middle of the twentieth century, most governments concerned with the size of their populations were interested in increasing them. Such population policies as existed—and many Western countries adopted them, explicitly or implicitly—were designed to bolster the birth rate by offering family allowances and banning contraception and abortion. National might and national virility demanded a high birth rate: a large population was traditionally regarded as a crude indication of importance in the league table of nation states.

In some of the new members of that league, particularly in Africa where populations were mostly small relative to their land area, and where people took it for granted that a high proportion of their children would not survive, having large families was the preferred policy both from a family's and a nation's point of view. As late as the early 1960s, these ideas were still endorsed by some respectable theorists who continued to assume that population increase was a help to the development process. But an entirely new combination of historical and demographic forces was beginning to operate, and what had been through the ages a problem of how to replenish the human stock was turning into its inverse reflection. A planet bursting at the seams with people appeared a real and frightening prospect.

The first large and populous country to wake up to the effects of its internal demographic revolution was India. As political leaders and economists mixed the ingredients for Five-Year Plans, trying to chart the country's future goals, needs and resources in a scientific and integrated fashion, population growth no longer appeared on the credit side of national wealth and vigour, but firmly in the debit column. By 1965, India's population had risen to 435 million from 300 million in 1935; every year, the population was increasing by around twelve million, or 2·3 per cent, a rate which meant that there would be close to 900 million Indian citizens by 1990. Accordingly, requirements for schools, health facilities, jobs, housing, water supplies, sanitation, and improvements in diet and quality of life were multiplying at rates which threatened to swamp all efforts for national social and economic advance. Thanks to its accelerated pace, population growth had become incompatible with successful development. No longer, almost by natural order, did it keep in step with rising prosperity.

Some of the countries of Asia where population growth was beginning to cause alarm were already densely peopled. Crowdedness in the cities and their unhygienic slums was a mushrooming public health hazard, and the lack of proper sanitation and housing a blot on the national image. But if the wretched conditions in which so many people on the lower rungs of society's ladder were obliged to live already constituted a development nightmare, how much worse would the situation become if unprecedentedly high rates of population growth were allowed to go unchecked? At its crudest, the argument in favour of population control was stark, the image the one that Malthus had conjured so presciently more than a century before: countries already hard put to feed their people could anticipate famine and mass starvation if numbers continued to grow at such a rate. As more attention began to be fosussed on the problem, the spectacle of Mankind increasing his offspring at such a pace as to devour his supply of non-renewable resources within a few generations, destroying the fragile environmental equilibrium sustaining a liveable human society, began to grip the public imagination. The Freedom from Hunger Campaign had done a great deal to make more people aware of the problems of low agricultural production and food shortage in the poor countries; now the image of too many mouths to feed was given new drama and poignancy by the demographers' rising tide of numbers. There was a population 'crisis'; a population 'explosion', a population 'time bomb'.

The fall in the death rate would be followed by a decline in the birth rate.

Such was the proven experience; and disease campaigns and other life-saving, health-giving measures were hastening the day. But not, it seemed, fast enough.

The experience of the industrialized countries suggested that the transition was likely to take a generation or more. In circumstances of demographic 'explosion', the process of development would begin to lag further and further behind. The pace at which the social architecture—jobs, health facilities, schools—could be built would never catch up with the numbers of people needing them; meanwhile, those resources which could be used for social investment might well be drained away by the pressure of indigence, the bottomless pit of want.

These calculations encouraged national leaders to try and identify ways of hastening the process along. The most obvious way was to raise people's income, the most guaranteeable precondition of a change in fertility behaviour; but raising the income of the poor was itself the object of the development process being threatened by population growth. As with other issues related to family health and food supply, the challenge was to help overcome a high birth rate as a typical manifestation of poverty without having first to resolve the poverty itself. In the age of the modern technological breakthrough, it was natural to turn to the contraceptive device as the mass therapy for mankind's over-indulgence in reproduction.

Since the early years of the twentieth century, and before, much pioneering work had been done by private individuals and philanthropic organizations to spread information about techniques of birth control. Since time immemorial, just as society had evolved beliefs, behaviour patterns, and taboos designed to support high fertility, it had also adopted means of dealing with unwanted pregnancies and births. Much of the humanitarian effort devoted to birth control had been undertaken in an effort to replace abortion, infanticide and child abandonment with more acceptable techniques. Early campaigners on behalf of women's rights claimed as fundamental the right of a woman to control her own fertility and avoid the servitude and risks of almost uninterrupted pregnancy and childbirth from puberty to menopause.

The first devices to prevent conception were actually introduced into European society in the eighteenth and nineteenth centuries by reputation-conscious madams, anxious to avoid the charge that their premises were the source of widespread venereal infection. Although many respectable people were at first unwilling to use mechanisms associated with prostitution, public health did at least require that the technology develop and improve, and it gradually came more widely into use by parents who wanted to make choices about the size and spacing of families without resorting to sexual abstinence.

The campaigners who extolled the virtues of the contraceptive device as a means of planning family size excited the opprobrium of Roman Catholic theologians, as well as opposition from other Christians and religious believers who objected to the idea of tampering artificially with the sacred process of creating new life in the womb. Here was an issue so inextricable from long-rooted patterns of social and cultural behaviour, as well as from fundamental conviction, that it inspired great passion and emotion. But none of this originally had anything to do with population growth, a subject which until the 1950s was quite unconnected with women's rights or public health, and was the exclusive preserve of demographers and statisticians.

Once development prospects began to be perceived as linked to, and even determined by, the phenomenon of a population 'crisis', attitudes about family planning began to change. The idea of limiting a woman's chances of pregnancy had been current long before the widespread use of contraceptives; but in many people's minds family planning and contraception became interchangeable terms. To consider either or both, parents had to want to limit the size of their families, or space the intervals between births. By this time, it was so taken for granted in most industrialized societies that this was a universally desirable object that little serious attention was paid to whether or not Third World people would see the matter in the same light. Mechanistic means of achieving results were for some time the predominant concern of those anxious to control the developing world's rate of population growth. Their strategy was to spread the doctrine of family planning and distribute contraceptives to its adherents.

Thus became identified the social and economic policy makers' interests with those of the public health and women's rights protagonists. The condom, the diaphragm, the spermicide—superceded by the pill, the loop, and sterilization—were promoted from the quiet seclusion of the personal closet to an altogether grander and more public role as instruments of social and economic design. What had previously been regarded as a matter only for an individual's or couple's private consideration, having little or nothing to do with the rest of the community, society or nation, now became a matter on which public figures pronounced and certain governments propagandized. To many, both secular and religious, in societies all over the world, this change was profoundly shocking. The two originally quite separate concepts of birth control and population policy were talked of as if they were synonymous, a confusion which served to exacerbate the skein of controversies which now surrounded not only the use of artificial methods of impeding conception, but with the causes and dimensions of the population problem, and with the idea that Third World countries should adopt policies which to some sounded like national castration.

Every political, religious, national and cultural group had a position for or against an overt policy of fertility restraint. Accusations of racial engineering were hurled from those in the developing world who pointed out that no Western country had ever introduced a government programme for reducing the birth rate. Socialist opinion, while advocating the right of women to a choice about childbearing, was suspicious of support for birth control programmes designed to reduce the numbers of the poor. Family planning, it was suggested, seemed to be Capitalism's latest ploy for solving problems by means other than the redistribution of wealth and the dismantling of the class society. Most vehement in its opposition was the Roman Catholic Church. Countries with predominantly Catholic populations, which included all of Latin America and, in Asia, the Philippines, might well accept that population growth was a serious problem; but they were at the same time scandalized by the policies of countries which advocated family planning *pro bono publico*, and which even paid for contraceptives and sterilization from the public purse.

Given the sensitivities the subject aroused, it was not surprising—though many found it inexcusable—that the organizations involved in international co-operation entered the debate relatively late, and only with great reluctance. Within the UN system, B. R. Sen, Director-General of FAO, pushing ahead with the Freedom from Hunger Campaign in the face of declining food production all over the developing world, was willing to draw the inevitable conclusion, and publicly suggest that it was not possible to go on repudiating family planning.

Within the UN itself, the Bureau for Social Affairs, whose demographers played a dispassionate role in analyzing the causes and consequences of population growth, was constantly trying behind the scenes to push both Unicef and WHO in the family planning direction. WHO was unwilling to take premature decisions about the safety of pills and intra-uterine devices, and tried to keep out of the controversy by remaining immersed in medical enquiry about the health effects of family planning techniques. Unicef, which had to consider the issue only within the context of mothers' and children's health, did not wish to run ahead of WHO, whose endorsement of any policy it adopted in the field of health was essential.

By the middle of the 1960s, the moment had come when the debate could no longer be postponed, either within Unicef or within the rest of the UN system. India and Pakistan had both made it clear that they would welcome assistance with their national family planning programmes. Here were the test cases for Unicef: the Executive Board could not make a decision about these specific requests without arriving at a view on family planning as a whole. In June 1965, Labouisse's first Executive Board session, the decision about whether or not to provide family planning assistance to India and Pakistan was deferred until 1966. Unicef's secretariat had a year in which to reflect, consult and put together its considered view on what the policy ought to be.

One delegation to Unicef's Executive Board had been raising the twin issues of population control and family planning for several years: the

Swedish. When they first brought these issues up in 1959, Unicef's literature was already beginning to reflect the economists' growing concern with population statistics, drawing attention to the ominous increase in the numbers of children in need, compared with the increase in the food supply. However, the reaction of the Swedish delegate, who intimated out loud and in public that this laid a responsibility on Unicef to engage somehow in measures for birth control, produced a shock wave of disapproval and even disgust among some Board delegates. Such a delicate matter had never been brought before them, even obliquely.

In the years that followed, Nils Thedin, leader of the Swedish delegation, continued to make similar statements before the Board. Sweden was trying, not only in Unicef but elsewhere in the UN family, to shame the various organizations into taking up what the Swedes regarded as a problem of the most vital importance to the future of Mankind. For a year or two, Thedin and his colleagues in UN circles found themselves all but ostracized by other delegates, so lacking in taste and statesmanship did their crusade appear. While contemporary analysis gave constantly heightened attention to the threat to development of unrestrained population growth, the international community, including Unicef, assumed an ostrich-like detachment. They responded either with silence or side-stepped the issue by stating that it was exclusively the concern of governments to decide not only for or against a population policy, but also whether it was right to give family planning advice and contraceptives to those who, because of their ignorance and poverty, either did not have an idea of planning their families or had no means of doing so.

This position was tinged with hypocrisy, for on other issues—on the needs of the preschool child, for example—Unicef took it upon itself to act as spokesman and advocate, trying to increase awareness of a problem as a prelude to offering help in solving it. With population growth and family planning, the reverse applied. Since 1961 and the Survey on the Needs of Children, it had been agreed that if a country could make out a strong case for certain strategic programmes as a priority for improving children's lives, then Unicef would be prepared to consider providing almost any reasonable kind of support. However, when India and Pakistan established as a priority for children's well-being a reduction in family size and asked for support to their family planning programmes, Unicef had a pre-determined reaction which was far from open-minded.

During the early 1960s, the mood within Unicef began to change. At Board sessions Nils Thedin gradually began to find an ally or two willing to reinforce the importance of family planning in health—its confirmation of the dignity of motherhood and the positive effects of family spacing on the life chances of the individual child. The emotional charge surrounding the issue seemed to be weakening. By 1965, pressure was coming not only from Sweden, but also from the US and elsewhere to raise the issue and debate it fully. Unicef could hardly be serious about its new emphasis on planning for the needs of children and youth at the national level if the twin issues of population growth and uncontrolled fertility were not to be directly tackled. The two post-Bellagio regional meetings on planning and children, which took place in Santiago and Bangkok in November 1965 and March 1966 respectively, raised them openly and addressed them seriously. Under the pressure of what was now being widely described as a population and development crisis, opinion was rapidly changing.

Population control *per se* was not a subject on which Unicef wished in any way to become embroiled. The question of whether governments should adopt policies designed to contain the birth rate as part of the balance between the production of national resources and their consumption was not within Unicef's competence to judge, nor mandate to pronounce upon. The only legitimate population crisis to concern Unicef was the one that took place in people's homes, particularly in the homes of the poor, and adversely affected the well-being of mothers and children and the quality of family life.

A family with a large number of children, particularly one already suffering from poverty, had acute difficulty in stretching its resources to give each child enough to eat, let alone to provide the educational and other kinds of attention each child needed to develop his or her potential in life. This predicament was more visible in urban shanty towns, where families crowded together in one- or two-room shacks felt their own 'population crisis' in a way quite unfamiliar in the elastic, expandable family compound typical of many rural areas. In the cities, where food and household items must all be bought for cash, children as a workforce for garnering produce from the natural environment were not a source of wealth but an economic burden—unless, of course, they were sent out to run errands, to beg, to steal, to pimp, or to otherwise 'work' at a very early age, which was indeed increasingly happening in the cities of Latin America and some of those in Asia. In such circumstances, where parents' ability to nurture and raise their children was being hampered by their lack of means to stop conception, it was becoming more and more difficult to make out a case against the provision of family planning services.

In the towns, people already had some incentive to take whatever measures they could to control their fertility. In the countryside, unless there was great pressure on land and family holdings being subdivided into extinction, children were still almost automatically listed on the credit side of the family balance-sheet. A workforce was needed to help plant, till, harvest the crop and herd the livestock; sons were needed because men ran the family as they ran everything else; daughters were needed to draw water, help bring up younger siblings, carry out chores. Until parents believed that the children they did have would survive and be able to care for them in their old age, they had little incentive to limit the size of their families. But if the arguments for family planning in the rural areas were not so strong on the grounds of overall family well-being, they were strong for other reasons.

All the evidence suggested that uncontrolled fertility had serious effects on the health of a woman's offspring, as well as on her own physical condition. When pregnancies were spaced at intervals over the span of child-bearing years, the chances of survival and good health for both mother and child were considerably enhanced. In some societies, this was intrinsically recognized by the custom of sexual abstinence during lactation; kwashiorkor, the protein deficiency condition in small children, was named for the effects of poor birth spacing: 'the disease of the child deposed from the breast' by the inopportune arrival of another.

Apart from abstinence, which was not a convenient system of birth control except in a polygamous society, breast feeding itself was the only available natural contraceptive; in some societies, breast feeding was prolonged partly to capitalize on this effect. Although it was true that in poor rural families, a large number of children were needed to support the domestic economy, it was also a myth to imagine that every poor rural mother looked upon every pregnancy as a blessing.

Frequent pregnancy could ruin a woman's health. Women became psychologically exhausted and prematurely aged by the endless treadmill of reproduction; in some cultures there were special names for such a condition. Rearing many small children was also taxing in parts of the world where women routinely carried out many agricultural tasks and men took no responsibility in any domestic area, leaving it to the women to provide the household's food, fuel and water. Where mothers feared not being able to feed and care for a newborn child, the evidence of history showed that they frequently took steps to avoid doing so in ways which themselves could be dangerous and injurious to health. Even into the 1960s and beyond, abortion was still the most commonly used form of family planning worldwide. Since it was usually performed without the sanction of law and often inexpertly, the admission to maternity wards of patients suffering from the ill-effects of an illegal abortion was common in many countries, and abortion was still a significant and unnecessary cause of maternal death.

In May 1966, having carefully examined and set out all the most up-to-date information on the implications of high birth rates and lack of birth spacing on the well-being of mothers and children, Harry Labouisse laid before the Unicef Executive Board a modest proposal about a possible role for Unicef in family planning. The delegates had convened in Addis Ababa for the session as a salute to the new importance of African countries. Emperor Haile Selassie received Unicef's dignitaries at the Imperial Palace; discussions on planning for the needs of African children proceeded harmoniously, but the debate on family planning eclipsed all else on the agenda. The first, cautious suggestion to be presented formally to the governing body of an organization in the UN system that multilateral funds should be spent on providing poor mothers with access to family planning produced the most bitter and most explosive confrontation in Unicef's twenty years of existence.

The thrust of the Unicef proposal was summed up in the phrase 'responsible parenthood'. Where 'family planning' carried connotations of an inflammatory kind, Labouisse, in presenting the secretariat's recommendations, tried to neutralize their effect by pointing to responsible parenthood as the context in which Unicef's involvement in family planning should be approached. Certain measures which helped indirectly to improve the quality of family life—improving the status of women, promoting literacy, raising the marriage age, expanding MCH services—also had the effect of moderating population growth. Many of these were directly in line with Unicef's objectives and already encompassed by existing programmes. The problem with all of them from the point of view of family planning was that they were several steps away from the actual decision by a couple to do something to avoid pregnancy, and therefore their effect on the birth rate was slow-acting.

In order to have something more direct to offer governments, it was proposed that Unicef help might suitably be used to establish family planning elements within expanded MCH services. Traditional types of assistance could be offered: training stipends, teaching aids, vehicles, equipment; but positively no contraceptives.

Conversely, where a government had set up a family planning service with a separate workforce from the MCH network, Unicef would offer the family planners other kinds of MCH training and equipment so as to allow them to serve the health needs of mothers and children more completely. No advice would be offered by Unicef on any family planning technique, nor would Unicef seek to persuade any country to adopt a family planning programme.

This was the first occasion of significance within the UN system on which governments were obliged to lay their positions on family planning and population control squarely on the table. Whatever the tact with which Unicef presented its suggestions, however carefully stressed the connection between health and family spacing and the disassociation of Unicef from any recommendation of artificial contraception, they unleashed a storm among the member governments of the Unicef Board which encompassed the entire range of controversy on the subject.

The strongest protagonists in the proposals' favour were the delegates of India and Pakistan. Both countries had submitted requests for family planning assistance which depended on the outcome of the debate on the principle; Dr Sushila Nayer, the Indian Minister of Health and Family Planning, had flown to Addis Ababa to take part in the debate. The strongest antagonists were those who represented the Roman Catholic view on impeding procreation. In between were the representatives of the Socialist countries, who suspected that the population crisis was concocted by Western capitalist propaganda. Their position had something in common with that of certain developing countries, most of which were Catholic and Latin American, which believed that the population problem would take care of the world and the nations would dedicate themselves more forcefully to economic progress. Then there were those who protested against modern contraceptive technology on the grounds of its unknown risks to health. Last but not least were a few countries in Africa which believed that the population crisis was a racist invention, and that contraception was an offence against family custom and an incitement to female promiscuity.

In spite of the fact that the Executive Director had specifically stressed that Unicef would not provide contraceptive supplies for any family planning programme—nor equipment with which they could be made, nor advice on any contraceptive technique—the crux of the dispute concerned the use of artificial devices to prevent pregnancy: the anathema of Catholic orthodoxy on human reproduction. It was not that delegates from predominantly Catholic countries deliberately misheard the Unicef case. Rather, their objection was to the endorsement of the use of condoms, pills and intra-uterine devices which was implied by Unicef support of any kind to a programme exhorting people to use these items.

Some of the delegates from Catholic countries were willing to support the idea of spreading information among women about the effects of repeated pregnancy on their own and their children's health; others wished such information to be limited to demographic data and trends. Some were opposed to Unicef's association with any information; whatever disavowal was now being made, they believed that it would be impossible to control what Unicef's name was or was not associated with. Visual aids and educational pamphlets used in a programme such as India's would inevitably advertise the use of contraceptives, and assistance from Unicef would therefore imply endorsement of their use, which in turn would imply the endorsement of the members of the Board. This was unacceptable to the delegates of Switzerland, Belgium, the Philippines, Peru, Brazil and others.

Many of these objections took the form of criticism that Unicef should presume, in the interests of maternal and child health, to adopt policies which WHO itself did not espouse. If Unicef's position on family planning was timid, WHO's was even more so. It was elaborated at such a high plane of ambivalence, in spite of the presence at the Board session of the Assistant Director-General Dr Lucien Bernard, that it was difficult to determine where exactly WHO stood. Consequently, the opposing sides both cited its position in their favour. Unicef had consulted with WHO while drawing up its proposals, but WHO had not subsequently offered any opinion on their contents, nor was it prepared to do so now. WHO's problem was that the only resolutions on family planning to be successfully negotiated through the World Health Assemblies of 1965 and 1966—in which the governments of 104 countries were represented as compared with thirty on Unicef's Board—were monuments to the caution required to avoid just such a confrontation as was now in progress.

Material aid to family planning programmes had been rejected by a substantial majority of the World Health Assembly on the grounds that the potential health hazards of the new contraceptive technology were as yet inadequately explored. WHO's role was currently confined to advice to governments, upon request, on programmes conducted within the framework of an existing health service. Under WHO auspices, various scientific groups were studying the clinical, chemical and physiological effects on human reproduction of the pill and the intra-uterine device. The preamble of the key WHO resolution stated that: 'Scientific knowledge with regard to human reproduction is still insufficient'. This was the phrase to which the opponents of contraception clung. In reply, the proponents pointed out that scientific enquiry into the biological impact of certain family planning techniques would never be complete, and that this had not inhibited certain countries from running effective family planning services for many years.

As the debate proceeded, its tone became increasingly heated. At one extreme was the statement of Dr Adeniyi-Jones, the delegate of Nigeria, who roundly condemned those who, for religious reasons were unwilling to provide family planning services for women desperate to avoid further pregnancies, and whose existing families would suffer because they were unable to make such a choice. People in the privileged sector of society, he pointed out to a hall full of them, were conspicuously successful in limiting their families to manageable proportions. It was cruelly unjust that those very individuals should be depriving others who were much less privileged of the opportunity to do the same. Board members, he went on, should take the responsibility of explaining to their governments that it would be out of keeping with the Universal Declaration of Human Rights to impose their own beliefs and attitudes on India and Pakistan by withholding family planning assistance.

At the other extreme was the delegate of Belgium, Hilaire Willot, who went so far as to say that if the proposals were approved, this 'would imply a distinct change in Unicef policy and a basic modification of the voluntary contract which has bound together its member States . . . A number of members would doubtless consider themselves released from their obligations'. Hans Conzett of Switzerland also talked of the loss in contributions which he believed would result if Unicef lent its support to the Indian family planning programme—a programme which he found particularly shocking because it included offering incentives to candidates for sterilization. In his view, support for such a programme would plunge Unicef's credit 'to zero' with little prospect of recovery.

There was strenuous objection, particularly from Nils Thedin of Sweden, to the use of economic pressure by any delegate. But strong-arm tactics, however unwelcome, were effective. Even family planning's strongest supporters were not willing to risk driving Unicef into impotent division over the issue. Although they seemed to have a slim majority in their favour, they conceded the field, and the decision was deferred until the following year. In the meantime, the WHO/Unicef Joint Committee on Health Policy was asked to study the matter and offer its opinion. The projects submitted for India and Pakistan were dismantled into their maternal and child health and family planning components. Unicef aid could train midwives, provide forceps and rubber gloves for safe deliveries, distribute iron and folates against anaemia and low birth-weight, give tetanus shots to mothers and newborns, extol the merits of long birth intervals and small families, but in no way be tarnished by even the remotest connection with a contraceptive device. That was the outcome of the 1966 debate.

At the time it was hard to imagine that the intransigence of family planning's adversaries could mellow.

During the course of the following year, Labouisse used his persuasive negotiating talents to bring the discordant views into some kind of consensus. In 1967, the Board took up the postponed discussion on the basis of the Joint Committee on Health Policy's report. Extreme care was given to the new presentation of the case. Any reference to family planning beyond its incontrovertible implications for maternal and child health was carefully avoided, and exemplary respect was paid to WHO's superior medical wisdom. The underlying assumption of the case was that any responsible medical practitioner providing care for mothers and children was properly concerned with fertility, pregnancy and birth spacing; and that family planning was therefore an integral part of a comprehensive health service. If this were the case, then it would be irrational not to support the family planning component while supporting all other antenatal and postnatal components.

This, with some difficulty, even the most resolute opponents were just able to swallow. There was to be no separate category of assistance to family planning: fertility was exclusively a medical concern. There must be not even a whiff of international approval for the policies of those governments who saw birth control as an instrument of economic and social regulation independently of its health implications. What the Board actually approved amounted only to increased support for maternal and child health services. In terms of what Unicef might offer, the progress in policy evolution was minute. But symbolically, a major step had been taken: the phrases 'family planning' and 'Unicef co-operation' had been joined.

Unicef had made a very tentative attempt to align itself with the growing body of opinion which saw population growth as one reason why poor people stayed poor and deprived children stayed deprived. It had wanted to enlist the new contraceptive technology actively on their behalf. The attempt was conclusively defeated, although attitudes did loosen up over the next few years. The 1966 UN General Assembly unanimously passed a resolution entitled 'Population Growth and Economic Development', calling for action to support governments undertaking programmes in the field of population. For some, this still meant demography. But within a year or two, the international mood had swung conclusively in the direction of those who had spent some years trying to persuade policy-makers to overcome their scruples about family planning. Under the influence of growing trepidation in the world at large, the family planners were gradually increasing their domination of the population issue. Those who had fought so hard to prevent any entry of the international community into fertility control had in retrospect been trying to plug their fingers in a dike which was gradually succumbing to the weight of an historical process.

In Unicef, the crack represented by the 1967 decision began to widen. WHO increasingly stressed that any measure for preventing or interrupting pregnancy must be integrated with maternal and child health services and supervised by the same professional personnel. The effort to make family planning services a part of health care, rather than a separate operation run by planners, economists or whoever was in charge of population policy, was one in which Unicef fully complied. By the end of the decade, the strong feelings which had so pervaded the debate between the nations on Unicef's Board only four years before had eased to the point where they were even willing to agree that Unicef might provide contraceptive supplies.

By this stage, over $3 million had been committed to programmes in twelve countries in Asia, the Middle East, Latin America and the Caribbean. In 1971, it was agreed that other social programmes than those run by health services — agricultural and home economics extension, literacy campaigns, women's education, community development — were suitable vehicles for family planning advice. In 1973, Unicef invited Mrs Titi Memet, then working in the Indonesian Ministry of Social Affairs, to become its special adviser on family planning, and more emphasis began to be placed on women's rights and women's status as part of the key to smaller family sizes.

By this time, however, the heat had been taken off both Unicef and WHO by the establishment of the UN Fund for Population Activities (UNFPA). The creation of a special trust fund for population work, in which the US and Sweden again played the predominant role, was announced by Secretary-General U Thant in 1967. To the relief of other UN organizations, the population issue was now notionally disentangled from their activities. Contributions to UNFPA were voluntary, so those governments with reservations need not support its work, nor threaten on pain of involvement with family planning to withdraw their assistance from other programmes. To the extent consistent with other organizations' policies, UNFPA carried out its programme in close collaboration with them. It provided Unicef, for example, with funds for family planning components of health programmes which Unicef was already supporting.

UNFPA inherited all the problems connected with population and family planning issues; but at least it could concentrate wholeheartedly on those problems and leave other organizations free from the controversies they provoked—and from the new generation of controversies that have taken their place in the 1980s.

By the early 1970s, the confidence with which the advocates of family planning had asserted that they could slow down the pace of population growth was beginning to evaporate.

Their expectations had been based on the assumption that the majority of people in the developing countries, with the possible exception of those in Africa, found large numbers of children a burden. In 1966, when Unicef had put together its case in favour of family planning, surveys from Latin America and Asia on parents' view of the ideal number of children had suggested between two and four. Dr Sushila Nayer had told the Unicef Board delegates in Addis Ababa that seventy per cent of Indian couples, both in urban and rural areas, wanted help in limiting family size. Such calculations turned out to be over-optimistic, but they encouraged the experts to believe that free contraceptives and advice need only be placed at the disposal of the population and customers would rush to help themselves. Once the major family planning programmes really began to expand, experience proved that this was far from the case. Like other exports from the technologically advanced societies to their poorer neighbours, modern contraceptive devices met with a decidedly mixed reception. Behaviour to do with such intimate matters is not susceptible to overnight change, and most people in poor societies were as yet far from attuned to the idea of limiting family size.

The field of population studies had been only recently removed from the slide rules and abstractions of the demographers, and it took time to discover what people's real attitudes were towards the revolutionary possibility of controlling what went on in their reproductive organs.

In most parts of the developing world, large families and frequent pregnancies were still part of the immutable fabric of life, taken as much for granted as the rising and setting of the sun. Many parents held an entirely fatalistic view of family size, assuming children to be the gift of the almighty; or simply felt 'the more the better'. Above all, it was important to bear sons, whose task it was in many societies to maintain parents in their old age, administer their burial rights and carry on the family lineage. Before people would abandon such ideas, they had to first believe that enough of the children—especially sons—born to the household would survive in good health into adulthood. Such a conviction might only come after a decade, or even a generation.

People also had to feel a 'population crisis' in their own household: the family landholding had to be subdivided into too many pieces; the dwelling had to be too cramped; the school fees or uniforms for several children too difficult to find; the cost of food, fuel, clothes and other essentials too high; the value of children's 'work' diminished by changing agricultural, lifestyle or employment patterns. Life-styles in many Third World countries were undergoing extraordinary shifts and upheavals, many exacerbated by burgeoning population growth and the high proportion of children and young people in the society. But to those caught up in these shifts, the overwhelming problem might not be perceived as family size, nor birth control the obvious solution. The likely response to subdivision of the land-holding or shortage of income was for one or more family members to seek their fortune in the town. The way to keep down the costs of education might well be to keep girl children out of school. In time, the computation of a variety of social and economic factors, backed up by the spread of information, was bound to make contraception more appealing to more people; but providing pills, loops and sterilizations free of charge was not on its own a quick route to population growth slow-down.

Some of the countries which took up family planning with enthusiasm threw too much effort into promoting their use to the exclusion of other social programmes. Pakistan began an all-out national family planning scheme towards the end of 1965. When Harry Labouisse visited both West and East Pakistan in December 1966, President Ayub Khan told him that population control was Pakistan's number one priority. The target was to reduce the birth rate from fifty to forty per 1000 by 1970, and the campaign was already in full spate. Every one of the country's twenty million fertile couples was to be reached, preferably with an IUD. Once an IUD was inserted, neither wife nor partner had any more contraceptive decisions or actions to take.

Pakistan's programme envisaged that IUD insertions would mainly take place as part of maternal and child health care. Lady doctors, midwives and lady health visitors were all given a special training. The country's *dais*—traditional midwives—were taught to round up the customers. Everyone, from doctors to *dais* and acceptors, were given special financial rewards.

But in many parts of the country there were no MCH clinics where mothers could go to receive their loops. As in the case of the mass campaigns against disease, impatience to achieve results led to the family planning campaign going off on its own limb, with its own staff and its own targets — and becoming detached from the mainstream of public health expansion. In many places, the campaign took on the atmosphere of a travelling circus: teams of family planners and tented camps, and injunctions through all available media channels to persuade women to line up and get their IUD inserted immediately. With no medical back-up to deal with the health problems which many IUD acceptors encountered, the massive campaign began to run into resistance and difficulty. Its final results were disappointing. The 1972 census showed no appreciable drop in the fertility rate, in spite of a total investment of $60 million over the five-year period.

In 1974, economists, demographers, social scientists, health officials and family planners met in Bucharest for the World Population Conference. This was one of the international meetings convened under the auspices of the UN to discuss critical problems facing Mankind. The urgent question was how to slow down the rate of population growth which, contemporary estimates suggested, would double the number of people in the world within twenty-five years, placing on earth eight billion people by the year 2000. The economists and planners no longer thought that the family planners held the answer to the problem. Disillusion had set in; there was a place in population control for pills and loops, but they were no substitute for development itself. Until the standard of living of the poor improved, and they could feel the economic advantages of the two- or three-child family, they would continue to have large numbers of offspring. Even where the idea of spacing births and avoiding constant pregnancy was catching on, most Third World parents wanted large families — families with double the number of children than most of their industrialized world counterparts.

WHO, supported by Unicef, worked hard at the Bucharest Population Conference to replace the link in people's minds between demographic trends and family planning, and replace it with the link between health care and family planning. The well-being of the existing children was the best persuasion that a mother need not bear another. Harry Labouisse, addressing the Conference, said: 'I want to invite you to look at the population problem not from the point of view of technical analyses and devastating predications regarding demography and national economies, but from the point of view of individual human beings, the family and the child . . . It is in the family, among parents and future parents, that the ultimate decisions are made, consciously or unconsciously, as to the number and spacing of children . . . I am therefore convinced that, to be really effective, national policies in the population field must be translated into specific measures that directly touch the lives of individual families, encouraging them to make, voluntarily, very personal decisions that will improve the quality of their own lives, while also being in accord with national policy.'

Many of the resolutions and plans of action adopted at the conference confirmed Unicef's own view of family planning as part of 'responsible parenthood'. The wheel had turned another circle. In less than a decade conventional wisdom regarding the population crisis had twice been turned on its head. The defeat which the Unicef exponents of family planning had suffered in the late 1960s in the effort to make it an important area of the organization's activity now left the policy exactly where expert international opinion said it should be. A mix of health and social ingredients akin to the list of measures thought to be conducive to 'responsible parenthood' were becoming accepted by many experts as the new orthodoxy on family planning and population control.

The evidence for this analysis could be found in an increasing number of countries or regions where a combination of effective social development and family planning programmes had made a dramatic impact on both the birth and population growth rates. These included Korea, Kerala (India), Taiwan, Malaysia and Singapore. In Sri Lanka, to take one case, the improvement in the spread of rural health services which began in the 1950s led to a drop in infant mortality from seventy-eight to forty-five per 1000 in twenty years, and an associated decline in the birth rate from thirty-nine to twenty-nine per 1000.

By the late 1970s, the demographers' more dramatic forecasts of population figures for the year 2000 were being gradually revised downwards. Fertility rates were declining all over Asia, the most populous part of the world. Because the parents of the next generation had already been born, another transition period was required before the population growth rate followed suit; but already in East Asia there were signs that this was happening. By the early 1980s, it had similarly slackened in the rest of Asia and by the 1990s, it is expected to have done so for the developing world as a whole.

Although the declines, like those in death rates before them, are the net result of a complex web of factors which vary from country to country and region to region, one vital precondition is a drop in the child and infant mortality rates; and there is also no doubt that those countries where there have been active and well-organized family planning programmes have experienced a faster fertility decline than others.

Apart from the eruption at Addis Ababa, which briefly mired Unicef in dispute—and constituted the most serious threat ever to its unruffled cohesion around the cause of children—the family planning issue was also significant in forming a link in the chain of Unicef's overall policy evolution. It brought into prominence two other areas. One was the pitiful and squalid conditions in the exploding cities of the developing world. Mass migration from the countryside to the city was becoming one of the most disturbing phenomena of the contemporary scene, born indirectly from the pressure of people on agricultural land and employment.

The other was women's rights. Amidst all the clamour about artificial contraception and whether it encouraged immorality, no-one had seriously resisted the notion that a woman had a right to a free choice about what should, or should not, happen in her womb. If Unicef supported family planning, however obliquely, this meant that for the first time it had implicitly recognized that women as women, and not just as mothers, were worthy of its attention. By the end of the first Development Decade, urbanization and women's rights were two of the new issues looming over the development horizon.

Main sources:

Notes on the biography and career of Henry Richardson Labouisse prepared by Sherwin Moe, 1983; interviews with Henry Labouisse and others by Jack Charnow for the Unicef History Project, 1983, 1984, 1985; articles and press cuttings concerning the career of Henry Labouisse from Unicef publications and other sources.

'Population and Family-planning Programs in Newly Developing Countries', an essay by J. Mayone Stycos in *Population: the Vital Revolution*, edited by Ronald Freedman, published by Aldine Publishing Company, Chicago, 1965. First published as a Doubleday Anchor Original in 1964.

Unicef Executive Board documentation 1965/66/67/70/71, in particular 'Family Planning: Report of the Executive Director on the Possible Role of Unicef'; statements to the Executive Board by Henry Labouisse, Dr Sushila Nayer, Dr Lucien Bernard, Dr Hans Conzett; summary records of meetings 25–27 May 1966; project recommendations for India and Pakistan; reports of the Board; report of the WHO/Unicef Joint Committee on Health Policy, February 1967.

People: An International Choice; the Multilateral Approach to Population, Raphael M. Salas, Executive Director, UN Fund for Population Activities, published by Pergamon Press, 1976.

Articles in *Unicef News*, and in the *New Internationalist* magazine.

Chapter 11

Earthquake, Wind and Fire

On 29 February 1960, the worst earthquake ever recorded on the African continent struck the city of Agadir on the Moroccan coast. There were two shocks, followed by a tidal wave. More than three-quarters of the city was reduced to rubble, and fire consumed most of the rest. Nearly one-third of the city's 45,000 people were thought to have perished, and the rest were left homeless and traumatized. Unicef was one among the many international organizations which immediately sent in relief supplies, adding its cargoes to the melée of tents, blankets, food and other supplies pouring in on behalf of the stricken population.

The earthquake at Agadir was only one of many disasters in various parts of the world in which Unicef continued to act in its original, emergency-relief capacity. During and after the postwar recovery period in Europe, there were the refugee crises in the Indian subcontinent and in the Middle East, earthquakes in Ecuador and Greece, wars in Korea and Vietnam, and the Hungarian uprising; in all of these situations Unicef helped care for children and mothers, often delivering its relief supplies through the local Red Cross or Red Crescent Society.

As the postwar period gave way to the era of development, Unicef became disenchanted with the role of instant saviour and band-aid supplier. After 1950, when directed by the UN General Assembly to concentrate on longer-term problems of children in the underdeveloped parts of the world, there was a purposeful withdrawal from the emergency role. In 1953, the word 'Emergency' was dropped from the organization's title. At the beginning of the 1950s emergency relief constituted eighty-five per cent of goods sent overseas; by the end of the decade, the proportion declined to an average of only seven per cent per year.

The earthquake at Agadir was particularly calamitous in the size of the shock, and the scale on which it shattered lives, homes and property. In its aftermath, international relief poured into the stricken area. Mobilized at short notice, without the benefit of proper assessments of needs and local conditions, an inevitable proportion of what was sent was questionably useful, became jammed in the overflowing relief pipeline, went unaccounted for, or duplicated what had been sent from elsewhere. The disorganization on the ground was relayed to the rest of the world via the international news media whose ubiquitous presence at major disaster scenes was becoming an integral part of the world's response. The publicity surrounding relief at Agadir attracted some notoriety to the international organizations involved. Within Unicef it provoked a debate on what the contemporary role in disasters ought to be.

As in many other organizations whose mainspring was humanitarian relief but which were now caught up with the challenge of development, the discussions reflected a common perception: that disaster relief and development co-operation were two quite different kinds of activity. A relief operation assuaged the distress caused by something unusual and devastating happening to a large number of people, until circumstances returned to normal and their lives could pick up from where they left off. The purpose of development co-operation, while it might also have the short-term effect of relieving distress, aimed to do the very opposite of leaving people in a position to lead the same lives they had previously led; it was intended to transform the circumstances of their lives into something permanently better. The difference between the two was the difference between charitable hand-outs and investment; and those humanitarian organizations whose purpose was not explicitly confined to emergency relief had spent the past decade working out that, as far as underdeveloped countries were concerned, investment was the more attractive proposition. Expenditures on instant succour vanished into a bottomless pit; and they deflected scarce resources away from tasks such as building up permanent maternal- and child-health networks, and attacking disease and malnutrition.

This viewpoint was encapsulated by the often-repeated Chinese proverb: 'Give a man a fish and you feed him for a day; teach him to fish and you feed him for life'. In March 1960, the Swedish delegation tentatively suggested to the Unicef Executive Board, meeting a month after the earthquake at Agadir, that Unicef had acted over-hastily in its anxiety to arrive swiftly on the scene, and might do well in the future to leave emergencies to others. But this idea provoked considerable opposition. However tidy their logic, the fact was then, and has remained since, that a retreat from disaster relief as a matter of policy was neither desirable nor practicable.

Any disaster—particularly the sudden calamity, but also the slow creeping kind whose demands may last months or even years—requires the mobilization of different skills and competences, often at very short notice. It would be impossible to find in any organization the full range of expertise required; and wasteful to try and create such an organization and keep it on permanent stand-by. Unicef had special organizational qualities and experiences to offer for disaster-relief operations. It had a record of offering relief to mothers and children on both sides of an armed conflict; its network of programme staff based in the field were in a position to signal the need for emergency aid for the victims of obscure disasters—an epidemic in the Maldive Islands, a landslide in the Andes Mountains, a cyclone in Mauritius. Its well-oiled supplies machinery, with stockpiles of goods already to hand in New York, Copenhagen, and other places where regular programmes were already underway, could be mobilized at a moment's notice.

At least as important a reason for continuing to be active in disaster relief was organizational credibility. Unicef's role in emergencies was important not only for the victims, but for the way the organization was perceived by many of its supporters, particularly the private individuals who gave generously to relieve suffering through the fund-raising drives of national committees. An international organization established to help mothers and children in distress could not stand aloof from the victims of a catastrophic earthquake or cyclonic tidal wave. In the television era, when it was becoming commonplace for film footage of disaster victims in distant lands to be beamed into living rooms all over the Western world, it was impossible for an organization such as Unicef to sustain its image and public reputation if it did not appear to be active at the moment when the sufferings of those it existed to help were bathed in the glare of publicity.

The sympathy and generosity of ordinary citizens, and the pressure they exerted directly or indirectly on their governments, were given new force by the media revolution; television itself became part of the dynamics of disaster relief. This was a mixed blessing. On the one hand, it meant that Unicef national committees and other nongovernmental organizations were able to focus attention on suffering in the developing world with an ease normally denied them; in their capacity as angels of mercy they were themselves a part of the news event. The disaster represented a rare opportunity to capitalize on public concern for children, latent under ordinary circumstances, as well as raise funds on their behalf.

The less fortunate side of all the attention was that it also turned the spotlight onto the efforts of the authorities on the scene of the disaster, and on their partners—the humanitarian aid organizations—just at the moment when they were jointly struggling hardest to mount programmes of assistance in the most adverse of circumstances. For a high proportion of the public in the West, the time of a disaster was almost the only time their attention was concentrated on the people of the Third World, or on their governments. What they saw in the brief span of time in which their own and the media's attention were engaged was actually the conditions of life and absence of administrative capacity in an underdeveloped society, suddenly illuminated by a sensational and cataclysmic event. The picture they received was, therefore, full of overly bright patches and empty spaces, and often thoroughly distorted.

An earthquake, cyclone, hurricane, even a drought, may strike a population in North America or Europe as devastatingly as that of an underdeveloped society. But sophisticated networks of roads, communications, security systems, health facilities, public works, and the greater resources of those affected, help to absorb the blow. Once food and water have been assured, the homeless given temporary shelter, the hospitals' emergency services mobilized, and the debris cleared away—all actions normally well within the capacity of local resources and management—the community can bathe its wounds and return to the regular routine of daily living. Not in a poor and underdeveloped society. The word 'under-developed' describes social and economic conditions in which, by definition, there are neither resources nor capacity to cope with a major disaster, and in which the victims' return to regular daily living may mean a return to a less spectacular, but scarcely less devastating, condition of misery and destitution.

In the nature of things, disasters always do most damage among the least well-off. Those who live on the poorest agricultural land, semi-arid stretches where no modernized farming enterprise would bother to venture, suffer hunger first in a drought. The oldest and most ramshackle dwellings collapse first in an earthquake or hurricane. The flood does not reach the better-off because they live on the higher ground. The poor are almost always, therefore, the worst affected victims of any disaster—in the Third World or elsewhere. In the Third World, they are also, by definition, the most difficult to reach. Whether the disaster is of the creeping kind, such as a drought leading to a famine, or the sudden kind, such as an earthquake or a cyclone, the burden of relief distribution falls on the local authorities. The poorer the area affected, the fewer are the means—in goods, in communications, in transport, and in personnel—at the authorities' disposal, and the weaker is their capacity to organize relief. They may not have the port or airport facilities, road networks or personnel to handle a deluge of assistance, however much needed and imploringly sought.

External assistance can fill the supply pipeline, provide trucks, supplement personnel with experienced logistics, health and communications experts. But except in the world's remotest areas, where there is still no more than a semblance of an administrative structure or in areas of conflict where effective administration has broken down, external assistance cannot substitute for local effort. It can only supplement. Its efficacy depends on the existing or expanded mobilization of internal resources, including the army, police, church and voluntary organizations, hospital and medical services, as well as the civilian administration. The fact is obvious. But it is almost always omitted from the descriptions of Third World disaster-relief operations offered to the public in the Western world. And because the public's views of places and peoples unfamiliar to them are principally informed by the oversimplified presentations on the television news programmes, the obvious is obscured.

In the case of the sudden calamity, when an entire population is plunged into trauma, left homeless, foodless, waterless, and prey to exposure and epidemic, the need for rescue teams and emergency supplies is most acute in the first twenty-four to forty-eight hours. Few international organizations are able to arrive on the scene and distribute relief within that period. In almost every case, they raise funds and despatch goods of which the overwhelming majority are actually distributed in the post-disaster, or rehabilitation, phase. In the case of a disaster where the victims had almost nothing before it occurred, this can offer an opportunity to set up housing, health services and public works which do not simply re-institute the miserable standards of living people knew before, but introduce some permanent improvement. The impact of the disaster often shocks an administrative structure into existence, or expands it, in ways that make development more possible thereafter.

In the case of a creeping disaster, such as a drought, a high proportion of the assistance sent is similarly allocated not to the immediate saving of lives, but to nutrition, water or health-care schemes almost indistinguishable from those which, in another area of the country not suffering from drought, would be described in quite different terms. Here is where relief and development purposes fuse. Whatever the theoretical tug of war between the two; whatever the curious dichotomy which places one in the forefront of public attention and the other in its nethermost recesses, they belong on the same continuum.

During the 1960s, views within Unicef continued to ebb and flow about the right degree of involvement in disaster relief. In a modest way, Unicef responded to many of the major emergencies of the first years of the decade: the 1960–62 Congo crisis; the earthquake at Skopje in Yugoslavia in 1963; the continuing war in Algeria and Vietnam, as well as to crises of lesser magnitude. As time went on, the sharp edges of the dichotomy between disaster relief and development co-operation began to blur. By the middle of the decade, implicity if not explicitly, most of Unicef's aid for emergencies was being directed not to relieving immediate distress but to post-disaster rehabilitation which chimed in more fittingly with the emphasis on development co-operation. A reserve fund of $100,000 existed for the Executive Director to use for disaster relief at his discretion, allowing for a sudden airlift of cholera vaccines or high-protein food supplements. But the mood generally was one of reluctance to let emergencies divert organizational energies and resources away from the longer-term task to which Unicef now attached overriding priority.

No-one could have foreseen that events of the late 1960s, followed by others in the 1970s and beyond, would wreak havoc on this careful balance of priorities.

In 1965, India suffered a failure of the monsoon rains. The drought, one of the worst of the century, covered a large belt of central and southern India. Crop damage was extensive and, by early 1966, there was widespread food scarcity. The national harvest shortfall was estimated at twenty million tons.

This food emergency came during an acutely difficult period for India. In 1964, shattered by the war with China, Jawaharlal Nehru, India's only Prime Minister since Independence, died. His passing marked the end of an era. Then, in 1965, war erupted with Pakistan. Beset by political and economic uncertainties, alarmed by the high rate of population growth and low rate of food production, India in the second half of the 1960s was in a period of deeper crisis than she had known since Independence. The new Prime Minister, Indira Gandhi, had based her political platform on the conquest of poverty, and the food emergency brought on by the failure of the rains represented a major setback. India has well-developed procedures for dealing with situations of food shortage and famine; but it took time for the Government to assess the state of grain stocks, calculate the needs and plan the necessary logistics for the wide-scale relief programmes required. Not until its own machinery was in position was it ready to respond to offers of outside assistance. Gradually, the elements were manoeuvred into place, but not before a clamour about 'famine' and the slow pace of the Indian response had begun to reach the outside world. The raw nerve of Indian national pride was touched.

The condition of children in an area suffering from food shortage is the barometer of its severity. Their bodies indicate long before those of adults the absence of certain kinds of nutrients, and the debility which makes them vulnerable to coughs, fevers and diarrhoeal infections. Through its network of field staff—and, in turn, their relationships with officials in district administrations and with church and other voluntary organizations active on the ground—Unicef was independently aware of the deterioration of children's health in certain States, and did its best to impress upon federal government officials and upon its partners in the international community how serious it believed the situation to be. It also diverted to drought-stricken areas stocks of dried milk powder and medical supplies which had already been provided within its regular programme of support.

By the early part of 1966 the situation appeared to be reasonably in hand. The US government had shipped eight million tons of wheat to help make up the harvest shortfall. Many other countries had responded with bilateral offers of aid, as had UN and voluntary organizations, including many Freedom from Hunger committees, Catholic Relief services, Oxfam, the Friends, Lutheran World Relief and many others. Unicef national committees in the Netherlands, Switzerland and Sweden were raising funds for nutrition projects.

In 1966, the monsoon failed again. Two successive years of drought was highly unusual and potentially disastrous. This time the drought was less widespread, but particularly intense in the two north-eastern States of Bihar and Uttar Pradesh, of which Bihar was the most vulnerable. Bihar was one of the poorest and most densely populated States in India. Nine-tenths of the fifty-three million inhabitants lived entirely from the land, and more than a quarter were the families of landless labourers—people with few reserves of any kind. Even in a normal year Bihar suffered from food shortage. Only a very small proportion of the land was irrigated and therefore unaffected by a poor monsoon. All the preconditions for a catastrophe were present.

From June onwards, when the rains should have come, a relentless sun beat down. In August, the North Bihar plains were hit with heavy floods, washing out the newly-planted seed. Meanwhile, miles upon miles of rice paddies in the south which should have been green were parched and bare. When no rain fell in September, famine began to threaten. The autumn crop produced only a quarter of its usual harvest, and in some districts it produced next to nothing. Because of the drought the previous year, there was no grain, either to eat or to sow: all had already been consumed.

The impact of any drought on agricultural production, food stocks, grain prices; the levels of water in rivers, ponds and wells; the condition of livestock; and the physical health of human beings—all these build slowly by imperceptible degrees over many weeks, months, sometimes even years. Its effects vary from place to place within the drought-stricken area, and from one population group to another. People have different degrees of economic resilience to gradually rising prices, depending on whether they have reserves of some kind: land, valuables, sources of income from elsewhere. At any given moment in the process of gradual deterioration towards the kind of widespread hunger, whose gaunt and terrible images are evoked by the word 'famine', opinions differ about the severity of what is going on, how many people it is affecting, and whether the situation warrants a red alert, orange alert, or is merely a false alarm. At such times, those trying to signal a red alert—which often include the representatives of aid organizations, as well as many local officials, health and other personnel—may find themselves walking a tight-rope if there is official resistance towards the idea that uncontrolled 'famine' is stalking the land. If the representatives of international humanitarian effort push too hard, they risk alienating the government at whose pleasure they operate, and thereby curtail their chance of helping the victims. If they stand back, keep silent and wait for circumstances to alter in favour of a relief programme in which they can join, they risk the accusation of inaction from their donor constituency. Juggling these considerations is one of the most delicate problems facing any organization involved in disaster relief.

In the case of the Bihar famine, Indian sensitivities meant that there were delays and some foot-dragging. But ultimately they crumbled in the face of India's own instinct for self-exposure. Towards the end of 1966, an outcry began in the Indian press about the failure of the Bihar authorities to notice the plight of their countrymen. This outcry was taken up in the international press. Thirty million of the poorest and most nutritionally-deprived people to exist anywhere in the world stared starvation in the face, and neither the Indian nor international officialdom appeared to be doing much to save them.

In November 1966, Prime Minister Gandhi turned the tide by touring famine-stricken Bihar and Uttar Pradesh to see the effects of the drought for herself. Now national pride was laid aside, and national and international relief began to flow to the stricken areas at a much faster pace. Unicef had already begun to make plans for a special emergency operation, taking on additional Indian staff and recruiting volunteers from Canada and the US. Before setting out on his own tour of the famine-stricken areas in November, Harry Labouisse visited Mrs Gandhi in New Delhi and committed Unicef to a programme of emergency assistance for six million children.

Mrs Gandhi asked Labouisse to avoid exaggerating the horrors of the situation in Unicef's fund-raising publicity, and not to reinforce the impression conveyed by some relief agencies that they alone had discovered the emergency and were the only people doing anything to alleviate it. Labouisse fully respected Mrs Gandhi's viewpoint. He understood how exasperating it was to countries whose moment of independence was still within recent memory to find themselves portrayed exclusively to outsiders in shocking, negative, poverty-stricken and helpless terms. It gave the false impression that their entire populations were on the brink of starvation, and that their own officials sat back, impotently wringing their hands, while emissaries from other countries sorted out their problems. Labouisse was keenly aware that Unicef's potential for action depended on a co-operative relationship with the Indian Government. In this, as in other major disaster situations, it was a hallmark of his leadership that everything must be done to avoid public statements which could hamper Unicef's negotiating position—and therefore its chances of helping the victims—with the relevant authorities.

Although not known for their efficiency, the Bihar authorities, with support from New Delhi, had begun to take the relief situation in hand. Food, some of it from consignments sent during the previous year's drought, was being moved into Bihar from elsewhere in India. More was brought in from overseas: an armada of ships brought another six million tons of US wheat across the seas. The total volume of fourteen million tons in 1966 and 1967 constituted an unprecedented movement of food from one country to another. Public works programmes were mounted, in which food was used in lieu of wages for manual labour. Thousands of fair-price shops were set up, through which grain was distributed at subsidized prices to almost the entire population of Bihar. Free rations were given to the elderly and infirm.

The feeding programme for children in which Unicef was active was primarily run by CARE, the American voluntary agency, through the State school system, and included rations for other siblings besides those formally registered at the schools. The US and Canadian Governments gave supplies of milk and high-protein foods. A new protein-rich mix, called CSM (corn-soy-milk, manufactured in the US), was one of the principal ingredients. A similar cereal mix using wheat, a high-protein Indian legume, powdered milk, and vitamins and minerals from Unicef was formulated by the Food Technology Institute in Mysore. The product's name, *bal ahar*, meant 'child's food' in Hindi. Fifty heavy-duty vehicles were redeployed by Unicef to distribute these foodstuffs and transport relief personnel, and 500 lightweight motor bicycles were provided to the Education Department for the use of school supervisors, now become school-feeding supervisors.

Every day, long lines of bony, dust-covered youngsters, each carrying a brass plate and a handful of dung or twigs for cooking fuel, would assemble in the school yards of drought-affected villages to receive a ladleful of gruel. This programme, whose outreach continued to spread throughout early 1967 into April and May as heat, dust and famine reached their peak, provided more than five million children in Bihar and one million in Uttar Pradesh with one good meal a day.

As the dry season came to its scheduled end, fears grew that with the rains would come epidemics. In a famine, disease threatens death more readily than hunger. Drugs, vaccines and multivitamins were despatched by Unicef in an effort to help prevent outbreaks of smallpox and cholera. As the drought deepened, wells and water sources dried up. The shortage of water became even more critical than the shortage of food.

Up to this time, Bihar had remained almost exclusively dependent for a water supply on the heavens and the River Ganges—sources which had proved very unreliable. There existed in Bihar a large underground reservoir of fresh water waiting to be tapped by the sinking of wells and boreholes. As part of the emergency programme, thousands of small mud-wells were dug, providing drinking water and irrigating small patches of land. Drilling rigs were brought in, some flown in by Unicef. Where digging and drilling could not penetrate hard rock below the surface, an elaborate system of transport by rail, road, bullock cart, and even human porterage, brought drinking water to distant villages.

Although thousands of children died in Bihar over the course of 1966 and 1967, the famine relief effort staved off the threatened tragedy of millions of deaths from starvation and disease. It had another positive aspect: for the first time it brought home to much of Indian officialdom the full dimensions of child malnutrition and its connection to national development. Studies undertaken in the famine area showed how the constant presence of hunger, a by-product of poverty, had weakened the strength, vitality, resistance to disease and mental alertness of entire generations of Bihari villagers. The relief effort revealed in all its starkness the effect of poor nutrition on children and nursing mothers, less spectacular in its death rate than a cholera outbreak, but nonetheless pernicious.

The cruel truth about the famine, according to a special report prepared at Mrs Gandhi's request, was that most of the children in Bihar were certain of one good meal a day for the first time in their lives. George Verghese, the Prime Minister's Information Advisor, wrote: 'In a "normal year", these people hover on the bread line. They are beyond the pale, nobody's concern, they starve. In a famine year, they eat. Their health is better and the children are gaining weight. For them this is a year of great blessing. This is the grim tragedy of the situation'.

There was more milk to drink in Bihar in 1967 than there had ever been before, or in the judgement of some, was likely ever to be again. Mineral and vitamin supplements had been consumed on an unprecedented scale. Vaccination against smallpox and cholera had reduced the incidence of these diseases to levels lower than before the famine. Whatever their initial resentment about the international spotlight cast on India's problems by the famine, the consciousness of senior government officials about the evils of child malnutrition was alerted. Many policies and programmes designed for its long-term alleviation were precipitated or stepped up. Verghese wrote: 'The famine has been a revelation, a trial, a shame; but also an opportunity and an awakening. It has transformed some of the inertia of the past into energy'.

One of the programmes to which the famine gave a boost was the applied nutrition programme which Unicef had been supporting since 1959. Since the days when Unicef officials had first waxed enthusiastic over fish ponds and fruit and vegetable gardens in Orissa State, this programme had expanded considerably. Charles Egger, who arrived in New Delhi to become the Regional Director in 1961, promoted it energetically at the central level; the success of the pilot programme and the attention it attracted from overseas caught the official imagination. In 1963, ambitious plans were set in motion to spread the programme progressively into other Indian States, and eventually into hundreds of thousands of villages throughout the country. By the end of that year small-scale farming on small plots had begun in 226 development blocks in twelve States. Many other international and bilateral aid organisations had become involved, including WHO, FAO, the Peace Corps, Freedom from Hunger Campaign committees, CARE, and the Ford and Rockefeller Foundations. By March 1966 Unicef had committed $8·25 million to the programme nationwide. Its fame helped gain child nutrition a first-time entry in the country's Five Year Plan. In the fourth Plan, covering the period 1966–1970, the Ministries of Health and Food and Agriculture (incorporating Community Development) were slated to devote $110 million to applied nutrition countrywide.

During the drought years of 1966 and 1967, applied nutrition projects were started as part of the emergency programme in the drought-affected

States. The water from the newly-dug wells and boreholes, while not large enough in volume for rice cultivation, could be used to water small vegetable plots and fruit orchards. This was a classic case of a developmental response to a disaster situation, a project with a longer-term and more enduring effect being set in place as a result of calamity. Many of the funds raised by Unicef's national committees found their way into seeds and hand tools, poultry incubators and fruit-tree nurseries, small-scale dairying and fishing equipment, intended to offer the families of India's poorest villages a nutritious food supplement for good times as well as bad.

A price was paid, however, for the haste with which applied nutrition programmes were extended. The urgency of the need encouraged the tendency, both in Unicef and among government officials, to overlook the fact that by no means all the experience so far was positive. In a special evaluation of the applied nutrition projects in various Indian States carried out in 1966, shortly before famine took hold of Bihar, James Hundley, an FAO/WHO/Unicef consultant, raised serious questions about the programme. Hundley feared that, as attention moved to new areas, the old projects might wither from lack of attention, resources and encouragement. He found little evidence that the effects of the programme had 'radiated' to neighbouring villages. He doubted whether the target of extending the programme to 1000 new blocks during the course of the next Five Year Plan was sensible without some radical revision of its methods and approaches. Hundley's prognostications were borne out by later events. But for the time being the impact of the famine temporarily forbade any delay.

Whatever the disappointments awaiting the outcome of some applied-nutrition schemes, the relief effort mounted during the Bihar famine had many positive sides. It showed the world that, with assistance, India could master the most serious consequences of natural calamity; and it fostered a commitment, particularly in India, to the conquest of hunger and malnutrition among children. It also helped to launch a massive effort to improve village water supplies and to lessen agricultural dependence on the vagaries of the weather.

The rains returned in 1968, and helped produce a bumper harvest. This was the first harvest in which the new hybrid seeds of the 'green revolution' helped to fill the national granary. Within a few years, India became a food-surplus instead of a food-deficit country, even though the twin problems of poverty and malnutrition remained. India has not since suffered a major famine, nor faced drought without sufficient grain in hand to avoid mass imports of food from elsewhere. The famine in Bihar provided a historical landmark. Although many people died, and most of them were children, in terms of what it might have been a great disaster was averted.

*   *   *   *   *   *

The colonial powers' hasty scramble in the late 1950s to leave most of the continent of Africa to its own political devices left a legacy with many inbuilt flaws. Decolonization was a precondition of African progress. But after the first flush of excitement at the dawning of Independence, few of the new States were able to settle down to a smooth and uneventful passage. Their political and administrative apparel was ill-fitting, and poorly designed for the task of economic and social transformation. Invented in the West at a very different stage of national evolution, it quickly showed a tendency to gape at the seams. One of the countries whose seams were most conspicuous was the Federal Republic of Nigeria. By the historical accident of British rule over three distinct but geographically adjacent regions, Nigeria came to independence as one nation whose only political cement had been supplied by Imperial domination. In 1958, existing rivalries between the peoples of the different regions were compounded by the discovery of oil in the east, the country of the Ibo.

Soon after Independence in 1960, turmoil began to overtake the fledgling institutions of government. In January 1966, the army took over in a military coup, which brought to power a predominantly Ibo leadership. A backlash of violence and reprisals against the Ibo led to another military coup, which brought to power a 31-year-old Christian Northerner, General Yakubu Gowon. Violence continued while Gowon tried to create a new federal structure, and the Ibo people began to retreat, physically and psychologically, into their eastern heartland. In May 1967, the fragile cement of unity cracked. Colonel Odumegwa Ojukwu, Military Governor of the eastern region, announced its secession and the creation of an independent republic called Biafra. In July, the federal forces of General Gowon attacked.

The Nigerian civil war, a profoundly bitter and bloody struggle, lingered on for two-and-a-half years until January 1970. Not only did it put the old colonial boundaries inherited by Africa to one of their severest tests. It did as much to the agents of international humanitarianism in the postwar era.

From the perspective of the UN, the civil war in Nigeria was an internal conflict in which, by the terms of its charter, it had no right to meddle unless invited to intervene by the Federal Government. But if the UN must stand to one side, some of its more prominent member states, notably the ex-colonial powers of Britain, France and Portugal—the one country in Europe determined to cling to its African possessions—were far from disengaged. Britain throughout was a strong supporter of the Federal Government and, despite intense domestic controversy, remained its major arms supplier. France and Portugal recognized the claim of Ojukwu and his followers to separate independent status and provided them with arms. The secession provoked disunity within Africa as well as outside it. At stake was the ability of the largest independent country in Africa to resist the forces of disintegration—forces which, as the Congo crisis had shown, were explosive elsewhere on the continent.

As the embattled eastern enclave shrank before the federal military advance during late 1967 and early 1968, and as Ojukwu appealed to the rest of the world for aid to the Biafran cause, humanitarian zeal was confronted with a series of dangerous political trip wires. This was a civil war whose bitterness was exacerbated by age-old regional tensions, and the unwillingness of either side to consider any compromise. The Nigerian Military Government, determined at all costs to salvage the nation's fragile political unity and to retain control over the lucrative eastern oilfields, instinctively distrusted the credentials of any rescue operation for 'Biafran' people. Gowon's government insisted that all aid to the victims of the civil war must be supplied to Nigerians, not to 'Biafrans'; meaning that there should be no relief pipeline into 'Biafra' outside the reach of federal control. This was unacceptable to Ojukwu, for whom sovereignty and recognition were vital issues, and who needed relief conduits for his arms supply. Encirclement and siege, with their corollary, the gradual starvation of a blockaded population, were weapons of war as old as warfare itself. The idea of a relief operation which parlayed its way through enemy lines to bring relief to innocent civilians had come of age only fifty years ago, during the first World War. In the historically, culturally and politically quite different circumstances of newly-independent Nigeria, the obstacles to a similar effort on the necessary scale turned out in the end to be insurmountable.

Unicef was legally as obligated as any other UN member organization to adhere to the principle of respect for sovereignty. This inhibited aid to any population group, including children, unless the recognized government of the country in question had issued an invitation. At the time of Unicef's creation, the founding fathers had insisted that no child should be seen as 'an enemy', disqualified from receiving Unicef aid; the critical phrase in the original resolution stated that assistance should be dispensed 'on the basis of need, without discrimination because of race, creed, nationality status or political belief'. By applying a certain elasticity of interpretation, Unicef had behaved for all practical purposes as if this clause, while not exempting it from the respect due to sovereignty, at least meant that it was not held up to quite the same rigorous standards of adherence as most other UN bodies. A record of working on both sides of armed civil conflict had been established since 1948 in China and the Middle East, and every time that the precedent was re-established it gained further *de facto* force.

The question of what actually constituted an 'invitation' to send in relief was left purposely vague; often Unicef simply manoeuvred to reach a tacit agreement that, while the invitation might never formally be issued, its lack of existence was not an impediment. In Nigeria, the question of whether the 'invitation' could be understood to extend to the population of secessionist Biafra was never satisfactorily resolved.

Towards the end of 1967, a few months after fighting began in July, came the first intimations of what was to follow, both in terms of food scarcity and of the problems any relief operation would confront. At that time, there were thought to be around twelve million people in the secessionist area, a rather higher number than usual because Ibo resident in other parts of the country had gone to their homeland to take refuge. In an area supporting more than its usual population, increasingly compressed by the federal advance, and blockaded by land and sea, supplies of food and medicine—specially the supply of protein foods such as fish and meat— began to come under serious strain. The International Committee of the Red Cross, the organization which has the longest tradition of acceptability as a neutral provider of humanitarian assistance in times of war, managed to bring in some medical relief supplies and a team of medical personnel.

Unicef asked the Red Cross to act as the channel into 'Biafra' for its own emergency supplies. Early in 1968, the ICRC, after many stops and starts, finally obtained the theoretical agreement of both sides to the provision of relief, an agreement which implicitly covered Unicef's participation. But it was many months before further negotiations actually permitted planes to fly in supplies from the island of Fernando Po in the Gulf of Guinea, and even then the federal authorities made it clear that the ICRC planes flew into rebel-held areas 'at their own risk'. On 21 May, the federal troops captured Port Harcourt and the airport where the relief planes had been landing. Permission to continue the flights was peremptorily withdrawn.

At this point, the surrender of the secessionist enclave appeared to be no more than weeks, or at most months, away. Enugu, its capital, and Port Harcourt, its vital link with the Gulf of Guinea and the outside world, were lost. Its area was significantly reduced. A series of peace negotiations began, mediated under the auspices of the British Commonwealth and the Organization of African Unity (OAU), while the federal forces remained poised for what looked like the final onslaught. The hope was that Ojukwu would withdraw the Biafran claim for sovereignty, thus avoiding the blood-shed and bitter legacy a federal conquest would entail. In the meantime, the federal blockade was strengthened. But the secessionists, both at the conference table and in the field of combat, continued to hold out. As the peace negotiations dragged on, the relief operation became a casualty. A few planes continued to land behind the lines. But the amounts they were able to bring in fell far short of requirements. Over the course of the summer, reports from relief personnel in the embattled enclave, reinforced by Ojukwu's pleas, described a sharply deteriorating food situation, wide-spread malnutrition among children, and sought the world's aid in relieving their plight. Accusations that the Federal Government was engaged in deliberate starvation of the Ibo people began to gain credence in the international press and the humanitarian community.

The success of the Biafran propaganda campaign in the West, a campaign that General Gowon failed hopelessly to counter, caused tremendous damage to the prospects of mounting a relief operation which both sides could regard as neutral. Popular sentiment in Europe, particularly in Britain where the Government faced widespread opposition to its pro-federal policy, rallied to the Ibo side. In mid-June, Leslie Kirkley, Director of the British voluntary agency Oxfam, spent a week in rebel-held territory touring villages and hospitals. Oxfam did its best to publicize the widespread child malnutrition he witnessed, the absence of food and medical supplies, and his prognostication of two million starvation deaths by September.

By early July 1968, the lack of an adequate relief operation was causing an international outcry. Passions ran extremely high, and mostly in favour of the Biafran cause. It was as if the predicament of the children in the seceded area conferred a moral superiority on their leaders. Sympathy with the plight of the Ibo was accompanied by the muddled assumption that those who were backing the unity of Nigeria accepted the starvation in the eastern enclave with indifference. The federal authorities were unfairly seen as exclusively to blame. In their view, the secession of would-be Biafra was the cause of the suffering, and the rebels led by Ojukwu were its perpetrators; the dying would end when the secession ended. Their position was backed at the international level by the OAU, whose position in turn was backed by the UN General Assembly. They therefore found the lack of neutrality among the would-be benefactors of these rebels quite incomprehensible.

In an atmosphere resounding with mistrust and ill-feeling, the ICRC's negotiations for a major relief effort became mired. The Federal Government declared itself willing to accept such an operation under ICRC auspices, if mounted through channels they controlled. These did not include an unsupervised airlift directly into secessionist territory from the Portuguese island of Sao Tomé and the Spanish-controlled Fernando Po. Portugal was a main shipper of arms to Ojukwu's forces, and Sao Tomé was known to be a principal route. The rebels, in turn, were not prepared to accept the loss of sovereignty implicit in a relief effort policed by the federal army. For two months, against the backdrop of the foundering peace negotiations first in Niamey, and later at the OAU in Addis Ababa, the ICRC tried unsuccessfully to convince both sides that, under its auspices, a relief operation for sick and hungry civilians could be carried out that would in no way promote the military fortunes of the other.

Unicef's Regional Headquarters for Africa happened to be located in Lagos. At this time, the Regional Director Dr Vedast Kyaruzi was a Tanzanian, and as Tanzania was one of the few African countries to recognize 'Biafra', Kyaruzi's personal position with the federal authorities was somewhat delicate. His deputy was Poul Larsen, a Dane and a long-time Unicef career officer, who therefore bore the brunt of the difficulties Unicef had to shoulder in Lagos on a day-to-day basis throughout the civil war. Before the international furore gained its full momentum, the Unicef Executive Board had carefully negotiated its way through a discussion on the Nigerian conflict at its session in mid-June 1968. Kyaruzi, who had attended in person, called guardedly for urgent relief. The utmost brevity and propriety was maintained in the language of discussion: this was a period of intense conflict in Vietnam, and Board members were becoming well versed in the niceties of talking about relief for children in highly sensitive situations.

The needs of those on both sides of the conflict, the needs of 'all Nigerian children', were given proportionately equal attention. Every possible nuance that could in any way indicate that Unicef had a viewpoint sympathetic to the rebels' cause was studiously avoided. The policy remained that all Unicef relief supplies for the emergency should be channelled through the ICRC. In spite of the problems the ICRC was confronting in getting any relief into the enclave, the best course was to hope that these would eventually be resolved, and to pretend that the agreement in principle they had reached with the opposing sides six months ago was still in force. Altogether, $400,000 was agreed by the Board as the sum that the Executive Director could use immediately at his discretion, with the understanding that more could follow when developments allowed.

When the storm broke in the international press, every party to the relief effort found itself buffeted in many directions. On the one hand, the public exposure of the threat to millions of children's lives was a tremendous advantage: it put pressure on the combatants to agree to the relief operation or face condemnation by world opinion. It also put pressure on the ICRC to throw more effort into the negotiations. On the other hand, given the popular bias towards one side, it sharpened the sensitivities that were already making it so difficult to mount full-scale relief.

UN Secretary-General U Thant now became involved. The United Nations, which had simply reiterated the OAU line up to this point, might not be able to take a stand on one side or the other of a civil conflict, but it could not hold up its humanitarian head if it took no stand on behalf of millions of children dying of starvation. At a meeting in Geneva, U Thant suggested to the heads of concerned UN member organizations that the organizations should assist where they could, but not without an invitation from the federal authorities. With the Nigerians poised on the brink of military victory, fearful of a UN intervention such as that undertaken in the Congo, such an invitation was hardly to be expected. Harry Labouisse told the Secretary-General that he did not consider that Unicef needed a specific invitation under its established mandate. Moreover, he felt that technically Unicef already had an invitation through the ICRC negotiations—assuming they were successful. As far as rebel-held territory was concerned, Unicef was the only card the UN had to play. Labouisse also informed the Secretary-General that he was shortly to undertake a personal mission to Lagos to help bolster both the ICRC negotiations and the arrangements for bringing in Unicef supplies. He was asked if he would be willing to act as the representative of the Secretary-General; but he felt that he should confine himself to representing Unicef given the sensitivities of the situation.

As time went by and still almost no relief went in, public pressure on the relief organizations to save the 'Biafran' babies became acute. Comparisons with Hitler's concentration camps and accusations about genocide were frequently voiced. For those private voluntary agencies for whom carefully worded expressions of neutrality were so much foot dragging and red tape, the need and the desire to act became overwhelming. They announced their intention of dropping relief supplies by parachute into Biafra independently of the ICRC and in spite of the lack of permission from the Nigerian authorities. Such actions, the authorities retaliated, would constitute a violation of Nigerian airspace, and would therefore be regarded as hostile. Statements, evasions and accusations unfolded along with events on an hour-by-hour, day-to-day basis in the full glare of worldwide publicity. Newspaper photographs of gaunt bodies and glazed expressions, photographs which established in the contemporary mind a Richter scale of mass-child emergency, fueled the war of words and passions.

Labouisse kept Unicef's name as far away as possible from the chorus of declamations. He believed that even a remote association of Unicef's name with the cause of 'Biafra' could prejudice Unicef's ability to provide assistance to all the children in need. This injunction to discretion was extremely difficult to observe given the fever pitch of press interest; and it was particularly frustrating for the Unicef national committees whose artery of support was the public now clamouring for action on an almost unprecedented scale.

In mid-July, Labouisse made a public appeal on behalf of Unicef for funds for emergency assistance for children and their mothers 'on both sides of the conflict'. A few days later, he left for Lagos accompanied by two aides. Simultaneously, the ICRC appointed as their Commissioner for Nigerian Relief Auguste Lindt, a long-time friend to Unicef and an ex-Chairman of the Executive Board, currently the Swiss Ambassador to Moscow.

While Labouisse was engaged in the critical process of diplomacy in Lagos, Charles Egger, recently arrived from India to take up the post of Deputy Executive Director for Programmes, went to Geneva to lend his weight, his experience and his Swiss nationality to the back-up for Lindt's ICRC mission. Gertrude Lutz, another Swiss national, was temporarily assigned to the ICRC as Unicef liaison officer. Willie Meyer, then serving as Unicef's representative in Dakar, Senegal, was sent to Fernando Po to try and get into the disputed territory. An extremely sick man with only weeks left to live, Meyer showed great fortitude in entering the rebel enclave twice to obtain an assessment of needs from on the ground. Dick Heyward in New York, surrounded by a team which included Sasha Bacic, Head of African programmes, and Ed Bridgewater, Chief of Supply Operations, pursued as clear-headedly as possible every source of funds and food they could think of. They devised a plan for the delivery of vast quantities of milk, protein-rich foods, drugs, vitamins and medical supplies over the coming months.

Calculating the size and content of the intended programme was a complicated business. Considerable movements of population, both before and after the outbreak of hostilities, made it difficult to establish any accurate numbers. Assessments of the harvest in the combat area—normally fertile and food-rich land—were also a matter largely for conjecture. The best estimate Heyward could come up with was that 5·5 million children and mothers were either totally dependent on relief or needed food supplements. For children under four, 7000 tons of milk and cereal mixes would be needed monthly, and for older children and mothers, 25,000 tons monthly. The total amounted to 1000 tons daily for all combat areas. This compared with 8000 tons for the Berlin airlift, but the terrain was difficult and the landing and communications facilities minimal.

It was clear that, under the circumstances, food supplies of this order of magnitude could never be brought in by airlift. Ambassador Lindt's negotiations for opening up sea ports and land routes through the embattled terrain were vital. At the moment they were successful, ships with food in sufficient quantity must be waiting off the coast. Accordingly, Heyward and his team chartered a cargo vessel, loaded it with 5000 tons of US-donated milk powder and high-protein food, and sent it to an as yet undesignated destination in the Gulf of Guinea. This was the first of many major Unicef consignments to the area.

Labouisse spent five weeks altogether in Lagos, and his visit had a crucial impact on Unicef's relief programme and on subsequent relations with the federal authorities. He met with General Gowon, and was convinced by the sincerity of the General's concern for the Ibo mothers and children. On his side, Gowon appeared convinced by the exclusively humanitarian concern of Unicef and its lack of partiality to the 'Biafran' cause—an impartiality he was not prepared to credit to most of the other humanitarian organizations. Labouisse managed to obtain from Gowon a commitment that planes carrying supplies from Unicef would not be shot down by federal troops; neither would shipments be searched. But although Gowon's suggestions about how to arrange relief movements overland across the line of battle sounded eminently reasonable to Labouisse, the fact was that negotiations for opening up routes either by land or air were no nearer a breakthrough. Auguste Lindt, in an intense process of shuttle diplomacy between the two sides, found the ground constantly shifting.

Land routes, cargo inspections, demilitarized zones, the choice of airstrips, the nationality of security staff—every detail was a stumbling block which fluctuated along with the military situation. By the middle of August, when 10,000 tons of food was stockpiled off the Nigerian coast and relief officials in the combat areas were reporting mounting starvation, Lindt was in a state of extreme frustration.

The ICRC was now under increasing pressure, attacked in Nigeria for partiality to the rebels, and in the rest of the world for its failure to bring them aid. Increasingly anguished reports coming out from the rebel enclave in early August indicated a death rate running into thousands every day. Red Cross Societies in various countries threatened to dissociate themselves from the ICRC effort unless it could find some means of gaining access to the starving. Anti-aircraft fire from federal troops meant that only an occasional flight with a few tons of protein food a day were getting in, not the 200 tons estimated as the minimum needed. The voluntary organizations—including the World Council of Churches, Caritas International, Oxfam, and a Scandinavian church aid consortium—now decided to mount their own separate airlift. They recruited as their squadron leader Count Carl-Gustaf von Rosen, a Swedish commercial pilot who performed heroic feats of hazardous flying to break the Nigerian blockade. Their base was Sao Tomé, the Portuguese island, and in the interests of humanity they decided to turn a blind eye to arms consignments which sometimes accompanied their cargoes. By September, their 'illegal' airlift was well under way.

At Unicef headquarters a decision had to be made about where to offload the 5000 tons of US food now approaching Nigerian waters, in view of the failure to open the hoped-for land route into the enclave from Port Harcourt. Heyward decided to ignore the protocols of intergovernmental relations and instructed the ship to proceed to Sao Tomé and offload part of the cargo—2000 tons—for onward passage via the 'illegal' airlift, and then go on to Lagos with the rest. In the event, the federal authorities chose not to regard the decision as a breach of Unicef's faith. This was partly because of the confidence in Unicef established by Labouisse in Lagos, partly because open contacts were maintained and frank information supplied to the Nigerian mission at the UN. Meanwhile, Auguste Lindt had decided that the ICRC must also begin its airlift into the beleaguered territory, notwithstanding the absence of an agreement signed by both sides.

In September, six ICRC planes were put into daily commission from Fernando Po. The federal authorities expressed their displeasure to both ICRC and Unicef. But the airplanes were not attacked. A total of over 3500 tons of supplies were taken in by the two airlifts during September. Flights could only be made at night, and landing conditions were primitive and hazardous. The supplies taken in amounted to a little more than half the lowest estimate of need, but they did prevent the death rate from climbing and the condition of the children began to stabilize. During the next few months, the airlifts managed to take in provisions of a similar and sometimes higher order of magnitude. Unicef was a major supplier of both.

At the same time, supplies continued to be sent to Lagos for the relief of areas outside the embattled enclave. In the south and east, areas from which the rebels had retreated, suffering was almost as acute. While in Lagos in early August, Labouisse and one of his aides had toured these areas. They had been deeply struck by the pitiful conditions in mission hospitals and refugee camps. The terrain was riverine, and the destruction of many bridges had made the movement of people and goods along waterways and roads even more tortuous than usual. Unicef therefore based two helicopters at Calabar which operated from dawn to dusk, carrying by sling a ton of goods at a time, on short-haul runs to areas close to the front.

By October, Unicef had spent around $1 million. Special appeals run by the national committees had raised $1·5 million, half of this in the Netherlands. Food, drugs and other contributions in kind from governments and private industry amounted to $10·6 million. However, as Labouisse pointed out to the Executive Board, any sense of achievement was dispelled by the reflection that all the combined efforts of the ICRC, church and voluntary organizations, and Unicef fell far short of meeting the needs. No comparable relief operation had ever had to be mounted independently of a government or governments mobilizing the resources of personnel and materiel which only they could command.

By now, it had also become apparent that Ojukwu and his followers, whatever their military prospects, were not willing to give up and would fight on to the end. Peace was many months away, and suffering and death were certain to continue even longer. Ambassador Lindt was still trying to find some way to remove the restrictions on relief that both sides were imposing. Labouisse invited governments to lend their weight to these diplomatic efforts, and to redouble their financial support.

Towards the end of the year, a major breakthrough was achieved. Unicef finally managed to impress upon the US State Department the stupendous costs of the relief operation, costs which the agencies could not cover indefinitely. Vice-President Hubert Humphrey took up the cause, and the US Government agreed to pay for the freight costs of food and medical supplies taken in by air from the offshore islands. Unicef and some of the agencies in the Joint Church Aid consortium could now claim reimbursement. This made a considerable difference to the financial security of the operation. It was also running more smoothly. Many of the organizations drew upon Unicef's capacity for supply procurement, and UNIPAC—the Unicef Procurement and Assembly Centre in Copenhagen—became the main purchasing and forwarding agency for both airlifts. In

January, the US Government provided eight additional cargo planes and, by the following April, the amount flown in had risen to 8000 tons a month. This kept on hold the nutritional state of the eight million people thought to be hemmed into the enclave.

Even though the amount of food and drugs carried in never reached the volume thought necessary, the grimmest prognostications about child deaths did not materialize. This was mainly due to the efforts of the head of Biafran paediatric services, Dr Aaron Ifekwunigwe. Force of circumstances inspired a superhuman response to the 1968 'epidemics' of child malnutrition. With the help of a Dutch nutritionist, Isabel Koeniggracht, and other local and foreign relief personnel, Ifekwunigwe managed to set up a special network of child-feeding stations in schools, church buildings and town halls at no more than two or three miles distance from one another. Since no particle of body-building food must be squandered, each child's nutritional condition was measured in order to select the neediest.

The system they used was crude but effective: they measured the children's upper arm circumference with what was known as a 'quac (Quaker Upper Arm Circumference) stick'. They dispensed rations of milk powder and CSM—corn-soy-milk—mixed with local produce: cassava, yam, bananas, and palm oil. They even ran an educational programme on nutrition for mothers and the guardians of the many thousands of children separated from their families by the turmoil of war. In mid-1969, Ifekwunigwe asked Unicef to develop a preparation that could be simply mixed with water and used to feed children with very advanced malnutrition. The result was K-Mix-2—based on casein, a milk derivative, skim milk, and sucrose. Once the worst was over, the patient could move onto a diet of CSM.

Ifekwunigwe's programme was one of the first instances where a child-nutrition programme in emergency circumstances was run on a truly scientific basis. Specific nutritional deficiencies were identified in the patients and treatment took account of local food habits. A distinction was made between the various stages of malnutrition and, according to the diagnosis, the child was hospitalized for feeding with K-Mix-2, treated as an out-patient with CSM, or enrolled at a programme in a school or health clinic where the mother received advice and supplementary rations. Immunization campaigns against smallpox, measles and tuberculosis were also organized, with vaccines supplied by Unicef. Thanks to Ifekwunigwe and his teams, the nutritional condition of the children in the enclave improved markedly during 1969. It was a prodigious achievement and many of its principles and practices, further refined, have since become the copybook format for child-feeding programmes in famine emergencies.

In mid-1969, the relief operation entered a new period of crisis. On 5 June an ICRC plane crossing the Nigerian coast just before dusk was shot down by a Nigerian fighter plane with the loss of four lives. ICRC flights were suspended. The church airlift continued, but at a reduced level and under great strain. Ten days later, Auguste Lindt was unceremoniously declared *persona non grata* by the Nigerian authorities. He had carried out a difficult, dangerous and thankless task with poise and aplomb, but tensions between the ICRC and the federal authorities had been growing for some time. On 30 June, the representatives of foreign relief organizations in Lagos were summoned to meet the federal authorities, and instructed that in future all their assistance for civilian victims in war zones must be channelled through the Nigerian Rehabilitation Commission or the Nigerian Red Cross, not through the ICRC.

An immediate problem was to find alternative ways to the airlifts of moving supplies into the rebel-held area. In a state of high emotion, the ICRC declared itself determined to go on with its relief operation. Negotiations about river and land corridors, and an air corridor for use in daylight, began again. Again, they collapsed. By mid-July, reports from Biafran-held territory described sudden and massive deterioration in the children's condition. The UN Secretary-General appealed to the combatants to allow the flights to begin again, but his efforts were in vain. The ICRC airlift was over.

Quietly, Unicef and the other relief organizations, backed by Clyde Ferguson, the US Commissioner for Nigerian Relief, began building up the independent church airlift. Towards the end of 1969, the tonnages of food imported had risen close to previous levels. But after more than two years of warfare and siege, starvation was beginning to take hold in the rebel enclave. A relief survey mission sent in by the US Government in October reported that the population generally was in the worst nutritional condition of any in reported medical history. This was not like the spectacular epidemics of child malnutrition which had horrified the world in mid-1968. This was slow, creeping debilitation, caused by long months of poor diet and continual hunger. In December it became clear that the final collapse of Biafra was imminent. On 10 January 1970, the war ended.

This was the moment at which so many of those sympathetic to the rebels' cause had forecast a bloodbath of revenge against the Ibo. No bloodbath took place. After a few days of unruliness, an uneasy calm took over. But there had been few preparations for the relief operation, for which the Nigerians now declared themselves and their own Red Cross Society solely responsible. Relations with most of the voluntary agencies and missions who had been operational in the rebel area had reached open rupture. But Unicef, thanks to the careful diplomacy of the past eighteen months, was still in federal favour. Labouisse's caution, his almost obsessive refusal to allow Unicef to be caught in the spotlight, had paid off. Among overseas humanitarian organizations, Unicef was in the unique position of being able to go into ex-rebel territory and contribute massively to the postwar relief and reconstruction effort.

Labouisse flew immediately to Lagos accompanied by Sasha Bacic, head of the Unicef Africa section and another aide. Within a few days of the cease-fire, he set off with Poul Larsen to assess needs in the Ibo heartland, an act of considerable courage given the forebodings of what was likely to occur there. Shortages of all kinds of food and essentials were extreme. A ship was immediately chartered by Unicef to provide coastal transport for fish, milk, medical supplies, trucks and ambulances, and a distribution network set up from Port Harcourt. A ship with CSM came in from Cotonou, Dahomey (Benin). Aircraft brought tons of other urgent supplies from Copenhagen. Vehicles were almost nonexistent in the area; with foresight, Unicef had ordered a fleet of trucks from England. Almost as critical were the conditions in hospitals and health centres, as well as the collapse of administration generally.

Meanwhile, all foreign journalists, and almost all relief and mission personnel, were ordered to leave. With the postwar calm balancing on a knife edge, General Gowon did not want any foreigners he distrusted in the area on the grounds that their presence might inflame the situation. Labouisse tried to persuade him to allow key hospital and health personnel to stay, but almost everyone from abroad was forced to depart and the area was effectively closed.

The Unicef team was allowed to remain. Sasha Bacic, a Yugoslav with wartime experience, was asked by Labouisse to act as Regional Director for Africa, and run the Unicef relief assistance programme in what had been the rebel territory. Bacic was capable of throwing the rule book out of the window and operating in unconventional circumstances on his own authority. In the administrative vacuum created by the end of the war, he requisitioned houses and warehouses, used whatever irregular methods were needed to unblock relief supplies from the overcrowded Port Harcourt docks, hired drivers and guards for the fleet of trucks under his supervision, and did everything he thought necessary to get relief supplies moving. The federal authorities allowed Unicef to assume an exceptional degree of operational responsibility for an organization whose usual role was to deliver supplies to government authorities and leave everything else to them. But Labouisse and Heyward knew that this course of action would have been quite inappropriate under the circumstances. Bacic was given free rein, and he used it.

Gradually, the new federal state which replaced 'Biafra' began to function administratively and the fears of a breakdown in security faded away. In April 1970, the Executive Board approved an allocation of over $7 million for rehabilitation in Nigeria. The submission was scrupulously put together to cover education, health and nutritional services in all parts of the country, 'including particularly areas affected by the civil war'. In the eastern States, Bacic hired contracters and architects to re-roof schools, re-equip them with benches and blackboards, and continued to supply the health centres and dispensaries now beginning to operate more normally with drugs and high-protein foods.

The period of most intense reconstruction lasted for around four months, during which Unicef liaised closely with the Nigerian Red Cross and the National Commission for Reconstruction. Towards the end of 1970, the operation was absorbed into local governmental machinery. By 1971, the programme had cast off its rehabilitation appearance, and become to all intents and purposes a programme of development co-operation indistinguishable from similar programmes elsewhere in Nigeria.

Controversy surrounded the Nigerian civil war and the huge international relief effort accompanying it. Its overall effectiveness, and the role within it of the various relief organizations, will forever remain subject to re-interpretation. The two years of tragedy inspired a great outpouring of energy and care from the international humanitarian community, and left its mark upon it. Whatever individual and organizational battles were fought, and whatever acts of true heroism were performed by both Nigerian and foreign relief workers in an effort to save the lives of mothers and children in the Ibo heartland, the sober reality was that around two million people starved—three quarters of whom were children under five years of age.

The late 1960s were the years of Bihar, the years of Nigerian civil conflict, and the years of Vietnam. Whatever the intention to steer a course closely along the path of development co-operation, disasters crept up or burst upon Unicef, demanding response. Discussions about whether they deflected resources and energy away from the longer-term, less dramatic tasks became academic. No-one could sit on the sidelines watching children die on the grounds that long-term programmes would solve the problem better. As the 1970s began; as cyclone and tidal wave battered the Bay of Bengal and civil war erupted in what was then East Pakistan; as refugees streamed towards Calcutta; as drought engulfed a great swathe of the African continent, leading to the notorious famine in Ethiopia and widespread hunger in the countries bordering the Sahara Desert; as the conflict in Indo China came to its messy conclusion . . . during these years disaster programmes and all they entailed became an inescapable fact of Unicef life. At the time of Bihar and Biafra, the emergencies seemed to be exceptions, temporary products of exceptional circumstances. Gradually, it began to seem as though the exception was becoming the rule.

Main Sources
Unicef Executive Board documentation, 1960–70: recommendations for emergency allocations; reports of the Executive Board; notes on criteria for Unicef aid in emergency situations; summary records; statements of Regional Directors; progress reports of the Executive Director.

Disaster Assistance: Appraisal, Reform and New Approaches, edited by Lynn H. Stephens and Stephen J. Green, published in the UNA-USA Policy Studies Book Series, New York University Press, 1979.

'Famine. A Symposium dealing with Nutrition and Relief Operations in Times of Disaster', symposia of the Swedish Nutrition Foundation IX, printed for the Swedish Nutrition Foundation by Almqvist & Wiksells, Uppsala, 1971.

Articles in *Unicef News* and other publications; for the events of the Nigerian Civil War, *The Economist*, London, and the *New York Times*.

Interviews undertaken for the Unicef History Project by Jack Charnow and others with Henry R. Labouisse, E. J. R. Heyward, Sasha Bacic, Poul Larsen, Charles Egger, Ed Bridgewater.

'Beyond the Famine' by B. G. Verghese, published under the auspices of the Bihar Relief Committee, New Delhi, 1967.

'Humanitarian Assistance in the Nigeria-Biafra Emergency', by Dan Jacobs, prepared for the Unicef History Project, July 1984.

Chapter 12

The Handpump Cometh

The drought in north-eastern India led Unicef into an area which gained tremendous importance as the 1970s progressed: supplies of clean, fresh, drinkable water for villages all over the developing world. In the early summer of 1967, Unicef airlifted nine high-powered Halco drilling rigs from England to India. Within two months they had pounded swiftly through soil and rock, bringing water to 222 villages in Bihar and Uttar Pradesh whose thirsty inhabitants had been faced with imminent evacuation to relief camps. Church of Scotland missionaries, led by John McLeod of Jalna, Maharashtra, had introduced modern hard-rock drilling techniques to India. But this was the first attempt to do so on a large scale, and it was a great success.

The despatch of the high-speed rigs was precipitated by the drought crisis, but at the same time many thousands of villages in hard-rock areas all over central and southern India, as well as in other parts of the world, were faced with an emergency of a more creeping kind. Population pressure, coupled in some places with environmental change, was lowering the water table. Where shallow digging through surface soil used to yield an adequate well, the ground water had now vanished into fissures and porous layers buried in inaccessible recesses of the rock. The 'folk' method of reaching it was to split the rock with fire and water, and dig painstakingly downwards for months at a time. Old-fashioned cable tool rigs took almost as long. But modern technology offered a revolutionary solution. The new rigs' air-driven percussion hammers could penetrate the rock swiftly and smoothly, bringing water to the surface in days—sometimes hours—instead of weeks.

Inspired by the success of the drilling experiment in Bihar, Unicef offered the Indian government support for a rural water supply programme in other hard-rock, drought-prone areas. Martin Beyer, a Swedish geologist working for a drilling company in Stockholm, was invited to travel to India in 1969 and assess the programme's viability. No drinking water drilling programme of these dimensions or in those conditions had ever been undertaken anywhere in the developing world before. His team reported favourably, and the programme began to take shape. Unicef ordered 125 of the new percussion rigs, from Halco of England and Atlas Copco of

Sweden, and began shipping them to India; a further 125 were ordered by the State governments, to be manufactured by Indian subsidiaries. In good conditions, each of the rigs could drill a tube-well over 150 feet deep in one day only. The well was capped with a concrete platform and a cast-iron handpump. Over the programme's four-year period, the plan was to supply 12,000 villages with clean drinking water. The cost of the rigs and other components to Unicef was $5·9 million, an extremely large—and exciting —investment by the standards of the time.

The Indian village water supply scheme was the first of its kind, but others soon followed. They too were spurred into place by disasters which opened the way to a longer-term response. On the night of 12 November 1970, a cyclone of unprecedented intensity in the Bay of Bengal struck the coast and off-shore islands in the low-lying delta region of what was then East Pakistan. In the worst natural catastrophe of the century, half a million people were drowned, crops on a million acres were totally destroyed, and most of the homes, fishing boats, and livestock in the flood path swept away by a tidal wave. More than 4·5 million people were affected, and a huge relief operation had to be mounted. At the moment of the disaster, a group of staff from the Unicef office in Dacca was visiting a deep-well installation on an island lying directly in the path of the storm. They took refuge and survived. Their rescue by coastal launch took them through the devastated area to Chittagong, which made possible an early assessment of the damage. As well as requirements for food and shelter, piping and parts were needed for fresh water tube-wells completely swamped by the flood waters.

In 1968, the Government of Pakistan had declared a target of providing one tube-well for each 200 people in the region, and Unicef had offered assistance in reaching this ambitious goal. At the time of the cyclone, some supplies and equipment had just been off-loaded in Chittagong. In the wake of the disaster, teams of public health engineers managed to use the equipment to repair and re-commission over 11,000 wells within a matter of months. The provision of fresh water therefore became by natural pro-gression the major emphasis of Unicef's proposed contribution to the eighteen-month reconstruction programme drawn up by the East Pakistan authorities. Labouisse wrote urgently around to Board members asking permission to go ahead with support, and set about raising $2·2 million in special contributions. This was the first time in Unicef's history in which its major external collaborator was the World Bank.

Before more than a few months, had passed, civil conflict erupted within East Pakistan. A mass exodus of refugees began. By June 1971, five million people had fled across the border into the Indian States of West Bengal, Tripura and Assam. Eventually, ten million people left their villages in search of sanctuary in India. The task of providing shelter, food and medical care for all these refugees, particularly during the months of the summer monsoon, presented the Indian authorities with problems of almost inconceivable magnitude. Extraordinarily, they managed, but with deepening misgivings about the prospects of repatriating or resettling this huge population influx. Meanwhile, within East Pakistan itself, effective administration broke down and the post-cyclone reconstruction programme was disrupted. Public health deteriorated, famine threatened, and cholera spread. While warfare continued, relief efforts within the breakaway State were reduced to a minimal level. On the Indian side of the borders, with the highest concentration in refugee camps around Calcutta, the programme of emergency relief continued, with the help of scores of local and international voluntary and UN organizations. Within the UN system, relief for the Bengal refugees was co-ordinated by the High Commissionor for Refugees (UNHCR). For many months during 1971, the crisis absorbed much of the energy of Unicef's staff in Calcutta and New Delhi, now under the directorship of Gordon Carter, a long-time career officer.

Unicef, with its experience in supply procurement and shipment, became UNHCR's quartermaster-general for shelter materials, high-protein foods, vehicles, sanitation supplies, drilling rigs and cooking utensils, spending altogether $33·7 million. Planes were lent by the US and Canadian Governments and, at the height of the rescue effort, at least one was in the skies with forty-two tons of Unicef cargo between the Western hemisphere and Dum Dum Airport in Calcutta in every twenty-four hours. In November 1971, another cyclone in the Bay of Bengal inflicted terrible damage on coastal territory, this time in the Indian State of Orissa. Emergencies in the hard-pressed subcontinent followed on the heels of one another with terrifying rapidity.

On 3 December, India intervened militarily in the civil war in East Pakistan on the side of the secessionists. The Pakistani forces surrendered to the Indian army on 16 December, and the exultant eastern Bengalis declared their independence in the new State of Bangladesh. But there was a bleak underside to their triumph. The world's newest country was also its poorest. 'Golden Bengal', the rich and fruitful land celebrated in the poetry of Tagore, had become a destitute land overburdened with people and poverty in which the inspiration of the freedom movement had now to be harnessed to the task of economic and social transformation. The ten million refugees—minus those of their families who had perished in the cruelties of flight or the squalor of the camps—streamed back across the borders and returned to their villages. For the next two years, the inexperienced Government of Bangladesh grappled with the immense problems of reconstruction with the help of a special UN relief office. UNROB—the United Nations Relief Office for Bangladesh—was set up in Dacca by Sir Robert Jackson, the UN's most experienced relief official, at the request of the new Prime Minister, Mujibur Rahman. Jackson, one of whose strengths was his understanding of what it took to make the various

UN organizations co-ordinate their efforts, headed an operation which administered around $1300 million in international assistance before removing itself at the end of 1973. During this extended emergency period, Unicef's representative in Bangladesh was Glan Davies; he was backed up by Robert Walker, a redoubtable character who alone among UN international staff had managed to hold on in Dacca and keep some kind of operation going throughout the civil strife. Altogether Unicef contributed $30·2 million to the joint UN programme, more than $10 million was for clean drinking water, to sink or repair 160,000 shallow tube-wells, and drill 1200 deeper ones in coastal areas where ground water near the surface was too saline to drink.

Unlike the situation in India and in many parts of the world where the amount of water available was the critical problem, Bangladesh suffered neither from aridity, drought, hard rock, nor water scarcity. On the contrary, the new country sat astride the confluence of two of the mightiest rivers in the world: the Ganges and the Brahmaputra. Their thousands of tributaries and secondary streams disgorged the melted snows of the Himalayas into a vast alluvial plain, presenting a spectacle of water in almost too great an abundance. The crowded habitation of the fertile, water-washed plains, the deep-rooted poverty and lack of hygiene, the seasonal floods which washed dirt and germs and humankind's unhealthy detritus across the landscape meant that almost all the water drunk by Bengali fisherfolk and farming families was contaminated with bacteria. People invariably took their drinking water from the open streams where animals wallowed and waste floated, and the caseload of diarrhoeas, dysentery, and the seasonal epidemics of cholera presented a public-health problem of nightmare proportions. During the postwar period, Unicef— alongside WHO—helped reconstruct and equip a skeleton network of health services and financed the production of intravenous fluids for cholera treatment. But over the longer term, the underlying causes of diarrhoeal disease had to be tackled by cheap and effective prevention. People must be discouraged from consuming bacteria-laden water by the provision of safer sources.

In 1974, disaster once again inundated the countryside of Bangladesh. The annual flood brought by the monsoon rose remorselessly, inch by watery inch, to an unprecedented level. In August and September, the rice crops on one third of the arable land were lost, grain stocks and homes were irreparably damaged, and millions of people were thrown once again onto the mercy of relief rations and temporary shelters. Meanwhile, worldwide inflation was causing steep rises in the cost of food and essential imports. The Unicef-assisted drinking water programme was subject to the hiatus affecting all development in a country whose name by now was internationally synonymous with distress. Delays and price increases necessitated re-scheduling of well-drilling targets, and Labouisse redoubled appeals to donor countries and Unicef Committees for special contributions. At the end of 1974, another $10 million was committed for materials and transport to sink thousands more wells in Bangladesh. The emergency years in the land of a thousand rivers had plunged Unicef up to its organizational neck in water.

Elsewhere in the world, the dynamics of other disasters were similarly deepening Unicef's involvement in an active, operational role in the provision of water for thirsty villages. In August 1973 Martin Beyer—now on Unicef's staff—was despatched to West Africa to look at another water shortage problem. Deepening drought was afflicting the mostly nomadic populations of the semi-desert Sahel region south of the Sahara. As a result of his visit, Unicef joined the UN Development Programme in providing vehicles and drilling rigs for a deep-well drinking water supply programme for Mali, Niger, Senegal and Upper Volta. This too was a part of the world where the underground water table could only be reached through hard layers of rock.

On the other side of the continent, Ethiopia had also fallen victim to the same trans-African belt of successive failure of the rains. In 1973 prolonged drought led to a disastrous famine in the central northern provinces. Tragic loss of life went unnoticed or ignored for months, and the international notoriety caused by the shocking revelation of the famine—a revelation engineered largely by the dogged persistence of Stephen Green, a Unicef programme officer based in Addis Ababa—led to a huge international rescue operation and profound political upheaval. Here again, once the immediate emergency had been met with child feeding, medical assistance and water supplies for relief camps, the post-emergency phase saw Unicef helping to drill boreholes, train engineers, set up maintenance workshops, and import rigs and piping.

The emergencies of the early 1970s definitively launched Unicef into the water supply business. When Martin Beyer returned from West Africa in 1973, he was invited to become a roving advisor on water programmes all over the world. Although the disasters had acted as a trigger, other forces had also been at work in plunging Unicef into this field, now rapidly consuming a larger amount of financial resources. The drama of the drilling rig and the magic of the water coursing from the tube-well were new weapons in the Unicef armoury; but they did not by any means constitute the opening salvo in the organization's attention to water and sanitation, merely the most spectacular to date.

In the heyday of the disease control campaigns in the 1950s and early 1960s, when Unicef was still functioning very much as the junior partner of WHO in the health field, it had become evident that two very important groups of diseases whose major victims were infants and children were not being tackled by the onslaughts on tuberculosis, yaws, malaria and leprosy. These were gastro-enteric infections, or diarrhoeas; and parasitical infections, or intestinal worms. A bout of diarrhoea in a small child—as long as it was not cholera or typhoid—did not appear to pose the same threat to life and health as malaria or tuberculosis. Appearances deceived: statistics from underdeveloped countries which had such statistics showed that gastro-enteric infections, which were especially lethal in association with poor nutrition, were so numerous that they often accounted for more than half the deaths of children under one year. Taken together, the disease rate from all causes associated with bad water and poor sanitation was much higher. Apart from gastro-enteric infections, trachoma and skin diseases such as scabies and yaws were easily spread by lack of personal hygiene in places where water for washing was in short supply. Other diseases were caused by parasites which lived in water, and were either imbibed—such as the guinea worm; or entered the skin through cuts or abrasions—such as bilharzia or schistosomiasis, carried by water snails. Another group of water-related diseases was spread by flying vectors whose habitat was a swamp or a river: malaria carried by mosquitoes, and river-blindness carried by flies.

The great gains over the previous century in public health in the industrialized countries had proved that only the massive provision of uncontaminated drinking water and proper disposal of human excreta, accompanied by public understanding of the virtues of cleanliness, could decimate the disease and death rate from water-related causes. Campaigns against specific diseases formed a highly visible and important part of public health; but taken over the longer term, essentially a smaller part than water and sanitation. The subject first came before the WHO/Unicef Joint Committee on Health Policy in 1952, and the following year the Committee made recommendations about how far Unicef should enter the field of water supply and environmental hygiene.

The enormity of the task to be done in cleaning up the rural Third World was even more daunting than that of tuberculin testing all its children or eradicating malaria. Given the limitations of Unicef's resources, it was not thought possible for the organization to do more than dabble its toe in the pool. In the early 1950s, certain actions were taken within carefully defined parameters: water supplies and sanitation in health-care facilities and schools, where the absence of clean water and latrines radically curtailed their contribution to child health and welfare. Some of the earliest programmes were in Central America; the first project to receive pumps, pipes, and some stipends for the training of sanitarians was in Panama in 1954. Within five years, Unicef assistance—in the usual forms of supplies and training stipends—and WHO technical approval had been given to thirty-three projects, eighteen of which were in Latin America and the rest in Africa, the Middle East, Europe, South-East Asia, and the Pacific.

In 1959, the World Health Assembly adopted a policy of greater emphasis on community water and sanitation facilities as a key to health, and WHO began to put pressure on Unicef to do more. The 1960 Executive Board addressed the question, and immersed the Unicef foot a little more deeply. Not only health centres, but also water supply schemes serving a community could in future receive support. The context must continue to be a health programme, but a building at which medical care was dispensed as the site of the supply was no longer an absolute criterion. Nevertheless, Unicef was still tentative about expanding its aid to water and sanitation. Their importance was self-evident, but it was hard to see how to make substantial progress without involving Unicef in huge expense; perceptions about water and sanitation schemes were still highly coloured by the notion of large public works. Into such schemes, Unicef resources could easily vanish like the drop in the proverbial bucket. This, all were agreed, was to be avoided. Therefore, any project to be assisted must belong to the familiar conceptual category of 'demonstration' and 'catalysis': the input would help establish a model for a much larger programme funded from the national budget or better-endowed bilateral or multilateral sources.

In some countries, the strategy worked. In Peru, a WHO/Unicef supported demonstration project in one small area led directly to government adoption of a national scheme to bring piped water by gravity into every village, financed by the government with the help of external loans. A similar outcome blessed a similar project in Taiwan. In Kenya, a modest programme with documented health and economic benefits among village children was taken up with great local enthusiasm, and looked set to move in the same direction. But not everywhere were results so impressive. A thorough survey undertaken at the request of the 1965 Executive Board included on-site evaluations in eight of the eighty countries with whose water authorities Unicef was by this time co-operating. In West Pakistan, an over-ambitious programme to provide water to a thousand rural communities had over-stretched the resources of an inexperienced public health engineering department, and much of the equipment brought in by Unicef was lying around unused. This was particularly embarrassing because this was the largest water programme Unicef had ever supported; it had been launched with great fanfare following the 1964 Bangkok Conference on the Needs of Children in Asia and, by 1969, it had consumed thirty per cent of the $16·7 million Unicef had spent on water and sanitation over the ten-year period.

Some adjustments were needed in the criteria for assistance in the public-health field. In certain countries, it was unrealistic to expect that a demonstration project on a small scale could blossom into a national village water grid. Some governments simply did not have the necessary resources, nor did they attach a high priority to rural water works and excreta disposal. Even if they were committed, there were simply not enough sanitary engineers and inspectors, and cadres took time to train.

Too many assumptions had been made about dovetailing sanitation and medical services. While both were critical to improved health, they required very different kinds of personnel who were often employed by different authorities. The paths of doctors and nurses running hospitals and health centres might never cross those of the engineers and surveyors constructing and supervising water systems and latrines. At a lower level in the public-health hierarchy, who did the sanitarian report to? Was he a technician or a health person, or was he both? Co-ordinating water with health at a conceptual level was easy; at a practical level there were all sorts of problems. And without such co-ordination, the health education which was vitally needed to persuade villagers to use a new water supply hygienically and dispose carefully of waste had a tendency to fall into the gap between the doctors' efforts to cure the sick and the engineers' efforts to build the means of sickness prevention. This dichotomy between water as engineering achievement and water as bringer of health haunted water supply and sanitation schemes then, and has continued to do so down the years.

Meanwhile, the customers for pipes and pumps, the villagers of the developing countries, were usually keen—sometimes desperate—for water. Water is life, more immediately essential to human survival even than food. The water schemes of the 1960s gave great currency to the terms 'self-help' and 'community participation', originally coined by the community develop-ment enthusiasts and becoming key tenets of development thinking. To cut down costs, free unskilled labour for digging wells or trenches for water pipelines and carting stones for catchment dams were designated as the villagers' contribution to 'their' schemes. Usually, enthusiasm for water was such that they willingly co-operated. In a parched land where the only stream is miles away across a burning plain or down the sides of a steep mountain gorge, and where every precious drop must be carried on a woman's head or, at best, a donkey's back, the benefits of a well or a standpipe in the village were keenly appreciated.

Such receptiveness on the part of most beneficiaries—a receptiveness the more welcomed because the meeting of minds between would-be helpers and would-be helped in the circumstances of many development projects was relatively rare—engendered high morale among government officials and those helping to drill, pump and gravity-feed. Unfortunately, the well-deserved sense of achievement sometimes obscured the fact that the villagers' appreciation usually had little or nothing to do with whether the children had diarrhoea or intestinal parasites. To the customers of the new supply, water was a convenience, not a health aid. In some places, people only used the new well in the dry season; when the open water course nearby their houses was still freely flowing, they continued to draw their water from there just as they had always done, however many cattle wallowed in it or other sources of pollution floated down from upstream. Some people objected to the tastelessness of clean water or found its strange temperature upsetting—even, in their opinion, unhealthy; they might only use the new source for bathing and other non-drinking purposes unless the hazards of the old source were satisfactorily explained to them. And if the villagers in many water-short communities had a tenuous sense of the connection between dirty water and health, still less convinced were they of the value of confining ordure to a special place within the family compound. Excreta is not a popular subject in any culture. The harbingers of public health began to discover that there were few places in the world where people could be easily persuaded to attach social caché to a latrine. They had a point: its aerobic ambiance tends to compare unfavourably with that of the open field, the sea shore, or the ditch.

The mixed results of the assistance offered by WHO/Unicef to water and sanitation schemes came under scrutiny in 1969. The persistently unhygienic behaviour of the Third World's farming people was noted in a call for more training for sanitarians and more emphasis on health education. There was still some hesitation about how far Unicef's resources should be invested in this branch of public health, but by now the die was cast. The Indian hard-rock drilling programme was under discussion, and other circumstances were gradually propelling Unicef towards deeper immersion. Many countries and bilateral and multilateral donors were waking up to the heavy economic toll poor water supplies were exacting from the agricultural labour force in terms of sickness and low farming output. Health authorities were also lamenting the severe drain on their thinly-stretched budgets represented by the need to cure preventable water-related disease. It was also becoming clear that some alternatives to the large-scale public works approach to mass problems of water and sanitation shortage were in urgent need of development, in order to fill the techno-logical gap between faucets and water closets laid on to every household, and nothing but the stream and the bush. Some pioneer work in small-scale rural drinking water and irrigation works had been undertaken by various voluntary organizations. But they did not have the resources for anything other than the micro-scale enterprise: a few wells here, a series of small catchment dams there. Missionaries with a mechanical bent were turning old automobile engines into prototype irrigation pumps for school vegetable gardens. But such efforts were truly localized. A lacuna in international co-operation with an important bearing on maternal and child health had become visible, and Unicef—with its practical bent—was ready to do something about it.

The changing climate of opinion was connected in part to the awareness awakening worldwide about the fragile relationship between Mankind and his environment. The word 'environment', like 'development' before it, was beginning to take on an expanded conceptual significance. Not only population pressure, but urban growth, industrial pollution, the depletion of fossil fuels, the disruption of ecosystems by the use of pesticides and artificial fertilizers: all were beginning to cause a worldwide panic. Some of the pioneers who brought the world's attention to its planetary constraints, notably the British economist Barbara Ward, regarded 'environment' and 'development' as two sides of the same coin. Rain water, sea water, river water; water for energy and for agriculture as well as for health and domestic comfort; water in all its life-giving power was an obviously over-lapping concern. Since time immemorial, Mankind had disposed of his wastes into the streams from which he also drew his drinking water. The cycle of biological reaction between fish, plants, oxygen and bacteria meant that moving bodies of water had remarkable natural self-cleansing powers. But, as was so clearly demonstrated in Bangladesh, population growth had begun to overstretch those powers. Drinking water supplies which might once have been 'safe', at least for a population which used them regularly and had developed some immunity to their particular hazards, were now becoming heavily polluted. This phenomenon began to concern not only the health specialists, but a new breed—the environ-mentalists—anxious to prove their credentials for improving life on earth. The human reservoir of knowledge about natural resources—their value, their preservation, and their utilization—began to increase sharply.

The drought- and flood-related crises of the early 1970s certainly helped to trigger the upsurge in demand for Unicef's involvement in water supplies and sanitation; but these other forces were also at work. In Afghanistan, Malawi, Bolivia, Burma, Tanzania, Sudan, Guatemala, Mexico, Nepal, Sri Lanka, Mongolia; in mountainous areas and in plains; in scrubland and in semi-desert; in sprawling slums and shanty towns: clean water was a problem independent of whether drought or epidemic might suddenly dramatize its deficiencies in quality or quantity. By 1973, references to the need for clean water and better sanitation were surfacing more forcefully within Unicef. They stemmed in part from the striking affirmation of water's key role in rural development emerging from the Lomé Conference, held in Togo under Unicef auspices in May 1972 with the aim of strengthening the capacities of West African governments to 'plan for the needs of children'.

The statements of national priority presented at Lomé by the planning ministers of eight francophone countries—who had tried hard to remove themselves from international orthodoxies—placed water supplies at the top of their lists. Interestingly, the village tap they all thought was critical to the needs of children rated attention less because of its relationship to health than because it was a determining factor in the whole environment affecting women's and children's conditions of life, economic situation and nutritional status. Millions of women throughout Africa spent hours of back-breaking labour every day hauling water in pots, jars and enamel basins from distant streams and open wells. Water's scarcity and the labour involved in fetching it meant that far too little was used for washing

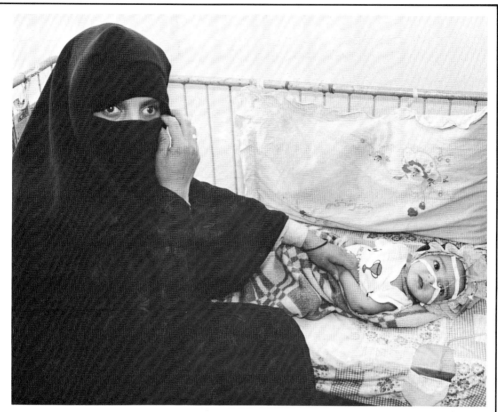

A mother and her
seriously sick child
at the Rawda Health
Centre in the Yemen
Arab Republic. They
had to travel from a
village 100 miles
away to find medical
help.
(*Unicef/Massey*)

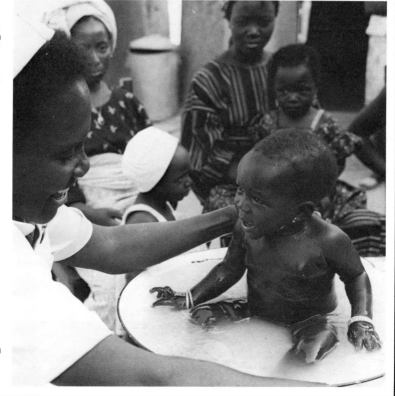

A centre for family
welfare and
mothercraft opened
in Zaria, Nigeria, in
1962 with the co-
operation of WHO,
FAO, the UN Bureau
of Social Affairs and
Unicef.
(*Unicef/Bernheim*)

At a mother-and-child health care clinic in Zinder, Niger, classes are given in nutrition and cooking.
(*Unicef/Watson*)

Opposite:
In 1966, Unicef helped Algeria produce a nutritious food mix from processed grain. Here, a little girl eats her lunch of Superamine.
(*Unicef/Wolff*)

Dhandlan, India, 1981: a day-care centre worker administers a dose of orange-flavoured vitamin A to a three-year-old boy at his own home while his grandmother looks on.
(*Unicef/Nagarajan*)

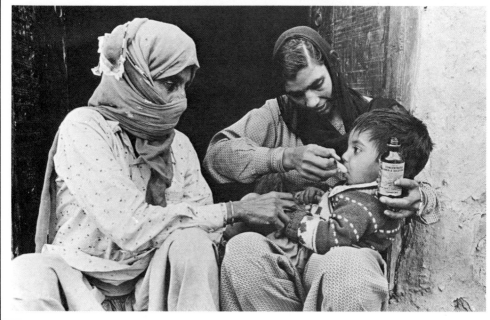

Selected by his own community, one of India's community health volunteers gives first aid and simple medicines, and looks for early signs of TB, leprosy and other diseases. (*Unicef/Nagarajan*)

An auxiliary nurse/midwife examines a pregnant woman in Dhandlan, India. (*Unicef/Nagarajan*) children and keeping domestic utensils and environment clean. Bound to a daily cycle of incessant drudgery, women had too little time and energy to spend on such matters. Nor on other domestic tasks, including cultivation of the family's food which, more often than not, was their exclusive responsibility. Without water in the village, the Lomé Conference suggested, not only was the drinking supply stagnant, but the entire rural economy.

This, within Unicef, was a new perspective to add to the health imperative for water supplies. It made another dent in the earlier resistance to large-scale support. In 1974, soon after Martin Beyer had set up his advisory service in Unicef headquarters and begun to travel ever further afield, Unicef expenditures on water supply and sanitation reached nearly $12 million for the year. Water was becoming more popular, both with aid donors willing to give special contributions, and with recipients. As the requests piled up, a new breed of technicians were joining Unicef's staff: hydrogeologists and master drillers. The survey requirements for hard-rock drilling and the operation of the new high-speed rigs required special technical and operational skills. As yet, such skills were mostly available only in countries with advanced technology. A new chapter in Unicef programming had opened, and its heroes were the rugged personalities prepared to work in remote and sometimes dangerous conditions in waterless corners of the globe.

Early in 1974, Hakan Landelius, the head of Radda Barnen, the Swedish Save the Children Fund, visited his compatriot Martin Beyer in New York. He had been travelling in India visiting projects assisted by Unicef with which Radda Barnen had a close association, and had observed that in most villages where the hard-rock drilling programme had provided new wells, the handpumps which brought the water to the surface had broken down. Gordon Carter and his Unicef team in New Delhi were trying to address this problem; meanwhile Unicef was on the point of committing a further $9 million for the rural water supply programme in India and Beyer was justifiably anxious. A spot survey carried out in the States of Tamil Nadu and Maharashtra had shown that, for all its high technology and its cost, the Indian rural drinking water programme had managed to provide three-quarters of the villages with nothing better than a hole in the ground and an inoperative pump on top of it.

The teams of drillers with their high-powered equipment had gone to the villages, performed their marvels, and disappeared. No-one had realized that the pumps they were installing were too fragile for sustained use by a whole community. The number of breakdowns had overwhelmed the resources of sewing-machine and bicycle-repair shops and others entrusted by state authorities with the job of pump maintenance. In many areas, it was not clear to villagers what steps they could effectively take to bring a handpump breakdown to the attention of those who might repair it. They waited for the miracle men who had put the pump there in the first place to reappear, and resorted to the waterholes they had been obliged to rely on in the past.

The cast-iron pumps used in the drinking water programme were poor quality copies of old-style European and American handpumps designed for use by a single family, long since out of use in the land of their birth and therefore unimproved for at least a generation. Their unsuitability for use by an entire village had already been registered by a handful of Indian officials and mission workers involved in small-scale water programmes. At Jalna in Maharashtra, Church of Scotland missionaries cum water engineers had already invented a tougher handpump made of steel. A mission at Sholapur improved upon the Jalna design and began to manufacture it to uniform professional standards. Other nearby projects began to copy these designs, and by 1974 several thousand durable pumps had been installed over tube-wells in Maharashtra. When Unicef water staff realized that continued well-drilling could not be justified unless something was done to improve handpump quality, they turned to the Sholapur pump. Two Unicef water engineers, Rupert Talbot and Ken McLeod, sought authorization to buy up several thousand Sholapur pump sections to allow State governments to replace the broken down cast-iron variety. This initiative— whose costs were met by Radda Barnen—convinced the Indian authorities of the need for a sturdier handpump for use in village water supply schemes. The handpump then developed by Unicef, in association with the government-run company of Richardson & Cruddas in Madras, was a refinement of the earlier Jalna and Sholapur pumps and was named by Unicef the India Mark II.

The India Mark II handpump is an unqualified success story, and a story in which Unicef is justifiably proud to have played a significant role. The main development phase took place between 1975 and 1977. The aim was to design a pump that would operate for a full year without breakdown; that could be manufactured entirely from components available in India; would cost less than $200; be easy to operate; maintainable in working condition by people with a minimum of engineering knowledge. It was important that the pumphead should be solidly encased so that nothing unhygienic could fall down the hole and pollute the water source; also that children playing with the pump could not easily damage the handle or block up the spout. Cast iron was abandoned in favour of mild steel. The fulcrum of the pump was a sealed ball bearing without need of oiling or greasing, and the pump rods were linked to the handle with a flexible chain. These critical design features were and are the crux of the India Mark II; over the years minor modifications have been incorporated to minimize maintenance.

Great effort was made to ensure that the India Mark II maintained its quality and did not lose its reputation to poor quality imitations entering the market at a lower price. At the same time it was important to assure that there were competitive manufacturers in different parts of the country. In 1979 the Indian Standards Institute brought out a very detailed standard with specifications for all components. Unicef, on its side, prepared a list of approved India Mark II handpump manufacturers. Any prospective supplier first had to give satisfaction that it was capable of manufacturing the pump; if this screening procedure was successfully accomplished, a trial order was placed, and the handpumps submitted for independent quality testing. Only after this process could the manufacturer be entered on the list of recognized suppliers. By 1984, thirty-six suppliers had qualified, of which there was one at least in every Indian State. Their combined production output in that year was 13,000 handpumps per month. By this stage, more than 600,000 had been installed in Indian villages, of which Unicef had procured 100,000 and State governments the rest. Handpump production was an established industry, and some suppliers had exported large quantities of India Mark II handpumps to countries in Africa and elsewhere in Asia for other village water programmes supported by Unicef.

Faulty handpump manufacture was not the only potential cause of breakdown. Correct installation, in which the engineering staffs of public health departments were trained, was also important. Unicef put together a manual with precise instructions: the three legs of the pump must be embedded in a concrete platform covering the tube-well so that dirty water could not trickle back into the source; a drain must lead away the water which inevitably collected around the pump base. An effective maintenance was also necessary: handpumps, whatever the excellence of their design, are bound to break down from time to time. What has since become known as the three-tier handpump maintenance system, and has been adopted widely throughout India, was pioneered in Tirunelveli and Thanjavur districts of Tamil Nadu State at the southern tip of the sub-continent. Tamil Nadu was the home of Richardson & Cruddas, and its Water Supply and Drainage Board pioneered the introduction of the India Mark II. The concept was championed by M. Francis, an energetic State government official who had a gift for mobilizing people and keeping them enthused.

The three-tier maintenance system was based on the idea of the designation of a bright young man in the village as the 'handpump caretaker'. He was to form the first link in the chain which would ensure that a handpump never broke down for more than a few days at a time. The caretaker must live near the pump, and ideally be a school-teacher, a shopkeeper, or someone with a little social standing. The first group of handpump caretakers from Tirunelveli were selected in 1976 in consultation with local village councils, and 100 or so candidates presented themselves at a two-day training camp. Out of this camp a pattern developed which was used elsewhere to set up the caretaker network as close as possible to the time when handpumps were installed. The caretakers were volunteers; their only badge of recognition was a certificate and a log sheet with their name at the top. They were armed with two spanners and some grease, and taught how to open the pump-head, check the action of the chain, grease and tighten nuts and bolts. If the pump suffered a serious breakdown, the caretakers used one of their pre-stamped and addressed postcards to summon the block engineer, the next of the three maintenance 'tiers'. If the problem turned out to be beyond the competence of the block engineer, he would call in the third tier: the district mobile repair team.

For some years, the village caretakers in Tamil Nadu were a model of successful community mobilization. Francis was seconded to Unicef, and became the mainstay of the training programme and its follow-up. He sustained the enthusiasm of the village caretakers by writing a monthly newsletter, sending them greetings for Tamil festivals, and organizing competitions and radio appearances for the best. Although the model was adopted elsewhere, it never quite reached the same star quality. In a land where each of hundreds of thousands of rural communities had its own environment to contend with and its own mysterious codes and dynamics, it takes an individual with the charisma of Francis to make widespread mobilization of villages behind such a programme truly effective. But even its moderate success, coupled with the sturdiness of the India Mark II, has prevented large-scale pump breakdown. The teams who drill the holes and install the pumps upon them are no longer visitors from another planet who perform a conjuring trick and vanish. They are accessible, and with some pushing, the village can command a re-appearance when they need one. Because the caretaker is unpaid, and because the pumps rarely suffer serious breakdown, the maintenance system is cheap: around $32 a year per pump.

Apart from his maintenance duties, the village handpump caretaker is supposed to act as an informal public-health worker. During his training, he is taught the message at the heart of all rural drinking water programmes: that clean water is the key to health, and that everything must be done to make sure the handpump water stays pristine pure all the way from spout to mouth. He is supposed to make sure that the concrete platform under the handpump is swept and dry, and the drainage channel flows free. He is also supposed to admonish those women using dirty pots, or who still resort to the old open well because it is closer to their homes.

But a man with a spanner and a can of grease is a mini-mechanic, not a ˙mini-nurse or doctor. The women in the village might heed a midwife who told them such things. But a young teacher or shopkeeper? What would he know about children's health? Male village caretakers tend to feel uncomfortable about interfering with the women's domain and are at best half-hearted in their public-health performance. In some States, including

Tamil Nadu and Maharashtra, women have also been selected as handpump caretakers to reinforce the health messages. But women are less keen on the mechanical role, and carry less clout when it comes to summoning the water authorities. In the end, the essential task is for the caretakers, male and female, to keep the handpump in working order and the water supply uncontaminated. Hopefully, time will prove to the villagers that handpump water is not only more convenient, but healthier.

Within water-supply and sanitation schemes, health education as a component was for a time somewhat overshadowed. The lustre of hard-rock drilling, the technical challenge of the cheap and durable village handpump, the feat of capping springs high on Himalayan mountainsides and in the southern and central African massifs: these were the consuming preoccupations of the engineers who dominated the rural water supply business during the 1970s. And rightly: without the hydrogeologists, the engineers and the master drillers there would be no new sources of drinking water in many parts of the world where the deadly partnership of drought and population increase was making the task of water collection more and more difficult. Some of the technicians recruited by Unicef during these years, who have spent their working lives in some of the wildest places on earth, were larger-than-life personalities—men whose dedication and whose spirit of adventure were redolent of the great tradition of humanitarian exploration in the nineteenth century. In post-revolutionary Ethiopia, a Yugoslav, Vlado Zakula, who had served the Emperor Haile Selassie's Government mining for gold, joined Unicef's staff to mine what to village people was as valuable: water. Moving heavy, sensitive equipment through difficult terrain from site to site presents problems requiring superhuman endurance and skill. Zakula's rig, and what it could mean in a relief camp or a village deep in areas where guerilla activity added to the hazards of his existence, became such an extension of his life that he camped alongside it wherever he felt its own life was in danger. Fausto Bertoni, an Italian, who joined Unicef's staff in Afghanistan and took similar hardships in his stride, became an almost legendary figure in villages from the Sudan to the Punjab. Men like Zakula and Bertoni trained scratch crews of local engineers to master modern drilling tech-nology and form the backbone of their country's water engineering depart-ments. They were the heroes of the rural water supply revolution.

When Unicef first became deeply involved in water and sanitation, the most important immediate task was seen by Martin Beyer and his growing cadre of water experts as the development of low-cost technological responses to the worldwide drinking water problem.

In the early 1970s, the latest buzz word in development circles was 'appropriate': 'appropriate technologies' for water supply and sanitation in

Third World villages meant something more modest and affordable than a national water grid with faucets in every home and flush toilets connected to a central sewage system. Public works on this scale remained, and still remain, absolutely beyond the reach of the budgetary capacities of the poorer developing nations, except in the cities, or in parts of the cities, where the risk of serious epidemic has to be taken into account. Other technological answers had to be found, some of which—like the highly sophisticated percussion-hammer drilling rigs—were the direct product of late twentieth century industrial invention; others—like the India Mark II handpump—were adaptations of devices which had been familiar in Europe and North America a generation or two ago.

Largely as a result of the popularity of E. F. Schumacher's proposition that 'Small is Beautiful', even technologies that had been around for a millennium or two now suddenly swept into vogue. Schumacher articulated to a mass audience the dawning realization that the large-scale industrial technology of the Western world, expensive both to build and maintain, was a hopeless misfit economically and otherwise in most parts of the rural Third World. The quest for new, more 'appropriate', technological responses to the problems of poverty and underdevelopment was graced by the moral overtones of its rejection of dehumanizing industrialization, itself a fashionable doctrine of the time. The fledgling village water and sanitation business became caught up with this new religion. Hydrological devices invented by the ancient Chinese for raising water from the depths of the earth; Cretan windmills with sails set for the prevailing breeze; solar stills which would use the sun's rays to convert salt water into fresh; all were grist to the new 'appropriate' mill. Some of the endeavours foisted on Third World villages under this banner belonged to the wilder shores of humanitarian boy scoutism. Others were more realistic.

Whatever its excesses of zeal, the new technological creed contained an essential truth. The place to start the search for appropriate responses to problems in the rural Third World was not necessarily among the pattern books of nineteenth-century mechanical devices in Europe and North America, nor among the texts of the ancients, but in the places where people had long since devised their own technological solutions: the villages themselves. Some of these solutions, as the development experts discovered to their surprise, turned out to be already remarkably 'appropriate'. Dick Phillips, a water programme officer in Unicef's Dacca office, contemplated the effectiveness of the local method of well drilling and, together with officials from the Directorate of Public Health Engineering, decided that with minor modifications, nothing could be more suitable for the Unicef-assisted well-drilling programme in Bangladesh. While in countries elsewhere, hard rock below ground was making drilling an ever more sophisticated adventure in which water must be as expensively mined as precious metal, the alluvial plains of Bangladesh consisted of layers of sand and clay deposited over the centuries by the great rivers. The soil was like a huge soft sponge which soaked up rainfall during the seasonal monsoon; the water table was no more than a few feet beneath the surface, but was usually heavily polluted at that depth. Deeper down, at 100 feet or so, it had been filtered through layers of sand and cleaned and purified in the process.

To drill a well to such a depth through the rock-free soil required nothing more than human energy. With the help of a bamboo scaffold and a lever, three or four drillers could 'pump' a galvanized iron pipe to the necessary depth within a day. The method was called sludging. One member of the team used his hand as a valve over the mouth of the pipe, flushing out silt and sludge so as to allow the pipe to descend. When one length of pipe was fully inserted, another length was screwed to its end, until a depth of around 100 feet had been reached. It was then removed, length by length, and replaced by a durable PVC water pipe covered by a filter to prevent sand and soil particles from entering the bore-hole. A handpump was then bolted to the pipe and mounted on a concrete platform. Because the clean water rose quickly to the level of the water table, only a small handpump which lifted by suction was required. As in India, a prototype pump was modified and made more durable at Unicef's initiative; once a standardized design was approved, Unicef helped to import pig-iron, limestone and coke to enable the pumps to be manufactured in local foundries. Even when prices rose in the mid-1970s, the entire cost to Unicef of supplying the materials for a finished tube-well averaged only around $75, half the cost of the finished installation.

The Directorate of Public Health Engineering built up a staff of well-drilling teams to carry out installation and maintenance, and every village wanting a tube-well taxed its members a few cents each to off-set part of the installation costs. Gradually, demand from the villages grew to the point where the drilling teams could not keep up, even at a rate of 50,000 new tube-wells each year. By 1978, over 300,000 tube-wells had been sunk with Unicef assistance, an average of one handpump with clean water for each 250 inhabitants of Bangladesh's rural areas, an achievement very close to the goal of one tube-well per 200 people set by the Pakistani authorities in 1968. The country's drinking water problem had moved a considerable distance towards being solved, in spite of the disasters which had so disrupted the country during a decade of turmoil.

The Indian and Bangladeshi water-supply programmes were the largest in terms of Unicef's involvement, but there were many others in which Unicef played a role closer to the pump-priming initiative envisaged in 1969. An example of a different kind of appropriate technological response to rural water shortage was a scheme in southern Malawi, which capitalized on natural energy sources to keep costs to a minimum. Its design required the capture of waterfalls into a main reservoir high on the 9000-foot slopes of Mount Mulanje, and the water's descent by gravity through a series of main and branch pipelines to 450 villages in the 100 square miles of the plains below. The Ministry of Community Development devised and carried out the plan, and Unicef provided all 148 miles of pipe.

The most impressive feature of this kind of scheme was the role played by the people of the villages in its construction. Here was 'self-help' in action on a spectacular scale. Each village turned out in force under the direction of its own committee to dig the miles of wide and narrow trench which would house the pipes bringing the water to their communal standpipe. This feat of intervillage organization and the provision of voluntary labour on such a scale for something other than famine relief works was a phenomenon common to many rural water-supply schemes. It reinforced the thesis which held that if villagers wanted something badly, if it was a 'felt need', they would turn out en masse to make it happen. On the lower slopes of Mount Mulanje, men dug trenches for miles over rocky and difficult terrain; women carted sand and stones for dam construction in baskets on their heads; elders organized community self-taxing schemes for water rates.

The day the water actually travelled the full twenty miles from the reservoir to the village at the furthest edge of the plain was a day of wonder and riotous celebration. The success of the scheme led to eleven other similar gravity-fed rural water systems in other highland areas of Malawi. Subsequently, an assessment of the country's surface water availability forced the authorities to the conclusion that a ground water drilling programme was also necessary. Drawing on the lessons of the Mulanje project, every effort was made to involve the villagers in the programme's execution. The site of each borehole was determined not only by the geological experts, but also by villagers, including the women, taking into account factors such as who owned the land and how steep would be the gradients up and down which water would be carried. Village committees were set up to oversee handpump maintenance and use.

While the popularity of water-supply schemes was being rapidly proven in countries all over the world, the same could not be said for sanitation. Everyone paid lip service to the necessity of providing for waste disposal as part and parcel of any scheme for water supply; in practice, no-one—neither public health nor engineering departments, village communities, nor donors from voluntary or intergovernmental organizations—showed a similar degree of enthusiasm for schemes to confine human excreta to places where the hazards it posed to health could be minimized. Even the Indian rural water-supply programme—such a success in many of its aspects—managed to achieve almost nothing in the context of sanitation. 'Excreta disposal has not been touched', it was reported in tones of frustration in 1974. Little could be expected to change without more health education; 'Just about impossible to obtain a collaboration between health educators and engineers', the same rapporteur lamented. While water was a deeply 'felt need', a latrine decidedly was not. While communities willingly organized themselves to dig a hole in the earth for a pipeline, they evinced little or no enthusiasm to do the same for a latrine.

This particular 'appropriate' response to the task of human waste disposal has had the utmost difficulty in passing the ultimate test: acceptability. Even where health education has managed to establish in sceptical minds the connections between dirt, germs, flies and infection, habits concerning the human being's most basic bodily function are deeply ingrained and not easily abandoned. Since no-one even wants to discuss the subject, it is difficult to encourage people to change their ways. In Bolivia, where between 1968 and 1977 Unicef supported a very popular well-drilling programme, the public health department in Santa Cruz resorted to the device of refusing to sink a community well unless latrines had already been built in three-quarters of the village houses. Latrine slabs were provided at cost by Unicef, and reluctantly householders complied. But when public-health officials later toured the community, they found that the latrines were mainly being used as chicken coops and larders for the cool storage of beer, not for their intended purpose.

The Bolivian experience was not uncommon. In spite of technical modifications which have made latrines environmentally more pleasant, and have turned them into safe natural fertilizer production units, the problem of acceptability remains. One possible key is an improvement in the status of rural women: in some societies modesty and a densely-inhabited rural landscape make for women's great discomfort in daylight hours. In other places, the attention of a free source of fertilizer may persuade the menfolk—who invariably control public works of any kind—that latrines have distinct advantages. In some urban parts of the developing world, attitudes have already changed. They have been forced to: the numbers of those willing to accept a life-long career in nightsoil disposal at the very bottom of the social heap have declined sharply since the days when Mahatma Gandhi took up their cause. But in rural areas, particularly where households are spaced at a reasonable distance from one another, the latrine may take some years to command an enthusiastic following. Until the human race is able to abandon its inhibitions about the subject, as it has done for sex and reproduction, excreta disposal is likely to remain the joker in the health-care pack.

By the mid-1970s, water supplies and sanitation had begun to command ever greater attention on the world stage from those caught up in the twin concerns of 'environment' and 'development'. In 1972, a UN Conference on the Human Environment met in Stockholm; this, the first of many grand global events staged to address the problems which had so far defeated

Mankind's best intentions—population growth, hunger, human settlements, women's rights—owed a large part of its genesis to Barbara Ward and the allies she had managed to assemble behind her particular vision of what was going sadly wrong with the planet Earth. Out of it came a new offshoot within the UN system: the UN Environment Programme.

In an attempt to make a convincing connection between the ills of underdevelopment and those of shrinking planetary resources, the Stockholm Conference declared that the 'pollution of poverty' was the worst of all pollutions. The prophets of the post-industrial world tried to convince the developing countries that condemnation of Mankind's voracious consumption of non-renewable resources did not conflict with their own demand for a greater share of the consumption process. The drive to improve man's habitat and keep his global village clean encompassed international outrage at the statistics concerning access to a supply of clean water and proper waste disposal. In the developing world, less than half the people drew their domestic water supply from a source which would pass a laboratory test for cleanliness; three out of four had no better facilities for excreta disposal than a disgusting bucket or a walk in the fields. The squalor of the crowded slums in so many mushrooming cities of the developing world presented a frightening picture of the hazards of epidemic and ill-health. The effect of all this unsanitariness on the disease and death rate of children was almost incalculable.

In 1976, the situation was brought to the attention of another UN conference: Habitat, the Conference on Human Settlements meeting in Vancouver, passed a resolution declaring that clean water should be provided for all the world's people by 1990 at the latest. Yet a third UN conference in March 1977 took up the same theme, with even greater emphasis. The delegates met in the Argentinian city of Mar del Plata to examine all the statistics associated with the consumption of water by humankind in the fourth quarter of the twentieth century, and consider what to do about them. With more bravado than realism, they elaborated an action plan costing $144,000 million in 1977 US dollar value which would provide clean water and sanitation for everyone in the world, and declared that 1981 to 1990 would be the International Drinking Water and Sanitation Decade during which the goal should be reached. They envisaged that developing countries would themselves supply most of the necessary investment; but that large amounts running into the thousands of millions would have to come from external funding sources.

During the 1970s, when not only Unicef but also many other bilateral and multilateral donors began to commit much larger investment flows to dams and reservoirs and public works all over the developing world, the engineers and other technicians were seen as the arbiters of global cleanliness. The underlying assumption was that the existence of a plentiful and clean water supply would perform a similar miracle on the rates of disease and death as had the public health installations of a century earlier during the industrialization of Europe and North America. Down the years, much rhetoric but too little practical attention had been paid to the need for health education alongside the water works. Now, on the threshold of a major push for 'drinking water and sanitation for all by the year 1990', doubts began to assail the underlying assumptions of previous years. Studies were published showing that a clean, protected water supply did not automatically confer health—in the narrow definition of the term—on village and slum inhabitants. Disease rates, particularly the gastro-enteric infections which so seriously affected children, had not plunged as far downwards as had been predicted. However 'appropriate' their technologies, however sophisticated their drilling rigs, however immaculate their design of gravity-fed water systems and handpumps, the technicians did not have all the answers. The health specialists began to re-assume ascendancy in water and sanitation.

Unicef had entered the world of water for one very specific reason: its impact on child health. The villagers and slum dwellers of the developing world had responded with enthusiasm to schemes to supply them with water, but for different reasons: they wanted rid of thirst, drudgery and inconvenience. No-one in the world wants to drink water that is dirty or foul-smelling, and most people instinctively appreciate the risks of ill-health that doing so carries. But germs and worms too tiny to be seen are not self-evidently harmful to those who do not know that they are there. If the water is clean, but the water pot dirty; if hands are not washed; if food is not covered; if human ordure is not confined; if compounds and streets are not swept: the water supply on its own will not do all it could to transform the health of children.

As the decade of the 1970s drew to a close, the critical question concerning water and sanitation had become how to ensure the maximum health advantages for children from the new water source. Whatever the water supply had not done, it had achieved a release of village women from back-breaking toil, an advantage sometimes underrated by those fixated purely on measuring declines in certain water-related disease rates. With more time and energy on their hands, women might well embark on other life- and health-improving activities around the home. This begged a wider question: what, actually, was 'health'? Was it merely the absence of debilitating disease and infirmity? Or was it, as the village women of the rural Third World might suggest, enough food for the children to eat, plentiful rainfall for a good harvest, and a shorter distance to walk to the well? On the plains below Mount Mulanje, as they celebrated the instalment of their new standpipe, the villagers might sing: 'Health is wealth'. The question of what good health truly consisted of, and how it might best be provided to far-flung communities all over the world, was itself undergoing a reappraisal.

Main Sources

Unicef Executive Board: general progress reports of the Executive Director; reports on programme developments in South-Central Asia; recommendations by the Executive Director for assistance to India and Bangladesh, and for relief and rehabilitation assistance for children and mothers affected by drought in the Sudano-Sahelian region of Africa and in Ethiopia; 1970–1976.

Reports by the WHO/Unicef Joint Committee on Health Policy: 'Environmental Sanitation Activities in Relation to Unicef', 1953–1959; 'Environmental Sanitation and its Relation to Child Health', WHO, 1952; 'Assessment of Environmental Sanitation and Rural Water Supply Programmes 1959–1968'.

Articles and reports in Unicef information materials and publications, in particular *Unicef News* and *Assignment Children*, 1965–85.

Information materials and publications prepared by the Unicef Water and Sanitation Service, New York.

Interviews with present and retired Unicef staff members, conducted by Jack Charnow for the Unicef History Project, 1983–85.

Only One Earth: The Care and Maintenance of a Small Planet, Barbara Ward and Rene Dubois; an unofficial report commissioned by the Secretary-General of the UN Conference on the Human Environment, published by W. W. Norton & Company Inc., New York, 1972.

'Children, Youth, Women, and Development Plans: The Lomé Conference', report of the conference of Ministers held on Lomé, Togo, May 1972; published by the Unicef Regional Office for West and Central Africa, Abidjan.

'Semi-industrial Projects Assisted by UNICEF in India', an assessment prepared for Unicef by Tata Economic Consultancy Services, Bombay; published by Unicef's Regional Office for South Central Asia, New Delhi, December 1984.

'Who puts the water in the taps? Community participation in Third World drinking water, sanitation and health', edited by Sumi Krishna Chauhan, published by Earthscan, the information service of the International Institute for Environment and Development, London, 1983.

Chapter 13

An Alternative Order

Towards the end of the 1960s, leading figures in government and international affairs launched a process of examination into why the results of the UN's first Development Decade had not lived up to expectations. In relation to the target set for the Decade—a minimum of five per cent growth in the Gross National Product in each developing country—results were extremely promising. Certain countries had not managed to reach the goal, but on average it had been surpassed: among the less well-off, the average was five per cent, and seven per cent among the middle-income countries. These were higher rates of growth than ever attained by the industrialized nations in their earlier history; slightly higher even than their rates for the same period. In spite of everything, however, the inescapable fact was the new wealth generated by these rates of growth had made little impact on the majority of people living in the developing world, most of whom continued to live in deepest poverty.

In the developing countries themselves there was a sense of disillusion that they were not moving ahead at the rate they should; among aid donors, there was a widespread feeling that their assistance programmes were ineffective. It began to seem that the transfer of technical know-how and financial investment from the rich world to the poor—at least in its current form—was not after all a very effective instrument for rapid development; it was only an effective instrument for increasing the growth rate of GNP, which, essential as it was, was not sufficient on its own. One reason for the upset in calculations was the high population growth rates, which meant that the fruits of progress had to be shared between many more people. Another was that capital and technical assistance had been invested in such a way that the fruits of progress were very unevenly distributed, both between countries and within them.

In accordance with conventional economic norms, investments had gone to the most promising countries and the most promising ventures, almost all of which were large-scale industrial or agricultural enterprises. The effect had been 'to he who hath shall more be given'. Among the developing countries, the poorer were falling further and further behind; within the countries, the same was happening to the people. Little of the increase in national wealth was trickling down to households in the lowest income groups, many of whom were experiencing the effects of land shortage, un- or underemployment, low prices for their agricultural produce, higher food and living costs, and were not receiving very much compensation in the form of improved community services—credit, jobs, water supply, health and education services—which might help them break out of the cycle of low income, low skills, and low expectations.

During the 1950s and 1960s, the membership of the UN had swelled from the fifty-one countries who signed the original charter in 1945, to 128 by the end of the first Development Decade. Almost all the new members were developing nations, and during the decolonization process the task of international co-operation in development had become the largest activity in the UN system. The UN now began to make preparations for a second Development Decade. With the experience of the first behind it, and with the benefit of the work being done by the increasing number of economists, planners, administrators and technical experts who had taken up careers in Third World development, the preparations made for the second Development Decade were much more thorough than they had been for the first.

One important contribution was a report produced by an international commission set up in 1968 at the request of the World Bank, and headed by Lester Pearson, ex-Prime Minister of Canada. Pearson's commission conducted a 'grand assize' on 'the consequences of twenty years of development assistance', and published their findings under the title *Partners in Development*. The commission noted that 'the climate surrounding foreign aid programmes is heavy with disillusion and distrust', but its analysis was that this reaction was unjustified. Its recommendations for a revised development strategy included an increase in the flow of international aid: the UN member organizations and their partners must renew their appeal on behalf of mankind, some of whose members still lived in conditions which amounted to a denial of human dignity. Two of the ten recommendations made by the report were in the social field: population growth rates should be slowed, and aid to education and research must be revitalized.

The UN adopted its official strategy for the second Development Decade at the General Assembly of 1970. Some of its ingredients were the classic precepts: rapid growth in the GNP of the developing countries, for which the target was raised from five to six per cent; and increased flows of international development assistance from the countries of the industrialized world, for which the target set was one per cent of GNP. But a new dimension of the strategy was a preoccupation with 'human development'. How the growth target set for the Decade was to be reached was now regarded as equally important as the target itself. The measures for reaching the target were spelled out in some detail, and they included putting a brake on population growth; the creation of jobs, particularly in the countryside from which people were emigrating in great numbers towards the cities; the provision of education, health, and nutrition services; and the participation of children and youth in the development process.

Gradually, a new climate of thinking was evolving. Now that it was clear that rapid economic growth did not automatically wash human misery away in its wake, it was necessary to pinpoint precise activities which would do something to reduce poverty and relieve distress without at the same time destroying the prospects for economic growth. Policies must be designed to have direct effects on the basic essentials of ordinary people's lives—food, housing, education, health; this was the only way to ensure that the benefits of local investment and international aid did not stop short before they reached into the lives of the poor. During the course of the next few years, economists and planners began to lay aside many familiar norms and reorientate their thinking. In the past, they had looked down on welfare considerations as 'consumption': their business was with investment in productive enterprise, in the build-up of technological and managerial capacity. They had not given much serious consideration to how their poor relations in the social sector spent the wealth they generated on housing, health, nutrition, or education. Now things began to change.

One institution whose policies both reflected and helped to shape new attitudes was the World Bank. In 1968 Robert McNamara became its President, and during his first five-year term there was a significant shift in the Bank's policies. Not only did it increase its lending to the least developed countries, but it tried to find investment opportunities that would spread their benefits widely, particularly among the least well-off.

In 1972, McNamara made what was regarded as a landmark statement in his annual address to the Board of Governors. He stated that the task confronting the governments of the developing countries was to reorientate their development policies to attack directly the personal poverty of the poorest forty per cent of their people. He did not suggest that they should abandon a policy of vigorous growth, but that growth targets should be set in terms of human needs such as nutrition, housing, health, literacy and employment. If this led to a reduction in the pace of growth, so be it. Social justice—reinforced by political prudence—demanded some sacrifice from the privileged few on behalf of the desperately poor majority. McNamara was only one of many leading contemporary figures to champion the idea of an all-out attack on poverty as the cornerstone of the 1970s development strategy. 'Redistribution with growth' and 'meeting basic needs' became the economic slogans of this new line of thought.

One effect of the growing interest of the policy-makers in human development was the discovery that, in their own little ways, some of the projects in the Third World which had been fostered and funded by the humanitarians—the voluntary agencies and organizations such as Unicef— had met the new development criteria rather successfully. These obscure participants in international development co-operation had never tried to do anything other than reach poor families with a modest improvement in their well-being: better food for their children and some gardening tools to grow it; a fully-equipped health post and an auxiliary nurse or a trained midwife to run it; a new classroom for the community school and some slates for the children to write on.

Where Unicef primarily concerned itself with these items at the level of national policies and programmes, the voluntary agencies with their smaller budgets and necessarily more limited focus usually dealt with them in the context of what had come to be known as the 'micro-project'. Most such organizations did not have the resources, clout, or expertise to fuss about Five-Year Plans or calculate the development potential of a hydro-electric dam or a textiles factory. They had focussed on the village, the community, the family and the children; and the counterpart organizations through which they assisted projects in the Third World—the local co-operative society, the women's club, the mission hospital, the village council—gave them a direct link with the poor whose lot they were trying to alleviate.

Unicef's exclusively humanitarian mandate was unique among those member organizations of the UN system concerned with long-term development. So, therefore, was the range of its experience with trying to meet the basic needs of the poor—experience enhanced by its relationships with the voluntary agencies. Some of its preoccupations—rural water supplies, applied nutrition projects—had clear implications for the rural economy independently of their health and welfare benefits. Unicef had made an attempt to influence Five-Year Plans and development strategies in favour of the child, with only a modest degree of success. Now a new legitimacy was conferred on these efforts. Doors opened where before they had been closed, or at best held condescendingly ajar. In its 1973 annual report, the World Bank commented warmly on its growing association with Unicef in fields such as training, nutrition and population. The post-civil war, rural-water supply programme in Bangladesh, which represented the first Unicef programme in association with the World Bank, had opened a new chapter in institutional partnerships.

While the development establishment pursued their search for alternatives to their old models for progress, another search for alternatives was also underway. Many people in Europe and North America were challenging the values of 'the good life' as defined by materialism and unfettered consumption. Leaders of the Christian Church preached that 'Enough is Enough'. Others agreed with E. F. Schumacher that 'Small is Beautiful', and criticized the assumption of power by large, impersonal, inaccessible institutions in extensive areas of people's lives. The ideas of self-reliance and community action which had gained popularity in the 1960s took on new force and depth of meaning. The pressure that Mankind was exerting on the planet's dwindling resources reinforced the idea of the global village in which the lifestyles of one section of humanity were interdependent with those of others. The high level of energy consumption by those in the West threatened the future of the whole human race, and the 'haves' therefore had an obligation to share the resources of a finite world more equitably with the 'have-nots'. An alternative development model, according to this view, was something everyone needed, not merely the less fortunate inhabitants of the poorer parts of the world. Many of the ideas generated by the debate about alternatives were about society as a whole; they were not exclusively about the Third World, the First World, or any other specific, notionally separate, 'world'.

No sooner had the second Development Decade opened than events occurred to inject new urgency into this ferment. If the 'population crisis' was the international theme to emerge most strongly in the late 1960s, followed very soon afterwards by the 'environmental crisis' in which the population crisis was itself a critical part, in the early 1970s these were temporarily eclipsed by two other crises with which they were closely connected: the 'oil crisis' prompted by the formation of the OPEC cartel; and the 'food crisis', caused by two disastrous world harvests in 1972 and 1974.

The UN responded with an agenda of international conferences designed to address the various interlocking world problems. The first, on the environment, took place in Stockholm in 1972; it was followed by others on population, in Bucharest in 1974; food, in Rome also in 1974; women, in Mexico, 1975; human settlements, Vancouver, 1976; employment, Geneva, 1976; water, Mar del Plata, 1977; desertification, Nairobi, 1977. Whatever the individual and collective outcomes of this series of international talking-shops, these conferences helped to clarify the issues, and establish where different international, governmental and organizational players stood; they were also an opportunity for public debate and the dissemination of information.

Meanwhile, at a moment when the international community had on its hands the fullest agenda in its entire experience, a series of natural and man-made disasters afflicted Third World countries in what seemed to be a remorseless round of catastrophe. It began with the cyclone in the Bay of Bengal which inundated East Pakistan in late 1970; was followed in the same area by civil war and the refugee exodus to India; continued with drought over large stretches of Africa during 1973–76, inflicting famine on some of the countries of the Sahelian zone, and on Ethiopia; included some of the world's worst-ever earthquakes—in Managua (1972) and Guatemala (1976)—as well as other natural disasters, military conflicts, and refugee crises. The toll of human misery from all these disasters created a demand on the international community for relief and rehabilitation operations on a scale never before undertaken.

The ferment of ideas, fuelled by events, reached its climax in the middle of the 1970s. The developing countries, now in a majority within the UN

General Assembly, had begun early in the Decade to call for fundamental change in the international economic order. To offset the effect of industrial man's reckless consumption of resources, they sought adjustments in international aid, trade and financial mechanisms to create a world in which every human being would have enough to live adequately. Their call was reinforced by religious and humanitarian leaders all over the world. In April 1974, a special session of the General Assembly was summoned—mainly at the insistence of the oil-rich Third World nations exerting their new economic and political muscle—and the UN adopted the first of its resolutions calling for a New International Economic Order.

The debates which led up to this resolution had important repercussions in Unicef. The world economic crisis and the world food shortage had serious implications for the health and well-being of the 400 to 500 million children who lived in the countries designated 'most seriously affected'. Harry Labouisse, addressing the Unicef Executive Board within two weeks of the end of the 1974 special session of the General Assembly, spoke in sober terms of a 'quiet emergency that, unfortunately, affects children at all times in many developing countries—a quiet emergency, as distinct from the widely-publicized emergencies associated with natural disasters and disasters related to war. Now these unpublicized, continuous emergencies have reached a new pitch, an amplitude requiring a new level of world co-operation'. In the twenty-five countries designated by the UN as 'least developed', in twenty-five others almost as poor and with very large child populations and in twenty very small countries with special needs, the current emergency circumstances would make it hard for their governments even to maintain existing services for children, let alone expand them.

Unicef Pakistan delegate, Professor Zaki Hasan, representing a developing country, spoke about the plight in which so many poorer developing countries now found themselves. His country was one of those most seriously affected by the current crisis. The cost of importing essential raw materials would multiply by five in the coming year, and Pakistan looked set to spend more than one half her export earnings simply on importing food, fertilizer, medicine and other essentials. 'To say the least', he concluded, 'the outlook is bleak for the children of Pakistan and other seriously affected countries'. He and others supported the Executive Director's suggestion that the Board should make a formal Declaration of an Emergency for Children as a way of calling the attention of the world community to the sufferings of children as a result of the crisis. Experience showed that social services were the first to be cut at such times, and children would be the first victims of deprivation. Unicef could expect urgent requests for vital drugs, medical equipment and transport—the kind of supplies normally associated with disaster relief—simply to help these countries keep on doing what they were already doing.

The food situation was causing particular anguish. The gaunt images of the 1973 famine in Ethiopia, in which at least 100,000 people had died before the local authorities and the international community had roused themselves sufficiently to put in place a full-scale relief operation, were still painfully fresh in many minds. Drought was still affecting other African countries, including those in the Sahelian zone in the western part of the continent, where livestock was perishing, water courses dwindling, the desert consuming arable land, and millions of people being thrown onto the mercy of relief. The effects of the climate were only the most visible cause of the world's food problems.

In the previous two years, a mixture of scarcity and demand had quadrupled the price of cereals. The world's food stocks were dangerously low, and the amount of surplus food available for emergency aid and development assistance was less than half its normal average. The price of oil had carried the price of fertilizer along in its wake, and of this too there was a world shortage. In the hardest hit countries, the cost both of growing food commercially and of buying it was becoming prohibitive. Without fuel for tractors and fertilizer for the fields, the new hybrid seeds could not yield the bumper harvests needed to refill the world's breadbasket and the 'green revolution' would stop in its tracks. Before the recent price rises, according to Unicef's figures, there were some ten million severely malnourished children in the world, and many millions more in a less serious condition. Their numbers seemed likely to increase rapidly over the months and years ahead.

While Unicef could not itself try and tackle directly the global problem of food availability, there were immediate actions to be taken to try to prevent child malnutrition from spreading. One was to encourage governments to set up early warning systems about crop damage, poor rainfall, rising prices in village markets and the general deterioration in children's weight or health. Another was to promote the applied-nutrition approach: school and village gardens, community fish-ponds and poultry projects.

Most of the people in the rural Third World still grew their own food supply, and ways had to be found to help them both to grow more food and to grow food of a more nutritious kind. Certain crops, protein-rich legumes for example, did not feature as extensively in the agriculturalists' calculations as cereals and livestock, because they did not command the profitability and status of grains. Greater efforts were needed to impress upon ministries of agriculture, rural extension workers and home economists that these crops had a special role to play in promoting maternal and child health and nutrition. Villagers also had to be shown how to store food better: rats and rot often consumed one-quarter of the harvest in the family food bin. Ignorance, too, was an important barrier to good nutrition. Some plants and local products were neglected as food for children because mothers did not understand that they had dietary value. The 'child emergency' demanded that Unicef encourage governments to adopt national-nutrition policies which took account of all these elements, and dovetailed with the spread of maternal- and child-health services and family-spacing techniques.

When the UN first took up the call for a New International Economic Order, the industrialized countries had not shown any great enthusiasm for the idea. They were reluctant to embark upon a process of reforming the monetary and trading system that they had invented and they controlled. There was no guarantee at all that any overhaul would actually help the poorest half of mankind. Meanwhile their own already hard-pressed economies—on whose health so many others depended—were likely to suffer. In 1975, yet another special session of the General Assembly—the seventh in UN history—was summoned to go over the ground again. By this time, the views of the key industrialized countries had begun to shift. A sense of deepening crisis about the fate of the least well-off countries, and the fate of the least well-off people within those countries, helped to prompt their change of heart.

They had also begun to see some merit in the thesis of global inter-dependence. The sudden rise in oil prices had underlined the fragility of international economic equations and shown how quickly they could be upset. The richer nations were still dependent on the raw materials of the poorer, particularly on their oil and their minerals. Meanwhile, the trade balance sheets showed that the poorest countries, almost all of which were dependent on agriculture and imported oil, were even more seriously damaged by economic crisis. The international market mechanisms were indeed discriminatory and, unless they could be adjusted, a prospect loomed of trying to mount relief operations for whole countries of people on the brink of disaster.

In September 1975, Henry Kissinger delivered a speech to the seventh UN special session which indicated that the industrialized world was ready to enter into serious negotiations with the developing nations on a restructuring of global institutions. It finally seemed that an alternative order was around the corner, one whose hallmark would be a new respect for the countries of the Third World and a concern for the needs of its poorer inhabitants.

Within Unicef, the 'child emergency' acted as a stimulus for the elaboration of its own alternative order, something more modest but as radical in its way—an alternative order that showed a recognition for what the poorer inhabitants of the Third World could themselves provide towards the effort to set development in motion. Labouisse, speaking to Executive Board delegates in 1974 about the nature of the 'quiet emergency' affecting children in the developing countries, used a term which began to take on great significance during the next few years. He said: 'From whatever angle we view the situation today, one essential conclusion emerges, namely, the need of these countries for vastly-increased assistance to help them maintain, and then enlarge as rapidly as possible the basic services reaching children'. The idea of 'basic services' and how they might be put in place, administered, staffed and paid for was to become the cornerstone of Unicef's strategy for the alternative order for children.

When the leading institutions in international development co-operation began to realize in the late 1960s that economic growth was paying few dividends among the poor, they began to cast around for ways to invest money profitably in the social sector. The area which had immediate appeal was education.

When Unicef had first opened the policy door to providing aid to education in 1961, the African countries had been the principal customers. In 1960, the literacy rate in the continent as a whole was only sixteen per cent. In some countries, less than ten per cent of children attended school. Many of these emerging nations had arrived at independence with no more than a handful of university graduates and a dearth of scientists and technicians of all kinds. The appetite for learning was voracious; a rapid turn-out of well-educated, well-qualified personnel to man all branches of government, industry and the professions was seen as a precondition of national development. Over the decade of the 1960s, education had been one of the largest growth industries in the average developing country. Public expenditure on schools, training institutes and universities had risen from around fifteen per cent to around twenty-five per cent of government budgets. Unicef's own support to education had also grown, particularly in Africa, where by 1965 schooling absorbed nearly half its overall assistance on the continent.

By the early 1970s, however, some of those who had helped to expand schools, training colleges, universities, and all the institutions of the modern educational system in developing countries began to diagnose a 'world educational crisis'. Foremost among them was Philip Coombs, an American economist who had served the Kennedy Administration as an Assistant Secretary of State for Education and was now head of the International Institute for Educational Planning, a division of UNESCO. Within the past generation, there had been a two-fold increase in both the proportion and the numbers of children attending school; this was, as Coombs put it, the bright side. However, he went on: 'The figures are silent about the dark side. They do not reveal the vast social waste and the human tragedy in the high rate of drop-outs and failures. They hide the large number of costly "repeaters". And, most important, they say nothing about the nature, quality and usefulness of the education received'.

In the early 1970s, as the economic crisis descended on the world like an ugly blanket, it was clear that the poorer developing countries could not afford to go on opening up new schools and classrooms and training more teachers at the same rate as they had done over the past two decades. Yet, even to keep the existing proportion of children in school, a high rate of expansion had to be maintained. The population profile of the developing countries was changing; year by year, the edges at the base of the pyramid were creeping wider, meaning that more than forty per cent of the people in many countries were now under fifteen years of age. If the growth rate in educational expenditure could not accommodate these children—and it was already showing signs of slowing down—the authorities could expect much disaffection from parents and students aspiring to the better life for which schooling was a necessary prerequisite.

If the authorities tried to keep pace with demand, the quality of education was bound to suffer; yet its existing quality was nothing to boast about. Not only were classrooms packed, teachers underqualified, textbooks in short supply, but what most of the children were learning was still largely irrelevant to the life most of them were destined to live. The entire educational structure was geared to providing the chosen ten per cent—those who managed to stay in school and fight their way up the educational ladder—with white-collar jobs in city offices. At the end of the line, most Third World adolescents emerged from their brush with academic learning with raised expectations, dashed hopes and disenchantment with rural life. Here was a recipe for profound social trauma.

A country's education system is a mirror image of its social values. The embryo education systems that the ex-colonies inherited from their Imperial masters were a mirror image of their masters' values. Some of their anachronisms were legendary: geography syllabuses which required African children to know the names of towns and rivers in Europe, and almost nothing of their own continent; history lessons where they learnt about the campaigns of the ancient Gauls and Britons, with no mention of the ancient Hause, Nuba, or Masai; home economics lessons where girls learnt how to match wallpapers and bake cakes, instead of learning about the protein content of legumes and eggs and how to protect the weanling against kwashiorkor. The students sat matriculation and examination papers set in Paris and London, and were steeped educationally in the values and mores of other cultures. The ultimate ambition was a scholarship which would allow the student to travel abroad, see and experience 'developed man' in the industrialized world, and join him in disregarding, intentionally or otherwise, the values of his own cultural background.

Whatever the shortcomings of the educational syllabus being taught in many ex-colonies, now that the countries were independent and equal few of their leaders wished to replace it with something more culturally home-grown. Most of those now in charge took for granted the virtues of Western-style education, the type they had themselves received. Few claimed, as Jomo Kenyatta had done in *Facing Mount Kenya*, written in 1938, that traditional rural societies had systems of 'education' more suited to their own environment than anything colonizers and missionaries wanted to put in its place. If the leaders of the new countries wanted to debate on equal terms with their ex-colonizers, they must have the same intellectual weapons and talk the same language—both literally and metaphorically. If they wanted to modernize, they needed modern skills and ideas. How else to impart them to the up and coming generation except by mimicking Western schools and Western syllabuses? They must, and quickly, turn out doctors, accountants, civil servants, lawyers and businessmen who were free of the old, out-worn, traditional values which used to sustain farm and tribe. Scientific understanding must replace superstition; initiative must replace resignation.

For the tiny minority who managed to make it through the most demanding educational forcing tube in history, well-paid jobs, often in the industrialized countries, awaited. But by far the majority of its products were the eighty per cent of primary school leavers who did not qualify for the narrow openings in secondary education, were stranded in the stagnant rural economy of the countryside, and had been equipped not with ideas and methods for transforming its fortunes, but with the mark of failure by the standards of sophisticated urban society. The content of what they had learned had failed them. In failing them, it failed their societies likewise. The cities of the developing world were full of young people with half a school certificate, few prospects of gainful employment, and a sometimes frightening, sometimes pathetic, determination not to pass up their slice of the action.

Back in the villages, many of their brothers and sisters—particularly their sisters—were still out of school. Either they had never been at all, or they had dropped out, often because their parents could not afford to do without their help in minding younger children, tending goats, fetching water and firewood, and other domestic and farming tasks essential to the family's survival. Some skimped and saved desperately—even uniforms, shoes and exercise books represented a major investment—to put a boy or two through school in the hope that he would be one of the lucky ones to make it to a big desk in the city and the kind of money that would save them all from destitution. Others shook their heads over the young layabouts who no longer respected their parents or the old beliefs, and who thought themselves too good to dirty their hands now that they 'knew book', in a phrase from rural Nigeria. In all its dimensions, the 'modern' education system, the boast of so many industrialized countries, was serving the vast majority of people in the Third World extremely badly. The transplantation of the Western educational model to the developing world, like the transfer of high technology, was not 'appropriate'. Alternatives must be found.

The search for alternatives within the formal school system had begun early in the 1960s. The most obvious place to start was with the primary school curriculum, changing its content to make it more attuned to the social, physical and economic environment in which the majority of students were likely to spend their future. The first programme of this kind to which Unicef lent support was in the early 1960s in Upper Volta, whose experimental Farm Schools taught agriculture alongside more conventional academic subjects. In Africa, and to some extent elsewhere, educational experiments of this kind became relatively common. Some were carried out by educational nonconformists who set up their own schools and raised financial support from nongovernmental agencies. Others were administered as part of a government service, sometimes part of youth and social services rather than education, and were carried out in their own separate institutions.

Kenya opened 'village polytechnics'; Thailand offered school drop-outs a second chance in Mobile Training Schools; Upper Volta had a network of Rural Education Centres. In Colombia, thousands of *campesinos* tuned into the radio programmes of Accion Cultural Popular, beamed to remote rural areas where group leaders passed out simple textbooks and led discussions. The aim of these experiments was to impart 'basic education', the knowledge and skills to make a modest, but better, living in a rural setting. In these schemes, and many others, Unicef was a keen supporter. So, increasingly, were other international donors: UNDP, UNESCO, the World Bank, the Ford Foundation, and many local and international voluntary organizations.

The most thorough and philosophically complete version of the same idea was introduced by President Julius Nyerere throughout the Tanzanian primary school system. 'Education for Self-Reliance' was the phrase he used to describe his educational policy, introduced shortly after his declaration of African socialism in 1967 and central to his entire political philosophy. Nyerere, who was a teacher by profession and was known familiarly to all Tanzanians as 'Mwalimu' ('teacher' in Swahili), wanted schools to promote co-operative rather than individual success, and to teach pupils how to transform from within, rather than to despise, the social and economic mores of traditional rural life. The school was a laboratory where new techniques and entrepreneurial activities benefiting the entire community could be pioneered. Every school should establish farming plots, and each class spend some of its school day hoeing and planting, feeding rabbits, building chicken coops and tending goats. Not only would the profits from these projects help offset the costs of the school, but the improved techniques they demonstrated would be passed back from classroom to family *shamba*. The schools would also serve the community by providing day care for toddlers and classes in adult literacy. The keynote was the participation of the villagers, their use of the school and the meshing of their needs with those of their children.

Unicef was an enthusiastic partner in helping to shape the new style primary school education in Tanzania, helping equip prototype 'community schools' and acting as a source of advisory and material assistance; its close co-operation in 'education for self-reliance' with the Tanzanian educational authorities still continues today.

In the early 1970s, the world educational crisis identified by Philip Coombs and others began to inspire a much more radical attack on the content and quality of existing educational systems. Some of the inspiration came from China: although no-one was invited to go and look at it, the cultural revolution showed how a rigid educational and class mould could be broken, and many Western progressives applauded from afar the idea of despatching the university professors off to the commune to do something useful. Another revolutionary creed was propounded by the Brazilian educator, Paulo Freire, who became an exile from his own country and a cult figure elsewhere. Freire described the ignorance of the poor as the result of their economic, social and political oppression, and the current educational system as an instrument for keeping them that way. The process of learning should not submerge them in a 'culture of silence', but instead bring them to reflect on their environment as a first step to changing it. 'There is no such thing as a neutral educational process', he wrote. Learning to read and write must be a means of self-liberation.

Many of Freire's ideas were very difficult; this only added to their popularity. So were those of Ivan Illich, whose *De-schooling Society*, published in 1970, advocated the removal of schools altogether. 'The mere existence of school', he wrote, 'discourages and disables the poor from taking control of their own learning'. The ideas of these two educational thinkers were very influential, not so much in helping elaborate alternative educational systems, but in exposing the human damage of those that existed and in challenging people and organizations who claimed to align themselves with the poor to think very deeply about what they were offering as solutions. Above all, they reinforced the thesis that people, however poor and ignorant, had good reasons for what they did, and that they might be right in rejecting or ignoring some of the solutions being offered. They went further: the active participation of people in any programme designed for their benefit was not only necessary for its success, but also a development strategy in its own right. Freire's idea of 'conscientization' was a new version of the 'psychological shock' proponents of community development in the late 1950s had wanted to use to dispel the apathy and fatalism inherent in uneducated rural attitudes. Community participation not only helped get trenches for water pipes dug and new village classrooms built, but the acts of digging and building and their results brought villagers to the realization that they were capable by their own efforts of transforming their destiny.

The impact of these ideas was by no means confined to the field of education *per se*; but education in its broadest sense was where the impact started. The world educational crisis meant that millions of children, particularly girl children and therefore the mothers of the next generation, were growing up without the knowledge and openness to new ideas normally inculcated in the classroom. This was a problem of direct concern to Unicef.

In 1971, Unicef commissioned Philip Coombs and his team from the International Council for Educational Development (ICED) to carry out a major research study into what more might be done, outside the formal school system, to help prevent the social and economic waste represented by the millions of half-lettered and unlettered children and adolescents who had either dropped out of school or had never managed to get there in the first place. The ICED was simultaneously undertaking a related study for the World Bank. The Bank was interested in increasing its investment in education, particularly in the kind of education which would promote its new goal: an attack on rural poverty. Unicef also asked the ICED to focus on the underprivileged, underserved rural areas; but its concern was with the plight of the educationally-dispossessed child, not on changing the rural economy.

Inevitably, these two major studies, both led by Coombs, had much in common. They, in turn, drew upon another contemporary study: that carried out by an International UNESCO Commission on the Development of Education, whose landmark report, 'Learning to Be', was published in 1972. The scope of the Unicef study was as broad as any similar exercise Unicef had ever commissioned; it included special case studies in a score of countries and looked at scores of others; it tackled shortcomings in the formal school system as an adjunct to its mainstream; it brought into its mainstream subjects—family diet, child-raising—normally regarded as adjuncts to education; it took more than two years to complete. The two reports it engendered, in 1973 and 1974, brought a new concept into Unicef's regular vocabulary: 'non-formal education'.

Non-formal education was not a new term. It had become increasingly used to distinguish other types of educational activities from those carried out in the formal academic hierarchy of school and college—a type already supported by Unicef. But this was the first effort to carry out a systematic analysis of what non-formal education was and what it should be, and what was being done in its name in programmes all over the world.

The first report took as its starting point the growing recognition that education was a lifelong process of learning, in which what people learned as children at their parents' knee, and what adolescents learned as they tried to find their way in the adult world, was as significant as the prescribed chunk of their lives they spent in the classroom. Learning did not begin and end with the clang of the school bell; nor need education. It could happen in the day-care centre, the marketplace, the village co-operative, the mosque, the church, the age-set group, the boy scouts, the girl guides, the women's club, the football team, the maternity ward, the under-fives clinic.

The report listed what it called a 'minimum package' of attitudes, skills and knowledge that every young person needed for a satisfying adulthood. The package included positive attitudes, including towards learning itself; basic literacy and numeracy; a scientific understanding about the person's own environment; and functional knowledge about raising a family, running a household, earning a living and taking part in civic life. The thesis was that non-formal education would supplement what everyone in any society picks up informally simply by living; that in the case of the unschooled rural child or adolescent, what they picked up in this way needed a supplement because without it they could not even aspire to change the misery of their circumstances, or know how to set about improving the quality of their own, and eventually their children's, lives.

Among the clients for non-formal education were the child of preschool age, whose physical growth, intellectual curiosity and emotional well-being would determine whether at a later stage he or she could make any use of classroom teaching. But by far the most important category were the adolescents and adults who had dropped out of school or never reached the classroom door. Among these the great majority were girls and women. In many rural areas, where modern education and modern aspirations were the exclusive preserve of boys, well over ninety per cent of girls reached maturity without knowing how to read a label on a bottle of medicine, write her child's name on his health card, count the number of eggs the hens had laid, or measure the distance between the rows of ground nuts in the plot she farmed.

This 'unfinished business' of the schools meant that other programmes for social improvement which depended on women to absorb their messages and put them into effect—health programmes which counselled the dangers of drinking dirty water, nutrition programmes which extolled the virtues of lentil soup and eggs, family planning programmes which explained the value of spacing births—would fall on unreceptive ears. Where there was no knowledge, there was no will for change, only an unquestioning dependence on beliefs and behaviour patterns handed down through generations of mothers and grandmothers with scarcely perceptible adaptations to the seamless continuity of rural life.

Women not only raised the children, but in many countries, particularly in Africa, were also responsible for providing the family's food, fuel, water supply and most items connected to children's welfare. A woman's interest in learning could be aroused by teaching her something that might help her fulfill more easily her regular functions. Whatever form her demand took, its satisfaction would start a process whereby she could begin to enjoy the ability to take in and use new ideas. This would bring her and others like her closer to the mainstream of society, opening a new chapter in their attitudes to health, welfare and the quality of family life.

The two complementary ICED reports on non-formal education were presented successively to the Unicef Executive Boards of 1973 and 1974. The first was hugely popular, and was printed and widely circulated to university departments and learning institutes all over the world. It represented a seminal contribution to ideas about the role of education in development, both in its formal school setting, and in its many non-formal settings elsewhere. The enthusiasm it engendered carried the authors rather further in the second than many were prepared to follow.

At the 1974 Board session, Coombs and his principal assistant, Manzoor Ahmed, from Bangladesh, raised more than a little dust. In spite of the fact that they stated the need for formal and non-formal educational systems to march hand-in-hand towards the objective of rural transformation, the 1974 report appeared to many of the Board delegates to go too far in its criticism of the schools, and to describe so optimistically the potential of non-formal education that its authors unintentionally conveyed the impression that they regarded it as a panacea.

UNESCO was decidedly frosty. 'Learning to Be', the 1972 report of its own Commission, had fully accepted the schools' shortcomings, particularly the rigidity and outdatedness of their curriculae, which prevented young people from learning the things 'that best suited their aptitudes'. But this did not mean that the whole formal education system was obsolete. Coombs and Ahmed were congratulated for providing 'a systematic conceptual framework for many *ad hoc* and unco-ordinated learning activities'. But UNESCO believed that they had somewhat overstated the case on behalf of non-formal education. However useful radio programmes, film-strips for youth clubs, after-school literacy classes for women and all sorts of other activities could be in filling in educational gaps and compensating adults who never had a chance to go to school, they were nonetheless a poor cousin to mainstream education. In the end, there could be no substitute for reforming the schools and pressing on with the expansion of the formal educational structure.

Whatever the shortcomings of schooling and its over-emphasis on paper qualifications which were no automatic passport to the good life, the reality was that not only did educational authorities rate conventional schooling more highly than any non-formal version, but the people of the developing world were voting for it with their feet. The parents who wanted education for their children wanted them to go to school, and they did not want them to spend their time there hoeing ground nuts and minding chickens which they could have done more usefully if they had stayed at home.

Students felt the same way. In the Serowe Brigades of Botswana, students bitterly protested a work schedule of carpentry and construction which left them too little time to prepare for their examinations. Those who took advantage of non-formal courses of instruction in Kenya's Village Polytechnics wanted a certificate upon completion; and when they got one, they set off for the city to look for a job as an auto mechanic or a factory worker.

International experts might argue that educational budgets were overstrained, and that the choice for many children who would otherwise have gone on to secondary school was not between formal and non-formal, but between non-formal and nothing at all. But in the villages and shanty towns, people who thought they knew second best when they saw it were not convinced. While city jobs paid more than the hard slog of casual labour in town or countryside, non-formal education was at best a limited tool for rural transformation.

Within a few years, the sting went out of the debate about non-formal education. In the meantime, the work of Coombs and his team, both for Unicef and for the World Bank and others, had put in place a conceptual framework for support to education outside the school system. Their wide circulation within the education community helped to create a favourable climate for non-formal education. During the next few years, youth clubs, radio programmes, women's groups, credit unions, community newspapers and co-operative societies enjoyed new prestige and financial support from Unicef and others.

By the time that Unicef next examined its role in basic education, in 1977, schooling and non-formal learning were moving closer together. Except in oil-rich developing countries, public expenditures on expanding networks of schools and colleges had levelled off. Coombs's original diagnosis—that rising numbers and increased costs would end by swamping the schools—proved to be correct. By this stage, more education ministries had accepted the need to use every kind of alternative to the conventional classroom, standard syllabus and examination routine in the effort to give their uneducated and untrained young adult population some kind of future hope and prospects. The classrooms of the rural Third World had not been abandoned. On the contrary: many had been co-opted into a wider developmental role. No longer did the land of primers and exercise books, blackboards and chalk, only belong to children at a certain age and stage. Nyerere had led where others followed. They were beginning to belong to everyone.

The ferment of ideas about formal and non-formal education was essentially a re-examination of what the up-and-coming generation needed in the way of knowledge, skills and learning, in order to join fully in the process of development, both for their own and their societies' sakes. It was, therefore, part of the reconsideration of the nature of development itself. Within Unicef, the quiet emergency which Labouisse described as confronting the children of the developing world prompted a series of reappraisals, of which education turned out only to be the first, and the one which helped prompt discussion about where and how all kinds of learning—including that about health, nutrition, hygiene and child care—took place.

In 1975, the year after the second report on non-formal education was presented to the Executive Board, Labouisse presented the results of two other important studies. One had been carried out by WHO with Unicef's participation; it outlined 'Alternative methods of meeting basic health needs'. The other had been carried out at Unicef's request by Dr Jean Mayer of the Harvard School of Public Health, and its subject was the priorities for child nutrition in developing countries.

As each of these successive studies helped to fill in the picture of the children's situation, and as so many of their findings converged, Unicef's version of the alternative order began to emerge. The neat dividing lines between what constituted educational services, health services, water supply and sanitation services, nutrition services, or social welfare services, were becoming increasingly blurred. All programmes designed to expand or improve such services had to be mutually reinforcing; their inputs, whether aimed primarily at social or economic advance, should be integrated.

This theme had first been sounded during the late 1950s when the community development approach was becoming popular. In due course, it had been reflected in Unicef by the concept of integrated services for the 'whole' child. This policy shift of the early 1960s had encouraged Unicef's growing network of country representatives and programme officers to seek out ways in which all the needs of the child could be served by programmes whose own components were interconnected. In the mid-1960s, it had seemed essential to go for commitment at the national level: involvement of the planning ministry, recognition in the Five-Year Plan. In many countries, it had taken time to convince officialdom of the need to plan for children as part of mainstream social and economic development, of the virtues of interministerial committees, and of the 'country' programme which brought all the elements of the picture together and addressed them together.

Even where governments had taken these initiatives for themselves, or been gradually persuaded into doing so, there were many cases where what was discussed and agreed at national level was scarcely reflected by what took place on the ground. Sometimes the plans still looked immaculate at regional, provincial or district level; but there some essential thread snapped. Personnel were overstretched; transport or fuel for going out into the countryside unavailable; trainers and teachers unenthusiastic; equipment ill-used or inappropriate. In one place a water supply had performed a miracle, but no health care could be had for miles in any direction; in another, the health centre functioned admirably, but the village children did not have enough to eat; in another, the women's club had a beautiful vegetable garden, but it was bound to wither in the dry season because they had no water.

The integration of services did not appear automatically to trickle down the administrative hierarchy, any more than did economic growth. The directors of agriculture and health might meet for an occasional co-ordinating session at district or provincial headquarters. But meanwhile, out in the villages, a rural extension worker and a nutrition advisor doing their rounds might travel the same beat in the same neighbourhood and never meet to discuss how their admonitions to their 'clients' clashed or complemented each other. The way services—health, nutrition, water, education—were structured was inhibiting their effectiveness. It was also somewhat bewildering, and sometimes time- and energy-wasting, to those the services were meant to serve. Villagers untaught in the ways of the modern world did not think of dividing their problems—lack of financial resources, low agricultural prices, a poor food crop, too many mouths to feed, a dried-up water source, lack of a community road—into compartments and bringing the relevant compartments to the relevant authorities. Until the first knot between the villagers and the appropriate authorities had been firmly tied, the services provided reached people, if they reached them at all, with an impact refracted through misperceptions, mis-apprehensions and misfits. Yet as far as Unicef was concerned, the child emergency demanded that the services reach mothers and children more quickly, with a greater impact, at a time when economic crisis had placed government budgets for social expenditure under heavy pressure.

To reach the villagers and tie the knot required a strategy for 'basic services'—not health, nutrition or education services—which covered and contained all these and others—water supply, sanitation, food conservation, family planning, support to women's activities—in an integrated package. Instead of putting the chief emphasis on improving the co-ordination between administration departments at levels above the village, the essence of the new perspective was to make the services dovetail more closely with the villagers' own uncompartmentalized view of their lives.

One lesson that the experiences of the 1950s and 1960s had brought home to all those trying to alleviate poverty in the Third World was that people's attitudes towards programmes, which governed the degree of their involvement, were fundamental to those programmes' success. People's energy, which in the earlier days of community development had been seen as something to be harnessed to a programme to help it along, now appeared to be the critical force which could make or break it. Something more than 'harnessing' was needed; something more subtle and complex, in which the villagers' views and ideas—their minds as well as their labour—were enlisted.

Where once the catchphrase had been 'community development', now it had become 'community participation'. During the previous few years, the various studies and reappraisals undertaken not only by Unicef but also by organizations, research institutes, and government and university departments throughout the Third World and within the international-development community had forced those involved to consider more carefully how the anonymous mass of the millions of people who lived in poverty actually went about their lives and why they made the choices they made. Until answers could be provided to such questions, within each country, region, province, district and community, it was impossible to solve the problem of how to reach directly into their lives and help them improve them. It was possible to arrive at a model of their basic needs at the round table conference, in the government planning department, at the research institute seminar. But without a picture of their 'felt needs', it was impossible to identify where the two might coincide, and what agent or agents could make the liaison.

During the early 1970s, considerable attention began to focus on certain micro-projects and mini-programmes which had shown success, often within a limited radius and sometimes under exceptional circumstances, at raising the quality of life for the poorest members of society. Many had grown out of spontaneous organization in villages or shanty towns, and were often led by charismatic individuals who had sought financial help from church and voluntary agencies. These groups had a direct contact with their constituency, and their relative freedom from rigid bureaucratic structures had allowed them to pioneer and experiment. Verghese Kurien's programme at Anand in Gujerat, whose village dairying co-operatives had provided a springboard for a national co-operative dairy movement and a range of improvements across the whole spectrum of rural life, was one such example. Plenty of others existed elsewhere in the developing world.

Many of these projects had begun in response to a crisis, or a sorely felt need of some kind. But whatever impulse had set them in motion, they usually moved rapidly into other activities. Almost by fluke, rather than design, they had taken on the character of the multi-purpose, integrated programmes now being held up as the development model. A community-health programme in the highlands of Guatemala stated as its top priority social and economic justice; land reform was next, malnutrition came fifth, and curative medicine was last on the list. A slum-housing programme in India did not stop at sympathetic architectural and urban planning, cement and construction materials for poor householders, water points and latrines; it worked just as hard to provide small loans for rickshaw drivers and *dhobis* (washermen and women), and set up health-care services for the under-fives. Nutrition recovery centres for children suffering from drought in the Sahel set people along a path which led to well-digging, village pharmacies, and road-building. It did not take the experts long to observe that the success of these ventures derived from their popularity with the communities concerned, who mobilized their own efforts behind them.

In some countries, the same ideas had already been adopted as part of government policy. Tanzania's 'education for self-reliance' was one element of 'ujamaa' (fellowship), Nyerere's doctrine of African socialism built upon traditional ideas of mutual self-help and community co-operation, and called upon people to build the nation from below. In Indonesia, General Suharto declared that the centrepiece of his new order was the traditional system of mutual help—*gotong-royong*—and extended budgetary aid directly to village development councils. In the Peruvian province of Puno, the Indians' traditional pattern of community ownership had been revived, and part of the revenues from silver mines and cottage industries used to pay for children's services run by the people.

The mobilization of the people which characterized these examples and many others came to something considerably more than organizing work parties to dig trenches across the hillside or putting school pupils to work in the fields. In these programmes, the people in the communities not only helped set the goals, but also took part in their planning and execution. Their views, opinions, and existing knowledge, as well as their labour, were reflected in what services the programme managers set out to provide, and how they were run. The people enlisted not merely as spectators or passive recipients of services designed to help them, but as operators and participants.

In many cases they did so through one of their own representatives. Certain community members had been selected for some training, and were now playing a leading part at the community level, answerable to the community for what they did, but under the technical supervision of those who were professionally employed to run the project or the service. In different places, these workers went under different names: health promoters, motivators, animateurs, monitrices, first-aiders, village-based workers. Whatever they were called, and whatever their specific function, they represented a whole new class of development personnel. They lived and worked in the community, undertook their tasks on a voluntary or semi-voluntary basis, received only a short period of training, and were seen as the front-line workers in the programmes which counted on their services. Not only did their use cut personnel costs to a minimum, but it filled the vital and elusive gap, culturally and administratively, between a programme and those it was meant to assist.

Independently of the growing recognition of the potential of community participation as part of a strategy for the attack on poverty, Unicef's own programme experiences in the Third World had offered many practical lessons along the same lines. Long ago, in Leo Eloesser's health-care programme in northern China, in Dr Kodijat's yaws campaign in Indonesia, in Mexico's effort to eradicate malaria, lay people had been recruited and given a little training to carry out simple tasks. Other examples of the importance of community organization were even closer to hand: the many rural water-supply schemes, especially those using villagers as hand-pump caretakers in Tamil Nadu and elsewhere; the Gujerat dairy co-operatives; the grass-roots women's group movement in Kenya; *animation rurale* in Senegal; *educacion inicial* in Puno; Mobile Training Centres in Thailand; *gotong-royong* in Indonesia; community schools in Tanzania.

The 'strategy for basic services'—the strategy whose promotion was to dominate Unicef's policy during the second half of the 1970s in the way that planning for the needs of children had dominated during the 1960s—was an important landmark in the evolution not only of Unicef's own philosophy, but also was a major contribution to the ideas about meeting human needs and establishing a new international economic order which had been circulating since the beginning of the second Development Decade. An approach which could be adapted to local social and economic circumstances; which had built into it a means of tapping the views, the resources and the latent energies of the individual community; and which attached to the existing health, education or rural extension services an outer, labour-intensive layer of personnel who acted as the conduit for ideas and material assistance under the technical supervision of the professionals . . . this approach had a great deal to recommend it. It did have to overcome suspicions that basic services were amateur and second-best; and it also had to overcome professional resistance to the idea that laymen and women with only a short period of training were quite adequately equipped to carry out simple technical tasks, give out pills and lotions, discuss the virtues of improved seeds and fertilizers, and the effect on health of drinking tube-well water from a pump instead of open water from a pond.

Elaborating the basic services approach to the Unicef Executive Board in 1975, Harry Labouisse told the delegates that he believed that it was possible, at the cost of only a few dollars a head per year, to provide a package of basic services which would meet the needs of every child in the world. He suggested that an increased level of development assistance, perhaps in the order of $2–3 billion annually, not an exorbitant sum, would be needed to implement the strategy on a global scale through all available channels. The strength of the approach lay in its modesty and efficacy: no cumbersome and expensive new machinery or institutions were needed; simply the extension of what existed already, using local individuals as their antennae to reach into the communities and encourage their active participation.

Labouisse saw in the approach a source of great optimism at a time when the negative images of hunger and famine were inculcating a sense of despair among government donors and the general public towards the attack on world poverty. 'It is my conviction', he said, 'that, if they really try, the poor and affluent countries working together are perfectly capable of meeting the children's basic requirements in a not-too-distant future. We know enough about what needs to be done and how it should be done. With adequate help from the world community, the most essential needs of the world's children could begin to be met in practical, justified ways at capital costs the world, as a whole, can afford, and at recurring costs which the countries and communities directly concerned could, in time, reasonably bear'. There was an essential proviso: the collective will needed to do the job.

Here was Unicef's own response to the global search for alternatives.

Main sources

The Poverty Curtain by Mahbub ul Haq, published by Columbia University Press, New York, 1976.

Rich World, Poor World by Geoffrey Lean, published by George Allen & Unwin, London, 1978.

One Hundred Countries, Two Billion People by Robert S. McNamara, published by Praeger, New York, 1973.

Report of the World Bank and IDA, Washington, 1973.

Helping Ourselves: Local Solutions to Global Problems by Bruce Stokes, published by the Worldwatch Institute/W. W. Norton, New York and London, 1981.

Partners in Development: Report of the Commission on International Development, Chairman: Lester B. Pearson, Praeger, New York, 1969.

Unicef Executive Board documentation; general progress reports of the Executive Director; summary records; reports of the Board; statements to the Board by Henry Labouisse and others; special reports and studies: 'Non-formal Education for Rural Development' by Philip Coombs and Manzoor Ahmed (also issued as 'New Paths to Learning', ICED, October 1973); 'Building New Educational Strategies to Service Rural Children and Youth', March 1974; 'Basic Services for Children in Developing Countries', March 1976.

The World Educational Crisis. A Systems Analysis by Philip H. Coombs, Oxford University Press, 1968; *The World Crisis in Education: The View from the Eighties* by Philip H. Coombs; Oxford University Press, 1985.

Articles in *Unicef News* (on the child emergency); articles in *Assignment Children* (on community participation and non-formal education).

Interviews undertaken for the Unicef History Project; monograph on Unicef and Education by H. M. Phillips, September 1985.

Chapter 14

Health for Some or Health for All?

The strategy for basic services, whose broad outline the 1975 UN General Assembly asked Unicef to fill in more precisely, received a full elaboration for the Executive Board session of March 1976. From philosophical, practical and programmatic perspectives, Unicef drew together the available information on how different attempts had been made in different locations and under different political circumstances to use some version of the basic services approach to transform the lives of the poor. The number of those living in conditions of absolute poverty was now 900 million, according to the World Bank, of whom 700 million were in the rural areas and 200 million in the urban slums. The dimensions of need, and the widening gap between the fortunes of the haves and the have-nots made ever more urgent the search for ways of reaching into their lives with some definite means of improvement.

Of all the services which could do most for children, and were most sought after by families and parents, the most important was a service that provided health. It was the clause 'for child health purposes generally' in its founding resolution that had allowed Unicef to transfer its attention from postwar emergency relief in Europe to development co-operation in the least well-off countries of Asia, Latin America and Africa. Whatever the determination since the early 1960s not to omit from the scope of its assistance the full range of the child's needs, the child's state of health and nutritional well-being remained, and always would remain, Unicef's quintessential concern. Although basic services envisaged a package of interlocking ingredients including water supply and sanitation, child nutrition, activities to improve the situation of women and girls, village technology and ways of filling the learning 'gap', the essential stimulus was above all the need to improve health services, particularly maternal and child-health services.

In many ways, the strategy for basic services was a direct extension in other areas of 'alternative approaches to health care', an analysis and a set of recommendations prepared under joint WHO and Unicef auspices during 1973 and 1974. The standard system of health-care delivery, which in most developing countries was essentially a facsimile of the Western model adapted for the specific health hazards of a tropical environment, had not escaped the challenges confronting the entire apparatus of international co-operation for development during the late 1960s and early 1970s.

Just as rising costs and expanding populations were putting under great strain the capacities of developing-country governments to meet their citizens' aspirations for educational qualifications, so were they in danger of falling further and further behind in meeting their needs for health care. In a meeting of the WHO/Unicef Joint Committee on Health Policy in Geneva in 1972, yet another disheartening review of the slow rate at which health care was reaching people led to a decision that WHO should examine existing experiences with alternative models of health services and try to come up with a more flexible formula. The realization was growing that, alongside the world economic crisis, the world food crisis, the environmental crisis, the population crisis and the educational crisis, there was also—for many of the same reasons—a world health-care crisis.

During the 1960s, many public-health professionals in the Third World, some of them members of the international health community working either for WHO or Unicef, began to have serious doubts about what was happening in the name of health care in many countries. Like the educationalists contemplating the content of their curricula and examination syllabuses, the public-health specialists began to feel a sense of acute discomfort about how badly suited to the social and economic context of most Third World communities was the type of service they were delivering. At a time when heart transplants and other breakthroughs in medical technology were stunning the world and opening up visions of conquering the most technically complex medical problems, millions of people—more than three-quarters of the people in many countries—were outside the reach of any modern health care at all. The kinds of sickness that they, or more usually their children, were suffering and dying from— diarrhoeas, fevers, measles, whooping cough, tuberculosis and influenza— no longer constituted any serious threat to their counterparts in the Western world and were viewed there in the most pedestrian terms. Yet mothers in many parts of Africa, Asia and Latin America frequently lost one or more of their children to a number of quite easily preventable or curable maladies, whose hazards were greatly increased by an unclean water supply, lack of proper sanitation, poor nutrition, or a combination of all of these.

Since the early 1950s, when Unicef first began in earnest to help developing countries expand their maternal and child-health services by equipping maternity wards and MCH centres and training midwives and paediatrics personnel, many countries had nearly doubled the numbers of their networks of health centres and subcentres. This was an impressive achievement; but in overall terms it had done no more than make a slightly larger dent in what remained a vast problem of potential or actual ill-health. The expansion of services had still scarcely reached mothers in the remote countryside; for them things had changed little since the heyday of the disease-control campaigns. Their encounters with medical services were still mostly confined to the rare occasions when they were told to bring their children to the chief's compound for a vaccination, or malaria-sprayers came by and drenched their homes with DDT.

Most of the fruits of government expenditures on building up the national health-care network were to be seen in the cities, where hospitals named after princesses and presidents built in the architectural image of the medical Hiltons of the industrialized world required the equivalent of a whole district preventive health budget just to keep their operating theatre lights, their laboratory equipment, their boilers and their X-ray machines in running order. Anomalies abounded: in one country which constitutionally declared health a fundamental human right, eighty per cent of one province's health budget went on one teaching hospital, while in outlying areas, there was only one general purpose dispensary to serve half-a-million people.

If the hide-bound educational system of schoolroom and paper qualifications unsuited to the realities of rural life was in a state of crisis, so was the health-care system it helped to bolster. Graduates of medical colleges identical in syllabus and surgical technology to their *alma maters* in the West did not want to live deep in the bush and practise their skills in hospitals with no fancy equipment and often not even a regular supply of electricity to provide hot water or power a refrigerator.

The caseload of coughs, colds and gastro-enteritis, and the lines of mothers with squalling children, might pack the hospital verandah from dawn to dusk. But the doctor had not received a fellowship to a famous university teaching hospital to give out syrups and instruct mothers to feed their children body-building eggs that they could not afford. Those who tried often found themselves overcome by mounting helplessness. As they dispensed pills and food supplements to mothers with scrawny infants, they knew that they would come back as long as their babies were still alive.

Long-lasting cure was very difficult to effect in a place where poverty and ignorance were the underlying diseases. The doctors' only weapon was disease prevention and health education for the mothers; but even for these they were ill-equipped. A course in advanced paediatrics does not help a doctor to convince a woman in an advanced stage of pregnancy that she should not give birth in a draughty and unhygienic hut; nor persuade the expectant mother with a year-old child that if she does not make up a special nutritious food mix for the first-born when the second arrives and then deprives him of the breast, he will soon show symptoms of kwashiorkor.

By the mid-1960s, some of the doctors who had studied tropical medicine in prestigious institutes from London to Calcutta and gone to, or returned to, the developing world to practise began to lift their eyes from the petri dish and ask themselves what they should do to make existing health-care policies more appropriate to the real health needs of the people. Derrick Jelliffe, Professor of Child Health in the Unicef-endowed chair at Makerere University Medical School in Uganda, convened a conference in 1964 with the assistance of WHO and Unicef to discuss with like-minded colleagues the many shortcomings of the health-care systems in which they performed. The title of the conference was 'Hospitals and Health Centres in Africa', and it covered everything that went on inside both types of institutions and what they supervised outside their own perimeter. Many of the participants were to become important figures in the subsequent revolution in attitudes towards the delivery of health care in developing countries: Jelliffe himself; David Morley of the London School of Hygiene and Tropical Medicine; Maurice King, a lecturer in microbiology at Makerere. King spent much of the next two years editing the papers presented at the conference into what he described as a 'Primer on the Medicine of Poverty'.

One of Makerere's recent medical graduates described to the conference the conditions he confronted in a district hospital: 'I would say that my problems were mainly these: overwork, lack of equipment, lack of staff, shortage of drugs, the absence of anyone to consult with, shortage of beds and the lack of diagnostic facilities. I had to look after the medical, surgical, maternity and children's wards. I used to see the outpatients; I had one major operating day each week; I had to collect blood for transfusions, do many police post-mortems and often attend court. In other words, I was needed in several places at the same time, and this used to make life a little bit difficult.

'We did not have any Balkan beams but I asked a carpenter to make one; he made two, but we did not have any pulleys so I asked the orthopaedic surgeon at the national hospital for some, but he could not spare any. I could not obtain any scalp vein needles, nor enough of the big ones for taking blood. There was a pressure lamp in the theatre which attracted flying arthropods; these frequently hit the lamp and fell into the operation wound . . . There was one laboratory assistant, but he could not do a blood urea, a blood sugar, test for urobilinogen in the urine, or count reticulocytes. He was also very busy and could not cope with all the stools I wanted him to look at . . . We were very short of beds; there were lots of floor cases, and often two children in the same cot. The premature babies had to be nursed in the general ward . . . There was no fence around the compound and visitors came in at any time.'

This description of conditions of work in the less well-appointed health institutions of the Third World was familiar to thousands of doctors who had served in similar or worse, and hardly raised an eyebrow in the ambience of the Makerere conference. King quoted it in his 'Primer on the Medicine of Poverty' because it helped to explain to those who did not know and could not picture trying to run a health service under such circumstances why it was almost impossible to make the existing health-care system function effectively, and why no competent medical practitioner would choose to serve in such a hospital unless he or she was a dedicated and highly-motivated individual.

King's 'Primer', which remained for some years a seminal work, argued that lack of financial resources and personnel not only presented a formidable challenge to medical care in developing countries, but gave it a distinctive quality. A doctor with 100,000 potential patients, not 3000 as was usual in an industrialized country, simply could not approach his tasks in the same way. Equally, if the money available for drugs, syringes, instruments, theatre equipment, blood transfusion, hospital furniture and laboratory supplies was one-fortieth of that available elsewhere, it could not be well spent if spent in the same manner.

Whatever medical resources existed must be applied to benefit the entire community. Tropical medicine, the branch of medical science developed by the old Imperial powers to deal with the specific health problems of their colonies, equipped its practitioners to diagnose and treat diseases unknown in cooler climates: yellow fever, trypanosomiasis (sleeping sickness), onchocerciasis (river blindness), schistosomiasis (bilharzia); as well as malaria, cholera, tuberculosis and smallpox, which had now retreated from the wealthier countries. But the vast majority of the case-load was more directly caused by poverty than by anything to do with the climate. The medical care dispensed by doctors, hospitals and health administrators must conform with prevailing social and economic reality. At the moment, it did not; but rising demand for cures, injections, pills and all the accoutrements of modern medicine together with population increase meant that staff and services were hopelessly overburdened. The results were inefficiency, poor quality and demoralization. King argued for a rethink and redesign from first principles of everything the members of his profession were doing in developing countries in the name of health— from training curriculae through medical technology and hospital archi-tecture to treatment of the under-fives.

What was needed was a systematic plan for the deployment of medical resources, not a motley collection of hospitals, mobile outreach, MCH centres and disease campaigns, some of which tripped over each other and many of which left large populations untouched by one or any of their ministrations. In 1965, WHO came up with a design for what it described as 'basic health services': a minimum standard of medical care, incorporating disease prevention alongside curative services, and working in the closest of partnerships with MCH.

Cleaning up village paths, weighing and immunizing babies—activities which were critical to the 'medicine of poverty' but whose health-promoting qualities were not so well understood by uneducated villagers—would piggyback on the popularity of cures, first aid and midwifery. The diagrammatic model of the basic health service looked like a planetary system, with the hospitals at the centre, a group of health centres dependent on them—and their satellites, rural health units and health posts, dependent on the health centres. Manned by a small team of professional health workers, the peripheral unit would directly serve the population around it—at its weekly under-fives and antenatal clinics, in its handful of beds for expectant mothers and others who needed nursing care—by instructing all its customers in hygiene, nutrition and preventive health, and by visiting their homes.

This planetary system offered a coherent plan for gradually extending medical facilities to reach everyone in due course with at least a basic health service in their own vicinity. The responsibility for simple curative work, MCH and health education in villages and schools was to be vested in the satellites. Cases of serious illness or major accident could be referred up the line from the village to the health centre and, if necessary, further up the line to the operating theatre in the hospital. Each link in the chain had its own functions, with the central administering hospital assuming responsibility for curative work outside the competence of the intermediary or peripheral units, and for co-ordinating and supervising the whole health infrastructure, including laboratory work and training programmes. The adoption of this health service model, at least as the target to be aimed for, was an important step in the direction of the ideas which, a few years later, were to crystallize into an alternative health-care approach.

In 1967, after the WHO/Unicef Joint Committee on Health Policy had given its seal of approval to 'basic health services', it examined a review of MCH, now regarded as the core of overall community health. Although there were encouraging signs that progress had been made in obtaining general agreement to underlying principles, progress in putting them into effect was much more patchy. There were examples to prove that the comprehensive MCH approach could achieve all that was claimed for it: in the Penonome district in Panama, infant mortality had dropped by a quarter in three years without any extra infusion of manpower, merely by its redeployment.

But such successes had to be seen as tiny islands in an ocean of want. In many places it was not even possible to measure the impact of whatever MCH service existed: no data on births or deaths existed; no systematic health records of any kind offered a picture of mother and child population, mortality, pattern of sickness, nutritional status, treatment success rate. Without basic data, the planning of the health service, including how best to deploy resources, was bound to be an erratic procedure. At many health centres and hospitals, the lines of mothers waiting on the verandah still overwhelmed doctors and nurses to the point where improvisation was the only rule. Without more personnel, preventive work remained a dream. Whatever its importance, it could not be carried out instead of diagnostic and curative work. Mothers came to the health centres when their children were ill, not when they thought they might be ill sometime in the future. They could not be sent packing with admonitions about washing their hands and cleaning their compounds or they would not come again.

The MCH review was discussed both by the Joint Committee and by the Unicef Executive Board. They applauded the way in which the comprehensive approach was gaining impetus. But they also deplored the standard of practice in many MCH programmes: syringes unsterilized; syrups dispensed for no clear medical reason; vaccines poorly stored and impotent; wards unswept; blankets unwashed; drugs inventories and immunization records unkept; health education non-existent. The further away from the central hospital, the fewer, less well-equipped, and less well-trained or supervised the MCH staff, the worse the picture became. Stoic and dedicated individuals wrought miracles in impossible circumstances; but in too many places, will and discipline evaporated. The other depressing realization was that, in spite of all the valuable efforts of the past years, far too few mothers and children were receiving any MCH care at all. At the present pace of setting up basic health services, generations would pass before everyone was reached.

A leap of imagination was needed. It was not tolerable to wait for generations before a baby who, by accident of birth, arrived into a world of poverty and could be saved from neonatal tetanus for the want of a clean knife and a vaccination; or that a weanling should die of diarrhoea because the parent thought that the loss of fluid from one end would be prevented if you denied it to the other; or that pills and injections costing only a few dollars should be denied a suffering child who could so easily be cured. That leap of imagination had already been taken by some medical pioneers in certain countries. It was to their example that WHO and Unicef now turned.

In spite of the hardships and the problems of providing medical care in parts of the world where the white-coated variety of the profession was a rarity, there were, as there have always been, certain dedicated individuals, some of them working in their own countries, others working as missionaries or in the tradition of Christian or voluntary service overseas, who chose to practise their calling where needs were greatest and facilities most lacking.

Such men and women took in their stride, or managed somehow to accommodate, the 'overwork, lack of equipment, lack of staff, shortage of drugs, the absence of anyone to consult with, shortage of beds and the lack of diagnostic facilities' that made medical practice in such places 'a little bit difficult'. They were mostly people of considerable independence of spirit, and often chose, if they could, to work outside the mainstream of their country's formal health-care establishment. By definition, therefore, the contact between the intergovernmental organizations with such projects was mostly informal. The individuals involved often sought out the appropriate personnel of WHO and Unicef for advice and support of whatever kind was applicable; sometimes the organizations sought them out. Many later joined the staff of one or other, or became their consultants. But at least in the early stages of their ground-breaking endeavours, their regular sources of material and technical assistance were nongovernmental. They were often provided by the more progressive overseas voluntary agencies— fund-raising organizations such as Oxfam and others—which worked mainly in co-operation with Christian-related counterpart groups in the developing countries.

For some decades, in their own quiet way, some of these pioneers had employed the same rationale as the Chinese had applied when they invented the cadre of personnel known as the 'barefoot doctors': if there were not enough doctors and nurses, not enough resources to provide even a modified version of the conventional health system, then they would have to start from other precepts and enlist people who were neither doctors nor nurses in a radically different health-care delivery system.

The majority of actions needed for the prevention and treatment of the most common types of illness were relatively straightforward. They were the kind of things an educated mother in an industrialized society would do without the advice of a doctor or nurse: bathing the baby regularly; keeping her own hands, nipples, and anything that came in contact with the baby's food or drink scrupulously clean; feeding her children a balanced diet; applying ointments and medicaments for minor ailments. In most Western countries, there was a structural division between the curative and preventive aspects of maternal and child-health services. Since most mothers had enough knowledge both to undertake most preventive actions without prompting and to seek professional advice when they required it, there was no need to make of the mother who had sought treatment for her sick child a captive audience for a lecture on weaning foods or careful excreta disposal. In the developing world, where the average rural mother was completely unlettered and rarely sought medical help unless her child was obviously ailing, her visits to the health centre were the only opportunity provided to the doctor or nurse in charge to impart to her the knowledge of how to prevent her children getting sick or underweight in the first place.

However, a price had been paid for fusing MCH curative and preventive care in developing countries. Seriously overworked medical personnel were wasting their time giving out cough lozenges and teaching mothers how to bath the baby. Given the right training, there was no reason why lay people could not dispense certain pills and know-how to their neighbours and the wider community—no reason why the better-informed village woman in Bangladesh or Botswana could not do the same for her children as her more privileged counterpart in the Western world.

Among many pioneers whose health projects began to attract attention were an Indian couple, both physicians: Drs Mabelle and Rajanikant Arole. Determined to work in a rural setting where needs were acute, the Aroles established themselves in 1970 at Jamkhed in Maharashtra State. Their aim was to provide comprehensive community health care to the 40,000 people in the surrounding villages. With the approval of village leaders and government officials, and financial backing from a non-governmental group with overseas and local funding, the Christian Medical Commission, they took on a team of staff and set up a health centre. The centre was only intended as a stepping stone to a programme with a much wider catchment than any static entity could provide; it made them locally known and won them the confidence of their staff and clients.

When they began to take mobile services—MCH, family planning, leprosy and tuberculosis treatment, immunization—out to the villages, the Aroles originally planned that an auxiliary nurse-midwife would be placed in each location to check up on cases, confer with mothers on child care and nutrition, round up children for immunization sessions, and make sure that practices promoting health became rooted in village mores. But they found it difficult to persuade young women to live out in the villages, and even when they did so their performance was poor. So instead, the Aroles found volunteers within the communities who, with training and supervision from the project staff, themselves could carry out the necessary functions. Before long, the use of ordinary people in the community as village health workers proved to be an inspired solution. They were cheaper since they did not require special housing or amenities. They were also much more effective.

City-trained health workers talked differently, dressed differently and had a different way of life from village people. There were problems of communication: villagers were sceptical that an outsider's dietary quirks or their insistence on drinking boiled water would not necessarily suit their own constitutions. But if someone of their own, whose judgement they trusted, tried to persuade them to change their ways, results would be different. The Aroles chose middle-aged women, respected community members whose credentials on child care would go unchallenged. Each spent two days a week being trained at Jamkhed. On a third, the mobile team would visit her community, treat cases of sickness, and go with her to call on newborns and pregnant women. She would hold meetings for child feeding, give talks on health education, and promote family planning on home visits. Her main tasks were, therefore, disease prevention and liaison with the curative work of mobile team and health centre. But she also had a kit with simple drugs, eye ointment, dressings and contraceptives. She was paid Rs. 30 a month. The Aroles believed that job satisfaction and enhanced status was more important than a cash incentive.

The employment and training of village women was only one of the distinctive features of the Aroles' project, but it was a feature it shared with all the health-care systems and individual health-care projects examined by WHO as part of the quest for a new health strategy. And it was the cumulative evidence of the effectiveness of laywomen and laymen in community care which marked the alternative approach to meeting basic health needs submitted to the Joint Committee on Health Policy in February 1975, almost three years after WHO was first presented with the challenge. The WHO study team had sought out examples where basic health care was being delivered to at least eighty per cent of the target population at a cost per head which even a country of very limited resources could afford. They went to Bangladesh, China, Cuba, Niger, Nigeria, Tanzania, Venezuela and Yugoslavia, as well as India. They had sought approaches which were woven into the social and economic environment; they had looked for elements which would be replicable on a wide scale in other cultural, social, economic and political settings. The synthesis of these experiences, and a strategy that encapsulated their essential features, was discussed at length by the senior officials of the two organizations; both Dr Halfdan Mahler, Director-General of WHO, and Harry Labouisse, Executive Director of Unicef, put in a rare appearance at the JCHP to emphasize the importance they attached to the direction in which health ideas were moving.

The study on alternative health care and its conclusions represented a major landmark in the reorientation of health policies at the international level. It reflected the evolution which had taken place in recent years in WHO's interpretation of its mandate for furthering standards of health care and promoting the role of health ministries throughout the world; health care and health-related activities were now measured not only against internationally-agreed standards of technical excellence, but against the development context in which they were to be performed. The new strategy for health care reflected this broader view, particularly as its central tenet—the mobilization of the community to take care of as many as possible of its own health needs via the village health worker—dethroned the medical profession from its position of control over every action carried out as a function of the official health service. In this sense, it was revolutionary.

In fact, its revolutionary character was the main problem faced by this alternative health-care concept. To those without professional vested interests, the concept sounded like inspired commonsense; but to some members of the medical profession, it sounded decidedly ominous. While they might have no objection to training the lay helper to demonstrate how to bath the baby or calculate the calories, proteins and vitamins in a weaning food mix, many doctors objected strenuously to the idea that anyone but a fully-trained health professional should handle any type of antibiotic drug, treat a malaria case, or give a vaccination. Once laymen with a few ounces of training got into the swagger of 'doctoring', it might lead anywhere. One 'alternative' health project in Savar, Bangladesh, whose director Dr Zafrullah Chowdhury was internationally well-known for bold departures, had actually trained—successfully, as it happened—semi-literate village girls to carry out female sterilizations. If such things were sanctioned by the medical establishment, argued some of its members, *ipso facto* the lay health worker would achieve something very close to quasi-professional recognition.

True, any remuneration for the lay health worker was supposed to come from the community—the client—rather than from the ministry of health; to this extent, there was no definitive recognition. But this was another mark of loss of control, a potential step backwards towards the days of witch doctors and herbal brews. To those who saw standards slipping dangerously as ignorant or unscrupulous villagers set themselves up as quacks and pill-merchants with the approval of the health-care service, the alternative health-care strategy sounded like the abandonment of everything they stood for in terms of professionalism.

This was far from the intention of the protagonists of the new concept, who did not envisage a fall-off in medical standards; on the contrary. Since much of the work done by the community health volunteer was intended to be preventive, the likelihood was that disease rates would decline and the remaining case-load of diarrhoeas, fevers and respiratory infections could be handled more effectively. The strategy envisaged the redeployment of professional medical personnel in such a way as to use a large part of their time for training and supervising the lower echelons of the service.

Village health workers would handle the mundane activities which previously swamped clinic staff and left them no time for running the kind of service which would help prevent the clinic being overcrowded in the first place. The idea of the planetary system of the basic health service, with its central hospitals, district health centres, and satellite subcentres stayed intact, and the village health workers added as an extra tier of satellites attached to the outermost edge of the formal structure. The lay person would work within the control of a supervisor, part of whose duties would be to organize extra training sessions or refresher courses as necessary, gradually building up the community health worker's knowledge and skills.

A final feature of the new approach was that health-promoting activities were seen as taking place in a number of ways other than in a clinic, or at the behest of a member—professional, auxiliary or lay—of the health-service team. If poor health was mainly an outcome of ignorance and poverty rather than the presence in a vulnerable population of virulent forms of epidemic disease, then all sorts of improvements could be health-promoting. More cash in the pocket, a better house to live in, a clean water supply, births more conveniently spaced, the availability of cheap and nutritious forms of food, improved household utensils for storing, preserving, or preparing food, and more information about what helped or hindered family well-being; a service producing any of these helped also to produce health. In practical terms, the new approach to health care and the basic services strategy dovetailed together.

The recommendations of WHO for the alternative order in health went to the World Health Assembly and the Unicef Executive Board in 1975. Many delegates commented that the analysis and the recommendations were not only welcome, but long overdue. The truth was that the ideas the study reflected and the revolutionary solutions it proposed would have been regarded by many as heresy only a few years before. Summing up the recommendations of the Joint Committee on Health Policy to the members of the Unicef Executive Board, Labouisse pointed out that while the new strategy was a marked reorientation of health-service policy, it would not mean any drastic change in the types of assistance already provided by Unicef to MCH services. Training stipends for traditional birth attendants and nursing auxiliaries; midwifery kits, and equipment for health centres and maternity wards; bicycles and motor vehicles for mobile clinics and supervisory rounds; all these and other familiar items on the Unicef shelf would be needed in greater quantity than before. The essential difference would be the role of community involvement in the health-service structure in which they were applied. Some of the more elaborate and expensive items would be less available than in the recent past; the new emphasis on community involvement meant that the ingredients of Unicef's co-operation had taken a turn back to basics, as had those of all the apostles of alternative visions.

The first step towards a global commitment to what was becoming known as 'primary health care' had been taken. WHO had developed a strategy for providing health, not just for some of the people in the world—those fortunate enough to live in industrialized societies or their replica within developing countries—but for everyone. The next step was to persuade the governments and the health ministries of the Third World that it was a workable strategy, and to help them put it into practice.

The gradual emergence of the alternative order in health care spelt not only a greater emphasis on basic MCH—antenatal care, maternity care, and paediatric care of the young child; but it had the potential for heightening the emphasis on child nutrition.

During the 1960s, Unicef's concern about the preschool child, in particular the prevalence of malnutrition in children aged between six months and three years, had been reflected in its calls for national planning for children's services. A determined effort had been made to push nutrition, the poor relation of health, agriculture and social services, into a more prominent position on the slate of government concerns, preferably by persuading countries to set up nutrition units within their ministries of planning. The production of food, the price of food and the consumption of nutritious food by children were subjects to be addressed on a national planning level embracing a variety of government sectors. In the decade leading up to the World Food Conference in 1974, this theme resounded through Unicef's statements on food and food emergencies.

At the same time, a parallel theme began to develop. In 1965, a report commissioned by the Joint Policy Committee on Health on the health aspects of nutrition programmes pointed out that, since applied nutrition programmes were intended to achieve health benefits among young children, they would be much more likely to achieve those benefits where they were run in conjunction with a health-service network already in place. Nutritional surveillance, nutrition education, rehabilitation of the nutritionally sub-normal: these were inseparable ingredients of any overall improvement in children's diet. No strategy for putting more good food into the mouths of young children would have much impact on their health unless their bodies were in a fit state to absorb the nutrients and utilize them.

This thesis was borne out by the experience of the applied-nutrition programme in India, which had tried to run all over the country before it was able to walk properly in its original locations. The model which had seemed so promising in Orissa and elsewhere yielded very uneven results as time went on. It was introduced in State after State, district after district, block after development block, without the modifications needed for each successive environment. In their search for the archetypal programme formula, the enthusiasts for applied nutrition allowed their unwieldy and unresponsive machine to roll on in the hope that, with some tinkering, it would yet prove to be the answer. But results did not markedly improve. As the first Decade of Development drew to a close, the puzzle of how to feed the hungry and malnourished child was still a long way from solution.

When the crises of the early 1970s prompted Unicef's Executive Board to declare a 'child emergency', the sense of anxiety about the nutritional condition of children all around the world became more acute. It seemed to many Board delegates that this, the most critical area of all, was being neglected. Year after year, in spite of the call for national food and nutrition policies, in spite of the frightening statistics which claimed that as many as 700 million children in the world suffered from some kind of nutritional deficiency with at least ten million close to starvation at any one time, Unicef appeared to be spending no more on nutrition programmes than when the emergency first began: only around twelve per cent of programme expenditure each year.

The role of Unicef in child nutrition, and the role of nutrition in national planning for meeting the needs of children, were still questions with incomplete answers. The only sure answers were about what had been tried and, for one reason or another, had been abandoned.

The main casualty was milk and its substitutes. Unicef's long love affair with the dairy cow was over. Dairy investments, even with subsidies, had not managed on any scale to bring milk within the reach of the poor at a price they could afford. The experimental high-protein foods had not yet quit the field, but only their most ardent devotees still refused to see that their cost was prohibitive to the low-income families whose children were most in need. As far as the poor were concerned, modern food-processing technology had a role limited to the production of K-Mix-II and other special concentrates for emergency child-feeding programmes.

The days of Unicef's involvement with the mass distribution of surplus dried skim milk powder had ended with the creation in the early 1960s of the World Food Programme (WFP), which took on the function within the UN system under the wing of FAO of redeploying the world's surplus foodstuffs. During drought and famine emergencies WFP was the key provider of grains and other staples, and it also provided large quantities of foods for supplementary feeding programmes and food-for-work schemes with a rehabilitation or developmental purpose. In the disaster relief operations in Bangladesh, Ethiopia, the Sahel and elsewhere during the early 1970s, Unicef collaborated closely with WFP on supplementary feeding for mothers and children, and established a working partnership for the future.

There were some specific micro-nutrient deficiency diseases for which the FAO/WHO/Unicef approach was to try and organize the mass consumption of the missing ingredient. In certain parts of the world—northern India, Pakistan and Nepal, for example—goitre, or iodine deficiency disease, was common among women. It could cause mental retardation, other handicaps, or even cretinism in their offspring. Adding iodine to salt, an item of everyone's diet, was a remedy widely attempted. It was not, however, a very efficient remedy in a country with no mass food marketing and distribution system. In most such countries, salt mining was a cottage industry outside the reach of governmental control, and few people in the countryside bought their supply in a packet from a shop. Trying to solve nutritional problems by the processing of foodstuffs had inbuilt limitations, therefore. People's nutritional condition could not be invisibly 'fixed'. A health education campaign was needed to help people understand the need to protect themselves by buying the 'improved' version.

The campaigns to combat night-blindness in children by widescale distribution of vitamin A were more successful; they were carried out through schools and health centres. Night-blindness was a common problem among children, particularly in parts of Asia; in the more serious cases, acute deficiency of vitamin A could lead to xeropthalmia, or total blindness.

For the want of a little knowledge and some green leafy vegetables or yellow fruit in their diet, thousands of children annually lost their eyesight. In 1971, Sir John Wilson, a champion of the blind whose affliction he shared, presented an eloquent case for mass vitamin A distribution to the Executive Board on behalf of the World Council for the Welfare of the Blind. With the technical agreement of WHO, Unicef thereafter began to provide large-dosage capsules for children in India, Indonesia, Pakistan, Bangladesh and elsewhere.

These campaigns to combat specific micro-nutrient diseases, important as they were, were not the main thrust of Unicef's concern. There were no additives or simple remedies for the child malnutrition associated with poverty. This remained the outstanding problem to which the school and home gardens and community poultry schemes of applied nutrition offered at best a partial solution.

By the early 1970s, the growing body of knowledge about the epidemiology of malnutrition and undernutrition was beginning to alter the way in which they were tackled. One important discovery was that 'the protein gap' was less critical a problem than 'the calorie gap'. A severely undernourished child needed food first, protein second; if fed protein, the child's metabolism would simply use the protein as if it were ordinary food energy. The nutrition scientists disagreed about the precise amount of protein needed, but they downgraded their previous estimates. Staple cereals—maize, millet, rice and wheat—had a reasonable protein content for adults and, supplemented with beans or other legumes, could provide for growing children. Only among people whose staples consisted of almost pure starch—such as plantains, cassava and yams—was lack of protein more serious a threat to their children's health than straightforward lack of food.

Derrick Jelliffe, Professor of Child Health at Makerere Medical College, cited evidence to support the thesis from different regions of Uganda. In the south, among the children of the Baganda people, the bloated stomachs and faded hair of kwashiorkor were often seen. The staple food of the Baganda was *matoke*, mashed plantain or cooking banana. Plantain contained only one per cent protein and was full of water and cellulose. It was therefore almost impossible for a small child to consume enough *matoke* to meet his or her full nutritional needs. The Baganda in general were much more prosperous than the Acholi people of the north; but Acholi children rarely suffered from kwashiorkor. Their staple was millet, whose protein content was seven per cent.

Applied nutrition programmes now began to concentrate on the family food supply, and on dispelling ignorance about the inadequacy for children of diets based exclusively on starchy crops. The 'backyard approach', as Jelliffe called it, did not have the space-age appeal enjoyed by the notion of cultivating micro-organisms on oil waste—one of the major new sources still being identified by the advocates of protein. But it was much more practicable. There were very few areas of the world where some combination of familiar cereals and legumes did not constitute a perfectly adequate diet, as long as children ate enough of it.

In many places, people had arrived at a suitable blend without the benefit of nutritional science. In Jamaica, they ate rice and peas. In Mexico, frijoles and tortillas. In Indonesia, rice and soya bean. In many African countries, pounded maize or yam was served with a fish, chicken or vegetable sauce. Cassava was treated as a famine crop; no-one ate an exclusive diet of cassava if they could avoid it. The backyard approach was based on existing dietary habits. It borrowed 'appropriate' technology — improved versions of traditional techniques — to increase yields of protein and vegetable crops; store the main food crop properly; preserve food by drying; and cook it in fuel-efficient ways.

On the face of it, this new, more balanced, calorie-protein picture appeared to make the task of feeding the hungry child much simpler: far fewer children than previously imagined needed extra protein in their diet. For most of the rest of the undernourished, a little extra of what they already ate would do. In practice, however, these more modest dietary changes proved almost as hard to achieve as the more radical and inappropriate ideas they had overtaken.

Special meals and gruels had to be prepared for the weanling child; special ingredients had to be put in the toddler's food to make it different from the family dish. The emphasis was now on helping mothers recognize and overcome malnutrition in their children by methods that were within their reach, physically and financially. But this began to underline once more to those trying to put it into practice that women's lives, specially in rural areas, did not easily accommodate such changes. The lot of rural women — the fatalism of their outlook; the drudgery of their labour-intensive day; the work in the fields which took them far from home; the effort involved in hauling fuel and water, boiling gruels and pounding special ingredients — was becoming increasingly perceived as not just an obstacle, but a major obstacle to improved family health and well-being.

Every new breakthrough in nutritional knowledge, every new scientific or practical approach appeared to lead only a very limited extra distance down the path towards relieving the hunger and listlessness of the mal-nourished child. As the child emergency deepened, nutrition continued its journey from sector to sector, discipline to discipline, pushed from agriculture to medicine, across to population and environment, up a few rungs into planning — and still progress only inched forward. Gradually it seemed after all that its most fruitful convergence was with health. The wheel had turned another circle; not back to the outworn idea that malnutrition was a 'disease' susceptible to some kind of medical cure, but the recognition of the very special relationship between sickness and poor nutrition in the small child, particularly in the child vulnerable to either because of poverty. Once again, the quest for alternatives helped to shed light on the dimensions of this relationship, and what to do about it.

When the Drs Arole arrived at Jamkhed in October 1970, Maharashtra was in the grip of drought. In their first contacts with village councils, they realized that the villagers' priorities were not health, but food and water. Since the Aroles interpreted 'health' in the broadest sense, and since they wanted to supply services which matched the villagers' own sense of their needs, they started with food. They obtained food for the under-fives and mothers, and the villagers organized community kitchens: a child nutrition programme had been born. Once established, the programme had to find ways of supplying its own food. Wells were dug, and those farmers who benefited gave land to grow food for the community. Meanwhile, the village health worker used the feeding programme for nutritional monitoring. She was taught by the project staff how to record the weight of the under-fives on a card and single out those whose failure to gain weight was a tell-tale sign of incipient or actual malnutrition. To these, she gave extra rations, and to their mothers extra pep talks. She could also watch out for new pregnancies, specially those where the mother's own nutritional condition might be a cause for alarm concerning her foetus.

In many of the new-style community-based health-care programmes, the volunteer workers spent a high proportion of their time on child nutrition as part of their MCH duties. From the perspective of a poor rural community, nutrition and health care were indistinguishable, even if the policy makers and district officials often tried to tidy them into different compartments: nutrition with agricultural and home economics extension; health care with medical practice. As the years had passed, the tidy compartmentalization had become much more blurred—at least at the theoretical level. From the villagers' point of view, they never had been compartmentalized. Their underlying problem was poverty; its symptoms —lack of food, water, medical care, security, cash income, knowledge, work—were computed differently in different places, regions and countries. But they were perceived by their victims as a seamless, interconnected whole, not as belonging to different 'sectors' in the way that governments, professions, academic disciplines and aid agencies are organized.

Community-based programmes, because they embrace the villagers' diagnosis as well as the experts', tend to reflect the seamlessness of the view from the village. The community volunteer, whether nominally employed as a health worker or as something else—family planning promoter, women's group leader, under-fives feeding monitor—frequently carries out almost identical tasks. In some places, the same person may be the community volunteer for several programmes conceived sectorally by the authorities, merely changing his or her hat on the day the respective officials come to visit. In the person's mind, the questions and answers do not change: merely the face of the inquiring official.

The only really significant differences of function are between those normally carried out by men, and those normally carried out by women. In a traditional rural society, sex roles are sharply defined. While the community volunteer may grow in self confidence as a result of some training and the enhanced standing it confers, it is unrealistic to expect him or her to depart radically from traditional preoccupations. Even if males and females are taught an identical curriculum, they tend to perform different tasks, identifying with those that belong naturally to their own sexual domain. Food preparation and child care are the domain of women; anything to do with land allocation, construction or engineering is the preserve of men. Male villagers are no more likely to talk to women about the virtues of breastfeeding and careful weaning than are women to organize street-cleaning parties or build latrines. This sexual divide can be awkward from an administrative point of view, and is often unrecognized by those whose enthusiasm for breaking down the sexual barriers which reinforce women's dependency is stronger than their respect for inbuilt cultural restraints. But it is a real divide, whereas the sectoral divide is artificial.

In Kasa, also in Maharashtra State, a nutrition programme based on a Primary Health Centre was initiated in 1974 under the direction of Professor P. M. Shah of the Institute of Child Health in Bombay. The project was sponsored by the Government of India, the Government of Maharashtra and the US nongovernmental organization, CARE. P. M. Shah's professional standing and existing links with WHO meant that the international health community took an interest in the Kasa nutrition project from the start.

The project was designed around the use of part-time social workers (PTSW), chosen by the communities as volunteers, and paid Rs. 80 a month. Like the Aroles, the project managers wanted the communities to employ middle-aged women with leadership qualities; but unlike the Aroles, they required them to be literate. The female literacy rate in Kasa was only ten per cent, and in some of the twenty-eight project areas there were either no literate women at all, or only a few young ones. This brought down the average age of the PTSW to twenty-two; and more than half were male. As a result of these two disadvantages, there was a heavy drop-out rate. The enthusiasm and openness of the young to change and to new ideas was offset by certain disadvantages. Their elders might not be willing to listen to their advice, which was discouraging. And many saw their new-found confidence and the pocketful of skills they had collected not as a means of serving the community, but as a first step along the route out of it.

The Kasa project not only illustrated some of the problems associated with deploying community workers successfully, but it also illustrated how overlapping conceptually were a community's health and a community's nutrition programme—and how inappropriate it was to separate them along a rigid sectoral divide. The duties of the PTSW were as follows: census-taking and record-keeping; regular weighing of children and nutrition education; monitoring of pregnancies and family-planning motivation; distribution of nutrition supplements and vitamin A capsules; monthly chlorination of open village wells; gathering children together for immunization by the nurse-midwife. After a year's experience on the job they were allowed to treat common illnesses with simple drugs, using a manual written in the local dialect. Although this was a nutrition project, the list of duties would have been identical for a community volunteer in a health or even an environmental sanitation project.

From Unicef's point of view, the volunteer village worker in all his, and especially her, different guises was the person in whom basic services for children fused: day-care with feeding, water supply with hygiene, diet supplements with weight monitoring, maternity care with family spacing, education with self-awareness and the desire to change life for the better. Paramount among these services were Unicef's two traditional and longest-running concerns: child health and child nutrition. The evidence that poor nutrition and childhood disease compounded each other in a particularly crushing partnership was now much more widely appreciated.

If a poorly-nourished child picked up a common infection, its effect on the child could easily bring on the symptoms of classic kwashiorkor or marasmus. Any fever from which the child was suffering, the loss of fluid or food from diarrhoea, the consumption of any remaining reserves of energy in trying to fight off the disease quickly turned a mild case of malnutrition into a severe one. The disease itself, meanwhile, took a much more serious course in a poorly-nourished child, whose weakened immune system could not withstand its invasion. Many children whose cause of death would have been clinically listed as measles, pneumonia or dysentery would not have died if they had picked up the infection when well-fed. In very small infants, breastfeeding made a vital contribution to their immunity. In children between six and thirty-six months old, studies were showing that nutritional attention alone reduced illness and death from diarrhoeal and respiratory disease. Conversely, prompt treatment of the dehydration caused by diarrhoea, regular health monitoring at the MCH clinic, immunization and attention to cleanliness could prevent the onset of severe malnutrition.

The world food crisis, induced by the disastrous harvests of 1972 and 1974, had a powerful effect for a brief span of time in concentrating the world's conscience on the problem of hunger. Its causes and remedies were exhaustively discussed at the 1974 UN World Food Conference in Rome. The debate brought home to those who had not already worked it out that hunger and food shortage were to do with poverty. The lack of food in the home of labourers or peasant farmers, and therefore by implication the nutritional status of their family, had to do with one simple circumstance: their inability to translate enough of the resources at their disposal into food or the means to buy it. The weather—in the form of drought—might play a part. But lack of land to grow food, lack of employment, lack of credit, lack of seed or fertilizer or irrigation, lack of cash income from some kind of realizable asset were more important.

This overall analysis offered Unicef and WHO few obvious channels for their own contribution. Yet they certainly could not abandon the field of hunger and malnutrition to the political economists, bankers, agriculturalists, plant technologists and civil engineers on the basis that the efforts of these groups of experts were the only ones which counted. Apart from any other consideration, such efforts might take a generation or more to show the permanent effect that everyone was waiting and hoping for. In the meantime, the fusion of nutrition with a broader definition of health care offered a way forward—perhaps at a secondary level, but at least at a level which could achieve results without the resolution of all the complex problems of poverty first. The alternative approach to health care, based upon the community worker, opened up the prospect of a network of mutually-reinforcing health and nutrition activities in the localities where deep-felt poverty was to be found.

In 1975, Dr Jean Mayer and a team from the Harvard School of Public Health presented to the Unicef Executive Board their report on priorities in child nutrition in developing countries. They strongly endorsed the new community worker approach. Primary health care and primary nutritional care were, to all intents and purposes, one and the same. This realization has guided Unicef's policy on child nutrition until the present day.

On 6 September 1978, delegates from 134 governments and sixty-seven UN organizations met at Alma-Ata, capital of the Kazakh Soviet Socialist Republic, to attend a six-day international conference on 'Primary Health Care', the name now used to designate the alternative order in health care. WHO and Unicef sponsored the conference, and it was preceded by a year-and-a-half of preparation by both organizations, including international meetings in Brazzaville, Washington, Alexandria, Manila, New Delhi, New York and Halifax. Dr Halfdan Mahler, Director-General of WHO, and Harry Labouisse, actively backed by their respective senior lieutenants, Tejado de Rivero and Dick Heyward, had committed themselves and their organizations to overcome the first hurdle confronting the new approach: international respectability.

The main document for the conference was a joint report by Halfdan Mahler and Henry Labouisse. The strength of its attack on the prevailing pattern of health care was remarkable. In both the developed and the developing countries, 'Health resources are allocated mainly to sophisticated medical institutions in urban areas', the report stated. 'Quite apart from the dubious social premise on which this is based, the concentration of complex and costly technology on limited segments of the population does not even have the advantage of improving health. Indeed, the improvement of health is being equated with the provision of medical care dispensed by growing numbers of specialists, using narrow medical technologies for the benefit of the privileged few. People have become cases without personalities, and contact has been lost between those providing medical care and those receiving it.'

The main architects of this damning indictment of the results brought about by postwar advances in medical technology were Mahler and de Rivero. They believed that medicine had blossomed into a colossal industry with powerful vested interests, and that these interests dictated health policy unwisely and with punishing discrimination against the poor.

According to the WHO constitution, established in 1949, the protection of health was 'a state of complete physical, mental and social well-being, and not merely the absence of disease'. Health care was a fundamental human right whose fulfilment was now projected as part of the social justice demanded by the new international economic order. In keeping with this fundamental analysis, several distinctly revolutionary statements swam through the conference without opposition: 'The promotion and protection of the health of the people is essential to sustained economic and social development and contributes to a better quality of life and to world peace' (Article III, the Declaration of Alma-Ata); 'The people have the right and duty to participate individually and collectively in the planning and implementation of their health care' (Article IV).

In the course of the past few years, Primary Health Care had become an ideology. Its principles, particularly that of community participation, had taken on the force of doctrine. For nearly two decades, development had been delivered to the people, for the people, at the people. The people had not thought a great deal of it; frequently, it had not appeared to take their own views, beliefs, and realities into serious account, rather treating them as a blank sheet on which someone else's idea of progress was to be written. Now the pendulum had swung heavily in their direction. In the alternative order, the critical elements of the people's wishes, their sense of their own needs, and their resources and energies were to be not just taken into account, not just harnessed to an engine of development designed and driven by someone else, but to be an integral part of programme formulation and development, growing and expanding with the programme itself

The alternative order in health was health by the people. The role of the professionals and the government service was to provide training, supervision, logistical back-up, material aid and technical advice. These ideas, echoing the spirit of the times, borrowing revolutionary fervour from 'conscientization' and 'deschooling', gained excitement and appeal from their very antagonism to the existing structure of the medical world. Opposition could be expected from health ministries, health insurance companies, pharmaceuticals industries—and the whole business of medicine, built as it was on quite opposite assumptions.

Alma-Ata took place because WHO and Unicef were keenly aware of the need to secure political commitment to the Primary Health Care approach. Every effort was made to counter anticipated resistance. It might be unrealistic to expect industrialized countries to recast their health-care systems; but by claiming that they should, and that primary health care was intrinsically superior, they forestalled criticism that they were trying to palm off a second-class system on the developing countries. They also suggested that any loss of income sustained by the medical industry would be more than made up by increased demand for simpler, more basic equipment and drugs. The two organizations worked hard to obtain the necessary statements of support; Alma-Ata was the testing ground.

In its own terms, the Alma-Ata conference was a triumph. It represented a watershed: the moment at which primary health care ceased being the provenance of a few brave medical pioneers in dusty villages and a group of international protagonists on their behalf, and instead became an approach to which most of the governments in the world had given their endorsement, and many ministries of health committed themselves to carrying out.

Within no more than three years of the first serious attempt to synthesize alternative health experiences, both analysis and prescription had been clasped to the international breast of a notoriously-conservative breed: administrative bureaucrats and their colleagues in the medical profession. This achievement by Mahler, Labouisse, de Rivero, Heyward and other key people on the WHO and Unicef staffs was remarkable. The Declaration of Alma-Ata required, after all, a revolutionary re-definition of health, a revolutionary re-definition of medicine, and a transformation of everything conventionally done in their name. The health establishment and the politicians from countries around the world met and agreed to all of this, at least in principle. Whatever reservations many harboured, the alternative order in health was declared. Its goal: 'Health for All by the Year 2000'.

Main sources
WHO/Unicef Joint Study on Alternative Approaches to Meeting Basic Health Needs of Populations in Developing Countries; report prepared for the WHO/Unicef Joint Committee on Health Policy, February 1975; paper on Basic Health Services prepared for the 1965 JCHP session; appraisal of MCH programmes prepared by the WHO for the 1967 session of the Unicef Executive Board; report on Community Involvement in Primary Health Care; A Study of the Process of Community Motivation and Continued Participation', prepared for the 1977 session of the JCHP.

Executive Director's progress reports and other documentation prepared for the annual sessions of the Unicef Executive Board; summary Records of Board proceedings and reports of the Executive Board.

Health by the People, edited by Kenneth W. Newell (in particular 'A Comprehensive Rural Health Project in Jamkhed (India)' by Mabelle Arole and Rajanikant Arole), published by WHO, 1975.

'The Origins and Policy Basis of WHO/Unicef Collaboration in the International Health Field: A Look at the Official Record (1946–1983)' prepared by WHO, June 1983. Also: 'A brief history of WHO/Unicef Joint Committee on Health Policy 1948–1983', prepared by Newton Bowles for the Unicef History Project, May 1983.

Medical Care in Developing Countries: A Symposium from Makerere, edited by Maurice King; based on a conference assisted by WHO/Unicef, and an experimental edition assisted by Unicef, published with a grant from the Ford Foundation by Oxford University Press, Nairobi, 1966.

Articles in *Les Carnets de l'Enfance/Assignment Children*, Unicef, in particular Issue 42, April/June 1978, published in preparation for the International Conference on Primary Health Care. Articles in *Unicef News*, in particular Issue 71, March 1972, and Issue 74, December 1972.

'The Nutrition Factor' by Alan Berg, published by the Brookings Institution, 1973; and 'Malnourished People: a Policy View' by Alan Berg, published in the Poverty and Basic Needs Series, World Bank, 1981.

'Primary Health Care: Report of the International Conference on Primary Health Care, Alma-Ata, USSR, 6–12 September 1978' (includes the joint report by the Director-General of WHO and the Executive Director of Unicef), published by WHO, Geneva, 1978.

Interviews undertaken for the Unicef History Project.

Chapter 15

The Year of the Child

On 9 January 1979, the hall of the UN General Assembly in New York was packed with an audience of an unfamiliar kind for a unique occasion. The British media personality David Frost was the Master of Ceremonies.

Performing live on a podium normally reserved for Heads of State, senior statesmen and distinguished diplomats were a galaxy of pop stars. Abba, the Bee Gees, Earth Wind and Fire, Olivia Newton-John, John Denver, Rod Stewart, Donna Summer and other famous names from the music world sang a 'Gift of Song' for the world's children. Held to launch the International Year of the Child, organized by the US Committee for Unicef, the concert was telecast in sixty countries around the world to an estimated audience of 250 million. In spite of a last-minute panic over Rod Stewart's rendering of 'Da Ya Think I'm Sexy?', which did not quite conform to the standard of decorum associated with activities in the General Assembly, the occasion was a triumph. All the artists who performed gave to Unicef the rights of a song, either the one they sang or another, and between the telecasts and the album sales, 'A Gift of Song' raised $4 million. 'Music for Unicef' launched the International Year of the Child in truly celebratory style.

For some of those present, the most dazzling aspect of the occasion was that the International Year of the Child had been launched at all. The idea of such a year, when mooted seven years before, had a distinctly mixed reception. It was the brainchild of Canon Joseph Moerman, Secretary-General of the International Catholic Child Bureau (ICCB) in Geneva. The UN had recently passed a resolution to bring under control the number of international years, decades and anniversaries, and the expensive international conferences associated with them. Member countries were beginning to feel that Years—for refugees, population, women, anti-apartheid, to name but a few—had already punctuateu the past two decades to the point of surfeit.

Canon Moerman took a different line. His view was that only a narrow slice of officialdom were weary of Years; people at large were not suffering from 'international year fatigue' because the torrent of words had barely reached them. He had observed that many organizations and individuals expressed compassion towards children but that, as an issue, the child was in danger of being drowned out by the clamour surrounding more fashionable debates. The lack of controversy concerning children, which worked to their advantage at times of political crisis, lost out in competition with highly-charged subjects like population control and women's liberation. Moerman felt that a year for children might generate a second wind, something beyond the routine of good works and passive good will.

Canon Moerman made his first overture to UN Secretary-General Kurt Waldheim in 1973, and Waldheim was positive. His approval was essential. Moerman recognized that no amount of support from religious and voluntary organizations could compensate for its lack from the UN and its member governments: to be nationally observed, any Year must have their imprimatur. At first Harry Labouisse at Unicef was concerned. If the UN declared a Year for children, the brunt of responsibility, not to mention cost, was very likely to fall on Unicef. He feared that the effort would interfere with Unicef's ongoing work and deflect resources away from its principal mission in the developing world. Few of the parades, galas and gracious appearances which were the main feature of such Years would have much to offer a child herding goats through the grasslands of Africa or living in a bamboo house in a Bangladesh village. Labouisse also feared that putting children on the global agenda invited politicization, a plague which he had spent his career at Unicef keeping its cause away from. The controversies surrounding women's rights and population invariably acted as a magnet for political divide, particularly at the international conferences which were the usual climax of a Year's celebrations. Why invite controversy when there was nothing politically contentious to debate? Central principles were not at stake. There was no grand divide, east-west or north-south, over children.

Labouisse despatched Charles Egger to Geneva to discuss the whole idea with Moerman; upon Egger's return, Labouisse's misgivings began to soften. Moerman—a Belgian Catholic priest—made it clear to Unicef that he was against any move to use a pro-child Year as a platform for anti-birth control or pro-motherhood lobbies. Egger had pointed out Unicef's strong reservations about any international conference about children, and discovered that Moerman was by no means wedded to the idea.

By 1975, Moerman had accumulated a strong phalanx of nongovernmental support. The idea of a Year for the Child appealed strongly to the International Union of Child Welfare which, more than a decade earlier, had led the crusade for the Declaration of the Rights of the Child. The Declaration was the internationally agreed synthesis of the essential rights and needs of children; but in many parts of the world, its fine sentiments were still far from realized in practice. At a time when the process of modernization was loosening, sometimes abruptly, the traditional ties of family life and forcing many Third World children to operate independently in an adult world at an early age, the rights of children needed all the extra push an IYC could give them. Other nongovernmental organizations of stature—the YWCA, the World Council of Churches, for example—began to join Moerman's band wagon. Some had consultative status with Unicef. The effect of their enthusiasm was felt, through the NGO Committee on Unicef and the medium of one or two strong supporters within Unicef: Jack Charnow, head of NGO liaison and Secretary to the Executive Board; and Jack Ling, Director of Information, who saw in the Year a forceful engine of public goodwill and voluntary fund-raising.

At the May 1975 Executive Board meeting, Mildred Jones of the YWCA, then the Chairman of the NGO Committee, made an appeal on the Year's behalf. She was followed to the rostrum by Moerman himself. Labouisse made it plain that he thought a successful international Year depended on the commitment of governments to offer more than rhetoric, to undertake adequate preparatory work and lend financial support; he also stated his opposition to an international conference. The response of the delegates was guarded. But over the course of the following year, attitudes began to change. Moerman's message began to penetrate not only the NGOs, but governments. Norway, whose representative, Aake Ording, had pushed thirty years ago for a UN Appeal for Children, now became a champion of a Year for the child. Holland was almost as keen, and the countries of eastern Europe were all in favour. So were many from the developing world: India, the Philippines, Colombia, Argentina, and several in Africa. Those who knew that they would have to foot a large part of the bill—the US, Britain, Federal Republic of Germany, Sweden—continued to stand politely back. But as usual, it was difficult to come out openly against something for children. By the 1976 Board meeting, Labouisse had managed to obtain recognition that Unicef would have to bear special strains— financial, in particular—if the IYC were declared, and to receive promises of special support. His condition that there should be no international conference was accepted. The IYC became a *fait accompli*, and it was agreed that Unicef would have to take the lead in much of its activity. The date for the Year was fixed for 1979, the twentieth anniversary of the Declaration of the Rights of the Child. Unicef now set out to make sure that the plans for it emphasized action, and that its administration and budget cause as little harm as possible to Unicef's regular programme of work.

The Declaration of the Rights of the Child provided an internationally sanctioned checklist of what was meant by the dictum: 'Mankind owes to the child the best it has to give'. The operative question for the Year to determine was whether and how far 'the best' was being delivered in countries around the world, and how much closer to 'the best' every country, rich and poor, might reach.

The proposals Labouisse and others engineered through the UN machinery established a character for the Year of the Child which was different from that of most previous UN Years. It borrowed certain essentials from World Refugee Year, 1959, for which Sherwood Moe, a long-time aide of Labouisse, had been a deputy representative of the UN Secretary-General. Although declared internationally, the style of its observance was to be left to each country to decide, at national or local level. Three main objectives were laid down for the Year: all countries should make a fresh appraisal of the situation of their children; they should be inspired into new efforts to do something for children whose situation needed improvement; better-off countries should be inspired to increase their aid contributions for those whose level of development was far less advanced. National IYC commissions would be set up by, or at the invitation of, governments, and organizations which normally had nothing to do either with the UN or with children would be invited to take part. Each national commission would decide on its own programme within certain guidelines, the main one being that IYC was for all children, not just the special cases, the handicapped or orphaned; nor just for the child victim of poverty and underdevelopment.

In the developing world, Unicef expected the IYC to be a vehicle for the promotion of basic services, a policy going forward for endorsement from the Executive Board to the same General Assembly that would proclaim the IYC. The IYC resolution passed the General Assembly on 21 December 1976. It emphasized that IYC should be a time for studying children's needs and launching programmes that were 'an integral part of economic and social development plans'. This theme dovetailed with the current deliberations on the new international economic order and reflected the ideas Unicef had propounded since the Bellagio conference of 1964. The resolution, rather more modestly, also underlined the moral purpose of the Year, by stating that the IYC would provide a 'framework of advocacy' for children. This, in the minds of its keenest protagonists, was the noble goal: to make governments and people hold up a mirror to their consciences and examine their failures on behalf of their children. In this context, IYC was to surprise everyone.

In 1977, preparations began in earnest. The resolution had recognized that Unicef's regular staff and budget were not expected to carry the administrative load or the budget for the Year and its preparations. Unicef's Executive Director was identified as responsible for IYC co-ordination, but it was understood that Labouisse might appoint a special representative, and solicit special contributions. Norway was the first to pledge a sum of $400,000. The total budget was set at $4 million. Later it was increased to $7·2 million. Labouisse wrote to all foreign ministers of UN member States, asking for contributions and suggesting that they set up national IYC commissions. He also contacted the otheragencies in the UN which could be expected to co-operate actively, and Unicef's own national committees. Then he began to set up the IYC Secretariat.

As Special Representative, responsible for IYC affairs, Labouisse wanted a woman and preferably one from a developing country. He interviewed several, and his choice was Dr Estefania Aldaba-Lim, Minister for Social Services and Development in the Philippines. Dr Lim was a person of considerable experience with the problems of children in her own country, having served for seven years as the Minister responsible for community development, particularly among the rural poor, and having taken a special interest in family well-being, child nutrition and the problems confronting out-of-school youth. Her competence and dynamic personality equipped her for an exacting role, which included a gruelling travel marathon to over sixty-five countries during the course of the next two-and-a-half years. Lim succeeded in enlisting the support of Heads of State, First Ladies, and senior government officials. Her visits and the publicity surrounding them, particularly in developing countries, succeeded in nudging many national IYC commissions into existence and action. She also did the rounds of ambassadors and heads of UN missions in New York and elsewhere, and her own enthusiasm for the Year was infectious. Lim's contribution made a vital difference to the way in which the IYC subsequently took off.

Under Lim, Labouisse placed two senior Unicef veterans as respective directors of the IYC Secretariat's two branches in New York and Geneva: John Grun, a Netherlander whose most recent tour of duty was Regional Director in New Delhi; and James McDougall, a New Zealander who had spent ten years as Regional Director in the Middle East. Their experience overseas and within Unicef provided a firm anchor for the less experienced IYC staff, most of whom were newcomers.

As preparations intensified, the magic of a Year for the Child began to reveal itself. Moerman's idea had touched the hidden spring that, in the business of human compassion, is quite unpredictable. In mid-1977, eighty-five international NGOs formed a special committee of their own for IYC with Canon Moerman at its head. Their network quickly grew; the number of national branches and subgroups of large international voluntary bodies such as the Jaycees, the Lions, Rotary, the YWCA and the Red Cross, as well as hundreds of small independent groups which did something for the Year, reached into the thousands by the end of 1979. On the governmental side, the response was equally electric. The optimists had hoped that around fifty countries would set up IYC commissions; by mid-April 1978, more than seventy had already done so; and by the end of 1979, there were 148 in existence.

The national IYC commissions were as diverse in character as any truly decentralized group of institutions with only a common theme to link them internationally. Some were government bodies with a cross section of membership from different ministries; others were private, with a membership drawn entirely from voluntary bodies; others were a mixture of the governmental and the nongovernmental. Some included representatives from national committees for Unicef, and a few—Hungary, Israel, and Norway—were identical with them. In many, the nongovernmental organizations, who mobilized their supporters and volunteer networks, were the life blood of the Year's impending activities. Some reached out to towns and provinces, setting up local IYC support groups to bring the Year right into people's homes.

To help the developing countries set up IYC commissions and embark on programmes, Unicef set aside a special fund of $3 million to be taken up on a project-by-project basis. One of the activities most strongly encouraged, both by Unicef offices and by Aldaba-Lim on her country visits, was for the relevant authorities to undertake a review of existing legislation on their children's status, and examine whether the health and social services adequately met their needs.

This exercise in 'pump priming' also meant that Unicef could help a national commission to hire a full-time secretary and develop information materials. The IYC Secretariat in Geneva published a series of discussion papers on various technical subjects, to serve as resource and information background on salient issues. Other member organizations of the UN family co-operated closely with the IYC preparations. ILO campaigned to enforce the child labour convention. World Health Day 1979 was dedicated to children by WHO, as was World Environment Day by the UN Environment Programme. UNITAR, the UN Institute for Training and Research, joined with the Columbia University Law School in publishing a two-volume survey on Law and the Child, based on monographs produced by lawyers and child welfare specialists in nearly sixty countries.

The success of IYC depended very heavily on the national commissions' programmes of action and the energy they injected into them. Some, unquestionably, only gestured in the direction of IYC observance: a stamp was issued and posters displayed in the capital city. Others took IYC much more seriously, as a lever for fundraising, for calls on government to do more for children, and as an umbrella for many different causes. Several undertook a national diagnosis of their children's situation, some for the first time ever (Guinea-Bissau, Saudi Arabia); others studied their nutritional condition (China, Haiti, Oman), set out to eradicate polio (Malawi), or immunize newborns (Bhutan). Some looked at more specific problem areas; the children of migrant labourers (Luxembourg), 'latchkey' children (UK), street children (Colombia); yet others tried to do more for the orphaned (Chad, the Philippines), the nomadic (Botswana), the victims of war (Nigeria, Lebanon), and refugee children (Finland). Many ran campaigns to start preschools (Benin), get children off the streets and into school (Ghana, Kenya), lowered the age of school entry (Gambia), or abolished elementary school fees (India). Some focussed on care of the handicapped (Vietnam, Korea) and the mentally disabled (Bahrain, Chile, Congo). Several started to put on the statute book a family code (Togo, Barbados), new legislation on adoption and legitimization (Indonesia), child abuse (USA), child neglect (Liberia), a law against child battering, including all forms of physical punishment including spanking (Sweden), and protection for minors (Dominican Republic). By any reckoning, the list of efforts and achievements was extraordinarily wide-ranging.

The volume of sound made on behalf of children around the world during the Year was almost deafening. As a subject for exhibitions, films, posters and all the visual arts, children are irresistible. Media events designed to increase public awareness of children's needs and rights took place in over 130 countries, ranging from a 100-foot banner proclaiming the International Year of the Child stretched across the road in a remote village in the highlands of Papua New Guinea, to a week-long assembly of gifted children in Sofia under the patronage of Bulgarian First Lady, Madame Zhivkova—and to sophisticated telethons and galas such as the concert in the General Assembly that formally launched the Year. Tens of thousands of articles were published and hundreds of television films were made. Newspapers by and for children were written; radio series on parents' education were produced; colloquia and seminars canvassed views by and about children. The millions of images and miles of press publicity celebrated on the one hand the joys of childhood; on the other, they exposed major problems of young people: drugs, vandalism, child labour, sexual abuse, teenage pregnancy.

The IYC Secretariat ran a referral service to put different organizations in touch to learn from each other's experiences. It had been expected that the organizations of the developing and developed worlds would express interest in markedly different concerns. The IYC discussion papers on Unicef's traditional programme areas—nutrition, health care, water supply, the young child—turned out to be equally sought by industrialized countries where pockets of severe deprivation could be found; while material on child exploitation, children with learning difficulties, urban children, children in the age of television was also keenly sought by people in developing countries. The problems of children turned out to be as universal as they are diverse.

During the International Year of the Child, Canon Moerman's 'second wind' for children unquestionably blew into corners unreached by other Years. The success of the Year astounded the Year-weary; a Year for the Disabled—1981—capitalized on the initial airing of this problem among children during the IYC, and Years for the Aged and for Youth have since been held. None before or since quite entered the hearts of humankind as completely as the Year of the Child.

Many governments increased their allocations to services for children, and set out on new courses of action which would ensure that their children rode the tide of IYC into the 1980s and beyond. Unicef itself benefited directly from the explosion of energy. The response to the Year forced Unicef to reach into its own pocket and advance $1·6 million to the costs, but it recouped its investment many times over. Private contributions to Unicef from all sources exceeded $50 million during 1979, nearly double the total for 1978. The goal of $200 million for Unicef's total income, set in 1977, was exceeded. Some of the extra generosity was inspired by the emergency in Kampuchea which broke upon the world in the last months of 1979, but IYC had a great deal to do with it.

The special genius of the IYC was to make it a do-it-yourself affair. This approach, on which both Moerman and Labouisse had been so insistent, paid off handsomely. Only because of it were so many subjects picked up, addressed and publicly examined in a way which made it impossible at year's end for them ever to look quite the same again. In October 1979, the Year's activities were discussed at the plenary session of the General Assembly. The debate was unique, not only because of its harmonious spirit. This was one of the very few times that an international Year was considered sufficiently important to warrant such attention. It was a land-mark in the continuing saga of trying to elevate the children's cause to the high table of international statesmanship.

Introducing the topic, the President of the General Assembly, Salim Salim of Tanzania, told the delegates, 'No issue touches us more closely, or has more direct bearing on the future of the world, than that of our children . . . For we are keenly aware that those who will inherit our world and manage it in the third millennium are the children of today, and that the shape of that world is being decided, now, by the way in which we are building their bodies and forming their minds'. During the next three-and-a-half days, eighty-six delegates described the ways in which IYC had been observed in their countries and how its momentum would be carried forward. As speaker followed speaker, Labouisse, always inclined to modesty, turned to John Grun, and said, 'You know, I do believe it's worked'.

The International Year of the Child had, indeed, worked.

Once the national commissions for IYC were set up in the industrialized countries, the Unicef national committees—except in the few cases where the committees were invited to be the IYC commission—no longer shouldered the main responsibility for the Year. Nonetheless, many recognized the opportunity it offered for raising Unicef's visibility in their countries, and worked closely with the national commissions in running special IYC campaigns.

Within each country, the Year's main focus was on their own children's problems, but in many industrialized countries this did not mean that the problems of children in developing countries were forgotten. Many focussed on the 'Third World child' in their own midst: the hungry child, the illiterate child, the refugee child, the immigrant child, the child suffering from neglect because mothers in straitened circumstances were forced to work long hours and had little time to spend on their families. Connections between the plight of such children and others even less fortunate in faraway communities were made almost effortlessly, particularly where television and newspaper series were run over several weeks. The IYC offered Unicef national committees a wonderful information vehicle, a vehicle most effectively used by those committees which, during the previous few years, had taken up a new activity: development education.

The concept of development education, a structured process of learning about change and upheaval in society, particularly in societies where poverty cried out for a more equitable distribution of wealth between rich and poor nations, rich and poor people, was a child of the alternative order. In the recent past, awareness in the industrialized countries about Third World problems had grown considerably. Many factors played a part: the Freedom from Hunger Campaign, the Development Decades, the famine emergencies, the Vietnam years, the fascination of the hippie generation for cultures of the East, international tourism, and the growing number of people involved in the international development industry. Public attention might be volatile, of short attention span, and often unsophisticated; but a new generation of young people were growing up in Europe and North America whose ideas about the societies of Asia, Africa and Latin America were free from many of the colonial perceptions of the past with all their overtones of superiority and racism. Under the influence of social critics such as Paulo Friere, Ivan Illich, E. F. Schumacher, and Barbara Ward, 'development' had become a new way of looking at the world and at all societal relationships, not merely a prepackaged set of skills, information and ideas to be shipped off to develop the poor.

Interest in the alternative society, with its implicit rejection of the material consumption patterns of the West and its dalliance with leftist political doctrine, instilled among a sizeable number of its adherents a sense of solidarity with the poor, both at home and overseas. Sometimes it took the form of romanticism; sometimes anger on behalf of the victims of apartheid or other liberation struggles; sometimes it erupted in boycotts of products produced in conditions of exploitation or insecurity, or inadequate environmental respect by certain countries or by certain multi-national companies. This amorphous collection of liberal humanitarians, political radicals and critics of the establishment, inspired by a compound of ethical, religious and political concerns, were a new force to be reckoned with. They were beginning to make an impression on how the problems of the Third World were conveyed to audiences in the West. Their inspiration had less to do with compassion than with social justice. They talked about the global village, the interdependent world. The image of the helpless African or Asian child, appealing for mindless generosity, offended them deeply. They believed it offended Africa and Asia as well.

The genesis of development education was in students' movements, relevant professions, and among the better-informed supporters of overseas aid organizations. It was encouraged by those European political parties who looked to public support for liberal international assistance policies. By 1974, UNESCO had begun to support it as a means of promoting international peace. A concept born of such various strands eluded clear definition; but its essence was to spread information, through schools and other learning institutions, and the media, about the process of world development. Its common property was a rejection of crude and simplistic messages, a desire to learn more about the complexities of trying to transform underprivileged societies, an ambivalence about whether development aid automatically conferred benefits, a zeal for new relationships between the developed and developing worlds; and for deeper understanding rather than a deeper dip into the pocket.

Within Unicef, these ideas first expressed themselves among certain European national committees who were unhappy with the information material they were given by Unicef headquarters as campaign tools. They believed that what Unicef was doing in the developing countries must be better communicated in order to win credibility with an increasingly demanding public. In November 1973, a group of their representatives held an information workshop at Eagle Hill, Denmark, under the chairmanship of Arne Stinus, the Executive Secretary of the Danish Committee. Stinus, a Danish parliamentarian with a reputation for trenchant campaigning on Third World issues, was a combative figure. The Eagle Hill report drew strongly on the influence of the representatives from the Nordic countries, where understanding about world development issues had already reached a relatively sophisticated level. They demanded of the Unicef Secretariat a greater sense of partnership in evolving information policy, more substantive treatment of development projects, and material that would enable them to run educational campaigns about children's needs in the developing world.

The Scandinavians believed that attitudes among children about their counterparts in other cultures and societies were being exclusively informed by stereotypes conveyed by the mass media. Their children were growing up with a superficial image of a world peopled by alien, helpless poor incapable of improving their own lives, and dependent on the charity of wealthier nations. Attempts to correct these negative impressions must start in the classroom during a young person's formative years. This meant attracting the attention of teachers and educational planners. The Nordic Unicef committees began to develop teacher's kits, slide sets, pamphlets and educational materials of various kinds. Some received financial or other support from their governments. The Finnish Committee, for example, began an annual distribution of a multi-media kit based on Unicef material to 8000 schools through the Education Ministry. In 1977, the foreign ministries of Denmark, Finland, Norway and Sweden co-financed with Unicef a trip for fifteen Nordic educators to Sri Lanka, the first of similar visits by teachers from industrialized countries to witness development in action.

Where the Nordic committees led, others soon followed. In Holland, in Italy, in France, in Canada, in the UK, and the US, the national Unicef committees began to try and take their message to the schools, particularly— as this was Unicef—to the classrooms of younger schoolchildren. Within and between committees, there was some debate about intentions and results. Was development education just a fancy name for information distributed at the time of a fundraising drive among children, like Trick or Treat in the US? Or was it pure education, untainted by any demand that children give their pocket money to the organization whose name was in the textbook or on the wall chart? Viewpoints differed. In France, a four-year experiment beginning in 1977 in seven schools was purely pedagogic: teachers and documentalists worked with pupils to create development education materials for the classroom. In Spain, a special ten-volume text-book series on the Rights of the Child was issued in collaboration with an educational publishing house and sent to 28,000 schools. Other committees which took up development education in its no-strings-attached form included the Dutch, the Belgian, the Swiss and the West German.

Not every committee was enthusiastic, and even Unicef's own information division was reluctant to make an unqualified commitment. Those who saw the principal goal of a Unicef committee as raising funds for children in developing countries had little time for development education unless it clocked up visible financial rewards. Others—the Italians, for example, under the leadership of a Napoleonic figure, Aldo Farina—rejected any dichotomy between fundraising and education; Farina was content with a less tangible currency—visibility for Unicef and its cause. A typical Farina coup was to persuade the organizers of the 1979 International Children's Book Fair in Bologna to mount it under the banner of IYC and give enormous publicity to Unicef. Interest snowballed throughout Italian schools. Farina's tactic was to make Unicef such a household word in Italy that whenever the plight of the disadvantaged child in a poor community came to the surface, it triggered an automatic association with Unicef. Farina's love of fairs, spectacles and public events exasperated more sedate Unicef officers. But in time his strategy paid off. In the early 1980s, in response to a campaign run by the Radical Party and supported through many channels, the Italian Government multiplied its overseas aid contribution dramatically, and became one of Unicef's most important donors. Farina's successful efforts at the grass roots helped to pave the way.

Most Unicef national committees capitalized heavily on IYC. The excitement generated by the Year gave many a 'second wind' along with their cause. For some, the Japanese for example, IYC raised the image of Unicef to a completely new level. During the first part of 1979, Mrs Sadako Ogata, then in the Japanese Foreign Ministry, was Chairman of the Unicef Executive Board, and in July, during the main week of celebrations for the Year, Harry Labouisse and his wife visited Japan to take part. In Japan, as in Italy, the IYC played a part in raising Unicef's profile not only among the public but in official circles. Indirectly, therefore, it opened up the possibility of the expanded resources for children's programmes from both voluntary and government sources—whether through Unicef or other conduits—that Labouisse had felt must be the benchmark of the Year's success.

When most of the IYC commissions closed down in the industrialized countries, the Unicef committees inherited their sponsors and supporters, a welcome infusion of fresh blood. As a result of the Year, these members of the Unicef family gained a boost to morale and income which helped them move forward into the next Development Decade with a renewed sense of partnership.

When the IYC speeches and celebrations were done, a more sober assessment awaited. At the beginning of 1979, the best estimates of child deprivation around the world suggested that fifteen million children born each year died unnecessarily before they reached their fifth birthday; that forty per cent of those who survived had been affected by some degree of malnutrition; four out of ten never went to school; seven out of ten were outside the reach of professional health care.

At the end of the IYC, in spite of all the activity, it could not be said that anything had happened to alter dramatically this overall picture. 'The International Year of the Child', wrote Labouisse, in a report issued at the end of 1979 on the situation of children in the developing world, 'was not intended to be a high point on the graph of our concern for children. It was meant to be a point of departure from which that graph would continue to rise'. Turning the rhetoric into programmes of lasting benefit for children was a more elusive goal, and there was a long and arduous way to go.

Unicef had hoped that the Year would give a fillip to basic services, that more governments would adopt this strategy as a means of reaching all their children with marked improvements in their lives. There were some positive indications. In March 1979, an IYC symposium hosted by Unicef's regional headquarters in Nairobi brought together ministers and senior representatives of eighteen eastern African countries, who had unanimously committed themselves to the basic-services approach. The phrases 'basic services' and 'community participation' were beginning to crop up all over the place, and a number of countries claimed to have reinforced or extended programmes during IYC which fell into the basic services category. During the debate in the General Assembly, the representatives of thirty countries stated that the provision of services for children was now an integral part of national economic and social policy.

Encouraging though these commitments were, at this stage they were mostly statements of intent. By its nature, development is a slow, evolutionary process, and any substantial restructuring of, for example, a country's health services into something resembling the primary health-care model could not be achieved quickly. Professional views change slowly. Annual budgets are many months in the making and national plans take years to prepare. The question at the end of the Year was whether the groundwork for action had been adequately laid, and whether mechanisms for carrying it forward were strong enough to survive the 31 December release of pressure.

Unicef was entrusted by the General Assembly with the inheritance of IYC. Grun and McDougall disbanded their staffs. Aldaba-Lim flew off on her last voyage as Special Representative. Canon Moerman put his mind to how the outpouring of interest from the NGO community during the Year could be sustained into the 1980s. The work of the NGO/IYC Committee was absorbed into Unicef's regular NGO Liaison Committee. Some of the IYC national commissions in developing countries remained in existence, while others handed over their functions to successor bodies. Although Unicef's mandate for the most disadvantaged children in the poorest societies remained essentially unchanged, the organization was now charged with providing a framework of advocacy on behalf of children everywhere, in the industrialized world as well as the developing world. One legacy was the heightened sense of the need to act as a spokesman for children and to keep as much information as possible moving down newly-sensitized channels. 'IYC follow-up' was a subject thoroughly examined at the 1980 Executive Board, and many well-intentioned pledges were made.

The fact was that IYC had run its course, and its momentum was by definition a temporary phenomenon. Some of its special publications lingered on, some of its networks continued, some of its research findings were circulated. But however hard its enthusiasts might plead that every year should be a year of the child, that kind of exuberant fellow-feeling linking groups with disparate interests and different energies could not be cultivated on a year-in, year-out basis. A Year is a year. Within Unicef, the information exchanges and referral services described as IYC follow-up spluttered half-heartedly into existence, and died for lack of sustenance. In Europe, under the regional directorship of Aida Gindy, a short-lived attempt was made to run a service for countries in the region seeking advice on programmes for children. It too withered for lack of serious interest and support. IYC was an event. It changed hearts and minds; it dented policies and programmes; it left a vital residue of goodwill both for children and for Unicef. But once it was over, it was over, and attention moved elsewhere.

When all the dust had settled, however, it was possible to detect some developments which emerged as IYC's direct result. Public and governmental awareness of the needs of children was much enhanced, as well as the knowledge of how to address these needs. Like the Year itself, this awareness grew out of the tenaciousness of certain nongovernmental organizations which took up the cudgels for certain themes. One such theme was the plight of children whose home and whose entire universe was encompassed by the streets of the expanding cities of the Third World.

During their own period of rapid industrialization, the cities of Europe and North America had similarly nurtured their scavenging 'waifs and strays', their street urchins, their gangs of miniature hooligans, abandoned by parents who could not or would not support them. The brutalizing hardship of their existence was familiar from the pages of Dickens, Hugo, and other nineteenth-century writers. The demands of survival could lead to crime, prostitution, violence and exploitation at the hands of the unscrupulous. In some European cities, in Marseilles and Naples for example, they could still be found, the human detritus of urban poverty, deprived of anything resembling normal childhood.

In the second half of the twentieth century, the process of rural exodus had wrought a transformation in the cities of the developing world, and it was accompanied by the uncontrolled growth of urban slums and shanty towns, hardship for most of the new city-dwellers, and the same breakdown of close-knit family life which the Western world had experienced a hundred years ago. In Bombay, Addis Ababa, Mexico City, Cairo and countless other cities, the children of the streets were such a familiar feature of the urban landscape that their presence and life-style was hardly a matter for comment. There were shoe-shine boys, parking boys, pathetic little beggars thrusting wizened limbs at passers-by, street-wise youngsters selling newspapers or chewing-gum through car windows, scruffy imps running errands in the market, *matatu* boys hanging precariously on the back of unlicensed taxis to collect customers and fares. The meteoric growth of the cities of Asia, Africa, and Latin America had propelled their populations of street children skywards.

Concerned individuals, voluntary organizations and government departments estimated that around seventy million children in the developing world fell under the broad definition of 'an irregular family situation', meaning that they lived wholly or virtually without parental support. Many helped to support their families, not by herding goats or gathering fuel as they would have in the rural areas, but by earning cash, casual work, running errands, petty trading, or straightforward theft. Forty million such children lived in Latin America where industrialization was more advanced than in most countries of Asia or Africa. This meant that one in five

Latin American and Caribbean youngsters lived in a state far from that of traditional dependency on family and kin. In Brazil, which harboured close to thirty million, around ten per cent were children whose living, eating, working, and sleeping place was the street, the market, the rubbish dump, the car park and the deserted building. The problem was enormous, and it was growing.

Rarely was it an overnight calamity which forced children—and they included girls as well as boys—into the mud and concrete jungle. A protracted civil war might add its quota of small parentless or abandoned people to the streets and alleyways of Managua or San Salvador. But the more remorseless pattern was one of economic, social and cultural upheaval. The cycle normally began with the family's departure from the countryside in search of a better livelihood in the city. There, the city's glittering promise was revealed in all its squalor: a tin and cardboard shack in a municipal wasteland, with no running water, no roads, pirated electricity, and an ever-present threat of neighbourhood violence. Any available regular work—usually petty trading or construction jobs—was bound to be far away in another part of town. In the new, exclusively money-based economic circumstances in which the family found itself, without familiar networks to sustain and support when times were bad, the effort to bring in enough money was horrendous. It often defeated the father, who might lapse into drunkenness or leave his wife and children to fend for themselves. Beyond the reach of the traditional sanctions which, in the countryside, required adults to obey the rules of marriage and meet their family responsibilities, values were destroyed and the bonds of kinship disintegrated.

An abandoned mother with several children to care for might resort to brewing illicit liquor and 'entertaining' men; her children would be sent off to work in a factory or in a kitchen, to scavenge, steal, pick up a few cents somehow or somewhere. 'Home' was a one-room shack with two beds for five or seven or ten people and only a ragged curtain between them for privacy. An unwanted child might easily decide to stop returning. Before long, he or she would lose contact, become a self-defender out among the bright lights and the money. Psychologically toughened and scarred, many took drugs to make the day seem nicer or the night less cold or the stomach less empty. In Brazil, it was estimated that three million children had reached the final point on the cycle, where they were completely without any kind of home or relative to care for them, open to exploitation by the most vicious elements of society.

At the beginning of 1981, Peter Tacon, a Canadian who had worked with street children in Latin America for ten years and was then working in postwar Nicaragua for the Canadian Save the Children Fund, joined Unicef's staff. He was assigned to travel throughout the Americas and examine existing programmes which helped the children of the streets and move them, not into penal or disciplinary institutions, but onto a track which opened up to them the possibility of lives as decent, contented, employed, law-abiding citizens while still living with their families, or with alternative family groups. By the end of the year, Tacon was in a position to make a proposal. The Brazilian Ministry of Social Assistance and Welfare had requested that Unicef share in the development of a two-year project in which the other partner was the government's National Child Welfare Foundation (FUNABEM), responsible for abandoned and delinquent children.

Brazil became the leading pioneer of humane solutions for its ragged outcasts. The 1982 session of the Executive Board agreed to the proposal that a regional advisory service be set up to research into, and exchange information about, the problems of street children in Latin America. Funds were provided by the Canadian Government and the Canadian Committee for Unicef. Tacon was assigned by Unicef to work closely with FUNABEM.

The project's underlying philosophy was that, no matter how beneficent its purpose, an institution was a solution of last resort for a child of the streets. The essence of the life lived on the street by children, whether they had chosen it or it had chosen them, was its freedom, its removal from a conventional framework of discipline. For children used to such an environment, a residential institution represented a prison where resistance to the rules of society which put him or her there would harden rather than diminish. FUNABEM started from a different perspective. They tried to intervene in the cycle of poverty and family disintegration which took the child onto the streets, before the link with the family snapped altogether and the child became truly abandoned. Their response therefore involved not only the children, but their families and communities as well. If the children retained a sense of belonging to a home and a neighbourhood, then they would not want to sever their connections. If they could, at the same time, continue to help their mothers to pay the rent and put food on the table, their families would feel no reserve about offering them the love and care they needed.

A growing number of Brazilian communities began to take up the challenge. One was the town of Cachoeira Paulista, a community of 30,000 inhabitants in the State of Sao Paulo. In 1983, a survey showed that one in four children in Cachoeira did not attend school because they were out earning to help support their families. The municipality set up kitchens in community centres to provide free meals twice a day for 1800 children between the ages of three and eighteen years.

The smallest children were looked after at preschools organized by volunteers given a short course. Sports and recreation were organized at the public schools for older children, who were also enrolled in workshops for weaving, ceramics, hand-painting on clothing, leatherwork and carpentry, and paid for their work. Orders for leather sandals and hand-made dolls helped make the programme economically viable. Odd jobs on the street, like shoe-shining, were organized so that children had their own regular stands with set prices and a cashier. Adolescents were offered work as municipal gardeners and cleaners. A group of monitors were employed to liaise with the parents, whose interest was aroused once the programme began. Community meetings examined the parents' own immediate problems and fostered neighbourhood solidarity. At the end of 1984, the town council estimated that the problem of its street children was close to being solved.

Colombia, Mexico and Ecuador were the first three countries to follow Brazil in a comprehensive examination of the problems of street children and try out on a systematic basis means other than institutionalization for turning their lives around. Unicef's regional advisory service found itself in much demand as town and city councils began to take up the problem all over the hemisphere. Many Latin American church and nongovernmental organizations have become increasingly active, and support has come from outside the region, particularly from the International Catholic Children's Bureau. In 1984, the Unicef Executive Board agreed to a further expansion of the programme.

The initiative taken by Latin America has been infectious. In Asia and Africa, the situation of street children in the Philippines, Thailand, Kenya, Mozambique, Sudan and Somalia is being actively studied, and new projects are coming forward.

Another group of children whose problems were widely aired during the IYC were those with disabilities: hearing, sight and speech impairments, physical and mental handicaps. Many children in the developing world were affected, as was painfully visible in any street or marketplace, where wasted limbs and sightlessness went with outstretched hands and begging bowls.

Once the days of postwar rehabilitation in Europe were passed, Unicef kept a distance from the disabled child. Their treatment, in which special kinds of surgery and rehabilitation were often needed, was expensive and normally available only in an urban institution. Homes for the mentally handicapped and special schools for the blind were too costly on a benefit per child basis to meet Unicef's criteria for assistance. Support for health and social care must be used in ways whereby the maximum number of children could be reached at relatively little cost per case. Tragic though wasted limbs and begging bowls might be, Unicef did not feel it could justify helping the few at the expense of the many. Until the health and nutritional status of the many improved, few developing countries could afford any large-scale conventional programme for the care of the disabled.

In the meantime, special care for special cases was regarded as a luxury best left to the specialist nongovernmental organizations.

Many of those organizations which had pioneered a revolution in attitudes and care towards the handicapped in the industrialized world were active in the developing countries. They and their national associates were beginning to realize that a different approach was needed to the problems of disability in poorer societies. In colonial times, good works in their nineteenth century image had been exported all over the world along with the Christian prayer book and other insignia of missionary devotion, and had left behind a sprinkling of special homes and institutions. At the very most they catered for only a tiny proportion of those in need. Many lived a precarious financial existence, dependent on charitable support from religious or other voluntary organizations overseas.

There were, too, reasons other than cost for questioning the relevance of institutions copied from the Western humanitarian example. Once admitted for a stay of any length in such a place, geographically distant and culturally alien from life at home, the child often became a complete stranger to his or her community, unable to re-integrate. Meanwhile, the opportunities for employment or for leading a reasonably normal life without the help of the extended family were almost nonexistent.

Organizations concerned with the disabled child therefore begn to look much more closely at disability prevention, and ways of helping the handicapped within their own homes and communities. Through its NGO Liaison Committee, Unicef had contacts with a number of these bodies, contacts which had occasionally flowered into co-operation. Sir John Wilson of the Royal Commonwealth Society for the Blind, whose representations in 1971 to Unicef and WHO on behalf of the World Council for the Welfare of the Blind had opened the way for their support to distribution of vitamin A as a blindness preventative, helped move the predicaments of all disabled groups a few degrees closer to Unicef's direct line of sight.

Certain MCH elements helped directly in the prevention of childhood disabilities: care for the mother during pregnancy and birth helped lower the chance of deformity in the foetus or the newborn; anti-leprosy and anti-trachoma campaigns, as well as immunization against polio, helped lower the rate of disabling disease; nutritional rehabilitation for the very young child helped prevent the irreversible effects of severe malnutrition. As the 1970s progressed, some people in Unicef had already begun to ask themselves whether there was something more Unicef could do for children with disabilities in the developing world. Jack Charnow, Secretary to the Board, had long been interested, and was aware of the progressive attitude of some of the NGOs at work in the field. An important push was given by the declaration by the UN General Assembly in 1976 of 1981 as an International Year for Disabled Persons. In 1978, as preparations for the IYDP began, the theme of 'full participation and equality' was established.

In 1979, Labouisse informed the Unicef Executive Board that he had commissioned a nongovernmental organization, Rehabilitation International, to undertake a special study of measures that might improve the quality of life for disabled children in parts of the world where the vast majority were outside the reach of any rehabilitative services. Norman Acton, Secretary-General of Rehabilitation International, an umbrella organization for those working directly with the disabled, had long been a close associate of Unicef. His Assistant Secretary-General, Susan Hammerman, played a central role in preparing the Unicef report.

For over a year, Rehabilitation International consulted with organizations all over the world. They also made field observations in various countries, including Bangladesh, Brazil, Jamaica, Mexico, the Philippines and Saudi Arabia. The critical characteristic of these visits was that, instead of spending their time in overcrowded and understaffed facilities for the disabled, Acton and Hammerman went to villages and urban slums to interview teachers, nurses, social workers—all those whose work brought them into regular contact with children. They sought out families with an impaired child or children and tried to find out what was happening in their lives. In case upon tragic case, by dint of gentle probing and careful persuasion, they found children unnecessarily banished from a family or community role because they carried the stigma of physical or mental impairment; an impairment which had become far more disabling than it would have been if a little knowledge and understanding could have taken the place of superstition and fear.

Rehabilitation International's report turned much of conventional wisdom on its head. First, the scale of the problem was far larger than many governments or international organizations had dared to contemplate: disability did not afflict a relatively small number of 'special cases'. Studies from different countries and regions showed that at least one in ten children was born with, or later developed, a physical, mental or sensory impairment. This meant, and the estimate was conservative, that of the world's 1·4 billion children, 140 million suffered from an impairment which could easily develop into a disability. Because of the deprived environment and parental ignorance which governed the fate of most impaired children born in the developing world, most of those who lived in poverty did become disabled. Thus, eighty per cent of disabled children were in the developing world.

The second important finding of the report was that special treatment for the handicapped was not the only nor the most important way of approaching the problem. Most impairments were not in themselves necessarily disabling. But if left unattended, or if their victim was kept isolated or over-protected, they could easily develop into serious handicaps. This happened far more often among the children in poor families than among those with more means and knowledge at their command. A child who had a minor defect of vision, for example, would, in an industrialized society, be given a pair of eye glasses and do as well in school as classmates with perfect sight. But in a village in Asia, that child might do poorly in school and drop out, and no-one might ever have realized why he or she was an uneducatable failure.

Similarly, a child with a partially defective limb would, in an industrialized society, be given special exercises to make the most of its muscles, and a caliper, so as to be able to move around and take part in all regular school activities. In a poor family in Asia or Africa, the limb was more likely to waste altogether from neglect and disuse, and the child become completely immobilized.

During their investigations, Acton and Hammerman discovered case upon case where a child with an impairment had been confined at home, sometimes out of sight, and kept away from school, play, visits to the health clinic, preschool learning, or supplementary feeding programmes. These reactions had interfered with normal growth in ways far more damaging than the original defect. Age-old fears prevented impaired children from receiving their fair share of mental, physical and emotional stimuli, while only their better-endowed brothers and sisters were taken to the health clinic, received vaccination shots, or went to school.

If families reacted harmfully to their child's affliction, most health and educational services were doing no better. Superstition, distaste or simple avoidance was pervasive among teachers, health-care workers and government officials. The impaired child, like the street child, was treated as a burden and an outcast, relegated to society's scrap-heap. Yet there were many ways well within the means of an existing network of basic services and its community volunteers which could brighten the prospects for the impaired child. With a little extra training, primary health-care workers could be taught to recognize the failure of a child to walk, talk or react to stimuli at the normal time in early life, and help a mother compensate for her child's disadvantage. Simple exercises could help a child's motor reflexes. Special feeding might prevent the loss of sight or stimulate physical and mental growth. Precautions could be taken to avoid accidents in the home without having to tie down an epileptic child or confine him or her in ways which restricted other sensory or motor learning. These ideas, which brought care for the child with an impairment out of the ghetto and incorporated it into existing health and educational services, were fundamentally different from the view which held that the child must be plucked from his or her normal environment and placed in a special institution.

This new strategy for the care of children with disabilities was presented to Unicef's Executive Board by Rehabilitation International in May 1980. Like the strategy for basic services, it was based upon a handful of pioneering experiments in various developing countries whose common threads were woven into a policy with widespread applicability. One of the pioneers who had proved that services for the impaired child did not have to be exorbitantly expensive was a Jamaican pathologist, Dr Molly Thorburn. In 1975, the Jamaica Council for the Handicapped started an early stimulation project for impaired children in Kingston. Thorburn set out to disprove the common conceptions that such children inevitably grow into dependent, non-productive adults and that their education can only be carried out by specialists.

Taking the community health aide as her model, she believed that women with a little education and a mature and understanding personality could be trained to carry out a home-teaching programme. Using a precision method which divided the process of child development from birth to six years old into small sequential steps, Thorburn trained her first batch of child development aides from candidates currently sweeping the streets in a government scheme for the unemployed. Each aide made regular weekly visits to the homes of around twelve children, working with the mother or grandmother and using simple toys and games to stimulate the child. Tests carried out two years after the project began showed that mildly and moderately impaired children had gained almost as many skills as a normal child would have done over the same period. Costs averaged only $151 per child per year: a very modest amount compared with residential and specialized care. The mothers in the programme were so encouraged by their children's progress that their own morale had radically improved.

The Jamaican example of an alternative approach to dealing with disabilities was one of as yet a bare handful in different developing countries. By 1980, a similar programme was underway in the Philippines with Unicef support, as were others in Panama, postwar Nicaragua and rural Mexico. All were still on a very small scale. The challenge, as expressed by Susan Hammerman, was to transform rehabilitation for the disabled child into a movement: 'many miracles for the few' must become 'few miracles for the many'.

The Rehabilitation International report to Unicef was a model of progressive wisdom, and its recommendations were regarded as a breakthrough. WHO joined the endorsement, and the Joint Committee on Health Policy discussed ways in which the two organizations could together promote its suggestions. Rehabilitation International continued their close association with Unicef as advisers on new initiatives for the prevention and early detection of childhood disabilities. Public awareness about the problems of the disabled, particularly their determination to overcome prejudice and minority status, was given a perceptible nudge during the International Year of Disabled Persons, 1981. But it will take many years, perhaps decades, before attitudes and practices towards the impaired child radically change throughout the world. The general extension of primary health care will make an important difference. Little by little, curricula in medical, social, and educational training programmes will be adjusted to include the range of simple measures which can prevent impairment deteriorating into disability and handicap. Like so many other issues allied to the business of social and economic development, these changes will probably take place by almost imperceptible degrees. But when reckonings come to be made, the approach first articulated by Rehabilitation International for Unicef, in the wake of the Year of the Child, will be seen as a turning point.

The celebration of the International Year of the Child left one other important legacy. In February 1978, the Polish Government submitted to the UN Commission on Human Rights a proposed text for a Convention on the Rights of the Child with a view to its adoption during 1979. Their text was based on the 1959 Declaration of the Rights of the Child, transformed into legal provisos. Canon Moerman, addressing the Commission, asked for a postponement of its consideration. While the observance of the rights of the child left much to be desired in many countries, he believed that changes in international law could not be rushed. A Declaration was a statement of principles, whereas a Convention was a legal instrument binding on any government which signed it. Its text, therefore, must be radically different. He suggested to the Commission that the IYC might throw up new insights into the nature of children's rights, and that discussions held during its course might pave the way for subsequent work.

At the end of 1978, the UN General Assembly decided that a working group within the Human Rights Commission in Geneva should be set up to draft a Convention, but that it should not be subject to any time limit for submitting the results of its deliberations. By implication, this might become a forceful tool, or it might become a symbolic gesture, depending on the attitude of the governments participating. The working group first met during 1979.

During IYC, many national commissions used the Declaration of the Rights of the Child as a main theme of educational campaigns. Many people became aware for the first time that children were so widely exploited in the labour force, and that the Declaration provided such flimsy protection against this and other forms of child abuse. Once the issue was raised, it did not lightly go away. But rights are an exceptionally tricky cause to handle, and not a cause that is easy to take up with inter-governmental mechanisms. Encouraging governments to meet children's needs by providing services is one thing; demanding that they respect children's rights and be legally held to account for any infringement is quite another. The first requires some tactful criticism of economic and social policy, and constructive suggestions for change in which programmes

Water supply
projects sparked
home-gardening
activities. Here in
Keur Momar Sarr,
Senegal, a women's
co-operative collects
water to cultivate
their home-grown
produce.
(*Unicef/Murray-Lee*)

The year 1981 was
the UN-proclaimed
International Year of
Disabled Persons.
The Year gave
special attention to
the prevention and
rehabilitation of
childhood disability.
(*Unicef/Solmssen*)

The problem of abandoned children living on the streets is acute in San Paolo, Brazil. These two had been living under this motorway bridge for five years before a Unicef-assisted programme reached them. (*Unicef/Edinger*)

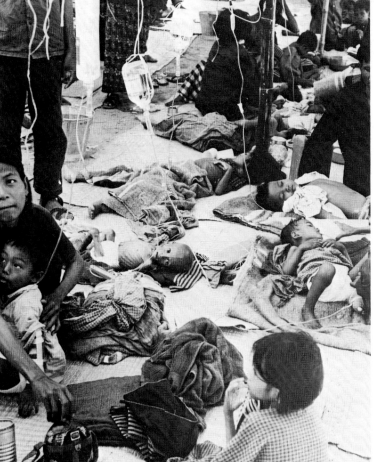

Opposite:
Part of the international effort to assist drought-stricken countries in Africa: Unicef's Goodwill Ambassador Liv Ullmann visiting the Sahel region to increase public interest in malnourished children. (*Unicef/Danois*)

Thailand 1979: the special malnutrition ward at a camp for Kampuchean refugees. Many small children arrived in a state of chronic hunger and disease. (*Unicef/Danois*)

Unicef's Executive Director James P. Grant at a refugee camp on the Thai/Kampuchean border. (*Unicef/Danois*)

The exploding shanty-towns of Third World cities: an open sewer is all there is for drainage in this densely-populated slum in Visakhapetnam, India. (*Unicef/Sprague*)

of international co-operation can play a part. The second treads on much more dangerous ground. Whatever Unicef might morally feel, it was not anxious to take up issues which might thrust it into the political arena, hamper its good relations with governments, and thereby undermine its chances of influencing and assisting health and educational programmes for children.

In February 1980, the Polish Government submitted a revised version of their original text to the Human Rights working group. Now the group began work in earnest, using this draft as their working document. It became clear that the issue of children's rights was not going to evaporate now that the IYC was over; the nongovernmental organizations were not willing to let the matter drop. During the IYC, under the chairmanship of Canon Moerman, they formed an umbrella organization, Defence for Children International, to maintain pressure at the international level on issues of children's rights. DCI began to build up a membership among organizations around the world and developed its own international programme, commissioning studies on child labour, sexual exploitation of children, abandoned children, children in adult prisons, and children caught up in the turmoil of war. It also provided a vehicle for co-ordinating the nongovernmental input into the Convention on the Rights of the Child, nudging and pushing its elaboration forward within the official international establishment.

Unicef, which had kept in the background when the original Declaration was drafted twenty years before, started by taking a back seat. But the tide of opinion began to flow too strongly to resist. Not only the Polish Government but others including the Canadian and the Swedish, were beginning to express active interest. By 1983, it began to seem as though there was enough genuine commitment to ensure that obstacles would be navigated rather than allowed to bog the process down. Within the Human Rights Commission, governments were making strenuous efforts to avoid ideological confrontation on the eternally difficult question of how far, and at what point, the machinery of the State should intervene in family affairs on behalf of a child at risk. Children were once more playing their one political card: their innocence of the political divide. It might take some years, but a Convention was in the offing. Such were the signals when the NGOs asked Unicef to take a more active part in the steps leading to the drafting and ratification of the Convention.

Unicef took up the challenge. In April 1983, Nils Thedin, delegate of Sweden and senior statesman on behalf of children, raised at the Executive Board an issue which had inspired in him a lifelong commitment ever since he witnessed the suffering of children during the Spanish Civil War. He proposed what sounded like an old man's dream: that children be declared 'a neutral, conflict-free zone in human relations'.

In a violent world, a world in which military strife and conflict increasingly invaded civilian life, children should be internationally protected — in their homes, in institutions, in the provision of health care, food, shelter and basic services. To Thedin, as to Moerman, and increasingly to others, it was no longer possible to draw a dividing line between meeting children's needs and protecting children's rights. The care and nurture of children, the humanitarian cause to which Unicef's existence had been devoted, could not stop short at measures to improve children's health and well-being.

The UN has always upheld that rights in the civil and political sphere, and those in the economic and social sphere, are equal, indivisible and interdependent. In the case of children, economic and social rights may provide a path to those in the civil sphere, rather than, as in the case of nations, the other way around. The 1984 Unicef Executive Board commissioned a study on children in specially difficult circumstances, a euphemism for the range of sensitive subjects which include victims of labour exploitation, abandonment, sexual abuse and conflict.

Unicef also began to put its weight behind the drafting of the Convention on the Rights of the Child. It is more than possible that, by the end of the decade, a Magna Carta for children will have passed into international law. Whether it does reach final draft and ratification, and whether governments all over the world genuinely try to abide by it, is a barometer of Mankind's aspirations for its children, and a minor test of twentieth century civilization.

Main sources

Unicef: 'International Year of the Child 1979 in Perspective', report prepared by Joan Bel Geddes, September 1981.

Unicef Executive Board: proposal for an International Year of the Child; note by the International Catholic Child Bureau and the International Union of Child Welfare, January 1975; proposal for an International Year of the Child; note by the Executive Director, March 1975; reports of the Unicef Executive Board, May 1975, May 1976; progress reports of the Executive Director, 1975–79.

Interview with Canon Joseph Moerman of the International Catholic Child Bureau conducted for the Unicef History Project by Edward B. Marks, October 1983; other interviews for the Unicef History Project, notes and memoranda of staff members and other principals.

Carnets de l'Enfance/Assignment Children: 'IYC a New Focus on Policies and Children', issue 47/48, Autumn 1978; 'The Disabled Child: A New Approach to Prevention and Rehabilitation'; issue 53/54, Spring 1981; *Unicef News:* issue 94/1977/4: 'Education in a Changing World', issue 97/1978/3: 'International Year of the Child 1979', issue 102/1979/4: 'IYC: End or Beginning?', issue 105/1980/3: 'Exceptional Children'.

Memorandum to national IYC commissions, national Unicef committees, Unicef field offices and NGOs on the IYC debate in the UN General Assembly, 15–18 October 1979, prepared by the Unicef Information Division, New York.

'Development Education in Unicef', by Jeanne Vickers; Unicef History Series, monograph I, April 1986.

'A Historical Perspective on National Committees for Unicef in Europe', by Doris Phillips, Unicef History Series, monograph II, May 1986.

'The Situation of Children in the Developing World', a report for Unicef at the conclusion of the International Year of the Child by Peter Adamson, Unicef Consultant, with a foreword by Henry R. Labouisse, Executive Director.

'My Child Now! An Action Plan on Behalf of Children without Families', by Peter Tacon, policy specialist for Unicef, 23 September 1981.

Unicef Executive Board: 'Childhood Disability: Its Prevention and Rehabilitation', report of Rehabilitation International to the Executive Board of Unicef, March 1980; other programme recommendations and special reports on programmes for alleviating childhood disabilities and for abandoned children, 1981–85.

'Children in Situations of Armed Conflicts; Exploitation of Working Children and Street Children', reports presented to the Unicef Executive Board, 1986.

Chapter 16

The Crisis in Kampuchea

The turmoil in Indo-China in the generation after the second World War was the most protractedly painful of all the post-colonial disentanglements. To the world at large, the high point of the South-East Asian drama was reached with the build-up and engagement of US military forces in Vietnam, and their subsequent withdrawal from the peninsula. But for the humanitarian organizations, the ultimate challenge came with the crisis which consumed Kampuchea during 1979 and 1980.

Many believed that a long train of nightmarish events had brought an entire nation to the brink of extinction, and that only a massive international rescue operation had any hope of saving it. The scale of the emergency was not the largest to date: more people were affected in Bangladesh following the civil war and natural calamities of the early 1970s, as during the long years of African drought. But in degree, the crisis in Kampuchea was more intense, a black hole among emergencies, terrible in its unfathomable currents. By the natural law of humanitarian relief, the more acute the human needs and the more tangled their political context, the more difficult the task of emergency assistance, and the more subject to error and public criticism. From the crisis in Kampuchea, nobody emerged unscathed.

On 7 January 1979, the Vietnamese Army entered Phnom Penh, the capital of Democratic Kampuchea, and overthrew the Khmer Rouge. The Khmer Rouge, under Pol Pot, had been in power since April 1975 and, over the course of nearly four years, they had carried out a ruthless revolutionary experiment. Within days of their victory they had emptied the cities at gunpoint, including the hospitals whose most severely-ill patients were propelled onto the streets in their beds. They had then proceeded to dismantle the country's intellectual and administrative structure; outlaw religious worship and all kinds of learning; abolish money; and force every man, woman, and child to live under a rigid system of collective farming. The most trivial infringement of the rules—wearing eye glasses, reading a book, eating at the wrong time of day—was subject to fearful punishment, even death.

Only a few outsiders were invited to witness the 'new miracle' of Democratic Kampuchea. The interpretation of their accounts and the contrasting

378

stories of refugees fleeing to Thailand fell victim to the ideological polarization which afflicted all viewpoints on events in the peninsula. Until the Khmer Rouge fell in January 1979, the full dimensions of their experiment had been largely a matter of conjecture in the rest of the world. As the scale of the atrocities suffered by the Kampuchean people was gradually revealed after the Vietnamese invasion, no-one could question that liberation had been necessary. But the Kampucheans' misfortune was that their liberator was their own traditional enemy, as well as one feared and disliked by many countries in Asia, and distrusted by their Western allies. The exodus of boat people from Vietnam was reaching its peak at this time, and international tempers had been inflamed by their treatment. Attitudes towards Vietnam's new client regime in Phnom Penh were sharply divided along the East-West axis, with the result that the People's Republic of Kampuchea, headed by Heng Samrin, failed to gain recognition as the country's legitimate authority by a majority of UN member States.

While Western diplomatic circles tied themselves in knots between revulsion against the Khmer Rouge and condemnation of Vietnamese aggression, the people in Kampuchea awoke as if from a long and hideous dream. During the first months of 1979, the agricultural camps were disbanded and people began to criss-cross the country, coming out of hiding, returning to their villages, looking for family members whom they had lost. Meanwhile, the Khmer Rouge forces retreated towards the border with Thailand and fighting continued in the north-west.

Kampucheans trapped by the continuing warfare, whatever their sympathies, began to flee across the Thai border, or to take refuge in makeshift camps nearby. The two dimensions of the Kampuchean crisis were beginning to crystallize. The number of Kampuchean refugees seeking sanctuary in or close to Thailand was growing, and their fate was inextricably tangled with Khmer Rouge action against the Vietnamese from bases near the Thai border. Within Kampuchea, a people was emerging from collective trauma, trying to piece together lives and families shattered by the Khmer Rouge, and a skeletal People's Revolutionary Council was trying to impose some kind of order. The Khmer Rouge had described 1975 as 'year zero'. Four years later, another 'year zero' had dawned.

Help from outside was essential. But since the rest of the world was antipathetic towards the Phnom Penh regime, it relied exclusively on the Vietnamese and their Socialist allies. In January 1979, the International Committee of the Red Cross (ICRC) and Unicef both began offering aid to Kampuchea, through their offices in Hanoi. These two organizations formed the natural vanguard of international humanitarian assistance in a situation enmeshed in political complications, as they had previously done during the Nigerian civil war and in other crises. Their respective mandates, and established precedent, exonerated them from taking factors other than human need into consideration. The UN itself and most of its system of agencies was inhibited by the principle that the normal procedure is for a member State to request their assistance. In the case of Kampuchea, the member State was Democratic Kampuchea under the Khmer Rouge and Pol Pot, not the new People's Republic under Heng Samrin.

The months went by and neither the ICRC nor Unicef received any positive reply from the Heng Samrin authorities. By May 1979, the handful of journalists and diplomats allowed to visit Kampuchea began to raise fears of impending famine. The tremendous dislocation of people in the early months of the year had coincided with the premonsoon and early monsoon planting season. Millions of acres of rice paddies had been left unplanted at a time when planting should be far advanced. Estimates of the probable consequences on the 1979 crop were pure guesswork. If anything resembling a survey had been undertaken, no-one in the international aid community was aware of it. Anxieties began to mount.

In May, Unicef held its annual Executive Board session in Mexico City. It decided to lend its support to the current ICRC attempt to send a survey mission to Kampuchea, and set up a special fund for a joint emergency programme. Labouisse instructed his representative in Hanoi, Bertram Collins, to step up his overtures to the Vietnamese to gain permission for a Unicef visit. In early July, the authorities in Phnom Penh at last asked for help from the UN. They wanted food for more than two million people—half the remaining population—who, they said, were threatened by famine. At the same time, word finally came from the Kampuchean ambassador in Hanoi that a representative from both Unicef and the ICRC would be welcomed in Phnom Penh. The two men selected by their respective chiefs were Jacques Beaumont from Unicef, a Frenchman with an astute grasp of political sensitivities and extensive relief experience in Indo-China, and François Bugnion, a lawyer and longtime ICRC delegate. Aware of the damage publicity could cause to such a tricky endeavour, Labouisse imposed complete discretion about the mission to Kampuchea. No announcement should be made; only those who had to be—UN Secretary-General Kurt Waldheim, for example—would be kept informed.

On 17 July, Beaumont and Bugnion flew to Phnom Penh from Ho Chi Minh City with suitcases full of medicines and visas valid for two days only. In the forty-eight hours allowed them by the Heng Samrin authorities, they had to try and assess the needs of a destitute country, and negotiate with a tiny handful of suspicious and inexperienced officials a relief operation more intricate, more wide-ranging and potentially larger than anything ever before undertaken. On their visit, a great deal depended.

Labouisse and his senior staff had experience in the delicate manoeuvres required to open doors to Unicef assistance in Communist Indo-China. At the 1967 Executive Board session, Dr Mande, the delegate of France, had raised the question of assistance to both parts of Vietnam, North as well as South. For many years up to this time the Board had routinely agreed to support maternity care, tuberculosis control and other typical Unicef-assisted projects in the South. The first allocations dated from 1952, when it had been intended that aid for children's hospitals would reach provinces throughout Vietnam. But after the country was 'temporarily' partitioned by the Geneva Accords in 1954, it had proved impracticable to extend help to the North. President Ho Chi Minh's regime in Hanoi was not recognized by the UN and he sought no relationship with any part of a body he regarded as a creature of the Western alliance.

During the late 1950s and early 1960s, Unicef continued to deliver maternity kits, BCG vaccines, dried milk powder, school books and furniture to the Government in Saigon, where their use was overseen by one of Sam Keeny's key lieutenants, Margaret Gaan. Difficult as it was to ignore the erupting turmoil, Gaan tried always to stress the longterm nature of whatever assistance was offered, to ensure that midwives were trained, paediatric wards equipped, and newborn babies visited in the villages whatever was going on politically and militarily. Up till 1965, Unicef spent more than $1·5 million on these programmes. But war increasingly intruded, disrupting health services and drawing medical staff away. From 1964, when the scale of the war accelerated sharply, Unicef also gave help for children who had been wounded, orphaned or abandoned. By 1967, it was no longer possible to pretend that the emergency was simply a background noise.

American bombing of North Vietnam began in February 1965. The theatre of military engagement had been extended, with all its international consequences. For Unicef, the critical aspect was that children were now suffering the direct effects of war in the North as well as in the South. Apart from questions of need, there were also the inevitable political ramifications, from which no humanitarian démarche in Indo-China was immune. A large proportion of Unicef's resources came from the US and its Executive Director was a US citizen. If Unicef failed to be even-handed towards all the children of Vietnam, it risked accusation of partiality. Senior delegates to the Executive Board from countries who disapproved of the war's escalation, notably Robert Mande of France and Nils Thedin of Sweden, were privately beginning to express anxiety to Labouisse; others who backed the North Vietnamese were unlikely to tolerate continued assistance to the children of one side only. Labouisse was deeply concerned to uphold the principle of non-discrimination and give humanitarian relief wherever it was needed. But there was a problem: the North Vietnamese had not requested help. Nor did they seem likely to do so. They did not believe that the UN was an impartial body and were in no hurry to become a supplicant for anything it offered.

For any UN organization, including Unicef, to send relief to any country there normally has to be an invitation from the government, or at least a nod in its direction. To send help to a country that does not want it can be interpreted as interference in its sovereign affairs. Principles aside, no agreement to the receipt of relief supplies means no consignee for their delivery nor any guarantee as to whether they will be distributed or to whom. In the case of North Vietnam, Unicef might have used the North Vietnamese Red Cross Society through the League of Red Cross Societies as a third party; but Hanoi's attitude towards the international nongovernmental establishment seemed no more favourable than towards the intergovernmental. Neither the League nor the International Committee of the Red Cross had been asked for relief; as a channel for Unicef supplies they too were inoperative.

Somehow, a way must be found to penetrate the psychological armour of the North Vietnamese. Early in 1967, Labouisse talked with the ICRC and the League, both trying to open a route to Hanoi. He hoped that if either was successful, Unicef supplies could go in on Red Cross coat tails. When they made no progress, Labouisse realized that an independent Unicef initiative should be tried.

When Dr Mande proposed in the Executive Board that Unicef should find a way of helping children in both theatres of the war, the way was officially cleared for Labouisse to take the first steps. The move also helped to pre-empt a political row in the Board over aid proposed for Saigon. Although the projects in the South to which approval was being sought were described as longterm—mere extensions of existing programmes—it took no great insight to realize that the reason they were being extended yet again was that war was constantly wrecking their progress. The USSR was outspokenly opposed to further aid, and the Polish delegate, Dr Boguslaw Kozusznik, had 'serious doubts'.

In this question of opening up Unicef contacts with North Vietnam, the role of the Executive Board was critical. The senior statesmen—Nils Thedin, Robert Mande, Senator Avocato Montini of Italy and Hans Conzett of Switzerland—knew how to raise highly controversial issues in a noncontroversial way. They and their predecessors had made it an unwritten rule of Executive Board proceedings that to introduce comments of a political nature was a shameful breach of etiquette.

In 1967, no subject generated more international heat than the war in Vietnam. Yet the discussion of Mande's proposal in the Unicef Board was almost serene. Even the US expressed cautious interest. The outcome was that Labouisse was instructed to 'study ways and means whereby the help of Unicef could be extended with the co-operation of Red Cross organizations, in emergency situations, to both parts of Vietnam'. Without this clear sanction from the Board, he would not have been able to proceed.

Labouisse's first step was to send an aide-memoire to the North Vietnamese authorities, suggesting that the Red Cross might help deliver Unicef assistance. He received no answer. At the end of the year, his diplomatic antennae picked up signals that the North Vietnamese were willing to discuss the idea. Charles Egger went to Paris in January 1968 and held discussions at the North Vietnamese mission. Another aide-memoire was sent. More silence. And there, for the time being, efforts stalled.

By the time the next Board session came round, the fortunes of the war in Vietnam had changed. In late January 1968, communist forces in the South mounted the Tet offensive. The ferocity of the fighting and its mounting unpopularity in the US were gradually pushing the combatants towards the conference table. By now Unicef's representative in Saigon, Bernard Klausener, was devoting all his energies to emergency relief. In the even more highly-charged political atmosphere, Labouisse brought Klausener to New York to present to the Executive Board a reassuring description of Unicef's work. Thousands of children were daily receiving milk from kitchens set up in and around Saigon by government social workers and Red Cross committees. Some Board members protested: not at the feeding of children, but that some of the supplies were being handed over to government authorities rather than to the Red Cross. More contentious yet was the fact that no progress had been made in arranging for aid to be sent to the North.

Since the Tet offensive, US bombardment of the North had reached a new intensity and suffering was thought to be acute. Certain delegates wanted to push Unicef into sending relief supplies to the Democratic Republic of Vietnam without the formal invitation and plan for distribution stipulated as a precondition. An important principle was at stake: if normal procedures were to be waived in one set of circumstances, they might have to be waived in others. At this time, Labouisse was equally embroiled in diplomatic manoeuvres to provide help to the victims of the Nigerian civil war. Without the most strict adhesion to regular practice, the ability of Unicef to give emergency relief according to its mandate could be permanently compromised. After a long wrangle in which draft resolutions and amendments poured down like confetti, the Board agreed to a compromise which essentially repeated the *status quo* — to study ways and means to send aid to both sides — established the year before. Dr Boguslaw Kozusznik, the Polish delegate, was one of those who did not feel that enough was being done to open up the channels for sending aid to North Vietnam. Along with some others, he abstained.

As a result of this debate, the seeds of a new manoeuvre were planted. Poland had shown itself determined that Unicef assistance reach North Vietnam; Kozusznik himself, through friendly contacts between the Socialist countries, might be able to obtain the necessary agreement by visiting Hanoi. Labouisse enthusiastically encouraged this proposal; but it took time. Hanoi's invitation to Kozusznik finally arrived the following spring. In May 1969, the Secretary-General of the League of Red Cross Societies visited Hanoi and arranged with local officials of the Red Cross Society to send in drugs and medical supplies. Kozusznik's visit followed shortly afterwards. He thereby took the first concrete step towards an agreement between the Hanoi authorities and Unicef, but his report was couched in terms which did not assuage US ambivalence about the idea of Unicef aid to North Vietnam. With suspicion still dominating the attitudes of both sides, the process of agreement was still far from complete. In the meantime, Unicef provided some assistance to the North through the channels set up by the Red Cross. Special contributions of $200,000 from the Netherlands and Switzerland were used. On Kozusznik's recommendation, the money was spent on cloth for children's clothing. It was a gesture, but it was something.

Throughout this period, peace negotiations were dragging on in Paris. In late 1972, it finally began to seem as though, in Kissinger's phrase, peace was at hand. Early in 1973, agreement was reached and a cease-fire declared. Within the UN, discussions began about a possible joint programme of Indo-Chinese rehabilitation, along the lines of that headed by Sir Robert Jackson in postwar Bangladesh. Labouisse then set up a special headquarters staff group for Indo-China whose task was to analyze the needs of children in all parts of the peninsula and start new initiatives. It was a particular response to a particular, and very sensitive, situation. The withdrawal of US troops from South Vietnam—the principal outcome of the Paris Agreement—did not at all mean that peace had arrived. The war had merely been handed back to its Indo-Chinese protagonists.

By now both Laos and Kampuchea were engulfed in their own offshoots of the Vietnamese turmoil. In his quietly unshakeable way, and in the knowledge that he would provoke great disapproval from the US, Labouisse reaffirmed the principle that Unicef aid was available to any administration, legally-constituted or otherwise, that wanted to do something for children in whatever territory it controlled. At the head of his Indo-China Peninsula Liaison Group, he placed a longtime career officer, Martin Sandberg, a Norwegian who had just concluded a tour as his representative in Indonesia. Jacques Beaumont of France was his deputy. In all its aspects—negotiating, estimating needs, drawing up programmes, public information (or non-information), fund raising—the group operated along special lines and reported direct to Labouisse. Dick Heyward and Charles Egger were also closely involved.

Discretion was vital. The first task was to try and find ways to provide assistance for children in all areas; this entailed making contact with groups occupying and administering territory not under government control: the Pathet Lao in Laos; the Khmer Rouge in what was then still Cambodia; and the Provisional Revolutionary Government (PRG) of South Vietnam. The conduit to all of these, and the most important administration in its own right, was the Government of the Democratic Republic of Vietnam.

A series of diplomatic moves were made in Paris and in Stockholm. In due course, Hanoi reacted.

At the end of June 1973, Sandberg and Beaumont flew to North Vietnam. For both men, to be the first UN officials ever to be received in Hanoi was an unforgettable experience. They explained how Unicef worked and tried to win the confidence of officials. These were introduced as members of the North Vietnam Red Cross; but they were also officials of various ministries. Negotiations opened with the presentation to Unicef of a shopping list of medical items. Treading carefully, Sandberg and Beaumont began to question the rationale behind the request: they wanted to show that Unicef expected to be brought into a discussion about the nature of programmes and not simply treated as a source of free imported goods. It was to take some years before this aspect of the Unicef *modus operandi* was fully appreciated. A list of emergency supplies was agreed, and the two Unicef officials flew back to New York with a tremendous sense of achievement. It was a breakthrough. After six years of treading on eggshells, Unicef had finally managed to open up a direct channel of aid to the children of North Vietnam.

Over the course of the next two years, Unicef gradually expanded its Indo-Chinese programme. The 1973 Executive Board agreed to expenditures of up to $30 million over two years, and the 1974 Executive Board raised the figure to $44 million to the end of 1975. Most of the resources were provided by special contributions; Federal Republic of Germany, Norway and Denmark were the most generous donors. The Board also committed some of Unicef's regular income, over the protest of the US, which tried to prevent any of its contribution going to children in North Vietnam. Until 1975, almost all Unicef aid went to education; many primary schools had been destroyed or damaged by bombardment. Jacques Beaumont paid periodic visits to Hanoi to check on progress, and he also opened up contacts there with representatives of the South Vietnamese PRG and the Khmer Rouge.

In Laos, although the situation remained unstable, programmes with some long-lasting benefit began to inch forward following the cease-fire negotiated in January 1973. A Unicef office was set up in Vientiane in September 1973. The following April, when a provisional government divided the country into two zones administered respectively by the Royal Lao Government and the Pathet Lao, Unicef was able to maintain working relationships with both sides and channel some assistance to both parts of the country. Local hospitals and maternal and child-health centres were reconstructed, and well-drilling and classroom repairs began.

The end of the war in Vietnam finally brought to a conclusion the long struggle for ascendancy in Laos. The country was reunified, the monarchy abolished, and the Lao Democratic Republic declared in December 1975. When a longterm plan for the development of health and education services throughout the country was prepared early in 1976, Unicef was poised to offer substantial assistance.

In South Vietnam and Cambodia, reasonable progress was sustained during 1973 and most of 1974. The Cambodian Government, first under Prince Sihanouk and later under Lon Nol, welcomed Unicef assistance. A Unicef office opened in Phnom Penh in November 1973 under Paul Ignatieff, a young Canadian; the Saigon office expanded under the leadership of Ralph Eckert, a Swiss national of long-standing Unicef experience. Amidst all the insecurity of ongoing warfare, efforts still went on to build classrooms, train teachers, organize kindergartens, run immunization campaigns and provide rehabilitation for wounded children. Some help was given to areas under the respective control of the Khmer Rouge opposition in Cambodia and the Provisional Revolutionary Government in South Vietnam, through their offices in Hanoi. But most went through 'normal' channels: the internationally-recognized governments clinging to control over shrinking territory.

At the end of 1974, hostilities began to intensify once again. In spring 1975 the North Vietnamese began their final offensive towards Saigon; simultaneously, the Khmer Rouge were driving towards Phnom Penh. In what had become a familiar and agonizing pattern, programmes originally designed to help restore permanent services for children ground to a halt and relief was hastily substituted. As the gunfire drew closer and closer, immediate needs for food and shelter for families desperately fleeing the countryside for the safety of the cities were all that counted.

At Unicef headquarters, the Indo-China Group assumed that sooner rather than later the fighting would cease, and programmes of rehabilitation would be needed. Contacts with the expected victors in both countries were already favourably established and aid had already been accepted by them. Sandberg and his colleagues estimated that up to $50 million would be needed for Unicef's part in the postwar rehabilitation in Cambodia and South Vietnam. In the uncertainty of events, they tried to make whatever preparations were practicable.

April 1975 saw the war come to its bitter conclusion, first in Phnom Penh and then in Saigon. Throughout the final weeks, Unicef stepped up emergency aid with airlifts of shelter materials, children's food and blankets, and medical supplies from stocks held at its main warehouse in Copenhagen and others in Bangkok and Singapore. On the ground, its staff worked with Red Cross medical teams and the UN High Commissioner for Refugees. UN Secretary-General Waldheim, responding to desperate appeals from Saigon, made an appeal for international aid to be channelled through Unicef and UNHCR. On 17 April, he announced that he had set up a special UN fund for Indo-Chinese relief under Sir Robert Jackson, who would co-ordinate the emergency programme for the whole UN system. When the North Vietnamese streamed into Saigon at the end of April, air access was suspended and all international aid came temporarily to a halt. Ralph Eckert, Unicef's representative in Saigon, stayed on in the hope of working out a rehabilitation programme with the new authorities. He waited in vain. A few weeks later the PRG asked him to close the office. All aid for the South would now be channelled through Hanoi.

The final victory of the Communist forces in the peninsula meant a re-arrangement of Unicef's activities. Previously there had been 'the Indo-Chinese emergency', in which *ad hoc* arrangements, mostly for emergency relief, were made from day-to-day with whomsoever was in control in a given area. Now this loosely-knit programme for an entire region must give way to a set of regular country programmes. Given the decisive political reorientation, the critical theatre of operations was now in North Vietnam. Building on the good relations established by Beaumont, Sandberg and the existing programmes of Unicef assistance, Labouisse managed to obtain the agreement of the North Vietnamese to a permanent Unicef set-up in Hanoi.

The 'Unicef mission'—a room in the hotel inhabited by the handful of foreign missions and delegations in Hanoi, with no separate telephone, vehicle or any office facilities—was opened in April just before hostilities ceased. Dr François Rémy, a Frenchman who had been with Unicef since the late 1960s and was then serving in North Africa, was asked by Labouisse to take charge; he was to be assisted by a young Welshman, Ian Hopwood. Rémy arrived in early July, by which time Hopwood was installed and relief supplies jointly administered by Unicef and UNHCR were on their way to the South. After visits to Saigon and the provinces worst affected by the long years of war, Rémy set in motion Unicef assistance for the rehabilitation of health and education services.

Until the reunification of Vietnam in July 1976, Rémy's dealings concerning Unicef assistance to the South were with the PRG. He and Hopwood found their relationship with the North Vietnamese much more difficult. For many weeks, they waited in their 'office' in Hanoi in the company of two veteran Vietnamese campaigners assigned to look after them, and received rare and inconclusive visits from Red Cross officials.

Now that the emergency was over, Rémy was unwilling to accept any more shopping lists for imported supplies. Over the course of the next three years, Unicef expected to spend around $20 million in the North. Different criteria had to be applied. Up to now, the main item on the list had been prefabricated primary schools from Switzerland. Rémy did not regard these as cost-effective. Hundreds more classrooms could be built if local materials and construction methods were used. The North Vietnamese did not appreciate Rémy's cancellation of further prefabricated schools, and took time to understand that no sinister motive inspired his wish to be involved in planning how Unicef's assistance would be used.

Rémy was deeply impressed by the way in which the North Vietnamese had, since independence in 1954, applied the policy of basic services, just now being articulated by Unicef. Even while waging a protracted war, they had brought medical care, unsophisticated though it was, to almost every mother in every rural hamlet. In two years, Rémy's eye, practised by years of service in the French colonial medical services in North Africa, saw only one case of serious undernutrition in a small child. The contrast with the South was dramatic, where such sights were commonplace. But health and nutrition services were carried out in the most threadbare circumstances. Rémy sought to use Unicef support to upgrade medical facilities, equipment, drugs and training, and similarly make modest improvements in day-care and primary schooling. In time, he penetrated Vietnamese reserve and won the confidence of officialdom. His place was taken in 1977 by a Guyanan, Bertram Collins, whose task it later became to try and smooth Unicef's path into a Kampuchea that had now become a client State of Vietnam.

In Cambodia, conquered by the Khmer Rouge and renamed the Democratic Republic of Kampuchea, the aftermath of the Vietnam war led in a very different direction. There too, until the encirclement of Phnom Penh during the final weeks before their triumphant entry on 17 April 1975, every attempt was made to maintain some kind of programme operations. Up until the last throes of the conflict when all was subsumed in emergency relief for the vast numbers of people flocking to Phnom Penh, classrooms continued to be built, teachers trained, text-books and note-books distributed, new kindergartens organized, playthings given out, drugs and diet supplements sent to hospitals, along with prosthetics for physically-handicapped children. Because of the conflict in the countryside, most of the work was confined to Phnom Penh and areas nearby. As government disintegrated, Unicef worked more closely with CARE, the US voluntary agency, and Save the Children of the UK.

In retrospect, the careful accounting of all the Unicef inputs seems pathetic; at the time there were clear indications from the Khmer Rouge that they would welcome Unicef's co-operation in their rehabilitation of the wartorn country. In the event, all was razed, abolished, burned, and everything to do with Western ideas or institutions made a cause for persecution in the months to come.

In the days following the Khmer Rouge takeover, the two Unicef officials who stayed to see things through—Paul Ignatieff, the representative, and Joseph Acar, a young Lebanese colleague—witnessed the evacuation at gunpoint of the entire city of Phnom Penh. Along with other remaining expatriates, they took refuge in the French Embassy compound. There, they did their best by arranging French passports and instant marriages to protect the lives of their twenty Cambodian colleagues by enabling at least some of them to leave the country: to no avail. In early May, the two men were driven by truck to the Thai border. Two weeks later, Ignatieff addressed the Executive Board. He tried to speak unemotionally about the events in Phnom Penh, and of the superb performance of the local staff they had left behind. He expressed his hope that the new authorities would soon invite Unicef to resume its aid for the stricken children of Cambodia.

The new authorities did no such thing. Unicef's presence in Democratic Kampuchea, like that of all other international UN and nongovernmental organizations, was not wanted. Pol Pot's revolutionary experiment in government was to be an entirely Khmer affair. It took an invasion by Vietnam in January 1979 to end the nightmare of national self-destruction, the most extraordinary infliction of suffering by a people on its own in the name of a 'better order' that can ever have been systematically carried out in the history of Mankind.

And then another chapter of agony began.

The two-day visit of Jacques Beaumont of Unicef and François Bugnion of the ICRC to Phnom Penh in mid-July 1979 must rank as one of the most bizarre and frustrating quests in the history of international relief. It was the second time in Beaumont's life that he had been the first UN official granted a tiny glimpse into a closed and mysterious country, believed to be the victim of tremendous suffering—but unwilling for its own reasons to display it, even to those trying to come to its aid.

If there were parallels with his 1973 trip to North Vietnam, the difficulties of interpretation were much more acute, as were those of winning the confidence of officials. Beaumont and Bugnion did not leave the capital. What they saw was the city's total dereliction; hospitals, with no drugs and almost no medical staff, flooded with patients; hunger in the faces of children in hopelessly overcrowded and filthy orphanages; people everywhere weak and still glazed with trauma. They were convinced that the grimmest predictions of disaster in the whole country had to be taken seriously. But they were unable to persuade President Heng Samrin to allow them the permanent presence in the country required to oversee the aid they wanted to bring in. Obliged to return to Vietnam without any agreement, they began to organize shipments of supplies with no certainty of ever being allowed back in.

At the time of Beaumont's and Bugnion's visit, officials of the new regime had declared that two-and-a-quarter million people in the People's Republic of Kampuchea—the country's new designation—were in imminent danger of starvation. They had appealed to the UN World Food Programme for urgent delivery of 108,000 tons of rice and quantities of other foodstuffs. This crude statement of need was the only one available to officials of the international organizations, and remained so for many months. By their calculations, it required a delivery and distribution rate of 1000 tons of food a day to save more than half the four million people said to have survived the rigours of Pol Pot's social experiment. Not until 13 October—three months to the day after Beaumont and Bugnion flew out of Phnom Penh after their first visit—was the machinery in place to start moving into the country a volume of food which even approximated to this amount. Every conceivable obstacle had blocked the progress of the two organizations' joint attempt to mount a relief programme corresponding to the tradition of political impartiality lying at the heart of their respective mandates.

Labouisse believed that navigating the obstacles in the way of mounting the major relief operation required for Kampuchea required an almost total information blackout on the Unicef/ICRC diplomatic manoeuvres and everything to do with them. ICRC was in full agreement. But events nearly derailed the entire enterprise.

In early September, mounting alarm in the international press about the prospect of famine in Kampuchea reached a crescendo. The British aid agency Oxfam fuelled the outcry by giving maximum publicity to the report of their own representative, Jim Howard, just returned from Phnom Penh with a tale of horror. Howard had seen what Beaumont—who had by now been twice to Phnom Penh—had seen. But where Unicef and ICRC opted for discretion in order to make possible a dialogue in Phnom Penh, Oxfam put Howard on the most public of platforms. His searing accounts were published everywhere.

As in the case of the Nigerian civil war, strong passions were aroused by the repeated use of the words 'genocide' and 'holocaust' to Khmer Rouge atrocities, only now being revealed in all their grisly detail. Moral outrage about these crimes, crimes from which the Kampuchean people had been released by the Vietnamese, had a potent influence on the way the world now responded to the threat of famine. An assumption developed that it was only the antipathy of the Western countries and their South-East Asian allies towards Vietnam which stood in the way of the desperately-needed rescue operation. The international organizations—UN and Red Cross—were perceived as dragging their feet and openly criticized. The need for absolute discretion, seen by Labouisse as vital to the still-undecided outcome of Beaumont's and Bugnion's overtures to the Heng Samrin regime, inhibited Unicef from any public defence. The situation for both Unicef and the ICRC was extremely uncomfortable.

The core of the problem lay in the refusal of most of the governments in the world to recognize the Heng Samrin regime as the legitimate government in Kampuchea. The fact of Khmer Rouge atrocity was weighed in the international balance, and found not to justify armed Vietnamese aggression. Some Asian countries were anxious to keep armed resistance against Vietnamese forces in the field. If a principal organ of that resistance was the Khmer Rouge, so be it. When the UN General Assembly opened in New York on 18 September, it spent three days discussing who should represent Kampuchea; finally, the Khmer Rouge representative took the seat.

To many around the world, with revelations about camps, mass graves and torture chambers fresh in their minds, the UN had forfeited all claim to morality. The Khmer people had desperately needed liberation and the Vietnamese Army had provided it. But the 'act of aggression' required to do so seemed to many to be all that the UN was prepared to notice. Scepticism that any UN organization could be trying its best to mount a relief operation in co-operation with the regime in Phnom Penh reached its peak. Ironically, this was the same session of the General Assembly which later spent three days extolling the merits of all the initiatives taken for humanity during the course of the International Year of the Child.

Labouisse and Charles Egger, chief lieutenant throughout the crisis, did not enjoy seeing Unicef's name dragged through the mud. But they and their counterparts at ICRC headquarters in Geneva were becoming increasingly agonized by the failure of Beaumont and Bugnion to obtain agreement from the authorities in Phnom Penh to the start of a major relief operation. On 9 September, the UN Secretary-General had designated Unicef the lead agency in the UN system for the delivery of relief to Kampuchea. This decision, about which both Labouisse and Egger expressed misgivings to Waldheim, was inspired by Unicef's record of providing relief on both sides of a civil conflict, which—from the perspective of the UN—over-rode the problem posed by the lack of recognition for the People's Republic of Kampuchea. Thus, although the World Food Programme would procure and ship the necessary food and although other UN organizations—notably FAO—would give vital assistance in the months to come, relief would enter the famine-stricken country under the joint Unicef/ICRC umbrella. But while, in UN eyes, Unicef's humanitarian mandate immunized it from the charge of political discrimination, the authorities in Phnom Penh took a very different view. They and their Vietnamese patrons placed a high premium on international respectability. The decision in the UN to seat the Pol Pot representative was a major setback; it coloured, not surprisingly, their attitude towards everything undertaken in the name of the UN.

Simultaneously with the events unfolding at the UN, Beaumont and Bugnion were once again in Phnom Penh, ignoring requests that they leave the country on the aircraft which had been allowed to land a few relief cargoes. On 28 September 1979, the two men were informed in writing for the first time that the Phnom Penh authorities accepted their plan for a relief operation and a continuing presence in the country on three conditions. The first was that they should submit detailed plans; this was perfectly agreeable. The second was that all distribution would be carried out by the authorities; this did not facilitate the free and independent monitoring they had been asking for, but this they felt they had to concede.

The third was that they undertake not to give any relief to Kampucheans, wherever situated, including in areas of the country still controlled by the Khmer Rouge, except through Phnom Penh. This was inadmissible. Unicef had always upheld the principle of giving aid to children on both sides of a conflict. Under the Geneva Conventions, the ICRC was similarly obligated. This was a condition which neither organization would ever accept.

At the time it seemed as though little more than a principle was at stake. Although it was known that there were Kampucheans trying to cross the border into Thailand, the Thai Army was holding them back and only a trickle were getting through. Back in July, at the time when Beaumont first went to Phnom Penh, the Khmer Rouge representatives at the UN in New York had paid a call on Labouisse. They had protested Beaumont's visit and objected to Unicef giving any aid through the 'illegal' government of Heng Samrin. They had also told Labouisse that there were mothers and children in the north-west of the country, just across the Thai border, who were suffering as acutely as any elsewhere. Labouisse replied that it was Unicef's policy to help all children in need that it could reach, no matter where they were; he also pointed out that Unicef had wanted to go on providing assistance for Kampuchean children during 1975–79, but had been forcibly ejected by the Pol Pot regime.

Following this encounter, Labouisse enjoined Roberto Esquerva-Barry, his Regional Director in Bangkok, to reconnoitre quietly the truth of the Khmer Rouge report of suffering children in the north-west, and see what Unicef could do. The first Unicef/Red Cross mission into Kampuchean territory under Khmer Rouge and other opposition control took place on 17 September. The pitiful condition of the thousands of women and children harboured there for whatever reason was profoundly shocking, matching in human misery any eyewitness account from Phnom Penh itself. Following this discovery, Labouisse authorized relief on a modest scale but instructed that no public statement should be issued concerning Unicef's action. He was fearful that if the authorities in Phnom Penh heard of it, they would pull the rug out from under Beaumont.

The widespread view was that, although some relief was clearly needed around the border, the main effort to save the Khmer people from extinction must go into Kampuchea itself. The Director-General of Oxfam, Brian Walker, who flew into Phnom Penh at the end of September in the third plane-load of relief goods sent by Oxfam, was put under pressure by the Heng Samrin regime to sacrifice the principle that Unicef and ICRC insisted upon. Walker finally agreed, as a condition of a relief effort being mounted by a consortium of voluntary agencies under Oxfam's leadership, not to feed Kampucheans up on the Thai border under the protection of the Khmer Rouge.

Walker was also prepared to disassociate the Oxfam relief operation from that run by Unicef and the ICRC. The fact that, however many voluntary organizations joined in, he could never command international resources on a remotely comparable scale to the combined weight of the UN and the international institutions of the Red Cross, seemed less important to Walker than to open up channels for the Oxfam consortium programme. The comparative strengths of the two sets of organizations were imperfectly understood by Heng Samrin's inexperienced officials. The satisfactory agreement they reached with Oxfam was yet another temporary setback to Beaumont and Bugnion's own negotiations. The international humanitarian community was splitting into two camps, and there was a clear danger that one group might be played off against the other.

Meanwhile, on 10 October the Vietnamese Army launched a new offensive against the Khmer Rouge resistance. Within seventeen days, 130,000 Kampucheans, the vast majority ordinary people trapped by the fighting, had fled across the border into Thailand. Another 120,000 were right behind them, only three miles away. They were sick, starving and in a lamentable state. On the principle that Unicef and the ICRC refused to concede in Phnom Penh hung the fate of these people, and hundreds of thousands more.

In Phnom Penh, Beaumont and Bugnion continued their nerve-wracking negotiations. In the end, the impasse on the Heng Samrin condition that no aid be given through opposition forces was broken by a formula to which neither side formally assented: they simply agreed to disagree, and understood, warily, that this constituted 'agreement' of a sort. Although the Kampuchean officials never withdrew the condition, and continued to protest to Unicef and ICRC representatives in Phnom Penh about what gradually developed into a major operation on and near the Thai border, the programme inside the country now began to go ahead in force. On 13 October, daily relief flights began, using an RAF Hercules loaned by the UK. The airlift out of Bangkok and Singapore gradually increased in volume as other countries lent planes, and at its peak flew five missions a day.

Also on 13 October, the first major Oxfam relief consignment—and the first of any to be sent by sea—arrived by barge from Singapore, under the redoubtable captaincy of Guy Stringer, Oxfam's Deputy Director. Stringer, who realized that the Phnom Penh officials did not after all intend to refuse aid from Unicef and ICRC, forgot about Oxfam's commitment not to work with the international heavyweights and made peace with his Unicef and ICRC colleagues. The danger of two competitive and overlapping programmes was averted.

During the next weeks, the various organizations managed to increase their staffs in Kampuchea and, for the first time, to visit a few areas outside Phnom Penh. Beaumont, sick and exhausted, had seen the Unicef mission through the perilous negotiating phase. He left Kampuchea, and John

Saunders, a recently retired and very experienced senior official of UNDP then took charge of UN relief operations in Kampuchea. Food and medical assistance began to flow in by air and sea, as well as some of the means to unload it and move it around the country. At last it seemed that the effort needed to avert catastrophe was underway.

In mid-October, along the border with Thailand, the trickle of refugees trying to cross the Thai border turned first into a stream, and then into a flood. Many thousands of sickly and emaciated mothers and children were using their last breath to reach help. On 17 October, the Thai Government, which had previously turned back the refugees, announced a change of policy. After obtaining the agreement of the UN Secretary-General to accept responsibility for providing them with food and shelter, they announced an 'open door' policy. Waldheim then asked Unicef and the World Food Programme to shoulder the urgent task of providing food and water to the populations under the control of Khmer Rouge and other resistance groups just across the Thai border, while UNHCR maintained holding centres for 'illegal immigrants' inside Thailand.

As the numbers mounted alarmingly through late October and November, reaching around 650,000 in early December, a programme of a type and magnitude Unicef had never previously organized was set in motion. The food for the people in both border camps and holding centres, much of which was purchased in Thailand, was provided by the WFP. Medical care—doctors and nurses, camp hospitals, medicines—was provided by the ICRC, and teams from many voluntary organizations. But the delivery of the means of survival to the border camp populations was Unicef's responsibility.

The task extended way beyond Unicef's normal mandate for mothers and children. But, in the light of the Secretary-General's request, it had no alternative. Ulf Kristofferson, a young Swede who had served Unicef in Phnom Penh before the Khmer Rouge takeover in 1975, became the major domo. His expertise was in moving supplies around, and he now deployed it to effect. He set up an office and warehouses in Aranyaprathet near the border, a sleepy nonentity of a place swiftly being transformed into a freak boom town. Kristofferson was tough, energetic and enterprising. He hired fleets of vehicles, took on 200 Thai staff, and enlisted 2000 helpers among the Khmer population in the camps to distribute food and water. Every day, huge convoys of food trucks and water tankers—sometimes over eighty vehicles to a convoy, carrying half a million litres of water and hundreds of tons of rice—moved out from Aranyaprathet to locations north and south.

In early December, one border camp became the site of a 'land bridge': tens of thousands of Kampucheans who had trekked to the border on foot, by bicycle or in ox-carts were given twenty kilos of rice and fifteen kilos of rice seed per person, and were swallowed back into the country. Thousands of tons of rice seed were funnelled across the border by this route during the next two months. For many of the farmers in the west and north-west of Kampuchea, this made it possible for them to plant and harvest a reasonable crop for the first time in several years. These operations went as much like clockwork as possible under the circumstances.

Much more of a nightmare was the problem of seeing that, in the camps, the food went into the hands of civilians, particularly the most needy, rather than to Khmer Rouge and other armed fighters. They controlled the camps, and their guns and orders were the only law in their land. To begin with, the civilian camp population figures they provided were taken on trust, as was their word about distribution. But profiteering and black-market dealings soared, partly on the basis of gold that many Kampucheans smuggled out of their homeland with them.

To reassert some control, Kristofferson sent his own teams into the camps to try and verify population figures, prevent the diversion of supplies, weigh and measure children and talk to mothers. On occasion, supplies were temporarily withheld from a camp to elicit co-operation from the warlords. In an area where illegal fortunes were being made, where the only other authority in the vicinity was the Thai Army, and with Vietnamese forces pressing on Khmer Rouge sanctuaries from only a few miles away, the operation was fraught with danger. Camps sometimes came under armed attack. Kristofferson, fortunately, thrived on a situation that would have driven many to the edge of breakdown. The extraordinary feat was that it worked as smoothly as it did, whatever the rate of diversion and loss.

By the end of the year, when the Unicef convoys were providing rations for 450,000 people, nutritional surveys had proved that the condition of the women and children had much improved. Despite the daily turmoil, the Unicef team also managed to arrange some schooling for 30,000 children in the camps, recruiting teachers from among the refugee Khmers. Whoever else had profited, the principal goal of saving helpless people's lives and reintroducing some degree of normalcy had been attained.

In October and November, when the refugee crisis was erupting, the real state of conditions in the Kampuchean countryside was still somewhat shrouded in mystery. Relief officials in Phnom Penh, whose numbers were heavily restricted, were still relying mainly on estimates provided by the authorities. At the end of November, the figure of two-and-a-quarter million people in need was raised to three million: three-quarters of the supposed population, minus those who had fled. But no relief official had yet been allowed to travel widely in the country to confirm this scale of need at first hand. Few Western journalists had been allowed into the country.

By contrast, the wretched condition of the refugees in Thailand was filmed, photographed and beamed all over the world by the international press corps based in Bangkok, whose access to the camps was unrestricted.

In the UK, a television film by Jon Pilger was screened at the end of October and unleashed a tidal wave of generosity towards the hapless Kampucheans. It was soon echoed by similar outpourings in other Western countries. On 19 October, as confident as he could be that Heng Samrin would not at this stage renege on the tacit 'agreement' Beaumont and Bugnion had reached with the Phnom Penh regime and at Labouisse's request, Secretary-General Waldheim launched a joint Unicef and ICRC appeal for funds at the UN in New York. Two weeks later, member States met for a special conference to pledge resources. The statements of many of the delegates were strongly influenced by the reports of journalists and embassy officials in Bangkok. Everyone had drawn the same conclusion: the misery of those at the border was typical of millions more inside the country. The country and its people were in their dying throes.

The relief officials in Phnom Penh, isolated from normal communications channels, were unaware of the mounting fracas. They were still trying to connect the pieces of a major programme—under the strain of continuing lack of confidence from the authorities and their Vietnamese advisors, and a lack of proper information in every respect. The destruction wrought in the country over the previous several years meant that almost nothing worked, and even the smallest task—unloading a bargeful of supplies—was problematic. Handling equipment, such as cranes and forklifts, was nonexistent. The weakened state of many of the Kampucheans on dock duty meant that supplies had to be packed in bags no heavier than fifty kilos; otherwise they could not be lifted. As well as equipment, hundreds of trucks had to be shipped or airlifted in to move supplies around the country. These problems emerged, and had to be addressed, in a cloud of incomplete understanding and conflicting assurances from Kampuchean officials, all of whom were functioning under conditions of similar confusion and duress.

Early in November, Labouisse made a personal visit to Phnom Penh in an effort to exert pressure on the various governments involved, and to unblock some of the logjams. Like others before and after him, he was deeply affected by experiencing at first hand how completely the Pol Pot regime had destroyed the social and economic fabric of their own country. He met Heng Samrin, who predictably raised the vexed question of the 'third condition'; again, it was left unresolved. There was some progress on other matters: suggestions for improving logistics and transport were well-received. At the conclusion of his visit, Labouisse went on to Hanoi, where Unicef's stock was relatively high thanks to its continuing programme of co-operation. Prime Minister Pham Van Dong gave Labouisse various undertakings to do with helping move supplies into and around Kampuchea; few materialized over the forthcoming months. This process of backing and advancing through diplomatic hoops was the most exhausting and frustrating of all the problems associated with Kampuchean relief.

By mid-December, the target of moving 1000 tons of food a day into the country was reached: by this stage the joint Unicef/ICRC programme had delivered 29,000 tons. Now a new problem arose. Warehouses in the port of Kompong Som, the main entry point for relief sent by sea, were choked with 35,000 tonnes of food. Vehicles were arriving from Unicef, Oxfam and from the USSR—eventually their total exceeded 1500—but there was little sign of their urgent deployment to prevent mass deaths from famine. The authorities had insisted that they would undertake distribution of relief, and furnish reports to Unicef and ICRC. There were no reports. John Saunders and François Bugnion, the one low-key, the other irate, remonstrated with Kampuchean officials and besought their respective headquarters to put diplomatic pressure where it might count.

As this new turn of events filtered into the press in early 1980, the organizations once more began to feel the heat of worldwide outrage, indirectly against themselves, directly against the authorities in Phnom Penh. The sense, earlier so potent, that, given their liberation of the Kampuchean people from genocidal fanatics, the Vietnamese deserved the benefit of the doubt about their intentions in Kampuchea, began to evaporate. The new regime had declared a famine and asked the world for help. The world had sent help, and most of it was sitting in warehouses. Many explanations were offered, few of them sympathetic to the Heng Samrin regime. Unicef and ICRC, trying to calm the storm, found it difficult to avoid charges of evasion and naivety.

Was there a famine in Kampuchea or was there not? In the world outside Phnom Penh—a world whose primary source of information was Bangkok—the answer to the question seemed almost less important than the sense of outrage that the Western world, so generous in the Khmer people's latest hour of need, had been duped. In Phnom Penh itself, the relief officials knew the answer to the question: at least on the scale threatened, the famine had retreated, at least for the time being. They had finally begun to travel in the countryside; they saw hunger, malnutrition, ill-health, rural breakdown on a severe scale; they also saw starvation. But not as much as expected; certainly not enough to justify earlier fears about widespread death. With all the intense public pressure and media exposure, some of which they continued to feel at second hand through their headquarters, they found it hard to persuade senior colleagues in New York and Geneva that, given all the circumstances, the situation was relatively in hand.

In a country whose whole social fabric had been through intense disruption; where trained and competent administrative people were few and far between; where no map was left extant in any government office in Phnom Penh at the end of the Pol Pot period; where there were no survey data or up-to-date statistical information, nor any means of printing and distributing them even if there were; it was not surprising to those with long experience of this kind of situation that the picture was more fluid, less clear-cut and a great deal less lurid than depicted in stories threatening 'two million dead by Christmas'.

The main reason that the famine was not as severe as forecast was that the tropical climate and natural productivity of Kampuchean soil produced food, willy nilly. People had cultivated maize, cassava, bananas and other crops in garden plots; and they harvested fish from the many rivers and from the large lake of Tonle Sap. They did manage, in addition, to grow some kind of a rice crop. In November, they brought in a harvest thought to approximate 300,000 tons, or one-third of the 900,000 tons needed: considerably more than the one-fifth earlier expected in a land where no estimates were accurate. So long as more food arrived within the next three months, disaster could be averted.

The policies of the Phnom Penh authorities was the other reason why famine on a mass scale was avoided. In normal times, a grain tax was traditionally levied on the farmers; the grain thus taken by the authorities was sold in the towns or for export to raise revenues. In November 1979, and during the two harvest seasons in 1980, the grain tax was suspended. Instead, following negotiations with Unicef and FAO, the Heng Samrin regime used relief food supplies to feed and pay government servants and party officials (rice was still the only medium of exchange in 1979 and early 1980). They also used the imported relief food for urban dwellers, putting it in the markets of the gradually re-emerging towns and cities. This meant that those who had planted rice kept their entire crop; there was no movement of food out of the countryside. It also alleviated the critical logistical problem of moving food around the country. The one stipulation made by the Unicef/FAO negotiators was that none of their rations go to the Vietnamese Army. For this purpose, grain sent by the USSR and other Socialist allies was used.

Although moving food from one area to another within the country continued to present great logistical problems for many months, the shortfalls in its distribution in the months before and after Christmas 1979 did not mean the difference between life and death for the entire country. The people in the worst-affected part of the country, the north-west, had suffered extreme hardship; and it was the pitiful condition they were in when they reached the Thai border which had led the world to imagine that there was a country full of starvelings behind them. The feeding operation run from Thailand which saved and recuperated many lives from this area also made a vital contribution by sending food and rice seed across the border via the land bridge. The stamina of the Kampuchean people also played its part, as did their ability—proved over the Pol Pot years—for survival in adversity.

While relief officials in Phnom Penh were beginning to feel as though the situation was under some degree of control, the roused passions of public, press and donor governments put the organizations' Western-based headquarters under great pressure. Unicef, in particular, was making heavy weather of the lead agency role the Secretary-General had thrust upon it. Not only were Labouisse, Egger and many other senior staff devoting much of their energies to the crisis, but the work of the whole organization was being affected. In one critical dimension, the lead agency role was hobbled from the start. Unicef did not have the power of the purse. When UN Secretary-General Waldheim and Labouisse launched the public appeal for Kampuchean relief on 19 October, the target was $110 million for a programme lasting six months. As events unfolded at breakneck speed during October and November, the amount was re-estimated at $250 million for a year.

At the special pledging conference called in early November, governments eventually came up with promises of $210 million altogether. But instead of setting up a special fund as he had done for Indo-China in 1975, the Secretary-General had invited governments to pledge separately to the main UN bodies involved: Unicef, UNHCR, WFP, FAO. The distribution of responsibility—particularly for what was going on in Thailand—was imperfectly understood by the donors. As a result, Unicef was continually forced to spend money it had not yet received, temporarily diverting other resources. During late 1979, Charles Egger spent much of his time chasing pledges and extra resources. When, in December 1979, the world's press began to report food piling up in Kompong Som while Kampuchea starved, donors who had pledged funds began to show a marked reluctance to part with them. The problems of the situation were compounded by the confusion over whether the famine had been stayed or not; nothing was easy to explain to a world whose understanding of the intricacies of relief in obscure countries is not sophisticated, and whose goodwill is fickle at best.

Difficulties were further compounded by the uncertainty surrounding the various responsibilities of Unicef, WFP, UNHCR and ICRC in the area around the Thai border where the Khmer resistance groups were encamped, and by the presence in Bangkok of people from nearly 100 different voluntary agencies, each with its own agenda, constituency and view of how and whom to help. After visiting the region in November, Mrs Rosalyn Carter, wife of the US President, appealed to the UN Secretary-General to appoint someone with the authority to bring order out of chaos. The Secretary-General appointed the veteran Sir Robert Jackson as special relief co-ordinator. Jackson had relationships stretching back over many years with Egger, Saunders and many of the senior diplomats and statesmen involved in the Kampuchean imbroglio. He also understood where UN feathers were likely to be ruffled and how to smooth them. Jackson thereupon made Bangkok his base and endlessly travelled the diplomatic circuit, throwing into the operation all his contacts and experience, not to mention his legendary panache.

With the new year came other changes. Harry Labouisse retired. His fifteen years at the head of Unicef had culminated with the triumph of the International Year of the Child, and, simultaneously, with the Kampuchean crisis and its extraordinarily taxing demands. Almost his last act as Executive Director was to write to President Heng Samrin asking him to place the highest priority on improving the distribution of relief food. On 1 January, his successor, James P. Grant, previously head of the Overseas Development Council in Washington, took over the leadership of Unicef, and inherited the thorniest international relief crisis since the Nigerian civil war.

As President of the ODC, Grant had been active since Waldheim's and Labouisse's appeal in October in exerting pressure on the US Administration to make a major contribution to Kampuchean relief. On 25 October, President Carter committed $39 million altogether, of which $30 million was for relief inside Kampuchea and $9 million for refugees on the Thai border. Grant saw this as the turning point in mobilizing generous contributions from European donors and the Japanese. However, in spite of his determination that Unicef continue to acquit itself effectively in its Kampuchean relief role, Grant was essentially a man with long-term development problems on his mind—what he called the 'silent emergency'. Like the rest of Unicef's senior staff and many Board members, he was dismayed by the extent to which Unicef had been plunged up to its operational neck in a 'loud emergency'. He believed that responsibility for the large and intricate operation Ulf Kristofferson had built up along the border with Thailand more properly belonged with the UNHCR.

The most serious problem was the cross-border operation to feed mothers and children under the protection of the armed Khmer opposition groups. These were not truly refugees since they had not fled their country; but while Unicef continued to provide for them, relationships between John Saunders, the representative in Phnom Penh, and the Heng Samrin authorities remained distinctly awkward. At a time when there were great problems with getting food moving around the country before the results of the November harvest were exhausted, Saunders felt that the cross-border programme jeopardized the more complex and even larger programme inside Kampuchea itself. All efforts to divest Unicef of the role of 'feeding the Khmer Rouge' proved in vain, however. The UNHCR pleaded that it already had its hands full with refugee camps and holding centres within Thailand, and with other refugee problems elsewhere in the world; and the Thai Government was adamant that Unicef should continue.

In late January, Grant visited both Phnom Penh and the base of the Thai and cross-border programme in Aranyaprathet, and what he saw of the programmes and the efforts of the staff serving under him overcame any previous lack of enthusiasm. From this point onwards he became wholeheartedly committed to fulfilling Unicef's mission to the maximum in both operational theatres, went actively after funds all over the world, and was an energetic spokesman on Kampuchea's behalf, using the limelight cast on Unicef to enhance its prestige.

On 7 January at the anniversary celebration of his installation in power, Heng Samrin responded to Labouisse's valedictory effort to get food moving out of Kompong Som. He announced that he had instructed his officials to attach the highest priority to mobilizing transport and food distribution. Indeed, over the coming weeks things did begin to improve. Still under the greatest pressure from all external quarters to expedite their programme, the relief teams in Phnom Penh were beginning to piece together fragmentary information from districts and provinces, and began to present a convincing account of supplies finally getting through. In Thailand, the numbers of people receiving food rations at the border hovered around the 600,000 mark at the beginning of 1980. During January, 5000 tons of food were funnelled across the land bridge into the north-west. Gradually, as food once more became available inside Kampuchea, many of the famine refugees began to return home.

On 14 February a special session of the Unicef Executive Board was summoned in New York. Grant presented a full and up-beat account of the situation he had explored both within Kampuchea and on the Thai border, and announced the outcome of discussions held in Bangkok under Jackson's auspices between all the senior UN agency representatives involved. It was now clear that the entire relief operation, and Unicef's lead agency role in Kampuchea, would have to continue at least through 1980, and probably well into 1981. The UN organizations and the ICRC began to make plans for the next twelve months. They had almost no breathing space. Current stocks of food in Kampuchea, together with the dry-season harvest of the late spring, would start to run out at the end of May, and then there would be nothing until the next main harvest in November 1980. Unless enough paddies were planted before the monsoon, then that harvest too would be seriously short.

The two critical requirements were food—240,000 tons of rice, according to FAO/WFP calculations—to tide the country over, and 40,000 tons of rice seed to plant during the coming months. In these two areas, Hans Page of FAO and his small staff played the essential role, working closely with the Phnom Penh authorities to draw up elaborate plans to purchase and ship in these huge volumes of food and seed.

The critical question once again was the handling and distribution capacity. Without opening up new port facilities and river routes, without more trucks, barges and better use of them, it was hard to see how the pipeline would not become hopelessly blocked. Once the monsoon began in the summer, many roads already in poor condition would become impassable. Unless the whole road, rail and river distribution network was somehow dramatically geared up, the spectre of famine would raise its head again and there would be another flight towards the Thai border.

Over the coming months, much of the effort both by the joint UN/ICRC effort in Phnom Penh and by the voluntary-agency consortium headed by Oxfam was invested in transport and logistics. The country's truck fleet was steadily increased, eventually to 1500 imported and donated vehicles. Tugs, barges and other rivercraft, as well as marine engineer services were also provided, and rail transport between Kompong Som and Phnom Penh was restored. While the full repairs required by the railroad were beyond the capacity of the international relief operation, they set up vehicle repair workshops for trucks, trains and boats. Unicef's most experienced transport officer, Horst Ruttinger from the Federal Republic of Germany, was despatched to Phnom Penh in April 1980. Unicef recruited a group of East German mechanics to help him, and Oxfam assigned another mechanic. Under Ruttinger's leadership, this team played a vital role in building up an efficient national trucking system over the spring and summer. Port bottlenecks were much alleviated by teams of dockers sent from the USSR who substantially improved the speed at which goods were offloaded; cranes, forklifts and conveyors were delivered; floating wharves were built; and port repairs were undertaken at both Phnom Penh and Kompong Som.

In spite of these improvements, the situation both in Kampuchea and on the Thai border, where military action continued, remained balanced on a knife-edge, sustaining the world's sense of urgency. The image of a country pounded to pieces had left a powerful imprint on the conscience of Mankind. Even though the worst prognostications of the autumn had turned out to be wrong, though the political knots remained tied, and though the picture from Phnom Penh remained ill-defined, the world wanted to do its best for the Khmer people. With the various means at its disposal, it tried.

The flood of generosity from the general public had reached over $60 million from western Europe, the US, Japan and Australasia by February 1980. Funds continued to flow into scores of voluntary agencies, those in the Oxfam-led consortium as well as others, and to Unicef national committees. But the really large sums had to come from governments. So far, $205 million had been swallowed up by the joint relief operation. Unicef was still overspent on its current relief efforts, and far from buoyant for the next stage and others beyond it. To finance the necessary operations to the end of the year, another $263 million was needed.

The confidence of the main donor governments in the programme was growing, but some were still unhappy that Unicef as lead agency had been obliged to go way out of its normal line. They were, however, persuaded that no better arrangement could be made. Unicef had demonstrated its efficacy in supplies procurement and delivery. It was true that distribution beyond a certain level—in the border camps, beyond camp overlords; and in Kampuchea, beyond the national authorities—was rarely under the control of the relief operation. During the spring months, before the monsoon began in earnest, every effort was made to influence both by negotiation and by practical measures the movement of supplies to their final destination. In March, a new logistical problem arose when part of the wharf at Phnom Penh collapsed: it was a symptom of how overstrained the severely-deteriorated port and transport system still were.

In May, with Jean-Pierre Hocke, the ICRC's Director of Operations, Grant again flew to Phnom Penh. The two men tried to reinforce Jackson's continuing efforts to put across to the authorities the fragility of the operation, its dependence on their ability to give answers to their donors, and the possibility that it would suddenly cease if distribution bottlenecks could not be unblocked. In spite of all the problems, the donor governments were reassured by the reports of Grant and Hocke. A thorough re-assessment of needs based on the much more precise information about food and seed availability in different parts of the country, and the promised opening-up of new ports and delivery routes from Vietnam gave an appearance for the first time of some margin of safety. In spite of all the diplomatic overtures of Grant, Hocke and Jackson, however, there were still extreme political difficulties in facilitating supply lines through areas of combat. The prospects of another famine scare were still very real. At a special conference called in Geneva in late May, the donors came up with another $116 million. Jackson's and Grant's relentless arm-twisting in capitals around the world had managed to keep the programme financially afloat: there was now at least enough money in hand to carry on until the post-monsoon harvest.

Within Kampuchea, the ports and transport systems improved markedly as the summer months progressed. Food delivery around the country remained sluggish. But the authorities attached a very high priority to the need to put much larger areas of land under rice cultivation, and with the help of Hans Page and his small FAO/WFP team, this countrywide exercise was planned and carried out with comparative efficiency. Due to delays in receiving funds and in purchasing and delivery delays the target of bringing in enough rice seed before the end of the planting season nearly fell by the wayside. At the last minute, 3000 tons of floating seed was brought in by airlift. With a superhuman effort of despatch and logistical precision, it was quickly moved out to the farmers in the countryside. By what seemed a miracle, two-thirds of the regular crop was planted, putting twice the 1979 area under cultivation. And in the meantime, for the second time in twelve months, the threat of widescale death from hunger in the pre-harvest months had been held at bay.

Once again, the resilience of the Kampuchean people, as well as the food-distribution programme, helped to deflect disaster. They supplemented their diet with other foods: fish, wild game, maize, manioc, sweet potatoes, beans. Nutritional surveys in a few parts of the country between August and December revealed some severe malnutrition, but nothing widescale, and the prospects of an adequate rice harvest were good. It finally seemed as though the country's agricultural and rural life was returning to normal, and that stop-gap emergency measures to import food could be scaled down. Towards the end of the year, the organizations involved in Kampuchean relief could begin to think in terms of the end of the emergency, and turn their attention instead to more conventional programmes of long-term rehabilitation and development.

John Saunders, who had seen the mission through its most gruelling and frustrating period of operation, left Phnom Penh in June, and was replaced by Kurt Jansson, a Finnish administrator similarly brought out of retirement after a long and distinguished UN career. From the summer months onwards, Jansson concentrated most of the efforts of his small handful of staff on the task of constant monitoring. They covered as much of the country as possible, visiting warehouses, ports and distribution points, and doing their best to work out with the authorities whatever means they could to improve the rate at which food moved about the countryside by truck, barge and rail. Jansson's reports to the donor governments were vital to allay the fears, constantly expressed in the media, that the food provided by the UN operation was going to feed the Vietnamese Army. He was able to satisfy them on this point.

For the ICRC, the time had come to bow out. In the normal course of events, their role was confined to emergencies. During the past fifteen months, as well as helping to run the entire programme on both sides of the border, they had provided vital emergency health services in Kampuchea's shattered hospitals as well as in the refugee camps. Their medical teams and other personnel were gradually withdrawn. But Unicef, which had hoped finally to be released from the role of lead agency, carried on. In the UN General Assembly of 1980, the representative of Democratic Kampuchea once again took the Kampuchean seat. Waldheim, confronted with the same political puzzle which had prompted his original designation of Unicef to shoulder the burden, wrote to Grant asking Unicef to continue as lead agency for Kampuchean relief throughout 1981. In spite of the misgivings of senior staff and Board delegates, there was no alternative but to accept. A more modest programme was envisaged for 1981, with a somewhat different emphasis. A budget of $200 million had been set. Now the plans for this programme became a source of contention.

Back in May 1980 Unicef's Executive Board had approved a quite separate, relatively modest programme of Unicef co-operation for the People's Republic of Kampuchea, to be carried out alongside the major emergency programme but concerned with the long-term health and education needs of the kind usually assisted by Unicef. One of the earliest Unicef team members to arrive in Phnom Penh was the young Welshman, Ian Hopwood, who had previously worked in Hanoi. When Grant made his first visit to Kampuchea in January 1980, he had been impressed by the tremendous enthusiasm shown both by the people and by the authorities to rebuild the schools destroyed under Khmer Rouge rule. Everywhere in the countryside he and Egger had seen classes being conducted in the most primitive of conditions, with pupils of twelve and thirteen years struggling to master the first rudiments of learning, without books, pencils, slates, benches or desks. Already, close to a million children were enrolled, although because of the recent past, less than a quarter of those instructing them had qualifications of any kind. Inspired by this evidence of the thirst to learn, and convinced that education would help salve psychological wounds and knit communities together again, Unicef had shipped in some basic primary-school supplies, and Hopwood pursued educational rehabilitation with vigour. At the May 1980 Executive Board session, most of the $2 million programme was for school supplies, the rest for health. To this programme, the Board had agreed without demur.

Now, however, in early 1981, when aid to education was proposed as a part of the main emergency relief programme, some of the donors objected. They were determined that Kampuchea should receive humanitarian relief and nothing else. They did not want their contributions to be spent on anything that would help rebuild the country's infrastructure. They did not recognize the People's Republic of Kampuchea; they did not want the Heng Samrin regime to stand on its own, or its allies', feet. To Robert Jackson, the debate was an echo from the days when UNRRA was helping postwar rehabilitation in the countries of eastern Europe and was accused in the West of ideological bias. At the regular meetings of donors for Kampuchean relief, which continued throughout 1981, he expressed exasperation. Time and again, he pointed out that to draw a line between 'relief' and 'rehabilitation' is impossible for all practical purposes. The delivery of relief—food, for example—could not be divorced from the state of the road along which it had to be driven. If the road network, and other parts of the social and economic infrastructure, was left to collapse, the task of delivering relief would become much more expensive and complicated.

Unicef's assistance to primary education provoked considerable complaint at these meetings, in spite of the fact that schools had become venues for supplementary feeding programmes for young children, and were playing an important part in the people's recovery from their long ordeal. Here was a classic example of how ambivalent can be the international community even in the late twentieth century towards an issue where humanitarian considerations clash with political and strategic interests. Undeterred, Unicef sought approval from its 1981 Executive Board for a larger programme of co-operation for health care, schools, orphanages, drinking water and nutrition. In this public forum at least, no dissenting voice was raised.

At the end of 1981, Unicef at last relinquished its lead agency role for

Kampuchean relief. Altogether, the joint UN and ICRC programme, in which Unicef had shouldered a lion's share of the administrative burden inside Kampuchea and much of it outside the stricken country, had provided some $634 million in assistance between October 1979 and December 1981. Unicef's own expenditures on Kampuchean relief within the overall programme were $49 million in 1980 and $22·7 million in 1981. Altogether, 300,000 tons of food aid had been distributed, as well as thousands of tons of rice seed, fertilizers, pesticides, agricultural equipment, vehicles, handling equipment, fuel and medical supplies. More than 6000 schools and 1000 clinics and hospitals had been re-opened. It was not perhaps quite the largest relief and rehabilitation programme ever undertaken, but it was the most complex, and the most all-encompassing for a single country.

On the border with Thailand, the relief operation for refugees and famine victims had cost the international community $132 million. By the end of 1981, many of those who had fled the west and north-west with their families and sought refuge under Khmer resistance protection, had returned home to their villages. Over 250,000 refugees still remained in the camps, and the task of providing for them was handed over to a special UN body—the UN Border Relief Operation (UNBRO)—created for the purpose.

The two-and-a-quarter years of the programme had imposed a heavy strain on Unicef, one from which both Grant, and Labouisse before him, had feared Unicef could not emerge without serious damage to its reputation for impartiality. Somehow it did so; and, largely due to the quality of leadership provided by the two Directors, it also emerged with heightened prestige in international circles.

During the course of 1980 and 1981, the world's attention began to shift to other humanitarian crises: the Pakistani side of the border with Afghanistan, and the Somalian side of the border with Ethiopia—in both of which huge refugee populations had congregated. Worse was to come, in the shape of famine across the African continent. If the Executive Board and James Grant could possibly avoid it, Unicef would not be designated lead agency again. Operationally, diplomatically and financially, the Kampuchean crisis was one of the stormiest and most difficult passages of Unicef's history. It was also one of which it could be justifiably proud.

Although the main chapters of the Kampuchean story were concluded at the end of 1981, and in spite of the country's remarkable recovery at the end of the emergency period, the real process of reconstruction had yet to begin. The 1981–82 monsoon was uneven and food aid and rice seed were still needed on a very considerable scale throughout 1982. The trauma suffered by the Kampuchean people was still a living memory from which it would take at least a generation to recover.

But the world's memory is short. Unicef and other organizations in the international community continue to support the process of Kampuchean recovery and rehabilitation. But the passions aroused throughout the world by the horrors endured by the Khmer people as an outcome of the years of turmoil in Indo-China have died away. It may, tragically, take another cataclysm to re-arouse them.

Main sources

'Kampuchea: Back from the Brink', a report by the International Committee of the Red Cross on its 15-month joint action with Unicef in Kampuchea and Thailand, ICRC, October 1981.

Unicef: 'Lessons to be Learned from the Kampuchea Emergency Operation', a confidential report (never formally issued) by Ron Ockwell, December 1982.

The Quality of Mercy: Cambodia, Holocaust and Modern Conscience, by William Shawcross, Simon & Schuster, New York, 1984.

Rice, Rivalry, and Politics: Managing Cambodian Relief, by Linda Mason and Roger Brown, University of Notre Dame Press, 1983.

Unicef Executive Board: documentation concerning emergency relief and rehabilitation assistance to services for mothers and children in the Indo-China peninsula throughout the period 1965 to 1981; Executive Director's progress reports; summary records; statements by Unicef representatives; and other specially-prepared papers.

40,000 enfants par jour: Vivre la cause de l'Unicef, by Dr François Rémy, published by Robert Laffont and Michel Archimbaud, Paris, 1983.

Interviews with many of the principals, undertaken by the Unicef History Project, 1983–85.

The Economist: articles concerning Indo-Chinese refugees, Kampuchea, and emergency relief to victims of the Kampuchean crisis 1979–1980 in Kampuchea and in Thailand; 7 July 1979 through September 1980.

Unicef: Kampuchea Emergency progress reports; a series of reports prepared during the period November 1979–end 1981 to keep donor governments informed of the relief situation inside Kampuchea and on the Thai-Kampuchean border.

Chapter 17

The Women and the Cities

When Harry Labouisse was asked whether he would be interested in becoming the Executive Director of Unicef in November 1964, the invitation came to him out of a clear blue sky. When James Grant received the same invitation in May 1979, the sky was cloudy and the invitation had taken years to deliver.

In 1975, at the conclusion of Labouisse's second five-year term, he informed UN Secretary-General Kurt Waldheim, whose task it was to appoint a successor, that he intended to stand down. Waldheim persuaded him to reconsider, and Hans Conzett—then the Chairman of the Executive Board—endorsed Waldheim's request. The Board had great confidence in Labouisse, and had no wish to see him depart although he was now over seventy years old. He agreed to stay, first through 1976, then through 1977. At the end of 1977, the resolution declaring 1979 the International Year of the Child was passed by the General Assembly, and once more Kurt Waldheim asked Labouisse to stay on. Continuity of leadership through the period leading up to, and including, the Year was the cogent argument Waldheim offered, but it masked another difficulty that he had no taste for resolving.

Although the US had taken the lead in creating and underwriting Unicef during its early years, the Nordic countries led by Sweden had steadily increased their influence over policy and their financial support during the previous decade. In 1977, the Swedish contribution was over $19 million, a contribution *per capita* of $2.33, then the highest in the world. Given their record, the Swedes found it objectionable that the US regarded Unicef's chief executive slot as its preserve. Nils Thedin, Board Chairman from 1971–73, had taken advantage of his contacts with the Secretary-General at that time to point out that his Ministry of Foreign Affairs would like the next head of Unicef to be Swedish. By 1977, it was clear that the US was far from enthusiastic to support a candidate of another nationality, while Sweden was exerting pressure at the highest levels. Waldheim, wishing to offend neither government, did not like to decide between the Swedish and the US candidates: Ernst Michanek and James Grant. In the years prior to 1979, both had taken part in their Governments' delegations to the Board, and lobbying became intense at meetings and in diplomatic circles.

It fell to the 1979 Board Chairman, Mrs Sadako Ogata of Japan, to prevail upon Waldheim—whose own re-election was in the offing—to make up his mind: the issue was becoming undesirably politicized. A careful diplomat, Ogata was determined to prevent the Board becoming totally preoccupied by the succession. Waldheim, under pressure from the US Secretary of State and the Swedish Minister of Foreign Affairs, pushed her to the limit, asking her to canvass Board members and delaying his decision. Finally in May, when the Board delegates were already assembled in Mexico City for the annual session, Waldheim announced his selection of James Grant. By a considerable margin, one that included the eastern Europeans, his candidacy was preferred by the member governments of the Board.

This was critical to Waldheim's decision. He was also aware that the UN's image in the US was declining, that Unicef was among its few well-known and popular institutions, and feared that if its directorship was lost to the US, the UN as a whole might suffer. But with Waldheim, as with the Board, the decisive factor in favour of Grant was his record. A lifetime of service to Third World development, including stretches in China, India, Sri Lanka and Turkey, gave him the edge. Michanek had an excellent record as the head of SIDA, the Swedish bilateral aid administration, but had no equivalent personal experience in developing countries.

James Pineo Grant was born in Peking in 1922. His grandfather had been a medical missionary in China. In the 1920s, his father, Dr John B. Grant of the Rockefeller Foundation, was developing a reputation as one of Asia's leading public-health pioneers, using his position on the faculty of the Peking Union Medical College to influence China's embryonic national-health policy. During the 1930s, he became a close associate of Dr Ludwik Rajchman, then chief of the League of Nations health section, who first visited Peking at Grant's instigation.

Grant senior shared Rajchman's still revolutionary view that, in areas where poverty was widespread, governments must shoulder the burden of promoting health, and that cost-effective programmes against low standards of public hygiene and communicable disease took precedence over elaborate curative care for the few who could afford it. After the Japanese invasion forced him out of China, Grant senior helped establish the All-India School of Hygiene and Public Health in Calcutta. As an advisor to WHO in the 1950s, he was on the same circuit as Sam Keeny, Unicef's Regional Director in Asia, and Fred Soper, malaria superstar. Like them, and Rajchman, he was one of the exceptional breed of men who made up the first generation of truly international public-health practitioners. No-one exerted on his son Jim a greater influence, both in his zeal for serving the greater good of Mankind and in his style of operation.

Jim Grant's childhood and part of his youth was spent in China, in an environment where leaps of professional imagination and the cultivation of friends in high places could make a major effect on the health of millions. After wartime military service in Burma and China, his fluency in Chinese equipped him to serve first on the staff of General George C. Marshall during his unsuccessful effort to reconcile China's warring factions, and then in 1946, at the age of 24, as a representative for UNRRA's relief programme to Communist-held areas. Later, after a law degree at Harvard and a few years of legal practice, Grant joined the ICA, predecessor of USAID. In 1956, he became an unusually young chief of mission to Ceylon (Sri Lanka), and in 1958 was recalled to Washington to become ICA's Deputy Director responsible for programmes and planning.

Except for a short spell at the Department of State under the Kennedy Administration, he thereafter never wavered from a career in the expanding field of development assistance. He served USAID in Turkey and Washington, and in 1969 became the first head of a new private organization, the Overseas Development Council, set up in Washington to foster US understanding of Third World problems. Under his leadership, the ODC quickly became a source of respected economic analysis and an influential voice in US development-assistance policy. Grant had learned from his father's example the importance of harnessing political allies to a cause. The Kennedy era and the first Development Decade brought with them a new political consciousness towards developing countries. Grant worked strenuously to validate that consciousness, enlist the interest of senior US policy-makers, and prevent the goals of Third World social and economic progress from sliding into the foreign policy background.

Throughout the international development community, the early 1970s were a time of reappraisal. Grant, active in many of the professional and intellectual fora where conventional wisdom was being thrown out of the window, was strongly influenced by ideas which were gradually taking shape within academic and policy-making circles. In 1976, while taking part in a Study Team set up by President Ford to examine the problem of world hunger and malnutrition, Grant and an ODC colleague, Morris D. Morris, decided that a new way was needed for measuring the effects of development policies on social well-being. The old yardstick—Gross National Product (GNP) divided by population—was a symptom of what was wrong with the traditional emphasis on economic growth. *Per capita* GNP was an efficient method for measuring a country's economic output, but it said little about the internal distribution of wealth or about the quality of life for its citizens. Some countries, and some regions within countries, had managed to make great improvements in social well-being without much economic growth. These success stories—in China, Sri Lanka, parts of India and elsewhere—offered some hope that the right mix of development strategies might uplift the lives of the poorest people in the poorest countries much faster than the slow process of wealth accumulation. To learn from such successes, it must first be possible to measure scientifically what they had achieved. In 1977, the ODC published its proposed yardstick: an index to measure a country's Physical Quality of Life (PQLI).

The PQLI computed infant mortality, life expectancy at age one and basic literacy, and ranked countries according to the well-being—or its absence—of their citizens by this index. Its efficacy as a measuring tool or guide to policy was contested in the circles where these things matter, but to Grant its public relations aspect was equally important. If arguing about the merits of PQLI prompted development planners and strategists to pay more attention to the lot of human beings and gained currency for the view that lowering infant mortality, increasing life expectancy and enhancing literacy were proper targets of development policy, then that was a valuable corrective in itself. Grant was riding against the current which now presented the eradication of the misery endured by much of Mankind as a very elusive target, fraught with imponderables and complexities. History taught that poverty, wretchedness, squalor and ill-health only ultimately succumbed to material prosperity—but some countries had flouted history and proved that much could be done without it. Grant believed that their experiences must be analyzed, synthesized and widely applied; that they offered Mankind an opportunity to bend the course of human history in the direction of the poor.

During the years immediately before his appointment as Executive Director of Unicef, Grant spoke and wrote tirelessly on this theme. His gospel was the 1976 Report to the Club of Rome, 'Reshaping the International Order', to which he was a contributor. This report called for a commitment to meeting certain global targets in infant mortality, life expectancy, literacy and birth rate by the end of the century. After the experience of the first two Development Decades, sobered observers regarded this kind of global goal setting as simplistic. Beset by its own problems, an inward looking Western world had less goodwill and an even shorter attention span towards the problems of the Third World poor than a decade ago. Even the humanitarian view was jaundiced by what seemed like scanty results from private and public generosity. Grant's sense of the need for political allies led him to popularize and sloganize in an effort to lift the development banner out of the disaffection in which it was trailing. If new, attractive and attainable goals could be set, they might generate sufficient political will to turn world poverty around.

In 1980, after years of sharpening these ideas, Grant became the leader of an international organization in the UN system—one that was popular, respected and dedicated to the well-being of the most vulnerable members of the human race. Unicef, if seemed, offered a sound programme philosophy, long practical experience, high international standing and a cause with strong popular appeal . . . all of which could be harnessed to a regeneration of the development crusade.

Not only the career background which impressed Waldheim and the Executive Board equipped Jim Grant for his new role at the head of Unicef. Like Pate and Labouisse before him, he was a human being dedicated to improving the lives of the world's least advantaged people, especially the children. This motivation inspired his action. His personal commitment—a more flamboyant and driving version than the quiet self-effacement of Labouisse—was an important ingredient in the credentials he brought to Unicef. Grant shared with Labouisse another important attribute: a wife who complemented his leadership superbly. Ethel Henck Grant quickly immersed herself in Unicef in the stalwart tradition of Martha Lucas Pate and Eve Curie Labouisse before her, and began to make her own special contribution.

By 1 January 1980, when Grant took over, Unicef had existed for thirty-three years, just over eighteen of them under Maurice Pate, and just under fifteen under Harry Labouisse. Although the organization had grown enormously and its programme philosophy had gone through various metamorphoses, its evolution had been relatively trouble-free. The main reason was the continuity of its leadership, the firm and steady hand of two successive Executive Directors whose personal style was unassuming but whose statesmanship was sure.

Under Pate, Unicef had earned a reputation for prompt and effective response to the distress call of the weakest members of humanity. During Labouisse's tenure, it had become recognized as an organization fully involved in the process of development, equipped to play a special role, if a modest one, alongside the UN and its specialized agencies, UNDP, the World Bank, and other members of the international big league. Labouisse himself had articulated in many fora the underlying idea behind Unicef's contemporary philosophy and programming actions: that helping children to lead healthier and more fruitful lives is a prerequisite for national progress. He had put his personal weight, and Unicef's, behind the basic services strategy, and worked closely with Dr Halfdan Mahler and WHO in endorsing and promoting the concept of primary-health care and 'Health for All'. He had enjoyed a very special sense of partnership with his two deputies, Dick Heyward and Charles Egger. He had championed children and Unicef without seeking the limelight, and without allowing the organization to compromise any of the clean bill of health its humanitarian reputation had already established for it in the 1950s.

One of Labouisse's outstanding achievements was to keep Unicef free of political currents. This was a principle which had governed Pate's leadership; but during Labouisse's it was a much harder principle to maintain. During the 1960s and 1970s competing political pressures became a much more dominant fact of life within the entire UN family. It required extraordinary staying power to navigate the complexities of post-colonial conflict in Nigeria and in Indo-China and somehow keep some sort of channel open to children. It was also difficult to resist pressure in an international community of nations so much enlarged by the end of Western Imperial adventures and in which so many of the old alliances were volatile. Labouisse never conceded to any pressures of this kind; this was with him an unbreakable principle of organizational and personal integrity. When the occasion demanded, he demonstrated a willingness to take risks and showed considerable personal courage. But a risk he never took was with Unicef's reputation. This made him seem at times unduly cautious and publicity-shy. But for him, the short-term advantage must always be sacrificed to the longer-term. What mattered was that the trunk of the Unicef tree grow solidly and well, and he did his best to protect it and allow it to do so.

Financially, Unicef had grown enormously in the previous fifteen years. Annual income had grown from $35 million in 1965 to over $250 million in 1979. The number of staff had grown from 774 to 2184 in the same period. The programme of co-operation which they helped to oversee had changed radically in character. Milk and disease control—the nutrition and health approaches which had characterized Unicef's first decade or two—were now gone for good, or subsumed in basic health services. Under Labouisse, family-planning programmes had received support for the first time; support to water and sanitation had expanded unrecognizably; the amount of Unicef assistance expended on training programmes for primary-health and other workers in the less sophisticated echelons of basic services had risen dramatically. These areas were all ones in which Labouisse had taken a personal interest.

He had travelled widely in the field, accompanied by his wife Eve who supplemented his role superbly. This very special Labouisse partnership had made a point of trying to witness in depth and at first hand the day-to-day problems of poverty and the programmes in which Unicef assistance was playing a part. These experiences had fortified his belief in the need for a conscious effort to avoid the accumulation of power at the centre of an organization, a natural tendency in any expanding bureaucracy. Like Pate before him, and like Heyward, he believed that it was important to decentralize organizational power and give Unicef representatives the freedom to adapt policies to local conditions. Programmes in which Unicef co-operated must be able to grow organically, according to priorities established in the developing countries. In 1975, a management survey undertaken by the Scandinavian Institute for Administrative Research (SIAR) had the effect of institutionalizing and strengthening these trends.

In January 1980, when Jim Grant took over from Labouisse, the change in leadership signalled the end of an era. Although some key figures in headquarters—in particular Dick Heyward, Charles Egger and Jack Charnow—were urged to stay on for the first two years of Grant's regime, there was a sense of expectancy about their forthcoming retirement and replacement by a younger generation. As well as these three, many other senior Unicef figures stationed elsewhere retired at or around this time: Gordon Carter, Glan Davies, Ralph Eckert, John Grun, Martin Sandberg, and others. These and many others had joined Unicef as young men and given it most of their working lives and more besides. They had helped to shape the Unicef Grant inherited, and their disappearance represented a more complete changing of the guard than had taken place at the time of Labouisse's arrival. Many left an indelible print on programmes and policies around the world—some in more than one country, continent or hemisphere.

Among them, the contribution of one man stood out in particular: that of Heyward. By 1980, he had served Unicef in the same position for thirty-one years, an extraordinary performance which combined supremacy over day-to-day operations with unchallenged intellectual leadership. The way in which Unicef's policies over the years constantly evolved to reflect the latest in technical understanding and growing experience within the international development community owed more to Heyward than to any other single individual. Almost every articulation of programme policy bore his imprint. His ability to apply contemporary understanding on development issues to the needs of children around the world was one of the organization's most valuable assets in its years of evolution through the first two Development Decades.

While Grant inherited the darkest and most entangled horror in the story of postwar international relief—the crisis in Kampuchea—he also inherited all the goodwill generated by the International Year of the Child. The euphoria generated by IYC and the extra lift it had given to Unicef's growing income had fuelled a vision of spectacular growth.

Jim Grant, in his first year of office, visited the capitals of major Unicef donor countries and showed himself an aggressive fund-raiser. But if income was really to climb by leaps and bounds, sources of revenue other than steady increments from traditional donors had to be found. In April 1980, a breakthrough occurred which made it seem as if the new lode had been discovered. At last, a line had opened to the oil wealth of the Arab world.

Since the early 1970s, particularly after OPEC action had raised the price of Middle-Eastern oil, Jim McDougall and François Rémy, successive Unicef Regional Directors in Beirut, had tried hard to interest Arab governments in contributing more than token amounts to Unicef's treasury. Labouisse had visited the Shah of Iran in 1972, and various approaches had been made to other heads of state, to little immediate avail. Then in 1979, by a curious chain of circumstances, Sabah Al Alawi, the Unicef liaison officer in Riyadh, struck up a close contact with a brother of King Khaled of Saudi Arabia, Prince Talal Bin Abdul Al Saud. Prince Talal had a long record of interest in social well-being, and had been instrumental in establishing the first school for girls in Saudi Arabia.

Prince Talal was an enthusiastic ham radio operator. In one of his typically flamboyant ventures, Aldo Farina, head of the Italian Committee for Unicef, had persuaded a world association of 'hams' to adopt Unicef for IYC. Prince Talal entered into the spirit of this idea, and sent off messages of solidarity with Unicef from his broadcasting studio to radio contacts around the world. Sabah Al Alawi made himself useful, and managed to interest the Prince more deeply in Unicef's work. In April 1980, at Grant's invitation, Prince Talal visited UN headquarters in New York, met Secretary-General Waldheim, and took up an honorary position as Unicef's Special Envoy. The Prince wanted to do something for the world's children. In the eyes of Grant and of Unicef, that something primarily consisted of tapping financial resources, as well as becoming a spokesman for Unicef on behalf of children. A year later, in April 1981, as a result of Prince Talal's initiatives, seven Arab governments joined forces in an Arab Gulf Programme for United Nations Development Organizations. Very large sums were spoken of and Unicef and UNDP expected to be the principal beneficiaries.

Inspired by the prospect of a large jump in income, Grant began to weave the ideas he had helped to develop at the Overseas Development Council into Unicef's fabric. He was strongly impressed by its field-based, programme-oriented nature, which offered a far larger and more solid canvas to work on than the research-based, public affairs nature of the ODC. He saw in Unicef's experience with trying to help extend basic services in developing countries a chance to build up a body of evidence and practical example which would help the world to realize by the year 2000 the targets set by the 1976 Report to the Club of Rome—particularly the reduction of infant mortality.

As a medium for his ideas, Grant decided to establish as a tradition the publication of an annual report on 'The State of the World's Children' on Unicef's anniversary. At the end of the International Year of the Child, Labouisse had issued a report on 'The State of the Children in the Developing World'. Grant took up this idea, and its principal architect, Peter Adamson, a British development writer, honed the report into an impressive international public information vehicle. Grant's first 'The State of the World's Children Report' issued in 1980 represented a fusion of the theme he had been pounding out for the last few years with Unicef's mandate for children and its experience of practical programming. He spoke of accelerating the all-out effort to improve the lives of children by reducing the ratio between money spent and benefits achieved. Because of rapid population growth, the numbers of the absolute poor—estimated at 780 million, of whom half were children under fifteen years old—were outstripping the pace of development on their behalf. The low-income route to social progress, tried and proven in a handful of countries, offered the world a chance it must not turn down. To help the world seize this chance, Unicef offered the basic-services strategy. It must be put into practice more widely, and at a faster pace.

Grant believed that in order to promote this process, Unicef needed an intellectual cadre that could analyze and synthesize the basic-services experience and translate it from programme to programme, country to country, organization to organization, using all the communications channels available in the penultimate decade of the twentieth century. He perceived this task as an extension of Unicef's existing work, building upon it and multiplying its overall impact. He used a number of metaphors to convey his ideas: Unicef must 'change gears'; the task ahead was to find out where and how 'the points could be switched'.

Grant's misfortune was that the invigoration of Unicef's effort, and the new phase in the growth of its programmes and intellectual capacity he envisaged, were being elaborated at a moment when global economic recession was causing many governments to slice back social-services programmes, as well as aid for the developing countries. The chill was beginning to reach the UN system, and many other UN organizations were talking grimly of retrenchment. By contrast, Unicef's Executive Board, meeting for its annual session in New York in May 1981, found itself addressing a budget for a considerably expanded programme of co-operation and a financial plan projecting a skyward expansion of income—from $313 million in 1980 to $710 million in 1984. This budget turned out to be unrealistic. The economic climate, not to mention the progressive sense of disenchantment with development issues which characterized the dawning of the third Development Decade, was unsuited to such dramatic plans. The Board made it plain that they disapproved, and modifications had to be made.

Grant, undaunted, reiterated the theme of 'more for less', and stepped up his fund-raising initiatives to both traditional Unicef donors and to sources—governmental and nongovernmental. During the summer of 1981, as the effects of global recession began to bite deeper, the need for austerity could no longer be ignored. The rise of the US dollar against other currencies had lowered the value of contributions pledged to Unicef for the current year by $40 million. In the face of the inevitable, a certain amount of trimming was required, both in programmes of co-operation and in plans for expansion.

The appointment of Prince Talal as Unicef's Special Envoy in April 1981 had very positive repercussions. Talal threw himself and his personal establishment into his role as international spokesman for the world's children, taking the task to heart and cultivating support for Unicef not only in the Arab world but in countries in every continent. In September 1981, at a ceremony in the UN Secretary-General's office, Prince Talal, in his capacity as President of the Arab Gulf Programme, pledged $40 million to Unicef from its resources, $25 million of which was for 1981. Grant had worked strenuously with the Prince to reach this happy conclusion; the sum compared well with the top Swedish and US annual contributions of around $35 million. It was, however, considerably less than the sums originally forecast and no longer represented the great financial leap forward many had been led to expect. Unavoidably, therefore, there was a slight sense of anticlimax.

During the next four years, Prince Talal travelled widely all over the globe at his own expense as an advocate for children and Unicef's cause. As Special Envoy, he visited Unicef-assisted programmes in Niger, Djibouti, Somalia, Senegal, Brazil, Bangladesh, Colombia, Costa Rica, Thailand and many other countries all over the developing world. He also visited many European capitals to persuade heads of government and leading figures to increase their country's contribution to Unicef and the cause of social development.

The Arab Gulf Programme, known as AGFUND, has continued to be an important Unicef donor, while its contributions to development through other UN member organizations have also expanded. When Prince Talal relinquished his role as Unicef Special Envoy in December 1984, Grant paid tribute to his dedication on behalf of children, and underlined the continuing partnership that the Prince's and Unicef's coinciding goals guaranteed. By the end of 1985, AGFUND had contributed to Unicef a total of $59·5 million.

The other significant lift to Unicef's resources was provided by the Italian Government, which announced in 1982 their heightened interest in helping to alleviate world hunger and malnutrition. This decision reflected an increased awareness among the Italian public about the problems of poverty and underdevelopment, an awareness that Aldo Farina, Director of the Italian Committee for Unicef—with his cultivation of allies for Unicef over the years and his enthusiasm for establishing Unicef's name as a household word in schools, in the entertainment industry, and everywhere obviously relevant or otherwise to the cause of Third World children—had done a great deal to engender.

A joint programme of WHO/Unicef support to nutritional improvement in a minimum of fifteen countries was approved by the 1982 Unicef Board, and the Italian Government agreed to cover its entire cost of $85 million over the period 1982–86, adding a further $15 million for providing certain countries in Africa with essential drugs. The first three countries to develop special programmes under this joint WHO/Unicef/Italian initiative were Mali, Sudan and Tanzania; their design reflected the cardinal tenet of the primary-health care era: that health and nutritional elements in programmes are inseparable, and that they in turn form part of a broad-ranging approach which embraces food production, conservation, and storage in the home, as well as education, environmental sanitation, and all the components in the basic-services package. The focus on Africa reflected growing concern throughout the international community with the emergencies which continually engulfed the African continent, setting back development prospects. Italy also became an important donor to emergency programmes in Africa, setting up in 1985 a Fund for Italian Emergency Aid, and committing up to $110 million towards programmes of joint co-operation with Unicef.

Since the early 1980s, there has been a slow but steady increase in Unicef's income, but not on the scale so optimistically anticipated at the height of IYC excitement. The new avenues of support which opened up during 1981 and 1982 helped to cushion Unicef rather than usher in a new growth phase on a par with that experienced during the late 1970s. The fact that Unicef's fortunes have kept buoyant during what has largely been an adverse financial and political environment for the UN as a whole is owed to a considerable extent to Grant's energetic capacity for fund-raising. The generosity of major government donors and the general public towards the drought emergencies in Africa has also played an important part. In 1985, Unicef's total income was $362 million, of which $94 million came from nongovernmental sources, including the sale of greeting cards—an increase of nearly $50 million over the past five years.

In 1981, the two-year period of the changing of the guard in Unicef ended. Two new Deputy Executive Directors had been appointed: Margaret Catley-Carlson, previously the Canadian delegate to the Board, in Heyward's place as Head of Operations; and Richard Jolly, previously Director of the Institute of Development Studies in the University of Sussex, England, in Egger's place as Head of Programmes. Grant had also brought on board, as a third Deputy for External Relations, Tarzie Vittachi, a Sri Lankan journalist and editor who had demonstrated as the Head of Information for the UN Fund for Population Activities a particular genius for popularizing complex development issues and getting them widely aired.

At year's end the three Unicef 'giants'—Heyward, Egger and Charnow—men who most potently symbolized an unbroken thread of organizational continuity and personified the established Unicef tradition, graciously took their final bow. Now the stage truly belonged to Grant and his new generation.

In 1980, the midpoint of the Decade for Women, Unicef undertook its first major examination of the role of women within the development process since the basic-services and primary-health care strategies were adopted in the mid-1970s. The request for such a report came from the 1978 Executive

Board, in response to a statement by Mrs Titi Memet, Unicef's family planning advisor, the most senior woman on its staff, and a keen advocate of women's issues.

Unicef's concern with women dated back to its moment of birth, but the movement for women's rights which gathered momentum in the 1970s in yet another manifestation of the quest for alternatives came to the situation of women from a very different direction. Unicef at this particular juncture was very much a male-dominated organization. The women who had made such a noteworthy mark on Unicef's first twenty years or so—Adelaide Sinclair, Charles Egger's distinguished predecessor as Deputy Executive Director for Programmes; Margaret Gaan, Sam Keeny's key lieutenant in Asia; Alice Shaffer, Unicef representative for a number of Latin American countries; Gertrude Lutz, whose career in Unicef began as Chief of Mission in Poland in 1949 and ended as Deputy Director in the office for Europe—had all retired by or in the early 1970s. Whether or not the temporary lack of a female stamp in Unicef's senior ranks at the time when the campaign for women's rights reached a crescendo made a difference to its outlook or not, the fact was that there was a good deal of ambivalence within the organization about its relevance to programmes of Unicef co-operation.

From its earliest forays into health campaigns and feeding programmes in the villages of Asia and Africa, Unicef had accepted as a matter of course that the well-being of children was inseparable from the well-being of their mothers. In maternal and child-health care, Unicef had a legitimate claim to have helped pioneer improvement in the lives of women; it had taken a lead in according due respect to the nurturing role of women, not only as mothers and home-makers, but also as healers and birth attendants.

From health care, Unicef assistance for women had broadened to training in what in the early days was described as 'mothercraft' and 'homecraft'. The support which, at Charles Egger's initiative, had been first offered to women's groups in east Africa in the late 1950s had initially been provided as a means of improving child nutrition and family welfare. But before long, the women's group or women's association had been seen in a more potentially significant light. The ideas which, in parts of French-speaking Africa, found their expression in *animation rurale*, suggested that the women's group not only provided a context in which women could learn new skills, but also gave them a new set of ideas about themselves, the kind of lives they were leading, and what to do about them.

Such awareness was the precondition of taking any kind of action to breach the rigid codes governing family and community life, most of which were designed to keep women in inferior and subservient roles, and in whose application women usually connived without question. Brought up in a narrow world of drudgery, male domination and constant child-bearing, women's willpower was sapped. Before they could take a small step forward, they needed to be able to conceive of other relationships than the fixed ones of kin, and achieve new worth and dignity in their own eyes. Changing the attitudes of government officials and national leaders towards women in such a way as to open up more opportunities and more protection for the fulfilment of their domestic and maternal roles would not help women who had no sense of their advantage. In a telling statement, an observer wrote of the 'bat women of Asia, clustered safely in the darkness of male domination and fluttering about fearfully when an opening door lets in some light'.

The growing sense that attitudinal change was needed—both by women and about women—in order for them to profit from the development process on their families' behalf was one of the reasons for the stress on reaching women and out-of-school girls through the mechanisms of non-formal education. In some parts of Asia and many parts of Africa a female illiteracy rate of seventy per cent in rural areas was still common in the early 1980s, and in some places rose as high as ninety per cent. Families who appreciated the benefits of schooling often appreciated them on behalf of a boy, who might find a salaried job behind a desk in town and handsomely repay the investment; but not on behalf of a girl. Her duties helping her mother in the house and in the fields were usually more economically important to the family. The disproportion between the numbers of boys and girls entering school reinforced the discriminatory process which kept men moving ahead while women remained in ignorance of the modern world. The theme that more girls should be in school was constantly repeated; but what ministries of education were actually doing, or able to do, to redress this balance was difficult to identify.

One study of village life undertaken in Africa in the early 1970s described the classic syndrome whereby the persistence of traditional education for girls reinforced women's marginalization: 'According to tradition, the (village) community entrusts the education of girls to the mother. The training focuses on routine procedures which girls will be expected to perform as wives, mothers, agricultural workers . . . The mother participates with a deep sense of responsibility, eagerness, and real interest . . . She is interested in being a good educator because certain rewards accrue to her such as enhanced status in her community and emotional satisfaction . . . While the mother is found sufficient by the village community for educating girls, nonetheless she suffers from a major handicap in that role—namely, the education she imparts is greatly limited to her own ignorance, and inability, due to illiteracy and isolation, to gather further information developed on scientific lines. Thus she transmits to her daughter only those traditions, superstitions, and ways of living that she knows, many of which are nonconducive to socio-economic development of the community.'

Although Unicef's view of the role of women in development widened over the years, there was a strong latent resistance to the idea that Unicef itself—which was after all created in the name of children rather than women—should be concerned with any other female role than that of the bearer and rearer of children. Resistance to picking up the cudgels on behalf of women *qua* women was reinforced by the fact that changes in the laws affecting women's status and employment—the primary goal of much of the women's rights movement in the industrialized societies—would have little effect on the lot of rural women in developing countries. The kind of discrimination experienced by women caught in the trap of poverty, ignorance and life-long labour was not easily susceptible to the passage of laws, however important it was to create a legal framework for equal rights. Unicef believed that the attitudinal change that must take place in society to improve the lot of women was more likely to be promoted by providing services to help her improve her maternal and domestic performance. Better health and nutrition for her children and herself were seen as inherently attractive to women, and as a first step to the opening up of their minds to a wider range of family life improvements.

By the late 1970s, certain champions of women's rights had intensified the debate concerning the lot of women in developing countries. The demand for equality in job opportunities and pay which characterized much of the clamour in the Western world spilled over into the developing world with a demand that more respect be given to the economic functions of women in rural society. A group of protagonists began trying to put across the message that, in communities living at the edge of survival, there was no division between women's role as mothers and their role as economic providers, and that any effort to help them as mothers was bound to be handicapped by a failure to take all their responsibilities into account. The long obsession with economic production as the gauge of development and its definition as something with a monetary value had obscured the fact that all the functions required of a woman in traditional society—including child-bearing—were critical to the family's means of support.

Since the days of Unicef's first support to homecraft and mothercraft in rural Africa, the enormous domestic load carried by many Third World women was well understood. What was different now was to describe this load in economic rather than social terms. In large parts of Africa, women undertook almost every task connected with growing and processing food, including planting, weeding, hoeing, harvesting, winnowing, storing the crops, and rendering them into cookable ingredients. Elsewhere their agricultural burden might not be as heavy, but the most casual inspection of the Third World countryside would show that nowhere was it light. They tended all small livestock, milked anything that could be milked, grew all the vegetables. Since most of this was done without money changing hands, none of it figured in the development statistics. In all traditional societies women also collected the family's water and fuel supply, carrying heavy pots to and from the river, gathering sticks, burning charcoal, or patting dung into cakes and drying it in the sun. They fashioned cooking pots from clay, plaited grasses into baskets, scraped out gourds, spun and wove wool and cotton. 'Handicrafts' like these were no pastime for creative expression, but the necessary manufacture of utensils for household use. None of these tasks counted in any national balance sheet as economic production unless their result was sold through some identifiable channel, even though the family would perish if they were not done.

The changes that modernization, or development, had wrought in the landscape over the past twenty years had tended to increase, rather than relieve, women's drudgery. Rising population had meant a heavier pressure of people on the land, which made it harder to grow enough food, further to walk to gather fuel, longer to fill the water pot from the trickle of water in the bottom of the well. It also swelled the casual labour force, making it harder for landless families—whose womenfolk routinely sought agricultural or construction site work—to make ends meet. Meanwhile, most of the opportunities for improvement had come the way of men. Agricultural development almost invariably meant cash crops, crops that could be sold by a national marketing board to pay the national import bill. Cash was for men, for the heads of household, the supposed providers. So agricultural extension workers visited the men, not the women, with advice about hybrid seeds, tools and fertilizers. Improved technology, training courses, credit to set up a mechanized mill or other food-processing business: all went to men.

Without education, women had no earning power. Yet the provision of everything needed to maintain the home and keep the children fed and clothed remained their responsibility. In a world in which it was becoming more and more difficult to manage without resource to cash, women were being thrust deeper and deeper into the cracks and crevices of society, losing status rather than gaining it. With all the demands upon them, it was scarcely surprising that when they leapt at the few opportunities they were offered, it was usually the ones that reduced their workload or improved their family comfort: a more convenient water supply, a tin roof for their hut, a chance to sell some handicrafts for cash. The lecture on nutrition or the injunction to bring a perfectly healthy toddler several miles to receive a vaccination shot which made him feverish and fretful rarely had the same appeal.

The priority need—the one women themselves felt—that their domestic load must be lightened first came forcefully home to Unicef in connection with water projects. The 1972 conference of government ministers held in Lomé, west Africa, on 'Children, Youth, Women and Development Plans' was one of the first occasions in which the importance of a sure supply of drinking water in transforming the situation of women was given forceful expression, and it was not a conclusion that Unicef, the convenor of the conference, had anticipated. Although improving family and child health was the underlying purpose of water and sanitation schemes, it began to emerge that their popularity with the women in the villages had more to do with convenience: their understanding of the connection between disease and impure water was very uncertain. As the years went by, Unicef's co-operation in water-supply programmes concentrated less on engineering and hardware, and more on women's involvement in public health. Without their participation and understanding, the full health benefits of water programmes could not be realized.

Another activity which helped to bring the role of women to the fore was applied nutrition. The only guarantee—and it was still only a partial guarantee—that green vegetables, eggs and milk grown on a family or a communal plot would find their way into the mouths of children rather than onto the local market was to equip women, not men, to cultivate them. In 1974, when the global food crisis was at its peak, Unicef turned its attention to household food processing and preparation. The tremendous outpouring of technologically-appropriate gadgets had mostly yielded improved tools for economic production: brick-making machines and better ploughshares. Unicef began to support the research and development of village technology for domestic labour-saving: bio-gas plants, fuel-efficient cooking stoves, rat-proof storage bins, the drying and canning of fruits and vegetables.

As the full weight of women's responsibilities became better understood, so did the interlocking elements of women's overall predicament. Many hopeful schemes were languishing because women were not fulfilling their expected roles as instruments of community development. More significantly from the point of view of the economic planners, they were compounding their problems by the large numbers of children they persisted in bearing. At a time when concern about population growth was dominated by frightening statistical estimates of the effect of exponential growth rates on dwindling planetary resources, Unicef helped to reinject the human dimension into the debate.

Labouisse's statement for the 1974 Population Conference in Bucharest argued persuasively that the population issue needed to be examined from the point of view of parents' decisions about family size. Apart from pride and joy in their children, parents in poor communities needed large numbers of children to swell the family workforce and ensure that enough survived to care for them in their old age. On the other hand, they were also beginning to worry about dividing shrinking landholdings into ever smaller portions among their male offspring and the expenses of schooling. But those who weighed up the pros and cons of family planning were usually men: the low status of women meant that they did not have much say in decisions about conception and pregnancy. No effect could be made on parental decisions about family size and spacing without taking these considerations into account and doing something about them.

The disappointing results of many family-planning campaigns opened the way to a new appreciation of women's status. Most modern contraceptive technology inhibited female, not male, fertility. Yet the women in poor societies, those who bore most of the world's children, were not stepping forward with alacrity to swallow pills and have loops inserted. Unless the male head of household began to feel children as an economic burden, rather than a value, he would not encourage his wife to go in for family planning. As women did all the work connected with rearing children, including carrying the economic burden for their food and dress, the men had little motivation to listen to the family planners. And a woman was most unlikely to oppose her husband; such an idea would not occur to her, however exhausted she was by child-bearing and however painful the prospect of another mouth to feed and little to put in it.

In certain places, in Kerala State in India, for example, the success of family-planning campaigns began to illustrate a connection between a woman's education and her susceptibility to family-planning advice. Some learning made a great difference to a woman's capacity to resist pressure from a husband or a mother-in-law. It also influenced how her children regarded her, and their attitude later in life towards the role of women. A sense of herself, of her own ability to do something and be something of her own encouraged her to consider spacing her children, of having a certain number rather than whatever number God and her husband conspired to send her. Once again, the attitudinal break-out from under heavy layers of fatalism was the trigger for behavioural change. Demographic researchers were beginning to establish that, apart from a leap in economic fortune, the factor correlating most closely with a drop in the birth rate was a rise in female literacy. Here was another means of advancing social goals without having to wait for the distant millennium of universal prosperity.

During the late 1970s, Unicef's practical emphasis for women continued to be on maternal and child-health care and nonformal education, within which responsible parenthood was an important strand. Women's lack of economic and decision-making power was still a problem Unicef felt reluctant to tackle specifically. There was support for vocational training and women's groups: sewing machines and cookery equipment were standard items in many country programmes. But the rationale behind their supply was not that they might permit women to enter the tailoring or catering business; rather that they could run up small garments for their children or ring nutritious changes in the family diet.

Attitudes were, however, rapidly changing. The Western ethnocentric view that women, no matter what their cultural environment or how perilous their hold on the means of survival, were primarily housewives who looked after children while their husbands went to work was finally being eroded. Concern about another social problem—the misery of life for increasing numbers of mothers and children in the slums and shanty towns of Third World cities—finally laid any residual prejudice to rest.

In 1971, the Executive Board had agreed to the expansion of Unicef's aid to children in poor urban areas based on a report prepared by Dr Constantina Sfilios-Rothschild, a sociologist well-known for her research on family affairs. There had earlier been resistance to this idea. Everyone had decried the way development investment had been skewed in favour of the cities, and Unicef had felt that all its aid was needed in the countryside.

Townspeople already had access to health care and education. The city's wealth was a magnet for the best services a country could provide; few doctors and teachers wanted to work in rural areas. Improving urban amenities could only aggravate the exodus of the poor from the countryside to town, an already alarming phenomenon. The proliferation of slums and shanty towns, *bidonvilles*, *favelas*, squatters' settlements of flimsy shacks in disused nooks or wasteland on the urban periphery, was being greeted everywhere with municipal horror, and often with municipal bulldozers. But for all the indications that they were not wanted, those shaking off the dust of agricultural life from their feet and exchanging it for the mud and putrefying garbage of the slum did not seem disposed to go away. Jobs, cash and amenities beckoned the new city dwellers and others following hard on their heels. They had come, in their hundreds and thousands, to stay. The squalor, the high cost of city life, the loss of traditional community ties and the resultant changes in family life, were a price they were willing to pay for a foothold on the ladder to the modern world.

By 1976, when HABITAT, the international conference on human settlements, was held in Vancouver, people had begun to talk about 'exploding cities'. The statistics of the demographic change were frightening in their implications. In 1960, only half the world's nearly two billion people were urban dwellers, by 2000, over two billion people would be living in the cities of the Third World alone; more than half of these would be living in poverty; more than half of those living in poverty would be women and children.

In many countries of Africa, Asia and Latin America, urban population was growing at double the national rate, and the slum population was growing at double the urban rate, not only because of migration from the rural areas but also because women in the slums continue to bear many children. This meant that, in cities like Lima, Lagos and Bombay, the numbers of people crammed into squalid huts and tenements were doubling well within a decade. City budgets were already overstretched. Even if the authorities could be persuaded to see the shanty-town dwellers as people with something to offer instead of as a blot on the municipal escutcheon, how could they provide basic physical amenities—roads, transport, garbage collection, sewage disposal, water points, street lights—not to mention jobs, schools and health care—for the swelling tide of urban humanity?

The answer was that they could not. During the 1970s, as new shanty towns mushroomed faster than fire, pestilence, and city bulldozers could clear them away, the apostles of alternative thinking began to present the nightmare of urban proliferation in a new light. They argued that the tenacity and ingenuity of slum-dwellers in solving their own problems was a resource to be husbanded, organized, and built upon.

Instead of trying to tear down their humble structures and banish them to somewhere even further out on the rim of society, city authorities should help squatters become legalized citizens and offer them incentives to upgrade their environment. Slum inhabitants were not parasites; they carted stones on building sites, swept streets, drove rickshaws and taxis. They were people on whom the city depended in many of its less salubrious and lowly-paid occupations. Vendors and petty traders were part of the city's economy, whether or not their modest transactions showed up in the municipal balance sheet. The authorities should drain land and install water pipes, offer leases and loans for building, lay out minimal 'sites and services'. With some security and a sense that officialdom was on their side instead of constantly threatening to evict them, people could be encouraged to form neighbourhood groups, volunteer their labour for garbage collection or road mending, become health workers or child minders. Built on community involvement, the new approach to eliminating the worst effects of urban poverty was a variation on the alternative order.

By 1975, Unicef was beginning to ask itself why the basic-services strategy was not being adopted faster in the cities. Anthony Kennedy, a Harvard-trained architect, was seconded to Unicef from the UN Centre for Housing, Building and Urban Planning and asked to explore the possibilities of Unicef assistance to slum children and youth. One of Unicef's first contributions to urban renewal was a self-help housing project in Lusaka, Zambia, in collaboration with the American Friends Service Committee and the World Bank. The Friends and Unicef were particularly concerned with training people to make the process of community participation work.

Another landmark programme was in India. In 1975, Kennedy recruited Dr William Cousins, an American sociologist who had spent several years working in Indian community development, to join Unicef's staff in New Delhi. Cousins, Dr Surya Rao and the staff of the municipality of Hyderabad, India's fifth largest city, designed an expansion of a project in Hyderbad's *bastis*—pocket slum neighbourhoods. Surya Rao and his team were veterans of India's community development experience, and they concentrated on building a spirit of *basti* co-operation before trying to upgrade housing and other physical amenities. They fostered welfare committees, youth clubs, school groups, and women's mutual aid. Their resources were extremely slim—a factor to which Surya Rao later attributed their success: they could not afford to do things for people, only with them, so activities had to meet genuine community needs.

The essential role of the Hyderabad team was to open up avenues between *basti* dwellers and the city's financial and administrative structure. If people knew how the system worked, they could make it work on their behalf. If they could build a modest hall or find an empty classroom, they could run a tailoring class or a day-care centre. If they knew how to get a license and market a product, they could set up a small business enterprise. Most important, they could obtain credit. No regular bank was prepared to administer loans of $10 or so, the amount a washerman or -woman needed to buy an iron or a handcart. By acting as intermediary, the project could manage an arrangement on their behalf. Although seventy per cent of the city population was Moslem and Moslem women do not easily leave the seclusion of the home, a number of mini-enterprises run entirely by women began to flourish. Hyderabad began to get recognition as a low-cost participatory exercise in slum improvement, which worked on a significant scale.

In 1976, Dr John Donohue took over Kennedy's role as advisor to Unicef on urban affairs; he had previously worked in the slums of Lima, as well as in Brazil. Once Unicef began in earnest to promote the basic-services strategy in urban areas, the debate about whether it was fitting to support women's efforts to earn money evaporated. Without particularly underlining the fact, more and more of the programmes developed between Unicef and municipal authorities and local-government groups emphasized support to women in all their roles. In the city, those had to include jobs and income. In the city, poor women were working, as poor women have always worked, not as an act of liberated choice, but for their families' bare survival. In the back alleys of the Third World city, women's rights meant a chance to do so while preserving some shred of female dignity, and hopefully the bonds of marriage as well.

Too often, the move to the city wreaked havoc on family life. The male head of household tried to find work where he could. But the effort of earning enough to maintain the family in its new setting—where money was needed to buy food, water, fuel, shelter materials, utensils, all of which had previously materialized from women's cashless engagement with field and furrow—was too much for him alone. Wives, and children too, must help out. The only jobs open to them were the most menial, the lowest-paid. Domestic service was the aristocracy of employment. Without skills, most women were obliged to make what little money they could by cooking food and selling it on the street—or by rising at dawn to walk miles to market, purchasing a head-load of vegetables and laying it out on a muddy corner to earn a few cents by trading. If their menfolk abandoned them—a growing trend: in some cities half the women were forced to become their children's only provider—they often slipped further down the social ladder, brewing illegal liquor and working the twilight hours in back rooms and tin-shack 'hotels'. More children came; more children with no male provider.

Coincidentally the report which deepened Unicef's understanding about the realities of childhood, upbringing and family life in slum communities was undertaken by a woman: Mary Racelis, then Professor of Sociology at the Ateneo de Manila University in the Philippines. Prepared at the request of the 1977 Executive Board, her report identified many features of poor urban communities which worked in favour of the basic-services strategy: their openness to change; their willingness to organize, sometimes militantly; their exposure to mass media; their proven ability to find their own solutions to their problems. Municipal authorities must harness this problem-solving capacity, channelling the vigour and imagination of slum people into community self-help. They must also improve entrepreneurial and job opportunities, and do what they could to prevent the disintegration of family life.

In 1978, Racelis succeeded Titi Memet as Unicef's senior advisor on family welfare, and led the study on women, children and development prepared for the 1980 Board session and the Copenhagen Women's Conference. Whatever residual doubts persisted about the emphasis to be given to women in other than nurturing roles, delegate after delegate to the Executive Board—including many from developing countries—singled out the importance of helping women as producers: to grow more food, learn more skills, earn more money, and play a larger part in the whole development process. Unicef's thinking on women had finally turned the corner.

In 1982 the Board again reviewed Unicef's urban experience in an extensive study prepared under Donohue's guidance. By this time, many municipal authorities around the world had become much more progressive in their attitude to their burgeoning slums, or at least resigned to their presence and prepared to try policies which cost much less than razing and relocation.

The previous five years had seen great growth in Unicef support for programmes helping urban mothers and children. In 1977, Unicef had been helping urban programmes in seven countries; by 1982, the number had risen to forty-three. For the review, case studies were undertaken of projects in Addis Ababa, Rio de Janeiro, Kuala Lumpur, Hyderabad, Mexico City, Lima, Colombo, and data collected from many others. These studies led to some important conclusions: the urban basic-services strategy was viable and was a means of extending facilities to the poorest families. It responded sensitively to the needs articulated by poor people, and the services provided were cheaper, more suitable, better understood and better maintained because the people were involved in the process. The Unicef Board indicated its support by approving regional advisory posts to expand this work.

Although the application of the basic-services strategy had included Unicef's traditional support to MCH and water supply, the striking feature of the programmes was their emphasis on the needs of working women: skills, credit and day-care services. The survey showed that women's needs were often so acute that mini-enterprises and day care were often the first points at which community organization would coalesce, paving the way for activities such as health campaigns to which the people themselves attached a lower priority.

The problems surrounding urbanization were at their most acute in Latin America where the process of industrialization was further advanced. By 1982, sixty-five per cent of Latin America's population was already living in large cities, which also accounted for ninety-five per cent of the region's population growth. Mexico City and Sao Paulo looked set to become the world's largest cities, with thirty-one million and twenty-six million respectively by the end of the century. The proportion of urban dwellers living in poverty was also rising, as high as sixty per cent in Bogota. The strains endured by those living under the pressure of this environment bred violence and hostility—a tough world for children. Poor standards of nutrition and hygiene, child abandonment, single-parent families, alcoholism, brutality, child exploitation: the ills of urban misery were endemic to Latin America.

Their corollary was some of the most imaginative adaptations of the basic-services strategy; parts of some cities had become the laboratory for new legal, administrative, and social arrangements. Brazil was experimenting with new approaches for children of the streets. Slum dwellers in Peru had established self-managed cities, the pueblos jovenes—young towns—of metropolitan Lima. In Vila, El Salvador, a local network of self-governing associations had managed to build and run a primary health-care system with a minimum of outside support: mainly construction materials from Unicef and advice and training from local officials. In the suburbios of Guayaquil, Ecuador, and in many other cities, day-care centres of utmost simplicity were run by mothers with a little special training. Other women became community health workers.

In many of the city slums, child malnutrition was a serious and growing problem. Because their food supply depended entirely on their cash supply, many mothers found it even harder in the town than in the countryside to feed their children an adequate diet. An alarming characteristic of the problem in the cities was the very early age at which babies began to suffer from malnutrition and its symbiotic partner, diarrhoea. During the 1970s, another aspect of galloping urbanization began to attract attention: the widespread replacement of breast-feeding by bottle-feeding. Few mothers living in squalid and poverty-stricken circumstances understood the need to keep the bottle sterile and boil the water used to mix the formula. Even fewer could afford to give it to their babies in the quantities described in instructions on the tin, which anyway they could not read. Not only were many of their infants undernourished but, deprived of the immunizing agents a breast-fed baby absorbs along with mother's milk, they were much more prone to pick up infections.

For some years, paediatricians and nutritionists had been warning the rest of the medical community of the disastrous effect on infant health of the worldwide decline in breast-feeding. Now, determined to try and arrest the decline, they began to examine the various causes of mothers' stampede towards the bottle. Among them were the changes in social attitudes associated with modern urban living. Many believed that favourable attitudes towards the bottle were being influenced by marketing campaigns for infant formulas. As the decade progressed, breast versus bottle grew into an international *cause célèbre*.

During the mid-twentieth century, great progress was made in the manufacture of breast-milk substitutes, bringing them closer to the composition and digestibility of human milk. This unquestionable scientific and technological advance was a boon to infant care for it meant that, where a newborn was orphaned or abandoned, or where a mother or her surrogate could not breast-feed, the baby could have not only a chance of survival but a good nutritional start in life.

Some better-off mothers in better-off societies took to bottle-feeding as the modern equivalent of the wet nurse their forebears had employed, either because the idea of suckling their own children offended them or because it was inconvenient and demanding on their time. Since the 1930s, certain medical and psychological practitioners in child development had railed against the abandonment of the breast, the biologically ideal child-feeding device and a means of bonding between mother and infant. This debate largely took place within the confined world of individual choices among educated mothers able to apply the latest paediatric advice, for whom the price of breast-milk substitutes was not an issue, and whose kitchens contained faucets, refrigerators, sterilizing gadgets, and sometimes nursemaids to operate them.

In the 1970s, the context of the debate changed. Now the decline in breast-feeding, suddenly much more pervasive and taking place in a broader range of social strata, was the result of urban growth in the poor world. For the poor urban mother, there were no mitigating effects, such as comfortable means, regular visits to the paediatrician, obedience to formula preparation instructions, or knowledge of the risks of dirty rubber teats and unboiled water. This decline had profound implications for the nutritional well-being of millions of newborn babies, and for other siblings following them into the world. Breast-feeding was also a natural, if imperfect, means of contraception. Given its nutritional and immunological advantages, its intimate bonding effect, its child spacing properties, and its lack of cost breast-feeding was infinitely preferable for poor mothers in poor societies. Even where mothers were thought to be too poorly nourished for good lactation, the first priority was to give them a food supplement, not give one in a bottle to their infants. But in spite of all the factors in breast-feeding's favour, mothers were moving in the opposite direction, even before they had taken up the advice about good weaning which nutritionists had been trying to put across to them for at least two decades. Why were they so perverse?

The reason was the way that poor urban mothers had to live. In the village, a mother could carry her baby with her to the fields, or to the well, or to the wood where she collected fuel. If the baby was hungry, she offered her nipple. In the city, this was much more difficult. If she was a factory worker, she would be extraordinarily lucky if there was a creche attached. Many women must travel long distances on a bus or walk a busy highway; the crowdedness and attitudes of other townspeople did not encourage her to breast-feed in public. If she undertook casual labour, an employer was most unlikely to be sympathetic to her suckling her baby on the job. The city environment was not attuned to breast-feeding. Everything favoured leaving the baby at home, in the charge of a granny or child-minder with a tin of formula and a bottle.

For most urban women of the slums, personal strain, social mores, economic constraints—even when much of what they earned was spent on infant food—appeared to offer them no choice. And very little in the new environment to which they were trying so hard to adjust supported the idea that breast was best. On the contrary, it supported just the opposite. Bottle-feeding was the modern thing. Domestic servants could see the evidence before their eyes. A bottle and a rubber teat were as much a sign of new-found status as the transistor radio which pelted out jingles and pop songs all day long. On the bus ride into town, sleek, smiling, bouncing babies loomed out of advertising billboards. They did not hang on a sagging breast; they chuckled over a formula brand name. The reasons for the decline in breast-feeding among the urban poor were not a mystery. They were there for anyone who chose to look.

The ill-effects on the young babies of the slum neighbourhood could be found in malnutrition wards in urban hospitals all over Asia, Africa and Latin America. A government-sponsored study in Sao Paulo, Brazil, which measured malnutrition among the preschool children of poor parents showed that thirty-two per cent of bottle-fed children were malnourished, compared to only nine per cent of breast-fed children. These kinds of findings began to be echoed from countries all over the world. Poor urban mothers could not afford enough formula to give their babies an adequate diet, and the result was that it was often over-diluted and the infant starved. The water used to dilute the formula was often contaminated, and the ignorance of the mother, or that of the granny or child-minder, meant that the need to use scarce and expensive fuel to boil the water was overlooked. As a result, the bottle-fed baby in a poor household had a much greater chance than the breast-fed of contracting a diarrhoeal infection, a risk enhanced because the baby had none of the immunological protection breast-feeding would have provided.

The MCH and nutritional reports prepared under WHO and Unicef auspices stressed from the earliest days of support to health care in the developing world the supreme desirability of breast-feeding against any other nutritional formula for the small infant. In the late 1960s, the trend of breast-feeding decline, particularly in the expanding cities, began to cause alarm. Within the WHO/FAO/Unicef Protein Advisory Group, concerned nutritionists began to consider how to counteract the weight of social pressure in favour of the bottle and reverse, or at least arrest, the trend. The first meeting between child development experts and representatives of the infant-formula manufacturers took place under Unicef and WHO auspices in Bogota, Colombia, in 1970. Others followed, in New York, Paris, and Singapore. WHO began to study comprehensively the patterns of breast-feeding in countries around the world.

In 1974, the World Health Assembly adopted a resolution calling on member States to do all they could to promote breast-feeding, including regulating the sales promotion of infant foods. Few did so. Suddenly, the issue moved out of the confined realm of official reports and professional papers, into the public eye. Following its exposure in *New Internationalist* magazine in 1973, the British voluntary aid organization War on Want brought out a pamphlet called 'The Baby Killers', accusing the Nestlé Corporation of rating the sales promotion of their products above the well-being of Third World infants. When a translation of the pamphlet appeared in Switzerland, Nestlé sued. In due course they won the case, but it was a Pyrrhic victory. The techniques they used to promote infant formula in the developing countries had been given a vociferous public pasting. The judge suggested that Nestlé should change its marketing practices. The company had not won the moral victory.

Another suit followed in 1976, taken out by the Sisters of the Precious Blood against a US infant-formula manufacturer, Bristol-Myers, provoking public outrage on the other side of the Atlantic. By this stage, the companies had formed their own producers' association, the International Council of Infant Food Industries (ICIFI), and written their own code of marketing ethics. But their actions appeared inadequate and did little to abate the hue and cry. In July 1977, a US activist group, the Infant Formula Action Coalition (INFACT), declared a boycott of all Nestlé products.

A decade before, when discussion about birth-control measures left the privacy of people's bedrooms and became a public policy debate, the protagonists of family planning spent a great deal of energy attacking the

Catholic establishment for its ban on artificial contraception. Now, as breast-feeding—a subject also associated with intimate human behaviour—became a matter of concern to politicians, economists and worldwide opinion, the debate became similarly overshadowed by one of its dimensions: the marketing of the formulas, rather than the socio-economic reasons why many mothers in slums and shanty towns could not nurture their children in a more natural and health-giving way. The reason, as with family planning, was ideological. This was the era when church and humanitarian groups concerned with Third World issues turned their spotlight onto the activities of multinational corporations. The promotion of infant foods, with all its emotive connotations, symbolized for many the kind of exploitation of the Third World poor of which the 'unacceptable face of capitalism' was capable. The formula companies had not adjusted their marketing policies to take into account the poverty, squalor and ignorance in which so many urban mothers lived. They promoted their products in hospital wards and maternity clinics, through doctors and through the medical profession, often dressing their salespeople in a white-coated imitation of a nurse's uniform. They insisted that their sales pitch was directed at the same socio-economic group in developing countries as it was for the competent, educated and well-enough-off mothers in the industrialized world. But poor women, as well as rich, went to the hospital to deliver their babies; poor women, as well as rich, heard jingles on the radio; poor women, as well as rich, saw hoardings in city streets. And poor women were far less able than rich to make a sensible judgement about the information offered by a woman wearing a nurse's uniform employed as an infant-formula salesperson.

Prejudicial as these things were to convincing a mother that breast was best, not only at birth but also for many months beyond, all the publicity generated a distorted impression that the main responsibility for the decline in breast-feeding lay with the baby-food companies. This, naturally, put them onto the defensive—a defensive which on the one hand encouraged them to change their practices, and on the other inhibited amicable dialogue with the breast-feeding protagonists. But studies did not show that mothers abandoned breast-feeding primarily because they heard a radio jingle or encountered a baby-food 'nursemaid' in the clinic. More often, they abandoned breast-feeding because nothing had been done to underline its important health and nutritional advantages. Many mothers, it turned out, thought that their breast-milk was too weak, or that they had too little of it. The entire range of health-care behaviour, consumer behaviour and social behaviour which was consciously or unconsciously discriminating against the breast needed to be examined.

If the formula companies had blotted their copybook, the medical profession had done little better. Perhaps because modern paediatrics had been dominated by men, lactation was a subject which was largely ignored in health-care training. Breast-feeding was thought of as a natural function, a somewhat embarrassing and unmentionable one like sex, for which no specific instruction was needed, either for nurses or for mothers. In the traditional family setting, where a woman often delivered her child in her mother's home under the eye of someone known to her through childhood, she could be easily helped to learn the tricks of getting the baby to suckle properly. In the city, a woman rarely had support of this kind. She went to hospital to deliver, among bustling strangers and odd contraptions. She was anxious, apprehensive and uncertain—not a psychologically useful frame of mind to help her establish intimacy and confidence with her new baby. Most hospitals compounded her unease. Often, the baby was not given to her to suckle until after a couple of days. If a mother had problems with her milk or her nipples, the nursing staff lost no time in compensating with bottle feeds. Around her, posters frequently displayed the bouncing health of the bottle-fed. Not surprisingly, an anxious mother soon gave up the struggle.

In 1975 Dr Natividad Relucio-Clavano, who had picked up ideas from leading breast-feeding protagonists while on a WHO fellowship in the UK, tore down the infant-formula posters from her maternity unit walls in Baguio General Hospital in the Philippines. Dr Clavano was one of the earliest paediatricians in the Third World to take such concrete action against the intrusion of the bottle. She firmly told the company 'nurse-maids' to leave the maternity ward and not to return. Until she took over at Baguio, the unit had been run along lines customary in Western teaching hospitals: newborn babies were isolated to cut back the risk of infection and routinely given supplementary feeds. But diarrhoea and other ailments were common in the nursery, and fewer and fewer mothers were still breast-feeding when they left the hospital.

Dr Clavano's knowledge of the scientific evidence of breast-milk's anti-infective properties prompted her to change the way the unit was run. Nursing began when mother and baby were still in the delivery room. Babies 'roomed-in' around the clock with their mothers. In time, artificial feeds were banished, even for the premature. Within two years, the mortality rate among newborns dropped by ninety-five per cent and infant infection by eighty-eight per cent. Dr Clavano's experiments proved conclusively to mothers and to the medical staff that breast was best. The Baguio maternity unit became a model to the health profession, and the site for training and re-orienting staff from all over the Philippines. Elsewhere in the developing world, other chiefs of maternity services were beginning to make similar adjustments in hospital routines.

Other initiatives took place to stem breast-feeding's decline under the pressure of continuing public controversy. In October 1979, WHO and Unicef held an international meeting on infant feeding. Over 150 representatives from governments, UN agencies, nutritional and paediatric experts, the infant-food industry, voluntary agencies and consumer groups met in Geneva. The meeting, whose content and form owed much to Dr Tejada de Rivero of WHO and Dick Heyward of Unicef, was a landmark. Not only did it provide a high-level forum in which all protagonists were represented, it examined its subject—infant and young child feeding—in all its dimensions instead of fixing on one or two.

The recommendations of the meeting were adopted by consensus and covered a wide and carefully noncontroversial range: medical practices to support breast-feeding and sound weaning; the effect of women's status on their feeding behaviour; the use of media in nutrition campaigns; teaching teenage children about breast-feeding in school. Last but by no means least, the meeting agreed that an international code for the marketing of breast-milk substitutes should be drawn up. Although many of the companies had by now somewhat modified their promotion to the general public, there were still important differences about what could reasonably be described as the provision of 'information' about their products to health workers and medical professionals.

In May 1981, a draft International Code of Marketing for Breast-milk Substitutes was presented to the World Health Assembly for its consideration. The Code had been revised several times in consultation with the various parties. Among its provisions was a ban on all infant-formula advertising and free distribution to the general public. Under the Code, except where it was used for medically-approved purposes in the hands of health personnel, infant formula would no longer have a place in hospitals and health centres, and no company employees in nursing uniforms would be permitted to enter their doors. At the same time, governments should take on the responsibility of giving out information about infant and young-child feeding for the benefit of mothers, families and all those professionally involved in nutrition. Although its subject was the marketing of breast-milk substitutes, in its broadest sense the Code was a policy checklist for countries trying to halt breast-feeding's downward trend. A government which tried sincerely to put the Code into effect would be obliged to undertake certain legislative and regulatory actions and commit itself to the promotion of breast-feeding as a public policy.

The long debate did not reach its climax without a further spasm of public controversy. Although they had originally supported the idea, when the Code reached its final draft, the infant-formula companies did not like it. In the weeks leading up to the World Health Assembly vote, they vigorously lobbied officials and legislators in many countries against its adoption. The voluntary, religious and consumer activists who had fought the companies so hard and so long lobbied just as hard in its favour.

The Code, obviously, did not carry the force of law: voting in its favour was an acceptance in principle, not a binding commitment on a government. In the event, the only country to vote against it was the US on the grounds that it was contrary to US laws on freedom and free enterprise. Japan abstained.

In the four-and-a-half years following the passage of the Code in May 1981, twenty-five countries had passed all or some of its provisions into law. In a further twenty countries, legislation on the Code was pending. In many other countries, the government had taken steps to control the distribution of infant formula, or introduced the Code as a voluntary means of controlling its marketing. Most baby-food manufacturers had accepted the Code's provisions in principle.

With the passage of the Code, one chapter in the struggle to protect breast-feeding was over. But there are others still far from complete. Some countries, such as Brazil and Papua New Guinea, had already begun vigorous national campaigns in the early 1980s to promote breast-feeding. They fully recognized that passing laws in support of the Code and making sure that they were applied was only one important element in the whole campaign. Many more were needed if poor mothers in the slums and shanty towns were to be persuaded to continue to breast-feed. To kick the bottle, they would need support and amenities of many kinds, as well as vital information. Creches, hygienic washrooms in public places, extra maternity leave, nursing support, media support, demanded an all-out effort. The historical tide in favour of the breast had yet to be turned.

Main Sources
Papers, speeches and published articles by James P. Grant during his Presidency of ODC and his Executive Directorship of Unicef; ODC publications; also published articles, press releases, and biographical sketches concerning his career.

Interviews with key Executive Board members and members of Unicef staff, undertaken for the Unicef History Project by Jack Charnow, 1983–1985.

Unicef Annual Reports 1980–86; Unicef Information Notes and United Nations press releases concerning the appointment of Prince Talal Bin Abdul Aziz Al Saud of Saudi Arabia as Unicef Special Envoy, and the activities of the Arab Gulf Programme for the United Nations Development Organizations.

Reports on 'The State of the World's Children', 1980–86, James P. Grant, Executive Director of Unicef.

Unicef Executive Board: progress Reports, reports of the Committee on Administration and Finance, summary records, reports of the Board, programme recommendations, special reports on women's programmes, on urban programmes, and statements made by Unicef Executive Directors to international conferences on Population, Women, etc. 1975–85.

'Women and World Development', edited by Irene Tinker and Michele Bo Bramsen, published by ODC, prepared under the auspices of the American Association for the Advancement of Science, 1976.

Women's Role in Economic Development by Ester Boserup, St. Martin's Press, N.Y., 1970.

New Internationalist magazine; issues on women and development, urban growth, the babyfoods controversies, 1973–1982.

Assignment Children, issues 55/56 and 57/58; *Unicef News*, issues 82, 104, 107, 110, 114; and other Unicef publications.

'Urban Basic Services: a Strategy for Coverage of the Urban Poor', paper prepared by William J. Cousins, Unicef Senior Urban Advisor, for a seminar on urban development in India organised by Association Dialogue Entres les Cultures, Paris, January 1986.

'Family Contexts of Breastfeeding' by Margaret Mead, keynote address at the International Conference on Human Lactation, New York City, 2 March 1977; published in *Breastfeeding and Food Policy in a Hungry World* edited by Dana Raphael, Academic Press, 1979.

Human Milk in the Modern World, Derrick B. Jelliffe and E. F. Patrice Jelliffe, Oxford University Press, 1978.

Joint WHO/Unicef Meeting on Infant and Young Child Feeding, Geneva, 9–12 October 1979; statement, recommendations, list of participants, Geneva, 1979; International Code of Marketing of Breast-milk Substitutes, Geneva, 1981.

Chapter 18

'The land is growing old'

In the early part of 1980, when the international airwaves were buzzing with alarm about whether the Kampuchean people would manage to plant in time for the monsoon, the weather in Africa was also causing anxiety. Poor rainfall was only part of the problem: dark economic, political and military clouds were as pervasive as drought and often interconnected. In April, the world was alerted—by a television report, in what had become the set pattern for the exposure of mass tragedy in the late twentieth century—to terrible starvation in a northern pocket of Uganda. The famine in Karamoja was a gruesome example of what could happen in a drought year when random events penetrated the closed world of a traditional society, upsetting its precarious contract with nature.

The 350,000 people of the semi-nomadic Karamajong had lived for generations by cattle-herding, raiding, and growing a little food in their arid homeland. They had little contact with any modern institutions—except for a few mission posts, a borehole here and there, and a rough road masquerading as a highway to the better developed parts of the country in the south. During the 1979 war in which President Idi Amin was ousted, his troops fled northwards; en route, they raided an armoury in the town of Moroti. Some of the stolen guns fell into the hands of Karamajong herdsmen, and replaced the spears they normally used for cattle-raiding. A series of violent encounters took place and most of the tribesmen lost their herds to the masters of the guns. When the worst drought in a century struck their land, their usual safety valve for times of hardship—trading cattle for food from farming people to the south and west—had disappeared.

At least 25,000 people died in Karamoja before the machinery of relief was mobilized. Most of the police posts, health centres, schools and other emblems of the flimsy administrative apparatus were abandoned when the area became unsafe. Gun-toting raiders terrorized the countryside. The various UN and voluntary agency partners in the belated and messy relief operation which finally took off in May 1980 had to build warehouses, repair roads and bridges, set up and staff health and feeding centres, operate and guard convoys of food vehicles. The bulk of the food came from WFP, most of the vehicles from Unicef. The awkward logistics and insecurity throughout Uganda—food supplies were occasionally ambushed

Ethiopia: an estimated 6.4 million people in 1986 became in need of food and other emergency assistance because of prolonged drought. At Sekoto, a town of 120,000 people, the eight available wells were open for a few hours each morning, so women lined up their earthenware jars the previous day. (*UN/Isaac*)

In one of the worst-affected drought areas, in Ethiopia, a mother comforts her severely-malnourished baby at a special feeding centre. (*UN/Isaac*)

Civil war, Lebanon, 1976. For these children, the only source of water was an inch of pipe protruding from a wall. (*Unicef/Hewett*)

Opposite:
An Egyptian mother feeding her baby. WHO and Unicef are strong supporters of breast-milk as the ideal nutritional mix for babies. Breast-feeding also has anti-infective and contraceptive properties, and fosters bonding between mother and child. (*Unicef/Wolff*)

Chad's campaign against seven diseases (diptheria, measles, polio, tetanus, tuberculosis, whooping cough and yellow fever) used local chiefs, musicians, radio announcements and banners to convince women to bring their children to vaccination posts. (*Unicef/Clifton*)

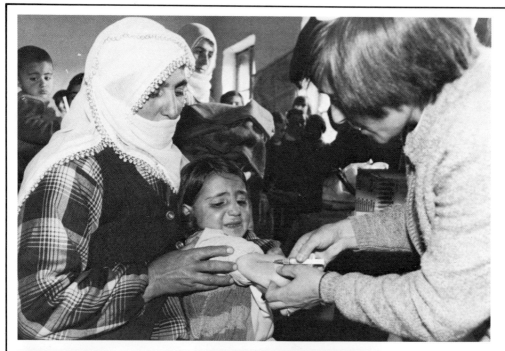

On 3 December 1985, Turkey completed its nationwide vaccination drive. More than 80 per cent of Turkey's five million under-fives were protected against immunizable disease.
(*Unicef/Isaac*)

A Pakistan father gives oral rehydration salts (ORS) to his child after making a simple mixture at home; dehydration caused by diarrhea kills about five million children a year in developing countries.
(*Unicef/Thomas*)

and some agency personnel lost their lives—made it one of the most difficult and acrimonious of relief operations.

By late 1980, 250,000 people, mostly women and children, were dependent on emergency relief and medical care; but the authorities and their international helpers had the famine under control. More than 15,000 children were receiving Unicef milk and food supplements at posts run by the British Save the Children Fund. The situation remained tenuous through most of 1981, during which the Unicef team, headed by Cole Dodge, an American who had gained his experience in Bangladesh and Ethiopia with Oxfam, set up an imaginative monitoring system to signal to the local authorities any lapse in children's health. Mothers brought their children to be weighed and measured regularly at bush clinics, and when their growth began to falter or decline, supplementary feeding was restarted.

Simultaneously, crisis deepened in the desert lands of the Horn of Africa, calling for another international rescue effort. In 1977, Somali forces had invaded south-eastern Ethiopia in an attempt to conquer the Ogaden, an area inhabited by Somali-speaking nomads but incorporated within Ethiopia's territory. The military campaign ended disastrously for Somalia in March 1978; but within the Ogaden guerilla warfare and armed resistance to Ethiopian forces continued. By early 1979, well over 100,000 nomads had fled hundred of miles from their homes in the Ogaden, driving their camels across the Somali border and pitching their sapling and hide tents in refugee camps.

Although the Somalis did not hesitate to care for their ethnic kin, the refugees were a heavy burden for an impecunious desert nation. Almost all the camp inhabitants were women and children whose menfolk were either waging war or trying to save their livestock by herding them in the vast desert grazing grounds. As 1979 gave way to 1980, the same drought which spelled starvation away to the south-west among the Karamajong began to cut a swathe all across the Horn. The failure of the rains to regenerate the pastures compounded the disruption of the fighting. By June, 1·5 million victims of hunger had sought food, safety and grazing in Somalia. At the peak of the influx, pathetic family groups were emerging from the desert haze at the rate of 1500 people a day.

Half the refugees—around 700,000—were kept alive by UN rations. Few of the thirty-five camps were close to a road system or health infrastructure of any sophistication. In places whose normal climate did not support sedentary life, vast concentrations of people had to be supplied with food, water, health and nutritional care. The entire UN and international voluntary agency community, co-ordinated by the UNHCR, was once again mobilized to help the Somali authorities. Only when the rains returned in 1981 and the pasture finally began to recoup did the Ogadenis begin to melt back towards their homeland.

In Ethiopia, every year, starting in 1971, was a food shortage year, threatening millions of people with worse than hunger. Since time immemorial, starvation has been a common feature of life in the Ethiopian countryside. Famines of terrible scale and severity have periodically wiped out large populations. As a result of the famine of 1973–74 in the northern provinces of Wollo and Tigre 300,000 people lost their lives. Such was the impact of this disaster on the regime of Emperor Haile Selassie that the elderly monarch was forced off his throne. To avoid another similar disaster, the post-revolution Government set up an early warning system for harvest prospects, and entrusted emergency operations to an expanded and powerful Relief and Rehabilitation Commission (RRC). Unicef provided some assistance towards this food monitoring system, and in the wake of the 1973–74 famine, increased its co-operation with water supply, health, nutrition, and other basic-services programmes.

As the decade progressed and rainfall was consistently low, the RRC's annual predictions of food scarcity in certain areas began to take on a numbing monotony. Annually, Ethiopia was forced to rely on large amounts of imported food aid, used for relief and food-for-work rehabilitation schemes; simultaneously, the Government was trying to exert its control over Eritrea and Tigre in the north and the Ogaden provinces—Sidamo, Bale, and Haraghe—in the south-east. It had also embarked on the long struggle for rural development in a countryside ground to dust by centuries of feudal neglect.

The 1980–81 famine in Karamoja illustrated one kind of contemporary African tragedy: a disastrous collision between an ancient equilibrium and the collapse of the post-colonial political system. The constant challenge of hunger in Ethiopia illustrated another: a conspiracy between climatic perversity, land shortage and agricultural backwardness. In a country with a modern system of food production, stockpiled resources, the organizational capacity to mount relief for the destitute, the means of regulating food prices and moving surpluses around, drought is a cause for anxiety but not—as in Ethiopia—of seemingly uncontrollable loss of human life.

The crowded landscape of northern Ethiopia is a topographical extravaganza of rugged escarpments, plunging gorges, table-top mountains and mighty rivers inhabited by people whose way of life and farming systems had scarcely altered since the days of King Solomon. Even in years when the weather was kind, the farming communities in the peaks and valleys of these highlands pursued a life of great hardship and declining prospects.

In recent decades, land hunger and population pressure had forced the people to over-graze, over-crop, deplete the woodland, and reduce the steep mountainsides to eroded infertility. Much of Ethiopia offered a testament to rural deprivation: few roads, no modern bunding or irrigation techniques, no tools or implements belonging to the post-mediaeval era, no fertilizers or agricultural incentives of any kind. Until the downfall of Selassie and the introduction of land reform, the only contact of most

Ethiopian peasants with authority was with a landlord who took away a portion—sometimes a very high portion—of the crop in rent. The process of impoverishment was already so far advanced that there was absolutely no margin left. In this environment a minor failure of the rains could cause widespread distress. A major failure could precipitate a whole society towards disintegration.

In 1979, the country's perennial state of drought suddenly took another downwards turn. The RRC estimated that over five million people faced the risk of famine, not only in the north, but in the provinces of the Ogaden; all these areas were still in a state of upheaval caused by guerilla warfare and banditry. In the south, hundreds of thousands of people left their homes and livelihoods and had thrown themselves on the mercy of RRC relief. In the face of the overpowering combination of drought and hostilities, government services in the area had virtually ceased to function.

In Bale province, the RRC had already set up farming settlements for 100,000 families from the northern highlands—people whose land and livelihood had been lost in the 1973 famine, and who had spent the past few years trying to establish themselves in very different savanna terrain. Now the RRC hurriedly set up settlements for another 166,000 families. With assistance from Unicef, the RRC introduced some extremely basic and extremely necessary services: water supply, health care by volunteer trainees, educational instruction of the most rudimentary kind for adults and children.

In 1981, the rains returned to Bale. At least the new settlements, like their predecessors, could begin to farm co-operatively as a means of support preferable to food handouts. However frail the initial viability of the resettlement schemes, the Ethiopian Government had begun to believe that in less populous parts of the countryside they comprised the fastest way of reducing pressure on the environmental desolation of the northern highlands. Neither this, nor any other solution, could have been introduced in time to avert the tragedy of 1984.

Across the other side of the continent, a number of countries were victim to a different kind of environmental crisis, but one with similar underlying characteristics. The countries of the Sahel, the southern fringe of the Saharan desert—Senegal, Mauritania, Mali, Burkina Faso (then Upper Volta), Niger and Chad—were also experiencing a disruption of the delicate relationship between man and nature. Here too the climate was conspiring with unnatural pressure on a very different environment. At the height of the long 1968–74 drought in the Sahel, thousands of nomadic herdsmen were forced to migrate southwards. Their waterholes dried up and their pastureland was baked to dust. Their wealth and food supply—their cattle—lay dead on the trail behind them. Slowly bringing up the rear was the onward, inexorable march of the Sahara desert itself, moving at an average rate of some three-and-a-half miles a year.

The length and the severity of the drought, combined with short-sighted livestock development policies, had deepened an environmental crisis beyond the point of recovery. Previous years of plentiful rainfall, borehole drilling, and cattle vaccination programmes intended to improve the trade in livestock—one of the region's few natural resources—had encouraged the pastoralists to build up their herds. When the rains failed, traditional ways of coping with hardship failed with them. There were no spare grazing lands to go to; all were already overused. The great press of animals around the boreholes stripped the vegetation; its loss further lowered the water table; the remaining trees and bushes withered; without the protection of grass and scrub the land could not hold back the sands of the desert, blowing down from the north on the hot, dry, *harmattan* wind.

When the rains returned to the Sahel from 1975 onwards, they fell sporadically, rarely in sufficient force to regenerate the pastures or the herds. By 1983, many of the desert tribesmen who once cut such fine figures in their indigo robes and self-possession were reduced to a half-life offering themselves for labour on farm or work site. The transformation of pastoralist to cultivator or even urbanite was brusque and traumatic: for those who endured such humility, it represented the destruction of an entire way of life.

In Mauritania, half the nomad population 'settled'. Society was turned upside down: within ten years, a country whose people were four-fifths nomadic, living on milk and animal products, became three-quarters sedentary, suffering the petty indignities of urban squalor. Of Moorish descent, the nomads mixed uneasily with the black agriculturalists of the river basins. In Mali, these too were in deep trouble: the Niger and Senegal Rivers reached their lowest flood level in decades, and by 1981, 800,000 people had set up makeshift dwellings on the edges of the towns.

Burkina Faso, like Mali and Mauritania, received no appreciable rainfall for a decade. Many of the young able-bodied succumbed to the lure of better prospects in Ghana and Ivory Coast. Chad, a country of geographical and ethnic extremes, stretching from the Sahara in the north to equatorial forest in the south, was riven not only by ecological disaster but also by civil war. Senegal, the most prosperous of Sahelian countries, watched its agriculture and its peanut exports go into precipitous decline. All the countries of the Sahel, some of which had been well able to provide most or all of their food requirements before the 1968–74 drought, were now dependent on imports and international charity.

In many of the countries of the Sahel as well as in Ethiopia and Somalia, in Sudan, and in Angola where drought and civil disturbance were exacting an equally terrible penance, rates of child death and disease were among the highest in the world before the 'loud emergencies' struck. One-quarter of babies born to Ethiopian mothers died before reaching their first birthday; in Burkina Faso, the equivalent figure was one-fifth; in Mali, thirty-five per cent; mostly from the dreaded diarchy of malnutrition and infection. In none of these countries was there a network of modern health services worthy of the name. If one in ten mothers at the moment of delivery received the attention of a fully-equipped and trained midwife, that was already a cause for national self-congratulation. With so little in the way of a social infrastructure, with the countries' economies so impoverished and with so many pressing emergencies compounding the day-to-day problems of keeping their administrations running, the ways in which international help was offered needed to be tailored to their special needs, otherwise it could not be absorbed.

Relief and development problems were all part of an interlocking conundrum, as Unicef and other international aid organizations tried to explain to constituencies which demanded instant solutions to long-term problems. The devastating effects of drought were a testament to development failure; yet children and families could not be allowed to starve while national and international development experts puzzled over where the administrations and their external advisors had gone wrong in country after African country. At the same time, experience was showing that no-one could afford to ignore some of the negative longer-term effects of measures taken to stave off immediate suffering; beneficent food aid given at the wrong season or in the wrong quantities could depress agricultural prices, reinforcing a country's dependency on relief; deep boreholes could upset a fragile ecological balance between nomadic pastoralists and their means of support, encouraging over-grazing and environmental degradation.

Within emergency programmes, Unicef stuck to the role it knew best and was best appreciated for: supplementary foodstuffs, milk and high-protein mixes for the severely undernourished children and mothers admitted to camps and feeding centres; extra rations for pregnant and nursing mothers; basic drugs, immunizations, and medical supplies; training and equipment for community health workers and child-health aides; drilling rigs and personnel for water supplies; kitchen utensils and shelter materials.

Within the camps whose populations seemed set to stay for the foreseeable future—in Somalia, in the planned settlements in southern Ethiopia, in the makeshift settlements of the Sahel—the basic-services strategy could offer a low-cost approach to the problems of relief and development at the same time. Unicef also tried to maintain its regular programme support for mothers and children not immediately caught up in the trauma of drought and severe food shortage, but whose own fate was wrapped up with those who were because services which rarely met the people's needs at the best of times were now under even greater strain. Late in 1980, a sense of urgency and impotence about the deepening anguish of Africa led Unicef to begin to consider how to step up existing programmes and offer the worst-affected countries more in the way of co-operation.

At this time, a new Unicef witness to the mounting tragedy, the Norwegian actress and film star, Liv Ullmann, visited famine victims in Ethiopia, Somalia and Djibouti. In late 1979, Ullmann had been one of a much-publicized group of international personalities who, under the auspices of the International Rescue Committee, had undertaken a 'march' to the Thai-Kampuchean border to draw attention to the plight of Kampuchean refugees. The sincerity with which she publicly expressed her wish to continue to do something helpful for suffering Mankind brought an invitation to her from Jack Ling, Director of Information at Unicef. Early in 1980, she took up an honorary appointment as a Unicef Goodwill Ambassador.

'Ambassador' Ullmann made her first visit to programmes in Bangladesh, India, Sri Lanka and Thailand early in 1980. To her advocacy for children she brought the luminous quality which had earned her such a following as an actress. She managed to combine the capacity to talk seriously to a Head of State with an instinctive rapport with the child of the slum or refugee camp, a child whose dirty hand she took in her own and whose wrinkled bottom she sat on her lap. Liv Ullmann was not only a woman of beauty and international renown, but an articulate and intelligent spokes-woman on children's behalf, sometimes a formidable one. She felt very personally the small, intimate tragedies she witnessed in a dusty encampment or a squalid shanty town, and she could communicate that feeling to television audiences, legislators, even to diplomats and bureaucrats. The plight of the children of Africa became Ullmann's cause. She travelled all over Europe and North America, making public appearances, describing the images which had seared her own imagination: the pathetic lines of mothers and children waiting patiently in the grey sand of the Ogaden; the small naked boy collecting scraps of food in a little can.

A special session of the Unicef Executive Board met to discuss the problems of Africa in late January 1981. Its main purpose was to obtain the Board's permission to step up aid to certain countries, including those in the Horn, Uganda, Angola, Sudan, and Chad; newly-independent Zimbabwe was also on the list, and the Sahelian countries were added soon after. The cost of these additional programmes was over $50 million. The argument in their favour was that these were not emergency programmes in the usual sense, but regular basic-services programmes made doubly urgent by the refugee migrations, by drought, by other 'exceptional circumstances'. Included in these were the effects on Africa of the deepening worldwide economic recession.

As if drought, conflict and food shortage were not enough, the worsening terms of global trade and other spin-offs from Western recession were inflicting further blows on Africa's depleted circumstances. A world in dark times meant a Third World in darker times. From inflation, declining commodity prices and poor international credit ratings children all over the world—and specially in Africa—were showing visible signs of suffering.

The effects of global recession on the condition of the world's most vulnerable inhabitants was becoming a major challenge of the third Development Decade.

In December 1980, the UN General Assembly adopted an International Development Strategy for the 1980s. The strategy reflected many of the 'alternative' lines of thought which had emerged during the previous decade. As far as Unicef was concerned, the important feature was the new emphasis on development as an integral process, combining economic with social and humanitarian dimensions.

During the past twenty years, there had been a gradual convergence between the idea of development as a process which raised the GNP, improved the national balance sheet and credit rating, built new roads and factories, and strengthened the country's administrative structure, and the idea of development as a crusade to end the hunger, poverty and ill-health endured by millions of the world's inhabitants. Unicef and many other international and nongovernmental organizations with a humanitarian purpose had helped to bring this convergence about, drawing upon the programmes of co-operation in which they were engaged to illustrate the importance of social and human dimensions to the success of the overall development process. Among the many antecedents to the new emphasis in the strategy for the third Development Decade were the General Assembly's endorsements of the Unicef Board's 'Child Emergency' declaration in 1974 and its basic services strategy in 1976. Also among them were the precepts of 'RIO', the 1976 Report to the Club of Rome on Reshaping the International Order. The strategy called for a rapid acceleration in efforts over the next ten years to reduce infant mortality below fifty per 1000 births; to overcome mass illiteracy; and to provide greater access to water and sanitation and primary health care.

The ink was barely dry on the General Assembly resolution adopting these goals before they began to appear unrealistic. The year of 1981 was not far advanced before the developing countries began to feel the full chill of world recession, as did the budgets of governments and organizations offering them aid. In many industrialized countries, growth had slumped and unemployment risen to higher levels than at any time since the Great Depression of the 1930s. Their economic misfortune soon reverberated in developing countries, particularly those dependent on richer trading partners to buy their primary products and finance investment in their manufacturing industries on concessional terms. In the early 1970s, when the prices of oil, food grain and fertilizers shot up, many countries both developed and developing had experienced economic shock. But except in Africa, most managed to sustain enough growth to keep their output and their incomes steady. The blight of the early 1980s was far more severe.

Industrial and agricultural output, employment opportunities and personal income went into reverse for the first time since the 1960s.

Forced to retrench, governments everywhere began to cut back on social services expenditure, all too often the first casualty in times of hardship. Programmes supported by Unicef began to feel the effect. Shortage of foreign exchange meant lower imports of vital drugs and medical supplies; fewer spare parts and fuel for such public works as water-supply installations; and deterioration in already weak transport systems. At the same time, better-off countries reduced their expenditures on foreign assistance, especially for anything which appeared to offer no obvious return on economic investment; they were also less willing to offer loans on slow, low repayment schedules. Some Third World countries which had reaped the temporary benefit of high oil prices and become punch drunk on credit and imports—countries such as Nigeria and Mexico—now found themselves descending into a trough of debt. In certain countries, merely the cost of debt servicing was absorbing half or three-quarters of annual export earnings.

Not only did the poor suffer first and most from the cutbacks in govern-ment programmes, but their own survival margins were reduced. Work was more difficult to find, earnings lower and the small amounts of cash people without any stable employment managed to glean by petty trading or casual hire bought much less. With less purchase on the means of subsistence, their health and nutritional margins also shrank. The most vulnerable are always the women and children; in villages and shanty towns all over the developing world, their well-being was the hidden casualty of the downward curves showing up in company reports, stock and commodities markets, and international lending institutions. In his 1981 *The State of the World's Children Report*, James Grant commented bleakly: 'Not for a generation have expectations of world development, and hopes for an end to life-denying mass poverty, been at such a low ebb'.

The gloomy outlook obscured the very real progress that had been made in the developing world over the previous three decades. Average incomes had doubled. Average life expectancy had risen from forty-two to fifty-four years. The proportion of people who could read and write had increased from thirty per cent to fifty per cent. Primary school enrolment had reached sixty-four per cent from forty-seven per cent in 1960. The death rate of infants and children under five had dropped markedly. Even the birth rate was declining, although not as markedly. The problem now was how to sustain, and accelerate, these rates of progress in dark times. As the recession deepened, the targets set for the third Development Decade, and the RIO targets for the end of the century—life expectancy of sixty years or more, infant mortality at fifty per 1000 births or less, seventy-five per cent literacy, time in school for every child in the world—began to sound like hopeless fantasy.

There was, however, a glimmer of hope. The new perspective which linked the social and humanitarian to the economic dimensions of development might come to the rescue of the weakest members of the world community. In years gone by, the deep distress among society's least well-off which followed an economic downturn had been regarded as inevitable, almost a part of natural law. Now it was at least permissible to suggest that, for sound economic and developmental reasons and not only out of humanitarian concern, a safety net must be provided to keep the poor from bearing the full brunt of misery; this should be a part not only of domestic but also of international development policy.

The ideas which had seen expression in Unicef's 1974 'Child Emergency' declaration now sounded almost conventional, even economically respectable. But the problem was that they only did so among a relatively small circle of those on the international development circuit. Among national policy-makers all over the developed and the developing world—whatever the indications were that the world's trading systems, financial systems, productive systems, and marketing systems required overhaul—the tendency was to take the same old belt-tightening measures which discriminated against, rather than protected, the poorest. Under duress, even if they held out no guarantee of success, tried methods were the best form of 'adjustment', of trimming the world's economic sails. Grant at Unicef began to look for ways of giving currency to the alternative view: that with the necessary leap of imagination, policy-makers could hold a safety net under mothers and children without damaging their development targets; in fact, the contrary.

The fears that the poor of the Third World were suffering the worst effects of the current global recession were borne out by a study undertaken by Unicef in conjunction with a team of economic planners at Cornell University. The study was organized by Richard Jolly, Unicef's new Deputy Executive Director for Programmes and a well-known economist in his own right. Derived from a number of case studies from countries around the world and published in 1983, Jolly's report described the human cost of a phenomenon still normally described by planners and policy-makers in narrowly economic terms—inflation and interest rates, debt and deficit. Although data from the least developed countries was also least developed and therefore most difficult to assess, there was clear evidence to show that there were parts of the world where, as an effect of recent economic trends, weight-for-age among children dropped; the number of babies born underweight, and therefore more vulnerable, had gone up; and the numbers of children being deserted by their parents because of poverty were soaring. These findings were nothing more nor less than what had been regarded previously as strong supposition; but their documentation, and their presentation in economic form—and, in due course, in economic fora—helped to sharpen the case.

Jolly and his team made two basic recommendations: adjustment, or belt-tightening, policies must not neglect the need to preserve minimum levels of nutrition and household income; and countries should embark on campaigns to help place a safety net under child health by concentrating resources on low-cost, high-effect interventions. The most tragic aspect of the response to world recession was that 'There seems to have been a systematic sacrifice of the "social" sectors to the "economic" in the erroneous belief that "social" means "uneconomic". The fact is that both by hard-headed economic calculation and by the most elementary tenets of human welfare, investment in the health, skills and well-being of children is the most essential investment of all'.

Up to the time he arrived at Unicef and for a year or two afterwards, Grant had constantly reiterated the theme that there were low-cost routes to social advance, tried and proven in certain parts of the world under widely different economic and political systems; that Unicef's basic-services strategy offered a mix of low-cost ways to improve the lives of the poorest communities by fusing their resources with technical expertise, and multiplying their impact by combining them in one package.

During 1982, Grant began to look around for a way to generate a global campaign based on these ideas. The basic-services strategy was gradually becoming more widely accepted, as was the concept of primary health care to which it was closely related; but implementation seemed to him distressingly slow in a world in which approximately 40,000 small children were still dying every day. Under the pressure of worsening prospects for the world's children in the early 1980s, the safety net needed to prevent the poorest from sinking into the pit of chronic ill-health and malnutrition would not be meshed unless more effort was made, nationally and internationally. That effort required a focus. The 'child emergency' had been the focus of the 1970s. Grant wanted to narrow the focus down more precisely.

On the one hand, any selection of health and nutritional activities to be singled out must have obvious, documentable benefits for children, both as separate measures and in tandem. On the other, they must be non-controversial or they would not gain the adherence of government partners in the developing world or donors in the industrialized world; and they must be easily communicable to the widest possible audience so as to generate the kind of support which would override economic objections, political disinterest and the sense of malaise currently afflicting the entire international development movement. In this context, Grant showed his special appreciation for the need to popularize any issue he wanted to put across. In an era when mass media exposure had the power to influence the course of history, the kind of international crusade needed to make a significant impact must be highly communicable and easily understood. The complexities of development theories, of the values of basic services and planning for the needs of children, might sit well with technicians, professional experts and policy specialists—none of whom Grant had any intention of ignoring. But something extra, something simpler and catchier, was needed to bring the debate into the public and political realm.

In September 1982, a group of health and nutrition experts from WHO, FAO, the World Bank, USAID and a number of other agencies and academic institutions, as well as Unicef itself, met in New York at Unicef's invitation. For two days, they examined the various ways to tackle the twin problems of child hunger and poor health around the world and what kind of success they were having. Technical aspects, communications aspects, costs, acceptability, marketability, government and professional attitudes: pros and cons of different strategies, from food subsidies to family spacing, fuel-efficiency to female literacy, were touched upon.

After the discussion had gone backwards and forwards for a day and a half, someone jotted down on a piece of paper an acronym for the four measures that seemed most promising: 'GOBI'. 'G' was for growth in the young child, which needed to be constantly monitored to see that it was progressing normally; 'O' for oral rehydration, a simple way of replacing the life-sustaining fluids lost in bouts of childhood diarrhoea; 'B' was for breast-feeding, whose decline needed to be arrested; 'I' was for immunization against childhood diseases. GOBI caught the imagination of Jim Grant; it stood for a package of part-nutritional, part-medical, low-cost measures already within the gamut of primary health care. All seemed suited for easy promotion to mothers via the information networks of the modern world which, in recent years, had begun to reach even into the humblest of Third World homes. Transistor radios graced almost every household; commercial companies had their outlets even in the remotest of markets and the crudest of village stores. If these media could be used to promote patent medicines and infant formula, they could also be used to promote primary health care for mother and child.

GOBI came to head the list of Grant's prescriptions for improving the lot of children. The ingredients for what was to become Unicef's call for a world-wide 'child survival and development revolution' were falling into place. The context in which Unicef launched the campaign for GOBI was *The State of the World's Children Report*, issued with maximum public fanfare in December 1982, the thirty-sixth anniversary of Unicef's creation.

While Grant was evolving a new strategy for tackling the 'silent emergency' of child death and disease around the world, another 'loud emergency' forced its way onto Unicef's agenda.

In early June 1982, Israeli troops entered southern Lebanon. As they advanced northwards towards Beirut, it became evident that an all-out military campaign was underway to deny permanently the use of Lebanese soil to armed Palestinian activity and to eliminate its leadership from their Lebanese haven. The campaign went on for months and plunged much of the country into turmoil. This chapter in the continuing conflict in the Middle East was not the first in which Unicef was involved, but it was the first in which its role was of special significance.

Beirut's geographical position and its pre-eminence at the hub of Middle Eastern banking and commerce had made it the natural choice for Unicef's Eastern Mediterranean Regional Office. For many years a handful of staff served programmes in countries stretching from Syria in the north to the southern tip of the Arabian peninsula and Sudan, and across north Africa as far as Morocco. With the exception of certain less well-off or very poor countries—the two Yemens and Sudan—Unicef's programme support for most of these countries was modest and had run along conventional lines: support for courses in midwifery or nutrition; help in procuring vaccines and drugs for disease campaigns; in the early days, a pilot milk plant or a weaning food factory in each country; the occasional push for girls' or women's training; and, in co-operation with the UN Relief and Works Agency (UNRWA), social welfare for children in the shabby settlements housing Palestinians uprooted from their land in 1948. Assistance was also given to Israel, for day-care services, weaning food development, and emergency relief in the West Bank and Gaza; although since 1966, Israel's primary relationship with Unicef became that of donor rather than recipient. This was co-ordinated with the Unicef National Committee for Israel, run by Mrs Zena Harman, a previous Executive Board Chairman and one of Unicef's longstanding senior affiliates.

After OPEC's action of 1973–74 and the sudden infusion of wealth into oil-producing Arab nations, Unicef tried to raise its visibility in the Middle East in the hope that Arab governments now engaged in an overnight development splurge would choose to profit from Unicef's international experience to help bring down their high infant mortality rates and upgrade their health and social services networks. In addition, those casting around for ways to use their wealth in the Third World would be encouraged to use existing multilateral mechanisms rather than create their own or con-centrate only on bilateral aid to other Moslem countries. The stepping up of Unicef's Middle Eastern activity was assigned to Jim McDougall, Regional Director from 1967 to 1976. Some of the North African countries began to respond. Others showed reluctance.

During the Lebanese civil war of 1975–76, the efforts of McDougall's expanding regional team were diverted into emergency relief. He despatched his staff to Beirut's bazaars to buy up drugs and dried milk for distribution to families made helpless and homeless. Other supplies were flown in from the UNIPAC warehouse in Copenhagen. Relief goods were distributed through local Red Cross teams, UNRWA, and the official Lebanese relief mechanisms: every effort was made to be even-handed to all parties and religious groups in the labyrinth of Lebanese allegiances, and adhere only to the principle of helping children in need.

In late 1976, the savagery of the fighting forced McDougall to evacuate the staff—except those Lebanese who preferred to stay—by convoy through the battle lines. His deputy, Rachid Koleilat, stayed on throughout the fighting, and managed to maintain a relief operation of a kind. For those who left and those who stayed the experience was traumatic; McDougall's health deteriorated under the strain of responsibility for staff members dispersed to Amman, Damascus, Cairo and Cyprus. His strong right hand at this time was a solid and unflappable Swede, Gullmar Anderson, another of that pioneering species who are often found in the ranks of today's international humanitarian organizations, always in trouble-spots which everyone else is trying to leave. For Anderson, as for many other UN staff in Beirut, the evacuation of 1976 was the first experience of a kind which later became almost routine.

The office was reopened early in 1977, and François Rémy took over. Political and military calm was never re-established in a city now divided into a Christian east and a Moslem west with a strip of no-man's-land between. Although Unicef's programme co-operation reverted to a more typical long-term character, the problems of working in a country unable to resist the forces of violent disintegration became an ever-present burden. It became increasingly difficult not to become demoralized or swept up in powerful currents of anger, and to keep lines open with all the quarrelling parties. Yet in this complex situation, neutrality was critical if children of all groups were to be reached.

In mid-1978, Lebanese relief officials estimated that 1·3 million people—well over a third of the country's population—were displaced, at least temporarily, and that half of these were children whose families were destitute. The area of greatest flux was next to the Israeli border, south of the Litani River and east of the ancient port city of Tyre, where constant flare-ups between Israeli and Palestinian fighters had recently erupted in all-out war. Caught in military cross-fire, villagers fled northwards to Sidon and Beirut to shelter with relatives until calm returned. On the city peripheries, they swelled the straggling camps and squatter settlements of a vastly augmented 'poverty belt'. Witness to the ebb and flow of so much suffering, it was hard for the Unicef office to concentrate its attention anywhere else in the region. The areas where need was greatest and which were militarily most contentious were one and the same.

In 1978, Unicef became involved in water-supply and health-care reconstruction carried out by the Lebanese Government in the war-created poverty belt around Beirut and in a wide arc through the countryside from north to south. Its contribution was technical and advisory; most of the finance came from USAID. As a result of this experience, in 1980 Unicef was asked by the Lebanese Government to take on the management of a

$47 million programme funded by Arab governments for the reconstruction of hospitals, schools and water systems in southern Lebanon. This was a reversal of the normal role; usually Unicef made some contribution in material or technical support for a project run by a government department or its contractees. In southern Lebanon, Unicef contracted local labour and ran the project while the Government paid the bills. Although the operational role was one it normally took pains to avoid, the circumstances of southern Lebanon demanded an exception. Unicef personnel and vehicles could move through an anarchic mosaic of politico-military enclaves with relative impunity. Faced with an almost total breakdown of services of all kinds, the needs of the people were clearly acute, and the programme could also create jobs and revitalize local industry.

In October 1980, Unicef set up an office in Qana, south of the Litani River, east of Tyre, and within easy reach of a battalion of UNIFIL forces (the UN Interim Forces in Lebanon), whose engineers were very helpful. The programme was placed under the supervision of Gullmar Anderson. Over the course of the next twenty months, contacts were awarded to local Lebanese firms and construction was completed at 143 sites. Work continued even when shells and rockets flew overhead during artillery duels: Anderson did not want to let the momentum of the programme slacken. Schools, hospitals and dispensaries were rebuilt and re-equipped. Wells were drilled, and pipelines laid from the Litani River to village standpipes and health centres where faucets had not run for years. Gastro-enteric infections and scabies, diseases connected to water availability, began to decline and cleanliness improved along with that vital ingredient of public health: morale. An important link in the water supply system for 200,000 people was a new pumping station in the hills near Tyre built over a large spring once used by Alexander the Great.

Unicef had just completed the installation of two new pumps at Ras el Ain when the Israeli campaign of June 1982 began. In the first days of the fighting, the pumphouse suffered a direct hit and the station was completely destroyed.

The scale of the war and resulting crisis began to emerge as the Israeli Army moved through southern Lebanon. François Rémy was away; Anderson took charge of the office in east Beirut and began to buy relief goods off the shelf and distribute them through the authorities and voluntary organizations. At Unicef headquarters in New York, a task force under Margaret Catley-Carlson, Deputy Executive Director for Operations, began to examine emergency supply routes into Lebanon. The port of Beirut was under fire, as were those at Tyre and Sidon. Damascus, capital of Syria, was only two hours by road from Beirut. Rémy therefore flew to Damascus to receive relief supplies—blankets, baby food, milk, utensils, drugs—airlifted from Unicef's supply centre in Copenhagen.

Within a few days, UN Secretary-General Javier Pérez de Cuéllar appealed for international emergency assistance at the urgent request of the Lebanese Government. On 15 June, Grant announced a ninety-day Unicef relief effort costing $5 million, and called upon national committees and donors to lend support. Rémy in Damascus, Anderson in Beirut, and staff in Qana were authorized to spend what they must on procuring and distributing relief in the areas affected by military activity. The same day, the first convoy of tents, blankets, food and medical goods left Damascus and arrived at Baalbek in the Bekaa Valley. This area was a traditional sanctuary for Palestinian refugees and was now inundated by 55,000 new arrivals fleeing the Israeli advance. Unable to proceed beyond areas under Syrian control, the convoy unloaded its forty-one tons of cargo for distribution.

By this stage, the Israeli forces had encircled west Beirut, home of its Moslem population, including the Palestinian camps and fighters of the Palestinian resistance movements. These settlements now bore the brunt of the Israeli onslaught. In the south, the fighting had left its share of casualties and destruction, but after a period of tension and delay, relief organizations including UNRWA and Unicef were able to deliver supplies and provide shelter to the 400,000 people left homeless by the destruction.

West Beirut presented a more difficult problem. Under the Geneva Conventions, relief cannot be denied to enemy civilians by one or other party to a conflict. A siege, however, does not make nice distinctions between combatants and civilians because its weapons include the closure of supply lines of food, water and other life-sustaining items. Bombs and shells can be targeted; the closure of supply lines cannot. For this reason, this ancient form of military campaign is difficult to accommodate to the codes of conduct applied in contemporary warfare. Unless the 200,000 'civilians' in west Beirut were prepared to sacrifice their homes, withdraw voluntarily, and leave the 'military' to their fate—which most were not—they faced peril and extreme hardship. For the next days and weeks, the bombardment and siege continued.

It was not a hermetically-sealed siege. Food supplies were available in west Beirut, although they were outside the means of many inhabitants. Two relief convoys, organized by Unicef but bringing in supplies from many UN agencies and using trucks from the UN peace-keeping forces, were allowed to enter west Beirut under Lebanese Army escort. The arrival of the first, on 22 June, gave the people an important psychological boost. Other convoys, organized by the Red Cross, as well as by the joint efforts of UN agencies, were also permitted entry as the weeks wore on. Relief personnel and journalists were also allowed to move across the divide between east and west. But as the siege continued inconclusively, movement into the west became more and more restricted, and as fears mounted that Israeli troops would launch a direct attack, the Palestinian fighters in the city mined the entry routes. The difficulty of moving backwards and forwards continually increased.

The critical shortage in west Beirut was water. By early July, the taps were dry: the main cock at the principal source of supply, the Ashrafiye pumping station in the eastern sector, had been turned off. A water engineer on Unicef's staff, Raymond Naimy, a Lebanese of Christian background, had envisaged this possibility. Before the siege began, he had armed himself with maps from the city water department showing the locations of old artesian wells. He also built up a store of pumps, rigs and spare parts. At the end of June, as thirst threatened and public health deteriorated, Naimy became the *de facto* water department of west Beirut.

With a scratch crew of fourteen, Naimy managed to set up an alternative water-supply system. He brought disused wells into commission, even drilled new wells in the city streets, and assembled groups of 1000-litre steel water tanks at strategic points. Two Unicef tankers made nonstop deliveries of water from the wells to the tanks while women and children lined up. When the electricity supply was also closed down, Naimy scoured apartment complexes for generators to keep his pumps operating. Naimy's team not only managed to keep the communal tanks topped up and family water jars from running dry; they laid on water at five temporary hospitals, and cleared 250 tons of garbage from the streets every day. A few cases of typhoid fever were reported, but no serious epidemics of gastro-enteric disease. Raymond Naimy was regarded as a local hero.

On 8 July 1982, Jim Grant arrived in Damascus to make his own tour and assessment of Lebanese relief needs. Accompanied by Rémy, he drove into west Beirut, visited emergency installations and talked with relief officials. He was deeply impressed by the dedication and energy of the Unicef staff, particularly those in west Beirut who remained in the beleaguered city and refused the offer of evacuation to somewhere safe. On 10 July, he drove to Tyre and Sidon to see the damage sustained in the south, including the ruins of the Ras el Ain pumping station, which he promised would be repaired.

On 14 July, Rémy returned to west Beirut. Angered by the closure of the mains water supply, he tried to use diplomatic pressure through the UN system to get the taps at the Ashrafiye pumping station turned on again. When this failed, he used the international press to make a public furore. This decision labelled him as partisan which was touchy for an organization dedicated to neutrality; he had taken a risk, but the taps were turned on. Rémy stayed on throughout the next two months, and with Naimy and other members of the Unicef team, was one of the earliest witnesses to the desolation in the Sabra and Chatila camps after the massacres of September. In October, after a long and exhausting tour of duty, he left Beirut. Charles Egger was invited out of retirement to replace him temporarily; his place was eventually taken by another longtime Unicef career officer, Victor Soler-Sala.

On 10 August, Grant launched a $60 million rehabilitation programme.

Its main emphasis was the reconstruction of water, health and education facilities in southern Lebanon. Under Anderson's leadership, Unicef simply picked up the original programme, dusted off the debris and began again.

In Beirut itself, as in much of southern Lebanon, the most agonizing price of the war was paid by thousands of families who had lost not only some of their members, their homes and all their possessions, but also any sense of physical and emotional security after such a long period of fighting flaring up again after each supposed peace agreement. Thousands of children had been orphaned. Thousands of children had been severely wounded, bearing irreparable damage in their bodies and minds. Many of them needed shelter, foster care, physical rehabilitation, hope, love. Amidst the continuing turmoil of Beirut, many unsung heroes are trying to help such children overcome the scars of growing up among constant and bewildering bloodshed. These children are also the target of Unicef assistance. And will remain so.

In a tiny, half-deserted cluster of huts that passes for a village, a widow twenty-three years old with three children sits in the sand and gazes at her last possessions: a straw tent, a metal pot, a few balls of white yarn, two goat skins, a few rags of clothes and a pair of rubber flip-flop sandals. Her face is the face of a woman of fifty, her expression one of fixed, trancelike resignation.

This image comes from a village called Tin Taylout, thirty miles north across the sand dunes from Timbuktu, a town with a rich and romantic past at a crossroads of trans-Saharan trade. In 1984 and 1985, Timbuktu became a mecca for a different kind of traveller: Western journalists in search of the unending, repetitious images of a continent in crisis. With minor variations, the picture of the young woman in circumstances reduced to zero, with a baby at the breast and two other toddlers to care for, could have come from any one of twenty-five countries on the continent. The year 1984 was the one in which the detested clichés of hunger and suffering clinging to Africa took on their grimmest reality in modern times.

Throughout 1984, as drought deepened not only in its usual trans-continental path across the Sahel and into the Horn of Africa but also in countries far to the south, food shortage was widely predicted and inter-national alarm bells rang. Every international organization whose business had anything to do with famine, including Unicef, tried—in fits and starts—to build up its operational capacity in Africa as far as resources would allow; thousands of food cargoes were despatched; medical teams were sent to relief camps; efforts to keep track of children's nutritional condition were increased.

Soul-searching conferences about mistaken development policies and fund-raising appeals for African emergencies became almost monotonous sign posts along the route to mass tragedy. Representatives of international aid organizations clamoured at foreign office doors for more attention to Africa's needs; journalists and well-known figures—Liv Ullmann among them—toured countries at the agencies' invitations and broadcast the needs of people living on little but parched land and empty promises. But aid on the scale required was slow in coming forward. In mid-1984, Unicef told its Executive Board that in response to special appeals it had made for Angola, Chad, Ethiopia, Ghana and Uganda totalling over $20 million, only $2·5 million had been pledged. By this time, thirty million people in Africa were suffering acutely, at least four million of whom had abandoned their homes and villages in the hope that they could find shelter and something to eat elsewhere. 'The land is growing old', said an old Somali woman in despair, offering her own version of the process of population pressure and soil erosion, now fatefully compounded by the longest absence of rain in living memory.

But it took, yet again, a television report to bring home to the world the enormity of the abyss into which millions had fallen and to ignite a response on a scale which came anywhere close to pulling them out. The short seven-minute film, made by cameraman Mohammed Amin and BBC reporter Michael Buerk, and screened throughout the day on BBC television in the UK on 23 October, began with these words: 'Dawn, and as the sun breaks through the piercing chill of night on the plain outside Korem, it lights up a biblical famine, now, in the twentieth century. This place, say workers here, is the closest thing to hell on earth'. 'This place' was the same barren, mountainous, over-peopled, over-farmed, over-grazed landscape which in 1973 had destroyed hundreds of thousands of lives from starvation, and brought a dynasty crashing in its wake. Hunger had not disappeared, in spite of governmental determination that such a calamity should not occur again. Another series of disastrous drought years had led to another, a bigger, tragedy.

A year after widespread hunger began to gnaw apart the fabric of life in northern Ethiopia, the words spoken by Michael Buerk and the images that accompanied them blew away public and official apathy to Africa's plight. In October 1984, it was the turn of Western television audiences to stare in glazed disbelief as children with ravaged faces and stick-like limbs died before their eyes. Once again, it was the vast outpouring of public generosity and public horror inspired by these images which forced Western governments into large-scale efforts and contributions. Those African governments which had hesitated to discover or confess the pitiable condition of some of their people now found the spotlight of international compassion cast upon them. As usual, the spotlight was remorseless in casting blame and failure on governments and international organizations which exist in order that such things should never happen.

The prolonged public attention on Africa's misery had a benefit beyond the generosity it inspired—attention and generosity fuelled by a remarkable effort led by the popular singer, Bob Geldorf. It prompted an unusually probing portrayal of the ultimate spectacle of underdevelopment in remote, rural regions in poor, economically backward, and usually invisible countries. Until the journalists set off on their pilgrimage to Timbuktu, many people did not know that the legendary city really existed; still less did they know that it was in a country called Mali where 150 children out of 1000, even in normal times, died before they reached their first birthday, and where the remorseless advance of the desert was swallowing arable land and people's ancestral homes.

Places like Korem in Ethiopia, which had hardly ever appeared on a map before, now entered many people's geographic vocabulary. When camel caravans set off from the Red Sea hills not with exotic loads of myrrh and sandalwood but with grain for starving nomad families in the Sudanese interior, over-used words such as poor, backward, neglected, developing took on new and dramatic meanings.

Over the years, the international aid community had become more experienced and more imaginative in its responses to disaster. The media and the public, too, had become more discerning: more exacting on the one hand, more willing on the other to take into account the complexities of operating relief programmes in places where port facilities and transport were lacking, road surfaces appalling, health personnel in very short supply, and security ill-assured. Even to those uninitiated in the scene and philosophy of development, whose response to Africa's tragedy was at the simple emotional level of saving children from starving to death, the way in which a 'loud emergency' had built to a climax from a 'silent emergency' was plainly evident.

All the obstacles which stood in the way of a militarily precise and efficient rescue operation were the same obstacles which development ought to be eradicating, and was not. In Africa, economic and environmental deterioration had set in at a pace so fast that, at least for the time being, the development process was quite unable to stem it.

There had been development in independent sub-Saharan Africa in the past generation, some of it very conspicuous development. Every country, however poor, could point to modern factories, dams and highways, hospitals and universities, and growing cadres of professional, administrative and technical experts. Much of this represented real progress. But the reverse side of the coin was the lack of investment in the rural areas, dependence on primary commodities with undependable market values, declining food production per inhabitant, mounting debt and growing unemployment. Development had brought modern goods and services within the reach of some people in every country. But in the process, others had moved closer to the abyss. Drought had merely helped to accelerate the crisis.

The tragedy of Africa in the 1980s is a crushing indictment of modern man's chosen course of self-improvement, a course which has failed the poorest and most vulnerable. The vast majority of such people are women and children. The women and children of Africa are losing an unequal battle against powerful elements over which they have no control.

Within the complex skein of Africa's crisis, and of the combination of political, economic, agricultural, fiscal and social responses it demands, Unicef has at most a cameo role to play. To co-ordinate the UN response through all its various agencies and institutions, Secretary-General Pérez de Cuéllar set up a special African emergency office in January 1985 under Bradford Morse, Administrator of UNDP. By the end of the year, nearly $3 billion in food and financial aid had been mobilized. Within the overall effort, Unicef's essential role was to highlight the ravages of the crisis on African women and children, and to use its programme co-operation to offset such ravages where it could.

At the end of 1982, in his *The State of the World's Children* report, James Grant launched a new Unicef global campaign to revolutionize children's prospects of survival and better health throughout the first, critical years of their lives by focussing on certain basic health-care measures. As drought strengthened its grip on Africa during 1983 and 1984, the most glaring priority for children was survival. But survival and better health are inseparable. In the relief camps of Korem, Bati, Mekelle and other famine staging-posts in northern Ethiopia in late 1984, an overwhelming impression was the sound: coughing, an endless cacophony of dry, muted coughing, and otherwise the silence of despair. One signal of starvation, of profound debilitation, is a cough, lungs pained and infected and unable to function. Another is the soundless loss of the body's life-sustaining fluid because, in its weakened state, the most minor germ takes hold of the body in a convulsive diarrhoeal purge. A third is the quick hold a fatal epidemic of almost any disease takes on the weakened bodies of children already suffering from advanced malnutrition. In other words, children do not usually die of 'starvation': they die of simple ailments which hunger makes mortal.

Alongside its traditional help with special child-feeding, supplies of essential drugs for medical relief, and drilling wells to provide water supplies in villages and relief camps, Unicef also made a special effort to help control diarrhoeal disease and offer support for health-care measures which would act as a buffer against the worst effects of prolonged hunger. In Burkina Faso, a crash immunization campaign against measles and tuberculosis reached two-thirds of the country's children through 'Vaccination Commando' teams. Tons of oral rehydration mix—sodium and potassium salts and glucose—were airlifted to Ethiopia to offset the body fluid losses from gastro-enteric outbreaks among relief-camp children.

In north-east Uganda, where drought had caused such devastation among the Karamajong four years before, regular weighing and measuring of the children to signal any worsening in their condition was still in operation, and it was working. Every few months, the results of careful plotting on their charts showed that it was time to begin distributing rations again. All the children were systematically inoculated against measles, a disease commonly associated with malnutrition.

Further south, in Botswana, harvest failure was as bad as anywhere on the continent. But a similar nutritional watchdog and food-ration system was in place. A Unicef survey in mid-1984 revealed that over seventy per cent of the country's preschool children attended health clinics monthly, and ninety-five per cent of children in rural areas possessed health cards with their growth curve plotted along them. With this kind of gain in spreading health services, Botswana could cushion children against hunger. This success in avoiding tragedy went widely unremarked: horror stories did not emerge from Botswana so it was not on the journalists' famine itineraries.

One programme supported by Unicef in Ethiopia which did not go unnoticed was a variation, on a small scale, of the food-for-work schemes which are a stock-in-trade of international relief. These employ people on public works—digging irrigation channels, bunding hillsides, cutting roads—and pay their wages in food. One of the unwritten rules of institutional humanitarian effort is not to give out cash directly. There is a paternalistic fear that it will be squandered, that the poor cannot be trusted to spend other people's money on what is in their own best interests. Yet it is by no means uncommon to find that, in areas where drought has reduced many families to destitution, there is still food for sale. The problem is that those who need it cannot afford to buy it. In Gondar province, the observation that trucks of food still plied their way to urban markets while rural people went hungry led to the notion that, with cash in hand, poor families might manage. Simple calculations indicated that the cost of shipping and trucking food into the province and getting it to the worst-hit communities was at least as high as giving out the equivalent of a social security benefit.

In late 1983, discussions between Unicef and the Ethiopian Relief and Rehabilitation Commission led to the decision that, in a few communities on an experimental basis, cash-for-work would be given out instead of food-for-work. The 1000 families involved built feeder roads, cleaned springs and prepared seed beds against the return of rain; with their pay, they were able to stay in their villages and maintain their families' minimal food and welfare needs. A survey after six months revealed that the idea was an unqualified success.

In Mali, on an equally small experimental scale, livestock doomed by drought were bought at a reasonable price and slaughtered before they perished on the hoof. Their nomad owners were employed in an enterprise to dry the meat and tan the skins, the food products were given out, and some floor-level family income was maintained.

In Africa in 1984, according to the best estimate that rough data can provide, five million children died from hunger, malnutrition and related sickness. This is a terrible toll, and it is only the most conspicuous statistic about a tragedy that left many millions more children in a permanently depleted physical and mental condition. Yet the figures of child death represent a rise of only twenty-five per cent over previous 'normal' years. It is intolerable that any child should die of hunger in the late twentieth century, and shocking that the 'normal' toll should be so high. But, given the dimensions in which the tragedy was conveyed, the margin between what is normal and what happens when Africa is visited by climatic calamity is almost startlingly narrow.

What surprised many observers, as it had done when the spotlight was more narrowly focussed on Kampuchea five years before, was the incredible resilience of people depicted as helpless and destitute. In April 1985 in Sudan, famine was thought to threaten nine million people. Catastrophe was predicted for the agricultural people of the western regions and failure to solve transport bottlenecks ground relief efforts nearly to a halt. Although thousands died and hundreds of thousands suffered, starvation on the expected scale did not occur. By extraordinary stoicism, by resorting to the roots and wild berries of the desert, people managed to survive almost unaided. Africa's food providers, most of whom are women, have a lesson to teach the experts.

Africa is the world's oldest continent, and its inhabitants are among the world's most accomplished survivors. The adaptation that many African peoples have made to the uneven intrusions of modernity—the demands of the cash economy, urbanization, the erosion of traditional societal and cultural norms—is far more imaginative than many outsiders and national policy-makers looking at local problems through Western-trained eyes are prepared to recognize. In Zimbabwe, at the end of 1984 and a ruinous drought, the peasant farmers brought in a maize crop regarded by the Ministry of Agriculture as a miracle: they had produced food which no-one thought it was possible to grow. They had planted at a critical moment when an inch of rain unexpectedly broke the drought; and they had taken advantage of fertilizers, pesticides, credit and specialized seeds, put at their disposal by a far-sighted agricultural policy. As a result, the small farmers had brought in Zimbabwe's biggest harvest in four years of independence.

In Africa, eighty per cent of the family food supply is sown, weeded, harvested and stored by women. Ironically, it is they and their helpers, their children, who most often go hungry. These women and children are Unicef's special constituency. Not only as consumers, but as producers, women and children are special players in the unfolding drama. The economic planners cannot afford to go on ignoring them.

In the words of the Somali woman: 'The land is growing old'. With the right approach, the land could grow 'young' again. The rural-development strategies which have failed Africa so conspicuously must be abandoned in favour of something better. In Tin Taylout village across the sand dunes from the fabled town of Timbuktu, there must be more for the children to inherit than a straw tent, a metal pot, a few balls of white yarn, two goat skins, a few rags of clothes, and a pair of rubber flip-flop sandals.

There must be, and there will.

Main Sources

Famine: A Man-made Disaster?, a report for the Independent Commission on International Humanitarian Issues, Vintage Books, New York, 1985.

Unicef Information Division: 'Emergencies in Africa', background kit prepared in 1982; *Unicef News*, in particular Issue 109/1981 and 120/1984; *Ideas Forum*, Issue 17/1984; Unicef annual reports, 1981 through 1985; press releases and information notes on African emergency issued during 1984 and 1985.

Unicef Executive Board: country programme profiles; recommendations of the Executive Director for emergency programmes in Lebanon; progress reports of the Executive Director; reports of the Executive Board; statements by Board Delegates; summary records, etc; 1975–1985.

The State of the World's Children; reports for 1980–81, 'From here to 2000'; and 1981–82, 'Children in Dark Times', by James P. Grant, Executive Director of Unicef.

'The Impact of World Recession on Children', a Unicef special study, published as Chapter IV of *The State of the World's Children*, 1984.

'Adjustment with a Human Face: Context, Content and Economic Justification for a Broader Approach to Adjustment Policy', paper by Richard Jolly, October 1985.

40,000 Enfants Par Jour: Vivre La Cause de L'Unicef by Dr François Rémy, published by Robert Laffont and Michel Archimbaud, Paris, 1983.

Interviews of key Unicef staff and Board delegates, prepared for the Unicef History Project, 1983–85.

'Within Human Reach: A Future for Africa's Children', a Unicef report prepared by Manzoor Ahmed and others, 1985.

Chapter 19

Towards a Revolution for Children

The conference at Alma-Ata in the Soviet Union in 1978 engraved on the international development agenda the goal of 'Health for All by the Year 2000'. A revolutionary definition of the purpose, content and organization of health services, elaborated as 'primary health care', had been submitted to ministers of health and senior health officials from 138 countries and had been unanimously approved.

The results of Alma-Ata were an achievement of which WHO and Unicef, its joint sponsors, could be justly proud. Dr Halfdan Mahler, Director-General of WHO, had provided the vision and the driving force, but he had counted heavily upon the support of Henry Labouisse, then Executive Director of Unicef. The long process of critical analysis and careful preparation which had come to fruition in the Declaration of Alma-Ata also owed a great deal to the work of Dr Tejada de Rivero, Assistant Director-General of WHO, and Dick Heyward, Senior Deputy Director of Unicef.

The Declaration was a vindication of the view that health-care services must cease to be a top-down delivery of medical consumables orchestrated by the patriarchs of medical wisdom. The health-care service must respond to the population's real health-care needs: it must function out in the countryside where most of the people were; it must concentrate on low-cost prevention rather than high-cost cure; most important—since it must enlist the people in its own performance—it must be sensitive to their sense of health priorities. Mahler, who twenty-five years earlier had gone to India as a young tuberculosis expert and had been what he called a 'circus director' running great immunization 'shows', had long since reached the conclusion that no 'show' could endure, that no health service could function effectively over time unless it corresponded to people's own sense of their health-care needs. Now those in charge of delivering health-care services in countries around the world had agreed; or at least they said they had agreed. Alma-Ata could be an important trigger for a process of organic change in health-service design, if commitment in principle at the international level could be transformed into national effort.

Like all turning points in the history of ideas, the Alma-Ata conference was symbolically very important but, in the process of transforming the health prospects of the poor throughout the world, it represented but one milestone along a very long route. The first steps along the way had been taken more than fifty years earlier by people such as Dr Ludwik Rajchman, Dr John Grant, and other pioneers in whose steps had followed a whole generation of 'alternative' health practitioners. The challenge was now to realize 'Health for All' in a much less extended time frame: the twenty-odd years left before the end of the century. It was one thing to name the goal, quite another to reach it, particularly as population growth was increasing the pressure on all development efforts.

During the period after the Conference, WHO and Unicef made strenuous efforts to maintain and build upon the momentum that Alma-Ata had inspired. At its 1979 session, their Joint Committee on Health Policy examined the many constraints facing the rapid adoption of PHC, and tried to work out how their collaboration could be further strengthened and put to work on its behalf. Whatever the surface unanimity at Alma-Ata, many national authorities continued to think that high technology was more effective than health services based in the community. Their commitment to the target of 'Health for All' might be real, but their commitment to PHC as the strategy for getting there was no more than skin deep. In some countries, programmes were launched which fell far short of the realization of PHC in its many nonclinical aspects. Links between the health ministries and the water supply and education sectors, or that dealing with the food supply or women's status, were tenuous at best, never mind national commitments to clean water and sanitation for all by 1990, or those targets for the Decade for Women which related to health and the quality of family life. There was a long way to go before the full promise of PHC and its implications for other areas than those conventionally defined as health care were fully understood.

One direction adopted by some of PHC's new adherents was to take up some parts of the strategy and conveniently overlook its more uncomfortable aspects. The Alma-Ata Conference identified a minimum list of activities to be included in PHC: health education; promotion of the family food supply and sound nutrition; safer water and basic sanitation; MCH, including family planning; immunization against the major infectious diseases; control of endemic disease; treatment of common complaints and injuries; and the provision of essential drugs. The simplest way to adopt PHC was to add these activities to the rim of the existing health service, and carry them out with the help of extra unpaid man- and womanpower from villages and shanty towns. According to this model, primary health care was not a revolution within the health-care system, but a low-cost extra attached to its edge. It did not demand any major change of budgetary emphasis away from the sophisticated curative services used by the better-off members of society towards the more mundane requirements of ordinary—poor—families. This kind of change in the use of resources for health was regarded by some as the litmus test of whether a country's health establishment was merely paying lip service to 'Health for All', or whether it was serious.

Naturally enough, few countries made significant adjustments overnight. Change of the kind demanded by genuine implementation of the PHC strategy could not move faster than that governing the elaboration of national plans and the allocation of national resources. The progress towards PHC's adoption in its revolutionary entirety was bound to be slow. But the fact was that a heartening number of semirevolutionary changes in health care were taking place which did improve the chances of the world's least well-off mothers and children.

True, some programmes carried out in the name of PHC looked like the old disease-control campaigns. The authorities at the centre launched the scheme with loud public fanfare; and health officials set off into the countryside; the village headmen called a meeting; harangues, line-ups and children's weigh-ins ensued. But there was a difference. Officials did not simply get back into their landrovers when their part of the job was done and drive away, leaving behind a bewildered group of mothers only half convinced that anything health-promoting had happened to their squawling toddlers. Now things were done differently; there was some kind of exchange of views between the officials and the people; some of their numbers went for training, and when they returned they had answers to certain problems and, with luck, a metal box with Unicef on it and pills and bandages which they shared around.

Whatever its shortcomings, this was the reality of primary health care in action in many parts of the world. Some of the concept's keenest supporters lamented that it was not being given a proper try; others more pragmatically concentrated on how to make sure that what was being done was better done. This might mean making sure that a national plan for PHC was not applied with dogmatic uniformity; that malaria control was not made the first priority in a place where respiratory infections and intestinal parasites were the commonest complaints. It might also mean avoiding the pitfall of overloading the community health-care worker: the new vogue for the lay volunteer not only in health but also in other basic services meant that every kind of programme, from family planning to water supply maintenance, was depending on her and him. Often, the same villagers turned up for the various training programmes and confusion set in about whether feeding the under-fives or keeping the new handpump clean was the priority.

Then there was the need to improve what was often no more than a nod in the direction of consultation with the community. The success of PHC ultimately depended on the willingness of the community to assume part of the responsibility for their own health care. This required instituting a genuine dialogue between health-care officials and village people. Where village councils and other traditional mechanisms for running village affairs had already been enlisted in applied nutrition schemes or other community development activities, primary health care constituted a variation on a familiar theme. Elsewhere, old ways died hard. Many rural people, and the officials who had any contact with them, were unused to other than top-down ways of doing things and did not easily shed the behaviour of a lifetime.

Even if attitudes had begun to change, it was difficult to develop a sufficiently flexible health structure to respond imaginatively to communities' different needs. Some authorities were reluctant to decentralize enough power down the line to those at one remove from the village itself; and if they did so, some had insufficient confidence to use it. Designing techniques to bring about community participation became a new branch of development science: 'project support communications' was part of Unicef's version. Jack Ling, then the Director of Information, had managed to institute 'PSC' as a legitimate Unicef activity during the 1970s. Under Tarzie Vittachi, Grant's immediate deputy on the external relations front, the notion that effective communications at all levels of society were an essential ingredient in successful programming began to take firmer root in Unicef. At WHO, Mahler invited Jack Ling to join his senior lieutenants, and help give the content of WHO's programme of education for health a thorough overhaul.

Dissecting the ingredients of two-way communication exposed cultural blockages inhibiting the transmission of even quite simple messages. Visual aids designed in the advertising studios of the television era were incomprehensible to people who were 'visually illiterate'. The conventional kind of illiteracy, or semiliteracy, among community-health trainees caused even more obvious problems. In many parts of the Third World, people use one language—their traditional tongue—in everyday speech, and learn to read and write in another. The language of administration and instruction is alien to the everyday life of home or village. Yet primary health care messages are, by definition, everyday messages: 'filter the water', 'watch the baby's growth', 'clean the kitchen utensils'. Where teaching was not in the local dialect, many took in and promoted little of what they were taught. Yet it was expensive, difficult, and it sometimes went against the grain, to produce teaching materials in a wide variety of tongues officially regarded as a throwback to the past.

Another problem which disturbed the primary health care practitioners was the turnover among those chosen by communities for training. Many signed up enthusiastically for what they thought was a course which would set them on the ladder to employment. When they found that they were to be remunerated not by the health services or the water department, but by their own communities, some became disenchanted. Unless the village council put its weight firmly behind this idea and set about collecting levies, the village health workers often did not receive their stipends. Some external assistance organizations, impatient to get primary health care underway and see some results, were prepared to underwrite the stipends the community said they could not afford. This established a pattern for the programme which was not sustainable. If at a later stage the funding organization—as was normal—withdrew and the government would not, or could not, pick up the salary bill, the programme was likely to collapse.

In places where traditional systems of mutual support and communal levies were common, the resistance to payment for the community health worker was mostly to do with lack of conviction about the value of the services she or he was offering. Some of those families who said they were too poor to pay were actually sceptical, or simply confused. The community health worker visited their homes and criticized the wives' household management and the husbands' resistance to family planning; but when their children were sick, they were often told to take them to the health centre just as they had in the past. After all the expectations, the community might feel that the service they were getting was not worth paying for. Without an incentive, the village health worker easily gave up. The training he or she had undertaken would be applied in the family compound, and maybe the neighbours would draw conclusions and decide to copy the example. The value was not lost, but neither was it quite what the PHC protagonists had in mind.

For many of these problems, solutions could be found if the people and the experts were able to sit down together and sort them out. Whether it was called community participation or something less ideologically frightening did not matter as long as some kind of two-way communications process took place. It was relatively easy, for example, to redress the anomalies that occurred when male health workers turned up for courses on breast-feeding, and women were taught to do things—mend handpumps, go home visiting on a bicycle, impose fines for littering—that the male-dominated community power structure would not approve. These and many other issues, microscopically important on the grand plan, but make or break in the untidy context of the hypothetically typical slum or village, provided a fertile ground for the continuing health-care debate.

As time went by, new information and experience accumulated about what made the critical difference between one kind of effort and another, what made injections and brightly-coloured antibiotics acceptable where latrines were not, why mothers in some communities loved getting together to give their toddlers a special meal and others found it a waste of time. While more countries put into practice some part of the primary health care philosophy, the doctrine became more diffuse and the programmes carried out in its name more various. Some found in the blurring of its pure lines evidence of genuine community choice and dawning political awareness. Others despaired that its force was slackening: where was the real primary health care programme, they asked? What they meant was: where was the ideal primary health care programme? Like so many ideal versions of human arrangements it did not exist. Some found the reality messy and untidy and were frustrated. Others were encouraged by the variety of activity going on under the PHC rubric and saw this as proof of the strategy's underlying viability.

If nuances of its operational character exercised the minds of primary health care exponents, there were other questions at the national policy level. It was difficult enough to convince ministries of health in developing countries that imitating the evolution of the medical consumer society in the West was not in the best interests of their people. But a ministry of health was by no means the end of the line. According to the conventional view, a ministry of health absorbed revenues for welfare purposes; it did not contribute directly to economic productivity. Therefore, it was not a recipient of a large slice of national resources; and, as recession deepened, it was likely to receive an even slimmer one.

Primary health care offered comparatively cheap techniques for making major gains in people's well-being. But extending the spread even of cheap techniques required funds and personnel. The cost of a shot of measles vaccine or a vitamin A capsule might in itself be trifling. But the vehicle to distribute it from the health centre to a community volunteer in a far-flung village, the driver, the fuel, not to mention the supervisor's salary, did not represent a negligible sum. Primary health care did not posit fewer resources for health care; it posited at least as many, better spent. Where it was an extra layer of the health system tacked onto its existing edge, the need for extra resources was even more acute. Unless political figures with greater clout than mere ministers of health could be persuaded that there were definite gains to be made from investing in social purposes it would be hard to prise the necessary cash from the national till.

Political will—that overworked phrase—was critically needed to put primary health care into place. At one extreme, primary health care needed the political will of the mother in the village or urban slum, standing up for the first time in her life at a meeting of the community elders to demand a clean water supply near her home or a health worker in her neighbourhood; at the other extreme, it required that national leaders heard those voices and recognized that denying them was not only a social and an economic cost, but that a political price might be paid as well.

In the early 1980s, with recession eating into budgets for social improvement the world over, the sense that progress towards the adoption and implementation of basic services would falter without some extra political push inspired James Grant to look for a way to reinvigorate the crusade. Something must be done to give PHC an extra boost, to lift it out of the crossfire of discussion about this part of the approach or that—a debate confined to the already converted—and move it onto the political agenda.

WHO, in attempting to give countries guidance on strategies for achieving health for all by the year 2000, had established certain indicators as a way of measuring how close to the target they were reaching. The two main yardsticks were life expectancy at birth, and the rate of infant mortality (IMR). A 'healthy' population—or a population in which disease and loss of life were becoming a decreasing burden on family and community—was one in which the minimum life expectancy at birth was sixty years, and the infant mortality rate was no higher than fifty deaths (within the first year of life) per 1000 live births. These indicators of the physical well-being of a population were internationally recognized in a number of fora; they echoed, for example, some of the targets set for the end of the century in the Club of Rome's report on 'Reshaping the International Order'.

The infant mortality rate reflects not only how many babies die; it also reflects the state of health of their mothers, during pregnancy, at the time of delivery, and afterwards; the cleanliness in the home or lack of it; the mothers' knowledge of sound child-rearing or lack of it; the availability of weaning food or lack of it; reasonable family income or lack of it; and a number of other factors that decide whether or not a young baby comes through the first, most dangerous, year of life. The next three to four years—the preschool years—are also a testing time, particularly in the period between one year and thirty months when the process of weaning to an adult diet is normally completed. Unicef had always been preoccupied with these age-groups: it existed to be so. But now, under the influence of Grant's thinking, the preoccupation began to be illuminated more brightly, and somewhat redefined.

In 1982, after three decades in which infant and child mortality rates had been halved worldwide, an average of 40,000 young children still died each day. These deaths were the result not of war or sudden calamity, but because of simple, easily preventable sickness. In the thirty years following the second World War, the child death rates in the poorest countries had declined, both because of general economic and social progress and as a result of the mass-disease campaigns. Since the mid-1970s the momentum of decline had slackened. The same vigour that had fuelled the onslaught on the mosquito and on scourges of tuberculosis, smallpox, syphilis and leprosy had yet to be galvanized against the pernicious combination of childhood infection and undernutrition.

Vigour was not the only essential. Unlike most of the dreaded diseases, there were no shots or pills to cure or protect against poor hygiene and too starchy a diet. The health service and its personnel could lecture, cajole, upbraid and entreat mothers to feed and care for their children differently—

within their existing means. But the actual health-promoting actions would have to be undertaken by them in their homes, not by the health service. Until more parents in villages and shanty towns began to undertake such actions, the 'silent emergency' of disease and death would continue, destroying children's lives and mothers' hopes because poverty and ignorance deprived them of an equal chance alongside children and mothers who just happened to be born into different circumstances.

Grant believed that the continuing death toll among young children was a scandal when, for the want of primary health care, many or most could be saved. He also believed that unless and until most were saved, and their parents convinced that their younger brothers and sisters would likewise survive, the chances that they would bear many fewer children were remote. Not only did better health and better nutrition feed off each other, but they could, and would, fuel a decline in the birth rate. Nowhere in the world has the birth rate dropped before the death rate has dropped; increased child survival could only contribute — eventually — to a decline in the birth rate. This computation of the necessary precondition for a slowing down of population growth fortified the argument for bringing the IMR below fifty per 1000 births in as many countries as possible.

Grant therefore began to focus on the idea of reducing the infant mortality rate as a deliberate target of efforts in which primary health care and basic services would provide the underlying strategy. In some countries, mostly in Africa, the IMR was close to 200 per 1000 births; a rate close to 150 was not uncommon in either Africa or Asia; the average for the developing countries as a whole was 100. Grant also saw a strategic value in establishing the reduction of infant deaths as a target behind which governments and their partners in the international community could rally. He believed that such a target was both politically appealing and politically neutral, and that it was possible to cultivate the idea that those developing countries who ignored the target would be put in the dock and pilloried internationally for failing to meet the ethical standards of the late-twentieth century.

In establishing the reduction of child deaths as a target not just for Unicef but for all the allies it could muster, Grant was shifting the emphasis from where it had been placed by WHO; as an indicator, the IMR was used to measure human progress or development. Grant was talking about survival, about so improving the overall level of child health as to lower the number of infant deaths. He believed that survival was a precondition of healthy development; and that, as a cause, child survival had a more emotive appeal so long as it did not reawaken fears of a population crisis.

To inspire the kind of worldwide movement Grant had in mind, the child survival techniques chosen for its cutting edge had to pass a number of critical tests. Their first and essential attribute was that they must be able to achieve dramatic gains in the survival rate of the children of the poor.

They must, therefore, address common maladies suffered by children virtually everywhere in the Third World, not only diseases confined to special epidemiological circumstances. A second and related criterion was that their impact must be measurable.

The target Grant had in mind was a reduction by at least half of the current death rate among children under five, from fifteen million a year to seven million, or from 40,000 a day to 20,000; this included the target of reducing IMR to fifty or less worldwide. The target was deliberately ambitious; its boldness would help create a political and psychological impetus for the campaign.

In the climate of world recession, with social services budgets and overseas aid programmes under stress, another critical attribute of any health care technique selected for special emphasis must be cost. No drastic re-apportionment of national or international resources into health could be anticipated, and to depend upon one would invite failure. The cost of any technique was not only a practical consideration, but an intrinsic part of its marketability; something whose hardware cost only a few dollars or cents per child was bound to have popular appeal. Unicef's limited budget could not possibly extend very far in helping governments reach all their children even with one health-giving ingredient. To mobilize international forces behind the child survival target, not only governments would have to deploy their personnel and resources, but also other allies—church, voluntary agency, industrial, media, any and every kind of formal and informal organization—would have to take part. As well as being inexpensive in themselves, the techniques must also be attractive, easy to understand and carry no religious or ideological stigma.

To identify the health care components which would meet all these criteria was a tall order. To try to do so at all was daring: the underlying thesis of primary health care was that it was a total concept with many interlocking parts, and that the only preselection of specific ingredients was one that should be made on the ground, in the country and the locality concerned, based on the priorities and problems articulated not just at national or even provincial level, but at subdistrict and community level.

Grant's thesis was predicated on the idea that selecting out some primary health care techniques and pushing those would allow others to piggy-back on them, which would in turn force the pace for the delivery of primary health care in its entirety. The circumstance that he believed made such a strategy practicable where it had not been so in the past was the tremendous spread of communications networks, particularly radio and television, and also the various mechanisms of nonformal education and the social organization that went with them. He believed that the combination of political will and public dissemination could achieve a critical mass; that the necessary information about primary health care techniques could reach mothers and families with enough persuasiveness for them not only to want to use them, but also even to demand them.

In mid-December 1982, in his third annual *The State of the World's Children* report, Grant gave the first public elaboration of the four techniques Unicef had espoused as the frontline of its campaign for a 'child survival and development revolution'. They had materialized from the meeting held three months before with leading international health and nutrition experts from WHO, FAO, Unicef, the World Bank and a number of academic institutions. Very quickly, the package became known by the mnemonic GOBI.

The first was a technique for monitoring the growth of the small child. To a very large extent, the problem of malnutrition in the Third World is an invisible problem. Except in the case of famine, only a very small proportion of children in the average village or shanty town—less than two per cent—display the tell-tale bleached hair and swollen stomach of kwashiorkor or are short of food to a skin-and-bone degree. Most of the malnourished are underweight; the signs of their depleted health are listlessness, dulled expressions, lack of urge to play and vulnerability to infection. But unless their weight is compared to what it ought to be at their age, it is easy for a mother—and even a health worker—to overlook these signals. In most cases, even in a very modest household, the means exist to adjust a child's nutritional intake. Ignorance, the ally of poverty, is more often the cause of child malnutrition than outright poverty itself.

The way to make sure that a child is growing and developing normally is systematic weighing, month by month; then—as in the schemes introduced in Karamoja, Uganda and Botswana—if a child appears to be dropping behind, extra rations can be given or the mother encouraged to give more nutritious food. The cheapest way of running this nutritional watch-dog system, and the way which makes the child's mother the principal watch dog, is to issue her with a simple chart for each child, and to bring her together with other mothers in the community for regular weighing sessions where she helps plot her child's weight on the chart.

In primary health care services in various parts of the world, this system had been known for many years; WHO and many nongovernmental pioneers—the Aroles at Jamkhed, for example—had helped to develop and refine it. An example of a programme where it had already been extensively used was a national nutrition programme in Indonesia. By 1982, two million mothers in 15,000 Indonesian villages had been given KMS—*Kartu Menuju Sehat*, meaning: 'towards good health cards'. Once a month, they attended a meeting at their local weighing post where their toddlers were put in a simple harness and hung from a market scale. The nutrition cadres—volunteers with some training—plotted a mark on a rainbow coloured chart for the child's weight opposite the child's age. The line joining the marks month by month showed immediately whether the child was on or off the road to health.

The hardware for such programmes—charts and scales—was inexpensive; and supervision were the main costs. The programmes were intended to educate mothers about the relationship between diet, growth and health in the young child, and enable them to bring their children through the vulnerable weaning period in safety. This was 'growth monitoring': the G in GOBI.

The second technique, and the one which offered the most exciting prospects, was oral—as opposed to intravenous—rehydration as a means of preventing childhood death from diarrhoea. Acute diarrhoea was the cause of five million child deaths in the world; it affected many millions of other children, often several times a year, sapping away their strength, halting their growth, and leaving them a steep climb back onto the road to health. Diarrhoeal disease was particularly prevalent in poor and crowded countries where the food and drinking water supply was often contaminated, such as Bangladesh. Unfortunately, many mothers, watching the fluids of their child's body drain away, made what to them was the logical assumption that the only way to stem the flow was to deny the child anything to eat or drink. Scientists had long realized that the loss of fluid, salts and minerals, which dehydrated the body and could send it into a shock from which death was only hours away, was a much more serious problem than the infection itself; the infection was usually washed away in the process. Drinking salty water was not an efficient solution: the liquid suffered the same fate, rushing through the digestive tract without reaching the body tissues, and the salt could even increase the loss of fluid. Rehydration only seemed possible by bypassing the digestive system intravenously.

In the 1960s, it was discovered that adding glucose—in the form of sugar—to salty water in the right proportion changed the metabolic process. However acute the diarrhoea, the body absorbed the sugar normally, and with the sugar as pathfinder, the body raised no objection to absorbing the rest of the minerals too.

During the early 1970s, when Bangladesh was wrestling with cyclones, war, newfound independence, social disruption and a soaring rate of diarrhoeal infection, the then Cholera Research Laboratory in Dhaka began to experiment with an 'oral rehydration solution'—ORS. WHO collaborated closely with the Laboratory's research, as with similar efforts being undertaken in other centres in Calcutta and elsewhere. In 1971, during the cholera outbreaks among the refugees from East Pakistan temporarily camped in West Bengal, WHO and Unicef first made available an ORS. Its formula made it suitable for the treatment of dehydration from diarrhoea of any cause in all age groups. The work of the Cholera Research Laboratory in Dhaka was important not only because it helped to establish the credibility of ORS within the medical world, but also because the lack of health services in Bangladesh meant that the wider 'laboratory'—the countryside—proved how suited the remedy was for administration by village mothers, aided only by the village health worker. If sachets of ORS and knowledge of how to brew it from ingredients in the home could be made available in Third World villages the ill-effects of diarrhoea would cease to be an overwhelming threat. The Cholera Research Laboratory, later renamed the International Centre for Diarrhoeal Disease Control, Bangladesh, and heavily supported by USAID, helped ORS to earn a place in the primary health care package.

In 1979, the government of Bangladesh launched a national oral re-hydration programme. With assistance from Unicef, ORS production centres were set up in four districts. Between them, by 1982, they produced 2·5 million ORS sachets. Over 98,000 village health workers had been given a day's training in how to manage a case of childhood diarrhoea with ORS. The ORS sachets were retailed at five cents (US), but they were given out free of charge to health centres and health personnel. Each village health worker received ten packets at the end of the training course, and if he or she kept a record of their use and reported on cases treated, replacements were provided by the family welfare worker.

In Teknaf, a remote rural area, a study had showed that oral rehydration solution had proved a successful treatment for ninety-five per cent of 3000 cases of diarrhoea. The children who had died had all been in families who lived far away from the health clinic.

Meanwhile the Bangladesh Rural Advancement Committee (BRAC), a nongovernmental organization set up after independence, had begun a community health outreach programme in Sylhet, another remote district. BRAC used Oral Replacement Workers—women between the ages of twenty and fifty who could read and write Bengali—to teach village mothers the recipe for making what they called *lobon-gur*, a home-made drink comprising water, salt and molasses. Home-made ORS began to join the curriculum of many PHC training schemes elsewhere.

The discovery of effective oral rehydration was a significant scientific breakthrough and was so recognized in the medical literature. In 1978, the prestigious British medical journal *The Lancet* described it as 'potentially the most important medical advance this century'. But for several years following its discovery, ORS suffered a classic fate at the hands of what Halfdan Mahler called the medical consumer society: its very cheapness and simplicity led to its widespread neglect.

The level of public health enjoyed in the Western world meant that diarrhoea, that mundane and socially uninteresting complaint, did not threaten the lives of children in North America and Europe. For those who did contract something virulent and become acutely dehydrated, the hospital bed and the drip inspired much more confidence than a remedy which could be administered at home. As a result, ORS was ignored by the Western medical establishment, and by the pharmaceutical industry. Investment in its manufacture initially had to come from governments and humanitarian organizations. Big business could make and market infant formula to the impoverished woman of the shanty town; but did not show any similar enthusiasm for making and marketing a salt and sugar drink to treat her baby's diarrhoea—diarrhoea which might in fact have been caused by mixing the baby's formula with dirty water. Such are the ironies of infant death around the world.

The third technique, the B in GOBI, was the protection of breast-feeding. Breast-feeding's rapid decline in the developing world and the controversy surrounding the marketing of infant formulas had prompted a closer scientific examination of its properties. Its perfect nutritional mix, individually tailored to the changing requirements of its specific consumer, was already well understood; now scientific investigation had produced more complete information about its immunological properties. The colostrum produced by a mother in the hours immediately after birth contained especially important antibodies, and mature breast-milk imparted protection against respiratory and intestinal infections. These findings strengthened the case against the bottle, in favour of the breast.

The bottle-fed babies of the poor were not only more prone to infection because of malnutrition (over-dilute formula), and because of germs in the formula (unclean water, bottle, and teats), but also had little resistance to their effects because they did not have the immunities imbibed with milk from the breast. Conclusive evidence was beginning to document the very marked difference in prospects of the breast-fed as compared with the bottle-fed baby. A 1980 study in Brazil revealed that bottle-fed babies in poor families were between three and four times as likely to be mal-nourished; another in Egypt showed that the death rate among breast-fed babies was five times lower. From India came data which showed that bottle-fed babies suffered twice as many respiratory infections and three times as many bouts of diarrhoea.

A number of countries had begun to take steps to stem the decline in breast-feeding, a movement which had picked up noticeable steam since the 1979 WHO/Unicef meeting on infant feeding in Geneva, and the passage by the World Health Assembly of the International Code of Marketing of Breast-milk Substitutes in 1981. In the industrialized world, new appreciation for the virtues of breast-milk had already prompted a comeback for nature's infant food supply. Educated mothers were insisting on breast-feeding, and seeking whatever medical support they needed to overcome any problems they encountered. Many countries had passed helpful laws on maternity benefits and leave.

Now the signs of a similar movement back to the breast were showing up in the developing world. In Papua New Guinea, where legislation banning the advertising and sale of infant formula was passed in 1977, bottle-feeding dropped from thirty-five per cent to twelve per cent within two years, and cases of serious undernutrition in small children dropped by nearly three-quarters. The challenge now was to repeat this kind of success elsewhere, to try and help other governments provide the support poor mothers needed, not only to understand the importance of breast-feeding and sound weaning, but to be able to put their understanding into effect. Breast-feeding was the cheapest of all primary health techniques: as long as a mother did not lose earning power by being around to do it, breast-feeding was free. Its forceful promotion was an obvious contender for the child survival revolution.

The fourth technique was immunization against six widespread communicable diseases. Measles, diphtheria, tetanus, tuberculosis, whooping cough and polio between them carried away over five million children's lives each year. While these diseases did not represent the entire gamut of non-diarrhoeal diseases to which Third World children were prone, they had an important feature in common: low-cost vaccines were available against them. Some of these vaccines had been improved by recent medical advance, and their potency was less susceptible to warm temperatures. The smallpox eradication drive had proved that it was possible to reach into even the furthest corners of a country and inoculate the potential victims of a killer disease with a heat stable vaccine. Enthused by that success, the international health community set about increasing immunization against the six others.

In 1977, the World Health Assembly had declared a goal of Universal Child Immunization by 1990. Many countries stepped up their immunization drives; Unicef assisted with vaccines, kerosene refrigerators, cold boxes and training for vaccination teams. But because some of the vaccines required three doses to assure a child complete protection—diphtheria, whooping cough, tetanus (injected in a combined vaccine, DPT), and polio—these drives required a considerable degree of organization. At the turn of the decade the typical immunization drive managed to reach no more than twenty per cent of the target with all the shots—three for DPT— needed to protect a child fully. In order to protect an entire population from a communicable disease, the reservoir of those who could catch it and infect others had to be reduced to a very low point. According to Unicef's calculations, this meant reaching an immunization coverage rate of at least eighty per cent; higher in certain cases. At current rates of progress, there was no way that the world's children would all be protected by 1990, or even 2000, from the threat of diseases a simple series of drops or injections could prevent. Something had to be done to drive up the immunization rates. Immunization was the fourth plank of the revolutionary platform, the I in GOBI.

When *The State of the World's Children* report heralding GOBI was published in December 1982, much use was made of marketing words such as 'new' and 'breakthrough'. Novelty and discovery were part of the revolutionary éclat. But none of the techniques was a brand new invention. That was part of their beauty: all of them had already earned a respectable place in the pharmacopeia of the late twentieth century; WHO, the high priesthood of international public health, had been promoting their use for years. Unicef itself had a great deal of experience with vaccine supply, ORS production and support for training schemes for health-care workers in all PHC techniques. There was plenty of room for more operational and sociological enquiry into their use, and for their further technological refinement. Indeed, part of Grant's purpose was to create the kind of demand which would give a boost to both. What genuinely was new about them was either the full recognition of their scientific properties or their arrival at a state of technological readiness for widescale application.

The State of the World's Children report did not claim that the four techniques offered a complete answer to all the problems of high infant mortality and childhood disease. Three other measures were also singled out for special attention: family planning; the distribution of food supplements to poorly nourished children and nursing mothers; and female literacy. Although these were equally regarded as critical to the overall improvement of child health, they did not pass as easily all Grant's tests of low cost, political acceptability, and potential for popular acclaim; they were not, in his view, as 'do-able'. 'Do-ability' was an all-important consideration. The essential precondition for do-ability was that the word could be made to spread, the demand come forward, and enough of a country's social apparatus would assert itself to achieve the target.

The kind of model Grant cited as an example of the 'child survival and development revolution' was the all-out Polio Control Operation launched in 1980 in Brazil. This operation had been personally backed by the President and supported by all government ministries, and it had succeeded in mobilizing 320,000 volunteers and vaccinating eighteen million children. In the style which had characterized Mexico's onslaught on malaria twenty years before, national vaccination days were publicized heavily in advance and planned with military precision. Every kind of organization, from church to army, schools to neighbourhood associations, took part. The 320,000 volunteers were taught how to drop the vaccine into the children's mouths; 90,000 immunization posts were set up; and in the run-up to each day, television, radio, and newspapers were packed with exhortations to parents.

Brazil's experience proved the final and essential part of Grant's thesis. In the 1980s, particularly in the countries of Latin America and Asia, the degree of social organization and the ubiquitousness of the mass media had transformed the prospects of success for a huge child survival push. Brazil's polio campaign was not the only example to prove the point. If so many women in poor communities around the world had heard of infant formula and found from somewhere the means to buy it, then they were not beyond the reach of information which—if it corresponded to something they felt a need for—was capable of changing their behaviour towards their children.

The public response to the publication of *The State of the World's Children* report in December 1982 was extremely positive. The report's message was hopeful, up-beat; instead of emphasizing problems, it emphasized solutions. Grant's judgement that the simplicity and cost-effectiveness of the GOBI techniques would have instant public appeal was borne out in media commentaries in the industrialized and in the developing world. Not since the very early days of Unicef, when all eyes were turned on the UN and its mission in the world, had any Unicef 'story' about the needs of children attracted such widespread attention.

Grant launched the report in Paris and London. To Prime Minister Pierre Mauroy, he presented a Haitian growth chart in Créole; later the same day, he presented a sachet of ORS to Prime Minister Margaret Thatcher. Theirs were the first of many endorsements by national and international leaders, an array which eventually included Ronald Reagan, Indira Gandhi, Zia ul Haq, J. R. Jawardene, Olof Palme, Mother Teresa, Robert McNamara and Javier Pérez de Cuéllar. The UN Secretary-General, listing the four GOBI techniques, commented: 'Innovative and cost-effective action along these lines would demonstrate that even in times of acute financial strain for social services and international co-operation, it is possible for the world to take imaginative steps to heal some of the most tragic wounds of underdevelopment and poverty. I appeal to national leaders, to communicators, to health care workers and to concerned institutions and individuals to support this action'.

When the Executive Board met for its annual session in May 1983, the delegates endorsed Grant's 'revolution'. They accepted the premise that the economic climate demanded a redoubling of effort for children without expecting a doubling of resources. They accepted the techniques; they were familiar from many previous discussions of programmes, and to some—the delegate from Bangladesh, for example—the efficacy of one or more was already well-established on home ground. They accepted the strategy that growing communications and organizational networks in developing countries could be harnessed to their promotion. They also acclaimed Grant's personal enthusiasm and commitment to a new drive on children's behalf. At the same session, they agreed that the infant mortality rate would be one of the more important factors taken into account when Unicef considered the level of its programme co-operation in a country.

There was a cloud on the horizon. The WHO/Unicef Joint Committee on Health Policy had met earlier in the spring, and reviewed a WHO study on the progress of primary health care worldwide. While they had applauded the actions of nearly fifty countries in drawing up specific primary health care plans and starting to train auxiliary workers, they had not been so happy to discover how few countries had significantly altered the structure of their health services and reallocated expenditures to correspond faithfully to the full dimensions of the primary health care model. When Grant first articulated his new campaign in December 1982, his stress on the dynamic potential of the GOBI package heightened the impact of the message on lay audiences; but among some professionals it gave the false impression that Unicef regarded the promotion of the four techniques as somehow separate from the promotion of primary health care. The failure to emphasize the all-important goal of 'health for all' rang alarm bells in WHO.

Dr Halfdan Mahler, WHO Director-General, had definite reservations about globally singling out certain health activities for a special campaign. Of course the ingredients of the GOBI package met WHO's approval, as the 1983 session of the Joint Committee on Health Policy confirmed: the value of growth monitoring, oral rehydration, the protection of breast-feeding and immunization were not at issue. But this was a testing time for PHC. Adoption of the strategy in its entirety was moving ahead, but not speedily and not systematically. Until the concept took better root, any signal that Unicef was deviating from the creed was upsetting.

Mahler viewed GOBI and the campaigning potential of the child survival revolution with caution. The reformed ex-ringmaster of medical circuses looked upon any programme whose ingredients were predetermined for all countries and circumstances as anathema: a throwback to the days of top-down programmes, designed for people instead of with them and by them. Primary health care had been developed as an alternative to the top-down approach, as a reaction to previous efforts to short-cut the systematic development of a health infrastructure.

But Grant had not abandoned primary health care. The quintessential ideas of PHC, which his own father had done so much to pioneer in the early years of international public health, were part of the warp and woof of his thinking. The idea behind the child survival revolution was to speed up both the acceptance of the PHC concept and its implementation by using top-down vigour to hasten an organic process. The systematic development of the health care service could only come about if people demanded that it be there for them to use. Only time would tell if this idea could work.

The child survival and development revolution had been successfully ignited. The next step was to gather the first generation of allies to the cause, and help get governments and supporting organizations poised to step up existing campaigns or launch new ones around the GOBI techniques.

During the course of the next year, Grant used his prodigious energy to become a peripatetic salesman of GOBI to presidents, princes and prime ministers around the world. Sometimes this meant bypassing ministers of health; but, with all its risks, this was seen as the quickest way to guarantee national commitment to an all-out effort. If the head of government gave the word for mobilization, it could then be addressed to people and organizations in all walks of life and not just to the officials in one or two ministries. It also guaranteed any campaign the support of the State-sponsored media: no international humanitarian organization or government ministry could afford to deluge a population with radio jingles or newspaper advertisements at prime time commercial rates.

From the beginning of 1983 through 1985 Grant personally visited thirty-nine heads of state or national government in countries as far apart geographically and ideologically as Colombia and South Yemen, Haiti and Sri Lanka, India and Burkina Faso, Nigeria and Cuba, Dominican Republic and China, Nicaragua and El Salvador. He pointed out to these national leaders that saving children's lives was one of the few completely apolitical actions which commanded the unqualified support of parents everywhere. He was trying to turn the nonpolitical nature of the children's issue to its own political advantage. He and senior Unicef colleagues also sought the active collaboration of international nongovernmental bodies. The International Paediatrics Association and the League of Red Cross Societies were among the first worldwide networks to give 'child survival' their ringing endorsement.

At the beginning of the campaign, Grant believed that among the four GOBI techniques it was the spread of oral rehydration, both in manufactured sachet form and as a recipe concocted at home, which held out the most immediate promise. Diarrhoeal disease was the leading cause of infant deaths in most developing countries, and the availability of a remedy costing no more than a few cents struck the loudest public chord.

When the GOBI campaign was launched, forty-nine countries had already embarked on WHO-assisted programmes for the national control of diarrhoeal disease, of which thirty-five were already operational. Unicef's most important contribution was to provide sachets of ORS mix, manufactured according to the WHO-approved formula, of which it was the largest worldwide supplier; and to give support to local ORS production. In 1982, the total ORS production from these two sources was forty-five million sachets, and the world total was close to sixty million. By the end of 1985, the world total was 250 million sachets, of which Unicef had bought or helped produce slightly less than a third, and slightly less than half of which had been manufactured in the developing countries. This was a clear sign that oral rehydration had taken off. The effect of putting ORS sachets, and the knowledge of how to make up a home-made version, into the hands of community health volunteers and mothers had saved half a million children's lives during the course of the previous twelve months, Unicef calculated.

What had happened, and where, in order to multiply four-fold the global demand for ORS? One critical event took place in Washington. USAID, previously lukewarm in its interest in diarrhoea, became enthused. The long-range prospect for reducing diarrhoeal infection was the improvement in public health which water supplies and sanitation could effect. USAID, along with UNDP, WHO, Unicef and the World Bank, were heavily committed to the goals of the International Water and Sanitation Decade, 1981–1990. The widespread use of ORS offered a stop-gap solution to a major public health problem.

Coupling the promotion of ORS with the health education campaigns now regarded by Unicef and others as *de rigeur* components of water supplies programmes appealed strongly to Peter McPherson, Director of USAID. In June 1983, USAID, WHO, Unicef and the International Centre for Diarrhoeal Disease, Bangladesh, co-sponsored the first International Conference on Oral Rehydration Therapy in Washington. UNDP and the World Bank also began to support oral rehydration therapy. In the course of the next two years, USAID virtually took over the torch for ORS, backing national campaigns against diarrhoeal infection around the world and receiving extra resources for doing so from the US Congress.

Two of the new national ORS campaigns started since the child survival revolution was launched were in Egypt and Haiti. In both cases, the heads of state put their weight behind them.

With support from USAID, the Egyptian ministry of health began extending its onslaught against diarrhoeal disease nationwide in 1983. Lectures and workshops were arranged in teaching hospitals, medical colleges and nursing schools, and pharmacists all over the country began to stock ORS sachets. One of the problems with the promotion of the commercial variety of ORS is that the product is so cheap that pharmacists do not make much of a profit on its sale. Unless mothers insist on buying it because they are sure that it is really what their ailing child needs, an ignorant—or unscrupulous—drug merchant may sell her instead a highly-coloured capsule which may look more exotic, is certainly more expensive, but is almost guaranteed to be an inferior treatment for diarrhoeal dehydration. In Egypt, the pharmacists were offered a thirty per cent profit margin on each sachet they sold, and free measuring cups which they could also sell to customers. By the end of the five-year programme, it is hoped that mothers will insist on ORS and that these subsidies will no longer be necessary.

In Haiti, where a national programme to promote *serum oral* also began in mid-1983, stall and shopkeepers were given their initial supplies. Its price—nationally set—was advertised along with its properties on the radio and television to dissuade salesmen from extravagant mark-ups. By mid-1985, eighty per cent of mothers in Port au Prince and thirty per cent of those in the countryside had heard of *serum oral* and begun to use it.

In spite of these and other encouraging results, at the end of 1985, the latest *The State of the World's Children* report estimated that 'only about 20 per cent of the world's families knew enough about oral rehydration to be able to use it'. However perfect the technique, it had not proved a swift and easy task to mobilize whole countries and communities behind its use. Part of the problem was that existing attitudes about treating diarrhoea, both among health professionals and among mothers, had to be worn down before behaviour could be changed. ORS did not arrive to fill a vacuum, except in the minds of the already convinced. Mothers, healers and doctors had long had their ways of treating something so commonplace, and no-one easily deserts the familiar, specially for something which seems almost too crude and simple to be true.

Another inhibition was the subject itself, as the promoters of latrines had long experienced. Mothers might happily discuss their children's ailments with other mothers; but as a topic for general discussion, or a subject for mass entertainment on radio and television, diarrhoea must rank very close to the bottom of the list. Presidents and princes do not happily speak to their peoples on such a subject; rare is the regime—like the then regime in Haiti—which chooses to give over the presidential palace to a song and dance extravaganza on the national bowel movements of the under-fives.

It is not possible to decree a national 'diarrhoea day': unlike vaccination days; it makes no sense to summon parents to bring all their children for a dose of ORS at an appointed hour. Whatever their enthusiasm for 'support communications', governments and humanitarian organizations cannot over more than a short period invest the kind of resources in commercial advertising that a major pharmaceutical, food products or soft drinks company can invest in promoting their products. The widespread use of ORS will take time to achieve. It is one thing to make ORS sachets available, or give out the recipe for making an oral rehydration mix with household ingredients, but there is no power in the world which will make the mother of a sick child use it unless she knows about it and is convinced of its efficacy.

That does not mean that Unicef has in any way lessened its support for ORS, as Grant reassured the second international conference on oral rehydration in December 1985. Of the four GOBI techniques, the O was expected to be the champion. But in terms of mobilizing national leaders, organizations and people, immunization turned out to lead the field. Where oral rehydration had taken a sudden leap forward, immunization had bounded ahead.

By the early 1970s, widespread immunization meant that diphtheria, whooping cough, tetanus, measles and polio no longer presented serious public-health problems in the industrialized world. By contrast, the first four of these diseases remained uncontrolled in most of the developing world, and polio was reaching the epidemic scale seen in Europe and North America in the prevaccination era. The cost of fully immunizing a child against these diseases and tuberculosis and smallpox, a cost which included the organization required to reach the child as well as that of the antigens, was estimated at only a few dollars. In 1973, WHO decided that routine protection should be made available to children worldwide, and initiated an Expanded Programme on Immunization (EPI).

At the World Health Assembly the following year, twenty-five countries expressed keen interest. Work began on helping their ministries of health put together national immunization plans, and Unicef offered to pay for vaccines, cold boxes and health worker training. Over the course of the next few years, UNDP also became involved. Successful efforts were made to improve the vaccines and the cold-chain technology, as well as the management of campaigns. When primary health care was adopted as the alternative order in health, immunization was high on the list of functions to be carried out as part of meeting basic health needs. By this time, smallpox had been eradicated so the list of candidates for expanded immunization programmes was reduced to six. In 1977, the World Health Assembly adopted a target of universal immunization by 1990 as part of the overall goal of health for all by the year 2000.

In 1979, reporting to the World Health Assembly on the progress of the Expanded Programme on Immunization, WHO lamented that in spite of the low cost of vaccinating children, less than ten per cent of the developing countries' newborns were receiving their shots. 'The diseases are so commonplace', the report observed, 'that parents and, sad to say, health workers and political leaders are still for the most part numbed into accepting this continuing tragedy'. By the early 1980s, some countries had made noticeable EPI gains: in 1982, the best results reported were in Malawi and Lesotho, where respectively, coverage had reached fifty-five and forty per cent. This was still a far cry from the coverage needed for universal immunization. But it was distinctly more encouraging than the picture in large countries with spread out populations such as Sudan and Zaire. In such countries, the logistical problems of keeping vaccines cool along all the links in the cold chain meant that any kind of regular immunization service did not extend beyond urban areas.

One of the familiar EPI problems reported by Unicef staff in the field lay with the way immunization was being organized. Some countries were running their programmes like the old disease-control campaigns, with an administration separate from the health services, special fleets of vehicles and inoculation staff. This divorced immunization from primary health care; but then in many countries health care services themselves, whether primary or other, were not yet widespread. Here was a familiar example of the chicken and egg health conundrum: which came first—disease control or the onward march of the entire health system? Everyone knew that attack—in the language of malaria control—must be followed by consolidation. But without a health service already in place—as was the case particularly in Africa—how could consolidation be achieved?

In some countries—Sudan and Zaire were just two classic examples—health-service coverage for the majority of the population was at least a generation away. On the other hand, to create a health-service infrastructure which depended heavily on the active participation of semitrained volunteers did require a starting place, and the kind of tasks associated with vaccination campaigns were eminently suitable. The lay vaccinator was by no means a new type of health personnel; he and she dated back to the smallpox and even the BCG campaigns. In countries which did not permit injections to be given except by fully-fledged health professionals, laymen could be assigned to other duties: gathering the candidates for vaccination together by house-to-house visiting, filling in health cards, checking registers of names. The school of thought that supported the child survival and development revolution believed that an immunization campaign, specially when accompanied by a thorough public education campaign on the merits of full immunization for every child, could act as a cutting edge or an entry point, paving the way for a primary health care service in its entirety.

Soon after the launch of the GOBI prescription for a revolution in children's health, Teresa Albañez, Unicef's Regional Director for the Americas, previously a senior official in the Venezuelan Government, arranged for Jim Grant to meet President Belisario Betancur of Colombia. Betancur swiftly became a national and international field marshal of the child survival revolution. Betancur was solidly committed to the political idea of community action for development, and Colombia's Ministry of Health had long been committed to the promotion of preventive as well as curative health services. One-quarter of its staff were auxiliaries, and 4500 health *promotores*—volunteers—worked alongside the auxiliaries to generate an idea of health in the community which had less to do with the magic of medicine than with the mundane business of disease prevention and self-care.

In 1979, the Colombian health ministry had launched an expanded programme of immunization. The following year, the Pan-American Health Organization (PAHO), WHO's American arm, had helped Colombian health officials to evaluate the progress of the EPI. They discovered that only twenty per cent of children had been reached with full immunization coverage. In order to improve the coverage rate, the ministry of health adopted a new strategy being used elsewhere in Latin America—*canalizacion* or 'channelling'. Health workers resident in the community prepared a map of the local area, and with the help of community and administrative leaders, undertook a house-to-house census of children in the target age-

group. They recorded which children had been vaccinated, for which
diseases, how many times, and which had not. The purpose of immunization was explained to parents and they were told when and to which
house in the district to bring their children for the requisite shots.

Between 1981 and 1983, *canalizacion* raised the percentage of children
under one year old fully protected against DPT, polio and measles from
around twenty-seven per cent to around forty-three per cent. In March
1983, President Betancur threw down a new challenge to the health
ministry: to raise the numbers immunized against DPT, measles and polio
by half in a series of national vaccination days.

Some of the health officials were alarmed that an attack of this nature
would harm the steady expansion of *canalizacion*. But political might had
its way, and the plan drawn up for a National Vaccination Crusade was
worked out in such a way that it dovetailed with an increase in house-to-
house visits and personal encounters with parents. The days were set: three
days, one month apart in June, July and August of 1984. On each day, each
child would receive three doses of vaccine: measles, polio and DPT. The
Crusade was intended not only to catch in its net the new candidates for
vaccination, but also to see that there was no drop in attendance from 'day'
to 'day': no Colombian mother must rest in the delusion which frequently
affects the outcome of immunization campaigns: that one shot is enough.

President Betancur adopted the strategy used in the Brazilian campaign
against polio of 1980—a strategy whose success Grant had underlined. A
mass mobilization of volunteer helpers was needed to make the campaign
truly take on the character of a Crusade. For the first time in Colombia,
new allies outside the normal health service staff were recruited to help the
Ministry of Health prepare, launch and carry out a health effort. The
concept of health had already been broadened intellectually in Colombia;
now the concept of who could be the bringer of health was to be similarly
broadened to match the intellectual idea. The Church, the Red Cross, the
National Police, industrial associations, labour unions, the boy scouts and
the entire school network were involved. From their multiple and various
ranks 120,000 volunteers were lined up to help the health officials and
health *promotores* handle the expected turnout. If every child in the target
group was to be reached, the turnout would top the 900,000 mark. To
make sure it reached close to that, a veritable media blitz was planned:
more than 10,000 television and radio spots were broadcast.

The symbolic child of the campaign was 'Pitin'. A cheerful impish
looking little fellow, he received his name as a result of a media campaign
run by Caracol, the country's leading radio network, and *El Tiempo*, the
leading morning—and opposition—newspaper. Pitin appeared in colour
on children's health cards, where weight was plotted and immunization
shots recorded, and on ORS sachets which were also widely promoted. He
also appeared on the television, in posters sitting on a policeman's knee

advertising *securidad infantil*, and in campaign literature for the volunteers. Pitin became a national celebrity. The media blitz reached saturation points in the days before the 'days', and shut down afterwards to give people a rest.

On the first and subsequent national days, President Betancur appeared on national television firing the first shot by giving a child the first vaccination. Jim Grant and Teresa Albañez of Unicef and Dr Carlyle Guerra de Macedo, the Director-General of PAHO/WHO, were at his side. Betancur maintained a close interest in the progress of each day, telephoning his regional governors as immunization returns came in. The atmosphere was one of national carnival. In coverage terms, the results of the three days exceeded the target. Over sixty per cent of the under-ones received a complete vaccination series for polio and DPT. The coverage for measles, for which one shot only was needed, and which constituted the major threat, was fifty-three per cent. *Canalizacion* helped to raise the count, and when this became noticeable, it was introduced in some areas which had previously been unconvinced of the need for house-to-house visiting.

In Colombia, a combination of political will, media blitz and social action had put health techniques at the disposal of thousands of families that had not previously taken advantage of them. A genuine revolution for child survival and development had become something tangible. Not only the nation's children, but the entire health apparatus had received a shot in the arm. As a result, the phase of attack was transformable into consolidation. Thousands of new recruits were ready to join the ranks of the health *promotores*; these, in turn, were 'channelling' into many more households; priests were giving premarital counselling on child health care and asking mothers who brought their children for baptism whether they had yet been vaccinated; boy scouts were sporting child-survival buttons and gaining points for health promotion; the primary school curriculum had been revised to emphasize health education and 200,000 teachers were talking about child survival to their students; Pitin was poised to conquer new pastures. This was the social mobilization behind child health that Grant and his deputy Tarzie Vittachi had envisioned, the push that would help to make the full parameters of the primary health care concept universally understood, bringing into the alliance for better health new partners from all sectors of government and society.

In December 1984, President Betancur launched a National Child Survival and Development Plan to bring about by 1989 an overall reduction in infant and child mortality from the national average of fifty-seven per 1000 births to forty. Not only was the onslaught against measles, polio, diphtheria, whooping cough and tetatnus to be stepped up 'until there are no more cases of vaccine-preventable disease in our country', but other, even more important, child health priorities would now be similarly attacked.

Immunization, in fact, ranked fourth on the list of the Ministry of Health's mother and child priorities. Now, coat-tailing on its success, more could be done for the others: diarrhoea, acute respiratory infections, low birth weight and other birth complications, malnutrition, and early stimulation for the young child. Moves on all these fronts now began on a scheduled basis, region by region, with the goal of covering the entire country by the end of 1986.

On the national vaccination days in 1984, and on their repeat days in 1985, health officials from many countries around the world visited Colombia to observe the Crusade in action and learn from its experience. These were the people who Grant and many of the Unicef country representatives around the world hoped would become the next generation of crusaders for the revolution worldwide. They included representatives from the Dominican Republic, Ecuador, El Salvador, Burkina Faso and Turkey. In all of these countries, crash national vaccination campaigns were also well into their planning stages.

The most striking immunization campaign was that in El Salvador, which on three 'days of tranquillity' in spring 1985 stopped the civil war so that shots of a different kind could be fired. Unicef and the Roman Catholic hierarchy managed to gain the agreement of guerilla leaders that a *de facto* cease-fire would hold. Children from all over the country were able to go in peace to vaccination posts, manned in some sectors by health workers of the El Salvador Red Cross and the ICRC. Mainly because the publicity for the campaign was more difficult to stage manage, the coverage did not reach the levels achieved in Colombia, but the effort was revolutionary in another sense. Children had been made 'a zone of peace'. For three sweet days, the health of the children of El Salvador became a reason for national reconciliation amid a long and bitter armed confrontation.

Among the four GOBI techniques, immunization had most caught the national and popular imagination. By mid-1965, a number of countries— Nigeria, Turkey, Pakistan, Bolivia, Nicaragua, Lesotho, Sri Lanka, Saudi Arabia and Zimbabwe—had begun to orchestrate the stepping up of their immunization programmes to reach eighty per cent of their children. Demand for vaccines worldwide was running at three times the 1983 rate. Unicef estimated that a million children's lives were being saved as a result. Always alert to the tide of political will and constantly on the look-out for the breakthrough which would turn a slogan into a movement, Grant began to zero in more strongly on the goal of 'Universal Child Immunization by 1990', one of the targets set by WHO as a stepping stone to 'health for all'.

Among the various PHC strands which must be woven to place a safety net under children, immunization had passed the test of do-ability with higher marks than the others. Immunization appealed to national leaders; it offered opportunities to mobilize many other parts of society than merely the health services; it had readily quantifiable targets; national immunization crusades could be run with the military precision of the old disease-control campaigns, with which they had a lot in common. Like the campaign against malaria, it might be easier to mount the initial attack than it was to achieve consolidation, but the example of Colombia and other similar campaigns was showing that the orchestrated use of communications networks of every kind could break the barrier between the first phase and the second. The gains achieved by social mobilization could offset some of the reservations about GOBI and the child survival revolution which still persisted in certain quarters.

With their Pitins, presidents, television spectaculars, magic shots, 'days of tranquillity', races and chases to arrive at targets, the immunization campaigns were surely shows in the same way that the old disease campaigns had been shows. A bad odour had clung tenaciously to 'shows' and the top-down approach ever since disease campaigns went out of fashion and the alternative order in health had been declared. Not only Mahler at WHO, but certain Unicef Board delegates and members of the international health community were not yet fully convinced that this use of immunization shows as a galvanizing process could speed up the rate at which Mankind reached the all-important target of health for all. The alternative order assumed that the people, the community, the district and the nation established its own priorities within the gamut of basic services they wished eventually to put in place. The child survival and development revolution, it was alleged, offered a premixed package of solutions to the problems of disease and death among infants and small children. Such an approach begged the question of whether the immunization or ORS campaign truly responded to the people's or the country's felt needs, or had been thrust upon them.

The response of certain countries to the challenge of universal immunization provided a partial answer. If they did not feel that immunizing children against diseases which could kill them or permanently affect their health was a need, they would not have responded so enthusiastically to the idea of a campaign. If the people at large had not been interested, they would not have rallied in their turn. If Colombia could manage to boost *canalizacion*—a primary health care strategy of an ideologically pristine variety—by launching an attack and following it up so successfully that better child health had become a part of national self-esteem, then there was hope that other countries could do the same.

In Colombia's case, much had depended on the existing health-care service, how it was oriented, how fully it was manned, and its ability to take advantage of the services of thousands of religious and lay volunteers brought to its doors by social mobilization. There are many countries, particularly in Asia and Latin America, where some of the same preconditions prevail. In Africa, the existing degree of organization within the health care system is rarely as sophisticated. The rule of development, that a higher level of development begets more development, makes it inevitable that the route to universal immunization will be travelled faster in some places than in others. Only time can tell how many countries, in which continents, can follow Colombia's example, not just in running a successful immunization 'show', but in reflecting the results of that show in the organic growth of the primary health care delivery system.

The target of universal child immunization by 1990 can only be reached if every country is prepared to take a priority which may not be at the top of its list of causes of infant mortality, and nonetheless make it a national priority over the immediate term. The argument for allocating a larger slice of the health budget to immunization than a country otherwise might have done is that other priorities—the reduction of diarrhoea, respiratory infection, malaria—will gain ground as a result.

The more optimistic health experts believe that universal child immunization by 1990 is not an impossible dream. Nothing creates success like success. Targets—ambitious but not hopelessly unrealistic targets—help to create the feeling that something can happen. If it can, it may. The effort to bring more countries to the point of commitment to the target continues.

Grant has achieved an extraordinary feat in creating a bandwagon that leaders of nations small and great have chosen to step on board on behalf of their children. The child survival revolution represents another landmark in the elevation of children's well-being to the high table of international statesmanship. In early 1985, Prime Minister Rajiv Gandhi of India announced that as a 'living memorial' to his mother, India would try to reach full immunization by 1990. Later in the same year, the Chinese Government announced a target of reaching, province by province, eighty-five per cent immunization by 1988. The two most populous countries in the world had joined the crusade.

The year 1985 was the fortieth anniversary year of the UN. In June 1985, Javier Pérez de Cuéllar, the Secretary-General, wrote to the presidents or prime ministers of all 159 UN member States suggesting that commitment to universal immunization by 1990 'would be a most fitting manifestation of world dedication to the United Nations'.

At a ceremony held at the UN in New York on 25 October 1985, at the conclusion of the two-week celebrations of the UN's fortieth anniversary, national leaders, ambassadors, UN officials and representatives of key international nongovernmental organizations met to sign a declaration. The declaration was read out to a packed conference room. Its essence was as follows: 'We the people of the United Nations, determined to save succeeding generations from the scourge of preventable disease and to promote social progress and better standards of life in larger freedom, unite our strength for the protection of our children and are resolved to achieve the United Nations goal of Universal Child Immunization by 1990'.

This goal, the declaration continued, was '. . . an essential step in the establishment of sustainable Primary Health Care services and structures for the continuing protection of the world's children and families, leading to achievement of the United Nations goal of Health for All by the year 2000'. This was the ultimate goal to which the governments represented at the Alma-Ata conference, and their partners in the international community, especially Unicef and WHO, had been committed since 1978. There was just fifteen years left in which to reach it.

The postwar, post-colonial span of forty years in which Unicef has existed has seen more progress for children than any previous period in history. Improvements in the lives and prospects for children are mainly due to the social and economic progress there has been for people; for families, for communities, for nations. But Unicef, the first arrangement between the nations to do something specially for children, has played a part. In the heat of many an emergency—silent, quiet, loud, or deafening—it has been there to remind the world that many of the victims are children; and that the children are more innocent, more vulnerable and more dependent than any other victims. By concentrating its own efforts on the children, it has in its way been able to redress the balance a little in their favour. That, at least is what it has tried to do.

No-one could have envisaged when they first sat down to compute rations of milk and fat for hungry children in postwar Europe that, forty years on, Unicef would be an organization fully engaged in the business of national and international development. Conceptually, philosophically, geographically, everything has changed. In the process, by fits and starts, the children's cause has gradually climbed higher on the international agenda. Today, even while the pace of economic and social progress is faltering and the poor are bearing the brunt of dark times, initiatives around the world—initiatives in which Unicef is active—are helping to place a safety net under children. A *magna carta* for children—a Convention on Children's Rights—is being drawn up for possible passage into international law; and efforts are being stepped up to declare children 'a zone of peace' in countries where warfare or civil strife is hampering their survival and development.

With all that has been achieved and all that is promising, there is no cause for self-satisfaction. All the declines in infant and child disease and death over the past generation have not relegated the image of the hungry child to the pages of history. The peaky-faced, underweight, listless child, whose smile is so perishable, is still with us in countries all over the world.

The attack on poverty, and the attacks on the symptoms of poverty—ill-health, undernutrition, ignorance, powerlessness—has launched a thousand crusades, a thousand fleets of ships and airplanes, a thousand campaigns, a thousand theories, a thousand careers in development planning; and yet the hungry child—the impetus and symbol for so many of these efforts—has often turned out to be a heartbreakingly difficult customer to reach. Too many such children are still sitting in a dusty compound or a muddy puddle, not able to enjoy the most basic of rights: enough to eat, today and every day; clean water to drink and wash in; a house with a rainproof roof and walls; knowledgeable care and medicine at times of pain and sickness; some simple toys to play with; a chance to go to school and learn; a chance, in short, to become a fully-developed human being with all a human being's full potential.

Sometimes it seems in the buzz and excitement of new discoveries, new humanitarian adventures, new ways of unlocking puzzles which have been there since the world began that development co-operation is a mysterious world of wonders and illusions; that the closer the paraphernalia of development gets to the child, the more elusive the child becomes. Why else, in the light of all the distance we have travelled, did many millions of children have to die this year and last year quite unnecessarily?

The answer is that we do not control the fate of that child, however much we would like to do so. In forty years, we have learned that the final step needed to reach the child cannot be taken by us or by any of our governmental or nongovernmental partners; it can only be taken by the child's mother or some other family member. That step will not be taken unless she has the financial means, the knowledge and the confidence to use them. Once the family's resistance to new ideas is penetrated, and the protective shield which keeps the child's life and health in bondage is broken down, change may be desired. That first step on the road to changing the child's and the family's fortunes may be taken. At that point we can do our best through, and with, our partners at national, subnational and community level to ensure that the road taken leads to a place where the family can solve at least some of their problems. For many of the world's children, that process has begun to occur; for others, it may not occur within this generation.

Forty years on, forging the link which makes it possible for people to change the way they see and do things in ways that they control remains the continuing riddle of development. The child of poverty, in the dusty compound or the muddy puddle, is still waiting for us to solve it.

Main Sources

Unicef: annual *The State of the World's Children* reports by James P. Grant, Executive Director, 1982–83, 1984, 1985, 1986, published in association with Oxford University Press, Oxford.

World Health magazine; issues and articles on primary health care and health for all, 1978–1981, WHO, Geneva; *Unicef News*, issues 108/1981/2, 114/1982/4, 118/1983/4, and 119/1984/1; *Les Carnets de l'Enfance/Assignment Children*, issues 61/62, 1983, and 65/68, 1984; *New Internationalist* magazine, issue 127, September 1983.

Unicef: 'Current Views on Nutrition Strategies', report of an informal consultation in Unicef Headquarters, New York, September 1982, prepared by Hossein Ghassemi, Unicef Senior Adviser in Nutrition, February 1983.

'Primary Health Care: World Strategy', second Hugh R. Leavell Lecture by James P. Grant, delivered at the III International Congress of the World Federation of Public Health Associations, Calcutta, February 1981; other speeches and statements by James P. Grant delivered during the period 1981–85.

Unicef Annual Reports for 1983, 1984, and 1985, Unicef Information Division.

Unicef Executive Board: reports of the Executive Director; reports of the Executive Board; statements to the Board; special studies and papers prepared for the Board, 1983–85; reports and special studies prepared for the Unicef/WHO Joint Committee on Health Policy, 1975–83.

National Vaccination Crusade, 1984, published by the Ministry of Health, Bogota, Colombia, 1985.

Unicef Total Income 1947–85
Real and Nominal Terms

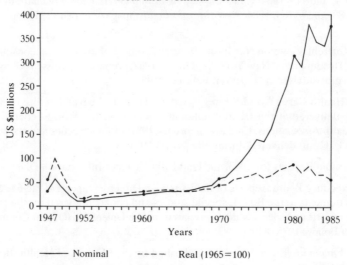

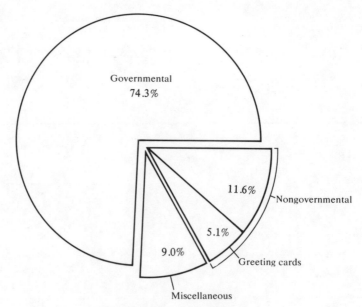

Unicef Income 1947–85 in Percentages by Source of Funds

Total Income in US dollars: $4,011,480,000

Expenditure on Programmes by Sector 1947–85

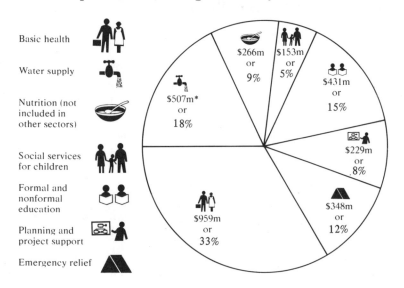

Basic health

Water supply

Nutrition (not included in other sectors)

Social services for children

Formal and nonformal education

Planning and project support

Emergency relief

\$266m or 9%

\$153m or 5%

\$431m or 15%

\$229m or 8%

\$348m or 12%

\$959m or 33%

\$507m* or 18%

* Expenditure for water supply incurred prior to 1970 is included in basic health.

Unicef Expenditure from Inception through 1985
($ million)

	1947–50	1951–59	1960–69	1970–79	1980–85	1947–85
Long-range aid:						
Health services	8.0	26.0	97.7	313.8	362.0	807.5
Mass disease control						
campaigns	12.3	56.7	82.2	*	*	151.2
Water and sanitation	*	*	*	156.3	350.8	507.1
Child nutrition	5.4	19.1	47.3	87.0	107.7	266.5
Social welfare services						
for children	*	*	9.1	49.3	94.9	153.8
Formal education	—	—	30.3	170.9	141.1	342.3
Nonformal education	—	—	2.4	27.7	58.2	88.3
General**	—	—	6.3	62.3	160.4	229.0
Total long-range aid	25.7	101.8	275.3	867.3	1 275.1	2 545.2
Emergency relief***	82.3	34.8	11.1	42.7	177.2	348.1
Total programme aid	108.0	136.6	286.4	910.0	1 452.3	2 893.3
Programme support services	0.3	14.1	42.4	158.1	293.6	508.5
Total assistance	108.3	150.7	328.8	1 068.1	1 745.9	3 401.8
Administrative costs	6.6	10.6	25.5	97.9	216.6	357.2
Total expenditures	114.9	161.3	354.3	1 166.0	1 962.5	3 759.0

* Included in health services.
** This assistance cannot be broken down into the above categories. It includes mainly planning and project preparation, project support services and project support communication.
*** Not including expenditure for rehabilitation of facilities damaged or destroyed in emergency situations which is distributed into appropriate categories of assistance. Emergency relief and rehabilitation combined would be $168 million during 1970–1979 and $279 million during 1980–1985.

Number of Institutions, Centres and Installations that have Received Unicef Equipment and Supplies*

	through 1959	1960–1969	1970–1979	1980–1985	Total through 1985
Child health					
District and referral hospitals	700	900	5 100	4 500	11 200
Urban health centres and institutions	600	2 300	7 400	9 200	19 500
Rural health centres	5 600	5 400	28 000	37 200	76 200
Sub-centres, village MCH centres	9 500	25 000	62 800	224 100	321 400
Total child health	16 400	33 600	103 300	275 000	428 300
Water systems**					
Open/dug wells and handpump installations	—	—	411 762	420 783	832 545
Engine driven pump installations	—	—	3 685	3 165	6 850
Piped and reticulated systems	—	—	5 081	5 385	10 466
Other***	—	—	1 655	27 069	28 724
Total water systems	—	—	422 183	456 402	878 585
Child nutrition					
Demonstration centres****	—	8 000	348 100	373 100	729 200
Support centres†	—	3 500	3 500	17 600	24 600
Training centres	—	500	3 100	8 300	11 900
Total child nutrition	—	12 000	354 700	399 000	765 700
Family and child welfare					
Child welfare centres	—	2 200	44 700	167 900	214 800
Women's institutions††	—	3 000	13 600	105 600	122 200
Centres for adolescents and youth	—	2 700	10 500	58 000	71 200
Training institutions	—	600	1 900	3 700	6 200
Total family and child welfare	—	8 500	70 700	335 200	414 400
Formal education					
Schools	—	45 500	528 900	393 700	968 100
Teacher training institutions	—	2 400	5 900	8 100	16 400
Other institutions	—	400	5 100	15 300	20 800
Total formal education	—	48 300	539 900	417 100	1 005 300
Pre-vocational training	—	1 000	5 000	5 623	11 623
Total	16 400	103 400	1 495 783	1 888 325	3 503 908

* Institutions receiving 'replacement' and other *ad hoc* supplies are not included.

** Data for water systems available only beginning with 1973; however data for 'other' installation available only beginning with 1978.

*** Including spring protection, rain water collection, water treatment plants, etc.

**** Including school gardens and canteens, nutrition centres, nutrition demonstration centres/clubs, community gardens.

† Including seed production units, fish hatcheries, poultry hatcheries, etc.

†† Including community centres, co-operatives, etc.

Number of Personnel Receiving Unicef Training Stipends in Countries with which Unicef Cooperates*

	through 1969	1970–1979	1980–1985	Total through 1985
Health				
Doctors	13 400	21 400	16 800	51 600
Nurses and midwives (including auxiliaries)	41 100	104 100	80 000	225 200
Traditional birth attendants	27 800	27 100	61 600	116 500
Other health and sanitation personnel	51 300	223 400	614 300	889 000
Total health personnel	133 600	376 000	772 700	1 282 300
Nutrition				
Village volunteers	146 200	449 500	1 324 200	1 919 900
Technical and admin. personnel	40 100	172 000	106 200	318 300
Total nutrition personnel	186 300	621 500	1 430 400	2 238 200
Family and child welfare				
Women's education and training	29 000	90 700	228 800	348 500
Other welfare personnel	62 000	245 700	550 500	858 200
Total family and child welfare personnel	91 000	336 400	779 300	1 206 700
Education				
Teachers	157 200	642 600	324 300	1 124 100
Other education personnel	400	91 000	156 800	248 200
Total education personnel	157 600	733 600	481 100	1 372 300
Pre-vocational training	2 900	13 000	58 600	74 500
Other				
Planning personnel	100	17 900	55 500	73 500
Statisticians	800	1 300	2 600	4 700
Transport personnel	300	700	1 800	2 800
Total other personnel	1 200	19 900	59 900	81 000
Total	572 600	2 100 400	3 582 000	6 255 000

* The information included in this table includes only those trainees who received Unicef stipends. In addition many more persons were trained within the training centres or institutions assisted with Unicef training supplies and equipment. A number of instructors in these institutions received Unicef assistance for salaries and honoraria, which are not included in this table.

Index

500